CHEVROLET *by the numbers*™

The Essential Chevrolet Parts Reference

1970–1975

By Alan L. Colvin

BENTLEY
PUBLISHERS

RB BENTLEY PUBLISHERS | AUTOMOTIVE BOOKS & MANUALS

Bentley Publishers, a division of Robert Bentley, Inc.
1734 Massachusetts Ave., Cambridge, MA 02138 USA
800-423-4595 • 617-547-4170

www.**BentleyPublishers**.com
Information that makes the difference®

WARNING—Important Safety Notice

In this book we have attempted to describe parts installed on Chevrolet vehicles, using examples which we believe to be accurate. However, the examples, instructions, and other information are intended solely as illustrations and should be used in any particular application only by personnel who are experienced in the repair and modification of Chevrolet vehicles and who have independently evaluated the repair or part. Installation of a part described in this book may render the vehicle unsafe for use in certain circumstances.

Do not use this book unless you are familiar with basic automotive repair procedures and safe workshop practices. This book illustrates parts which may be substituted for other parts originally installed on the vehicle; it is not intended to function as, or be a replacement for, a service manual. It is not a substitute for full and up-to-date information from the vehicle manufacturer or aftermarket supplier, or for proper training as an automotive technician. Note that it is not possible for us to anticipate all of the ways or conditions under which vehicles may be serviced or modified or to provide cautions as to all of the possible hazards that may result.

We have endeavored to ensure the accuracy of the information in this book. Please note, however, that considering the vast quantity and the complexity of the information involved, we cannot warrant the accuracy or completeness of the information contained in this book.

While we have attempted to create a useful reference, the author and publisher warn Chevrolet enthusiasts that car and parts verification is an unregulated field. We cannot be held responsible for any investment or purchase made on the basis of the information contained in this book. Use caution and common sense when buying cars or restoration parts.

FOR THESE REASONS, NEITHER THE PUBLISHER NOR THE AUTHOR MAKES ANY WARRANTIES, EXPRESS OR IMPLIED, THAT THE EXAMPLES, INSTRUCTIONS, OR OTHER INFORMATION IN THIS BOOK ARE FREE OF ERRORS OR OMISSIONS, ARE CONSISTENT WITH INDUSTRY STANDARDS, OR THAT THEY WILL MEET THE REQUIREMENTS FOR A PARTICULAR APPLICATION, AND WE EXPRESSLY DISCLAIM THE IMPLIED WARRANTIES OF MERCHANTABILITY AND OF FITNESS FOR A PARTICULAR PURPOSE, EVEN IF THE PUBLISHER OR AUTHOR HAVE BEEN ADVISED OF A PARTICULAR PURPOSE, AND EVEN IF A PARTICULAR PURPOSE IS INDICATED IN THE BOOK. THE PUBLISHER AND AUTHOR ALSO DISCLAIM ALL LIABILITY FOR DIRECT, INDIRECT, INCIDENTAL, OR CONSEQUENTIAL DAMAGES THAT RESULT FROM ANY USE OF THE EXAMPLES, INSTRUCTIONS, OR OTHER INFORMATION IN THIS BOOK. IN NO EVENT SHALL OUR LIABILITY WHETHER IN TORT, CONTRACT, OR OTHERWISE EXCEED THE COST OF THIS BOOK.

This book is only intended for persons who are seeking specific information about Chevrolet vehicles. It is not for those who are looking for general information on automobile repair. Exploded views are not to be used as a guide for vehicle disassembly. REPAIR AND MODIFICATION OF AUTOMOBILES IS DANGEROUS UNLESS UNDERTAKEN WITH FULL KNOWLEDGE OF THE CONSEQUENCES.

Before attempting any work on your vehicle, read the Warnings and Cautions on the inside front cover. Review the Warnings and Cautions each time you prepare to work on your vehicle.

Copies of this manual may be purchased from selected booksellers, automotive accessories and parts dealers, or directly from the publisher by mail. Robert Bentley books are also available in bulk quantity for industrial or sales-promotion use. For details write to Special Sales Manager at the publisher's address.

The publisher encourages comments from the readers of this book. These communications have been and will be considered in the preparation of this and other manuals. Please write to Robert Bentley Inc., Publishers, at the address listed on the top of this page. This book was published by Robert Bentley, Inc., Publishers. Chevrolet has not reviewed and does not warrant the accuracy or completeness of the technical specifications and information described in this book.

Library of Congress Cataloging-in-Publication Data

Colvin, Alan, 1959–
Chevrolet by the numbers : the essential Chevrolet parts reference, 1970-1975 / by Alan Colvin.
p. cm.
Includes index.
ISBN 0-8376-0927-5 : $29.95
1. Chevrolet automobile--Parts--Catalogs. I. Title.
TL215.C5C62 1994
629.222--dc20
94-19733
CIP

Bentley Stock No. GC75

GM Part No. 24502564

04 03 02 01 10 9 8 7 6

The paper used in this publication is acid free and meets the requirements of the National Standard for Information Sciences-Permanence of Paper for Printed Library Materials. ♾

Chevrolet By The Numbers™: The Essential Chevrolet Parts Reference, 1970–1975

Manufactured in the United States of America

On the Front Cover: 1) Blueprint, courtesy of General Motors Corporation; 2) Casting number, photo by Alan Colvin; 3) Engine and car, photos by Steve Reyes.

On the Back Cover: From the top 1) 1970 Chevelle SS 454, photo by Randy Lorentzen; 2) 1975 Corvette Coupe, courtesy of General Motors Corporation; 3, 4) 1970 Z28 Camaros, photos by Ron Sessions; 5) 1971 Nova 396, photo by Randy Lorentzen; 6) detail of Chevelle SS 454, photo by Randy Lorentzen.

Table Of Contents

CHEVROLET *by the numbers*™
1970–1975

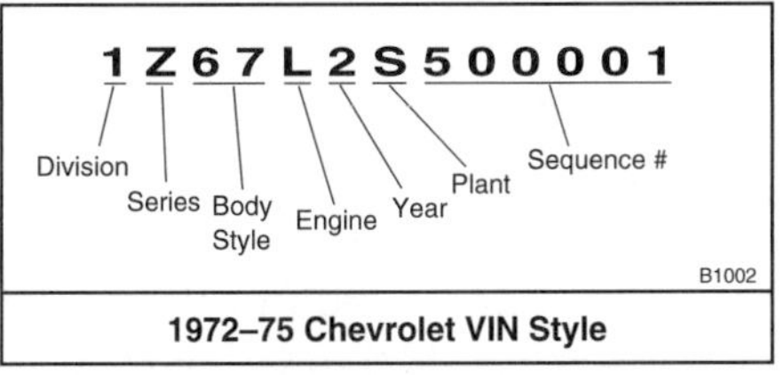

1972–75 Chevrolet VIN Style

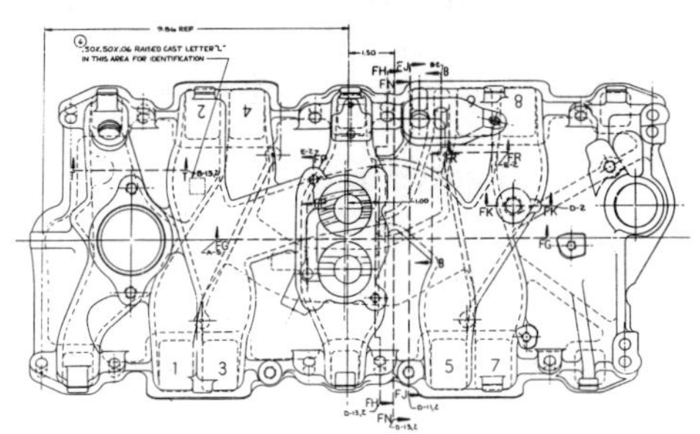

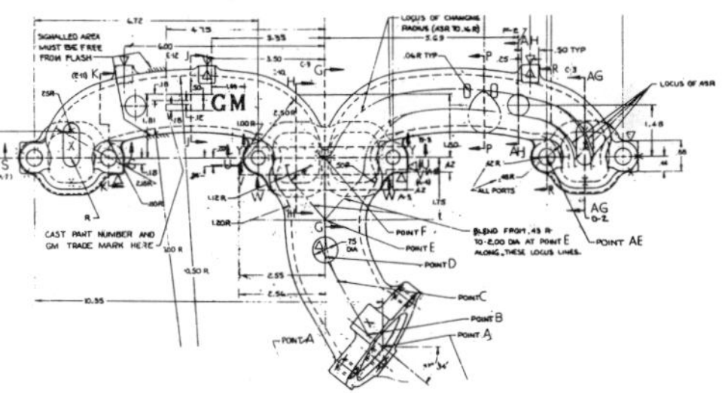

Dedication

I want to dedicate this book to my Lord and Savior, Jesus Christ. Only He could give me the strength, courage and endurance to complete such a task. It is my prayer that everyone who reads this book will come to have an understanding and faith in Him as I have.

I want to thank my wife, Julé, for enduring the many hardships necessary to complete this book series. We have grown stronger, wiser and more considerate through this process more than any other time in our marriage. Julé, I love you.

I also want to thank my publisher, Robert Bentley Publishers, Inc. To David Bull and my editor, John Kittredge, thank you for your professionalism, your courage when I missed deadlines and your understanding heart in the face of sometimes seemingly insurmountable odds. I sincerely appreciate you for making me look like the author I wished I could be.

Finally, I want to thank the many people who shared their time and expertise to make this book project complete. Someone once said that "nobody knows everything" and I can truly testify to that statement. This project would not have been completed if not for all of my friends and acquaintances helping in their own special way. I hope all of you feel as much a part of this book project as I do. It wouldn't have happened without all of you.

Take Care.

Introduction

The author at his desk.

THE ORIGINAL IDEA FOR THIS BOOK was conceived almost twenty years ago, when I first got into the car restoration hobby. As I began to search for parts to restore a 1957 Chevrolet (my first car), I quickly realized that there was no single, comprehensive source of casting information to which I could turn to determine the authenticity of the parts I needed. (By casting information, I mean the series of identification numbers Chevrolet cast into each part. These "casting numbers" are used as the basis for all parts identification in this book.) I have always been a "pack-rat" and had saved thousands of car magazines. From these I gleaned some information, but by and large, I still could not identify most of the parts I needed. I realized I had to create my own parts reference source book.

After years of research, hundreds of phone calls and thousands of conversations with various fellow club members, I developed what came to be known as my "little black book of numbers." This book enabled me to quickly identify parts and their application by their casting numbers. I took this little book wherever I went, many times to the spring and fall swap meets in Carlisle, Pennsylvania. Practically every time I would be looking in my book to identify a part, someone would tap on my shoulder and offer to buy the book; one fellow offered me several hundred dollars.

I couldn't sell the book as I had no copies and the information was irreplaceable, but it did make me think that if these people were that interested, others would be also. I didn't realize, however, that it would be another ten years before the project would start to take shape. In the meantime, I was continually on the lookout to buy any factory information that would help further my quest for casting numbers.

In the beginning of this research process, I located several sets of old documents written by the Automotive Engine Rebuilders Association. From them I began to compile a basic list of casting numbers. I also used years and years of Hemmings Motor News.

Once I had a master parts list, I began to cross-reference this with other engine rebuilder catalogs. As I progressed, I realized that there were potential problems. First, there was the possibility of wrong information and printing typos in my resource material. Also, several of my source lists were geared to making a part applicable for as many years as possible for interchange purposes. Thus, a part could be listed as applicable from 1969 through 1972, when in fact it was *originally* used only in 1969.

Alan's "little black book."

INTRODUCTION

In the spring of 1991, I came to a crossroads. I realized that my methods were not going to give me the accuracy I wanted. I could either give up, or press on to the next level. Because I have a great love for the car hobby, I decided that, above all, I wanted to create a series of books readers would want, need, and enjoy reading while at the same time learning about the identification of drivetrain components. To be able to accomplish this task, I knew that verifiable, documented parts and their history were paramount to the book's goals. To secure this legitimate "paper trail," traceable back to the original sources, it was clear that I had to take the next step and contact General Motors for their records.

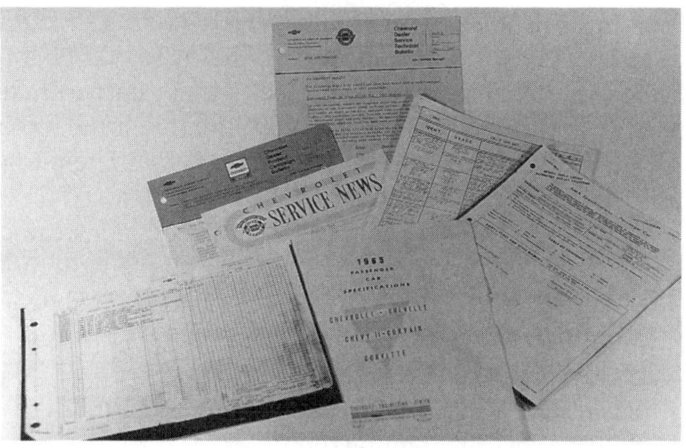

A small sampling of the various reference materials.

There followed several months of letters and phone calls to many of my General Motors contacts, after which I was granted clearance to conduct extensive research in numerous GM divisions. (The GM of today is not the same corporation that existed from 1955 through 1975. GM has been split up several times over the years, creating a giant quagmire of old records in various locations and separate legal departments.) These clearances allowed me to gain invaluable information in the form of original parts blueprints, twenty years of Chevrolet Engineering Specifications, twenty years of Automobile Manufacturer's Association (AMA) Specifications, and numerous original parts lists. I spent months poring over information from several different General Motors divisions, including AC Rochester in Rochester, New York, the GM Powertrain Division in Warren, Michigan, the Tonawanda Engine Plant in Buffalo, New York, the Flint Engine Plant in Flint, Michigan, Delco-Remy in Anderson, Indiana, the Saginaw Final Drive and Forge Division in Saginaw, Michigan, and also the Chevrolet-Pontiac-Canada Group in Sterling Heights, Michigan. I also collected a great deal of information from the Chevrolet Archives in Warren, Michigan, and from the National Automotive History Collection in the Detroit Public Library. Original documents pertaining to Saginaw and Muncie transmissions were obtained directly from the Muncie Transmission plant in Muncie, Indiana.

I spent several weeks in Chevrolet's Central Office Records Retention Area: hundreds of file drawers full of original photos, specifications and engineering data, sitting in a sub-basement, surrounded by a twenty-foot-high woven wire fence and padlocked gates. *Very Restricted*. This area is sealed off to everyone except specific Chevrolet employees or special VIPs. Unfortunately, much of the engineering data from the 1950s that was stored on microfilm in this facility has been destroyed due to Chevrolet's ten-year records retention policy. While this was a major disappointment to me, most of the other records were fortunately still available—thousands of Chevrolet documents which have never left that room. I was allowed to photocopy many of these records, in the process disabling one *HUGE* photocopying machine. Some of these records were so old and brittle that it was necessary to copy them over in longhand to keep from damaging them. Many times I felt as if I were holding Chevrolet's Dead Sea Scrolls in my hands, in my own time-warp, looking down a long corridor of rich Chevrolet history.

In another building several miles from the Chevrolet Tech Center I reviewed hundreds of original parts blueprints, many copies of which are used to illustrate this book. There are no actual blueprints stored at this facility. All original blueprints have been photographed, reduced and placed in aperture card files. I should note that the aperture card files were arranged in such a way that if I had no prior knowledge of the Chevrolet parts system and a listing of casting numbers, it could have taken me years to extrapolate any useful information.

By this time I had numerous questions about original General Motors parts that could only be answered by the Chevrolet engineers who created those parts, but most of the engineers have now retired. My next step was to try to locate these men. Once I did, they graciously spent hours of their own time researching old documents and contributing from their own archives.

I also spent hours talking to experts in the field. These ranged from business owners, to auto shop teachers, to various club, organization and society members. Some of these experts specialized in certain models, while others specialized in certain years. I also used years and years of information that I had collected in the form of Chevrolet Service News Bulletins, original parts books, and Chevrolet Technical Service Bulletins.

My research brought me in to contact with many original equipment manufacturers (OEMs). Many of these OEMs had retained their early parts lists and blueprint material. Once I had fulfilled their clearance requirements, I was able to obtain their documents as well. Among these manufacturers were the Carter Carburetor Division of Federal-Mogul and Kelsey-Hayes Wheel Corp, Romulus, Michigan.

As I pulled all of this information together, I had to do a tremendous amount of cross-referencing and double checking. As I built upon the lists, all of the casting numbers were then verified by at least three or four different sources. The various original blueprints that I obtained serve to identify and verify specific parts and numbers as no other method can. Also, after the individual chapters were completed, they were sent out to various experts to check for accuracy.

The Chevrolet Parts System

To fully understand how I have set this book up, you first must have a basic concept of the Chevrolet Parts System. Although I do not include every step in my explanation, it should familiarize you with the process.

All early Chevrolet parts have a seven-digit part number, for example 3700000. Chevrolet Central Office in Warren, Michigan, controlled the Parts Numbering System and created a large numerical "bank" that each Engineering Group in Chevrolet had access to. All Chief Engineers could "pull" a group of numbers in blocks to assign to a specific assembly under design. If a cylinder head assembly required 40 part numbers, a group of 40 numbers was pulled out of the system and assigned to that engineer for that cylinder head.

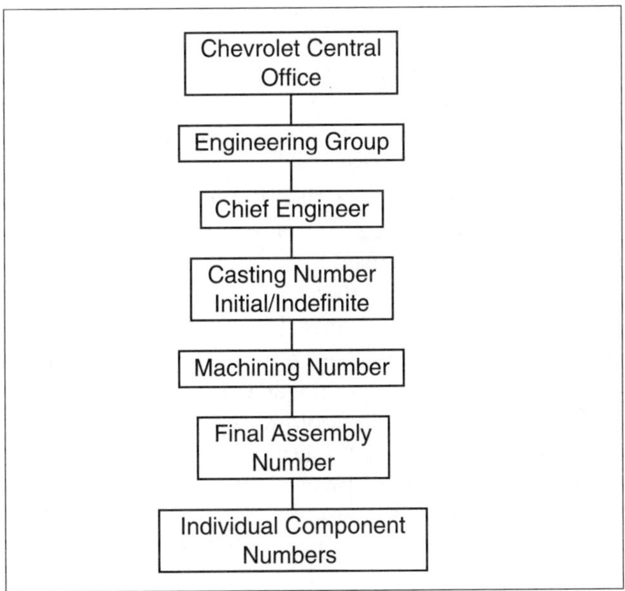

Chevrolet parts numbering system.

In most cases, the first number of that group was the *casting* number (or *identification* number) for that part. This number would stay with the part indefinitely, until the part was superseded by a design change. The next number in the sequence was usually the machine number. This number was assigned to the part of the complete assembly that required a machining process, such as a raw cylinder head casting. The next number in the total sequence would usually be the final assembly number, which contained all of the component parts of the complete assembly. The final numbers that composed the complete assembly would be each individual component, such as valves, guides, springs, etc. Please see the following diagram to understand the sequence of component parts numbering.

This system was not infallible. There are several documented cases where the system was changed slightly or numbers were switched around in the sequence. After all, Chevrolet Motor Division was in the business to sell cars, not classics. GM had specific policies to keep assembly plant lines in motion. They routinely substituted an originally designed part with another part that would serve the same correct function until the original part was again delivered to the plant and reinstated on the assembly line. This is typically how many odd parts end up on totally unrestored vehicles.

Although no complete casting number list has been found in Chevrolet's Archives, casting numbers were tracked by Chevrolet Service and Engineering for changes in design and model usage in both service and production. Both the Chevrolet Technical Service Bulletins (TSBs) and the Chevrolet Service News show these changes. Many times these changes were tied to a specific change-over date and Vehicle Identification Number (VIN). However, Chevrolet Service Parts created a separate set of problems.

Chevrolet Service constantly changed the part numbers offered over their dealership service counters. Example: A new part number 3700001 is issued by the engineering group for a cylinder head in model year 1955. The casting number on this head is 3700000. This cylinder head is used for three model years, and in the process has ten different part numbers assigned to it because it is used for ten different applications with different valve sizes, springs, etc. In model year 1959, Chevrolet Service decides that they can manufacture one *new* cylinder head that will fit all of these applications. They assign it a new part number 3800001. Now, in the 1959 Parts Catalog only one head is shown to cover ten applications, whereas in the 1958 Parts Catalog each application and head had its own number. Since this is a completely new cylinder head it now has a new casting number, too: 3800000.

See the problem here? Chevrolet Service was in business to supply correct parts for repairing Chevrolet vehicles, not to create archives for restoring these cars back to originality. Much information can be taken from old parts books, but keep in mind why they exist. If Chevrolet Service could replace ten parts (and part numbers) with one new part, that's exactly what they did.

INTRODUCTION

Matching Numbers

One of the most misused and misunderstood phrases in the restoration hobby is "numbers matching." Everyone, from those who have large collections of cars to people who have only a vague interest in the hobby, has their own interpretation of what constitutes a numbers matching car. Many hobbyists use the term loosely with no clue to what it actually means.

"Numbers matching" simply means a car which not only appears in original factory condition, but in which all pertinent identification numbers, as well as all casting numbers and dates, are correct for that specific model and pre-date the final assembly date of the car. (The term probably originated in the Corvette restoration hobby. It seems these cars were the first to be restored back to true originality.) It is important to also make the distinction that a car is only original once, period.

There are more and more "manufactured" cars turning up in collectors' hands, cleverly documented to be original numbers matching vehicles. What I mean by "manufactured" is that the car has been rebuilt with correct casting numbers to appear original and to match the documentation to be included in the sale of the car.

To say that this situation is creating a major problem in the hobby is a vast understatement. Thousands of dollars are being invested into many matching number cars which in fact are complete forgeries, built for the primary purpose of selling an incorrect car as a documented original. Many enthusiasts are unsure as to what composes a correct car. Much of the information that has been published to date in this area has been incorrect in several aspects.

Checking A Car

Knowledge is the ultimate weapon in the fight against counterfeit Chevrolet muscle cars. Before you ever set out to acquire or restore any Chevrolet vehicle, become as informed as you can about the specific model you are interested in. This is your best defense to keep from being ripped off. Next, check *all* pertinent identification numbers. The total amount of numbers will vary from year to year, but there are some basic ones.

The first and most important number is the Vehicle Identification Number (VIN). Depending upon what year of Chevrolet you are interested in, the VIN and its plate can tell you many things. The VIN will typically specify the designated engine type, model series, model year, assembly plant and sequence number. When looking at a VIN, also check the rivets or the tackweld attaching it to the body. Are they similar to other unrestored models like this car? Do the rivets show signs of age or do they look new? Does the tag itself look new? VIN styles sometimes changed drastically from year to year, so do your research. Also remember that many secondary VINs were stamped in various body locations through the years. This was done to help law enforcement agencies identify stolen parts and/or cars. Once you start learning these secondary VIN locations, you can feel confident you are becoming more knowledgeable about your specific model.

After you validate the VIN, the next detail you should check is the vehicle trim tag. Trim tags are usually found on the firewall or cowl area of all Chevrolet vehicles. The trim tag contains information concerning the specific model, trim, assembly plant, paint code, and some option information. The *body* build date is also stamped as well. The body build date is very important in that all casting and stamping numbers on the car should *precede* the body build date. There are a few documented cases in which the drivetrain has been installed after a body build date, but this scenario is rare.

One fallacy concerning matching numbers is that if the engine stamping numbers correspond to the VIN, then the car is a matching numbers car and the remainder of the cars identification numbers would be correct and original as well. This is not correct. In today's car restoration hobby, you cannot trust the cars total originality on only the engine block stamping alone.

Get to know what sort of codes and stampings to look for on parts. For example, there are two stampings on an engine block. The first stamping is the engine assembly build date code. The second code was the VIN designation stamping. Check all casting and stamping numbers as well on the block, cylinder heads, intake manifold, exhaust manifolds, distributor, carburetor, and so on. Learn what size typeface and specific coding is correct for your model year. Not all parts were stamped in the same area.

Finally, there is paperwork. Broadcast sheets, build sheets, original invoices, window stickers, bills of sale, and protect-o-plates used to be what the hobby regarded as irrefutable proof that a car was original and was being represented as correct. This is no longer the case. All of these documents can and are being reproduced today. There are even people advertising that they can make the documents look old to replicate original documents. Due to this fact, all documents are now being regarded as false until proven otherwise. This is very unfortunate for the hobby.

How To Use This Book

This brings me to the primary purpose of this book: to acquaint you with the direct correlation of *casting numbers* to the identification of drivetrain parts for the purpose of validating and restoring early Chevrolet vehicles. In a book of this type, the accuracy of each casting number and model-usage listing is very important. There are so many numbers on any given Chevrolet vehicle, it can overwhelm the average enthusiast. I have tried to make this book as easy to use as possible, while maintaining the accuracy needed to set this book apart from other so called "restoration guides."

Casting Number Charts

This book is arranged for two primary purposes. The first is to be able to quickly find a specific casting number or application, whichever is applicable to a reader's needs at the time. All casting number information is in numerical order so you can quickly find a casting number if you only have the part. The casting number is critical because it does not change across model applications. (If there are deviations in the casting number usage, they are noted in the book.) For example, the same engine or transmission used in 1955 on a Corvette and a Passenger car in many cases has the same casting number. Part numbers will only help if the part you are looking for is in the original box. Any part can be put into a box with a rare part number on it, but the casting number will always be on the part. You won't find many 30 year old drivetrain parts still in the original box. The casting number is always the number you want to refer to when checking parts at a swap meet or on a car you intend to buy.

The second purpose is to allow you to quickly find a model year application heading and efficiently find whatever model year and car type you have, while cross referencing back to the casting number lists. Included in the back of this book is a page on which you can fill in all pertinent information about your car so you can turn to that one page for quick reference while searching for parts.

Model Identification

The table below is a breakdown of Chevrolet passenger car model lines and body styles in those model lines. Please note that Chevrolet created new terminology in 1970 with alphanumeric model designations (A body, etc.), but models and body style categories remained the same.

Model Year

It is very important to understand the difference between the calendar year and the model year for a given car. A calendar year is just that, from January 1 through December 31. The model year is the period of time a Chevrolet model was produced and available to the general public. This is also sometimes called the production year. This period usually ran from August through June of the following calendar year. For example, production for 1965 models actually started in August 1964. Mid-year changes usually occurred around January or February.

All charts in this book reflect dating by the model year, not the calendar year. Also note that for a car built early in a model year, many parts correct for that car would be dated from the previous calendar year.

Date Coding

Almost all Chevrolet parts have some kind of date coding cast or stamped into the part. Date codes, contrary to current popular belief, were not used to make today's restorations easier. Chevrolet needed a way to track engineering and production changes, relative to model usage. Date codes on parts allowed changes to be documented and recorded. Many of the references in

1970 Through 1975 Model Identification

1970		1971		1972		1973		1974		1975	
Model	**Body Style**	**Model**	**Body Style**	**Model**	**Body Style**	**Model**	**Body Style**	**Model**	**Body Style**	**Model**	**Body Style**
B Body	Biscayne Bel Air Caprice Impala Impala Custom Brookwood Townsman Kingswood Kingswood Estate	*Passenger (B Body)*	Biscayne Bel Air Caprice Impala Impala Custom Brookwood Townsman Kingswood Kingswood Estate	*Passenger (B Body)*	Biscayne Bel Air Caprice Impala Impala Custom Brookwood Townsman Kingswood Kingswood Estate	*B Body*	Bel Air Caprice Caprice Estate Impala	*B Body*	Bel Air Caprice Caprice Estate Impala	*B Body*	Bel Air Caprice Caprice Estate Impala
Corvette	Sting Ray	*Corvette*	Sting Ray	*Corvette*	Sting Ray	*Y Body*	Corvette	*Y Body*	Corvette	*Y Body*	Corvette
X Body	Nova	*Nova (X Body)*	Nova Ventura II	*Nova (X Body)*	Nova Ventura II	*X Body*	Nova Nova Custom	*X Body*	Nova Nova Custom	*X Body*	Nova Nova Custom
A Body	Chevelle Malibu Monte Carlo El Camino El Camino Custom Nomad Greenbrier Concours	*Chevelle (A Body)*	Chevelle Malibu Monte Carlo El Camino El Camino Custom Nomad Greenbrier Concours	*Chevelle (A Body)*	Chevelle Malibu Monte Carlo El Camino El Camino Custom Nomad Greenbrier Concours	*A Body*	Deluxe Malibu Malibu Estate Monte Carlo S Laguna Laguna Estate El Camino El Camino Custom	*A Body*	Malibu Malibu Classic Malibu Estate Monte Carlo S Laguna El Camino El Camino Classic	*A Body*	Malibu Malibu Classic Malibu Estate Monte Carlo S Laguna El Camino El Camino Classic
Camaro	Standard	*Camaro* (F Body)	Standard	*Camaro (F Body)*	Standard	*F Body*	Camaro Camaro LT	*F Body*	Camaro Camaro LT	*F Body*	Camaro Camaro LT

Chevrolet Technical Service Bulletins (TSBs) and *Chevrolet Service News* to document parts changes were made by build date or casting date.

Date Code Chart

Part	Code Type	Month Code Range	Location
Block*	Casting	A to L	Rear/side of block
Heads	Casting	A to L	Top of head, between rocker studs
Carburetor Carter Holley Rochester	 Stamped Stamped Stamped	 A to M 1 to 0, A, B A to M	 Tag or base Air horn Tag or body
Intake Manifold	Casting	A to L	Top/bottom
Exhaust Manifold	Casting	A to L	Front/back
Water pump	Casting	A to L	Front face
Distributor	Stamped	A to L	Tag or base
Alternator	Stamped	A to L	Riveted tag, or housing
Transmission Saginaw/Muncie Muncie 4-speed Borg Warner	 Casting See text Casting	 A to L A to L A to L	Maincase, extension housing, or sidecover
Rear Axle	Casting	A to L	Center sec.
Wheels	Stamped	01 to 12	Rim at valve stem
*Some documented blocks have been found with a December "M" month code.			

There are two types of date coding. The first is referred to as the casting date code, and is the most common. On most parts such as blocks, cylinder heads, intakes and exhaust manifolds, this date code represents the *calendar* date of part *manufacture*.

The second type of date code is found on distributors and alternators. This code is stamped into the part and represents the *calendar* date of final *assembly*, since the entire part is made of many small parts which are not dated.

Many date codes do not use the letter "I" because it is easily confused with the number "1." As a result, the December code would be "M" instead of "L."

Conclusion

As you can see, this book is quite different from any other ever offered to the Chevrolet restoration hobby. What makes this book different from similar books, parts books, and interchange manuals is that all of these books fall short in incorporating the correct, verifiable information that is paramount to this project. A generic *interchange* manual can rely only on what the manufacturer originally supplied to them for information. The interchange manuals have no hands-on experience, no access to original parts blueprints, and no references who are experts in their respective automotive field. Many other books have not done the proper research to tie all of these factors together. Many have been rushed to the market to capitalize on a market that needs this information, without regard to authenticity and factory produced proof to back their efforts. All of the research that was done to produce this book relates directly back to Chevrolet's original records.

You will find this book to be very beneficial for a number of reasons. First of all, it provides the Chevrolet restorer with one comprehensive source to turn to in order to restore a car with the correct original drivetrain parts. Second, this book will help clarify the application of parts you may already have on hand. With this book you can discover parts that are correct for your car, but were manufactured for other Chevrolet models as well. For example, the owner of a Chevrolet Impala, which is possibly not as "collectible" in many cases as a Corvette, will find that he can use many Corvette parts to correctly restore his car. A Corvette owner, by using this book, now has a new parts "avenue" that could save time and money over normal Corvette restoration circles. Finally, I hope this book helps put a stop to misrepresentation in the sale of parts.

I want to express my sincere thanks to all of those GM employees who assisted me in gaining access to all Chevrolet restricted facilities. The actual worth of the original documentation obtained from these facilities will be immeasurable to the Chevrolet restoration hobby for decades to come.

I hope this series of books will help preserve the rich history of Chevrolet, by forever documenting the chronological and numerical history of drivetrain parts of these great cars for generations of car enthusiasts to come.

Chapter 1
Vehicle Identification

1. Introduction

Just as there are numbers that identify each component installed on a vehicle, there are numbers that relate to the whole vehicle to identify such things as model, engine, accessories and trim. These numbers are the Vehicle Identification Number (VIN), Trim Tag numbers, and Model Identification number.

Fig. 1-1. Typical trim tag locations (arrows) on all models except Corvette. Model identification number is printed on trim tag. On 1970 through 1971 models, the first five digits of the VIN are also the model identification number.

2. Vehicle Identification Number (VIN)

The Vehicle Identification Number (VIN) is probably the most important number on a car. If you do not know how to decode a VIN number on a particular Chevrolet, you will be unable to verify other components or numbers. The table below gives VIN locations.

1970 Through 1975 VIN Location

Model	Location
All except Corvette	Top of instrument panel, driver's side. Visible through windshield
Corvette	Inner vertical surface of driver's side windshield pillar, visible through windshield

2.1 1970 Through 1971 VIN Decoding

All 1970 through 1971 Chevrolet passenger cars including Corvette use a VIN consisting of 13 alpha-numeric characters. See Fig. 1-2.

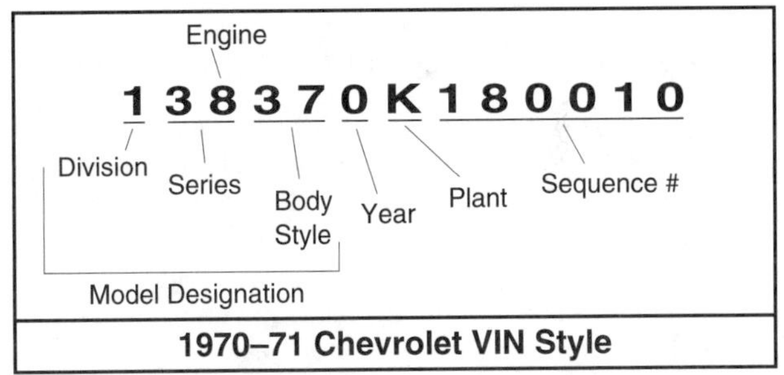

Fig. 1-2. Typical VIN for 1970 through 1971 Chevrolet models. See text for how to decode digits.

The 1st digit of the VIN signifies the General Motors Division for that particular car. In Chevrolet vehicles this digit will always be a "1."

The 2nd and 3rd digits indicate the vehicle series as well as the engine for the car. If the 3rd digit of the VIN is odd (1, 3, 5, 7) then the original engine would have been a 4- or 6-cylinder. If the 3rd digit is even (2, 4, 6, 8) then the original engine was a V-8.

The 4th and 5th digits indicate the body style for the car. For example if it is a 2-door sport coupe or a 2-door sedan.

> NOTE—
> On 1970 through 1971 models, the first five digits of the VIN also comprise the Model Identification number. For more information, see **10. Model Identification** in this chapter.

The 6th digit signifies the model year of that particular car. This number only specifies the model year, not the calendar year in which the car was actually built. For example, all early 1970 model year vehicles built prior to January 1, 1970, would still have the digit "0" on the VIN plate.

1970–1971 Model Year Code

Number Code	Model Year
0	1970
1	1971

The 7th digit, a letter, signifies the final assembly plant where the car was manufactured.

The final 6 digits represent the continuous sequence number of that specific vehicle at each assembly plant.

Some 1970–1971 VIN tags also include the dealer delivery date (DD) in the upper right hand corner.

2.2 Canadian VIN System

There were hundreds of thousands Chevrolet vehicles built in Canada from 1970–1975, and many of these cars were imported into the United States over the years. Although the Chevrolet model lines were virtually identical, the VIN numbering systems were not. I have decided to show the Canadian VIN numbering system here. The table below lists the cars built both in Canada and the United States.

Model Year	Model Line	Plant
1970–75	Passenger car	Ste. Therese (aft. 1966)
1970–75	Chevelle	Oshawa

Example:

1. VIN 1366701100001 = 1970 Chevelle 2-door Convertible (Oshawa)
2. VIN 1644702100001 = 1970 Chevrolet 2-door Custom Coupe (Ste. Therese)

The first 5 digits are the model identification number (Chevrolet division number is first digit). The next digit is the model year designation. The next digit is the final assembly plant code (1 = Oshawa, or 2 = Ste. Therese). The last 6 digits are the sequential number of that particular car.

Vehicle Identification and Accessory Codes

I would like to take the opportunity here to express some of my thoughts concerning the history and future of the restoration hobby. For as long as I can remember I have had an infatuation with the automobile. I started drawing and playing with cars at a very early age. My love for the automobile continued throughout my adolescence and into my adulthood. I bought my first car at the age of 15. After several nice cars, including a 1970 SS Monte Carlo and a couple of 1969 Camaros, I began to go to swap meets and car shows. I took my extra parts to sell or trade. Finally, after several years of buying and selling, I decided to start my own full-time business and began traveling the country, mostly in the Super Chevy Show circuit.

One conclusion that I have reached over the years is that the hobby that existed when I began is no longer. In the beginning it was primarily a used parts business. If your car needed a new interior, you searched junk yards and Hemming's Motor News until you found a good used interior. Soon, however, the hobby began to turn into a "restoration" market as more and more entrepreneurs saw the opportunity to make money. Don't get me wrong, all of us have benefitted from the restoration market in some way, myself included. However, the restoration market has now grown so strong that many restorers believe any part can be regarded as a reproduction part. This is where I beg to differ.

As I compiled this book over the last few years, I often pondered the thought of how I would discuss the data plates and the accessory codes on them. I spent hundreds of hours researching accessory codes and almost as many hours talking to most of the major car clubs about their own data plate projects. As I compiled all of this information and came up with new and exciting revelations on the accessory codes, one thought kept coming to me: I was creating the most comprehensive Chevrolet restoration book available but, if I included the accessory codes, it could become the "Complete Guide on How to Build a Bogus Car."

As the time grew closer for the deadline of this book, I knew I had to make a decision. I could publish all of the accessory codes and be known for how smart I was, or I could keep the information and devise a way to verify cars at a later date. I have decided to keep the information. Let me explain further.

I believe that the data plate should not be regarded as a reproduction part. A proper restoration is one which has been done to match the codes on the plate, not one in which the plate has been altered to match the restored car. Unfortunately, there are people out there who will supply anyone with a product, no matter what the cost to the rest of the hobby. In my opinion, the data plate is the last positive identifier of the originality of any car.

Other pieces of documentation, such as protect-o-plates, build sheets, order forms, or window stickers, do not dis-

continued

2.3 1972 Through 1975 VIN Decoding

All 1972 through 1975 Chevrolet vehicles use a VIN containing 13 alpha-numeric characters. This is the same as 1970–75 vehicles, however, the 1972 and later VIN changed to include a letter code for the model series and a letter code for engine usage. See 1-1.

The 1st digit in the VIN represents the General Motors division for that particular car. In Chevrolet vehicles the division number will always be a "1."

The 2nd digit represents the vehicle series. The digit is always a letter code.

The 3rd and 4th digits represent the body style of the car. These digits will always be numbers.

The 5th digit is the engine designation. Note that the 1972 model year was the first year a VIN number could validate a specific engine to the car model.

The 6th digit is the model year designation. This number only specifies the model year, not the calendar year in which the car was actually built. For example, all early 1972 model year vehicles built prior to January 1, 1972, would still have the digit "2" on the VIN plate.

The 7th digit, a letter, designates the final assembly plant where the car was manufactured.

The last six digits of the VIN are the build sequence number of that particular car from that assembly plant.

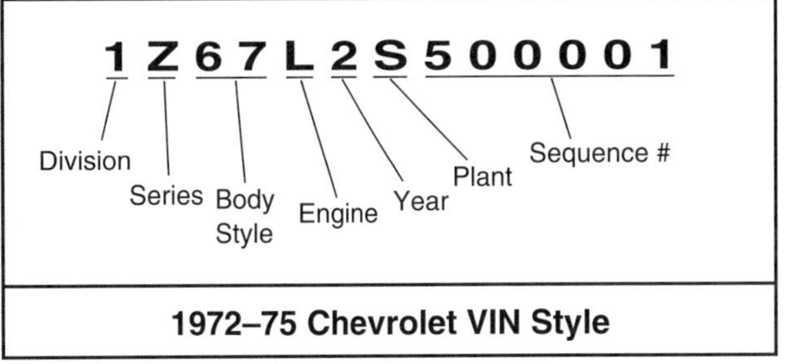

Fig. 1-3. Typical VIN for 1972 through 1975 Chevrolet models. See text for how to decode digits.

1972–1975 Model Year Code

Number Code	Model Year
2	1972
3	1973
4	1974
5	1975

close the unknown codes that the data plate contains. These other pieces of documentation have been reproduced because the information that is on them is available. In the past, if a car still had its original protect-o-plate, it was worth more. Now, however, since reproductions are available, any car can have a protect-o-plate. Does this make the car with an original protect-o-plate worth more or less? I believe that it makes it worth less because it brings in an element of doubt as to the car's originality. In my eyes, a correct original car should be able to stand on its own merit, without a protect-o-plate or window sticker.

If the data plate had other basic information like brake adjustment instructions, rather than model, paint, trim and option codes, it would be reproduced and sold for probably $20.00. What makes the same plate with different information worth $250.00 to $300.00? Simple. The increased value that the information on the tag adds to the car.

For example, when you look at a car that has air conditioning, you can clearly see that it has air conditioning. The same holds true for a car that is painted red, you can see it is a red car. This extra equipment obviously adds value to the car. When the *codes* on the data plate agree that it is red and has air conditioning, that also adds value to the car. Not only because the numbers and letters on the data plate happen to match the options on the car, it is also because of what the presence of those codes implies: that the car was originally ordered with those options. As long as the tag is the original to that car, those codes can and should be used to document and verify the originality of the car. In this case, they verify the increased value of the car. But in the case of a reproduction data plate, that increased value is false. What do you call it? You can pick the word yourself.

Do you now understand why a restamped data plate is worth $250.00? The data plate accessory codes are not known to the general public. In my research I have found that some codes were specific to certain assembly plants. Many assembly plants used several types of plates over a period of several years while other plants used just one. If the *correct* codes and specific details were furnished in this book, all of the cars out there would become "maybes." Are you confident enough to trust the data plate? I have run across several "restored" cars with *reproduction* data plates that have codes so wrong they stand out like a sore thumb to a knowledgeable person. Until the hobby decides that this is wrong and learns to police itself, I cannot in good faith publish the accessory codes.

(Note: I would like to especially thank Verne Frantz, Jr., President of the Jersey Late Greats, Inc., for his help in this area. This club is currently offering a decoding service for 1958–64 full-size Chevrolets and can be contacted at the address in the back of this book. I would like to establish a similar national data plate validation service for all 1955–75 Chevrolet cars. If you have an interest in this type of service, please contact me through my publisher.)

1970 VIN CHARTS

3. 1970 VIN CODE CHARTS

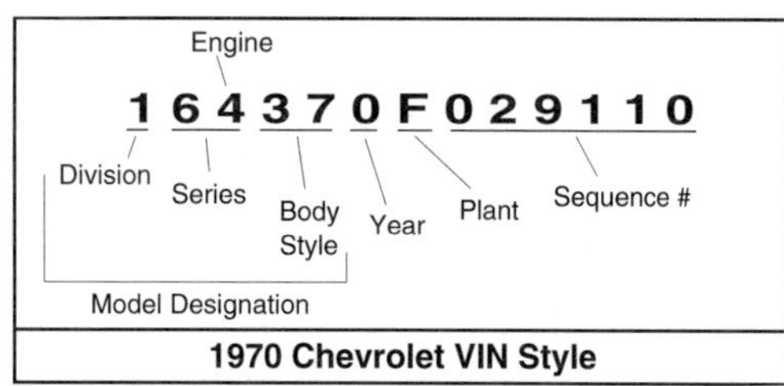

1970 Chevrolet VIN Style

Example: 1970 Impala VIN 1 64 37 0 F 029110

- 1 = Division: Chevrolet
- 64 = Series: Impala, V-8 engine (4 is even number)
- 37 = Body Style: 2-door sport coupe
- 0 = Model Year: 1970
- F = Final Assembly Plant: Flint, Michigan
- 029110 = Sequence Number: 29,110th car built at that plant in that year

1970 VIN Model Series Codes

Series Code	Series
11	Nova, 4 cyl
13	Nova, 6 cyl
14	Nova, 8 cyl
23	Camaro, 6 cyl
24	Camaro, 8 cyl
31	Nomad, 6 cyl
32	Nomad, 8 cyl
33	Chevelle / El Camino, 6 cyl
34	Chevelle / Greenbrier / El Camino, 8 cyl
35	Concours / Malibu / El Camino, 6 cyl
36	Concours / Malibu / El Camino, 8 cyl
38	Concours / Monte Carlo, 8 cyl
53	Biscayne, 6 cyl
54	Biscayne / Brookwood, 8 cyl
55	Bel Air, 6 cyl
56	Bel Air / Townsman, 8 cyl
63	Impala, 6 cyl
64	Impala / Kingswood, 8 cyl
66	Caprice / Kingswood, 8 cyl
94	Stingray

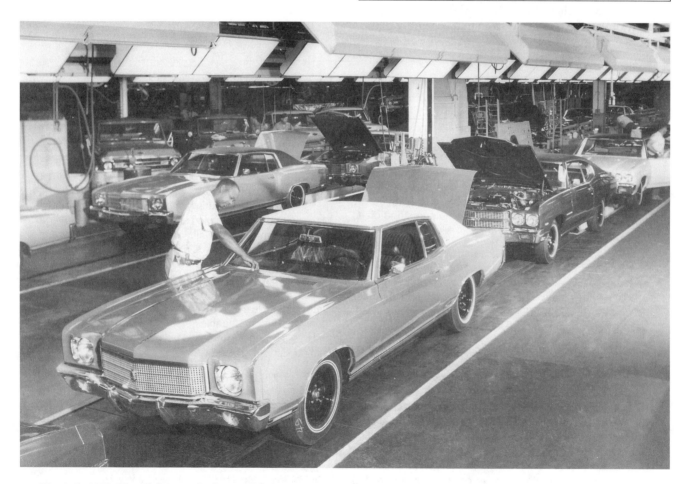

Fig. 1-4. 1970 Chevelle/Monte Carlo assembly line. Note that models came down the line in intermittent order.

1970 VIN CHARTS

1970 VIN Body Style Codes

Body Style Code	Body Style
11	2-door Sedan
27	2-door Sport Coupe
36	4-door Station Wagon, Six Passenger
37	2-door Sport Coupe
39	4-door Sport Sedan
46	4-door Station Wagon, Nine Passenger
47	2-door Sport/Custom Coupe
57	2-door Sport Coupe
67	2-door Convertible
69	4-door Sedan
80	2-door Sedan Pickup
87	2-door Sport Coupe

Fig. 1-5. ***Top****: 1970-1/2 Z28 Rally Sport Camaro.* ***Bottom:*** *1970 Chevelle SS 396.*

1970 VIN Assembly Plant Codes

Letter Code	Assembly Plant	Body Type*
A	Atlanta, Georgia	4
B	Baltimore, Maryland	4**, 6
C	Southgate, California	1
D	Atlanta, Georgia (Doraville)	1
F***	Flint, Michigan	4**, 6
J	Janesville, Wisconsin	1
K***	Kansas City, Missouri	4
L***	Los Angeles, California	4**, 5 (aft. Jan), 6
N	Norwood, Ohio	5
R***	Arlington, Texas	1 (bef. Dec.) 4 (aft. Dec.)
S	St. Louis, Missouri	1,2
T	Tarrytown, New York	1
U	Lordstown, Ohio	1
W	Willow Run, Michigan	3
Y	Wilmington, Delaware	1
1	Oshawa, Canada	1,4
2	St. Therese, Canada	1

*1 = Passenger car, 2 = Corvette, 3 = Nova, 4 = Chevelle, 5 = Camaro, 6 = Monte Carlo
**Includes El Camino production
***Designation change from 1969

1970 VIN Begin Sequence Numbers

Model	Begin Sequence Number	Plant
Chevy II	100001	Willow Run
Camaro	500001	Los Angeles, Norwood
Chevelle/ Monte Carlo	100001 100001 (Dec. 1969) 200001 (Jan. 1970)	All except Arlington Arlington
Chev/Pass	100001	All
Corvette	400001	St. Louis

Fig. 1-6. 1970 Corvette Coupe.

4. 1971 VIN CODE CHARTS

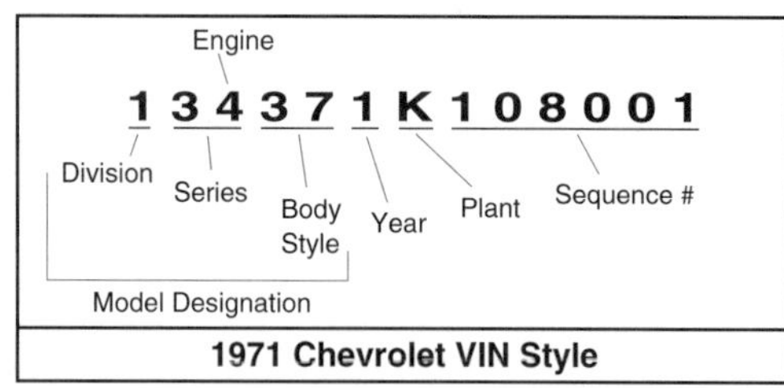

Example: 1971 Chevelle VIN 1 34 37 1 K 108001

- 1 = Division: Chevrolet
- 34 = Series: Chevelle, V-8 engine (8 is even number)
- 37 = Body Style: 2-door sport coupe
- 1 = Model Year: 1971
- K = Final Assembly Plant: Kansas City, Missouri
- 108001 = Sequence Number: 8001st Chevelle built at Kansas City in that model year

> NOTE—
> In the 1971 model year all serial sequence numbers returned to the 100001 start number in all plants excluding the Camaro. Chevrolet dictated that all sequence numbers would be separate if more than one model were built in one assembly plant. Also, Canadian production began with 100001 on all models except the Chevelle/Monte Carlo models, which started at a 500001 sequence number.

1971 VIN Model Series Codes

Series Code	Series
13	Nova / Ventura II / Acadian, 6 cyl
14	Nova / Ventura II / Acadian, 8 cyl
23	Camaro, 6 cyl
24	Camaro, 8 cyl
31	Nomad, 6 cyl
32	Nomad, 8 cyl
33	Chevelle / Greenbrier / El Camino / Sprint, 6 cyl
34	Chevelle / Greenbrier / El Camino / Sprint, 8 cyl
35	Concours / Malibu / El Camino / Sprint, 6 cyl
36	Concours / Malibu / El Camino / Sprint, 8 cyl
38	Concours / Monte Carlo, 8 cyl
53	Biscayne, 6 cyl
54	Biscayne / Brookwood, 8 cyl
55	Bel Air, 6 cyl
56	Bel Air / Townsman, 8 cyl
63	Impala, 6 cyl
64	Impala / Kingswood, 8 cyl
66	Caprice / Kingswood, 8 cyl
94	Stingray

*Fig. 1-7. **Top right**: 1971 Monte Carlo. Note square parking lamps in bumper. **Bottom**: 1971 Chevelle SS, with split parking lens and "Trans Am" Rally wheels.*

1971 VIN CHARTS

1971 VIN Body Style Codes

Body Style Code	Body Style
27	2-door Sport Coupe
35	4-door Station Wagon, Six Passenger
36	4-door Station Wagon, Six Passenger
37	2-door Sport Coupe
39	4-door Sport Sedan
45	4-door Station Wagon, Nine Passenger
46	4-door Station Wagon, Nine Passenger
47	2-door Sport/Custom Coupe
57	2-door Sport Coupe
67	2-door Convertible
69	4-door Sedan
80	2-door Sedan Pickup
87	2-door Sport Coupe

Fig. 1-8. 1971 Rally Nova, with new style Rally wheel and special striping.

1971 VIN Assembly Plant Codes

Letter Code	Assembly Plant	Body Type*
B	Baltimore, Maryland	4**, 6, 7
C	Southgate, California	1
D	Atlanta, Georgia (Doraville)	1
J	Janesville, Wisconsin	1
K***	Kansas City, Missouri	4**, 6, 7
L	Los Angeles, California	4*, 5, 6, 7
N	Norwood, Ohio	5
R	Arlington, Texas	4
S	St. Louis, Missouri	1,2
T	Tarrytown, New York	1
W	Willow Run, Michigan	3
Y	Wilmington, Delaware	1
1	Oshawa, Canada	1,4, 6

*1 = Passenger car, 2 = Corvette, 3 = Nova, 4 = Chevelle, 5 = Camaro, 6 = Monte Carlo
**Includes El Camino production
***Designation change from 1970

1971 VIN Begin Sequence Numbers

Model	Begin Sequence Number	Plant
Chevy II	100001	Willow Run
Camaro	500001	Los Angeles, Norwood
Chevelle, Monte Carlo	100001	All except Oshawa
	500001	Oshawa
Chev/Pass	100001	All
Corvette	100001	St. Louis

Fig. 1-9. 1971 Impala convertible.

1972 VIN CHARTS

5. 1972 VIN CODE CHARTS

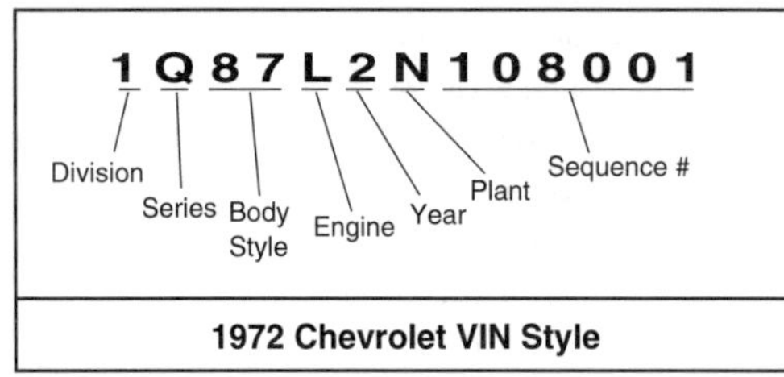

Example:

- 1 = Division: Chevrolet
- Q = Series: Camaro
- 87 = Body Style: Sport Coupe/Camaro
- L = Engine: 350/255HP
- 2 = Model Year: 1972
- N = Assembly Plant: Norwood
- 108001 = Sequence number: 8001st Camaro built at Norwood in that model year

1972 VIN Model Series Codes

Code	Model Series
B	Chevelle Nomad Wagon
C	Chevelle & El Camino/GMC Sprint
D	Malibu & Custom El Camino/GMC Sprint
H	Monte Carlo & Concours Station Wagon
K	Biscayne & Brookwood Station Wagon
L	Belair & Townsman Station Wagon
M	Impala & Kingswood Station Wagon
N	Caprice & Kingswood Estate Station Wagon
Q	Camaro
X	Nova
Z	Corvette

Fig. 1-10. *1972 Corvette Stingray 454 Coupe.*

1972 VIN CHARTS

1972 VIN Body Style Codes

Code	Body Style
27	Sport Coupe/Nova
35	Station Wagon/Chevrolet (2 seat)
36	Station Wagon/Chevelle (2 seat)
37	Sport Coupe/Corvette
39	4-door Sport Sedan/ Chevrolet, Chevelle
45	Station Wagon/Chevrolet (3 seat)
46	Station Wagon/Chevelle (3 seat)
47	Sport Coupe/Chevrolet
57	Sport Coupe/Chevrolet, Monte Carlo
67	Convertible/Chevrolet, Corvette Chevelle
69	4-door Sedan/Chevrolet, Nova, Chevelle
80	Pick-Up Delivery/El Camino, Sprint
87	Sport Coupe/Camaro

1972 VIN Engine Codes

Code	Cubic Inches	Type	Carburetor	Net HP
B	140	L4	1BBL / 2BBL	80 / 93
D	250	L6	1BBL	110
F	307	V-8	2BBL	130
H	350	V-8	2BBL	165
J	350	V-8	4BBL	175
K	350	V-8	4BBL	200
L	350	V-8	4BBL	255
R	400	V-8	2BBL	170
U	402	V-8	4BBL	240
V	454	V-8	4BBL	230
W	454	V-8	4BBL	270

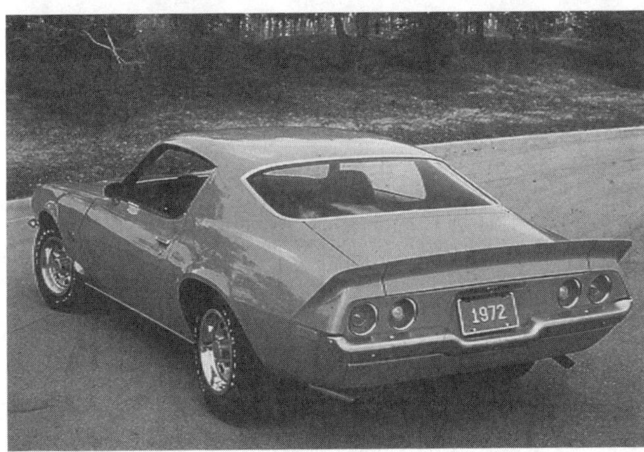

Fig. 1-11. 1972 Camaro SS.

1972 VIN Assembly Plant Codes

Letter Code	Assembly Plant	Body Type*
B	Baltimore, Maryland	4**, 6, 7
C	Southgate, California	1
D	Atlanta, Georgia (Doraville)	1
J	Janesville, Wisconsin	1
K	Kansas City, Missouri	4**, 6, 7
L***	Los Angeles, California	3, 4**, 6, 7
N***	Norwood, Ohio	5, 3 (3 after Feb)
R	Arlington, Texas	4
S	St. Louis, Missouri	1,2
T	Tarrytown, New York	1
W	Willow Run, Michigan	3
Y	Wilmington, Delaware	1
1***	Oshawa, Canada	1, 4**, 6

*1= Passenger car, 2 = Corvette, 3 = Nova, 4 = Chevelle, 5 = Camaro, 6 = Monte Carlo, 7 = GMC Sprint
**Includes El Camino production
***Designation change from 1971

1972 VIN Begin Sequence Numbers

Model	Begin Sequence Number	Plant
Chev/Pass	100001	All
Corvette	500001	St. Louis
Nova	100001	Los Angeles, Willow Run
	300001 (Feb. 1972)	Norwood
Chevelle, Monte Carlo	500001	All
Camaro	100001	Norwood

*Fig. 1-12. **Top:** 1972 Caprice Coupe. **Bottom:** 1972 Monte Carlo.*

1973 VIN CHARTS

6. 1973 VIN CODE CHARTS

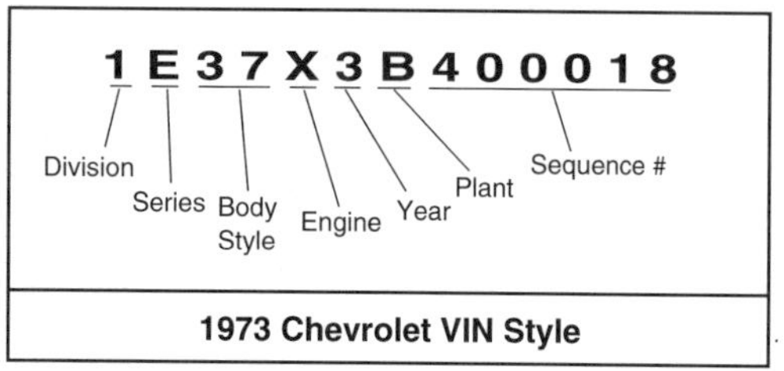

Example:

- 1 = Division: Chevrolet
- E = Series: Chevelle Laguna
- 37 = Body Style: 2-door Sport Coupe
- X = Engine: 454/215HP
- 3 = Model Year: 1973
- B = Assembly Plant: Baltimore
- 400018 = Sequence number: 18th Chevelle built at Baltimore in that model year

NOTE—
Sometime between VIN sequence number 407497 and 408746 the type size was enlarged on 1973 Corvette VIN plates. This type size was carried through the 1975 model year.

1973 VIN Model Series Codes

Code	Model Series
C	Chevelle Deluxe, El Camino/GMC Sprint
D	Chevelle Malibu, El Camino Custom & Sprint
E	Chevelle Laguna
G	Chevelle Malibu Estate Station Wagon
H	Chevelle Laguna Estate Station Wagon, Monte Carlo
K	Belair
L	Impala
N	Caprice Classic and Estate Station Wagon
Q	Camaro
S	Camaro Type LT
X	Nova
Y	Nova Custom
Z	Corvette

Fig. 1-14. 1973 Malibu, with new body style

Fig. 1-13. 1973 Caprice Classic 454.

1973 VIN CHARTS

1973 VIN Body Style Codes

Code	Body Style
17	2-door Hatchback Coupe/Nova
27	2-door Coupe/Nova
29	4-door Sport Sedan/Chevelle
35	4-door Station Wagon, 2 seat/Chev., Chevelle
37	2-door Sport Coupe/Corvette, Chevelle
39	4-door Sport Sedan/Chevelle
45	4-door Station Wagon, 3 seat/Chevrolet
47	2-door Custom Coupe/Chevrolet
57	2-door Sport Coupe/Chevrolet, Monte Carlo
67	2-door Convertible/Chevrolet, Corvette
69	4-door Sedan/Chevrolet, Nova
80	2-door Pick-Up Delivery/El Camino, Sprint
87	2-door Sport Coupe/Camaro

1973 VIN Engine Codes

Code	Cubic Inches	Type	Carburetor	Net HP
A	140	L4	1BBL	72
B	140	L4	2BBL	85
C*	250	L6	1BBL	95
D	250	L6	1BBL	100
F	307	V-8	2BBL	115
H	350	V-8	2BBL	145
J	350	V-8	4BBL	190
K	350	V-8	4BBL	175
R	400	V-8	2BBL	150
T	350	V-8	4BBL	245 (Z28) 250 (L82)
X	454	V-8	4BBL	215
Y	454	V-8	4BBL	245
Z	454	V-8	4BBL	270

*low compression export

1973 VIN Assembly Plant Codes

Letter Code	Assembly Plant	Body Type*
B	Baltimore, Maryland	4**, 6, 7
C	Southgate, California	1
D	Atlanta, Georgia (Doraville)	1
J	Janesville, Wisconsin	1
K	Kansas City, Missouri	4**, 6, 7
L***	Los Angeles, California	3
N***	Norwood, Ohio	5 (Aft. 10/72)
R***	Arlington, Texas	4**, 6
S	St. Louis, Missouri	1,2
T	Tarrytown, New York	1
W	Willow Run, Michigan	3
Y	Wilmington, Delaware	1
Z	Fremont, California	4**, 6, 7
1***	Oshawa, Canada	1, 4**, 6

*1= Passenger car, 2 = Corvette, 3 = Nova, 4 = Chevelle, 5 = Camaro, 6 = Monte Carlo, 7 = GMC Sprint
**Includes El Camino production ***Designation change from 1972
Note: In 1973, all final assembly plants producing Chevelles also produced Monte Carlos.

1973 VIN Build Sequence Numbers

Model	Begin Sequence Number	Plant
Chev/Pass	100001	All
	800001*	Doraville
	900001**	Southgate
Corvette	400001	St. Louis
Nova	100001	Los Angeles, Willow Run
Chevelle, Monte Carlo	400001	All except Oshawa
Chevelle	400001	Oshawa
Monte Carlo	600001 (after Feb. 1973)	Oshawa
Camaro	100001 (after Oct. 1972)	Norwood

**Indicates special run of 229 cars built at Southgate plant with catalytic converter, from April, 1973 through June, 1973

Fig. 1-15. 1973 Nova hatchback coupe.

1974 VIN CHARTS

7. 1974 VIN CODE CHARTS

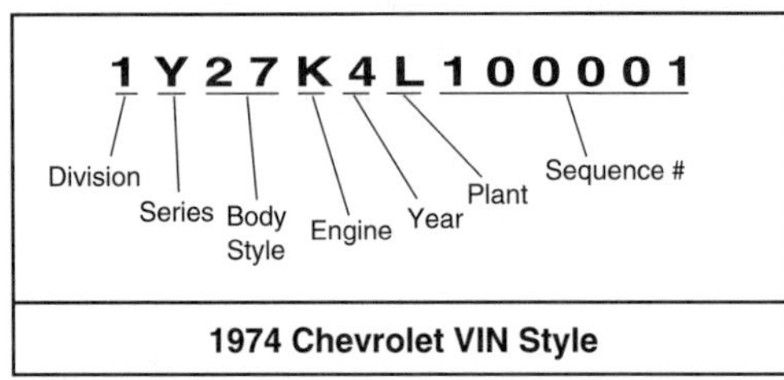

Example:

- 1 = Division: Chevrolet
- Y = Series: Nova Custom
- 27 = Body Style: 2-door Coupe
- K = Engine: 350/185HP
- 4 = Model Year: 1974
- L = Assembly Plant: Los Angeles
- 100001 = Sequence number: 1st Nova built at Los Angeles in that model year

1974 VIN Model Series Codes

Code	Model Series
C	Chevelle Malibu, El Camino
D	Chevelle Malibu Classic, El Camino Classic
E	Chevelle Laguna
G	Chevelle Malibu Classic Estate Wagon
H	Monte Carlo
K	Belair
L	Impala
N	Caprice Classic, Caprice Estate Wagon
Q	Camaro
S	Camaro Type LT
X	Nova
Y	Nova Custom
Z	Corvette

Fig. 1-17. *1974 Chevelle Laguna SS.*

Fig. 1-16. *1974 Camaro Z28.*

1974 VIN CHARTS

1974 VIN Body Style Codes

Code	Body Style
17	2-door Hatchback Coupe/Nova
27	2-door Coupe/Nova
29	4-door Sport Sedan/Chevelle
35	4-door Station Wagon, 2 seat/Chevrolet, Chevelle)
37	2-door Sport Coupe/Corvette, Chevelle
39	4-door Sport Sedan/Chevelle
45	4-door Station Wagon, 3 seat/Chevrolet
47	2-door Custom Coupe/Chevrolet
57	2-door Sport Coupe/Chevrolet, Monte Carlo
67	2-door Convertible/Chevrolet, Corvette
69	4-door Sedan/Chevrolet, Nova,
80	2-door Pick-Up Delivery/El Camino
87	2-door Sport Coupe/Camaro

1974 VIN Engine Codes

Code	Option	C.I.	Type	Carb.	Net HP
A	L13	140	L4	1BBL	75
B	L11	140	L4	2BBL	85
C*	L90	250	L6	1BBL	95
D	L22	250	L6	1BBL	100
H	L65	350	V-8	2BBL	145
J	L45	350	V-8	4BBL	195 (Corv.)
K	L48	350	V-8	4BBL	185 (All exc. Corv.)
L	LM1	350	V-8	4BBL	160
R	LF6	400	V-8	2BBL	150
T	Z28	350	V-8	4BBL	245 (Camaro)
	L82	350	V-8	4BBL	250 (Corv.)
U	LT4	400	V-8	4BBL	180
Y	LS4	454	V-8	4BBL	235 (All exc. Corv.)
Z	LS4	454	V-8	4BBL	270 (Corv.)
*Low compression export					

1974 VIN Assembly Plant Codes

Letter Code	Assembly Plant	Body Type*
B	Baltimore, Maryland	4, 6, 7
C	Southgate, California	1
D**	Atlanta, Georgia (Doraville)	1, 4, 6, 7 (4, 6, 7 after Jan.)
J	Janesville, Wisconsin	1
K**	Kansas City, Missouri	3, 4, 6, 7 (3 after Jan.; 7 Aug.–Oct. only)
L	Los Angeles, California	3
N	Norwood, Ohio	5
R	Arlington, Texas	4, 6, 7
S	St. Louis, Missouri	1, 2
T	Tarrytown, New York	1
W	Willow Run, Michigan	3
Y	Wilmington, Delaware	1
Z	Fremont, California	4, 6, 7
1	Oshawa, Canada	1, 4, 6
*1= Passenger car, 2 = Corvette, 3 = Nova, 4 = Chevelle, 5 = Camaro, 6 = Monte Carlo, 7 = GMC Sprint **Designation change from 1973		

1974 VIN Build Sequence Numbers

Model	Begin Sequence Number	Plant
Chev/Pass	100001	All
Corvette	400001	St. Louis
Nova	100001	Los Angeles, Willow Run, Kansas City (after Jan. 1974)
Chevelle, Monte Carlo	400001	All except Doraville & Oshawa
	400001	Doraville (after Jan, 1974)
Monte Carlo	600001	Oshawa
Camaro	100001	Norwood
Monza	100001	Ste. Therese

Fig. 1-18. *1974 Nova SS 350.*

Fig. 1-19. *1974 Corvette.*

1975 VIN CHARTS

8. 1975 VIN CODE CHARTS

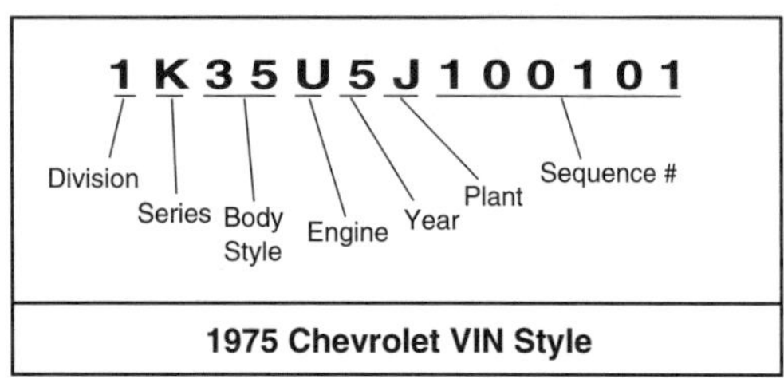

Example:

- 1 = Division: Chevrolet
- K = Series: Bel Air
- 95 = Body Style: 4-door Station Wagon
- U = Engine: 400/175HP
- 5 = Model Year: 1975
- J = Assembly Plant: Janesville
- 100101 = Sequence number: 101st Bel Air Wagon built at Janesville in that model year

1975 VIN Model Series Codes

Code	Vehicle/Body Style
C	Chevelle Malibu, El Camino
D	Chevelle Malibu Classic, El Camino Classic
E	Chevelle Laguna
G	Chevelle Malibu Classic Estate Wagon
H	Monte Carlo
K	Belair
L	Impala
M	Monza Town Coupe
N	Caprice Classic, Caprice Estate Wagon
Q	Camaro
R	Monza 2 + 2
S	Camaro Type LT
X	Nova
Y	Nova Custom
Z	Corvette

Fig. 1-21. 1975 Caprice.

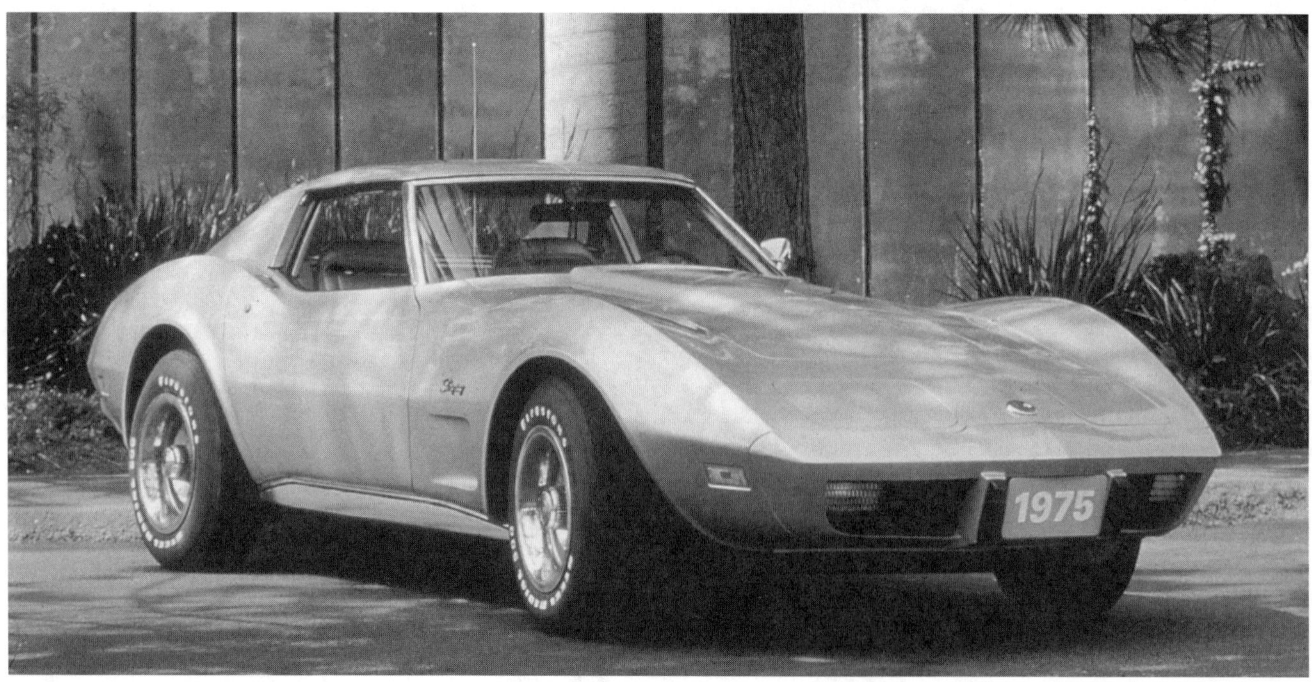

Fig. 1-20. 1975 Corvette Stingray.

1975 VIN CHARTS

1975 VIN Body Style Code

Code	Body Style
07	2-door Hatchback Coupe, Monza 2 + 2
17	2-door Hatchback Coupe/Nova
27	2-door Coupe/Nova, Monza Towne Coupe
29	4-door Sport Sedan/Chevelle
35	4-door Station Wagon, 2 seat/Chevrolet, Chevelle)
37	2-door Sport Coupe/Corvette, Chevelle
39	4-door Sport Sedan/Chevelle
45	4-door Station Wagon, 3 seat/Chevrolet
47	2-door Custom Coupe/Chevrolet
57	2-door Sport Coupe/Chevrolet, Monte Carlo
67	2-door Convertible/Chevrolet, Corvette
69	4-door Sedan/Chevrolet, Nova,
80	2-door Pick-Up Delivery/El Camino
87	2-door Sport Coupe/Camaro

1975 VIN Engine Codes

Code	Option	C.I.	Type	Carburetor	Net HP
A	L13	140	L4	1BBL	78
B	L11	140	L4	2BBL	87
D	L22	250	L6	1BBL	105
G	LV1	262	V-8	2BBL	110
H	L65	350	V-8	2BBL	145
J	L45	350	V-8	4BBL	165
L	LM1	350	V-8	4BBL	155
T	I82	350	V-8	4BBL	205
U	LT4	400	V-8	4BBL	175
Y	LS4	454	V-8	4BBL	215

Fig. 1-22. 1975 Camaro.

1975 VIN Assembly Plant Codes

Letter Code	Assembly Plant	Body Type*
B	Baltimore, Maryland	4, 6, 7
D**	Atlanta, Georgia (Doraville)	4, 6, 7
J	Janesville, Wisconsin	1
K**	Kansas City, Missouri	3, 6
L	Los Angeles, California	3
N	Norwood, Ohio	5
R	Arlington, Texas	4, 6, 7
S	St. Louis, Missouri	1, 2
T**	Tarrytown, New York	3
W	Willow Run, Michigan	3
Y	Wilmington, Delaware	1
Z	Fremont, California	4, 6, 7
1	Oshawa, Canada	4, 6
2	Ste. Therese, Canada	7, 8

*1= Passenger car, 2 = Corvette, 3 = Nova, 4 = Chevelle, 5 = Camaro, 6 = Monte Carlo, 7 = GMC Sprint, 8 = Monza
**Designation change from 1974

NOTE—
All plants producing Chevelles also produced Monte Carlos. The Kansas City final assembly plant produced the Monte Carlo and Nova models only. Monte Carlo production did not begin in the Kansas City plant until September of 1974.

1975 VIN Build Sequence Numbers

Model	Begin Sequence Number	Plant
Chev/Pass	100001	All
Corvette	400001	St. Louis
Nova	100001	All
Chevelle	400001	All
Camaro	500001	Norwood
Monte Carlo	400001	All

CHAPTER 1

9. TRIM TAG INFORMATION

In this section I will explain the information found on 1970 through 1975 Chevrolet firewall trim tags. It is imperative to know how to interpret this information on your own car or a car you intend to purchase, because it allows you to verify the model and the original paint and trim combinations for the car.

There were two basic trim tag designs: the first was for 1970 through 1975 cars except Corvette; the second for 1970 through 1975 Corvettes. All trim tags were attached by rivets. The position of the trim tag changed from year to year and model to model. See the headings below by year and model for individual trim tag locations and decoding of trim tag information.

> **NOTE—**
> Although theoretically there was one style of trim tag used for each model year, there were a number of different trim tag designs, and many final assembly plants used more than one style of trim tag. This information is not being disclosed

9.1 1970 Through 1975 Trim Tags

This trim tag design was first brought into production during the 1969 model year on only a few models, including the Camaro. By 1970, it was used by almost every division in General Motors. This trim tag is 3-1/2" long x 2-1/8" tall. The words "Body by Fisher" are stamped across the top and the sentence, "General Motors Corporation certifies to the dealer that this vehicle conforms to all U.S. Federal Motor Vehicle Safety Standards applicable at time of manufacture.", is stamped across the bottom half of the trim tag. There are ten specific positions where information is listed on this trim tag. See Fig. 1-1. Trim tag locations are given below.

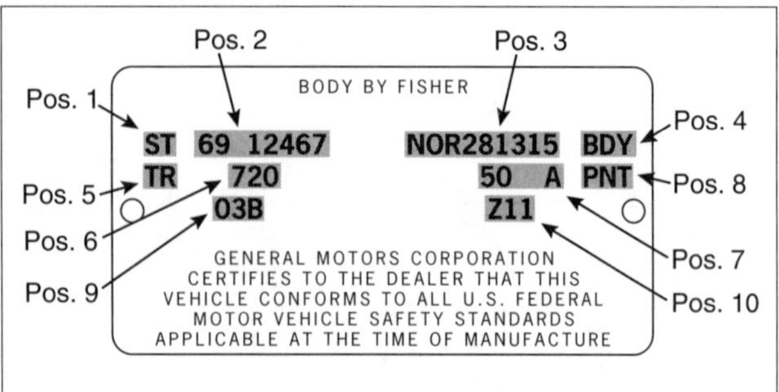

Fig. 1-23. *Example of typical late 1969 through 1975 trim tag, showing positions where model and trim information is listed.*

1970–1975 Trim Tag Location

Model	Year	Location
Passenger Cars	1970–71	In engine compartment, upper left hand corner of cowl plenum
	1972–75	In right upper horizontal surface of cowl plenum
Chevy II	1970–71	In engine compartment, vertical upper left hand corner of cowl plenum
	1972–73	In engine compartment, horizontal upper left portion of cowl plenum
	1974–75	In engine compartment, on vertical surface of shroud, behind brake booster
Chevelle	1970–75 (including Monte Carlo)	In engine compartment, horizontal upper left hand corner of the cowl plenum
Camaro	1970–75	In engine compartment, left upper portion of horizontal surface of cowl plenum
Monza	1975	In engine compartment, left upper portion of horizontal surface of cowl plenum

Position #1: The letters "ST." ST is short for "STYLE." This refers to the model year and model identification number in position #2.

Position #2: Model year and model identification. This code is two sets of numbers separated by a blank space. The first two numbers designate the model year of the car. The second group of five numbers is the model identification number of the car. A full description of the model identification number breakdown can be found later in this chapter.

> **NOTE—**
> • On all 1969 through 1971 trim tags, the engine identification portion of the model identification number always indicates a V-8 engine. No 6-cylinder engine identification numbers are stamped on any trim tag. Engine verification must be made by checking the VIN.
>
> • While the VIN style changed in 1972 to include a letter code for engine identification, the model identification number on the trim tag retained the earlier style of all numbers. Trim tag style changed to match VIN style in 1973. See Fig. 1-30 (p.20) for later model identification style.

Position #3: The assembly plant letter code and the sequential number of that body style produced at that assembly plant. The assembly plant code is two or three alphanumeric digits.

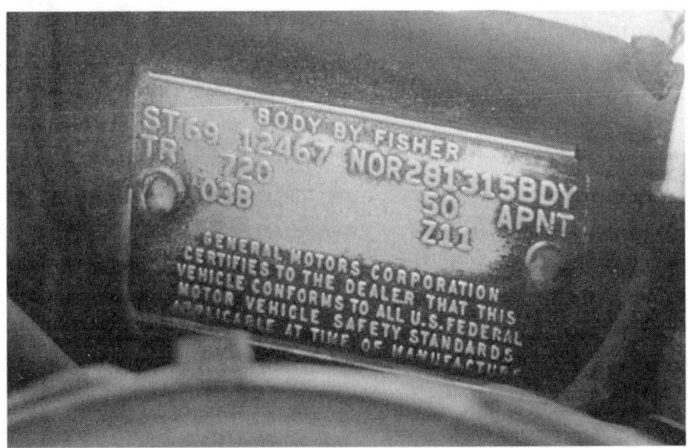

Fig. 1-24. 1969 Z11 Camaro convertible trim tag shown to illustrate late 1970 tag.

1970—1975 Assembly Plant Codes

Letter Code*	Plant Location	Years
A	Atlanta, Georgia	1970
B	Baltimore, Maryland	1970–75
BC	Southgate, California	1970
BF	Fremont, California	1970
BL	Van Nuys, California	1970
BT	Arlington, Texas	1970
BW	Wilmington, Delaware	1970
BZ	Fremont, California	1971
C	Southgate, California	1971–74
D	Doraville, Georgia	1970–75
FL2	Flint, Michigan	1970
J	Janesville, Wisconsin	1971–75
JAN	Janesville, Wisconsin	1970
K	Kansas City, Missouri	1971–75
KAN	Kansas City, Missouri	1970
L	Van Nuys, California	1971–75
LOR	Lordstown, Ohio	1970
N	Norwood, Ohio	1971–75
NOR	Norwood, Ohio	1970
OS	Oshawa, Canada	1970–71
R	Arlington, Texas	1971–75
S	St. Louis, Missouri	1972–75
ST	St. Therese, Canada	1970–71
STL	St. Louis, Missouri	1970–71
T	Tarrytown, New York	1971–75
TA	Tarrytown, New York	1970
W	Willow Run, Michigan	1972–75
WRN	Willow Run, Michigan	1970–71
Y	Wilmington, Delaware	1971–75
Z	Fremont, California	1973–75
1	Oshawa, Canada	1972–75
2	St. Therese, Canada	1975
*1972 and later plant codes changed to match VIN code		

The body sequence number is four to six digits. This number was a factory tracking code, with no correlation to the VIN sequence number. All car bodies came down the final assembly line a random style order. This order would be adjusted depending upon the actual sales demand of a particular style.

Position #4: The letters "BDY." This refers to the assembly plant and sequential number in Position #3.

Position #5: The letters "TR." This refers to the interior trim combination information in position #6.

Position #6: The interior trim code. All trim codes are a three-digit number that is specific to each car model. Sometimes there is another three-digit code that follows the trim code and begins with an "A," such as "A51." This code designates the modular seat code. For all 1972–73 cars, the seat code appears in this position. In 1974, this is the location of the modular seat code for GMAD assembly plants only. For all other 1974–75 models, the modular seat code was stamped immediately following the body build date code (position #9). The trim codes can vary greatly from year to year and are sometimes specific to a particular model. Please see the appendix for a complete breakdown of all interior trim codes.

1972 Through 1975 Seat Codes

Year	Code	Seat Style
1972	A51	Bucket seats
	A52	Bench seats
1973	A51	Bucket seats
	A52	Bench seats
	AN7	Swivel bucket seats
	AT8	50/50 Bench seats
1974–75	AN6	Adjustable driver seat back (F/H car)
	AN7	Swivel bucket (A car)
	AT8	50/50 bench/Adj. Pass recl. Caprice
	AG7	6-way power (B car)
	A42	6-way power (A/B car)
	A44	2-way manual bucket (H car)
	A51	Bucket seats (H/F/X cars)
	A52	Bench seats (A/B/X cars)
	A57	Auxiliary right seat (H car)
	A61	Bucket seats (H car)
	A65	Bench w/arm rest (A car)
	Y02	Custom (H car)

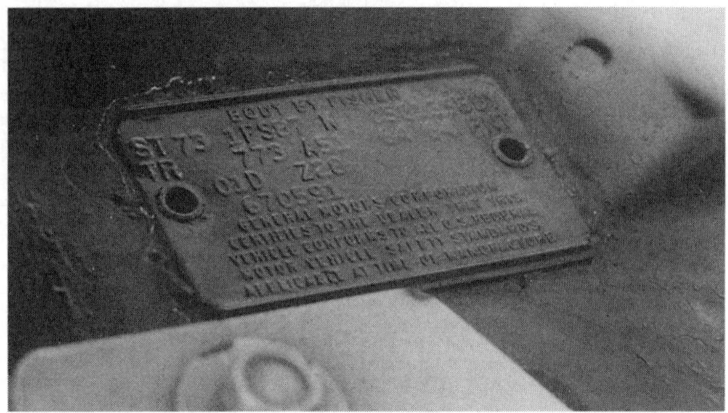

Fig. 1-25. 1973 Z28 Camaro trim tag.

Position #7: The exterior paint code. This paint code is two to four digits and is sometimes followed by a letter. The first two digits represent the lower body color, and the second two digits the upper body color. If a single letter is also present, it designates the vinyl top or convertible top color. Some assembly plants placed hyphens between letters and numbers, while other plants did not. Also noted on some trim tags was a dash or hyphen to indicate special paint.

Position #8: The letters "PNT." This refers to the exterior paint codes in position #7.

Position #9: The body build date code. This position denotes a month and week code. The body build date represents the date of the final body assembly only. Many restorers believe that this date represents the final assembly date of the complete vehicle, but this is incorrect. The body build date was moved from the top of the trim tag to the bottom of the trim tag in the 1969 model year.

Month Codes

01 = January	07 = July
02 = February	08 = August
03 = March	09 = September
04 = April	10 = October
05 = May	11 = November
06 = June	12 = December

Week Codes

A = First Week	E = Fifth Week
D = Fourth Week	C = Third Week
B = Second Week	

Example: 06C = June/Third Week

Position #10: The accessory options codes. These codes can be either near the body build date (position #9) or underneath the exterior paint codes (position #7), depending on the year and application. These codes were added to the trim tag while the car was in the Fisher Body section of the final assembly plant, prior to moving on to the Chevrolet final drive line assembly section. The codes defined the specific changes that were to be made to the body by the Fisher Body assembly line workers in order for it to accept particular Chevrolet driveline options. Not all options were coded on the trim tag, and these codes varied from plant to plant and model to model. For more information on accessory codes, see the introduction to this book.

Fig. 1-26. 1974 Nova trim tag.

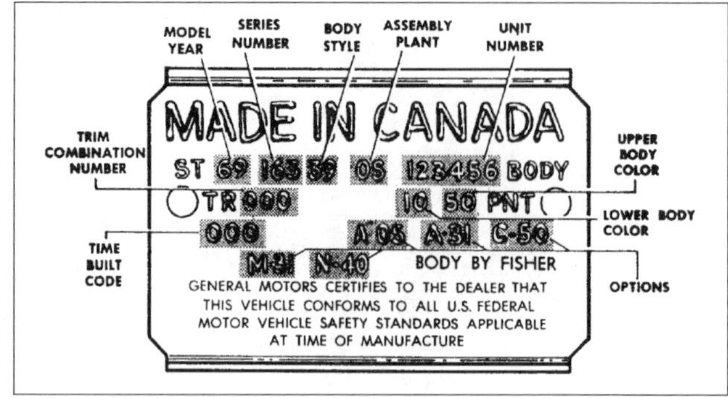

Fig. 1-27. 1969 Canadian trim tag.

9.2 1970 Through 1975 Corvette Trim Tags

The 1968–75 Corvette trim tag is different from the 1965–67 Corvette trim tag. In the top right corner of the trim tag is the body build date code. The body build date code consists of an alphanumeric code representing the month followed by two numbers representing the day of the month. On the left side of the trim tag is the word "Trim", which designates the interior trim code of that particular car. The actual trim code is to the right of the word "Trim" and consists of a 3 digit numerical code. Following the trim code and to the right is the car's exterior paint code. This code consists of a three digit numerical prefix, followed by the word "PAINT" to designate the paint code. Please see later in this chapter for a complete breakdown of all trim and paint combination codes.

Fig. 1-28. 1968–75 Corvette trim tag.

1970–1975 Corvette Trim Tag Location

Model	Year	Location
Corvette	1970–75	In left hand door hinge pillar

Early in the 1973 model year, the trim tag typeface size was changed from 1/4" to 3/8".

Body Build Date Month Codes

1970 St. Louis

A	January 1970
B	February
C	March
D	April
E	May
F	June
G	July

1971 St. Louis

A	August 1970
B	September
C	October
D	November
E	December
F	January 1971
G	February
H	March
I	April
J	May
K	June
L	July

1972 St. Louis

A	August 1971
B	September
C	October
D	November
E	December
F	January 1972
G	February
H	March
I	April
J	May
K	June
L	July

1973 St. Louis

A	September 1972
B	October
C	November
D	December
E	January 1973
F	February
G	March
H	April
I	May
J	June
K	July

1974 St. Louis

A	August 1973
B	September
C	October
D	November
E	December
F	January 1974
G	February
H	March
I	April
J	May
K	June
L	July

1975 St. Louis

A	August 1974
B	September
C	October
D	November
E	December
F	January 1975
G	February
H	March
I	April
J	May
K	June
L	July

10. MODEL IDENTIFICATION NUMBER

In this section I will explain the use and decoding of the Chevrolet Model Identification numbers from 1970 through 1975. Model identification is just as important to the hobbyist as the Vehicle Identification Number (VIN) because almost all specific information about a car depends on the model number. The options that are allowed on certain cars relate back to the specific model, along with interior trim and paint combinations as well.

Decoding the Model Identification number can be a little tricky, primarily because of VIN changes across the range of years and because its location changes.

On 1970 and 1971 cars, the Model Identification number is the first five digits of the VIN. While it seems that the Model Identification number also appears on the firewall trim tag, this is not the case. While most of the trim tag digits match the VIN, the engine identification code on the trim tag always indicates that the car has a V-8 engine, whether or not it actually does. Only the VIN will confirm the correct engine.

On 1972 cars, the Model Identification number is listed on the firewall trim tag. On 1972 models the trim tag engine code identification should match the car's original engine.

> NOTE—
> While the 1972 VIN style changed, the trim tag style (and Model Identification number on it) did not.

On 1973 through 1975 cars, the Model Identification number is also listed on the firewall trim tag.

1970 Through 1972 Model Identification

The basic numerical groups used for all passenger cars are as follows:

- 10000 Series = Corvair
- 11000 Series = Chevy II
- 13000 Series = Chevelle
- 15000 Series = Chev/Pass
- 16000 Series = Chev/Pass
- 19000 Series = Corvette

The model identification number will always consist of five digits. See Fig. 1-29. The first digit will always be a "1" and this designates the division, Chevrolet. The next two digits represent the vehicle series. If the third digit of the model number is odd, 1,3,5, or 7 the base engine is a 4- or 6-cylinder. If the third digit of the model number is even, 2, 4, 6 or 8, the base engine is a V-8.

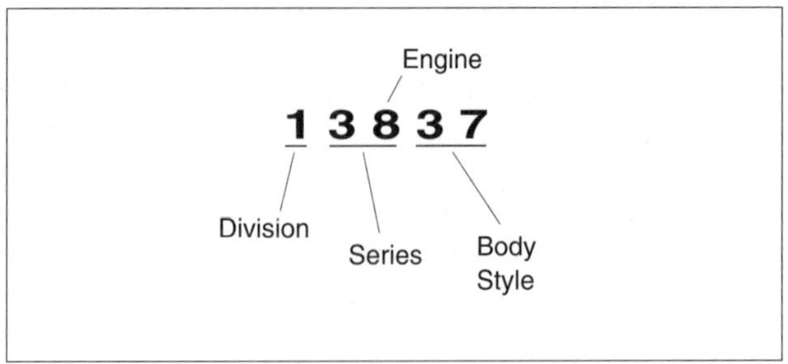

Fig. 1-29. 1970 through 1972 Model Identification number style. On 1970 and 1971 models, number is first five digits of Vehicle Identification Number (VIN). On 1972 models, this number is listed on firewall trim tag.

1973 Through 1975 Model Identification

In 1973 the model identification system changed again. Again, there are five digits in the model number. See Fig. 1-2. The first digit represents the division, which is Chevrolet. The next digit is a letter code, which represents the vehicle car line. The third digit is another letter representing the vehicle series. The last two digits represent the body style of that car.

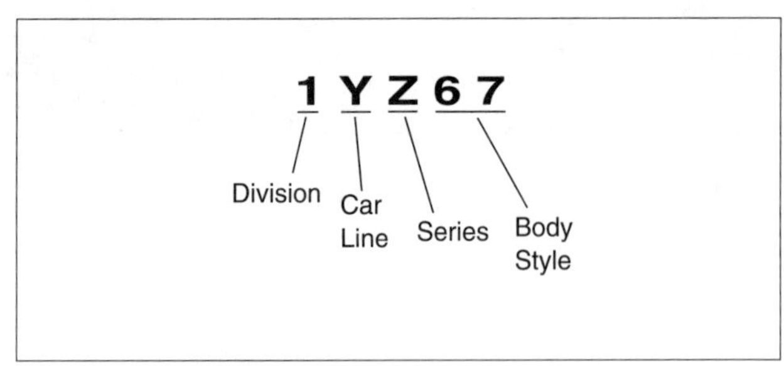

Fig. 1-30. 1973 through 1975 Model Identification number style.

1970 Model Designation

Model	Model #	Description	Style
Passenger	15311	2-door Sedan	Biscayne, 6 cyl
	15369	4-door Sedan	Biscayne, 6 cyl
	15411	2-door Sedan	Biscayne, 8 cyl
	15436	4-door Station Wagon, 6 Pass, 2 seat	Brookwood, 8 cyl
	15469	4-door Sedan	Biscayne, 8 cyl
	15511	2-door Sedan	Bel Air, 6 cyl
	15569	4-door Sedan	Bel Air, 6 cyl
	15611	2-door Sedan	Bel Air, 8 cyl
	15636	4-door Station Wagon, 6 Pass, 2 seat	Townsman, 8 cyl
	15646	4-door Station Wagon, 9 Pass, 3 seat	Townsman, 8 cyl
	15669	4-door Sedan	Bel Air, 8 cyl
	16337	2-door Sport Coupe	Impala, 6 cyl
	16339	4-door Sport Sedan	Impala, 6 cyl
	16369	4-door Sedan	Impala, 6 cyl
	16436	4-door Station Wagon, 6 Pass, 2 seat	Kingswood, 8 cyl
	16437	2-door Sport Coupe	Impala, 8 cyl
	16439	4-door Sports Sedan	Impala, 8 cyl
	16446	4-door Station Wagon, 9 Pass, 3 seat	Kingswood, 8 cyl
	16447	2-door Custom Coupe	Impala, 8 cyl
	16467	2-door Convertible	Impala, 8 cyl
	16469	4-door Sedan	Impala, 8 cyl
	16636	4-door Station Wagon, 6 Pass, 2 seat	Kingswood Es, 8 cyl
	16639	4-door Sport Sedan	Caprice, 8 cyl
	16646	4-door Station Wagon, 9 Pass, 3 seat	Kingswood Es, 8 cyl
	16647	2-door Sport Coupe	Caprice, 8 cyl
Corvette	19437	2-door Sport Coupe, 2 Pass	Stingray
	19467	2-door Convertible, 2 Pass	Stingray
Nova	11127	2-door Sport Coupe	Nova, 4 cyl
	11169	4-door Sedan	Nova, 4 cyl
	11327	2-door Sport Coupe	Nova, 6 cyl
	11369	4-door Sedan	Nova, 6 cyl
	11427	2-door Sport Coupe	Nova, 8 cyl
	11469	4-door Sedan	Nova, 8 cyl
Chevelle	13136	4-door Station Wagon, 6 Pass, 2 seat	Nomad, 6 cyl
	13236	4-door Station Wagon, 6 Pass, 2 seat	Nomad, 8 cyl
	13327	2-door Pillar Coupe	Chevelle, 6 cyl
	13336	4-door 2 seat Greenbrier	Chevelle, 6 cyl
	13337	2-door Sport Coupe	Chevelle, 6 cyl
	13369	4-door Sedan	Chevelle, 6 cyl
	13380	2-door Sedan Pickup, Regular	El Camino, 6 cyl
	13427	2-door Pillar Coupe	Chevelle, 8 cyl
	13436	4-door Station Wagon, 6 Pass, 2 seat	Greenbrier, 8 cyl
	13437	2-door Sport Coupe	Chevelle, 8 cyl
	13446	4-door Station Wagon, 9 Pass, 3 seat	Greenbrier, 8 cyl
	13469	4-door Sedan	Chevelle, 8 cyl
	13480	2-door Sedan Pickup, Regular	El Camino, 8 cyl
	13536	4-door Station Wagon, 6 Pass, 2 seat	Concours, 6 cyl
	13537	2-door Sport Coupe	Malibu, 6 cyl
	13539	4-door Sport Sedan	Malibu, 6 cyl
	13567	2-door Convertible	Malibu, 6 cyl
	13569	4-door Sedan	Malibu, 6 cyl
	13580	2-door Sedan Pickup Deluxe	El Camino, 6 cyl
	13636	4-door Station Wagon, 6 Pass, 2 seat	Concours, 8 cyl

continued on next page

1970 Model Designation (continued)

Model	Model #	Description	Style
Chevelle (cont'd)	13637	2-door Sport Coupe	Malibu, 8 cyl
	13639	4-door Sport Sedan	Malibu, 8 cyl
	13646	4-door Station Wagon, 9 Pass, 3 seat	Concours, 8 cyl
	13667	2-door Convertible	Malibu, 8 cyl
	13669	4-door Sedan	Malibu, 8 cyl
	13680	2-door Sedan Pickup Deluxe	El Camino, 8 cyl
	13836	4-door Station Wagon, 6 Pass, 2 seat	Concours Est, 8 cyl
	13846	4-door Station Wagon, 9 Pass, 3 seat	Concours Est, 8 cyl
Monte Carlo	13857	2-door Sport Coupe	Monte Carlo V-8
Camaro	12387	2-door Sport Coupe	Camaro, 6 cyl
	12487	2-door Sport Coupe	Camaro, 8 cyl

1971 Model Designation

Model	Model #	Description	Style
Passenger	15369	4-door Sedan	Biscayne, 6 cyl
	15435	4-door Station Wagon, 6 Pass, 2 seat	Brookwood, 8 cyl
	15469	4-door Sedan	Biscayne, 8 cyl
	15569	4-door Sedan	Bel Air, 6 cyl
	15635	4-door Station Wagon, 6 Pass, 2 seat	Townsman, 8 cyl
	15645	4-door Station Wagon, 9 Pass, 3 seat	Townsman, 8 cyl
	15669	4-door Sedan	Bel Air, 8 cyl
	16357	2-door Sport Coupe	Impala, 6 cyl
	16369	4-door Sedan	Impala, 6 cyl
	16435	4-door Station Wagon, 6 Pass, 2 seat	Kingswood, 8 cyl
	16439	4-door Sports Sedan	Impala, 8 cyl
	16445	4-door Station Wagon, 9 Pass, 3 seat	Kingswood, 8 cyl
	16447	2-door Custom Coupe	Impala, 8 cyl
	16457	2-door Sport Coupe	Impala, 8 cyl
	16467	2-door Convertible	Impala, 8 cyl
	16469	4-door Sedan	Impala, 8 cyl
	16635	4-door Station Wagon, 6 Pass, 2 seat	Kingswood Es, 8 cyl
	16639	4-door Sport Sedan	Caprice, 8 cyl
	16645	4-door Station Wagon, 9 Pass, 3 seat	Kingswood Es, 8 cyl
	16647	2-door Sport Coupe	Caprice, 8 cyl
Corvette	19437	2-door Sport Coupe, 2 Pass	Stingray
	19467	2-door Convertible, 2 Pass	Stingray
Nova	11327	2-door Sport Coupe	Nova, 6 cyl
	11369	4-door Sedan	Nova, 6 cyl
	11427	2-door Sport Coupe	Nova, 8 cyl
	11469	4-door Sedan	Nova, 8 cyl
	21327*	2-door Sport Coupe	Ventura II, 6 cyl
	21369*	4-door Sedan	Ventura II, 6 cyl
	21427*	2-door Sport Coupe	Ventura II, 8 cyl
	21469*	4-door Sedan	Ventura II, 8 cyl
	71327**	2-door Sport Coupe	Acadian, 6 cyl
	71369**	4-door Sedan	Acadian, 6 cyl
	71427**	2-door Sport Coupe	Acadian, 8 cyl
	71469**	4-door Sedan	Acadian, 8 cyl

continued on next page

1971 Model Designation (continued)

Model	Model #	Description	Style
Chevelle	13136	4-door Station Wagon, 6 Pass, 2 seat	Nomad, 6 cyl
	13236	4-door Station Wagon, 6 Pass, 2 seat	Nomad, 8 cyl
	13336	4-door, 2 seat	Greenbrier
	13337	2-door Sport Coupe	Chevelle, 6 cyl
	13369	4-door Sedan	Chevelle, 6 cyl
	13380	2-door Sedan Pickup, Regular	El Camino, 6 cyl
	13436	4-door Station Wagon, 6 Pass	Greenbrier, 8 cyl
	13437	2-door Sport Coupe	Chevelle, 8 cyl
	13446	4-door Station Wagon, 9 Pass, 3 seat	Greenbrier, 8 cyl
	13469	4-door Sedan	Chevelle, 8 cyl
	13480	2-door Sedan Pickup, Regular	El Camino, 8 cyl
	13536	4-door Station Wagon, 6 Pass	Concours, 6 cyl
	13537	2-door Sport Coupe	Malibu, 6 cyl
	13539	4-door Sport Sedan	Malibu, 6 cyl
	13567	2-door Convertible	Malibu, 6 cyl
	13569	4-door Sedan	Malibu, 6 cyl
	13580	2-door Sedan Pickup Deluxe	El Camino, 6 cyl
	13636	4-door Station Wagon, 6 Pass, 2 seat	Concours, 8 cyl
	13637	2-door Sport Coupe	Malibu, 8 cyl
	13639	4-door Sport Sedan	Malibu, 8 cyl
	13646	4-door Station Wagon, 9 Pass, 3 seat	Concours, 8 cyl
	13667	2-door Convertible	Malibu, 8 cyl
	13669	4-door Sedan	Malibu, 8 cyl
	13680	2-door Sedan Pickup Deluxe	El Camino, 8 cyl
	13836	4-door Station Wagon, 6 Pass, 2 seat	Concours Est, 8 cyl
	13846	4-door Station Wagon, 9 Pass, 3 seat	Concours Est, 8 cyl
	53380***	2-door Sedan Pickup	Sprint, 6 cyl
	53480***	2-door Sedan Pickup	Sprint, 8 cyl
	53580***	2-door Sedan Pickup Custom	Sprint, 6 cyl
	53680***	2-door Sedan Pickup Custom	Sprint, 8 cyl
Monte Carlo	13857	2-door Sport Coupe	Monte Carlo, 8 cyl
Camaro	12387	2-door Sport Coupe	Camaro, 6 cyl
	12487	2-door Sport Coupe	Camaro, 8 cyl
*Pontiac division number. **GM of Canada division Number. ***GMC Truck division number. Numbers supplied for reference.			

1972 Model Designation

Model	Model #	Description	Style
Passenger	15369	4-door Sedan	Biscayne, 6 cyl
	15435	4-door Station Wagon, 6 Pass, 2 seat	Brookwood, 8 cyl
	15469	4-door Sedan	Biscayne, 8 cyl
	15569	4-door Sedan	Bel Air, 6 cyl
	15635	4-door Station Wagon, 6 Pass, 2 seat	Townsman, 8 cyl
	15645	4-door Station Wagon, 9 Pass, 3 seat	Townsman, 8 cyl
	15669	4-door Sedan	Bel Air, 8 cyl
	16357	2-door Sport Coupe	Impala, 6 cyl
	16369	4-door Sedan	Impala, 6 cyl
	16435	4-door Station Wagon, 6 Pass, 2 seat	Kingswood, 8 cyl
	16439	4-door Sports Sedan	Impala, 8 cyl
	16445	4-door Station Wagon, 9 Pass, 3 seat	Kingswood, 8 cyl
	16447	2-door Custom Coupe	Impala, 8 cyl

continued on next page

1972 Model Designation (continued)

Model	Model #	Description	Style
Passenger (cont'd)	16457	2-door Sport Coupe	Impala, 8 cyl
	16467	2-door Convertible	Impala, 8 cyl
	16469	4-door Sedan	Impala, 8 cyl
	16635	4-door Station Wagon, 2 seat	Kingswood Es, 8 cyl
	16639	4-door Sport Sedan	Caprice, 8 cyl
	16645	4-door Station Wagon, 3 seat	Kingswood Es, 8 cyl
	16647	2-door Sport Coupe	Caprice, 8 cyl
Corvette	16669	4-door Sedan	Caprice, 8 cyl
	19437	2-door Sport Coupe, 2 Pass	Stingray
Nova	19467	2-door Convertible, 2 Pass	Stingray
	11327	2-door Sport Coupe	Nova, 6 cyl
	11369	4-door Sedan	Nova, 6 cyl
	11427	2-door Sport Coupe	Nova, 8 cyl
	11469	4-door Sedan	Nova, 8 cyl
	21327*	2-door Sport Coupe	Ventura II, 6 cyl
	21369*	4-door Sedan	Ventura II, 6 cyl
	21427*	2-door Sport Coupe	Ventura II, 8 cyl
	21469*	4-door Sedan	Ventura II, 8 cyl
Chevelle	13136	4-door Station Wagon, 6 Pass, 2 seat	Nomad, 6 cyl
	13236	4-door Station Wagon, 6 Pass, 2 seat	Nomad, 8 cyl
	13337	2-door Sport Coupe	Chevelle, 6 cyl
	13369	4-door Sedan	Chevelle, 6 cyl
	13380	2-door Sedan Pickup, Regular	El Camino, 6 cyl
	13436	4-door Station Wagon, 6 Pass, 2 seat	Greenbrier, 8 cyl
	13437	2-door Sport Coupe	Chevelle, 8 cyl
	13446	4-door Station Wagon, 9 Pass, 3 seat	Greenbrier, 8 cyl
	13469	4-door Sedan	Chevelle, 8 cyl
	13480	2-door Sedan Pickup, Regular	El Camino, 8 cyl
	13537	2-door Sport Coupe	Malibu, 6 cyl
	13569	4-door Sedan	Malibu, 6 cyl
	13636	4-door Station Wagon, 6 Pass, 2 Seat	Concours, 8 cyl
	13637	2-door Sport Coupe	Malibu, 8 cyl
	13639	4-door Sport Sedan	Malibu, 8 cyl
	13646	4-door Station Wagon, 9 Pass, 3 seat	Concours, 8 cyl
	13667	2-door Convertible	Malibu, 8 cyl
	13669	4-door Sedan	Malibu, 8 cyl
	13680	2-door Sedan Pickup Deluxe	El Camino, 8 cyl
	13836	4-door Station Wagon, 6 Pass, 2 seat	Concours Est, 8 cyl
	13846	4-door Station Wagon, 9 Pass, 3 seat	Concours Est, 8 cyl
	53380*	2-door Sedan Pickup	Sprint, 6 cyl
	53480*	2-door Sedan Pickup	Sprint, 8 cyl
	53680*	2-door Sedan Pickup Custom	Sprint, 8 cyl
Monte Carlo	13857	2-door Sport Coupe	Monte Carlo, 8 cyl
Camaro	12387	2-door Sport Coupe	Camaro, 6 cyl
	12487	2-door Sport Coupe	Camaro, 8 cyl
*Pontiac division number. **GMC Truck division number. Numbers supplied for reference.			

1973 Model Designation

Model	Model #	Description	Style
Passenger	1BK35	4-door Station Wagon, 6 Pass, 2 seat	Bel Air
	1BK45	4-door Station Wagon, 9 Pass, 3 seat	Bel Air
	1BK69	4-door Sedan	Bel Air
	1BL35	4-door Station Wagon, 6 Pass, 2 seat	Impala
	1BL39	4-door Sport Sedan	Impala
	1BL45	4-door Station Wagon, 9 Pass, 3 seat	Impala
	1BL47	2-door Custom Coupe	Impala
	1BL57	2-door Sport Coupe	Impala
	1BL69	4-door Sedan	Impala
	1BN35	4-door Station Wagon, 6 Pass, 2 seat	Caprice Estate
	1BN39	4-door Sport Sedan	Caprice Classic
	1BN45	4-door Station Wagon, 9 Pass, 3 seat	Caprice Estate
	1BN47	2-door Sport Coupe	Caprice Classic
	1BN67	2-door Convertible	Caprice Classic
	1BN69	4-door Sedan	Caprice Classic
Corvette	1YZ37	2-door Coupe	Corvette
	1YZ67	2-door Convertible	Corvette
Nova	1XX17	2-door Hatchback Coupe	Nova
	1XX27	2-door Coupe	Nova
	1XX69	4-door Sedan	Nova
	1XY17	2-door Custom Hatchback Coupe	Nova Custom
	1XY27	2-door Custom Coupe	Nova Custom
	1XY69	4-door Custom Sedan	Nova Custom
Chevelle	1AC29	4-door Sport Sedan Deluxe	Deluxe
	1AC35	4-door Deluxe Station Wagon, 2 Seat	Deluxe
	1AC37	2-door Sport Coupe Deluxe	Deluxe
	1AC80	2-door El Camino Pick-Up Delivery	El Camino
	1AD29	4-door Sport Sedan Malibu	Malibu
	1AD35	4-door Station Wagon Malibu, 2 Seat	Malibu
	1AD37	2-door Sport Coupe Malibu	Malibu
	1AD80	2-door El Camino Custom Pick-Up Delivery	Custom
	1AE29	4-door Sport Sedan Laguna	Laguna
	1AE35	4-door Laguna Station Wagon, 2 Seat	Laguna
	1AE37	2-door Sport Coupe Laguna	Laguna
	1AG35	4-door Malibu Estate Station Wagon, 2 Seat	Malibu Estate
	1AH35	4-door Laguna Estate Station Wagon, 2 Seat	Laguna Estate
	5AC80*	2-door GMC Sprint Pickup Delivery	GMC Sprint
	5AD80*	2-door GMC Sprint Custom Pickup Delivery	Sprint Custom
Monte Carlo	1AH57	2-door Sport Coupe	Monte Carlo
Camaro	1FQ87	2-door Sport Coupe	Camaro
	1FS87	2-door Type LT Coupe	Camaro
*GMC Truck division number. Numbers supplied for reference.			

1974 Model Designation

Model	Model #	Description	Style
Passenger	1BK35	4-door Station Wagon, 6 Pass, 2 seat	Bel Air
	1BK45	4-door Station Wagon, 9 Pass, 3 seat	Bel Air
	1BK69	4-door Sedan	Bel Air
	1BL35	4-door Station Wagon, 6 Pass, 2 seat	Impala
	1BL39	4-door Sport Sedan	Impala
	1BL45	4-door Station Wagon, 9 Pass, 3 seat	Impala
	1BL47	2-door Custom Coupe	Impala
	1BL57	2-door Sport Coupe	Impala
	1BL69	4-door Sedan	Impala
	1BN35	4-door Station Wagon, 6 Pass	Caprice Estate
	1BN39	4-door Sport Sedan	Caprice Classic
	1BN45	4-door Station Wagon, 9 Pass, 3 seat	Caprice Estate
	1BN47	2-door Sport Coupe	Caprice Classic
	1BN67	2-door Convertible	Caprice Classic
	1BN69	4-door Sedan	Caprice Classic
Corvette	1YZ37	2-door Coupe	Corvette
	1YZ67	2-door Convertible	Corvette
Nova	1XX17	2-door Hatchback Coupe	
	1XX27	2-door Coupe	
	1XX69	4-door Sedan	
	1XY17	2-door Custom Hatchback Coupe	
	1XY27	2-door Custom Coupe	
	1XY69	4-door Custom Sedan	
Chevelle	1AC29	4-door Sport Sedan Deluxe Malibu	
	1AC35	4-door Deluxe Station Wagon, 2 Seat Malibu	
	1AC37	2-door Sport Coupe Deluxe Malibu	
	1AC80	2-door El Camino Pick-Up Delivery	
	1AD29	4-door Sport Sedan Malibu	
	1AD35	4-door Station Wagon Malibu, 2 Seat Classic	
	1AD37	2-door Malibu Classic	
	1AD80	2-door El Camino Custom Pick-Up Delivery	
	1AE29	4-door Sport Sedan Laguna Type S3	
	1AE37	2-door Sport Coupe Laguna Type S3	
	1AG35	4-door Malibu Estate Station Wagon, 2 Seat	
	5AC80*	2-door GMC Sprint Pickup Delivery	
	5AD80*	2-door GMC Sprint Classic Pickup Delivery	
Monte Carlo	1AH57	2-door Sport Coupe Monte Carlo	
Camaro	1FQ87	2-door Sport Coupe	
	1FS87	2-door Type LT Coupe	
*GMC Truck division number. Numbers supplied for reference.			

1975 Model Designation

Model	Model #	Description	Style
Passenger	1BK35	4-door Station Wagon, 6 Pass, 2 seat	Bel Air
	1BK45	4-door Station Wagon, 9 Pass, 3 seat	Bel Air
	1BK69	4-door Sedan	Bel Air
	1BL35	4-door Station Wagon, 6 Pass, 2 seat	Impala
	1BL39	4-door Sport Sedan	Impala
	1BL45	4-door Station Wagon, 9 Pass, 3 seat	Impala
	1BL47	2-door Custom Coupe	Impala
	1BL57	2-door Sport Coupe	Impala
	1BL69	4-door Sedan	Impala
	1BN35	4-door Station Wagon, 6 Pass, 2 seat	Caprice Estate
	1BN39	4-door Sport Sedan	Caprice Classic
	1BN45	4-door Station Wagon, 9 Pass, 3 seat	Caprice Estate
	1BN47	2-door Sport Coupe	Caprice Classic
	1BN67	2-door Convertible	Caprice Classic
	1BN69	4-door Sedan	Caprice Classic
Corvette	1YZ37	2-door Coupe	Corvette
	1YZ67	2-door Convertible	Corvette
Nova	1XX17	2-door Hatchback Coupe	
	1XX27	2-door "S" Coupe	
	1XX69	4-door Sedan	
	1XY17	2-door Custom Hatchback Coupe	
	1XY27	2-door Custom "LN" Coupe	
	1XY69	4-door Custom "LN" Sedan	
Chevelle	1AC29	4-door Sport Sedan Deluxe	
	1AC35	4-door Deluxe Station Wagon, 2 Seat	
	1AC37	2-door Sport Coupe Deluxe Malibu	
	1AC80	2-door El Camino Pick-Up Delivery	
	1AD29	4-door Sport Sedan Malibu Classic	
	1AD35	4-door Station Wagon Malibu, 2 Seat	
	1AD37	2-door Sport Coupe Malibu Classic Landau	
	1AD80	2-door El Camino Custom Pick-Up Delivery	
	1AE37	2-door Sport Coupe Laguna Type S-3	
	1AG35	4-door Malibu Estate Station Wagon, 2 Seat Classic	
	5AC80*	2-door GMC Sprint Pickup Delivery	
	5AD80*	2-door GMC Sprint Classic Pickup Delivery	
Monte Carlo	1AH57	2-door Sport Coupe Monte Carlo "S"	
Camaro	1FQ87	2-door Sport Coupe	
	1FS87	2-door Type LT Coupe	
Monza	1HM27	2-door Notchback Towne Coupe	
	1HR07	2-door Hatchback 2+2 Coupe	
*GMC Truck division number. Numbers supplied for reference.			

11. Interior/Exterior Trim Charts

The following charts are reproduced from the original Chevrolet Engineering Specifications for each model year. In some cases, the interior and/or exterior options could have changed during the production year.

1970 Trim Combinations

BISCAYNE 153-400 SERIES
BEL AIR 155-600 SERIES

SERIES	MODEL	TYPE SEAT	Black Cloth	Black Vinyl	Medium Blue Cloth	Medium Blue Vinyl	Dk. Green Cloth	Medium Gold Cloth	Medium Gold Vinyl
Biscayne	69	Std. Bench		802		815			843
Bel Air	69	Std. Bench	803	804	818	819	848	836	

RPO	EXTERIOR COLORS	Black Cloth	Black Vinyl	Medium Blue Cloth	Medium Blue Vinyl	Dk. Green Cloth	Medium Gold Cloth	Medium Gold Vinyl
19	Tuxedo Black	X	X	X	X	X	X	X
14	Cortez Silver	X	X	X	X	X		
34	Misty Turquoise	X	X					
10	Classic White	X	X	X	X	X	X	X
28	Fathom Blue	X	X		X			
75	Cranberry Red	X	X					
25	Astro Blue	X	X		X			
50	Gobi Beige	X	X			X	X	X
48	Forest Green	X	X			X	X	X
45	Green Mist	X	X			X		
58	Autumn Gold	X	X			X	X	X
63	Desert Sand	X	X			X		
55	Champagne Gold	X	X				X	X
78	Black Cherry	X	X					
17	Shadow Gray	X	X	X	X			

RPO Lwr.	RPO Upr.	TWO-TONES	Black Cloth	Black Vinyl	Medium Blue Cloth	Medium Blue Vinyl	Dk. Green Cloth	Medium Gold Cloth	Medium Gold Vinyl
25	10	Astro Blue / Classic White	X	X	X	X			
34	10	Misty Turquoise / Classic White	X	X					
25	28	Astro Blue / Fathom Blue	X	X	X	X			
55	10	Champagne Gold / Classic White	X	X			X	X	X
58	10	Autumn Gold / Classic White	X	X			X	X	X
28	25	Fathom Blue / Astro Blue	X	X	X	X			
63	10	Desert Sand / Classic White	X	X					

CAPRICE 16600 SERIES

MODELS		SEAT TYPE	Black Knit Cloth	Med. Blue Cloth	Dark Green Knit Cloth	Med. Gold Cloth	Turquoise Cloth	Dark Blue Knit Cloth	Sandalwood Cloth
47	39	Std. Bench	813	822	855	840	845	826	870

RPO	EXTERIOR COLOR	Black	Med. Blue	Dark Green	Med. Gold	Turquoise	Dark Blue	Sandalwood
19	Tuxedo Black	X	X	X	X	X	X	X
14	Cortez Silver	X	X	X		X	X	X
34	Misty Turquoise	X				X		X
10	Classic White	X	X	X	X	X	X	X
28	Fathom Blue	X					X	X
75	Cranberry Red	X						X
25	Astro Blue	X					X	X
50	Gobi Beige	X		X	X			X
48	Forest Green	X		X	X			X
45	Green Mist	X		X				X
58	Autumn Gold	X		X	X			X
63	Desert Sand	X		X				X
55	Champagne Gold	X			X			X
78	Black Cherry	X						X
17	Shadow Gray	X	X					X

RPO Lwr.	RPO Upr.	TWO-TONES	Black	Med. Blue	Dark Green	Med. Gold	Turquoise	Dark Blue	Sandalwood
25	10	Astro Blue / Classic White	X	X				X	X
34	10	Misty Turquoise / Classic White	X				X		X
25	28	Astro Blue / Fathom Blue	X	X				X	X
55	10	Champagne Gold / Classic White	X		X	X			X
58	10	Autumn Gold / Classic White	X		X	X			X
28	25	Fathom Blue / Astro Blue	X	X				X	X
63	10	Desert Sand / Classic White	X						X

IMPALA 163-400 SERIES

69	37	47	39	67	SEATS Std. Bench	Black Cloth	Black Vinyl	Medium Blue Cloth	Medium Blue Vinyl	Saddle Vinyl	Dark Green Cloth	Dark Green Vinyl	Med. Gold Cloth	Med. Gold Vinyl	Turquoise Cloth	Sandalwood Vinyl	Red Vinyl
X					X	805	806	820	821		860		837		844		
			X		X	805	806	820	821		860	861	837		844	828	
	X				X	805	806	820	821	830	860	861	837		844	828	866
		X			X	805	806	820	821	830	860	861	837	841	844	828	
				X	X	805	806	820		830	860	861	837		844		866

RPO	EXTERIOR COLOR	Black Cloth	Black Vinyl	Medium Blue Cloth	Medium Blue Vinyl	Saddle Vinyl	Dark Green Cloth	Dark Green Vinyl	Med. Gold Cloth	Med. Gold Vinyl	Turquoise Cloth	Sandalwood Vinyl	Red Vinyl
19	Tuxedo Black	X	X	X	X	X	X	X	X	X	X	X	X
14	Cortez Silver	X	X	X	X	X	X	X			X	X	X
34	Misty Turquoise	X	X								X	X	
10	Classic White	X	X	X	X	X	X	X	X	X	X	X	X
28	Fathom Blue	X	X		X							X	
75	Cranberry Red	X	X			X						X	X
25	Astro Blue	X	X		X							X	
50	Gobi Beige	X	X			X	X	X	X	X		X	
48	Forest Green	X	X			X	X	X	X	X		X	
45	Green Mist	X	X			X	X	X				X	
58	Autumn Gold	X	X			X	X	X	X	X		X	
63	Desert Sand	X	X			X	X	X				X	
55	Champagne Gold	X	X			X			X	X		X	
78	Black Cherry	X	X			X						X	X
17	Shadow Gray	X	X	X	X	X						X	

RPO Lwr.	RPO Upr.	TWO-TONES @	Black Cloth	Black Vinyl	Medium Blue Cloth	Medium Blue Vinyl	Saddle Vinyl	Dark Green Cloth	Dark Green Vinyl	Med. Gold Cloth	Med. Gold Vinyl	Turquoise Cloth	Sandalwood Vinyl	Red Vinyl
25	10	Astro Blue / Classic White	X	X	X	X							X	
34	10	Misty Turquoise / Classic White	X	X								X	X	
25	28	Astro Blue / Fathom Blue	X	X	X	X							X	
55	10	Champagne Gold / Classic White	X	X			X	X	X	X	X		X	
58	10	Autumn Gold / Classic White	X	X			X	X	X	X	X		X	
28	25	Fathom Blue / Astro Blue	X	X	X	X							X	
63	10	Desert Sand / Classic White	X	X			X						X	

FOLDING TOP COLOR
White–Regular Production
Black–RPO

@–Not available on Convertible models.

STATION WAGON SERIES

	Seat Type	Black Vinyl	Med. Blue Vinyl	Saddle Vinyl	Dark Green Vinyl	Med. Gold Vinyl
Brookwood	Std. Bench	802	815	831	–	
Townsman	Std. Bench	804	819	838	–	839
Kingswood	Std. Bench	806	821	830	861	841
Kingswood Estate	Std. Bench	806	821	830	861	841

RPO	EXTERIOR COLOR	Black	Med. Blue	Saddle	Dark Green	Med. Gold
19	Tuxedo Black	X	X	X	X	X
14	Cortez Silver	X	X	X	X	
34	Misty Turquoise	X				
10	Classic White	X	X	X	X	X
28	Fathom Blue	X	X			
75	Cranberry Red	X		X		
25	Astro Blue	X	X			
50	Gobi Beige	X		X	X	X
48	Forest Green	X		X	X	X
45	Green Mist	X		X	X	
58	Autumn Gold	X		X	X	X
63	Desert Sand	X		X	X	
55	Champagne Gold	X		X		X
78	Black Cherry	X		X		
17	Shadow Gray	X	X	X		

RPO Lwr.	RPO Upr.	TWO-TONES*	Black	Med. Blue	Saddle	Dark Green	Med. Gold
25	10	Astro Blue / Classic White	X	X			
34	10	Misty Turquoise / Classic White	X				
25	28	Astro Blue / Fathom Blue	X	X			
55	10	Champagne Gold / Classic White	X		X	X	X
58	10	Autumn Gold / Classic White	X		X	X	X
28	25	Fathom Blue / Astro Blue	X	X			
63	10	Desert Sand / Classic White	X		X		

* – Except Kingswood Estate

1970 Trim Combinations

VINYL ROOF COLORS

		VINYL ROOF COLORS				
RPO	EXTERIOR COLOR	Black	White	Dark Blue	Dark Green	Dark Gold
19	Tuxedo Black	X	X			
14	Cortez Silver	X	X	X		
78	Black Cherry	X	X			
10	Classic White	X	X	X	X	
17	Shadow Gray	X				
75	Cranberry Red	X	X			
25	Astro Blue	X	X	X		
55	Champagne Gold	X	X			X
58	Autumn Gold	X	X			X
50	Gobi Beige	X	X			X
45	Green Mist	X	X		X	
48	Forest Green	X	X		X	
63	Desert Sand	X	X			
34	Misty Turquoise	X	X			
28	Fathom Blue	X	X	X		

Roof Sail Panel Moldings for 164-16647 models one color keyed to vinyl roof colors.

WINDSHIELD PILLAR MOLDING COLORS

INTERIOR TRIM COLOR	PILLAR MOLDING COLOR
Black	Black
Medium Blue	Dark Blue
Dark Blue	Dark Blue
Medium Saddle	Dark Saddle
Dark Green	Dark Green
Medium Turquoise	Dark Turquoise
Medium Red	Dark Red
Medium Gold	Dark Gold
Medium Sandalwood	Dark Sandalwood

All pillar moldings are painted metal except painted padding on metal for Convertible models.

SEAT BELT AND SHOULDER BELT COLORS

	STANDARD (a)	DELUXE (b)
INTERIOR TRIM	Seat Belts, Shoulder Belts, Roof Rail Retainers, Belt Retractor Colors	
Black	Black	Black
Medium Blue	Dark Blue	Dark Blue
Dark Blue	Dark Blue	Dark Blue
Medium Saddle	Black	Medium Saddle
Medium Turquoise	Black	Dark Turquoise
Medium Red	Black	Medium Red
Dark Green	Dark Green	Dark Green
Medium Gold	Medium Gold	Medium Gold
Sandalwood	Black	Medium Sandalwood

(a) Seat Belt and Shoulder Belt Buckles are plastic, same color as belts.

(b) Seat Belt and Shoulder Belt Buckles and brushed finish (includes Passenger-Driver Mini-Buckles).

CORVETTE

			INTERIOR TRIM COLORS & RPO NUMBERS					
Models		Trim	Black	Saddle	Red	Bright Blue	Green	Brown
37	67	Vinyl	Prod.	418	407	411	422	417
37	67	Deluxe*	403	424	—	—	—	—

RPO	EXTERIOR COLOR	Black	Saddle	Red	Bright Blue	Green	Brown
10	Classic White	X	X	X	X	X	X
14	Cortez Silver	X	X	X	X	X	X
15	Laguna Gray	X	X	X	X	X	X
26	Mulsanne Blue	X			X		
27	Bridgehampton Blue	X			X		
44	Donnybrooke Green	X	X			X	X
51	Daytona Yellow	X				X	
62	Ontario Orange	X					
72	Monza Red	X	X	X			X
77	Marlboro Maroon	X	X				X

Convertible Folding Top Colors:
Black—Production; White—RPO; Sandalwood—RPO; RPO C08 Vinyl Roof Option; Removable Hardtop—Black Pebble Grain

*Includes leather seat trim, special cut-pile carpeting on floor and lower side walls, wood grain insert on floor console, wood grain insert with bright die cast molding on door sidewall

CHEVY NOVA 111-113-11400 SERIES

APPLICATION	MODEL 27	MODEL 69	TRIM	Black	Dark Green	Med. Blue	Med. Gold	Sandal-wood
Standard	X	X	Cloth		745	735	740	
			Vinyl	731				
RPO ZJ1 (Custom Interior)	X	X	Cloth		744	736	741	
			Vinyl	732				747
RPO A51 (Bucket Seats)	X		Vinyl	733			742	746

(Interior colors and RPO numbers columns apply to the exterior color and two-tone tables below.)

Vinyl Roof: Black	Vinyl Roof: White	Vinyl Roof: Dark Blue	Vinyl Roof: Dark Green	Vinyl Roof: Dark Gold	RPO	EXTERIOR COLORS	Black	Dark Green	Med. Blue	Med. Gold	Sandal-wood
X	X				19	Tuxedo Black	X	X	X	X	X
X	X	X			14	Cortez Silver	X	X	X		X
X	X				34	Misty Turquoise	X				X
X	X	X	X		10	Classic White	X	X	X	X	X
X	X	X			28	Fathom Blue	X		X		X
X	X				75	Cranberry Red	X				X
X	X	X			25	Astro Blue	X		X		X
X	X			X	50	Gobi Beige	X	X		X	X
X	X		X		48	Forest Green	X	X		X	X
X	X		X		45	Green Mist	X	X			X
X	X			X	58	Autumn Gold	X	X		X	X
X	X				63	Desert Sand	X				X
X	X			X	55	Champagne Gold	X	X		X	X
X	X				78	Black Cherry	X				X
X					17	Shadow Gray	X	X	X		X

RPO Lwr.	RPO Upr.	TWO-TONES	Black	Dark Green	Med. Blue	Med. Gold	Sandal-wood
25	10	Astro Blue / Classic White	X		X		X
34	10	Misty Turquoise / Classic White	X				X
25	28	Astro Blue / Fathom Blue	X		X		X
28	25	Fathom Blue / Astro Blue	X		X		X
55	10	Champagne Gold / Classic White	X	X		X	X
58	10	Autumn Gold / Classic White	X	X		X	X
63	10	Desert Sand / Classic White	X				X

WINDSHIELD PILLAR MOLDING COLORS

INTERIOR TRIM COLOR	PILLAR MOLDING COLOR
Black	Black
Medium Blue	Dark Blue
Dark Green	Dark Green
Medium Gold	Dark Gold
Medium Sandalwood	Dark Sandalwood

SEAT BELT AND SHOULDER BELT COLORS

	STANDARD (a)	DELUXE (b)
INTERIOR TRIM	Seat Belts, Shoulder Belts, Roof Rail Retainer, Belt Retractor Colors	
Black	Black	Black
Medium Blue	Dark Blue	Dark Blue
Dark Green	Dark Green	Dark Green
Medium Gold	Medium Gold	Medium Gold
Medium Sandalwood	Black	Medium Sandalwood

(a) Seat Belt and Shoulder Belt Buckles are plastic, same color as belts.

(b) Seat Belt and Shoulder Belt Buckles are brushed finish (include Passenger-Driver Mini-Buckle).

CHAPTER 1

1970 Trim Combinations

MALIBU 135-13600 SERIES

MODELS 37	39	67	69	TRIM Bench	Bucket	INTERIOR TRIM COLOR AND RPO NUMBERS Black	Med. Blue	Saddle	Dark Green	Med. Gold	Turquoise	Ivory	Red
X	X		X	Cloth		753	762		782	776			
	X		X	Cloth							779		
X	X	X	X	Vinyl		755							
		X		Vinyl			764						
X		X		Vinyl				770				790	787
X	X			Vinyl					795				
	X			Vinyl						777			
X		X			Vinyl	756		771				791	788
		X			Vinyl		765						
X					Vinyl				796				

RPO	EXTERIOR COLORS	Black	Med. Blue	Saddle	Dark Green	Med. Gold	Turquoise	Ivory	Red
19	Tuxedo Black	X	X	X	X	X	X	X	X
14	Cortez Silver	X	X	X	X		X	X	X
34	Misty Turquoise	X					X	X	
10	Classic White	X	X	X	X	X	X	X	X
28	Fathom Blue	X	X					X	
75	Cranberry Red	X		X				X	X
25	Astro Blue	X		X				X	
50	Gobi Beige	X		X	X	X		X	
48	Forest Green	X		X	X	X		X	
45	Green Mist	X		X	X			X	
58	Autumn Gold	X		X	X	X		X	
63	Desert Sand	X		X				X	
55	Champagne Gold	X		X	X	X		X	
78	Black Cherry	X		X				X	X
17	Shadow Gray	X	X	X	X			X	X

RPO Lwr.	RPO Upr.	TWO-TONE @	Black	Med. Blue	Saddle	Dark Green	Med. Gold	Turquoise	Ivory	Red
25	10	Astro Blue / Classic White	X	X					X	
34	10	Misty Turquoise / Classic White	X					X	X	
25	28	Astro Blue / Fathom Blue	X	X					X	
28	25	Fathom Blue / Astro Blue	X	X					X	
55	10	Champagne Gold / Classic White	X		X	X	X		X	
58	10	Autumn Gold / Classic White	X		X	X	X		X	
63	10	Desert Sand / Classic White	X		X				X	

FOLDING TOP COLOR
White–Regular Production
Black–RPO

@–Not available on Convertible models.

VINYL ROOF COLORS

RPO	EXTERIOR COLOR	VINYL ROOF COLORS Black	White	Dark Blue	Dark Green	Dark Gold
19	Tuxedo Black	X	X			
14	Cortez Silver	X	X	X		
78	Black Cherry	X	X			
10	Classic White	X	X	X	X	
17	Shadow Gray	X				
75	Cranberry Red	X	X			
25	Astro Blue	X	X	X		
55	Champagne Gold	X	X			X
58	Autumn Gold	X	X			X
50	Gobi Beige	X	X			X
45	Green Mist	X	X		X	
48	Forest Green	X	X		X	
63	Desert Sand	X	X			
34	Misty Turquoise	X	X			
28	Fathom Blue	X	X	X		

WINDSHIELD PILLAR MOLDING COLORS

INTERIOR TRIM COLOR	PILLAR MOLDING COLOR
Black	Black
Medium Blue	Dark Blue
Medium Saddle	Dark Saddle
Dark Green	Dark Green
Ivory	Black
Medium Turquoise	Dark Turquoise
Medium Red	Dark Red
Medium Gold	Dark Gold

SEAT BELT AND SHOULDER BELT COLORS

INTERIOR TRIM	STANDARD (a)	DELUXE (b)
	Seat Belts, Shoulder Belts, Roof Rail Retainer, Belt Retractor Colors	
Black	Black	Black
Medium Blue	Dark Blue	Dark Blue
Medium Saddle	Black	Medium Saddle
Dark Green	Dark Green	Dark Green
Ivory	Black	Black
Medium Turquoise	Black	Dark Turquoise
Medium Red	Black	Medium Red
Medium Gold	Medium Gold	Medium Gold

(a) Standard Seat Belt and Shoulder Belt Buckles are plastic, same color as belts.
(b) Seat Belt and Shoulder Belt Buckles are brushed finish (includes Passenger-Driver Mini-Buckle).

STATION WAGON SERIES
EL CAMINO SERIES

SERIES	BODY STYLE 36	46	80	SEAT TRIM Bench	Bucket	INTERIOR COLORS AND RPO TRIM NUMBERS Black	Saddle	Blue
Nomad	X			Vinyl		750	772	759
Greenbrier	X	X		Vinyl		752	773	761
Concours	X	X		Vinyl		755	770	764
Concours Estate	X	X		Vinyl		755	770	764
Standard El Camino			X	Vinyl		752	773	761
Custom El Camino			X	Vinyl		755	770	764
Custom El Camino			X		Vinyl	756	771	765

VINYL ROOF COLORS @ Black	White	Dark Blue	Dark Green	Dark Gold	RPO	EXTERIOR COLORS	Black	Saddle	Blue
X	X				19	Tuxedo Black	X	X	X
X	X	X	X		10	Classic White	X	X	X
X	X	X			14	Cortez Silver	X	X	X
X	X				75	Cranberry Red	X	X	
X	X				78	Black Cherry	X	X	
X	X			X	55	Champagne Gold	X	X	
X	X			X	58	Autumn Gold	X	X	
X	X			X	50	Gobi Beige	X	X	
X	X				63	Desert Sand	X	X	
X	X		X		45	Green Mist	X	X	
X	X		X		48	Forest Green	X	X	
X	X				34	Misty Turquoise	X		
X	X	X			25	Astro Blue	X		X
X	X	X			28	Fathom Blue	X		X
X					17	Shadow Gray	X	X	X

@ Vinyl Roof for El Camino Only

MONTE CARLO 13800 SERIES

MODEL 57	67	SEAT TRIM Bench	Bucket	INTERIOR COLORS AND RPO TRIM NUMBERS Black	Saddle	Dark Green	Blue	Dark Blue	Gold	Sandalwood
X		Knitcloth		748		780		767		
X		Cloth					758		774	792
	X	Vinyl		754	778	785	768			
X			Knitcloth	749						
X	X		Vinyl	757	769					
X			Vinyl			784				

VINYL ROOF COLORS @ Black	White	Dark Blue	Dark Green	Dark Gold	RPO	EXTERIOR COLOR	Black	Saddle	Dark Green	Blue	Dark Blue	Gold	Sandalwood
X	X				19	Tuxedo Black	X	X	X	X	X	X	X
X	X	X	X		10	Classic White	X	X	X	X	X	X	X
X	X	X			14	Cortez Silver	X	X	X	X	X		X
X	X				75	Cranberry Red	X	X					X
X	X				78	Black Cherry	X	X					X
X	X			X	55	Champagne Gold	X	X	X			X	X
X	X			X	58	Autumn Gold	X	X	X			X	X
X	X			X	50	Gobi Beige	X	X	X			X	X
X	X				63	Desert Sand	X	X					X
X	X		X		45	Green Mist	X	X	X				X
X	X		X		48	Forest Green	X	X	X			X	X
X	X				34	Misty Turquoise	X						X
X	X	X			25	Astro Blue	X			X	X		X
X	X	X			28	Fathom Blue	X			X	X		X
X					17	Shadow Gray	X	X	X	X	X		X

FOLDING TOP COLOR
White-Reg. Production
Black-RPO

RPO	TWO-TONES @ Lower	Upper	Black	Saddle	Dark Green	Blue	Dark Blue	Gold	Sandalwood
25-10	Astro Blue	Classic White	X			X	X		X
34-10	Misty Turquoise	Classic White	X						X
25-28	Astro Blue	Fathom Blue	X			X	X		X
28-25	Fathom Blue	Astro Blue	X			X	X		X
55-10	Champagne Gold	Classic White	X	X	X			X	X
58-10	Autumn Gold	Classic White	X	X	X			X	X
63-10	Desert Sand	Classic White	X	X					X

WINDSHIELD PILLAR MOLDING COLORS

INTERIOR TRIM COLORS	PILLAR MOLDING COLOR
Black	Black
Medium Blue	Dark Blue
Dark Blue	Dark Blue
Medium Saddle	Dark Saddle
Dark Green	Dark Green
Medium Gold	Dark Gold
Medium Sandalwood	Dark Sandalwood

SEAT BELT AND SHOULDER BELT COLORS

INTERIOR TRIM	STANDARD (a)	DELUXE (b)
	Seat Belts, Shoulder Belts, Roof Rail Retainer, Belt Retractor Colors	
Black	Black	Black
Medium Blue	Dark Blue	Dark Blue
Dark Blue	Dark Blue	Dark Blue
Medium Saddle	Black	Medium Saddle
Dark Green	Dark Green	Dark Geeen
Medium Gold	Medium Gold	Medium Gold
Medium Sandalwood	Black	Medium Sandalwood

(a) Seat Belt and Shoulder Belt Buckles are plastic, same color as belts.
(b) Seat Belt and Shoulder Belt Buckles are brushed finish (includes Passenger - Driver Mini-Buckle).

1970 Trim Combinations

CAMARO

Series	Trim	INTERIOR COLORS AND RPO NUMBERS: Black	Sandalwood	Saddle	Bright Blue	Dark Green
	Vinyl	711	710	726	715	723
RPO 287 Custom Interior	Knit Vinyl	712	730	727	716	724
	Pattern Cloth	713/725*	—	—	714	720

VINYL ROOF COLORS: Black	White	Dark Green	RPO	EXTERIOR COLOR	Black	Sandalwood	Saddle	Bright Blue	Dark Green
X	X	X	10	Classic White	X	X	X	X	X
X	X		14	Cortez Silver	X	X	X	X	X
X	X		17	Shadow Gray	X	X	X		X
X	X		25	Astro Blue	X	X			
X	X		26	Mulsanne Blue	X	X	X	X	
X	X		43	Citrus Green	X	X			X
X	X	X	45	Green Mist	X	X	X		X
X	X	X	48	Forest Green	X	X	X		X
X	X		51	Daytona Yellow	X				X
X	X		53	Camaro Gold	X	X			X
X	X		58	Autumn Gold	X	X	X		X
X	X		63	Desert Sand	X	X	X		X
X	X		65	Hugger Orange	X	X			
X	X		67	Classic Copper	X	X	X		
X	X		75	Cranberry Red	X	X	X		

*Pattern cloth black & white for trim #713; all black for trim #725

1971 Trim Combinations

BISCAYNE 153-15400 SERIES
BEL AIR 155-15600 SERIES
IMPALA 163-16400 SERIES
CAPRICE 16600 SERIES

SERIES	MODEL 69	39	47	57	67	Black Cloth	Black Vinyl	Dark Blue Cloth	Dark Blue Vinyl	Sandalwood Cloth	Sandalwood Vinyl	Dark Jade Cloth	Dark Jade Vinyl	Medium Maize Cloth	Medium Maize Vinyl	Dark Saddle Vinyl
Biscayne	X					–	802	–	810	–	818	–	–	–	–	–
Bel Air	X					803	804	811	812	–	819	832	–	829	–	–
Impala	X					805	806	813	814	–	–	834	835	830	–	825
		X	X	X		805	806	813	814		820	834	835	830	827	825
					X	–	806	–	–	–	–	–	835	–	827	825
Caprice		X	X			807	–	815	–	821	–	836	–	828	–	–

CODE NO.	EXTERIOR COLOR	Black	Dark Blue	Sandalwood	Dark Jade	Medium Maize	Dark Saddle
11	Antique White	X	X	X	X	X	X
13	Nevada Silver	X	X	X			
16	Silver Steel	X		X			
19	Tuxedo Black	X	X	X	X	X	X
24	Ascot Blue	X	X	X			
29	Command Blue	X	X	X			
39	Sea Aqua	X		X			
42	Cottonwood Green	X		X	X		
49	Antique Green	X		X	X	X	X
52	Sunflower Yellow	X		X	X		X
55	Champagne Gold	X		X	X	X	X
61	Sandalwood	X		X	X		X
67	Classic Copper	X		X			
75	Cranberry Red	X		X			
78	Rosewood Metallic	X		X			

CODE NO. Lwr.	Upr.	TWO-TONES	Black	Dark Blue	Sandalwood	Dark Jade	Medium Maize	Dark Saddle
24	11	Antique White / Ascot Blue	X	X	X			
29	11	Antique White / Command Blue	X	X	X			
39	11	Antique White / Sea Aqua	X		X			
42	11	Antique White / Cottonwood Green	X		X	X		
49	11	Antique White / Antique Green	X		X	X	X	X
55	11	Antique White / Champagne Gold	X		X	X	X	X

Convertible Top: Black or White with any exterior color.

Wheels: Argent Silver with all exterior colors.

VINYL ROOF COLORS

CODE NO.	EXTERIOR COLOR	VINYL ROOF COLORS: Black	White	Dark Blue	Dark Green	Dark Brown
11	Antique White	X	X	X	X	X
13	Nevada Silver	X	X	X		
16	Silver Steel	X	X			
19	Tuxedo Black	X	X	X	X	
24	Ascot Blue	X	X	X		
29	Command Blue	X	X	X		
39	Sea Aqua	X	X			
42	Cottonwood Green	X	X		X	
49	Antique Green	X	X		X	
52	Sunflower Yellow	X	X			
55	Champaigne Gold	X	X			
61	Sandalwood	X	X			X
67	Classic Copper	X	X			X
75	Cranberry Red	X	X			
78	Rosewood Metallic	X	X			X

STATION WAGON SERIES

MODELS	Seat Trim	INTERIOR TRIM COLORS & RPO NUMBERS: Black	Dark Blue	Dark Jade	Medium Maize	Medium Saddle	Dark Saddle
Brookwood	Vinyl	802	810	–	–	823	–
*Townsman		804	812	–	–	824	–
Kingswood / Kingswood Estate		806	814	835	827	–	825

CODE NO.	EXTERIOR COLOR	Black	Dark Blue	Dark Jade	Medium Maize	Medium Saddle	Dark Saddle
11	Antique White	X	X	X	X	X	X
13	Nevada Silver	X	X				
16	Silver Steel	X				X	
19	Tuxedo Black	X	X	X	X	X	X
24	Ascot Blue	X	X				
29	Command Blue	X	X			X	
39	Sea Aqua	X					
42	Cottonwood Green	X		X			X
49	Antique Green	X		X	X	X	
52	Sunflower Yellow	X		X		X	X
55	Champagne Gold	X		X	X		X
61	Sandalwood	X		X		X	X
67	Classic Copper	X				X	
75	Cranberry Red	X				X	
78	Rosewood Metallic	X					

CODE NO. Lwr.	Upr.	TWO-TONE COLORS	Black	Dark Blue	Dark Jade	Medium Maize	Medium Saddle	Dark Saddle
24	11	Antique White / Ascot Blue	X	X				
29	11	Antique White / Command Blue	X	X			X	
39	11	Antique White / Sea Aqua	X					
42	11	Antique White / Cottonwood Green	X		X			X
49	11	Antique White / Antique Green	X		X	X	X	
55	11	Antique White / Champagne Gold	X		X	X		X

*–Except Kingswood Estate models.

WHEELS: Argent Silver with all exterior colors.

CORVETTE

	Interior Trim	INTERIOR TRIM COLORS & RPO NO'S.: Black	Dark Saddle	Red	Dk. Brt. Blue	Dark Green
Standard	Vinyl	400	417	407	412	423
Custom*	Leather	403	420	–	–	–

*Special "Firemist" colors.

CODE	EXTERIOR COLOR	Black	Dark Saddle	Red	Dk. Brt. Blue	Dark Green
10	Classic White	X	X	X	X	X
13	Nevada Silver	X		X	X	X
26	Mulsanne Blue	X			X	
27	Bridgehampton Blue	X			X	
48	Brands Hatch Green	X	X			X
52	Sunflower Yellow	X	X			X
76	Mille Miglia Red	X		X		
91*	War Bonnet Yellow	X	X			X
97*	Ontario Orange	X	X			X
98*	Steel Cities Gray	X				

Convertible Top: Black or White with any exterior color.

Vinyl Top: Used with auxiliary top only, Black with any exterior color.

*–Includes leather seat trim, special cut pile carpeting on floor and lower door side walls. Wood grain insert on floor console. Wood grain insert with bright die cast molding on door side wall.

1971 Trim Combinations

CHEVY NOVA 113-11400 SERIES

Models 27	Models 69	Interior Trim	Front Seat Type	Black Cloth	Black Vinyl	Dark Blue Cloth	Dark Blue Vinyl	Dark Jade Cloth	Dark Jade Vinyl	Sandalwood Vinyl	Dark Saddle Vinyl
X	X	Std.	Bench	750	751	756	757	759	760	763	–
X	X	Custom	Bench	752	753	–	–	761	–	764	–
X		Custom	Bucket	–	754	–	–	–	–	–	767

Vinyl Roof: Black	White	Blue	Green	Brown	Code No.	Exterior Color	Black	Dark Blue	Dark Jade	Sandalwood	Dark Saddle
X	X	X	X	X	11	Antique White	X	X	X	X	X
X	X	X			13	Nevada Silver	X	X		X	
X	X	X	X		19	Tuxedo Black	X	X	X	X	X
X	X	X			24	Ascot Blue	X	X		X	
X	X	X			26	Mulsanne Blue	X	X		X	
X	X		X		42	Cottonwood Green	X		X	X	
X	X		X		43	Lime Green	X		X	X	X
X	X		X		49	Antique Green	X		X	X	X
X	X				52	Sunflower Yellow	X		X	X	X
X	X				53	Placer Gold	X			X	X
X	X			X	61	Sandalwood	X		X	X	X
X	X			X	62	Burnt Orange	X			X	
X	X			X	67	Classic Copper	X			X	
X	X				75	Cranberry Red	X			X	
X	X			X	78	Rosewood Metallic	X			X	

Code No. Lwr.	Code No. Upr.	Two-Tones	Black	Dark Blue	Dark Jade	Sandalwood	Dark Saddle
26	11	Antique White / Mulsanne Blue	X	X		X	
43	11	Antique White / Lime Green	X		X	X	X
49	11	Antique White / Antique Green	X		X	X	X
53	11	Antique White / Placer Gold	X			X	X
61	11	Antique White / Sandalwood	X		X	X	X
62	11	Antique White / Burnt Orange	X			X	

STATION WAGON SERIES
EL CAMINO SERIES

Series	Body Style 36	Body Style 46	Body Style 80	Front Seat Type	Seat Trim	Black	Dark Jade	Sandalwood	Medium Saddle	Dark Saddle
Nomad	X			Bench	Vinyl	702	–	712	719	–
Greenbrier	X	X		Bench	Vinyl	703	–	713	720	–
Concours	X	X		Bench	Vinyl	705	731	–	–	721
Concours Estate	X	X		Bench	Vinyl	705	731	–	–	721
Standard El Camino			X	Bench	Vinyl	703	–	713	720	–
Custom El Camino			X	Bench	Vinyl	705	731	714	–	721
				Bucket		706	732	715	–	722

Vinyl Top*: Black	White	Blue	Green	Brown	Code No.	Exterior Color	Black	Dark Jade	Sandalwood	Medium Saddle	Dark Saddle
X	X	X	X	X	11	Antique White	X	X	X	X	X
X	X	X			13	Nevada Silver	X		X		
X	X	X	X		19	Tuxedo Black	X	X	X	X	X
X	X	X			24	Ascot Blue	X		X		
X	X	X			26	Mulsanne Blue	X		X	X	
X	X		X		42	Cottonwood Green	X	X	X		
X	X		X		43	Lime Green	X	X	X		X
X	X		X		49	Antique Green	X	X	X	X	X
X	X				52	Sunflower Yellow	X	X	X	X	X
X	X				53	Placer Gold	X		X		X
X	X			X	61	Sandalwood	X	X	X	X	X
X	X			X	62	Burnt Orange	X		X		
X	X			X	67	Classic Copper	X		X	X	
X	X				75	Cranberry Red	X		X	X	
X	X			X	78	Rosewood Metallic	X		X		

(*)–El Camino and Custom El Camino only.

MONTE CARLO 13800 SERIES

Model	Front Seat Type	Black Cloth	Black Vinyl	Dark Jade Cloth	Dark Jade Vinyl	Dark Blue Cloth	Sandalwood Cloth	Dark Saddle Vinyl
57	Bench	708	–	734	–	728	717	–
	Bucket	707	710	733	729	727	716	723

Vinyl Top: Black	White	Blue	Green	Brown	Code No.	Exterior Color	Black	Dark Jade	Dark Blue	Sandalwood	Dark Saddle
X	X	X	X	X	11	Antique White	X	X	X	X	X
X	X	X			13	Nevada Silver	X		X	X	
X	X	X	X		19	Tuxedo Black	X	X	X	X	X
X	X	X			24	Ascot Blue	X		X	X	
X	X	X			26	Mulsanne Blue	X		X	X	
X	X		X		42	Cottonwood Green	X	X		X	
X	X		X		43	Lime Green	X	X		X	X
X	X		X		49	Antique Green	X	X		X	X
X	X				52	Sunflower Yellow	X	X		X	X
X	X				53	Placer Gold	X			X	X
X	X			X	61	Sandalwood	X	X		X	X
X	X			X	62	Burnt Orange	X			X	
X	X			X	67	Classic Copper	X			X	
X	X				75	Cranberry Red	X			X	
X	X			X	78	Rosewood Metallic	X			X	

Code No. Lwr.	Code No. Upr.	Two-Tones	Black	Dark Jade	Dark Blue	Sandalwood	Dark Saddle
26	11	Antique White / Mulsanne Blue	X	X	X		
43	11	Antique White / Lime Green	X	X			X
49	11	Antique White / Antique Green	X	X			X
53	11	Antique White / Placer Gold	X	X			
61	11	Antique White / Sandalwood	X	X		X	
62	11	Antique White / Burnt Orange	X	X		X	

CHEVELLE 133-13400 SERIES
MALIBU 135-13600 SERIES

Series	Model 37	Model 39	Model 67	Model 69	Front Seat Type	Black Cloth	Black Vinyl	Dark Blue Cloth	Dark Blue Vinyl	Dark Jade Cloth	Dark Jade Vinyl	Sandalwood Cloth	Sandalwood Vinyl	Dark Saddle Vinyl
Chevelle	X			X	Bench	701	703	724	–	736	–	–	–	–
Malibu				X	Bench	704	705	725	–	730	–	–	714	721
		X			Bench	704	705	725	726	730	731	718	714	–
	X				Bench	704	705	725	–	730	731	718	714	721
	X				Bucket	–	706	–	–	–	732	–	715	722
			X		Bench	–	705	–	–	–	731	–	–	721
			X		Bucket	–	706	–	–	–	732	–	–	722

Code No.	Exterior Color	Black	Dark Blue	Dark Jade	Sandalwood	Dark Saddle
11	Antique White	X	X	X	X	X
13	Nevada Silver	X	X		X	
19	Tuxedo Black	X	X	X	X	X
24	Ascot Blue	X	X		X	
26	Mulsanne Blue	X	X		X	
42	Cottonwood Green	X		X	X	
43	Lime Green	X		X	X	X
49	Antique Green	X		X	X	X
52	Sunflower Yellow	X		X	X	X
53	Placer Gold	X			X	X
61	Sandalwood	X		X	X	X
62	Burnt Orange	X			X	
67	Classic Copper	X			X	
75	Cranberry Red	X			X	
78	Rosewood Metallic	X			X	

Code No. Lwr.	Code No. Upr.	Two-Tone	Black	Dark Blue	Dark Jade	Sandalwood	Dark Saddle
26	11	Antique White / Mulsanne Blue	X	X		X	
43	11	Antique White / Lime Green	X		X	X	X
49	11	Antique White / Antique Green	X		X	X	X
53	11	Antique White / Placer Gold	X			X	X
61	11	Antique White / Sandalwood	X		X	X	X
62	11	Antique White / Burnt Orange	X			X	

Convertible Top: Black or White with any exterior color.

CAMARO

Series	Trim	Black	Dark Blue	Dark Jade	Dark Saddle	Sandal-Wood	White/Black
Standard	Vinyl	775	776	778	779	777	–
Custom Z87	Cloth	785	786	787	792	–	789

Vinyl Roof: Black	White	Blue	Green	Brown	Code No.	Exterior Color	Black	Dark Blue	Dark Jade	Dark Saddle	Sandal-Wood	White/Black
X	X	X	X	X	11	Antique White	X	X	X	X	X	X
X	X	X			13	Nevada silver	X	X			X	X
X	X	X	X		19	Tuxedo Black	X	X	X	X	X	X
X	X	X			24	Ascot Blue	X	X			X	X
X	X	X			26	Mulsanne Blue	X	X			X	X
X	X		X		42	Cottonwood Green	X		X		X	X
X	X		X		43	Lime Green	X		X	X	X	X
X	X		X		49	Antique Green	X		X	X	X	X
X	X				52	Sunflower Yellow	X		X	X	X	X
X	X				53	Placer Gold	X			X	X	X
X	X			X	61	Sandalwood	X		X	X	X	X
X	X			X	62	Burnt Orange	X				X	X
X	X			X	67	Classic Copper	X				X	X
X	X				75	Cranberry Red	X				X	X
X	X			X	78	Rosewood Metallic	X				X	X

1972 Trim Combinations

BISCAYNE 153-15400 SERIES *
BEL AIR 155-15600 SERIES *
IMPALA 163-16400 SERIES *
CAPRICE 16600 SERIES

SERIES	MODEL					INTERIOR COLORS AND CODE NUMBERS: Black			Dark Blue		Light Covert		Dark Saddle	Dark Green			Medium Pewter	
	69	39	47	57	67	Cloth	Knit	Vinyl	Cloth	Vinyl	Cloth	Vinyl	Vinyl	Cloth	Knit	Vinyl	Cloth	Vinyl
Biscayne	X							802		809		816						
Bel Air	X					803		804	810	811		817		828				
Impala	X					805		806	812		815	818	826	829		830		
		X	X	X		805		806	812	813	815	818	826	829		830	834	835
					X			806				818	826					
Caprice		X	X			807	838		814		819			831	833		836	
	X						838		814		819				833		836	

CODE NO.	EXTERIOR COLOR	Black	Dark Blue	Light Covert	Dark Saddle	Dark Green	Medium Pewter
11	Antique White	X	X	X	X	X	X
14	Pewter Silver	X			X	X	X
18	Dusk Gray Metallic	X					X
19	Tuxedo Black	X	X	X	X	X	X
24	Ascot Blue	X	X				
28	Fathom Blue	X	X				
43	Gulf Green	X		X		X	
48	Sequoia Green	X		X	X	X	
50	Covert Tan	X		X	X	X	
54	Desert Gold	X		X			
57	Golden Brown	X		X			
62	Driftwood	X			X		
68	Midnight Bronze	X		X	X		
69	Aegean Brown	X			X		
75	Cranberry Red	X			X		

CODE NO.	TWO-TONE Lower	Upper	Black	Dark Blue	Light Covert	Dark Saddle	Dark Green	Medium Pewter
24-11	Ascot Blue	White	X	X				
28-11	Fathom Blue	White	X	X				
43-11	Gulf Green	White	X		X		X	
48-11	Sequoia Green	White	X		X	X	X	
54-11	Desert Gold	White	X		X			
57-11	Golden Brown	White	X		X			

Convertible Top: Black or White with any exterior color.
Wheels: Lower body color with hub caps, black with wheel covers.

* 153-155-16300 Series not merchandised after January 1, 1972.

STATION WAGON SERIES

SERIES	Model		INTERIOR TRIM AND CODE NUMBERS: Black		Dark Blue	Light Covert	Dark Saddle	Dark Green
	35	45	Cloth	Vinyl	Vinyl	Vinyl	Vinyl	Vinyl
Brookwood	X			802			824	
Townsman	X	X		804			825	
Kingswood	X	X		806	813	818	826	830
Kingswood Estate	X	X	808	806	813	818	826	830

COLOR CODE	EXTERIOR COLOR	Black	Dark Blue	Light Covert	Dark Saddle	Dark Green
11	Antique White	X	X	X	X	X
14	Pewter Silver	X			X	X
18	Dusk Gray Metallic	X				
19	Tuxedo Black	X	X	X	X	X
24	Ascot Blue	X	X			
28	Fathom Blue	X	X			
43	Gulf Green	X		X		X
48	Sequoia Green	X		X	X	X
50	Covert Tan	X		X	X	X
54	Desert Gold	X		X		
57	Golden Brown	X		X		
62	Driftwood	X			X	
68	Midnight Bronze	X		X	X	
69	Aegean Brown	X			X	
75	Cranberry Red	X			X	

CODE NO.	TWO-TONE LOWER	UPPER	Black	Dark Blue	Light Covert	Dark Saddle	Dark Green
24-11	Ascot Blue	White	X	X			
28-11	Fathom Blue	White	X	X			
43-11	Gulf Green	White	X		X		X
48-11	Sequoia Green	White	X		X	X	X
54-11	Desert Gold	White	X		X		
57-11	Golden Brown	White	X		X		

WHEELS: Lower body color with hub caps, black with wheel covers.

CODE NO.	EXTERIOR COLOR	VINYL ROOF COLORS: Black	White	Medium Green	Medium Blue	Light Covert
11	Antique White	X	X	X	X	X
14	Pewter Silver	X	X	X		
18	Dusk Gray Metallic	X	X			X
19	Tuxedo Black	X	X	X	X	X
24	Ascot Blue	X	X		X	
28	Fathom Blue	X	X		X	
43	Gulf Green	X	X	X		
48	Sequoia Green	X	X	X		X
50	Covert Tan	X	X			X
54	Desert Gold	X	X			X
57	Golden Brown	X	X			X
62	Driftwood	X	X			
68	Midnight Bronze	X	X			X
69	Aegean Brown	X	X			
75	Cranberry Red	X	X			

CORVETTE

	Interior Trim	INTERIOR TRIM COLORS AND CODE NUMBERS: Black	Dark Saddle	Red	Dark Bright Blue
Standard	Vinyl	400	417	407	412
Custom**	Leather	404	421		

COLOR CODE	EXTERIOR COLOR	Black	Dark Saddle	Red	Dark Bright Blue
10	Classic White	X	X	X	X
14	Pewter Silver	X	X	X	X
27	Targa Blue	X			X
37	Bryar Blue	X			
47	Elkhart Green	X	X		
52	Sunflower Yellow	X	X		
76	Mille Miglia Red	X	X	X	
91*	War Bonnet Yellow	X	X		
97*	Ontario Orange	X	X		
98*	Atlanta Gray	X	X	X	

*–Special "Firemist" color

Convertible top: black or white with any exterior color.

Vinyl top, used with auxiliary top only, black with any exterior color.

Wheels: Argent with hub caps and wheel covers.

**–Includes leather seat trim, special cut pile carpeting on floor and lower door side walls. Wood grain insert on floor console. Wood grain insert with bright die cast molding on door side wall.

NOVA 113-11400 SERIES

MODEL 27	MODEL 69	Interior Trim	Front Seat	INTERIOR TRIM COLORS AND CODE NUMBERS: Black Cloth	Black Vinyl	Dark Blue Cloth	Dark Green Cloth	Dark Green Vinyl	Light Covert Cloth	Light Covert Vinyl	Med. Tan Vinyl	White Vinyl
X		Standard	Bucket		751							767
X			Bench	750	751	756	759	760	765	763		
	X		Bench	750	751	756	759	760		763		
X		Custom	Bench	752	753		761			764		
X			Bucket		753						766	
	X		Bench	752			761			764		

COLOR CODE	EXTERIOR COLOR	Black	Dark Blue	Dark Green	Light Covert	Med. Tan	White
11	Antique White	X	X	X	X	X	X
14	Pewter Silver	X		X		X	X
24	Ascot Blue	X	X				X
26	Mulsanne Blue	X	X				X
36	Spring Green	X					X
43	Gulf Green	X		X	X		X
48	Sequoia Green	X		X	X	X	X
50	Covert Tan	X		X	X	X	X
53	Placer Gold	X			X		X
56	Cream Yellow	X			X	X	X
57	Golden Brown	X			X	X	X
63	Mohave Gold	X			X	X	X
65	Orange Flame	X					X
68	Midnight Bronze	X			X	X	X
75	Cranberry Red	X					X

COLOR CODE	TWO-TONE LOWER	UPPER	Black	Dark Blue	Dark Green	Light Covert	Med. Tan	White
26-11	Mulsanne Blue	White	X	X				X
43-11	Gulf Green	White	X		X	X		X
48-11	Sequoia Green	White	X		X	X	X	X
57-11	Golden Brown	White	X			X	X	X
63-11	Mohave Gold	White	X			X	X	X

WHEELS: Body color with hub caps, black with wheel covers and argent with RPO rally wheels.

VINYL ROOF COLORS

COLOR CODE	EXTERIOR COLOR	VINYL ROOF COLORS: Black	White	Medium Green	Light Covert	Medium Tan
11	Antique White	X	X	X	X	X
14	Pewter Silver	X	X	X		
24	Ascot Blue	X	X			
26	Mulsanne Blue	X	X			
36	Spring Green	X	X			
43	Gulf Green	X	X	X		
48	Sequoia Green	X	X	X	X	
50	Covert Tan	X	X		X	
53	Placer Gold	X	X		X	
56	Cream Yellow	X	X		X	
57	Golden Brown	X	X		X	
63	Mohave Gold	X	X		X	X
65	Orange Flame	X	X		X	
68	Midnight Bronze	X	X		X	X
75	Cranberry Red	X	X			

1972 Trim Combinations

CHEVELLE 133-13400 SERIES
MALIBU 135-13600 SERIES

SERIES	MODEL 37	67	39	69	Front Seat	INTERIOR TRIM COLORS AND CODE NUMBERS: Black Cloth	Black Vinyl	Dark Green Cloth	Dark Green Vinyl	Medium Tan Vinyl	Dark Blue Cloth	Light Covert Cloth	Light Covert Vinyl	White Vinyl
Chevelle	X				Bench	702	701	711	710	719	723			
				X	Bench	702	701	711		719	723			
Malibu				X	Bench	703	704		713	720	724	730	732	
			X		Bench	703	704		713		724	730	732	743
	X				Bench	703	704		713	720	724	730	732	743
	X				Bucket		704		713	720			732	743
		X			Bench		704		713					743
					Bucket		704		713					743

COLOR CODE	EXTERIOR COLOR	Black	Dark Green	Medium Tan	Dark Blue	Light Covert	White
11	Antique White	X	X	X	X	X	X
14	Pewter Silver	X	X	X			X
24	Ascot Blue	X			X		X
26	Mulsanne Blue	X			X		X
36	Spring Green	X					X
43	Gulf Green	X	X			X	X
48	Sequoia Green	X	X	X		X	X
50	Covert Tan	X	X	X		X	X
53	Placer Gold	X				X	X
56	Cream Yellow	X		X		X	X
57	Golden Brown	X		X		X	X
63	Mohave Gold	X		X		X	X
65	Orange Flame	X					X
68	Midnight Bronze	X		X		X	X
75	Cranberry Red	X					X

TWO-TONE* COLOR CODE	LOWER	UPPER	Black	Dark Green	Medium Tan	Dark Blue	Light Covert	White
26-11	Mulsanne Blue	White	X			X		X
43-11	Gulf Green	White	X	X			X	X
48-11	Sequoia Green	White	X	X	X		X	X
57-11	Golden Brown	White	X		X		X	X
63-11	Mohave Gold	White	X		X		X	X

Wheels: lower body color with hub caps, black with wheel covers, argent with RPO Rally wheels, dark gray with SS Trans-Am wheel.

* Not available on Convertible models.

STATION WAGON SERIES
EL CAMINO SERIES

SERIES	BODY STYLE 36	46	80	Seat Trim	INTERIOR TRIM COLORS AND CODE NUMBERS: Black	Dark Green	Medium Tan	Light Covert
Nomad	X			Vinyl	705		721	
Greenbrier	X	X		Vinyl	701	710	719	
Concours	X	X		Vinyl	704	713	720	
Concours Estate	X	X		Vinyl	704	713	720	
Std. El Camino			X	Vinyl	701		719	
Custom El Camino			X	Vinyl	704		720	732

COLOR CODE	EXTERIOR COLOR	Black	Dark Green	Medium Tan	Light Covert
11	Antique White	X	X	X	X
14	Pewter Silver	X	X	X	
24	Ascot Blue	X			
26	Mulsanne Blue	X			
36	Spring Green	X			
43	Gulf Green	X	X		X
48	Sequoia Green	X	X	X	X
50	Covert Tan	X	X	X	X
53	Placer Gold	X			X
56	Cream Yellow	X		X	X
57	Golden Brown	X		X	X
63	Mohave Gold	X		X	X
65	Orange Flame	X			
68	Midnight Bronze	X		X	X
75	Cranberry Red	X			

TWO-TONE* COLOR CODE	LOWER	UPPER	Black	Dark Green	Medium Tan	Light Covert
26-11	Mulsanne Blue	White	X			
43-11	Gulf Green	White	X	X		X
48-11	Sequoia Green	White	X	X	X	X
57-11	Golden Brown	White	X		X	X
63-11	Mohave Gold	White	X		X	X

*– Available only on El Camino models.

Wheels: lower body color with hub caps, black with wheel covers, argent color with RPO rally wheels and dark gray with SS Trans-Am wheel.

VINYL ROOF COLORS

COLOR CODE	EXTERIOR COLOR	VINYL ROOF COLORS: Black	White	Medium Green	Medium Tan	Light Covert
11	Antique White	X	X	X	X	X
14	Pewter Silver	X	X	X		
24	Ascot Blue	X	X			
26	Mulsanne Blue	X	X			
36	Spring Green	X	X			
43	Gulf Green	X	X	X		
48	Sequoia Green	X	X	X		X
50	Covert Tan	X	X			X
53	Placer Gold	X	X			X
56	Cream Yellow	X	X			X
57	Golden Brown	X	X			X
63	Mohave Gold	X	X		X	X
65	Orange Flame	X	X			X
68	Midnight Bronze	X	X		X	X
75	Cranberry Red	X	X			

MONTE CARLO 13800 SERIES

MODEL	Front Seat Type	INTERIOR TRIM COLORS AND CODE NUMBERS: Black Cloth	Black Vinyl	Dark Blue Cloth	Dark Green Cloth	Dark Green Vinyl	Med. Pewter Cloth	Dark Saddle Vinyl	Light Covert Cloth	Light Covert Vinyl
57	Bench	706	708	725	715		740	735	731	734
	Bucket	706	708			717	740	735		

COLOR CODE	EXTERIOR COLOR	Black	Dark Blue	Dark Green	Med. Pewter	Dark Saddle	Light Covert
11	Antique White	X	X	X	X	X	X
14	Pewter Silver	X		X	X	X	
24	Ascot Blue	X	X				
26	Mulsanne Blue	X	X				
36	Spring Green	X					
43	Gulf Green	X		X			X
48	Sequoia Green	X		X		X	X
50	Covert Tan	X		X		X	X
53	Placer Gold	X				X	X
56	Cream Yellow	X				X	X
57	Golden Brown	X					X
63	Mohave Gold	X				X	X
65	Orange Flame	X				X	
68	Midnight Bronze	X				X	X
75	Cranberry Red	X				X	

TWO-TONE COLOR CODE	LOWER	UPPER	Black	Dark Blue	Dark Green	Med. Pewter	Dark Saddle	Light Covert
26-11	Mulsanne Blue	White	X	X				
43-11	Gulf Green	White	X		X			X
48-11	Sequoia Green	White	X		X		X	X
57-11	Golden Brown	White	X					X
63-11	Mohave Gold	White	X				X	X

VINYL ROOF COLORS

COLOR CODE	EXTERIOR COLOR	VINYL ROOF COLORS: Black	White	Medium Green	Medium Tan	Light Covert
11	Antique White	X	X	X	X	X
14	Pewter Silver	X	X	X		
24	Ascot Blue	X	X			
26	Mulsanne Blue	X	X			
36	Spring Green	X	X	X		
43	Gulf Green	X	X	X		
48	Sequoia Green	X	X	X		X
50	Covert Tan	X	X			X
53	Placer Gold	X	X			X
56	Cream Yellow	X	X			X
57	Golden Brown	X	X			X
63	Mohave Gold	X	X		X	X
65	Orange Flame	X	X			X
68	Midnight Bronze	X	X		X	X
75	Cranberry Red	X	X			

CAMARO 12000 SERIES

SERIES	INTERIOR TRIM COLORS AND CODE NUMBERS: Black Cloth	Black Vinyl	Dark Blue Cloth	Dark Blue Vinyl	Dark Green Cloth	Dark Green Vinyl	Medium Tan Vinyl	Light Covert Cloth	Light Covert Vinyl	White Vinyl
Standard		775		776		777	778		779	780
Deluxe Z87	785		786		787			788		

COLOR CODE	EXTERIOR COLOR	Black	Dark Blue	Dark Green	Medium Tan	Light Covert	White
11	Antique White	X	X	X	X	X	X
14	Pewter Silver	X		X	X		X
24	Ascot Blue	X	X				X
26	Mulsanne Blue	X	X				X
36	Spring Green	X					X
43	Gulf Green	X		X		X	X
48	Sequoia Green	X		X	X	X	X
50	Covert Tan	X		X	X	X	X
53	Placer Gold	X				X	X
56	Cream Yellow	X			X	X	X
57	Golden Brown	X			X	X	X
63	Mohave Gold	X			X	X	X
65	Orange Flame	X					X
68	Midnight Bronze	X			X	X	X
75	Cranberry Red	X					X

Wheels: Body color with hub caps, black with wheel covers, argent with RPO rally wheels, and dark gray with Z28 Trans-Am wheels.

VINYL ROOF COLORS

COLOR CODE	EXTERIOR COLOR	VINYL ROOF COLORS: Black	White	Medium Green	Light Covert	Medium Tan
11	Antique White	X	X	X	X	X
14	Pewter Silver	X	X	X		
24	Ascot Blue	X	X			
26	Mulsanne Blue	X	X			
36	Spring Green	X	X			
43	Gulf Green	X	X	X		
48	Sequoia Green	X	X	X	X	
50	Covert Tan	X	X		X	
53	Placer Gold	X	X		X	
56	Cream Yellow	X	X		X	
57	Golden Brown	X	X		X	
63	Mohave Gold	X	X		X	X
65	Orange Flame	X	X		X	
68	Midnight Bronze	X	X		X	X
75	Cranberry Red	X	X			

1973 Trim Combinations

1973 CHEVROLET "B" INTERIOR – EXTERIOR COLOR COMBINATIONS

MODEL	Seat Type	INTERIOR TRIM Black Cloth	Black * Sport Cloth /Black	Black * Sport Cloth /Red	Black Knit Cloth	Black Vinyl	Black Knit Vinyl	Medium Blue Cloth	Midnight Blue Cloth	Midnight Blue Knit Cloth	Midnight Blue Vinyl
Bel Air – 1BK00 Sedan (69)	Bench	803					804	810			
Station Wagons (35-45)											
Impala – 1BL00 Sedan (69)		805	802	802		806			812		813
Sport Sedan (39)		805	802	802		806			812		813
Sport Coupe (57)		805	802	802		806			812		813
Custom Coupe (47)		805	802	802		806			812		813
Station Wagons (35-45)						806					813
Caprice Classic – 1BN00 Sedan (69)					840					843	
	50-50				840					843	
Sport Sedan (39)	Bench				840					843	
	50-50				840					843	
Custom Coupe (47)	Bench				840					843	
	50-50				840					843	
Convertible (67)	Bench										
Station Wagons (35-45)	Bench					806					813
EXTERIOR COLOR	Color Code										
White C/O	11	X		X		X		X		X	
Black C/O	19	X		X		X		X		X	
Medium Blue Metallic	24	X				X		X		X	
Bright Blue Metallic	26	X				X		X		X	
Dark Blue Metallic	29	X				X		X		X	
Dark Brt. Green Metallic	42	X				X					
Light Green Metallic	44	X				X					
Dark Green Gold Metallic	46	X				X					
Dark Green	48	X				X					
Chamois	56	X				X					
Yellow Orange Metallic	60	X				X					
Silver Taupe Metallic	64	X		X		X		X		X	
Taupe Metallic	66	X				X					
Brown Metallic	68	X				X					
Red Metallic	74	X		X		X					
Yellow Beige	81	X				X					
TWO TONE Lower / Upper	Color Code										
Med. Blue Met. / White	24-11	X				X		X		X	
Dk. Blue Met. / White	29-11	X				X		X		X	
Lt. Green Met. / White	44-11	X				X					
Dk. Green Gold Met. / White	46-11	X				X					
Dark Green / White	48-11	X				X					
Chamois / White	56-11	X				X					

* Accent carpet color. Obtained by specifying trim number plus Accent Carpet RPO number 19F – Black, 75F – Red, or 24F – Blue.

NOTE: Excepting models with vinyl roof or convertible top, solid exterior color and non-recommended interior trim combinations may be had when RPO ZP2 override is specified.

EXTERIOR COLOR – VINYL ROOF COMBINATIONS

BODY LOWER COLOR CODE	PAINT COLOR	OPTIONAL VINYL ROOF COLOR Black	White	Med. Green	Med. Blue	Light Neutral	Chamois	Maroon
11	White	X	X	X	X		X	X
19	Black	X	X			X	X	
24	Medium Blue Metallic	X	X		X			
26	Bright Blue Metallic	X	X					
29	Dark Blue Metallic	X	X		X			
42	Dark Bright Green Metallic	X	X					
44	Light Green Metallic	X	X	X				
46	Dark Green Gold Metallic	X	X			X		
48	Dark Green	X	X	X		X		
56	Chamois	X	X				X	
60	Yellow Orange Metallic	X	X			X		
64	Silver Taupe Metallic	X	X					X
66	Taupe Metallic	X	X			X	X	
68	Brown Metallic	X	X			X		
74	Red Metallic	X	X			X		X
81	Yellow Beige	X	X				X	

1973 CHEVROLET "B" INTERIOR – EXTERIOR COLOR COMBINATIONS

MODEL	Seat Type	INTERIOR TRIM Light Neutral Cloth	Light Neutral Vinyl	Light Neutral Knit Vinyl	Dark Green Cloth	Dark Green Knit Cloth	Dark Green Vinyl	Dark Green Knit Vinyl	Dark Saddle Vinyl	Dark Saddle Knit Vinyl	Dark Ox-blood Knit Cloth	White * Vinyl /Black	White * Vinyl /Red	White * Vinyl /Blue
Bel Air – 1BK00 Sedan (69)	Bench				828			827						
Station Wagons (35-45)				817						825				
Impala – 1BL00 Sedan (69)		815	818		829		830							
Sport Sedan (39)		815	818		829		830							
Sport Coupe (57)		815	818		829		830							
Custom Coupe (47)		815	818		829		830							
Station Wagons (35-45)			818				830		826					
Caprice Classic – 1BN00 Sedan (69)		841				842					836			
	50-50	841				842					836			
Sport Sedan (39)	Bench	841				842					836			
	50-50	841				842					836			
Custom Coupe (47)	Bench	841				842					836			
	50-50	841				842					836			
Convertible (67)	Bench		818				830					816	816	816
Station Wagons (35-45)	Bench		818				830		826					
EXTERIOR COLOR	Color Code													
White C/O	11		X			X			X		X	X	X	X
Black C/O	19		X			X			X		X	X	X	X
Medium Blue Metallic	24		X									X		X
Bright Blue Metallic	26		X									X		X
Dark Blue Metallic	29		X									X		X
Dark Brt. Green Metallic	42		X			X						X		
Light Green Metallic	44		X			X						X		
Dark Green Gold Metallic	46		X			X						X		
Dark Green	48		X			X			X			X		
Chamois	56		X			X			X			X		
Yellow Orange Metallic	60		X						X			X		
Silver Taupe Metallic	64		X			X			X		X	X	X	X
Tauge Metallic	66		X						X			X		
Brown Metallic	68		X						X			X		
Red Metallic	74		X								X	X	X	
Yellow Beige	81		X			X			X			X		
TWO TONE Lower / Upper	Color Code													
Med. Blue Met. / White	24-11		X											
Dk. Blue Met. / White	29-11		X											
Lt. Green Met. / White	44-11		X			X								
Dk. Green Gold Met. / White	46-11		X			X								
Dark Green / White	48-11		X			X			X					
Chamois / White	56-11		X			X			X					

* Accent carept color. Obtained by specifying trim number plus Accent Carpet RPO number 19F – Black, 75F – Red, or 24F – Blue.

Note: Excepting models with vinyl roof or convertible top, solid exterior color and non-recommended interior trim combinations may be had when RPO ZP2 override is specified.

EXTERIOR–INTERIOR COLOR COMBINATIONS

NEW OR C/O	EXTERIOR COLORS	COLOR CODE	PAINT COMB.	STANDARD ALL-VINYL 400 Prod.	413	415	425	418	CUSTOM LEATHER 404	416	422
TRIM COMBINATIONS: Folding Tops: Black, White; Soft Trim Roof Cover RPO C08 – Black Used with C07 Aux. Top				Black C/O	Med. Blue	Med. Saddle	Dk. Oxblood	Dk. Saddle	Black C/O	Med. Saddle	Dk. Saddle
C/O	White	10	910	X	X	X	X	X	X	X	X
N	Silver Metallic	14	914	X	X	X	X	X	X	X	X
N	Med. Brt. Blue Metallic	22	922	X	X	X			X	X	
C/O	Dark Blue Metallic	27	927	X	X	X	X		X	X	
C/O	Dark Green Metallic	47	947	X		X			X	X	
N	Dark Blue Green Metallic	45	945	X		X	X	X	X	X	X
N	Bright Yellow	52	952	X	X			X	X		X
N	Yellow Metallic	53	953	X	X				X		
N	Orange Metallic	80	980	X	X	X		X	X	X	X
C/O	Red	76	976	X	X	X	X	X	X	X	X

1973 Trim Combinations

NOVA

INTERIOR – EXTERIOR COLOR COMBINATIONS

MODEL	Seat Type	INTERIOR TRIM — Black: Cloth	Black: @ *† Sport Cloth /Black	Black: @ *† Sport Cloth /Red	Black: % Knit Vinyl	Black: *† Perforated Vinyl /Black	Black: *† Perforated Vinyl /Red
Standard - 1XX00							
Coupe (27)	Bench	755			751		
	Bucket				751		
Hatchback (17)	Bench	755			751		
	Bucket				751		
Sedan (69)	Bench				753		
Custom - 1XY00							
Coupe (27)	Bench		752	752			
	Bucket		752	752		754	754
Hatchback (17)	Bench		752	752			
	Bucket		752	752		754	754
Sedan (69)	Bench		750	750			
EXTERIOR COLOR	Color Code						
Antique White C/O	11	X		X	X	X	X
Light Blue Metallic	24	X			X	X	
Dark Blue Metallic	26	X			X	X	
Midnight Blue Metallic	29	X			X	X	
Dark Green Metallic	42	X			X	X	
Light Green Metallic	44	X			X	X	
Green-Gold Metallic	46	X			X	X	
Midnight Green	48	X			X	X	
Light Yellow	51	X			X	X	
Chamois	56	X			X	X	
Light Copper Metallic	60	X			X	X	
Silver Metallic	64	X		X	X	X	X
Dark Brown Metallic	68	X			X	X	
Dark Red Metallic	74	X		X	X	X	X
Medium Red	75	X		X	X	X	X
Medium Orange Metallic	97	X			X	X	
TWO TONES + LOWER / UPPER	COLOR CODE						
Dark Blue Met. / White	26-11	X			X	X	
Lt. Green Met. / White	44-11	X			X	X	
Green-Gold Met. / White	46-11	X			X	X	
Light Yellow / White	51-11	X			X	X	
Chamois / White	56-11	X			X	X	
Med. Orange Met. / White	97-11	X			X	X	

@ Black and white herringbone pattern.
% Two-Color pattern.
$ Three-tone interior provided (Medium Chamois/Medium Dark Chamois/Dark Chamois)
* Accent carpet color indicated by "/Color". Obtained by specifying trim number plus RPO number (RPO 19F for Black or 75F for Red)
† RPO AK1 Shoulder Harnesses/Seat Belts not avilable with Accent Carpeting. Optional Color Keyed floor mats available in Accent Carpeting colors.
+ Two-Tone color not available on Hatchback models.

NOVA

INTERIOR – EXTERIOR COLOR COMBINATIONS

MODEL	Seat Type	INTERIOR TRIM — Light Neutral: Cloth	Light Neutral: % Knit Vinyl	Light Neutral: Perforated Vinyl	Dark Green: Cloth	Dark Green: % Knit Vinyl	Medium Chamois: % $ Knit Vinyl	Medium Blue: Cloth
Standard - 1XX00								
Coupe (27)	Bench				759	760	767	756
	Bucket		763					
Hatchback (17)	Bench				759	760	767	756
	Bucket		763					
Sedan (69)	Bench				758	757		772
Custom - 1XY00								
Coupe (27)	Bench	764			761			
	Bucket			771				
Hatchback (17)	Bench	764			761			
	Bucket			771				
Sedan (69)	Bench	769			770			
EXTERIOR COLOR	Color Code							
Antique White C/O	11		X		X		X	X
Light Blue Metallic	24		X					X
Dark Blue Metallic	26		X					X
Midnight Blue Metallic	29		X					X
Dark Green Metallic	42		X		X			
Light Green Metallic	44		X		X			
Green-Gold Metallic	46		X		X			
Midnight Green	48		X		X		X	
Light Yellow	51		X					
Chamois	56		X		X		X	
Light Copper Metallic	60		X					
Silver Metallic	64		X		X		X	X
Dark Brown Metallic	68		X					
Dark Red Metallic	74		X					
Medium Red	75		X					
Medium Orange Metallic	97		X					
TWO TONES + LOWER / UPPER	COLOR CODE							
Dark Blue Met. / White	26-11		X					X
Lt. Green Met. / White	44-11		X		X			
Green-Gold Met. / White	46-11		X		X			
Light Yellow / White	51-11		X					
Chamois / White	56-11		X		X		X	
Med. Orange Met. / White	97-11		X					

	VINYL TOP COLOR	EXTERIOR COLOR
S	Black	All
S	White	All
S	Medium Green	11, 44, 48
S	Medium Blue	11, 24, 26, 29
S	Light Neutral	46, 48, 60, 74, 75, 97
S	Chamois	11, 56
	Maroon	11, 64, 74

S–Optional Sun Roof Colors.

1973 CHEVELLE AND EL CAMINO 'A' INTERIOR – EXTERIOR COLOR COMBINATIONS

MODEL	Seat Type	INTERIOR TRIM — Black: Cloth	Black: * Vinyl /Black	Black: * Vinyl /Red	Black: Knit Vinyl	Medium Blue: Cloth	Medium Blue: Vinyl	Lt. Neutral: Knit Vinyl	Lt. Neutral: Vinyl
Deluxe – 1AC00									
Sport Sedan (29)	Bench	702			701				
Sport Coupe (37)	Bench	702			701			733	
Station Wagon (35)	Bench				701				
El Camino (80)	Bench				701			733	
Malibu 1AD00									
Sport Sedan (29)	Bench	703	704	704		724	705		732
Sport Coupe (37)	Bench	703	704	704		724	705		732
	Bucket		704	704			705		732
Station Wagon (35)	Bench		704				705		732
El Camino (80)	Bench		704				705		732
	Bucket		704						732
Malibu Estate 1AG00									
Station Wagon (35)	Bench		704				705		732
Laguna 1AE00			Perf. V	Perf. V			Perf. V		Perf. V
Sport Sedan (29)	Bench	712	707	707		723	719		734
Sport Coupe (37)	Bench	712	707	707		723	719		734
	Bucket		707	707			719		734
Station Wagon (35)	Bench		707				719		734
Laguna Estate 1AH00									
Station Wagon (35)	Bench		707				719		734
EXTERIOR COLORS	Color Code								
White C/O	11	X		X	X	X		X	
Black C/O	19	X		X	X	X		X	
Medium Blue Metallic	24	X			X	X		X	
Bright Blue Metallic	26	X			X	X		X	
Dark Blue Metallic	29	X			X	X		X	
Dark Brt. Green Metallic	42	X			X			X	
Light Green Metallic	44	X			X			X	
Dark Green-Gold Metallic	46	X			X			X	
Dark Green	48	X			X			X	
Chamois	56	X			X			X	
Yellow-Orange Metallic	60	X			X			X	
Silver Taupe Metallic	64	X		X	X	X		X	
Taupe Metallic	66	X			X			X	
Brown Metallic	68	X			X			X	
Red Metallic	74	X		X	X			X	
Yellow-Beige	81	X			X			X	
TWO TONE** Lower / Upper	Color Code								
Med. Blue Met. / White	24-11	X			X	X		X	
Dk. Blue Met. / White	29-11	X			X	X		X	
Lt. Green Met. / White	44-11	X			X			X	
Dk. Green-Gold Met. / White	46-11	X			X			X	
Dark Green / White	48-11	X			X			X	
Chamois / White	56-11	X			X			X	

* Accent carpet color. Obtained by specifying trim number plus Accent Carpet RPO number 19F – Black, or 75F – Red.
** Two tone paint not available for Station Wagon models.

NOTE: Solid exterior color combinations (except vinyl top) may be obtained with non-recommended interior combinations when ZP2 override is specified.

MODEL	Seat Type	INTERIOR TRIM — Dark Green: Cloth	Dark Green: Vinyl	Dark Green: Knit Vinyl	Dark Saddle: Vinyl	Dark Saddle: Knit Vinyl	Dark Oxblood: Cloth	Dark Oxblood: Vinyl	Med. Chamois: Cloth	Med. Chamois: Vinyl
Deluxe – 1AC00										
Sport Sedan (29)	Bench	711		710						
Sport Coupe (37)	Bench	711		710						
Station Wagon (35)	Bench					722				
El Camino (80)	Bench *									
Malibu 1AD00										
Sport Sedan (29)	Bench	730	713							721
Sport Coupe (37)	Bench	730	713		720				716	721
	Bucket				720					721
Station Wagon (35)	Bench		713		720					
El Camino (80)	Bench		713		720					
	Bucket				720					
Malibu Estate 1AG00										
Station Wagon (35)	Bench		713		720					
Laguna 1AE00			Perf. V		Perf. V			Perf. V		
Sport Sedan (29)	Bench	726	727				714	709		
Sport Coupe (37)	Bench	726	727		717		714	709		
	Bucket				717					
Station Wagon (35)	Bench		727					709		
Laguna Estate 1AH00										
Station Wagon (35)	Bench		727					709		
EXTERIOR COLORS	Color Code									
White C/O	11		X		X		X		X	
Black C/O	19		X		X		X		X	
Medium Blue Metallic	24									
Bright Blue Metallic	26									
Dark Blue Metallic	29									
Dark Brt. Green Metallic	42		X							
Light Green Metallic	44		X							
Dark Green-Gold Metallic	46		X							
Dark Green	48		X		X				X	
Chamois	56		X		X				X	
Yellow-Orange Metallic	60				X					
Silver Taupe Metallic	64		X		X		X		X	
Taupe Metallic	66				X				X	
Brown Metallic	68				X					
Red Metallic	74						X			
Yellow-Beige	81		X		X				X	
TWO TONE** Lower / Upper	Color Code									
Med. Blue Met. / White	24-11									
Dk. Blue Met. / White	29-11									
Lt. Green Met. / White	44-11		X							
Dk. Green-Gold Met. / White	46-11		X							
Dark Green / White	48-11		X		X				X	
Chamois / White	56-11		X		X				X	

* Accent carpet color. Obtained by specifying trim number plus Accent Carpet RPO number 19F – Black, or 75F – Red.
** Two tone paint not available for Station Wagon models.

NOTE: Solid exterior color combinations (except vinyl top) may be obtained with non-recommended interior combinations when ZP2 override is specified.

1973 Trim Combinations

CHEVELLE

EXTERIOR COLOR–VINYL ROOF COMBINATIONS

BODY LOWER		OPTIONAL VINYL ROOF COLOR						
COLOR CODE	PAINT COLOR	Black	White	Med. Green	Med. Blue	Light Neutral	Chamois	Maroon
11	White	X	X	X	X		X	X
19	Black	X	X			X	X	
24	Medium Blue Metallic	X	X		X			
26	Bright Blue Metallic	X	X					
29	Dark Blue Metallic	X	X		X			
42	Dark Bright Green Metallic	X	X					
44	Light Green Metallic	X	X	X				
46	Dark Green Gold Metallic	X	X			X		
48	Dark Green	X	X	X		X		
56	Chamois	X	X				X	
60	Yellow Orange Metallic	X	X			X		
64	Silver Taupe Metallic	X	X					X
66	Taupe Metallic	X	X			X	X	
68	Brown Metallic	X	X			X		
74	Red Metallic	X	X			X		X
81	Yellow Beige	X	X				X	

1973 MONTE CARLO "SPECIAL A" INTERIOR – EXTERIOR COLOR COMBINATIONS

MODEL	Seat Type	INTERIOR TRIM: Black		Light Neutral		Dark Green		Dark Oxblood	Midnight Blue
		Knit Cloth	Vinyl	Cloth	Vinyl	Knit Cloth	Vinyl	Knit Cloth	Knit Cloth
Monte Carlo – 1AH00 Sport Coupe (57)	Bench	706		731		715		740	725
	Bucket	706	708		735	715	728	740	725
EXTERIOR COLOR	Color Code								
White C/O	11	X		X		X		X	X
Black C/O	19	X		X		X		X	X
Medium Blue Metallic	24	X		X					X
Bright Blue Metallic	26	X		X					X
Dark Blue Metallic	29	X		X					X
Dark Brt. Green Metallic	42	X		X		X			
Light Green Metallic	44	X		X		X			
Dark Green-Gold Metallic	46	X		X		X			
Dark Green	48	X		X		X			
Chamois	56	X		X		X			
Yellow Orange Metallic	60	X		X					
Silver Taupe Metallic	64	X		X		X		X	X
Taupe Metallic	66	X		X					
Brown Metallic	68	X		X					
Red Metallic	74	X		X				X	
Yellow-Beige	81	X		X		X			

NOTE: No Two Tones Available.

NOTE: Solid exterior color combinations (except vinyl top may be obtained with non-recommended interior combinations when ZP2 override is specified.

EXTERIOR COLOR – VINYL ROOF COMBINATIONS

BODY LOWER		OPTIONAL VINYL ROOF COLOR						
COLOR CODE	PAINT COLOR	Black	White	Med. Green	Med. Blue	Light Neutral	Chamois	Maroon
11	White	X	X	X	X		X	X
19	Black	X	X			X	X	
24	Medium Blue Metallic	X	X		X			
26	Bright Blue Metallic	X	X					
29	Dark Blue Metallic	X	X		X			
42	Dark Bright Green Metallic	X	X					
44	Light Green Metallic	X	X	X				
46	Dark Green Gold Metallic	X	X			X		
48	Dark Green	X	X	X		X		
56	Chamois	X	X				X	
60	Yellow Orange Metallic	X	X			X		
64	Silver Taupe Metallic	X	X					X
66	Taupe Metallic	X	X			X	X	
68	Brown Metallic	X	X			X		
74	Red Metallic	X	X			X		X
81	Yellow Beige	X	X				X	

CAMARO

INTERIOR–EXTERIOR COLOR COMBINATIONS

MODEL	Seat Type	INTERIOR TRIM + Black: *† @ Cloth No. 1 /Black	*† @ Cloth No. 2 /Black	*† @ Cloth No. 1 /Red	*† @ Cloth No. 1 /Blue	*† @ Cloth No. 2 /Blue	*† Vinyl /Black	*† Vinyl /Red	*† Vinyl /Blue
Standard - 1FQ00 Coupe (87)	Bucket	776	774	776	776	774	775	775	775
Type LT - 1FS00 Coupe (87)	Bucket	785	786	785	785	786	773	773	773
EXTERIOR COLOR	Color Code								
Antique White C/O	11	X	X	X	X	X	X	X	X
Light Blue Metallic	24	X	X		X	X	X		X
Dark Blue Metallic	26	X	X		X	X	X		X
Midnight Blue Metallic	29	X	X		X	X	X		X
Dark Green Metallic	42	X					X		
Light Green Metallic	44	X					X		
Green Gold Metallic	46	X					X		
Midnight Green	48	X					X		
Light Yellow	51	X					X		
Chamois	56	X					X		
Light Copper Metallic	60	X					X		
Silver Metallic	64	X	X	X	X	X	X	X	X
Dark Brown Metallic	68	X					X		
Dark Red Metallic	74	X		X			X	X	
Medium Red	75	X		X			X	X	
Medium Orange Metallic	97	X					X		

+ All vinyl material is solid color.
@ Cloth No. 1 Black & White pattern, Cloth No. 2 Black & Blue pattern.
* Accent carpet color. Obtained by specifying trim number plus Accent Carpet RPO number (RPO 19F for Black, 75F for Red, or 24F for Blue).
† RPO AK1 Shoulder Harnesses/Seat Belts not available with Accent Carpeting. Optional color keyed floor mats available in Accent Carpeting colors.
B Black and green pattern.
$ Three-tone interior provided (Medium Chamois/Medium Dark Chamois/Dark Chamois)

INTERIOR – EXTERIOR COLOR COMBINATIONS

MODEL	Seat Type	INTERIOR TRIM + Light Neutral	Dark Green		Dark Saddle	Medium Chamois
		Vinyl	B Cloth	Vinyl	Vinyl	$ Vinyl
Standard - 1FQ00 Coupe (87)	Bucket	779		777	778	780
Type LT - 1FS00 Coupe (87)	Bucket	788	781			
EXTERIOR COLOR	Color Code					
Antique White C/O	11	X	X		X	X
Light Blue Metallic	24	X				
Dark Blue Metallic	26	X				
Midnight Blue Metallic	29	X				
Dark Green Metallic	42	X	X			
Light Green Metallic	44	X	X			
Green Gold Metallic	46	X	X			
Midnight Green	48	X	X		X	X
Light Yellow	51	X				
Chamois	56	X	X		X	X
Light Copper Metallic	60	X			X	
Silver Metallic	64	X	X		X	X
Dark Brown Metallic	68	X			X	
Dark Red Metallic	74	X				
Medium Red	75	X				
Medium Orange Metallic	97	X			X	

VINYL TOP COLOR	EXTERIOR COLOR
Black	All
White	All
Medium Green	11, 44, 48
Medium Blue	11, 24, 26, 29 •
Light Neutral	46, 48, 60, 68, 74, 75, 97
Chamois	11, 56
Maroon	11, 64, 74

1974 Trim Combinations

1974 CHEVROLET "B" INTERIOR-EXTERIOR COLOR COMBINATIONS

MODEL	Seat Type	INTERIOR TRIM: Black Vinyl	Black Vinyl	Black & White Sport Cloth	Black & White Sport Cloth	Black & White Sport Cloth	Black & White Sport Cloth	Black Perf. Vinyl	Black Perf. Vinyl	Black Perf. Vinyl	Black Perf. Vinyl	Black Perf. Vinyl
	Carpet* Color	19F	75F	19F	75F	24F	53F	19F	75F	24F	53F	66F
Bel Air – 1BK00												
Sedan (69)												
Station Wagon (35-45)												
Impala – 1BL00												
Sedan (69)	Bench			802	802	802	802	806	806	806	806	806
Sport Sedan (39)				802	802	802	802	806	806	806	806	806
Custom Coupe (47)				802	802	802	802	806	806	806	806	806
Sport Coupe (57)				802	802	802	802	806	806	806	806	806
Station Wagon (35-45)								806	806	806	806	806
Caprice Classic – 1BN00												
Sedan (69)	Bench	808	808									
Sedan (69)	50-50	808	808									
Sport Sedan (39)	Bench	808	808									
Sport Sedan (39)	50-50	808	808									
Sport Coupe (47)	Bench	808	808									
Sport Coupe (47)	50-50	808	808									
Convertible (67)	Bench							806	806	806	806	806
Caprice Estate – 1BN00												
Station Wagon (35-45)	Bench							806	806	806	806	806
EXTERIOR COLOR	Color Code											
White C/O	11	X	X	X	X	X	X	X	X	X	X	X
Black C/O	19	X	X	X	X	X	X	X	X	X	X	X
Medium Blue Met. C/O	24	X	–	X	–	X	–	X	–	X	–	–
Bright Blue Met. C/O	26	X	–	X	–	X	–	X	–	X	–	–
Dark Blue Met. C/O	29	X	–	X	–	X	–	X	–	X	–	–
Bright Aqua Met.	36	X	–	X	–	–	–	X	–	–	–	–
Medium Green	44	X	–	X	–	–	–	X	–	–	–	–
Bright Green Met.	46	X	–	X	–	–	–	X	–	–	–	–
Dark Green Met.	49	X	–	X	–	–	–	X	–	–	–	–
Cream-Beige	50	X	–	X	–	–	X	X	–	–	X	–
Colonial Gold	55	X	–	X	–	–	–	X	–	–	–	–
Golden Brown Met.	59	X	–	X	–	–	–	X	–	–	–	–
Silver Taupe Met. C/O	64	X	X	X	X	X	–	X	X	X	–	–
Russet Orange Met.	66	X	–	X	–	–	–	X	–	–	–	X
Dark Taupe Met.	69	X	–	X	–	–	–	X	–	–	–	–
Red Metallic	74	X	X	X	X	–	–	X	X	–	–	–
TWO TONE: Lower / Upper	Color Code											
Medium Blue Met. / White	24-11	X	–	X	–	X	–	X	–	X	–	–
Dark Blue Met. / White	29-11	X	–	X	–	X	–	X	–	X	–	–
Bright Aqua Met. / White	36-11	X	–	X	–	–	–	X	–	–	–	–
Medium Green / White	44-11	X	–	X	–	–	–	X	–	–	–	–
Dark Green Met. / White	49-11	X	–	X	–	–	–	X	–	–	–	–
Colonial Gold / White	55-11	X	–	X	–	–	–	X	–	–	–	–
Russet Orange Met. / White	66-11	X	–	X	–	–	–	X	–	–	–	X
Red Metallic / White	74-11	X	X	X	X	–	–	X	X	–	–	–

*–Carpet selection. Obtained by specifying trim number plus Carpet RPO number: 19F – **Black**, 24F – Accent Blue, 75F – Accent Red, 53F – Accent Gold, 66F – Accent Russet.

1974 CHEVROLET "B" INTERIOR-EXTERIOR COLOR COMBINATIONS

MODEL	Seat Type	INTERIOR TRIM: Black Knit Cloth	Black Knit Cloth	Black Cloth	Black Cloth	Black Cloth	Black Cloth	Black Cloth	Medium Saddle Perf. Vinyl	Medium Saddle: Saddle & Black Sport Cloth	Dk. Oxblood Knit Cloth	Med. Taupe Knit Cloth
	Carpet * Color	19F	75F	19F	75F	24F	53F	66F	65F	65F	73F	69F
Bel Air – 1BK00												
Sedan (69)				803	803	803	803	803				
Station Wagon (35-45)												
Impala – 1BL00												
Sedan (69)	Bench			805	805	805	805	805	849			
Sport Sedan (39)				805	805	805	805	805	849			
Custom Coupe (47)				805	805	805	805	805	849	858		
Sport Coupe (57)				805	805	805	805	805	849	858		
Station Wagon (35-45)									849			
Caprice Classic – 1BN00												
Sedan (69)	Bench	840	840								857	896
Sedan (69)	50-50	840	840								857	896
Sport Sedan (39)	Bench	840	840								857	896
Sport Sedan (39)	50-50	840	840								857	896
Sport Coupe (47)	Bench	840	840								857	896
Sport Coupe (47)	50-50	840	840								857	896
Convertible (67)	Bench											
Caprice Estate – 1BN00												
Station Wagon (35-45)	Bench								849			
EXTERIOR COLOR	Color Code											
White C/O	11	X	X	X	X	X	X	X	X		X	X
Black C/O	19	X	X	X	X	X	X	X	X		X	X
Medium Blue Met. C/O	24	X	–	X	–	X	–	–	–		–	–
Bright Blue Met. C/O	26	X	–	X	–	X	–	–	–		–	–
Dark Blue Met. C/O	29	X	–	X	–	X	–	–	–		–	–
Bright Aqua Met.	36	X	–	X	–	–	–	–	–		–	–
Medium Green	44	X	–	X	–	–	–	–	–		–	–
Bright Green Met.	46	X	–	X	–	–	–	–	–		–	–
Dark Green Met.	49	X	–	X	–	–	–	–	X		–	–
Cream-Beige	50	X	–	X	–	–	X	–	X		X	X
Colonial Gold	55	X	–	X	–	–	–	–	–		–	–
Golden Brown Met.	59	X	–	X	–	–	–	–	X		–	–
Silver Taupe Met. C/O	64	X	X	X	X	X	–	–	X		X	X
Russet Orange Met.	66	X	–	X	–	–	–	X	X		–	–
Dark Taupe Met.	69	X	–	X	–	–	–	–	X		–	X
Red Metallic	74	X	X	X	X	–	–	–	X		X	–
TWO TONE: Lower / Upper	Color Code											
Medium Blue Met. / White	24-11	X	–	X	–	X	–	–	–		–	–
Dark Blue Met. / White	29-11	X	–	X	–	X	–	–	–		–	–
Bright Aqua Met. / White	36-11	X	–	X	–	–	–	–	–		–	–
Medium Green / White	44-11	X	–	X	–	–	–	–	–		–	–
Dark Green Met. / White	49-11	X	–	X	–	–	–	–	X		–	–
Colonial Gold / White	55-11	X	–	X	–	–	–	–	–		–	–
Russet Orange Met. / White	66-11	X	–	X	–	–	–	X	X		–	–
Red Metallic / White	74-11	X	X	X	X	–	–	–	X		X	–

*–Carpet selection. Obtained by specifying trim combination number plus carpet RPO number: 19F – Black, 24F – Accent Blue, 53F – Accent Gold, 65F – Dark Saddle, 66F – Accent Russet, 73F – Dark Oxblood, 75F – Accent Red, 69F – Dark Taupe.

NOTE: Solid exterior color combinations (except vinyl top or convertible top) may be obtained with non-recommended interior combinations when ZP2 override is specified.

1974 Trim Combinations

1974 CHEVROLET "B" INTERIOR-EXTERIOR COLOR COMBINATIONS

MODEL	Seat Type	INTERIOR TRIM										
		Light Neutral				Medium Green				Midnight Blue		
		Cloth	Vinyl	Knit Vinyl	Perf. Vinyl	Knit Cloth	Knit Vinyl	Cloth	Perf. Vinyl	Cloth	Perf. Vinyl	Knit Cloth
	Carpet * Color	60F	60F	60F	60F	44F	44F	44F	44F	29F	29F	29F
Bel Air – 1BK00												
Sedan (69)	Bench	815		817			851	852				
Station Wagon (35-45)				817			851					
Impala – 1BL00												
Sedan (69)	Bench	821			819			853	855	847	813	
Sport Sedan (39)		821			819			853	855	847	813	
Custom Coupe (47)		821			819			853	855	847	813	
Sport Coupe (57)		821			819			853	855	847	813	
Station Wagon (35-45)					819				855		813	
Caprice Classic – 1BN00												
Sedan (69)	Bench		841			850						843
Sedan (69)	50-50		841			850						843
Sport Sedan (39)	Bench		841			850						843
Sport Sedan (39)	50-50		841			850						843
Sport Coupe (47)	Bench		841			850						843
Sport Coupe (47)	50-50		841			850						843
Convertible (67)	Bench				819				855			
Caprice Estate – 1BN00												
Station Wagon (35-45)	Bench				819				855		813	
EXTERIOR COLOR	Color Code											
White C/O	11	X				X				X		
Black C/O	19	X				X				X		
Medium Blue Met. C/O	24	–				–				X		
Bright Blue Met. C/O	26	–				–				X		
Dark Blue Met. C/O	29	X				–				X		
Bright Aqua Met.	36					–				–		
Medium Green	44	X				X				–		
Bright Green Met.	46	X				X				–		
Dark Green Met.	49	X				X				–		
Cream Beige	50	X				X				–		
Colonial Gold	55	X				–				–		
Golden Brown Met.	59	X				–				–		
Silver Taupe Met. C/O	64	X				–				–		
Russet Orange Met.	66	X				–				–		
Dark Taupe Met.	69	X				–				–		
Red Metallic	74	X				–				–		

TWO TONE Lower	Upper	Color Code	Light Neutral	Medium Green	Midnight Blue
Medium Blue Met.	White	24-11	–	–	X
Dark Blue Met.	White	29-11	X	–	X
Bright Aqua Met.	White	36-11		–	–
Medium Green	White	44-11	X	X	–
Dark Green Met.	White	49-11	X	X	–
Colonial Gold	White	55-11	X	–	–
Russet Orange Met.	White	66-11	X	–	–
Red Metallic	White	74-11	–	–	–

*–Carpet selection. Obtained by Specifying trim combination number plus carpet RPO number: 29F – Midnight Blue 44F – Dark Green, 60F – Midnight Neutral.

NOTE: Solid exterior color combinations (except vinyl top or convertible top) may be obtained with non-recommended interior combinations when ZP2 override is specified.

EXTERIOR COLOR – VINYL ROOF COMBINATIONS

BODY LOWER		OPTIONAL VINYL ROOF COLOR									
EXTERIOR COLOR	Color Code	Black	White	Med. Blue	Med. Green	Cream-Beige	Silver Taupe*	Red Met.	Brown	Russet *	Med. Saddle*
White C/O	11	X	X	X	X	X		X	X	X	X
Black C/O	19	X	X			X	X	X			X
Medium Blue Met. C/O	24	X	X	X							
Bright Blue Met. C/O	26	X	X	X							
Dark Blue Met. C/O	29	X	X	X							
Bright Aqua Met.	36	X	X								
Medium Green	44	X	X		X						
Bright Green Met.	46	X	X		X						
Dark Green Met.	49	X	X		X						X
Cream-Beige	50	X	X			X			X		X
Colonial Gold	55	X	X			X					
Golden Brown Met.	59	X	X			X			X		X
Silver Taupe Met. C/O	64	X	X				X	X	X		
Russet Orange Met.	66	X	X							X	X
Dark Taupe Met.	69	X	X			X	X		X		X
Red Metallic	74	X	X					X			

* Not available on Impala Custom Coupe 1BL47 or Caprice Coupe 1BN47.

CORVETTE

TRIM COMBINATIONS				STANDARD ALL-VINYL						CUSTOM LEATHER		
				400 Prod.	406	408	413	415	425	404	407	416
Folding Tops: Black, White; Soft Trim Roof Cover RPO C08 – Black Used with C07 Aux. Top				Black C/O	Silver	Lt. Neutral	Dark Blue C/O	Med. Saddle C/O	Dk. Ox-blood C/O	Black C/O	Silver	Med. Saddle
NEW OR C/O	EXTERIOR COLORS	COLOR CODE	PAINT COMB.									
C/O	White	10	910	X	X	X	X	X	X	X	X	X
C/O	Silver Metallic	14	914	X	X		X	X	X	X	X	X
C/O	Med. Brt. Blue Metallic	22	922	X	X		X			X	X	
N	Gray Metallic	17	917	X	X	X	X	X	X	X	X	X
N	Dark Green Metallic	48	948	X	X	X		X		X	X	X
N	Bright Yellow	56	956	X	X	X		X		X	X	X
N	Brown Metallic	68	968	X	X	X		X		X	X	X
N	Red Metallic	74	974	X	X	X		X	X	X	X	X
C/O	Red	76	976	X	X	X		X	X	X	X	X
C/O	Orange Metallic	80	980	X	X	X		X		X	X	X

1974 Trim Combinations

1974 CHEVROLET NOVA 'X' INTERIOR – EXTERIOR COLOR COMBINATIONS

MODEL	Seat Type	INTERIOR TRIM: Black & White Check – Cloth	Black – Perf. Vinyl	Black – • Cloth /Black	Black – • Cloth /Red	Black – • Cloth /Blue	Black – • Perf. Vinyl /Black	Black – • Perf. Vinyl /Red	Black – • Perf. Vinyl /Blue	Black – • Sport Cloth /Black	Black – • Sport Cloth /Red	Midnight Blue – Perf. Vinyl	Midnight Blue – Cloth	Medium Saddle – Perf. Vinyl
Standard – 1XX00	Bench	750	825									826		
Coupe (27)	Bucket		825											
	Bench	750	825									826		827
Hatchback (17)	Bucket		825											827
Sedan (69)	Bench	750	825									826		
Custom – 1XY00	Bench			751	751	751	754	754	754	752	752		771	
Coupe (27)	Bucket						754	754	754	752	752			
	Bench			751	751	751	754	754	754	752	752		771	
Hatchback (17)	Bucket						754	754	754	752	752			
Sedan (69)	Bench			751			754							
EXTERIOR COLORS	Color Code													
Antique White C/O	11	X	X	X	X	X	X	X	X	X	X	X		X
Bright Blue Metallic C/O	26	X	X	X	–	X	X	–	X	X	–	X		–
Midnight Blue Metallic C/O	29	X	X	X	X	X	X	X	X	X	X	X		–
Aqua Blue Metallic	36	X	X	X	–	–	X	–	–	X	–	–		–
Lime Yellow	40	X	X	X	–	–	X	–	–	X	–	–		–
Bright Green Metallic	46	X	X	X	–	–	X	–	–	X	–	–		–
Medium Dark Green Metallic	49	X	X	X	–	–	X	–	–	X	–	–		X
Cream Beige	50	X	X	X	–	–	X	–	–	X	–	–		X
Bright Yellow	51	X	X	X	–	–	X	–	–	X	–	–		X
Light Gold Metallic	53	X	X	X	–	–	X	–	–	X	–	–		–
Sandstone	55	X	X	X	–	–	X	–	–	X	–	–		–
Golden Brown Metallic	59	X	X	X	–	–	X	–	–	X	–	–		X
Silver Metallic C/O	64	X	X	X	X	X	X	X	X	X	X	–		X
Bronze Metallic	66	X	X	X	–	–	X	–	–	X	–	–		X
Medium Red Metallic	74	X	X	X	X	–	X	X	–	X	X	–		X
Medium Red C/O	75	X	X	X	X	–	X	X	–	X	X	–		–

TWO-TONE PAINT – Lower	Upper
Midnight Blue Metallic	White for all applications
Aqua Blue Metallic	
Medium Dark Green Metallic	
Light Gold Metallic	
Bronze Metallic	
Medium Red Metallic	

VINYL TOP COLOR	EXTERIOR COLOR
Black	All
White	All
Medium Blue	11, 26, 29
Medium Green	11, 46, 49
Cream Beige	11, 50, 53, 55, 59
Silver Taupe	64
Maroon	11, 64, 74
Brown	11, 50, 59, 64
Russet	11, 66
Medium Saddle	11, 49, 50, 59, 66

•–Accent carpet color. Obtained by specifying trim number plus Accent Carpet RPO number: 19F – Black, 75 – Red, or 24F – Blue.

NOTE: Solid exterior color combinations (except vinyl top) may be obtained with non-recommended interior combinations when ZP2 override is specified.

1974 CHEVROLET NOVA 'X' INTERIOR – EXTERIOR COLOR COMBINATIONS

MODEL	Seat Type	INTERIOR TRIM: Medium Green – Perf. Vinyl	Medium Green – Cloth	Medium Green – Perf. Vinyl	Medium Green – † Perf. Vinyl /Black	Medium Green – † Cloth /Black	Green & Black Sport Cloth	Black & Green Check – Cloth	Black & Green Check – † Cloth /Black	Lt. Neutral & Black Check – Cloth	Lt. Neutral & Black Check – † Cloth /Black	Light Neutral – Perf. Vinyl	Light Neutral – Perf. Vinyl	Light Neutral – † Perf. Vinyl /Black	Light Neutral – † Perf. Vinyl /Black
Standard – 1XX00	Bench	828			828			756	756	764	764	829		829	
Coupe (27)	Bucket	828			828							829		829	
	Bench	828			828			756	756	764	764	829		829	
Hatchback (17)	Bucket	828			828							829		829	
Sedan (69)	Bench	828			828			756	756	764	764	829		829	
Custom – 1XY00	Bench						755						766		
Coupe (27)	Bucket			759									766		
	Bench						755						766		
Hatchback (17)	Bucket			759									766		
Sedan (69)	Bench		757			757							766		766
EXTERIOR COLORS	Color Code														
Antique White C/O	11		X			X		X		X	X	X		X	
Bright Blue Metallic C/O	26		–			–		–		–	X	–		X	
Midnight Blue Metallic C/O	29		–			–		–		–	X	X		X	
Aqua Blue Metallic	36		–			–		–		–	–	–		–	
Lime Yellow	40		X			X		X		–	–	–		–	
Bright Green Metallic	46		X			X		X		X	X	X		X	
Medium Dark Green Metallic	49		X			X		X		X	X	X		X	
Cream Beige	50		–			–		–		X	X	X		X	
Bright Yellow	51		–			–		–		X	X	X		X	
Light Gold Metallic	53		–			–		–		X	X	X		X	
Sandstone	55		–			–		–		X	X	X		X	
Golden Brown Metallic	59		–			–		–		X	X	X		X	
Silver Metallic C/O	64		–			–		–		X	X	X		X	
Bronze Metallic	66		–			–		–		X	X	X		X	
Medium Red Metallic	74		–			–		–		–	X	X		X	
Medium Red C/O	75		–			–		–		X	X	X		X	

† – "Big Four" Module [Carpet, package shelf (or load area), instrument panel upper and lower, and cowl kick pad] may be obtained by specifying the trim combination number plus Big Four Module number: 19X – Black.

NOTE: When the Big Four Module is offered on any model within a series (e.g., 1XY27-17), the order must specify the module number for each trim combination available in that style even if an accent Big Four color is not available with each specific interior color. Module numbers are: 19X – Black, 29X – Midnight Blue, 44X – Dark Green, 60X – Midnight Neutral, 65X – Dark Saddle.

NOTE: Solid exterior color combinations (except vinyl top) may be obtained with non-recommended interior combinations when ZP2 override is specified.

1974 Trim Combinations

1974 CHEVELLE AND EL CAMINO 'A' INTERIOR – EXTERIOR COLOR COMBINATIONS

		INTERIOR TRIM Black					
	Seat Type	Cloth	Cloth	Cloth	Cloth	Sport Cloth	Perf. Vinyl with Green Seats
Model	Carpet Color	19F*	75F*	24F*	66F*	19F	19F
Malibu – 1AC00 Sport Sedan (29)	Bench	701	701	701	701		894
	Bucket						
Sport Coupe (37)	Bench	701	701	701	701		894
	Bucket						
Station Wagon (35)	Bench						
	Bucket						
El Camino (80)	Bench	701	701	701	701		894
	Bucket						
Laguna Type 'S3' – 1AE00 Sport Coupe (37)	Bucket	703				704	
Malibu Classic – 1AD00 Sport Sedan (29)	Bench	702	702				
	Bucket	702	702				
Sport Coupe (37)	Bench	702	702				
	Bucket	702	702				
Station Wagon (35)	Bench						
	Bucket						
El Camino Classic (80)	Bench	702	702				
	Bucket	702	702				
Malibu Classic Estate – 1AG00 Station Wagon (35)	Bench						
	Bucket						
EXTERIOR COLORS	Color Code						
White C/O	11	X	X	X	X	X	X
Black C/O	19	X	X	X	X	X	X
Medium Blue Metallic C/O	24	X	–	X	–	X	–
Bright Blue Metallic C/O	26	X	–	X	–	X	X
Dark Blue Metallic C/O	29	X	–	X	–	X	–
Bright Aqua Metallic	36	X	–	–	–	X	–
Medium Green	44	X	–	–	–	X	X
Bright Green Met.	46	X	–	–	–	X	X
Dark Green Metallic	49	X	–	–	–	X	X
Cream-Beige	50	X	–	–	–	X	X
Colonial Gold	55	X	–	–	–	X	–
Golden Brown Met.	59	X	–	–	–	X	–
Silver Taupe Met. C/O	64	X	X	X	X	X	–
Russet Orange Met.	66	X	–	–	X	X	–
Dark Taupe Metallic	69	X	–	–	–	X	–
Red Metallic	74	X	X	–	–	X	–

TWO TONE Lower	Upper	Color Code	Cloth 19F*	Cloth 75F*	Cloth 24F*	Cloth 66F*	Sport Cloth 19F	Perf. Vinyl with Green Seats 19F
Medium Blue Met.	White	24-11	X	–	X	–	X	–
Dark Blue Met.	White	29-11	X	–	X	–	X	–
Bright Aqua Met.	White	36-11	X	–	–	–	X	–
Medium Green	White	44-11	X	–	–	–	X	X
Dark Green Met.	White	49-11	X	–	–	–	X	X
Colonial Gold	White	55-11	X	–	–	–	X	–
Russet Orange Met.	White	66-11	X	–	–	X	X	–
Red Metallic	White	74-11	X	X	–	–	X	–

* – Carpet selection. Obtained by specifying trim number plus Carpet RPO number: 19F – Black, 75 F – Accent Red, 24F – Accent Blue, 66F – Accent Russet.

NOTE: Solid, exterior color combinations (except vinyl top) may be obtained with non-recommended interior combinations when ZP2 override is specified. Two Tones are not available on Wagons or on the Laguna.

EXTERIOR COLOR–VINYL ROOF COMBINATIONS

BODY LOWER		OPTIONAL VINYL ROOF COLOR									
EXTERIOR COLOR	Color Code	Black	White	Med. Blue	Med. Green	Cream-Beige	Silver Taupe	Maroon	Brown	Russet	Med. Saddle
White C/O	11	X	X	X	X	X		X	X	X	X
Black C/O	19	X	X			X	X	X			X
Medium Blue Met. C/O	24	X	X	X							
Bright Blue Met. C/O	26	X	X								
Dark Blue Met. C/O	29	X	X	X							
Bright Aqua Met.	36	X	X								
Medium Green	44	X	X		X						
Bright Green Met.	46	X	X								
Dark Green Met.	49	X	X		X						X
Cream-Beige	50	X	X			X			X		X
Colonial Gold	55	X	X			X					
Golden Brown Met.	59	X	X			X			X		X
Silver Taupe Met. C/O	64	X	X				X		X		
Russet Orange Met.	66	X	X							X	X
Dark Taupe Met.	69	X	X			X	X		X		X
Red Metallic	74	X	X					X			

1974 Trim Combinations

1974 CHEVELLE AND EL CAMINO 'A' INTERIOR – EXTERIOR COLOR COMBINATIONS

		INTERIOR TRIM						
		Black						
	Seat Type	Perf. Vinyl	Perf. Vinyl	Perf. Vinyl	Vinyl	Vinyl	Vinyl with White Seats	Perf. Vinyl
Model	Carpet Color	19F*	75F*	66F*	19F*	75F*	19F	19F
Malibu – 1AC00								
Sport Sedan (29)	Bench	891	891	891				
	Bucket	891	891	891				
Sport Coupe (37)	Bench	891	891	891				
	Bucket	891	891	891				
Station Wagon (35)	Bench	891	891	891				
	Bucket	891	891	891				
El Camino (80)	Bench	891	891	891				
	Bucket	891	891	891				
Laguna Type 'S3' – 1AE00 Sport Coupe (37)	Bucket							708
Malibu Classic – 1AD00								
Sport Sedan (29)	Bench				707	707	747	
	Bucket				707	707	747	
Sport Coupe (37)	Bench				707	707	747	
	Bucket				707	707	747	
Station Wagon (35)	Bench				707	707		
	Bucket				707	707		
El Camino Classic (80)	Bench				707	707	747	
	Bucket				707	707	747	
Malibu Classic Estate – 1AG00 Station Wagon (35)	Bench				707	707		
	Bucket				707	707		
EXTERIOR COLORS	Color Code							
White C/O	11	X	X	X	X	X	X	
Black C/O	19	X	X	X	X	X	X	
Medium Blue Metallic C/O	24	X	–	–	X	–	X	
Bright Blue Metallic C/O	26	X	–	–	X	–	X	
Dark Blue Metallic C/O	29	X	–	–	X	–	X	
Bright Aqua Metallic	36	X	–	–	X	–	X	
Medium Green	44	X	–	–	X	–	X	
Bright Green Met.	46	X	–	–	X	–	X	
Dark Green Metallic	49	X	–	–	X	–	X	
Cream-Beige	50	X	–	–	X	–	X	
Colonial Gold	55	X	–	–	X	–	X	
Golden Brown Met.	59	X	–	–	X	–	X	
Silver Taupe Met. C/O	64	X	X	–	X	X	X	
Russet Orange Met.	66	X	–	X	X	–	X	
Dark Taupe Metallic	69	X	–	–	X	–	X	
Red Metallic	74	X	X	–	X	X	X	
TWO TONE: Lower / Upper	Color Code							
Medium Blue Met. / White	24-11	X	–	–	X	–	X	
Dark Blue Met. / White	29-11	X	–	–	X	–	X	
Bright Aqua Met. / White	36-11	X	–	–	X	–	X	
Medium Green / White	44-11	X	–	–	X	–	X	
Dark Green Met. / White	49-11	X	–	–	X	–	X	
Colonial Gold / White	55-11	X	–	–	X	–	X	
Russet Orange Met. / White	66-11	X	–	X	X	–	X	
Red Metallic / White	74-11	X	X	–	X	X	X	

* – Carpet selection. Obtained by specifying trim number plus Carpet RPO number: 19F – Black, 75F – Accent Red, 24F – Accent Blue, 66F – Accent Russet.

NOTE: Solid, exterior color combinations (except vinyl top) may be obtained with non-recommended interior combinations when ZP2 override is specified. Two Tones are not available on Wagons or on the Laguna.

1974 CHEVELLE AND EL CAMINO 'A' INTERIOR – EXTERIOR COLOR COMBINATIONS

		INTERIOR TRIM									
		Midnight Blue				Medium Green				Dark Oxblood	
	Seat Type	Cloth	Perf. Vinyl	Vinyl	Vinyl with White Seats	Cloth	Perf. Vinyl	Perf. Vinyl with Lt. Neut. Seats	Vinyl	Perf. Vinyl	Cloth
Model	Carpet Color	29F	29F	29F	29F	44F	44F	44F	44F	73F	73F
Malibu – 1AC00											
Sport Sedan (29)	Bench					723	793	830			
	Bucket							830			
Sport Coupe (37)	Bench		897			723	793	830			
	Bucket							830			
Station Wagon (35)	Bench							830			
	Bucket							830			
El Camino (80)	Bench		897			723	793	830			
	Bucket							830			
Laguna Type 'S3' – 1AE00 Sport Coupe (37)	Bucket									719	720
Malibu Classic – 1AD00											
Sport Sedan (29)	Bench	732			785	724			728		743
	Bucket				785				728		743
Sport Coupe (37)	Bench	732			785	724			728		743
	Bucket				785				728		743
Station Wagon (35)	Bench			735					728		
	Bucket			735					728		
El Camino Classic (80)	Bench	732			785	724			728		
	Bucket				785				728		
Malibu Classic Estate – 1AG00 Station Wagon (35)	Bench			735					728		
	Bucket			735					728		
EXTERIOR COLORS	Color Code										
White C/O	11		X		X	X		X	X	X	
Black C/O	19		X		X	X		X	X	X	
Medium Blue Metallic C/O	24		X		X	–		–	–	–	
Bright Blue Metallic C/O	26		X		–	–		–	–		
Dark Blue Metallic C/O	29		X		X	–		–	–	–	
Bright Aqua Metallic	36		–		–	–		–	–	–	
Medium Green	44		–		–	X		X	X	–	
Bright Green Met.	46		–		–	X		X	X	–	
Dark Green Metallic	49		–		–	X		X	X	–	
Cream-Beige	50		–		–	X		X	X	X	
Colonial Gold	55		–		–	–		–	–	–	
Golden Brown Met.	59		–		–	–		–	–	–	
Silver Taupe Met. C/O	64		–		–	–		–	–	X	
Russet Orange Met.	66		–		–	–		–	–	–	
Dark Taupe Metallic	69		–		–	–		–	–	–	
Red Metallic	74		–		–	–		–	–	X	
TWO TONE: Lower / Upper	Color Code										
Medium Blue Met. / White	24-11		X		X	–		–	–	–	
Dark Blue Met. / White	29-11		X		X	–		–	–	–	
Bright Aqua Met. / White	36-11		–		–	–		–	–	–	
Medium Green / White	44-11		–		–	X		X	X	–	
Dark Green Met. / White	49-11		–		–	X		X	X	–	
Colonial Gold / White	55-11		–		–	–		–	–	–	
Russet Orange Met. / White	66-11		–		–	–		–	–	–	
Red Metallic / White	74-11		–		–	–		–	–	X	

* – Carpet color. 29F – Midnight Blue, 44F – Dark Green, 73F – Dark Oxblood.

NOTE: Solid, exterior color combinations (except vinyl top) may be obtained with non-recommended interior combinations when ZP2 override is specified. Two Tones are not available on Wagons or on the Laguna.

1974 Trim Combinations

1974 CHEVELLE AND EL CAMINO 'A' INTERIOR – EXTERIOR COLOR COMBINATIONS

		INTERIOR TRIM						
		Lt. Neutral				Medium Saddle		
	Seat Type	Cloth	Perf. Vinyl	Vinyl	Perf. Vinyl	Vinyl	Perf. Vinyl	Cloth
Model	Carpet * Color	60F	60F	60F	60F	65F	65F	65F
Malibu – 1AC00 Sport Sedan (29)	Bench		892					
	Bucket		892					
Sport Coupe (37)	Bench		892					
	Bucket		892					
Station Wagon (35)	Bench		892					
	Bucket		892					
El Camino (80)	Bench		892					
	Bucket		892					
Laguna Type 'S3' – 1AE00 Sport Coupe (37)	Bucket						718	731
Malibu Classic – 1AD00 Sport Sedan (29)	Bench	722		714		740		
	Bucket			714		740		
Sport Coupe (37)	Bench	722		714		740		
	Bucket			714		740		
Station Wagon (35)	Bench			714		740		
	Bucket			714		740		
El Camino Classic (80)	Bench	722		714		740		
	Bucket			714		740		
Malibu Classic Estate – 1AG00 Station Wagon (35)	Bench			714		740		
	Bucket			714		740		
EXTERIOR COLORS	Color Code							
White C/O	11	X		X		X		
Black C/O	19	X		X		X		
Medium Blue Metallic C/O	24	–		–		–		
Bright Blue Metallic C/O	26	–		–		–		
Dark Blue Metallic C/O	29	–		–		–		
Bright Aqua Metallic	36	X		X		–		
Medium Green	44	X		X		–		
Bright Green Metallic	46	X		X		–		
Dark Green Metallic	49	X		X		X		
Cream-Beige	50	X		X		X		
Colonial Gold	55	X		X		–		
Golden Brown Metallic	59	X		X		X		
Silver Taupe Metallic C/O	64	X		X		X		
Russet Orange Met.	66	X		X		X		
Dark Taupe Metallic	69	X		X		X		
Red Metallic	74	–		–		X		

TWO TONE Lower	Upper	Color Code			
Medium Blue Met.	White	24-11	–	–	–
Dark Blue Met.	White	29-11	–	–	–
Bright Aqua Met.	White	36-11	X	X	–
Medium Green	White	44-11	X	X	–
Dark Green Met.	White	49-11	X	X	X
Colonial Gold	White	55-11	X	X	–
Russet Orange Met.	White	66-11	X	X	X
Red Metallic	White	74-11	–	–	X

* – Carpet color. 60F – Midnight Neutral, 65F – Dark Saddle.

NOTE: Solid exterior color combinations (except vinyl top) may be obtained with non-recommended interior combinations when ZP2 override is specified. Two Tones are not available on Wagons or on the Laguna.

1974 LAGUNA EXTERIOR COLOR – INTERIOR COLOR, VINYL TOP, AND STRIPE COMBINATIONS

					INTERIOR TRIM						
					703	704	708	719	720	718	731
ITEM	EXTERIOR BODY COLOR–LOWER	EXTERIOR BODY COLOR–UPPER	(1) RPO C08 VINYL TOP COLOR	(2) BODY SIDE AND FRONT STRIPE COLOR	Black Cloth	B/W Sport Cloth	Black Vinyl	Oxblood Vinyl	Oxblood Cloth	Saddle Vinyl	Saddle Cloth
1	WA3967 White	WA3967 White	White	4533 Red Met.	X	X	X	X (*)	X (*)	–	–
2	WA3967 White	WA3967 White	White	4223 Golden Brown Met.	–	–	–	–	–	X	X
3	WA3967 White	---	Maroon	4533 Red Met.	X	X	X	X (*)	X (*)	–	–
4	WA3967 White	---	Med. Saddle	4223 Golden Brown Met.	–	–	–	–	–	X	X
5	WA848 Black	WA848 Black	Black	4533 Red Met.	X	X	X	X (*)	X (*)	–	–
6	WA848 Black	WA848 Black	Black	4223 Golden Brown Met.	X	–	X	–	–	X (*)	X (*)
7	WA848 Black	WA848 Black	Black	3967 White	X	X (*)	X	–	–	–	–
8	WA848 Black	---	Maroon	4533 Red Met.	X	X	X	X (*)	X (*)	–	–
9	WA848 Black	---	Med. Saddle	4233 Golden Brown Met.	X (*)	–	X (*)	–	–	X	X
10	WA848 Black	---	White	3967 White	X	X	X	–	–	–	–
11	WA4533 Red Met.	WA4533 Red. Met.	Maroon	3967 White	X	X	X	X (*)	X (*)	X	X
12	WA4533 Red Met.	---	White	3967 White	X	X	X	X (*)	X (*)	–	–
13	WA4533 Red Met.	---	Black	3967 White	X	X	X	X	X	–	–
14	WA4319 Silver Taupe Met.	WA4319 Silver Taupe Met.	Silver Taupe	4533 Red Met.	X	–	X	X (*)	X (*)	–	–
15	WA4319 Silver Taupe Met.	WA4319 Silver Taupe Met.	Silver Taupe	3967 White	X	–	X	–	–	–	–
16	WA4319 Silver Taupe Met.	---	Maroon	4533 Red Met.	X	–	X	X (*)	X (*)	–	–
17	WA4319 Silver Taupe Met.	---	Black	3967 White	X	–	X	–	–	–	–
18	WA4319 Silver Taupe Met.	---	Black	4533 Red Met.	X	–	X	X	X	–	–
19	WA4518 Dk. Taupe Met.	WA4518 Dk. Taupe Met.	Brown	3967 White	X	–	X	–	–	X (*)	X (*)
20	WA4518 Dk. Taupe Met.	---.	Med. Saddle	3967 White	–	–	–	–	–	X	X
21	WA4501 Russet Orange Met.	WA4501 Russet Orange Met.	Russet	3967 White	X	–	X	–	–	X (*)	X (*)
22	WA4501 Russet Orange Met.	---	Med. Saddle	3967 White	–	–	–	–	–	X (*)	X (*)
23	WA4501 Russet Orange Met.	---	Black	3967 White	X	–	X	–	–	X	X
24	WA4501 Russet Orange Met.	---	Black	3967 White	X	–	X	–	–	–	–

(1) Vinyl top is forced option until new quarter upper is available.
(2) Stripe color prefix is WU for urethane front end and WA for sides
(*) Preferred colors for dealer introduction.
TOTALS
6 Exterior Body Colors
7 Vinyl Top Colors
3 Stripe colors
3 Interior Colors (7 RPO's.)
(3) Stripe I.D. – 11A White, 59A Golden Brown Met., 74A Red Met.

1974 Trim Combinations

1974 MONTE CARLO 'S' INTERIOR – EXTERIOR COLOR COMBINATIONS

MODEL	Seat Type	INTERIOR TRIM								
		Black		Medium Green		Midnight Blue		Medium Saddle	Light Neutral	Dark Oxblood
		Knit Cloth	Vinyl	Knit Cloth	Vinyl	Knit Cloth	Vinyl	Vinyl	Vinyl	Knit Cloth
Monte Carlo – 1AH00 Sport Coupe (57)	Bench	705	709	726	730	734	737		716	744
	Bucket	705	709	726	730			742		744
EXTERIOR COLORS	Color Code									
White C/O	11	X	X	X		X		X	X	X
Black C/O	19	X	X	X		X		X	X	X
Medium Blue Met. C/O	24	X	X	–		X		–	–	–
Bright Blue Met. C/O	26	X	X	–		X		–	–	–
Dark Blue Met. C/O	29	X	X	–		X		–	–	–
Bright Aqua Metallic	36	X	X	–		–		–	–	–
Medium Green	44	X	X	X		–		–	X	–
Bright Green Metallic	46	X	X	X		–		–	X	–
Dark Green Metallic	49	X	X	X		–		X	X	–
Cream-Beige	50	X	X	X		–		X	X	X
Colonial Gold	55	X	X	–		–		–	X	–
Golden Brown Metallic	59	X	X	–		–		X	X	–
Silver Taupe Met. C/O	64	X	X	–		–		X	X	X
Russet Orange Met.	66	X	X	–		–		X	X	–
Dark Taupe Metallic	69	X	X	–		–		X	X	–
Red Metallic	74	X	X	–		–		X	–	X

NOTE: Solid exterior color combinations (except vinyl top) may be obtained with non-recommended interior combinations when ZP2 override is specified. Two Tone paint is not available on the Monte Carlo.

EXTERIOR COLOR – VINYL ROOF COMBINATIONS

BODY LOWER		OPTIONAL VINYL ROOF COLOR						
EXTERIOR COLOR	Color Code	Black	White	Med. Blue	Med. Green	Cream-Beige	Maroon	Brown
White C/O	11	X	X	X	X	X	X	X
Black C/O	19	X	X			X	X	
Medium Blue Met. C/O	24	X	X	X				
Bright Blue Met. C/O	26	X	X					
Dark Blue Met. C/O	29	X	X	X				
Bright Aqua Met.	36	X	X					
Medium Green	44	X	X		X			
Bright Green Met.	46	X	X					
Dark Green Met.	49	X	X		X			
Cream-Beige	50	X	X			X		X
Colonial Gold	55	X	X			X		
Golden Brown Met.	59	X	X			X		X
Silver Taupe Met. C/O	64	X	X					X
Russet Orange Met.	66	X	X					
Dark Taupe Met.	69	X	X			X		X
Red Metallic	74	X	X				X	

CAMARO

INTERIOR–EXTERIOR COLOR COMBINATIONS

MODEL	Seat Type	INTERIOR TRIM								
		Medium Saddle			Saddle & Black Check	Green & Black Check	Medium Green	Medium Red	Medium Taupe	
		Cloth	Vinyl	Knit Vinyl	Cloth	Cloth	Vinyl	Vinyl	Cloth	Knit Vinyl
Standard – 1FQ00 Coupe (87)	Bucket		798		796	786	787	792		
Type LT – 1FS00 Coupe (87)	Bucket	797		799					783	784
EXTERIOR COLORS	Color Code									
Antique White C/O	11		X		X	X	X	X	X	
Bright Blue Metallic C/O	26		–		–	–	–	–	–	
Midnight Blue Metallic C/O	29		–		–	–	–	X	–	
Aqua Blue Metallic	36		–		–	–	–	–	–	
Lime Yellow	40		–		–	X	X	–	–	
Bright Green Metallic	46		–		–	X	X	–	–	
Med. Dark Green Metallic	49		X		X	X	X	–	–	
Cream Beige	50		X		X	–	–	–	X	
Bright Yellow	51		X		X	–	–	–	X	
Light Gold Metallic	53		–		–	–	–	–	–	
Sandstone	55		–		–	–	–	–	–	
Golden Brown Metallic	59		X		X	–	–	–	–	
Silver Metallic C/O	64		X		X	–	–	X	X	
Bronze Metallic	66		X		X	–	–	–	–	
Medium Red Metallic	74		X		X	–	–	–	–	
Medium Red C/O	75		–		–	–	–	X	–	

NOTE: Solid exterior color combinations (except vinyl tops) may be obtained with non-recommended interior combinations when ZP2 override is specified.

INTERIOR–EXTERIOR COLOR COMBINATIONS

MODEL	Seat Type	INTERIOR TRIM									
		Black & White Check			Black				Black	Light Neutral	
		• Cloth /Black	• Cloth /Red	• Cloth /Blue	Cloth	• Vinyl /Black	• Vinyl /Blue	Knit Vinyl	• Vinyl with Red Seat Welts/Red	Cloth	Vinyl
Standard – 1FQ00 Coupe (87)	Bucket	775	775	775		777	777		779		781
Type LT – 1FS00 Coupe (87)	Bucket				776			778		780	
EXTERIOR COLORS	Color Code										
Antique White C/O	11	X	X	X	X	X	X	X	X	X	
Bright Blue Metallic C/O	26	X	–	X	X	X	X	X	X	–	
Midnight Blue Metallic C/O	29	X	X	X	X	X	X	X	X	X	
Aqua Blue Metallic	36	X	–	–	X	X	–	X	–	–	
Lime Yellow	40	X	–	–	X	X	–	X	–	–	
Bright Green Metallic	46	X	–	–	X	X	–	X	–	X	
Med. Dark Green Metallic	49	X	–	–	X	X	–	X	–	X	
Cream Beige	50	X	–	–	X	X	–	X	X	X	
Bright Yellow	51	X	–	–	X	X	–	X	–	X	
Light Gold Metallic	53	X	–	–	X	X	–	X	–	X	
Sandstone	55	X	–	–	X	X	–	X	–	X	
Golden Brown Metallic	59	X	–	–	X	X	–	X	–	X	
Silver Metallic C/O	64	X	X	X	X	X	X	X	X	X	
Bronze Metallic	66	X	–	–	X	X	–	X	–	X	
Medium Red Metallic	74	X	X	–	X	X	–	X	X	X	
Medium Red C/O	75	X	X	–	X	X	–	X	X	X	

VINYL TOP COLOR	EXTERIOR COLOR
Black	All
White	All
Medium Blue	11, 26, 29
Medium Green	11, 46, 49
Cream Beige	11, 50, 53, 55, 59
Silver Taupe	64
Maroon	11, 64, 74
Brown	11, 50, 59, 64
Russet	11, 66
Medium Saddle	11, 49, 50, 59, 66

•–Accent carpet color. Obtained by specifying trim number plus Accent Carpet RPO number: 19F–Black, 75F–Red, or 24F–Blue.

NOTE: Solid exterior color combinations (except vinyl top) may be obtained with non-recommended interior combinations when ZP2 override is specified.

1975 Trim Combinations

1975 CHEVROLET 'B' INTERIOR–EXTERIOR COLOR COMBINATIONS

MODEL	Seat Type	INTERIOR TRIM: Black — Vinyl	Black — Perf. Vinyl	Black — Cloth	Black — Knit Cloth	Medium Sandstone — Vinyl	Medium Sandstone — Perf. Vinyl	Medium Sandstone — Knit Vinyl	Medium Sandstone — • Knit Cloth	Medium Sandstone — Cloth	Medium Green — • Perf. Vinyl	Medium Green — • Knit Cloth
Bel Air – 1BK00												
Sedan (69)	Bench			19C				55V		55C		
Station Wagon (35-45)								55V				
Impala – 1BL00												
Sedan (69)	Bench		19W		19D		55W		55D		44W	44D
Sedan (69)	50-50				19D		55W					
Sport Sedan (39)	Bench		19W		19D		55W		55D		44W	44D
Sport Sedan (39)	50-50				19D		55W					
Sport Coupe (57)	Bench		19W		19D		55W		55D		44W	44D
Sport Coupe (57)	50-50				19D		55W					
Custom Coupe (47)	Bench		19W		19D		55W		55D		44W	44D
Custom Coupe (47)	50-50				19D		55W					
Station Wagon (35-45)	Bench		19W				55W				44W	
Station Wagon (35-45)	50-50						55W					
Caprice Classic – 1BN00												
Sedan (69)	Bench	19H			19B	55H			55B			44B
Sedan (69)	50-50	19H			19B	55H			55B			44B
Sport Sedan (39)	Bench	19H			19B	55H			55B			44B
Sport Sedan (39)	50-50	19H			19B	55H			55B			44B
Sport Coupe (47)	Bench	19H			19B	55H			55B			44B
Sport Coupe (47)	50-50	19H			19B	55H			55B			44B
Convertible (67)	Bench						55W					
Convertible (67)	50-50						55W					
Caprice Estate – 1BN00												
Station Wagon (35-45)	Bench		19W				55W				44W	
Station Wagon (35-45)	50-50						55W					

EXTERIOR COLOR		Color Code	Black	Medium Sandstone	Medium Green
White C/O		11	X	X	X
Silver Metallic		13	X	–	–
Light Graystone		15	X	–	–
Black C/O		19	X	X	X
Medium Blue		24	X	–	–
Bright Blue Metallic		26	X	–	–
Dark Blue Metallic		29	X	–	–
Medium Green C/O		44	X	–	X
Dark Green Metallic		49	X	X	X
Cream-Beige C/O		50	X	X	–
Sandstone		55	X	X	–
Dark Brown Metallic		59	X	X	–
Light Saddle Metallic		63	X	–	–
Persimmon Metallic		64	X	X	–
Red		72	X	X	–
Red Metallic C/O		74	X	–	–
TWO TONE Lower	Upper	Color Code			
Medium Blue	White	24-11	X	–	–
Bright Blue Metallic	White	26-11	X	–	–
Dark Blue Metallic	White	29-11	X	–	–
Medium Green C/O	White	44-11	X	–	X
Dark Green Metallic	White	49-11	X	X	X
Sandstone	White	55-11	X	X	–
Dark Brown Metallic	White	59-11	X	X	–
Persimmon Metallic	White	64-11	X	X	–
Red Metallic C/O	White	74-11	X	–	–

NOTE: Solid exterior color combinations (except vinyl top or convertible top) may be obtained with non-recommended interior combinations when ZP2 override is specified.

1975 CHEVROLET "B" INTERIOR – EXTERIOR COLOR COMBINATIONS

MODEL	Seat Type	INTERIOR TRIM: Dark Blue — Cloth	Dark Blue — Knit Vinyl	Dark Blue — Perf. Vinyl	Dark Blue — • Knit Cloth	Dark Saddle — Sport Cloth	Dark Saddle — Perf. Vinyl	Dark Oxblood — Knit Cloth	White — Perf. Vinyl with Black †	White — Perf. Vinyl with Dk. Blue †	White — Perf. Vinyl with Dk. Oxblood †	White — Perf. Vinyl with Dk. Green †
Bel Air – 1BK00												
Sedan (69)	Bench	26C										
Station Wagon (35-45)			26V									
Impala – 1BL00												
Sedan (69)	Bench			26W	26D	63E	63W					
Sedan (69)	50-50			26W		63E	63W					
Sport Sedan (39)	Bench			26W	26D	63E	63W					
Sport Sedan (39)	50-50			26W		63E	63W					
Sport Coupe (57)	Bench			26W	26D	63E	63W		11W	02W	07W	04W
Sport Coupe (57)	50-50			26W		63E	63W					
Custom Coupe (47)	Bench			26W	26D	63E	63W		11W	02W	07W	04W
Custom Coupe (47)	50-50			26W		63E	63W					
Station Wagon (35-45)	Bench			26W		63E	63W					
Station Wagon (35-45)	50-50			26W		63E	63W					
Caprice Classic – 1BN00												
Sedan (69)	Bench				26B			73B				
Sedan (69)	50-50				26B			73B				
Sport Sedan (39)	Bench				26B			73B				
Sport Sedan (39)	50-50				26B			73B				
Sport Coupe (47)	Bench				26B			73B				
Sport Coupe (47)	50-50				26B			73B				
Convertible (67)	Bench					63E	63W		11W	02W	07W	04W
Convertible (67)	50-50					63E	63W					
Caprice Estate – 1BN00												
Station Wagon (35-45)	Bench			26W		63E	63W					
Station Wagon (35-45)	50-50			26W		63E	63W					

EXTERIOR COLOR		Color Code	Dark Blue	Dark Saddle	Dark Oxblood	White with Black †	White with Dk. Blue †	White with Dk. Oxblood †	White with Dk. Green †
White C/O		11	X	X	X	X	X	X	X
Silver Metallic		13	X	–	X	X	–	–	–
Light Graystone		15	–	X	X	X	–	–	–
Black C/O		19	X	X	X	X	–	–	–
Medium Blue		24	X	–	–	X	X	–	–
Bright Blue Metallic		26	X	–	–	X	X	–	–
Dark Blue Metallic		29	X	–	–	–	X	–	–
Medium Green C/O		44	–	–	–	X	–	–	X
Dark Green Metallic		49	–	X	–	–	–	–	X
Cream-Beige C/O		50	–	X	–	X	–	–	–
Sandstone		55	–	X	–	X	–	–	–
Dark Brown Metallic		59	–	X	–	X	–	–	–
Light Saddle Metallic		63	–	X	–	X	–	–	–
Persimmon Metallic		64	–	X	–	X	–	–	–
Red		72	–	–	–	X	–	–	–
Red Metallic C/O		74	–	–	X	X	–	X	–
TWO TONE Lower	Upper	Color Code							
Medium Blue	White	24-11	X	–	–	X	X	–	–
Bright Blue Metallic	White	26-11	X	–	–	–	X	–	–
Dark Blue Metallic	White	29-11	X	–	–	–	X	–	–
Medium Green C/O	White	44-11	–	–	–	X	–	–	X
Dark Green Metallic	White	49-11	–	X	–	–	–	–	X
Sandstone	White	55-11	–	X	–	X	–	–	–
Dark Brown Metallic	White	59-11	–	X	–	X	–	–	–
Persimmon Metallic	White	64-11	–	X	–	X	–	–	–
Red Metallic C/O	White	74-11	–	–	X	X	–	X	–

NOTES:

11W † – White Vinyl interior with Black Instrument Panel upper and lower, carpet, Cowl Kick Panel, and Package Shelf.

02W † – White Vinyl interior with Dark Blue Instrument Panel upper and lower, Cowl Kick pad, Carpet, and Package Shelf.

07W † – White Vinyl interior with Dark Oxblood Instrument Panel upper and lower, Cowl Kick pad, Carpet and Package Shelf.

04W † – White Vinyl interior with Dark Green Instrument Panel upper and lower, Carpet, Cowl Kick Panel, and Package Shelf.

NOTE: Solid exterior color combination (except vinyl top or convertible top) may be obtained with non-recommended interior combinations when ZP2 override is specified.

1975 Trim Combinations

1975 CHEVROLET – 1BL47 & 1BN47 RPO Z03 LANDAU
EXTERIOR COLOR/STRIPE/VINYL TOP APPLICATION

EXTERIOR COLOR	VINYL TOP COLORS (CB4)						
	White	Black	Dark Blue	Medium Green	Sandstone	Maroon	Silver Metallic
White	Black (19A)	Black (19A)	Dark Blue (29A)	Med. Green (44A)	Sandstone (55A)	Red (78A)	–
Silver Metallic	White (11A)	Black (19A)	Dark Blue (29A)	–	–	Red (78A)	Black (19A)
Light Graystone	White (11A)	Black (19A)	–	–	–	–	–
Black	White (11A)	White (11A)	–	–	Sandstone (55A)	–	Silver (15A)
Medium Blue	White (11A)	Black (19A)	Dark Blue (29A)	–	–	–	–
Bright Blue Metallic	White (11A)	Black (19A)	Dark Blue (29A)	–	–	–	Silver (15A)
Dark Blue Metallic	White (11A)	White (11A)	Med. Blue (24A)	–	–	–	Silver (15A)
Medium Green	White (11A)	Black (19A)	–	Dark Green (49A)	–	–	–
Dark Green Metallic	White (11A)	Med. Green (44A)	–	Med. Green (44A)	Sandstone (55A)	–	–
Cream Beige	White (11A)	Black (19A)	–	–	Black (19A)	–	–
Sandstone	White (11A)	Black (19A)	–	–	Black (19A)	–	–
Dark Brown Metallic	White (11A)	Sandstone (55A)	–	–	Sandstone (55A)	–	–
Light Saddle Metallic	White (11A)	Black (19A)	–	–	–	–	–
Persimmon Metallic	White (11A)	Black (19A)	–	–	Sandstone (55A)	–	–
Red	White (11A)	Black (19A)	–	–	–	–	–
Red Metallic	White (11A)	Black (19A)	–	–	–	White (11A)	Silver (15A)

STRIPE IDENTIFICATION

11A	White	WA 3967
15A	Silver	WSA 4814
19A	Black	WA 848
24A	Med. Blue	WA 4631
29A	Dk. Blue	WSA 4811
44A	Med. Green	WA 4516
49A	Dk. Green	WSA 4810
55A	Sandstone	WA 4635
78A	Red	WAS 4815

EXTERIOR COLORS – VINYL ROOF COMBINATIONS

VINYL TOP COVER (Material - Levant Grain)	EXTERIOR COLOR AVAILABILITY
Silver Metallic	Silver Metallic
	Black
	Bright Blue Metallic
	Dark Blue Metallic
	Red Metallic
Black C/O	All available colors
White C/O	All available colors
Dark Blue	White
	Silver Metallic
	Medium Blue
	Bright Blue Metallic
	Dark Blue Metallic
Medium Green C/O	White
	Medium Green
	Dark Green Metallic
Sandstone	White
	Black
	Dark Green Metallic
	Cream-Beige
	Sandstone
	Dark Brown Metallic
	Persimmon Metallic
Maroon – Production Name	White
	Silver Metallic
Dark Red – Sales Name	Red Metallic

CONVERTIBLE TOP AVAILABILITY
Model 1BN67 – White or Black

NOVA

EXTERIOR COLORS – VINYL ROOF COMBINATIONS

VINYL TOP COVER (Material - Levant Grain)	EXTERIOR COLOR AVAILABILITY	MODEL AVAILABILITY	
		1XX 1XY	LNX
Silver Metallic	Silver Metallic	X	X
	Bright Blue Metallic	X	–
	Dark Blue Metallic	X	–
	Red Metallic	X	X
	Red	(a)	–
Black C/O	Light Graystone	–	X
	Dark Green Metallic	–	X
	Red Metallic	–	X
	All available colors	X	–
White C/O	White	–	X
	Light Graystone	–	X
	Dark Blue Metallic	–	X
	Dark Green Metallic	–	X
	Sandstone	–	X
	Medium Blue	–	X
	Red Metallic	–	X
	All available colors	X	–
Dark Blue	White	X	X
	Silver Metallic	X	X
	Medium Blue	X	X
	Bright Blue Metallic	X	–
	Dark Blue Metallic	X	X
Medium Green C/O	White	X	–
	Medium Green	X	–
	Dark Green Metallic	X	–
Sandstone	White	X	X
	Dark Green Metallic	X	X
	Cream-Beige	X	X
	Sandstone	X	X
	Dark Sandstone Metallic	X	X
	Persimmon Metallic	X	–
Cordovan – Production Name	White	X	–
	Cream-Beige	X	–
	Light Saddle Metallic	X	–
Dark Brown – Sales Name	Persimmon Metallic	X	–
Maroon – Production Name	White	X	X
	Silver Metallic	X	X
Dark Red – Sales Name	Red Metallic	X	X
Red	White	X	–
	Red	X	–
	Silver Metallic	(a)	–

(a) – Vinyl Top usage for Nova SS (RPO Z26) only.

1975 CORVETTE INTERIOR–EXTERIOR COLOR COMBINATIONS

TRIM COMBINATIONS			STANDARD ALL-VINYL						CUSTOM LEATHER				
			19	26	60	65	73	14	192	652	142	262	732
NEW OR C/O	EXTERIOR COLORS	COLOR CODE	Black	Dark Blue	Lt. Neutral	Med. Saddle	Dark Ox-blood	Silver	Black	Med. Saddle	Silver	Dark Blue	Dark Ox-blood
C/O	White	10	X	X	X	X	X	X	X	X	X	X	X
N	Silver Metallic	13	X	X	–	X	X	X	X	X	X	X	X
C/O	Red	76	X	–	X	X	X	X	X	X	X	–	X
C/O	Red Metallic	74	X	–	X	X	X	X	X	X	X	–	X
N	Med. Brt. Blue Metallic	22	X	X	–	–	–	X	X	–	X	X	–
N	Dark Steel Blue	27	X	X	–	–	–	X	X	–	X	X	–
N	Flame Red	70	X	–	X	X	–	–	X	X	–	–	–
N	Bright Yellow	56	X	–	X	X	–	–	X	X	–	–	–
N	Bright Green Metallic	42	X	–	X	X	–	X	X	X	X	–	–
N	Medium Saddle Metallic	67	X	–	X	X	–	–	X	X	–	–	–

1975 Trim Combinations

1975 CHEVROLET NOVA 'X' INTERIOR–EXTERIOR COLOR COMBINATIONS

		INTERIOR TRIM												
		Black								Medium Sandstone				Med. Green
MODEL	Seat Type	Vinyl	• Vinyl /Red	Perf. Vinyl	• Perf. Vinyl /Red	Cloth	• Cloth /Red	Sport Cloth	• Sport Cloth /Red	Vinyl	● Perf. Vinyl	Cloth	● Knit Cloth	Knit Cloth
Standard – 1XX00	Bench	19V	19V			19C	19C			55V		55C		
Coupe (27)	Bucket	19V	19V							55V				
	Bench	19V	19V			19C	19C			55V		55C		
Hatchback (17)	Bucket	19V	19V							55V				
Sedan (69)	Bench	19V	19V			19C	19C			55V		55C		
Custom – 1XY00	Bench			19W	19W			19E	19E					44D
Coupe (27)	Bucket			19W	19W			19E	19E					
	Bench			19W	19W			19E	19E					44D
Hatchback (17)	Bucket			19W	19W			19E	19E					
Sedan (69)	Bench			19W	19W						55W		55D	44D
Luxury – 1XY00 Coupe (27)	Bucket												55G	
Sedan (69)	Bucket												55G	
EXTERIOR COLOR	Color Code													
White C/O	+11	X	X	X	X	X	X	X	X		X			X
Silver Metallic	+13	X	–	X	–	X	–	X	–		–			–
Light Graystone	+15	X	–	X	–	X	–	X	–		–			–
Medium Blue	+24	X	–	X	–	X	–	X	–		–			–
Bright Blue Metallic	26	X	–	X	–	X	–	X	–		–			–
Dark Blue Metallic	+29	X	–	X	–	X	–	X	–		–			–
Medium Green C/O	44	X	–	X	–	X	–	X	–		–			X
Dark Green Metallic	+49	X	–	X	–	X	–	X	–		X			X
Cream-Beige C/O	+50	X	–	X	–	X	–	X	–		X			X
Bright Yellow C/O	51	X	–	X	–	X	–	X	–		–			
Sandstone	+55	X	–	X	–	X	–	X	–		X			–
Dark Sandstone Met.	+58	X	–	X	–	X	–	X	–		X			–
Light Saddle Met.	63	X	–	X	–	X	–	X	–		–			–
Persimmon Met.	64	X	–	X	–	X	–	X	–		X			–
Red Metallic C/O	+74	X	–	X	–	X	–	X	–		–			–
Red C/O	75	X	X	X	X	X	X	X	X		X			–
TWO TONE Lower / Upper	Color Code													
Medium Blue / White	24-11	X	–	X	–	X	–	X	–		–			–
Bright Blue Met. / White	26-11	X	–	X	–	X	–	X	–		–			–
Dark Blue Met. / White	29-11	X	–	X	–	X	–	X	–		–			–
Medium Green C/O / White	44-11	X	–	X	–	X	–	X	–		–			X
Dark Green Met. / White	49-11	X	–	X	–	X	–	X	–		X			X
Sandstone / Cream-Beige	55-50	X	–	X	–	X	–	X	–		X			–
Dark Sandstone Met. / Cream-Beige	58-50	X	–	X	–	X	–	X	–		X			–
Persimmon Met. / White	64-11	X	–	X	–	X	–	X	–		X			–
Red Metallic C/O / White	74-11	X	–	X	–	X	–	X	–		–			–
Red C/O / White	75-11	X	X	X	X	X	X	X	X		X			–

NOTE: Solid exterior color combinations (except vinyl top) may be obtained with non-recommended interior combinations when ZP 2 override is specified.

+ The Nova LN is available in ten of the 16 exterior colors released for the Nova. The Nova LN colors are identified by the smybol +.

• – Carpet Selection: Accent Red – 75F.

1975 CHEVROLET NOVA 'X' INTERIOR–EXTERIOR COLOR COMBINATIONS

		INTERIOR TRIM													
		Dark Blue			Dark Saddle			Med. Gray-stone	Dark Oxblood		White				
MODEL	Seat Type	Vinyl	Cloth	Knit Cloth	Vinyl	Sport Cloth	Perf. Vinyl	Knit Cloth	Perf. Vinyl	Knit Cloth	† Perf. Vinyl /Black	† Perf. Vinyl /Dk. Blue	† Perf. Vinyl /Dk. Green	† Perf. Vinyl /Dk. Oxblood	• Perf. Vinyl /Red
Standard – 1XX00	Bench	26V	26C		63V										
Coupe (27)	Bucket				63V										
	Bench	26V	26C		63V										
Hatchback (17)	Bucket				63V										
Sedan (69)	Bench	26V	26C		63V										
Custom – 1XY00	Bench			26D		63E	63W		73W		11W	02W	04W	07W	11W
Coupe (27)	Bucket						63W				11W	02W	04W	07W	11W
	Bench			26D		63E	63W		73W		11W	02W	04W	07W	11W
Hatchback (17)	Bucket						63W				11W	02W	04W	07W	11W
Sedan (69)	Bench			26D											
Luxury – 1XY00 Coupe (27)	Bucket			26G				16G		73G					
Sedan (69)	Bucket			26G				16G		73G					
EXTERIOR COLOR	Color Code														
White C/O	+11		X			X		X	X		X	X	X	X	X
Silver Metallic	+13		X			–		–	X		X	–	–	–	–
Light Graystone	+15		–			X		X	X		X	–	–	–	–
Medium Blue	+24		X			–		–	–		X	X	–	–	–
Bright Blue Metallic	26		X			–		–	–		X	X	–	–	–
Dark Blue Metallic	+29		X			–		–	–		–	X	–	–	–
Medium Green C/O	44		–			–		–	–		X	–	X	–	–
Dark Green Metallic	+49		–			X		X	–		–	–	X	–	–
Cream-Beige C/O	+50		–			X		–	–		X	–	–	–	–
Bright Yellow C/O	51		–			X		–	–		X	–	–	–	–
Sandstone	+55		–			X		–	–		X	–	–	–	–
Dark Sandstone Met.	+58		–			X		–	–		X	–	–	–	–
Light Saddle Met.	63		–			X		–	–		X	–	–	–	–
Persimmon Met.	64		–			X		–	–		X	–	–	–	–
Red Metallic	+74		–			–		X	X		X	–	–	X	–
Red C/O	75		–			X		–	–		X	–	–	–	X
TWO TONE Lower / Upper	Color Code														
Medium Blue / White	24-11		X			–		–	–		X	X	–	–	–
Bright Blue Met. / White	26-11		X			–		–	–		X	X	–	–	–
Dark Blue Met. / White	25-11		X			–		–	–		–	X	–	–	–
Medium Green C/O / White	44-11		–			–		–	–		X	–	X	–	–
Dark Green Met. / White	49-11		–			X		X	–		–	–	X	–	–
Sandstone / Cream-Beige	55-50		–			X		–	–		X	–	–	–	–
Dark Sandstone Met. / Cream-Beige	58-50		–			X		–	–		X	–	–	–	–
Persimmon Met. / White	64-11		–			X		X	–		X	–	–	–	–
Red Metallic C/O / White	74-11		–			–		X	X		X	–	–	X	–
Red C/O / White	75-11		–			X		–	–		X	–	–	–	X

NOTE: Solid exterior color combinations (except vinyl top) may be obtained with non-recommended interior combinations when ZP2 override is specified.

+ The Nova LN is available in ten of the 16 exterior colors released for the Nova. The Nova LN colors are identified by the symbol +.

• – Carpet Selection: Accent Red – 75F is available by specifying RPO number 11W + 75F.

NOTES: 11W † – White Perforated Vinyl interior with Black Instrument Panel upper and lower, carpet, Cowl Kick Pad, and Package Shelf.
02W † – White Perforated Vinyl interior with Dark Blue Instrument Panel upper and lower, Cowl Kick pad, Carpet, and Package Shelf.
07W † – White Perforated Vinyl interior with Dark Oxblood Instrument Panel upper and lower, Cowl Kick pad, Carpet and Package Shelf.
04W † – White Perforated Vinyl interior with Dark Green Instrument Panel upper and lower, Carpet, Cowl Kick Pad, and Package Shelf.

1975 Trim Combinations

1975 NOVA 'SS' 1XA17-27 (RPO Z26)
COLOR/STRIPING AVAILABILITY
BODY SIDE STRIPE COLOR RECOMMENDATIONS*

EXTERIOR BODY COLOR		VINYL TOP COLOR									
		None	Black	White	Silver	Dk. Blue	Green	Sandstone	Cordovan	Maroon	Red
White	11	Red (75A)	Black (19A)	Red (75A)		Black (19A)	Black (19A)	Gold (52A)	Gold (52A)	Black (19A)	Red (75A)
Silver	13	Red (75A)	Black (19A)	Red (75A)	Red (75A)	Black (19A)				Black (19A)	Red (75A)
Lt. Graystone	15	White (11A)	White (11A)	White (11A)							
Med. Blue	24	White (11A)	White (11A)	White (11A)		White (11A)					
Brt. Blue Met.	26	White (11A)	White (11A)	White (11A)	Silver (13A)	White (11A)					
Dk. Blue Met.	29	White (11A)	White (11A)	White (11A)	Silver (13A)	White (11A)					
Med. Green	44	White (11A)	White (11A)	White (11A)			White (11A)				
Dk. Green Met.	49	Gold (52A)	Gold (52A)	White (11A)			White (11A)	Gold (52A)			
Cream Beige	50	Gold (52A)	Gold (52A)	White (11A)				Gold (52A)	Gold (52A)		
Brt. Yellow	51	Black (19A)	Black (19A)	Black (19A)							
Sandstone	55	White (11A)	White (11A)	White (11A)				White (11A)			
Dk. Sandstone Met.	58	Gold (52A)	Gold (52A)	White (11A)				Gold (52A)			
Lt. Saddle Met.	63	White (11A)	White (11A)	White (11A)					White (11A)		
Persimmon Met.	64	White (11A)	White (11A)	White (11A)				White (11A)	White (11A)		
Red Met.	74	White (11A)	White (11A)	White (11A)	Silver (13A)					White (11A)	
Red	75	White (11A)	Black (19A)	White (11A)	Silver (13A)						White (11A)

TWO-TONE EXTERIOR COLORS				Stripe
Lower		Upper		
Med. Blue	24	White	11	White (11A)
Brt. Blue Met.	26	White	11	White (11A)
Dk. Blue Met.	29	White	11	White (11A)
Med. Green	44	White	11	White (11A)
Dk. Green Met.	49	White	11	White (11A)
Sandstone	55	Cream-Beige	50	White (11A)
Dk. Sandstone Met.	58	Cream-Beige	50	Gold (52A)
Persimmon Met.	64	White	11	White (11A)
Red Met.	74	White	11	White (11A)
Red	75	White	11	White (11A)

STRIPE I.D.		
11A	White	WA3967
13A	Silver	WA4322
19A	Black	WA848
52A	Gold	WA4817
75A	Red	WA4330

*NOTE: RPO ZP2 override will provide for any available color stripe selection.

1975 NOVA LN – COLOR/STRIPE/INTERIOR USAGE CHART
WITH AND WITHOUT VINYL TOP APPLICATION
(RPO Z11 – 1XY69 OR 1XY27)

EXTERIOR BODY COLOR	BODY SIDE DUAL PIN STRIPE COLOR	WITH VINYL TOP RPO C09	WITHOUT VINYL TOP	INTERIOR TRIM – CLOTH			
				Medium Sandstone 55G	Dark Blue 26G	Medium Graystone 16G	Dark Oxblood 73G
White - (WA 3967)	Oxblood	–	X	–	–	X	X
		White	–	–	–	X	X
		Maroon	–	–	–	X	X
	Gold	–	X	X	X	–	–
		White	–	X	X	–	–
		Blue	–	–	X	–	–
		Sandstone	–	X	–	–	–
Silver Metallic (WA4322)	Oxblood	–	X	–	–	–	X
		Silver Metallic	–	–	–	–	X
		Maroon	–	–	–	–	X
	White	–	X	–	X	–	–
		Silver Metallic	–	–	X	–	–
		Blue	–	–	X	–	–
	Gold	–	X	X	–	–	–
		Silver Metallic	–	X	–	–	–
Light Graystone (WA4630)	Oxblood	–	X	–	–	–	X
	White	–	X	–	–	X	–
		Black	–	–	–	X	–
		White	–	–	–	X	–
Dark Blue Metallic (WA 4633)	White	–	X	–	X	X	–
		White	–	–	X	X	–
		Blue	–	–	X	X	–
Dark Green Metallic (WA 4634)	White	–	X	–	–	X	–
		White	–	–	–	X	–
		Black	–	–	–	X	–
	Gold	–	X	X	–	–	–
		Sandstone	–	X	–	–	–
Sandstone (WA4635)	White	–	X	X	–	–	–
		White	–	X	–	–	–
		Sandstone	–	X	–	–	–
Red Metallic (WA 4533)	White	–	X	–	–	X	X
		Silver Metallic	–	–	–	–	X
		Black	–	–	–	–	X
		Maroon	–	–	–	X	X
		White	–	–	–	X	–
Medium Blue (WA 4631)	White	–	X	–	X	X	–
		White	–	–	X	X	–
		Blue	–	–	X	X	–
Cream Biege (WA 4527)	Gold	–	X	X	–	–	–
		Sandstone	–	X	–	–	–
Dark Sandstone Metallic (WA 4648)	Gold	–	X	X	–	–	–
		Sandstone	–	X	–	–	–

NOTES:

(1) TOTALS
10 Exterior Body Colors
6 Vinyl Top Colors
3 Body Stripe Colors
4 Interior Colors

(2) Stripe I.D. – Paint
11A White (WA 3967)
52A Gold (WA 4326)
73A Oxblood (WA 3595)

(3) No Two Tones available

(4) The combinations shown are the only combinations available.

EXTERIOR COLORS – VINYL ROOF COMBINATIONS

VINYL TOP COVER (Material - Levant Grain)	EXTERIOR COLOR AVAILABILITY
Silver Metallic	Silver Metallic
	Black
	Bright Blue Metallic
	Dark Blue Metallic
	Red Metallic
Black C/O	All avilable colors
White C/O	All available colors
Dark Blue	White
	Silver Metallic
	Medium Blue
	Bright Blue Metallic
	Dark Blue Metallic
Medium Green C/O	White
	Medium Green
	Dark Green Metallic
Sandstone	White
	Black
	Dark Green Metallic
	Cream-Beige
	Sandstone
	Dark Brown Metallic
	Persimmon Metallic
Cordovan – Production Name	White
	Cream-Beige
	Light Saddle Metallic
Dark Brown – Sales Name	Persimmon Metallic
Maroon – Production Name	White
	Silver Metallic
Dark Red – Sales Name	Red Metallic

1975 Trim Combinations

1975 CHEVELLE AND EL CAMINO 'A' INTERIOR–EXTERIOR COLOR COMBINATIONS

MODEL	Seat Type	INTERIOR TRIM Black Vinyl	Black Knit ● Vinyl	Black Perf. Vinyl	Black Cloth	Black Sport Cloth	Black Knit Cloth	Medium Sandstone Vinyl	Medium Sandstone Knit ● Vinyl
Malibu – 1AC00									
Sport Sedan (29)	Bench		19V		19C				55V
Sport Coupe (37)	Bench		19V		19C				55V
	Bucket								
Station Wagon (35)	Bench		19V						55V
	Bucket								
El Camino (80)	Bench		19V		19C				55V
	Bucket								
Laguna Type 'S-3' – 1AE00									
Sport Coupe (37)	Bench			19Z		19E			
	Bucket			19Z		19E			
Malibu Classic – 1AD00									
Sport Sedan (29)	Bench	19W					19D	55W	
Sport Coupe (37)	Bench	19W					19D	55W	
	Bucket	19W					19D	55W	
Station Wagon (35)	Bench	19W						55W	
	Bucket	19W						55W	
El Camino Classic (80)	Bench	19W					19D	55W	
	Bucket	19W					19D	55W	
Malibu Classic Estate – 1AG00									
Station Wagon (35)	Bench	19W						55W	
	Bucket	19W						55W	

EXTERIOR COLORS	Color Code	Black	Medium Sandstone
White C/O	11	X	X
Silver Metallic	13	X	–
Light Graystone	15	X	–
Black C/O	19	X	X
Medium Blue	24	X	–
Bright Blue Metallic	26	X	–
Dark Blue Metallic	29	X	–
Medium Green C/O	44	X	–
Dark Green Metallic	49	X	X
Cream-Beige C/O	50	X	X
Sandstone	55	X	X
Dark Brown Metallic	59	X	X
Light Saddle Metallic	63	X	–
Persimmon Metallic	64	X	X
Red	72	X	X
Red Metallic C/O	74	X	–

TWO TONE Lower	Upper	Color Code	Black	Medium Sandstone
Medium Blue	White	24-11	X	–
Bright Blue Metallic	White	26-11	X	–
Dark Blue Metallic	White	29-11	X	–
Medium Green C/O	White	44-11	X	–
Dark Green Metallic	White	49-11	X	X
Sandstone	White	55-11	X	X
Dark Brown Metallic	White	59-11	X	X
Persimmon Metallic	White	64-11	X	X
Red Metallic C/O	White	74-11	X	–

NOTE: Solid exterior color combinations (except vinyl top) may be obtained with non-recommended interior combinations when ZP2 override is specified. Two Tones are not available on Wagons.

1975 CHEVELLE AND EL CAMINO 'A' INTERIOR–EXTERIOR COLOR COMBINATIONS

MODEL	Seat Type	INTERIOR TRIM Dark Blu. Vinyl	Dark Blu. Knit Vinyl	Dark Blu. Cloth	Dark Blu. Knit Cloth	Dark Saddle Vinyl	Dark Saddle Perf. Vinyl	Dark Saddle Sport Cloth
Malibu – 1AC00								
Sport Sedan (29)	Bench		26V	26C				
Sport Coupe (37)	Bench		26V	26C				
	Bucket							
Station Wagon (35)	Bench							
	Bucket							
El Camino (80)	Bench		26V	26C				
	Bucket							
Laguna Type S-3 – 1AE00	Bench						63Z	63E
Sport Coupe (37)	Bucket						63Z	63E
Malibu Classic – 1AD00								
Sport Sedan (29)	Bench	26W			26D			
Sport Coupe (37)	Bench	26W			26D	63W		
	Bucket	26W				63W		
Station Wagon (35)	Bench	26W				63W		
	Bucket	26W				63W		
El Camino Classic (80)	Bench	26W			26D	63W		
	Bucket	26W				63W		
Malibu Classic Estate – 1AG00								
Station Wagon (35)	Bench	26W				63W		
	Bucket	26W				63W		

EXTERIOR COLORS	Color Code	Dark Blu.	Dark Saddle
White C/O	11 †	X	X †
Silver Metallic	13 †	X	–
Light Graystone	15	–	X
Black C/O	19 †	X	X †
Medium Blue	24	X	–
Bright Blue Metallic	26 †	X	–
Dark Blue Metallic	29	X	–
Medium Green C/O	44	–	–
Medium Green Metallic	49	–	X
Cream-Beige C/O	50	–	X
Sandstone	55	–	X
Dark Brown Metallic	59	–	–
Light Saddle Metallic	63	–	X
Persimmon Metallic	64 †	–	X †
Red	72	–	–
Red Metallic C/O	74 †	–	–

TWO TONE Lower	Upper	Color Code	Dark Blu.	Dark Saddle
Medium Blue	White	24-11	X	–
Bright Blue Metallic	White	26-11	X	–
Dark Blue Metallic	White	29-11	X	–
Medium Green C/O	White	44-11	–	–
Dark Green Metallic	White	49-11	–	X
Sandstone	White	55-11	–	X
Dark Brown Metallic	White	59-11	–	–
Persimmon Metallic	White	64-11	–	X
Red Metallic C/O	White	74-11	–	–

NOTE: Solid exterior color combinations (except vinyl top) may be obtained with non-recommended interior combinations when ZP2 override is specified. Two Tones are not available on wagons or on the Laguna Type S-3.

† – The The Laguna Type S-3 is available in 6 colors. Available colors are identified by the symbol †. Exterior body colors, vinyl top colors, lower body paint stripe colors, rear bumper guard colors, and front and rear impact strips are color coordinated with each other and with interior color availability.

CHAPTER 1

1975 Trim Combinations

1975 CHEVELLE AND EL CAMINO 'A' INTERIOR–EXTERIOR COLOR COMBINATIONS

MODEL	Seat Type	INTERIOR TRIM: Medium Green Knit Vinyl	Dark Oxblood Knit Cloth	Dark Oxblood Knit Cloth	Dark Oxblood Sport Cloth	Dark Oxblood Perf. Vinyl	White Perf. † Vinyl /Black	White Perf. † Vinyl /Dk. Oxblood	White † White Vinyl with B&W Sport Cloth /Black	White † White Vinyl with B&W Sport Cloth /Dk. Oxblood
Malibu – 1AC00										
Sport Sedan (29)	Bench	44V								
Sport Coupe (37) *	Bench	44V								
	Bucket									
Station Wagon (35)	Bench									
	Bucket									
El Camino (80)	Bench	44V								
	Bucket									
Laguna Type S-3 – 1AE00	Bench				73E	73Z	11Z	07Z	11E	07E
Sport Coupe (37)	Bucket				73E	73Z				
Malibu Classic – 1AD00										
Sport Sedan (29)	Bench		44D	73D						
Sport Coupe (37)	Bench		44D	73D						
	Bucket			73D						
Station Wagon (35)	Bench									
	Bucket									
El Camino Classic (80)	Bench		44D	73D						
	Bucket			73D						
Malibu Classic Estate – 1AG00 Station Wagon (35)	Bench									
	Bucket									

EXTERIOR COLOR	Color Code	Medium Green	Dark Oxblood	White Perf. Vinyl /Black	White Perf. Vinyl /Dk. Oxblood	White Vinyl with B&W Sport Cloth /Black	White Vinyl with B&W Sport Cloth /Dk. Oxblood
White C/O	11 †	X	X †	X †	X †	X †	X †
Silver Metallic	13 †	–	X †	X †	X †	X †	X †
Light graystone	15	–	X	X	–	X	–
Black C/O	19 †	X	X †	X †	X †	X †	X †
Medium Blue	24	–	–	X	–	X	–
Bright Blue Metallic	26 †	–	–	X †	–	X †	–
Dark Blue Metallic	29	–	–	–	–	–	–
Medium Green C/O	44	X	–	X	–	X	–
Dark Green Metallic	49	X	–	–	–	–	–
Cream-Beige C/O	50	–	–	X	–	X	–
Sandstone	55	–	–	X	–	X	–
Dark Brown Metallic	59	–	–	X	–	X	–
Light Saddle Metallic	63	–	–	X	–	X	–
Persimmon Metallic	64 †	–	–	X †	–	X †	–
Red	72	–	–	X	–	X	–
Red Metallic C/O	74 †	–	X †	X †	X †	X †	X †

TWO TONE Lower	Upper	Color Code	Medium Green	Dark Oxblood	White
Medium Blue	White	24-11	–	–	–
Bright Blue Metallic	White	26-11	–	–	–
Dark Blue Metallic	White	29-11	–	–	–
Medium Green	White	44-11	X	–	–
Dark Green Metallic	White	49-11	X	–	–
Sandstone	White	55-11	–	–	–
Dark Brown Metallic	White	59-11	–	–	–
Persimmon Metallic	White	64-11	–	–	–
Red Metallic	White	74-11	–	X	–

NOTE: Solid exterior color combinations (except vinyl top) may be obtained with non-recommended interior combinations when ZP2 override is specified. Two tones are not available on wagons or on the Laguna Type S-3.

11Z † – White perforated vinyl interior with Black Instrument Panel upper and lower, carpet, Cowl Kick Pad, and Package Shelf.

07Z † – White perforated vinyl interior with Dark Oxblood Instrument Panel upper and lower, carpet, Cowl Kick Pad, and Package Shelf.

11E † – Black and white sport cloth in a White vinyl interior with Black Instrument Panel upper and lower, Carpet, Cowl Kick Pad, and Package Shelf.

07E † – Black and White sport cloth in a White vinyl interior with Dark Oxblood Instrument Panel upper and lower, Carpet, Cowl Kick Pad, and Package Shelf.

† – The Laguna type S-3 is available in 6 colors. Available colors are identified by the symbol †. Exterior body colors, vinyl top colors, lower body paint stripe colors, rear bumper guard colors, and front and rear impact strips are color coordinated with each other and with interior color availability.

MONTE CARLO

EXTERIOR COLORS – VINYL ROOF COMBINATIONS

VINYL TOP COVER	EXTERIOR COLOR AVAILABILITY	MODEL AVAILABILITY 1AH57
Silver Metallic	Silver Metallic	X
	Black	X
	Bright Blue Metallic	X
	Dark Blue Metallic	X
	Red Metallic	X
Black C/O	Light Graystone	–
	Red Metallic	–
	All available colors	X
White C/O	White	–
	Light Graystone	–
	Dark Blue Metallic	–
	Dark Green Metallic	–
	Sandstone	–
	Medium Blue	–
	Dark Sandstone Metallic	–
	Red Metallic	–
	All available colors	X
Dark Blue	White	X
	Silver Metallic	X
	Medium Blue	X
	Bright Blue Metallic	X
	Dark Blue Metallic	X
Medium Green C/O	White	X
	Medium Green	X
	Dark Green Metallic	X
Sandstone	White	X
	Dark Green Metallic	X
	Cream-Beige	X
	Sandstone	X
	Dark Sandstone Metallic	–
	Dark Brown Metallic	X
	Russet Orange Metallic	–
Maroon – Production Name Dark Red – Sales Name	White	X
	Silver Metallic	X
	Light Graystone	X
	Red Metallic	X
	Black	X
Red	White	–
	Red	–

C/O Levant Grain will be used for Monte Carlo

1975 MONTE CARLO 'SPECIAL A' INTERIOR–EXTERIOR COLOR COMBINATIONS

MODEL	Seat Type	INTERIOR TRIM: Black Knit Cloth	Black Vinyl	White † Vinyl /Black	White † Vinyl /Dk. Blue	White † Vinyl /Dk. Green	White † Vinyl/Dk. Oxblood	Medium Sandstone Knit Cloth	Medium Sandstone Vinyl	Dark Blue Knit Cloth	Dark Blue Vinyl	Dark Oxblood Knit Cloth	Medium Green Knit Cloth
Monte Carlo 'S' – 1AH00	Bench	19B	19H	11H	02H	04H	07H	55B	55H	26B	26H	73B	
Sport Coupe (57)	Bucket	19B	19H	11H	02H	04H	07H	–	55H	26B	26H	73B	
Monte Carlo Luxury	50-50	19N	–	–	–	–	–	55N	–	26N	–	73N	44N
Sport Coupe (57)	Bucket	19N	–	–	–	–	–	55N	–	26N	–	73N	44N
EXTERIOR COLORS	Color Code												
White C/O	11	X		X	X	X	X	X		X		X	X
Silver Metallic	13	X		X	–	–	–	–		X		X	X
Light Graystone	15	X		X	–	–	–	–		–		X	–
Black C/O	19	X		X	–	–	–	X		X		X	X
Medium Blue	24	X		X	X	–	–	–		X		–	–
Bright Blue Metallic	26	X		X	–	–	–	–		X		–	–
Dark Blue Metallic	29	X		–	X	–	–	–		X		–	–
Medium Green C/O	44	X		X	–	X	–	–		–		–	X
Dark Green Metallic	49	X		–	–	X	–	X		–		–	X
Cream-Beige C/O	50	X		X	–	–	–	X		–		–	–
Sandstone	55	X		X	–	–	–	X		–		–	–
Dark Brown Metallic	59	X		X	–	–	–	X		–		–	–
Light Saddle Metallic	63	X		X	–	–	–	–		–		–	–
Persimmon Metallic	64	X		X	–	–	–	X		–		–	–
Red	72	X		X	–	–	–	X		–		–	–
Red Metallic C/O	74	X		X	–	–	X	–		–		X	–

NOTE: Solid exterior color combinations (except vinyl top) may be obtained with non-recommended interior combinations when ZP2 override is specified. Two tone paint is not available on the Monte Carlo.

NOTES:

11H † – White Vinyl interior with Black Instrument Panel upper and lower, carpet, Cowl Kick Pad, and Package Shelf.

02H † – White Vinyl interior with Dark Blue Instrument Panel upper and lower, Cowl Kick pad, Carpet, and Package Shelf.

07H † – White Vinyl interior with Dark Oxblood Instrument Panel upper and lower, Cowl Kick pad, Carpet and Package Shelf.

04H † – White Vinyl interior with Dark Green Instrument Panel upper and lower, Carpet, Cowl Kick Pad, and Package Shelf.

1975 Trim Combinations

1975 EL CAMINO "CONQUISTA" INTERIOR–EXTERIOR COLOR COMBINATIONS

EL CAMINO – CONQUISTA – CUSTOM 1AD80 (RPO D91 and BX8)	SEAT TYPE	Black Vinyl	Black Knit Cloth	Medium Sandstone Vinyl	Dark Blue Vinyl	Dark Blue Knit Cloth	Dark Saddle Vinyl	Medium Green Knit Cloth	Dark Oxblood Knit Cloth
	BENCH	19W	19D	55W	26W	26D	63W	44D	73D
	BUCKET	19W	19D	55W	26W		63W		73D

HOOD & CENTER BODY COLOR	ROOF & LOWER BODY COLOR	Color Code	Black	Medium Sandstone	Dark Blue	Dark Saddle	Medium Green	Dark Oxblood
Bright Blue Metallic	Dark Blue Metallic	29-26-29	X	–	X	–	–	–
Medium Green	Dark Green Metallic	49-44-49	X	X	–	X	X	–
Cream-Beige	Sandstone	55-50-55	X	X	–	X	–	–
Sandstone	Dark Brown Metallic	59-55-59	X	X	–	X	–	–
Red ·	Red Metallic	74-72-74	X	–	–	–	–	X
White	Silver Metallic	13-11-13	X	–	X	–	–	X
White	Light Graystone	15-11-15	X	–	–	X	–	X
White	Black	19-11-19	X	X	X	X	X	X
White	Medium Blue	24-11-24	X	–	X	–	–	–
White	Bright Blue Metallic	26-11-26	X	–	X	–	–	–
White	Dark Blue Metallic	29-11-29	X	–	X	–	–	–
White	Medium Green	44-11-44	X	–	–	–	X	–
White	Dark Green Metallic	49-11-49	X	X	–	X	X	–
White	Cream-Beige	50-11-50	X	X	–	X	–	–
White	Sandstone	55-11-55	X	X	–	X	–	–
White	Dark Brown Metallic	59-11-59	X	X	–	–	–	–
White	Light Saddle Metallic	63-11-63	X	–	–	X	–	–
White	Persimmon Metallic	64-11-64	X	X	–	X	–	–
White	Red	72-11-72	X	X	–	–	–	–
White	Red Metallic	74-11-74	X	–	–	–	–	X

NOTE: RPO BX3 Exterior Ornamentation -- Woodgrain, RPO B84 Body Side Molding, RPO C09 Vinyl Roof Cover, RPO D99 Special Two Tone Paint on 1AD80, 5AD80, RPO YE7 GMC "SP" Package on 5AD80, and RPO Z15 "SS" Package on 1AD80 are not available with RPO D91.

1975 MALIBU CLASSIC
LANDAU STRIPE
(1AD37–RPO Z03)

EXTERIOR COLOR	CODE NO.	WA848 BLACK	WA3967 WHITE	WA4553 GOLD MET.	WA4409 RED
White C/O	11	X		X	X
Silver Metallic	13	X	X		
Light Graystone	15	X	X		
Black C/O	19		X	X	X
Medium Blue	24	X	X		
Bright Blue Metallic	26	X	X		
Dark Blue Metallic	29	X	X	X	X
Medium Green C/O	44	X	X		
Dark Green Metallic	49	X	X	X	
Cream Beige C/O	50	X	X	X	
Sandstone	55	X	X	X	
Dark Brown Metallic	59	X	X	X	
Light Saddle Metallic	63	X	X		
Persimmon Metallic	64	X	X	X	
Red	72	X	X	X	
Red Metallic C/O	74	X	X	X	

1975 MONTE CARLO LANDAU
COLOR/STRIPE/MOLDING/VINYL TOP APPLICATION
(RPO Z03 – 1AH57)

EXTERIOR COLOR	Color Combination Identification	White	Black	Dark Blue	Medium Green	Sandstone	Maroon	Silver Metallic
White	Stripe	Black	Black	Dark Blue	Med. Green	Sandstone	Red	–
	Molding	White	Black	Dark Blue	Med. Green	Lt. Beige	Maroon	–
Silver Metallic	Stripe	White	Black	Dark Blue	–	–	Red	Black
	Molding	White	Black	Dark Blue	–	–	Maroon	Sil. Metallic
Light Graystone	Stripe	White	Black	–	–	–	Red	–
	Molding	White	Black	–	–	–	Maroon	–
Black	Stripe	White	White	–	–	–	Red	Silver
	Molding	White	Black	–	–	–	Maroon	Sil. Metallic
Medium Blue	Stripe	White	Black	Dark Blue	–	–	–	–
	Molding	White	Black	Dark Blue	–	–	–	–
Bright Blue Metallic	Stripe	White	Black	Dark Blue	–	–	–	Silver
	Molding	White	Black	Dark Blue	–	–	–	Sil. Metallic
Dark Blue Metallic	Stripe	White	White	Med. Blue	–	–	–	Silver
	Molding	White	Black	Dark Blue	–	–	–	Sil. Metallic
Medium Green	Stripe	White	Black	–	Dark Green	–	–	–
	Molding	White	Black	–	Med. Green	–	–	–
Dark Green Metallic	Stripe	White	Med. Green	–	Med. Green	Sandstone	–	–
	Molding	White	Black	–	Med. Green	Light Beige	–	–
Cream Beige	Stripe	White	Black	–	–	Black	–	–
	Molding	White	Black	–	–	Light Beige	–	–
Sandstone	Stripe	White	Black	–	–	Black	–	–
	Molding	White	Black	–	–	Light Beige	–	–
Dark Brown Metallic	Stripe	White	Sandstone	–	–	Sandstone	–	–
	Molding	White	Black	–	–	Light Beige	–	–
Light Saddle Metallic	Stripe	White	Black	–	–	–	–	–
	Molding	White	Black	–	–	–	–	–
Persimmon Metallic	Stripe	White	Black	–	–	–	–	–
	Molding	White	Black	–	–	–	–	–
Red	Stripe	White	Black	–	–	–	–	–
	Molding	White	Black	–	–	–	–	–
Red Metallic	Stripe	White	Black	–	–	–	White	Silver
	Molding	White	Black	–	–	–	Maroon	Sil. Metallic

1975 CHEVROLET CAMARO 'F' INTERIOR–EXTERIOR COLOR COMBINATIONS

MODEL	Seat Type	Black Vinyl	Black • Vinyl /Red	Black Vinyl with White Seats	Black Vinyl with White Seats /Red•	Black Cloth	Black • Cloth /Red	Medium Graystone Knit Cloth
Standard – 1FQ00 Coupe (87)	Bucket	19V	19V	91V	91V	19C	19C	
Type LT – 1FS00 Coupe (87)	Bucket	–	–	–	–	–	–	16D
EXTERIOR COLORS	**Color Code**							
White C/O	11	X	X	X	X	X	X	X
Silver Metallic	13	X	–	X	–	X	–	–
Light Graystone	15	X	–	X	–	X	–	X
Medium Blue	24	X	–	X	–	X	–	–
Bright Blue Metallic	26	X	–	X	–	X	–	–
Dark Blue Metallic	29	X	–	X	–	X	–	X
Medium Green C/O	44	X	–	X	–	X	–	–
Dark Green Metallic	49	X	–	X	–	X	–	X
Cream-Beige C/O	50	X	–	X	–	X	–	–
Bright Yellow C/O	51	X	–	X	–	X	–	X
Sandstone	55	X	–	X	–	X	–	–
Dark Sandstone Met.	58	X	–	X	–	X	–	–
Light Saddle Met.	63	X	–	X	–	X	–	–
Persimmon Met.	64	X	–	X	–	X	–	–
Red Metallic C/O	74	X	–	X	–	X	–	X
Red C/O	75	X	X	X	X	X	X	–

NOTE: Solid exterior color combinations (except vinyl top) may be obtained with non-recommended interior combinations when ZP2 override is specified. Two Tones are not available on the Camaro.

• – Carpet selection: Accent Red – 75F.

1975 CHEVROLET CAMARO 'F' INTERIOR–EXTERIOR COLOR COMBINATIONS

MODEL	Seat Type	Dark Saddle Vinyl	Dark Saddle Knit Vinyl	Dark Saddle Knit Cloth	Dark Saddle Leather	Medium Sandstone Vinyl	Medium Sandstone Knit Vinyl	Medium Sandstone Cloth	Medium Sandstone Knit Cloth	Dark Oxblood Knit Cloth	Dark Oxblood Leather
Standard – 1FQ00 Coupe (87)	Bucket	63V				55V		55C			
Type LT – 1FS00 Coupe (87)	Bucket		63W	63D	632		55W		55D	73D	732

EXTERIOR COLORS	Color Code	Dark Saddle	Medium Sandstone	Dark Oxblood
White C/O	11	X	X	X
Silver Metallic	13	–	–	X
Light Graystone	15	X	–	X
Medium Blue	24	–	–	–
Bright Blue Metallic	26	–	–	–
Dark Blue Metallic	29	–	–	–
Medium Green C/O	44	–	–	–
Dark Green Metallic	49	X	X	–
Cream-Beige C/O	50	X	X	–
Bright Yellow C/O	51	X	–	–
Sandstone	55	X	X	–
Dark Sandstone Met.	58	X	X	–
Light Saddle Metallic	63	X	–	–
Persimmon Metallic	64	X	X	–
Red Metallic C/O	74	–	–	X
Red C/O	75	X	X	–

NOTE: Solid exterior color combinations (except vinyl top) may be obtained with non-recommended interior combinations when ZP2 override is specified. Two Tones are not available on the Camaro.

1975 Trim Combinations

CAMARO

EXTERIOR COLOR – VINYL ROOF COMBINATIONS

VINYL TOP COVER (Material - Levant Grain)	EXTERIOR COLOR AVAILABILITY
Silver Metallic	Silver Metallic
	Bright Blue Metallic
	Dark Blue Metallic
	Red Metallic
Black C/O	All available colors
White C/O	All available colors
Dark Blue	White
	Silver Metallic
	Medium Blue
	Dark Blue Metallic
	Bright Blue Metallic
Medium Green C/O	White
	Medium Green
	Dark Green Metallic
Sandstone	White
	Dark Green Metallic
	Cream-Beige
	Sandstone
	Dark Sandstone Metallic
	Persimmon Metallic
Cordovan – Production Name Dark Brown – Sales Name	White
	Cream-Beige
	Light Saddle Metallic
	Persimmon Metallic
Maroon – Production Name Dark Red – Sales Name	White
	Silver Metallic
	Red Metallic
Red	White
	Red

MONZA "2+2" AND MONZA "S" INTERIOR – EXTERIOR COLOR COMBINATIONS

		INTERIOR TRIM												
		Dark Blue		Medium Sandstone		Dark Saddle			Dark Oxblood			Black		
MODEL	Seat Type	Knit Cloth	Vinyl	Knit Cloth	Vinyl	Knit Cloth	Vinyl	Leather	Knit Cloth	Vinyl	Leather	Knit Cloth	Vinyl	Leather
'H' Special – HR07 Hatchback (07)	Bucket	26G	26Z	55G	55Z	63G	63Z	632	73G	73Z	732	19G	19Z	192
EXTERIOR COLORS	Color Code													
White C/O	11	X		X			X			X			X	
Medium Graystone Metallic	16	–		X			X			X			X	
Silver Blue Metallic	21	X		–			–			–			X	
Bright Blue Metallic	26	X		–			–			–			X	
Dark Green Metallic	49	–		X			X			–			X	
Cream-Beige C/O	50	–		X			X			–			X	
Bright Yellow C/O	51	–		–			X			–			X	
Medium Red C/O	75	–		X			X			–			X	
Burgundy Metallic	79	–		X			–			X			X	
Orange Metallic	80	–		X			X			–			X	

NOTE: Solid exterior color combinations (except vinyl tops) may be obtained with non-recommended interior combinations when ZP2 override is specified.

MONZA TOWNE COUPE INTERIOR–EXTERIOR COLOR COMBINATIONS

		INTERIOR TRIM									
		Black			Light Buckskin			Dark Firethorn		White	
MODEL	Seat Type	Vinyl	Cloth	Leather	Vinyl	Cloth	Leather	Vinyl	Cloth	† White Vinyl /Black	† White Vinyl /Dark Firethorn
Monza Deluxe 1HM27 Notchback (27)	Bucket	19H	19N	193	64H	64N	643	71H	71N	11H	07H
EXTERIOR COLOR	Color Code										
White C/O	11		X			X		X		X	X
Silver Metallic 1975	13		X			–		X		X	X
Medium Graystone Metallic 1975	16		X			X		–		X	–
Black C/O	19		X			X		X		X	X
Silver Blue Met. 1975	21		X			–		–		X	–
Bright Blue Met. 1975	26		X			X		–		X	–
Dark Blue Met. 1976	35		X			X		–		X	–
Firethorn Met. 1976	36		X			X		X		X	X
Bright Green Met. 1975	45		X			X		–		X	–
Dark Green Met. 1975	49		X			X		–		X	–
Cream – Beige C/O	50		X			X		X		X	–
Bright Yellow C/O	51		X			–		–		X	–
Russet Orange Met. C/O	66		X			X		–		X	–
Red C/O	75		X			X		–		X	–
Mahogany Met. 1976	37		X			X		X		X	X
Orange Metallic 1975	80		X			X		–		X	–

NOTES: 11H – White vinyl interior with Black Instrument Panel upper and lower, Carpet, Cowl Kick Panel and Package Shelf.
07H – White vinyl interior with Dark Firethorn Instrument Panel upper and lower, Carpet, Cowl Kick Panel, and Package Shelf.

Chapter 2

Engine Code Identification

1. INTRODUCTION

In this chapter I will describe the specific types of engine codes and how they were originally stamped on a particular engine. I will begin by discussing code location and format, and end with a listing of the engine code suffixes, which indicated which engine/transmission combination was used in a particular body style in a specific year.

The engine code was stamped at the engine assembly plant. In order to identify the engine with the vehicle in which it was installed (to reduce theft) all engines also had part of the Vehicle Identification Number (VIN) number stamped on them. Through Tech Service Bulletins, Chevrolet did indicate which engines were to receive the VIN stamp, however, it is possible that other engines could also have been stamped.

1.1 Code Location

The engine assembly code and portion of the VIN code were stamped on a block pad, located immediately forward of the right hand cylinder head. See Fig. 2-1.The engine code is positioned on the left side of the block pad, while the VIN is stamped on the right side of the pad. See Fig. 2-2.

To further deter theft, on some engines the VIN code was also stamped on the block at the transmission flange. See Fig. 2-3.

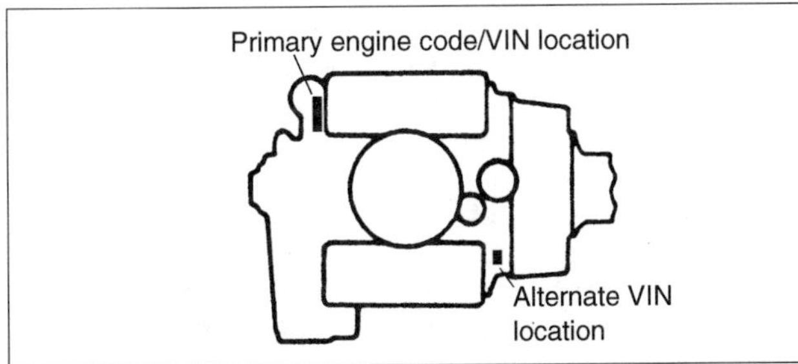

Fig. 2-1. *Eight-cylinder engine code locations.*

Fig. 2-2. *Block pad for 1968 427/435HP Corvette engine shows position of codes: engine code on left side of pad and VIN information on right side of pad. Note how cylinder head plug obscures left side of pad. Also note that VIN letters are 1/8" high. 1968 was first year when all plants used uniform size for VIN code letters.*

Fig. 2-3. *Position of alternate VIN number location at transmission flange on block. This is a 1969 396 Kansas City Chevelle VIN number stamping.*

1970 Through 1975 Engine Development

1970: There was a drastic reduction in the number of engine variations in 1970. The 302, 327, 396 and 427 engines were dropped. The 302 Z28 Camaro engine was replaced with the new 350 LT1 engine, which was available only in the Z28 Camaro (360HP) or the Corvette (370HP). The main difference between these two engines was the exhaust manifolds. The 396 now had a .030 overbore, making it in essence a 402, but was still marketed as a 396. Also, this was the only year for the famous 454/450HP LS6 engine, considered by many to be the all-time most powerful Chevrolet engine available to the general public.

Another new addition to the Chevrolet engine lineup was the small block 400. This low-rpm, high-torque engine was used in Chevrolet and Monte Carlo platforms. With this engine, Chevrolet achieved its largest production displacement of all small block engines. The new small block 400 was often confused with 402 big block engine. In some cases on Passenger cars, the engine emblem "400" on the front fender was used to designate both engines. This confusion also carried over to Chevrolet parts books and literature.

The most striking feature of this engine was the overbore (4.125) necessitating the joining (Siamesing) of the cylinders. This meant that coolant no longer circulated between each cylinder, and overheating became a real threat. To help eliminate steam and air pockets, six holes were drilled in the cylinder block decks. The corresponding cylinder heads and head gaskets also had these steam hole provisions. (See Fig 3-7.) The 400's stroke and main journal size were increased as well. This crankshaft, with the main journals turned down, was combined with the 350 cubic inch block in later years by various engine builders to become the "383," the standard motor of circle track racing. 1970 was the last year for gross horsepower ratings.

1971: 1971 was the year that could be described as "the beginning of the end." Although all engine applications were generally maintained for 1971, emissions regulations began to take hold and many performance cars were being eliminated. All compression ratios began to drop as well, which significantly affected performance of all engines. Horsepower levels were now given in net horsepower, measured with standard intake and exhaust manifolds and with accessories connected. All big block engines, excluding the LS6, now carried a 2-bolt main configuration.

1972: 1972 is regarded as the last year of performance for most of Chevrolet engines. The 350/255HP engine was the hottest small block still available in 1972. This engine, featuring a solid lifter camshaft, Holley carburetor, aluminum intake and a 4-bolt mains, was only available in the Z28 and Corvette. The 402 was available for the last time in the Camaro, Passenger Car and Chevelle. All basic engine options were maintained, but horsepower levels continue to drop due to emissions regulation and lower compression.

1973: In 1973, meeting emissions was primary. Engine design centered on meeting smog regulations, not on performance. The 350/245HP engine, which was the best small block offering Chevrolet had, now had a hydraulic camshaft, a Rochester carburetor and a cast iron intake that was the same used on base 4BBL 175HP engines. The 402 engine was now gone. The 454/215HP engine was the only big block engine available in the Passenger Car and Chevelle. This same engine was used in the Corvette, but it had a 245 HP rating due to a change in exhaust manifolds. This is the last year for the 307 engine.

1974: The 1974 engine lineup continued basically untouched from the prior model year. The 350/145HP engine became the standard base V-8 engine for all model lines excluding the Corvette, replacing the 307 from 1973. Almost all engines throughout 1974 were shared, with none being specific to any one model line. The 350/245HP engine was continued in the Z28 Camaro and Corvette, but with HEI (High Energy Ignition) added. The only big block available across all model lines was the 454/235HP engine. (270HP in Corvette applications). This was the last year the Corvette could be ordered with the 454 engine.

1975: The 1975 model year was the end of the high performance era. Chevrolet killed all high performance cars, including the Z28 Camaro for 1975, except for the Corvette, which carried the 350/205HP L82 engine option. This engine had the only 4-bolt main block available. It also had the standard high-performance 2.02 intake/1.60 exhaust cylinder heads. The engine used the same cast iron intake as all other 350 and 400 4BBL engines. The big block 454 was still available in the Passenger Car, Chevelle and Monte Carlo models. This engine was basically a carryover from 1974.

The major change for 1975 was the new 262 V-8. This smog engine was designed for the Nova and Monza because the only small block engines still available (the 350 and 400) were too large in displacement to power the Monza chassis. This 2-bolt block was a completely new casting carrying a 3.671" bore. The cast iron crankshaft had the same main and rod bearing journal sizes as a 350 crankshaft, with the primary difference being the new 3.10" stroke. The cylinder heads resembled a 350 head with 1.72/1.50 valve sizes, but with very small combustion chambers. In the end, Chevrolet built this engine for 1975 and 1976 only, since it was so "smogged" up with pollution controls that it couldn't perform. Unfortunately, this engine seemed to point the way to Chevrolet's future: it would be almost two decades before a high performance small block would again be offered to those ordering a Chevrolet vehicle other than a Corvette.

1.2 Engine Code Format

The engine code characters to be stamped were in general fitted into a metal holder and locked in place by an Allen key. The holder was then placed over the block number pad and struck with a dead blow hammer. All 1970 through 1975 engine codes consist of eight alphanumeric characters. See Fig. 2-4. All engine code characters are 3/16" high.

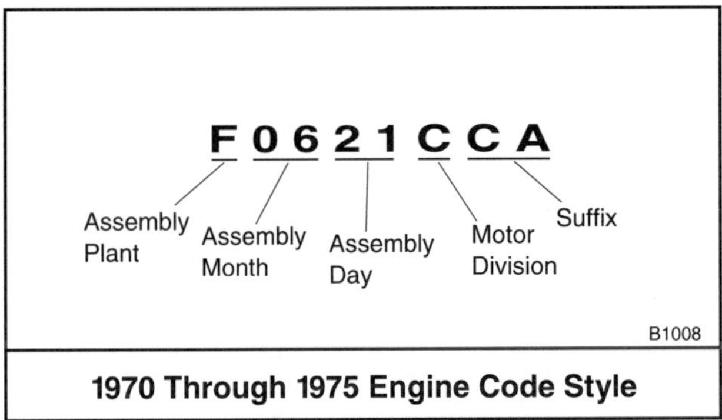

Fig. 2-4. *Example of 1970 through 1975 engine code. Format is the same as 1965–69, with addition of letter "C" before engine suffix.*

The first letter in the engine code designates the engine assembly plant. Although multiple plants began building engines for Chevrolet in 1967, this letter code is always one letter.

The next two digits designate the engine assembly month code. If the month code is January through September, the month code will be preceded with a "0" and still remain a 2-digit code. For example, "04" means April. "11" means November.

The next two digits after the month code designate the day of the month the engine was assembled. It will always be a 2-digit number. For example, "14" means the 14th day of the month.

The sixth digit, the letter "C" designates a Chevrolet passenger car. (Truck applications had the letter "T" in this position.) This digit was new beginning in the 1970 model year.

The last two letters of the engine code designate the engine code suffix. The engine code suffix gives the intended application for that engine in the model year that it was built. All engine codes have C as the first letter of the suffix.

1.3 VIN Code Format

The VIN information consists of the divisional identification number, model year, assembly plant designation and vehicle serial (or sequence) number. Example: 19J000025 is the engine installed on the twenty-fifth Chevrolet built at Janesville in 1969. VIN letters were in general 1/8" high.

> NOTE—
> For more information on reading the VIN code, see Chapter 1.

2. ENGINE SUFFIX CODES

The following tables list all engine suffix codes for 1970 through 1975. The tables are designed for access either by suffix code or by application.

When trying to identify an engine block, the engine code suffix should be the last part of the stamping you check. Often, when trying to match numbers, human instinct takes over and the suffix is the first part of the engine code you look at because it contains much information about engine specifications.

Unfortunately, when you look at the suffix code first you tend to overlook other vital aspects that should be checked on the engine, such as cross-referencing casting dates on the block, cylinder head, intake and so on. Many engines over the years used the same suffix codes for totally different applications. Unless you check the casting dates, you could be easily duped into buying an incorrect part for your application.

Engine Assembly Plant Codes

Year	Engine Plant Designation	Notes
1970 1971	F - Flint Motor Plant K - McKinnon Industries S - Saginaw Service T - Tonawanda Engine Plant V - Flint Engine Plant	All final car assembly plants stamped the Chevrolet division, model year, plant designation, and continuous sequence number portion of the Vehicle Identification Number.
1972 1973 1974 1975	F - Flint Motor Plant K - McKinnon M - G.M. of Mexico T - Tonawanda Engine Plant V - Flint Engine Plant	All final car assembly plants stamped the Chevrolet division, model year, plant designation, and continuous sequence number portion of the Vehicle Identification Number.

Abbreviations used in the following tables:

A/C	Air Conditioning	N.B.2.	Equipment required on CA vehicles, consisting of a complete A.I.R. system and camshaft with longer valve overlap
A.I.R.	Air Injection Reactor		
Alum.	Aluminum		
BBL	Barrel		
COPO	Central Office Production Order	Perf.	Performance
H.D.	Heavy Duty	P/S	Power Steering
HP	Horsepower	Spec.	Special
Hyd.	Hydraulic	T/I	Transistorized Ignition
L.C.	Low Compression	YF5	Equipment required on CA vehicles, consisting of a complete A.I.R. system and camshaft with longer valve overlap
Mech.	Mechanical		

NOTE—
Due to 1969 build-out schedule revisions after production change-over at the Tonawanda plant, some 1970 402 engine suffix codes were used on late 1969 396 engines. Example: a 1969 396/325HP, normally code JA would be CJA, which is also the code for a 1970 402/325HP engine. This is verified through *Chevrolet Service News*, January 1970. These engines are noted on the next page by an asterisk.

1970 Engine Code Suffix Identification

Model	Engine	Horsepower	Transmission, Options	Suffix
Passenger	350	250	3-, 4-Speed	CNO
		300	Manual, Police/Taxi	CNP
		250	3-, 4-Speed	CNQ
		300	Turbohydramatic 350	CNR
			Powerglide Police/Taxi	CNS
			Turbohydramatic 350, Police/Taxi	CNT
		250	Powerglide	CNU
			Turbohydramatic 350	CNV
			Powerglide, Police/Taxi	CNW
			Turbohydramatic 350, Police/Taxi	CNX
			L.C. Engine	CNY
			Powerglide/Torque Drive, L.C. Engine	CNZ
	400	265	Turbohydramatic 350, 400	CGR
	454	345	Police/Taxi, Turbohydramatic 400	CGS
		390	Police/Taxi, H.D. Turbohydramatic 400	CGT
			Turbohydramatic 400	CGU
		345	Turbohydramatic 400	CGV
Corvette	350	300	4-Speed, Rochester 4-BBL	CTD
			Turbohydramatic 400, Rochester 4-BBL	CTG*
			4-Speed, Rochester 4-BBL	CTL
			Turbohydramatic 400, Rochester 4-BBL	CTM
		350	4-Speed, Rochester 4-BBL, Perf. Cam	CTH*
			4-Speed, Rochester 4-BBL, Perf. Cam, A/C	CTJ*
			4-Speed, Rochester 4-BBL, Perf. Cam	CTN
			4-Speed, Rochester 4-BBL, Perf. Cam, A/C	CTO
			4-Speed, Rochester 4-BBL, Perf. Cam, T/I	CTP
			4-Speed, Rochester 4-BBL, Perf. Cam, A/C, T/I	CTQ
		370	4-Speed, Holley 4-BBL, T/I, LT1 (late, after 3/24/70)	CTK*
			4-Speed, Holley 4-BBL, T/I, LT1, w/o P.S. (early)	CTU
			M22 4-Speed, ZR1 Perf. Package, LT1 Engine	CTV
	454	390	Turbohydramatic 400, Rochester 4-BBL, Hyd. Lifters	CGW
			4-Speed, Rochester 4-BBL, Hyd. Lifters, T/I	CRI
			Turbohydramatic 400, Rochester 4-BBL, Hyd. Lifters, T/I	CRJ
			4-Speed, Rochester 4-BBL, Hyd. Lifters	CZU
Nova	307	200	Manual	CNC
			4-Speed	CND

*New code introduced during the 1970 model year, replacing the earlier listed code

continued on next page

1970 Engine Code Suffix Identification (continued)

Model	Engine	Horsepower	Transmission, Options	Suffix
Nova (cont'd)	307 (cont'd)	200 (cont'd)	Powerglide	CNE
			Turbohydramatic 350	CNF
			L.C. Engine	CNG
			Powerglide, L.C. Engine or Torque Drive	CNH
	350	250	3-, 4-Speed	CNI
		300	3-, 4-Speed	CNJ
		300	Powerglide	CNK
		250	Powerglide	CNM
		250	Turbohydramatic 350	CNN
		300	Turbohydramatic 350	CRE
	402	375	3-, 4-Speed	CKO
		375	Manual, H.D. Clutch	CKQ
		350	Turbohydramatic 400, High Perf.	CTW
		350	3-, 4-Speed, High Perf.	CTX
		375	Turbohydramatic 400	CTY
		350	Manual, H.D. Clutch, High Perf.	CTZ
Chevelle	307	200	3-, 4-Speed	CNC
			4-Speed	CND
			Powerglide/Torque Drive	CNE
			Turbohydramatic 350	CNF
			L.C. Engine	CNG
			Powerglide/Torque Drive, L.C. Engine	CNH
	350	250	3-, 4-Speed	CNI
		300	3-, 4-Speed	CNJ
		300	Powerglide/Torque Drive	CNK
		250	Powerglide/Torque Drive	CNM
		250	Turbohydramatic 350	CNN
		300	Turbohydramatic 350	CRE
	402	330	Turbohydramatic 400	CKN*
		375	3-, 4-Speed	CKO*
		375	Turbohydramatic 400, Alum. Heads	CKP*
		375	H.D. Clutch	CKQ*
		330	3-, 4-Speed	CKR*
		330	H.D. Clutch	CKS*
		375	3-, 4-Speed, Alum. Heads	CKT*
		375	H.D. Clutch, Alum. Heads	CKU*
		350	Turbohydramatic 400, High Perf.	CTW*
		350	3-, 4-Speed, High Perf.	CTX*
		375	Turbohydramatic 400	CTY*
		350	H.D. Clutch, High Perf.	CTZ*
	454	360	Turbohydramatic 400	CRQ
		450	Turbohydramatic 400, Spec. High Perf.	CRR
		360	3-, 4-Speed	CRT
		450	4-Speed, Spec. High Perf.	CRV
Monte Carlo	350	250	3-, 4-Speed,	CNI
		300	3-, 4-Speed	CNJ
		300	Powerglide/Torque Drive	CNK
		250	Powerglide/Torque Drive	CNM
		250	Turbohydramatic 350	CNN
		300	Turbohydramatic 350	CRE

continued on next page

1970 Engine Code Suffix Identification (continued)

Model	Engine	Horsepower	Transmission, Options	Suffix
Monte Carlo (cont'd)	400	265	Turbohydramatic 350	CRH
			4 Speed	CZX
	402	330	Turbohydramatic 400	CKN
			3-, 4-Speed *	CKR
	454	360	Turbohydramatic 400	CRN
Camaro	307	200	Manual	CNC
			4-Speed	CND
			Powerglide	CNE
			Turbohydramatic 350	CNF
	350	250	3-, 4-Speed	CNI
		300	3-, 4-Speed	CNJ
		300	Powerglide	CNK
		250	Powerglide	CNM
		250	Turbohydramatic 350	CNN
		300	Turbohydramatic 350	CRE
		360	Manual, Z-28	CTB
		360	Turbohydramatic 400, Z-28	CTC
	402	350	3-, 4-Speed	CJF
		375	3-, 4-Speed	CJH
		350	Turbohydramatic 400	CJI
		375	Turbohydramatic 400	CJL
		375	3-, 4-Speed	CKO
		350	Turbohydramatic 400, High Perf.	CTW
		350	3-, 4-Speed, High Perf.	CTX
		375	Turbohydramatic 400	CTY

* To date, no documented original 4-speed SS Monte Carlos have been found. Original GM order forms indicate that SS Monte Carlos could only be built with the TH400 automatic

1971 Engine Code Suffix Identification

Model	Engine	Horsepower	Transmission, Options	Suffix
Passenger	350	245	3-, 4-Speed	CLT
		245	Powerglide/Turbohydramatic 350	CGC
		245	Turbohydramatic 350/400, Police/Taxi	CGJ
		270	L.C. Engine	CJA
		245	Manual, Police	CJB
		270	Turbohydramatic 350	CJD
		270	Turbohydramatic 400, Police	CJH
	400	255	Powerglide	CAJ
			Turbohydramatic 350/400	CLK
	402	300	Turbohydramatic 400	CLB
			Turbohydramatic, Police	CLR
	454	365	Turbohydramatic 400, High Perf.	CPD
			Turbohydramatic 400, Police	CPG
Corvette	350	270	Turbohydramatic (M40), Rochester 4-BBL	CGT
			Turbohydramatic (M40), Rochester 4-BBL	CJK*
			4-Speed, Rochester 4-BBL	CJL
		330	M22 4-Speed, ZR1 Perf. Package, LT1 Engine	CGY
			4-Speed, Holley 4-BBL, LT1 Engine	CGZ
	454	365	4-Speed, Rochester 4-BBL, Hyd. Lifters	CPH
			Turbohydramatic (M40), Rochester 4-BBL, Hyd. Lifters,	CPJ

*Engine code CJK indicates a new code during the 1971 model year, replacing the earlier listed CGT code

continued on next page

1971 Engine Code Suffix Identification (continued)

Model	Engine	Horsepower	Transmission, Options	Suffix
Corvette (cont'd)	454 (cont'd)	425	4-Speed, Alum. Heads, Mech. Lifters, Holley 4-BBL	CPW
			Turbohydramatic (M40), Alum. Heads, Mech. Lifters, Holley 4-BBL	CPX
Nova	307	200	3-, 4-Speed	CCA
			Powerglide/Turbohydramatic 350	CCC
	350	245	3-, 4-Speed	CGA
		245	Powerglide	CGC
		270	Turbohydramatic 350	CJD
		270	3-, 4-Speed	CJG
Chevelle	307	200	3-, 4-Speed	CCA
			Powerglide/Torque Drive/ TH 350	CCC
	350	245	3-, 4-Speed	CGA
		245	Turbohydramatic 350	CGC
		270	Turbohydramatic 350	CJD
		270	3-, 4-Speed	CJJ
	402	300	3-, 4-Speed	CLA
			Turbohydramatic 400	CLB
			3-Speed Heavy Duty (MC1)	CLS
	454	365	3-, 4-Speed, High Perf.	CPA
		365	Turbohydramatic 400	CPD
		425	3-, 4-Speed	CPP
		425	Turbohydramatic 400 (10 engines built)	CPY
		425	Turbohydramatic 400/ 4-Speed (Four engines built)	CPZ
Monte Carlo	350	245	3-, 4-Speed	CGA
			Powerglide/Turbohydramatic 350	CGC
	350	270	3-, 4-Speed	CJG
	402	300	4-Speed	CLA
			Turbohydramatic	CLP
	454	365	Turbohydramatic 400	CPD
		425	4-Speed (M-22)	CPZ
			Turbohydramatic	CPY
Camaro	307	200	3-, 4-Speed	CCA
			Powerglide/Torque Drive/Turbohydramatic 350	CCC
	350	245	3-, 4-Speed	CGA
		245	Turbohydramatic 350	CGC
		330	Manual, Z-28	CGP
		330	Turbohydramatic 400, Z-28	CGR
		270	Turbohydramatic 350	CJD
		270	3-, 4-Speed	CJG
	402	300	3-, 4-Speed	CLA, CLC**
			Turbohydramatic 400	CLB, CLD**
**Unverified				

1972 Engine Code Suffix Identification

Model	Engine	Horsepower	Transmission, Options	Suffix
Passenger	350	165	Turbohydramatic, N.B.2., Police/Taxi	CAR
			L.C. Engine	CBL
			Turbohydramatic 350/400, N.B.2.	CDB
			Turbohydramatic 350/400	CKB
			Turbohydramatic 350/400, Police/Taxi	CSH

continued on next page

1972 Engine Code Suffix Identification (continued)

Model	Engine	Horsepower	Transmission, Options	Suffix
Passenger (cont'd)	400	170	Turbohydramatic 350/400, N.B.2.	CAT
			Turbohydramatic 350/400, Police	CDL
			Turbohydramatic 350/400, N.B.2., Police	CDM
			Turbohydramatic 350/400	CKP
	402	240	Turbohydramatic 400	CLB
			Manual, Police	CLR
			Manual, A.I.R.	CTB
			Manual, A.I.R., Police/Taxi	CTJ
	454	240	Turbohydramatic 400, A.I.R., Police/Taxi	CRY
		270 230 (Station wagon)	Turbohydramatic 400	CPD
			Manual, Police (Unverified)	CPG
			Turbohydramatic 400, A.I.R.	CRW
Corvette	350	200	4-Speed, Rochester 4-BBL, N.B.2.	CDH
			Turbohydramatic 400, Rochester 4-BBL, N.B.2.	CDJ
			4-Speed, Rochester 4-BBL	CKW
			Turbohydramatic 400, Rochester 4-BBL	CKX
		255	4-Speed, Mech. Lifters, Holley 4-BBL	CKY
			M22 4-Speed, ZR1 Perf. Package, LT1 Engine	CKZ
			4-Speed, Mech. Lifters, Holley 4-BBL, A.I.R.	CRT
	454	270	4-Speed, Rochester 4-BBL, Hyd. Lifters	CPH
			Turbohydramatic 400, Rochester 4-BBL, Hyd. Lifters	CPJ
			4-Speed, Rochester 4-BBL, Hyd. Lifters, A.I.R.	CSR
			Turbohyd. 400, Rochester 4-BBL, Hyd. Lifters, A.I.R.	CSS
Nova	307	130	3-, 4-Speed, N.B.2.	CAY
			Powerglide, N.B.2.	CAZ
			Turbohydramatic 350, N.B.2.	CAZ, CMA
			3-, 4-Speed	CKG
			Powerglide	CKH
			Turbohydramatic 350	CTK
	350	165	Manual, N.B.2.	CDA
			3-, 4-Speed	CKA
			Turbohydramatic, N.B.2.	CMD
			Turbohydramatic 350	CTL
		175	Turbohydramatic 350, N.B.2.	CDD
			3-, 4-Speed, N.B.2.	CDG
			Turbohydramatic 350	CKD
			3-, 4-Speed	CKK
			Turbohydramatic, A.I.R.	CRK
			Manual, A.I.R.	CRL
Chevelle	307	130	3-, 4-Speed, N.B.2.	CAY
			Powerglide, N.B.2.	CAZ
			3-, 4-Speed	CKG
			Powerglide	CKH
			Turbohydramatic 350, N.B.2.	CMA
			Turbohydramatic 350	CTK
	350	165	Turbohydramatic, Police	CAR
			3-, 4-Speed, N.B.2.	CDA
			Manual	CKA
			Turbohydramatic 350, N.B.2.	CMD
			Turbohydramatic, Police	CSH
			Turbohydramatic 350	CTL

continued on next page

1972 Engine Code Suffix Identification (continued)

Model	Engine	Horsepower	Transmission, Options	Suffix
Chevelle (cont'd)	350 (cont'd)	175	Turbohydramatic 350, N.B.2.	CDD
			3-, 4-Speed, N.B.2.	CDG
			Turbohydramatic 350	CKD
			3-, 4-Speed	CKK
	402	240	3-, 4-Speed	CLA, CLS
			Turbohydramatic 400	CLB
			Manual, A.I.R., Police/Taxi	CTA
			Turbohydramatic, A.I.R.	CTB
			H.D. 3-Speed, A.I.R.	CTH
			Turbohydramatic, A.I.R., Police/Taxi	CTJ
	454	270	3-, 4-Speed	CPA
			Turbohydramatic 400	CPD
			Turbohydramatic, A.I.R.	CRW
			Manual, A.I.R.	CRX
Monte Carlo	350	165	3-, 4-Speed, N.B.2	CDA
			Powerglide, N.B.2	CDB
			3-, 4-Speed	CKA
			Powerglide	CKB
			Turbohydramatic 350, N.B.2	CMD
			Turbohydramatic 350	CTL
		175	Turbohydramatic 350, N.B.2	CDD
			Turbohydramatic 350	CKD
	402	240	Turbohydramatic 400	CLB
			Turbohydramatic 400, A.I.R.	CTB
	454	270	Turbohydramatic 400	CPD
			Turbohydramatic 400, A.I.R.	CRW
Camaro	307	130	3-, 4-Speed, N.B.2.	CAY
			Powerglide, N.B.2.	CAZ
			3-, 4-Speed	CKG
			Powerglide	CKH
			Turbohydramatic 350, N.B.2.	CMA
			Turbohydramatic 350	CTK
	350	165	3-, 4-Speed	CKA
			Turbohydramatic, N.B.2.	CMB
			3-, 4-Speed, N.B.2.	CMH
			Turbohydramatic, A.I.R.	CRD
			Manual, A.I.R.	CRG
			Turbohydramatic 350	CTL
		175	Turbohydramatic 350, N.B.2.	CDD
			3-, 4-Speed, N.B.2.	CDG
			Turbohydramatic 350	CKD
			3-, 4-Speed	CKK
		255	4-Speed	CKS
			Turbohydramatic 400	CKT
	402	240	3-, 4-Speed	CLA
			Turbohydramatic 400	CLB
			Manual, A.I.R.	CTA
			Turbohydramatic 400, A.I.R.	CTB

1973 Engine Code Suffix Identification

Model	Engine	Horsepower	Transmission, Options	Suffix
Passenger	350	145	Turbohydramatic, N.B.2.	CKK/CLT
			Turbohydramatic 350/400	CKL/CLV
			Turbohydramatic, Police	CKS
			Turbohydramatic 350, Wagon	CLU
			Turbohydramatic, N.B.2., Police	CLW
			Turbohydramatic 350, Police Wagon	CLX
		175	Turbohydramatic, N.B.2.	CKD
			Turbohydramatic 400	CKJ
			Turbohydramatic 350/400, Police	CKM
			Turbohydramatic, N.B.2., Police	CKR
	400	150	Turbohydramatic 350/400	CSA
			Turbohydramatic 350/400, Police	CSB
			Turbohydramatic 350, N.B.2., Police	CSC
			Turbohydramatic 350/400, N.B.2.	CSD
			Turbohydramatic 350, N.B.2., Wagon	CSJ
			Turbohydramatic 350, Wagon	CSK
			Turbohydramatic 350, N.B.2., Police Wagon	CSL
			Turbohydramatic 350, Police Wagon	CSM
	454	245 215 (Station wagon)	Turbohydramatic 400, N.B.2.	CWD, CWH
			Turbohydramatic 400, N.B.2., Police	CWJ
			Turbohydramatic 400, Police	CWK
			Turbohydramatic 400	CWL
			Turbohydramatic 400, Police	CWU
			Turbohydramatic 400, N.B.2., Police	CWW
Corvette	350	190	4-Speed	CKZ
			Turbohydramatic 400	CLA
			4-Speed, N.B.2	CLB
			Turbohydramatic 400, N.B.2.	CLC
		250	Turbohydramatic 400	CLD
			Turbohydramatic 400, N.B.2.	CLH
			4-Speed	CLR
			4-Speed, N.B.2.	CLS
	454	275	4-Speed	CWM
			Turbohydramatic 400	CWR
			Turbohydramatic 400, N.B.2.	CWS
			4-Speed, N.B.2.	CWT
Nova	307	115	Manual	CHB
			Turbohydramatic, N.B.2.	CHC
			Manual, N.B.2.	CHD
			Turbohydramatic	CHH
	350	145	Manual	CKA
			Manual, N.B.2.	CKC
			Turbohydramatic, N.B.2.	CKK
			Turbohydramatic 350	CKW
		175	Manual	CKB
			Turbohydramatic, N.B.2.	CKD
			Manual, N.B.2.	CKH
			Turbohydramatic 350	CKU
Chevelle	307	115	Turbohydramatic	CHA
			Manual	CHB
			Turbohydramatic, N.B.2.	CHC
			Manual, N.B.2.	CHD

continued on next page

1973 Engine Code Suffix Identification (continued)

Model	Engine	Horsepower	Transmission, Options	Suffix
Chevelle (cont'd)	350	145	Manual	CKA/CKB
			Manual, N.B.2.	CKC
			Turbohydramatic, N.B.2.	CKK
			Turbohydramatic 350/400	CKL
		175	Manual	CKB
			Turbohydramatic, N.B.2.	CKD
			Manual, N.B.2.	CKH
			Turbohydramatic 400	CKJ
			Police	CKM
			Police, N.B.2	CKR
			Turbohydramatic 400, Wagon	CMM
	454	245	Turbohydramatic 400	CWB
			Manual, N.B.2.	CWC
			Turbohydramatic 400, N.B.2.	CWD
			Manual	CWR
Monte Carlo	350	145	Manual	CKA
			Manual, N.B.2.	CKC
			Turbohydramatic	CKK
			Turbohydramatic 350/400	CKL
		175	Turbohydramatic, N.B.2.	CKD
			Turbohydramatic 400	CKJ
		245	Turbohydramatic 400	CWB
			Turbohydramatic 400, N.B.2.	CWD
Camaro	307	115	Manual	CHB
			Turbohydramatic	CHH
			Manual, N.B.2.	CHJ
			Turbohydramatic, N.B.2.	CHK
	350	145	Manual	CKA
			Turbohydramatic 350	CKW
			Turbohydramatic, N.B.2.	CKX
			Manual, N.B.2.	CKY
		175	Manual	CKB
			Turbohydramatic, N.B.2.	CKD
			Manual, N.B.2.	CKH
			Turbohydramatic 350	CKU
	350	245	4-Speed	CLJ
			Turbohydramatic 400	CLK
			Turbohydramatic 400, N.B.2.	CLL
			Manual, N.B.2.	CLM

1974 Engine Code Suffix Identification

Model	Engine	Horsepower	Transmission, Options	Suffix
Passenger	350	145	Turbohydramatic 350, Police/Taxi	CMD
			Turbohydramatic 350/400	CMR
		160	Turbohydramatic 400, YF5	CKD
			Turbohydramatic 400	CMH
			Turbohydramatic 400, Police	CMJ
			Turbohydramatic 400, YF5, Police	CMK

continued on next page

1974 Engine Code Suffix Identification (continued)

Model	Engine	Horsepower	Transmission, Options	Suffix
Passenger (cont'd)	400	150	Turbohydramatic 400, HEI	CSU
			Turbohydramatic 400, HEI, Police	CSW
			Turbohydramatic 400, 2-BBL	CTA
			Turbohydramatic 400, Police, 2-BBL	CTB
		180	Turbohydramatic 400, HEI, Wagon	CSY
			Turbohydramatic 400, HEI, Police Wagon	CSZ
			Turbohydramatic 350/400, YF5	CTC
			Turbohydramatic 400, Wagon	CTD
			Turbohydramatic 400, HEI, YF5, Police	CTH
			Turbohydramatic 400, Police Wagon	CTJ
			Turbohydramatic 400, YF5, Police	CTK
	454	235	Turbohydramatic 400, Police	CWU
			Turbohydramatic 400, YF5, Police	CWW
			Turbohydramatic 400, YF5	CWY
			Turbohydramatic 400	CXA
			Turbohydramatic 400, YF5, Police	CXB
			Turbohydramatic 400, YF5	CXC
			Turbohydramatic 400, HEI, Police	CXT
			Turbohydramatic 400, HEI	CXU
Corvette	350	195	4-Speed	CKZ
			Turbohydramatic	CLA
			4-Speed, YF5	CLB
			Turbohydramatic, YF5	CLC
		250	Turbohydramatic, some YF5	CLD
			4-Speed, some YF5	CLR
	454	270	4-Speed, some YF5	CWM
			Turbohydramatic 400	CWR
			Turbohydramatic 400, YF5	CWS
Nova	350	145	Turbohydramatic 350	CMA
			3-Speed	CMC
		160	Turbohydramatic 350, YF5	CKD
			Manual, YF5	CKH
		185	Manual	CKB
			Turbohydramatic 350, YF5	CKD
			Manual, YF5	CKH
			Turbohydramatic 350	CKU
Chevelle	350	145	Manual	CMC
			Turbohydramatic 350/400	CMR
		160	Turbohydramatic 350, YF5	CKD
			Manual, YF5	CKH
	400	150	Turbohydramatic 400,2 BBL	CTA
		180	Turbohydramatic 350	CSU
			Turbohydramatic 350/400, YF5	CTC
	454	235	4-Speed	CWA
			Turbohydramatic 400, YF5	CWD
			Turbohydramatic 400	CWX
			4-Speed, HEI	CXM
			Turbohydramatic 400, HEI	CXR
			Turbohydramatic 400, HEI, YF5	CXS

continued on next page

1974 Engine Code Suffix Identification (continued)

Model	Engine	Horsepower	Transmission, Options	Suffix
Monte Carlo	350	145	Manual	CMC
			Turbohydramatic	CMR
		160	Turbohydramatic, YF5	CKD
			Manual, YF5	CKH
	400	150	Turbohydramatic	CTA
		180	Turbohydramatic, YF5	CTC
			Turbohydramatic 400, HEI	CSU
	454	235	Turbohydramatic 400, YF5	CWD
			Turbohydramatic 400	CWX
			Turbohydramatic 400, HEI	CXR
			Turbohydramatic 400, HEI, YF5	CXS
Camaro	350	145	Turbohydramatic 350	CMA
			Manual (Unavailable In California)	CMC
		160	Turbohydramatic 350, YF5	CKD
			Manual, YF5 (Available In California Only)	CKH
		185	Manual	CKB
			Turbohydramatic 350, YF5	CKD
			Manual, YF5	CKH
			Turbohydramatic 350	CKU
		245	4-Speed, Z-28	CLJ
			Turbohydramatic 400	CLK
			4-Speed, some YF5	CMS
			Turbohydramatic 400, Z-28, some YF5	CMT

1975 Engine Code Suffix Identification

Model	Engine	Horsepower	Transmission, Options	Suffix
Passenger	350	145	Turbohydramatic 350/400, Federal	CMJ/CLR
		155	Turbohydramatic, California	CMM/CLH
			Turbohydramatic, Police/Taxi, California	CTM
			Turbohydramatic, Police/Taxi, Federal	CTW
	400	175	Turbohydramatic 350/400, N.B.2., Police/Taxi, California	CSA
			Turbohydramatic 350/400, N.B.2.	CSB
			Turbohydramatic 350/400, N.B.2., California	CTL
			Turbohydramatic 350/400, N.B.2., Police Wagon	CTM
			Turbohydramatic 350/400, Federal	CTU
			Turbohydramatic 350/400, Police	CTW
			Turbohydramatic 350/400, Wagon	CTY
			Turbohydramatic 350/400, Police/Taxi Wagon	CTZ
	454	215	Turbohydramatic, A.I.R., Federal	CXX
			Turbohydramatic, Police/Taxi, A.I.R., Federal	CXY
Corvette	350	165	4-Speed, Federal	CHA
			Automatic, Federal	CHB
			Turbohydramatic, California	CHZ
		205	4-Speed, Federal	CHC
			Automatic, Federal, California	CHR

continued on next page

1975 Engine Code Suffix Identification

Model	Engine	Horsepower	Transmission, Options	Suffix
Nova	262	110	Manual, California	CZJ
			Turbohydramatic, California	CZK
			Manual, A.I.R., Federal	CZL
			Turbohydramatic, A.I.R., Federal	CZM
	350	145	Manual, Federal	CMU
			Turbohydramatic 350, Federal	CRX
		155	Turbohydramatic 350, A/C, Federal	CHW
			Manual (M20), Federal	CMB
			Turbohydramatic, California	CML
Chevelle	350	145	Manual, Federal	CJU
			Turbohydramatic 350, California	CJZ
			Turbohydramatic 350/400, Federal	CMJ
			Manual, Federal	CMU
	350	155	Turbohydramatic, California	CMM/CMH
	400	175	Turbohydramatic 350/400, N.B.2., California	CSB
			Turbohydramatic 350/400	CSC
			Turbohydramatic 350/400, N.B.2.	CSD
			Turbohydramatic 350/400, N.B.2., Wagon	CSM
			Turbohydramatic 350/400, Federal	CTU
			Turbohydramatic 350/400	CTX
	454	215	Turbohydramatic, A.I.R., Federal	CXW
Monte Carlo	350	145	Manual, Federal	CMU
			Turbohydramatic, Federal	CRX
		155	Manual, California	CMF
			Turbohydramatic, California	CMH
	400	175	Turbohydramatic, California	CSB
			Turbohydramatic, Federal	CTL
	454	215	Turbohydramatic, Federal	CXW
Camaro	350	145	Manual, Federal	CMU
			Turbohydramatic 350, Federal	CRX
		155	Turbohydramatic 350, A.I.R., Federal	CHW
			Manual (M20), Federal	CMB
			Turbohydramatic, California	CML
Monza	262	110	Turbohydramatic, A.I.R., Federal	CZU
			Manual, A.I.R., Federal	CZT
			Turbohydramatic, California	CZB
			Manual, California	CZA
	350	125	Turbohydramatic 350, Federal	CHY
			Turbohydramatic 350, California	CKF

Chapter 3

Engine Block Identification

1. Engine Block Identification

There were at least 12 different engine blocks installed in cars from 1970 through 1975. At the same time, there were only 6 basic engine displacements, so in many cases there are a number of blocks that may at first appear correct for a specific engine application.

There are a number of ways to identify an engine block. The main ones are the block casting number, the block casting date, and the engine code stamping. On big blocks, the crankshaft main bearing cap bolt pattern (2- or 4-bolt) can be determined by checking the oil filter mounting area.

All original blocks have a special grain which was machined into the surface of the block. The grain pattern is a series of very fine straight lines, called "broach" marks, running from front to back along the top of the block deck. The original equipment that left these marks is no longer in use, although there are rumors that the service can be bought in certain engine circles. Most modern milling machines use a rotary cutter which leaves a swirl broach pattern. Still, there are several ways in which to try to duplicate the original grain pattern. Also be aware that there are many people who are providing original GM stamping equipment to restorers for the sole purpose of restamping blocks.

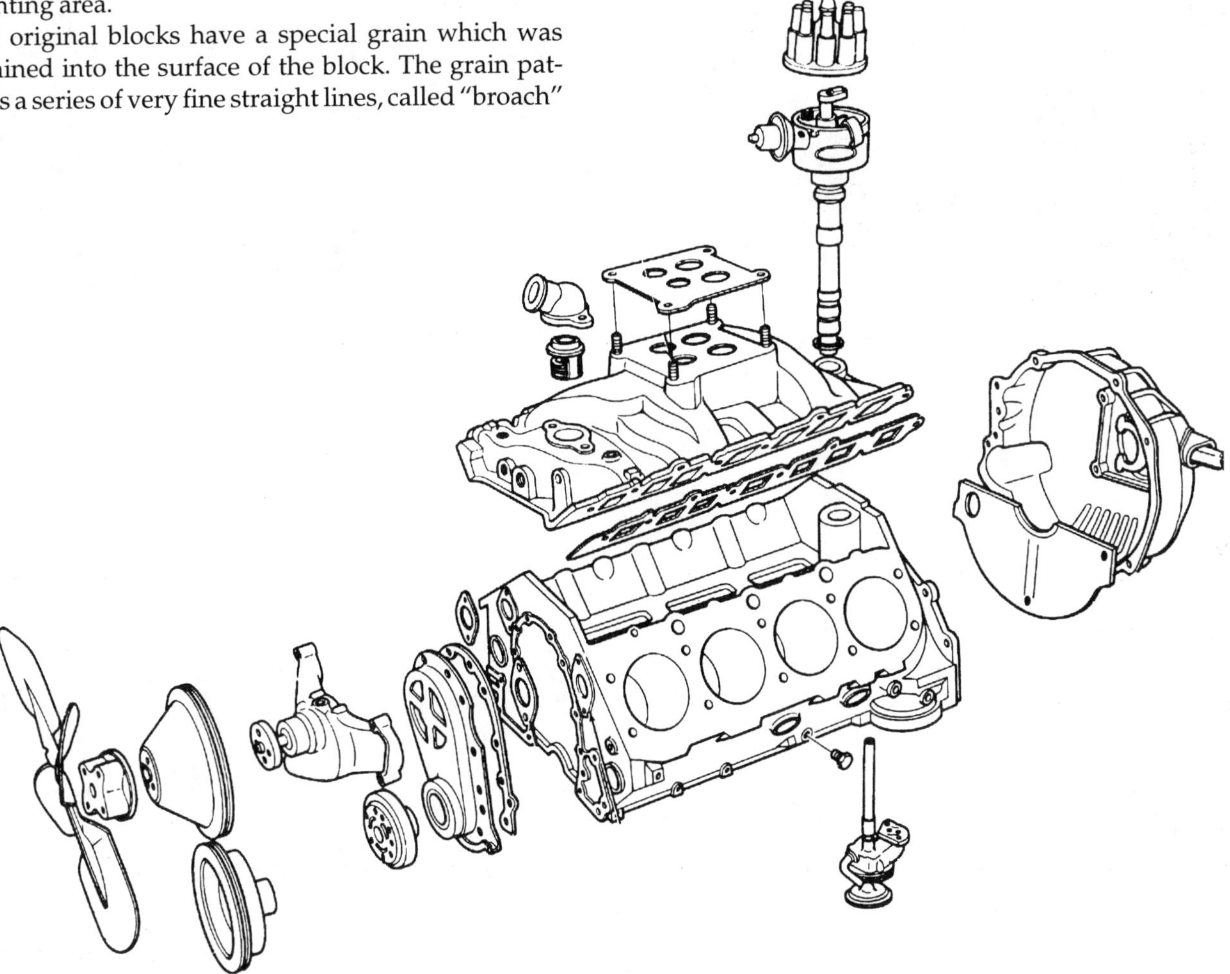

Fig. 3-1. *1972 400 V-8 engine block assembly, showing intake manifold, water pump, and distributor.*

1.1 Block Casting Number and Casting Date

The block casting number is the most important identification because it will probably be the last number on a block to be altered or changed to counterfeit or misrepresent a block. The casting number is usually found at the rear left side of the block, on top of the bellhousing flange. See Fig. 3-2. In some cases, during a production changeover, blocks had the original casting number ground off and a new casting number hand stamped into the block.

The casting date can usually be found at the rear of the block to the right of the casting number. See Fig. 3-3. Some blocks have the casting date on the long side of the block, near the freeze plug. These blocks are identified in the Notes under each casting number listing.

The casting date code is in alphanumeric sequence. The first digit will usually be a letter code, which specifies the month the block was cast. The remaining digits in the date refer to the day of the month and year of the block casting. Some casting dates have been found with all three digits represented as numbers such as "345", which decodes as March 4, 1965. These types of dates are not common in restoration circles.

It is important to note that there were two main plants casting parts for Chevrolet engines during this time period: Flint, Michigan, and Tonawanda, New York. Tonawanda cast all components for engines assembled there. Most Tonawanda engine component castings, including most W-block components, will have a "T" cast into the surface of the part to designate it as a Tonawanda casting. In addition, all Tonawanda cast parts will have a 2-digit year date code to indicate the year the part was cast. Some parts for the Flint plant (engine blocks, cylinder heads and intake manifolds) were cast in Saginaw, Michigan. These parts would have the sin-

Fig. 3-2. Casting number location for block #3963512.

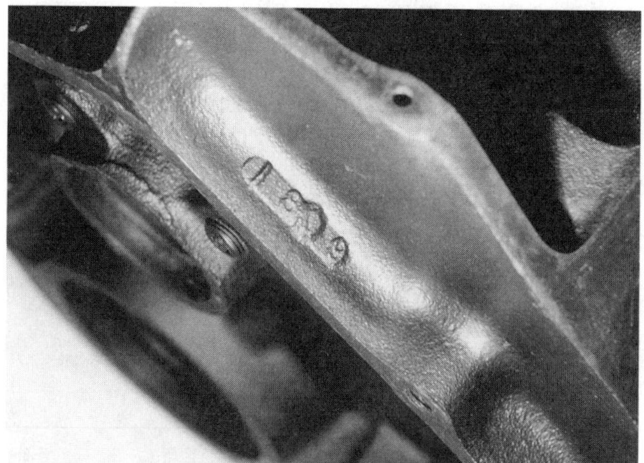

Fig. 3-3. Casting date position for block #3963512. Date reads I 8 9 (September 8, 1969).

1970 Through 1975 Engine Applications

Size	Year	Bore (in.)	Stroke (in.)	Main Journal Dia. (in.)	Rod Journal Dia. (in.)	Intake Valve Size	Exhaust Valve Size	Main Bearing Cap	Notes
Small Block									
262	1975	3.671	3.10	2.45	2.1	1.72	1.50	2-bolt	Emissions engine, Nova and Monza only
307	1968–73	3.875	3.25	2.45	2.1	1.72	1.50	2-bolt	Early emission engine. 283 bore, 327 crank
350	1967–75	4.0	3.48	2.45	2.1	1.94 / 2.02	1.6	2-, 4-bolt	Multi-usage, revised stroke 327. 1967 Camaro only
400	1970–72	4.125	3.75	2.65	2.1	1.94	1.60	4-bolt	Low rpm, high torque Siamesed cylinders
	1973–75	4.125	3.75	2.65	2.1	1.94	1.50	2-bolt	
Big Block									
402	1970–72	4.126	3.76	2.7495 / 2.7488	2.20	2.06 / 2.19	1.72 / 1.88	2-, 4-bolt	.030 overbored 396, internally balanced
454	1970–72	4.251	4.00	2.7495 / 2.7488	2.20	2.06 / 2.19	1.72 / 1.88	2-, 4-bolt	Only externally balanced big block, replaced 427 engine
	1973–75	4.251	4.00	2.7495 / 2.7488	2.20	2.06 / 2.19	1.72 / 1.88	2-bolt	

gle-digit year date code. Engines assembled in Flint with the single-digit year code were used in both passenger and Corvette applications.

Example: I 8 2

- I = Month: September
- 8 = Day: 8th day
- 2 = Year: 1972

Engine Block Month Codes (1st Letter)

A - January	E - May	I - September
B - February	F - June	J - October
C - March	G - July	K - November
D - April	H - August	L - December

NOTE—
When checking date codes of specific engine parts, always remember the following. First verify the build date of your car. (Refer to Chapter 1 for more information on build dates.) The date codes of the various engine components should generally be dated one to three months prior to the car build date. This time lapse allows for assembly of that engine, transport to the car assembly plant and installation in your car.

NOTE—
It has been documented that in the period leading up to a possible strike engines were built and stockpiled up to a six-month supply. The one- to three-month rule would not apply to these engines.

1.2 Casting Clock Code

Sometime during the 1964 model year, a casting clock code was added to some Saginaw blocks, intake manifolds, and exhaust manifolds to indicate the hour of the shift in which the part was made. This clock code is approximately 2 inches in diameter, and it is usually found at the rear face of the block, near the casting number.

The clock circle is made up of ten dots, each representing one hour of a specific shift. There is a second dot outside of the circle, which represents the beginning of a ten-hour shift. The Saginaw foundry usually operated in two shifts, the first from 7:00 AM to 4:00 PM, the second from 4:00 PM until midnight. Parts cast at the start of a shift would have the single clock hand pointing toward the double-dot hour position. Parts cast four hours into a shift would have the hand pointing to the fourth dot clockwise from the double dot. The screw head in the center of the clock designated the shift. A flat-head screw meant first shift, and a round-head screw the second shift.

Fig. 3-4. Block #3791362. Note date clock immediately to right of casting number. Clock indicates time of day block was cast (in this case 9:00 AM, 1st shift). This clock was not uniformly used across all blocks.

1.3 Engine Code Stamping Number

Many restorers believe that the engine code stamping number is more important than the casting date because the engine code number contains more information pertaining to the "original" use of the block. It is also very easy to locate and verify. However, for these same two reasons, many original blocks are restamped with a non-original code to represent a rare or desirable block for resale. There are several locations in which a restorer/buyer can look on the stamp pad that may clue that person in to an altered or misrepresented block.

NOTE—
See Chapter 2 for a thorough discussion of identifying engine codes.

1.4 Big Block Crankshaft Bearing Cap Configurations

On all Chevrolet big block engines, the method of crankshaft bearing cap retention (2- or 4-bolt caps) can be identified without pulling the engine apart or removing the oil pan. Just check the three exterior holes above the oil filter boss. See Fig. 3-5 and Fig. 3-6.

All 2-bolt blocks have the front hole drilled 5/16". It is not drilled or tapped into the oil galley. The center hole is drilled and tapped a 3/8" pipe thread into the oil galley. The rear hole above the oil filter has a 1/2" USS coarse-thread hole that is not drilled into the oil galley.

On 4-bolt blocks, the front hole (toward the front of the engine) has a 3/8" pipe thread hole drilled through the oil galley. The center hole has a 1/2" pipe thread hole drilled through to the top of the oil galley. The rear hole above the oil filter has a 1/2" USS coarse-thread hole, which is *not* drilled into the oil galley.

Fig. 3-5. Two-bolt big block, showing rear oil filter area and 3 holes to be checked to determine crankshaft bolt pattern. (Pointer indicates location where portion of Vehicle Identification Number (VIN) is stamped on some engines. See Chapter 2.)

Fig. 3-6. Four-bolt big block showing rear oil filter area and holes to be checked.

NOTE—
The drilling configuration on the 4-bolt block was done to provide for an external oil cooler if needed in racing applications.

Engine Assembly Order

The following is the assembly order for engines at the Flint and Tonawanda assembly plants. This order of assembly is general in scope. Small variations were usually made from model year to model year.

Flint Order	Tonawanda Order
Raw castings enter plant	Raw castings received (all major engine parts cast at Tonawanda)
Block machining (broaching) in 1 to 2 days:	Block washed
Block starts down line, upside down. Bore sizes on oil pan rail broadcast ahead to piston hook up area	Oil gallery plugs
Galley plugs	Transmission alignment pins
Camshaft	Camshaft
Main bearing caps removed, crankshaft installed, caps reinstalled	Main bearing caps removed, crankshaft installed, caps reinstalled
Flywheel and pressure plate	Flywheel and pressure plate
Cam and crank sprockets, timing chain	Cam and crank sprockets, timing chain
Piston hook-up and installation	Piston hook-up and installation
Front engine cover and seal	Front engine cover and seal
Harmonic balancer	Harmonic balancer
Oil pump shaft and oil pump	Oil pump shaft and oil pump
Windage tray bolts (if applic.)	Windage tray bolts (if applic.)
Oil pan and hardware	Oil pan and hardware
Clutch housing	TDC determined, timing pointer
Engine turned upright	Engine turned upright
TDC determined, timing pointer	Cam lifters
Cam lifters	Cylinder heads
Cylinder heads	Rocker arms, balls (studs already in head)
Rocker arms, balls, studs	Valves adjusted
Intake manifold	Intake manifold
Valves adjusted	Water outlet
Rocker covers	Water pump
Misc. brackets and switches	Build date/suffix code stamped
Build date/suffix code stamped	Spark plugs
Water test with vacuum gauge	Distributor
Oil cavity test	Misc. brackets
Painted	Exhaust manifolds
Distributor	Bench check (vacuum test)
Coil and plug wires	Rocker covers
Spark plugs	Paint
Temperature switches	Hot test
Hot test	Water and oil drained
Water and oil drained	Racked & readied for shipping
Exhaust manifolds	
Spark plug wire supports, heat shields, other misc. brackets	
Component verification	
Racked & readied for shipping	

2. ENGINE BLOCK CASTING NUMBERS

The following information is in a table format, arranged by casting number in numerical order for quick and easy reference. The Model column specifies the model in which the casting number was available. The Year(s) used column specifies the model year in which the block was used. The Engine and Horsepower columns dictate which engine and what horsepower the block was used for. The final column tells whether the crankshaft was retained in the block by a 2-bolt or 4-bolt main configuration.

NOTE—
The letter "N" on bearing caps indicates a cast nodular iron main bearing cap. The lack of an "N" indicates a standard forged crankshaft bearing cap. Most high performance blocks used nodular iron main bearing caps.

NOTE—
Main bearing configurations are derived from original Flint and Tonawanda records. In many cases, due to scheduling and parts availability, a 4-bolt block was used in a 2-bolt application. 2-bolt blocks were never substituted for 4-bolt blocks, due to the potential warranty problems. Many times during a production run, a 2-bolt block might have been drilled for a 4-bolt application, with no factory documentation to verify this.

Block #3951509

Year	Model	Engine	Horsepower	Main	Notes
1970	Passenger, Monte Carlo	400	265	4-bolt	This block was produced by the Flint Engine Plant from 1970 through the 1971 model year. It was then dropped for the 1972 and 1973 model years. It was reinstated for the 1974 model year and was used through the 1975 model year. The Tonawanda Engine Plant was also producing 400 engines, and they used the #3951511 block casting. The only difference between the Flint and Tonawanda block were small casting locators, which were specific to each plant's machining equipment. All 400 engines produced for 1970–71 should be 4-bolt. All 1972 and later 400 blocks should be 2-bolt. Service blocks were usually 2-bolt.
1971	Passenger	400	255	4-bolt	
1974	Passenger Chevelle Monte Carlo	400	150, 180	2-bolt	
1975	Passenger Chevelle Monte Carlo	400	175	2-bolt	

Block #3951511

Year	Model	Engine	Horsepower	Main	Notes
1970	Passenger, Monte Carlo	400	265	4-bolt	This block was used on all Tonawanda 400 engines during the 1970 and 1971 model years. The Flint Engine Plant used the #3951509 400 block during these model years. The only differences between the two blocks were small casting locators, specific to each plant's machining equipment. This block was replaced by #330817 block for 1973. All #3951511 blocks should be 4-bolt. Service blocks were usually 2-bolt.
1971	Passenger	400	255	4-bolt	

Fig. 3-7. Brand new for the 1970 model year was the 400 engine block. It was similar to the 350, but with a different bore and stroke. As a result, most of the internal parts were new, including crankshaft, pistons, rings, and rods. Head gaskets were not interchangeable, due to the water jacket holes shown above on the 400.

Block #3963512[Δ]

Year	Model	Engine	Horsepower	Main	Notes
1970	Passenger	454	345, 390	2-bolt	This block is identical with #3935440 (a 396 block released in late 1968 and early 1969) except for cylinder wall and water jacket revisions. Production of this block began in October, 1968 and continued through the 1971 model year. This block was very special because it was used as a 427 and 454 block simultaneously during the 1969 and 1970 model years. This block has huge reliefs cast into the block for crankshaft clearance. A 454 crankshaft would not clear the #3955270 (a 427 block produced in early 1969) cylinder walls so, consequently, this block was introduced in the 1969 427s in full anticipation that the 454 would be released for the 1970 model year. This block had the standard "high tower" distributor boss and a casting date located on the side of the block until it was redesigned on November 17, 1969. It was then recast with a much shorter tower and the casting date was moved to the rear bellhousing flange.
	Chevelle	454	360	2-bolt	
			450	4-bolt	
	Corvette	454	390	2-bolt	
	Monte Carlo	454	360	2-bolt	
			450*	4-bolt	
1971	Passenger	454	365	2-bolt	
	Corvette	454	365	2-bolt	
			425	4-bolt	
	Chevelle	454	365	2-bolt	
			425	4-bolt	ΔThis block was used in the 1969 model year.
	Monte Carlo	454	365	2-bolt	
			425	4-bolt	
					*Unverified application.

Fig. 3-8. 4-bolt main design of #3963512 block.

Fig. 3-9. #3963512 block showing short distributor tower design.

Block #3969854[Δ]

Year	Model	Engine	Horsepower	Main	Notes
1970	Chevelle	402	330, 350	2-bolt	This block was used for all 402 applications from the 1970 model year until the #3999290 block was released. It is unclear at this time when this took place, but it is believed to have been sometime during the 1972 model year. The block was used in both 2- and 4-bolt applications in 1970 only. In 1971 and 1972 the block was produced only in a 2-bolt main configuration. The only block to receive 4-bolt mains in 1971 was the 454/450HP LS6. The block has the "short tower" distributor boss located in the lifter galley area. The casting date is found at the rear of the block on top of the bellhousing flange, near the casting number.
			375	4-bolt	
	Camaro	402	350	2-bolt	
			375	4-bolt	
	Nova	402	350	2-bolt	
			375	4-bolt	
1971	Passenger	402	300	2-bolt	
	Chevelle	402	300	2-bolt	ΔThis block was used in the 1969 model year.
	Camaro	402	300	2-bolt	
1972	Passenger	402	240	2-bolt	
	Chevelle	402	240	2-bolt	
	Camaro	402	240	2-bolt	

Block #3970010$^{\Delta}$

Year	Model	Engine	Horsepower	Main	Notes
1970	Passenger	350	250	2-bolt	This block was a completely new design for small block engine cases. It came into production sometime in late April or early May of 1969 and was used through 1975. It was produced in 2- and 4-bolt main configurations and these applications varied greatly from year to year. In the 1969 model year, Chevrolet documentation shows the block was used only in a 4-bolt configuration. This block saw extensive truck usage as well. Some #3970010 blocks have been verified with a December "M" month letter code. It is unknown why this was done. $^{\Delta}$This block was used in the 1969 model year.
			300	4-bolt	
	Chevelle	350	250	2-bolt	
			300	4-bolt	
	Nova	350	250	2-bolt	
			300	4-bolt	
	Yenko Duece	350	360	4-bolt	
	Camaro	350	250	2-bolt	
			300, 360	4-bolt	
	Monte Carlo	350	250	2-bolt	
			300	4-bolt	
	Corvette	350	300, 350, 370	4-bolt	
1971	Passenger	350	245, 270	2-bolt	
	Chevelle	350	245, 270	2-bolt	
	Nova	350	245, 270	2-bolt	
	Camaro	350	245, 270	2-bolt	
		Z/28	330	4-bolt	
	Monte Carlo	350	245, 270	2-bolt	
	Corvette	350	270	2-bolt	
			330	4-bolt	
1972	Passenger	350	165	2-bolt	
	Chevelle	350	165, 175	2-bolt	
	Nova	350	165, 175	2-bolt	
	Camaro	350	165, 175	2-bolt	
		Z/28	255	4-bolt	
	Monte Carlo	350	165, 175	2-bolt	
	Corvette	350	200	2-bolt	
			255	4-bolt	
1973	Passenger	350	145, 175	2-bolt	
	Chevelle	350	145, 175	2-bolt	
	Nova	350	145, 175	2-bolt	
	Camaro	350	145, 175	2-bolt	
		Z/28	245	4-bolt	
	Monte Carlo	350	145, 175	2-bolt	
	Corvette	350	175	2-bolt	
			250	4-bolt	
1974	Passenger	350	145, 160	2-bolt	
	Chevelle	350	145, 160	2-bolt	
	Nova	350	145, 160, 185	2-bolt	
	Camaro	350	145, 160, 185	2-bolt	
		Z/28	245	4-bolt	
	Monte Carlo	350	145, 160	2-bolt	
	Corvette	350	195	2-bolt	
			250	4-bolt	
1975	Passenger	350	145, 155	2-bolt	
	Chevelle	350	145, 155	2-bolt	
	Nova	350	145, 155	2-bolt	
	Camaro	350	145, 155	2-bolt	
	Monte Carlo	350	145, 155	2-bolt	
	Monza (CA)	350	145	2-bolt	
	Corvette	350	165	2-bolt	
			205	4-bolt	

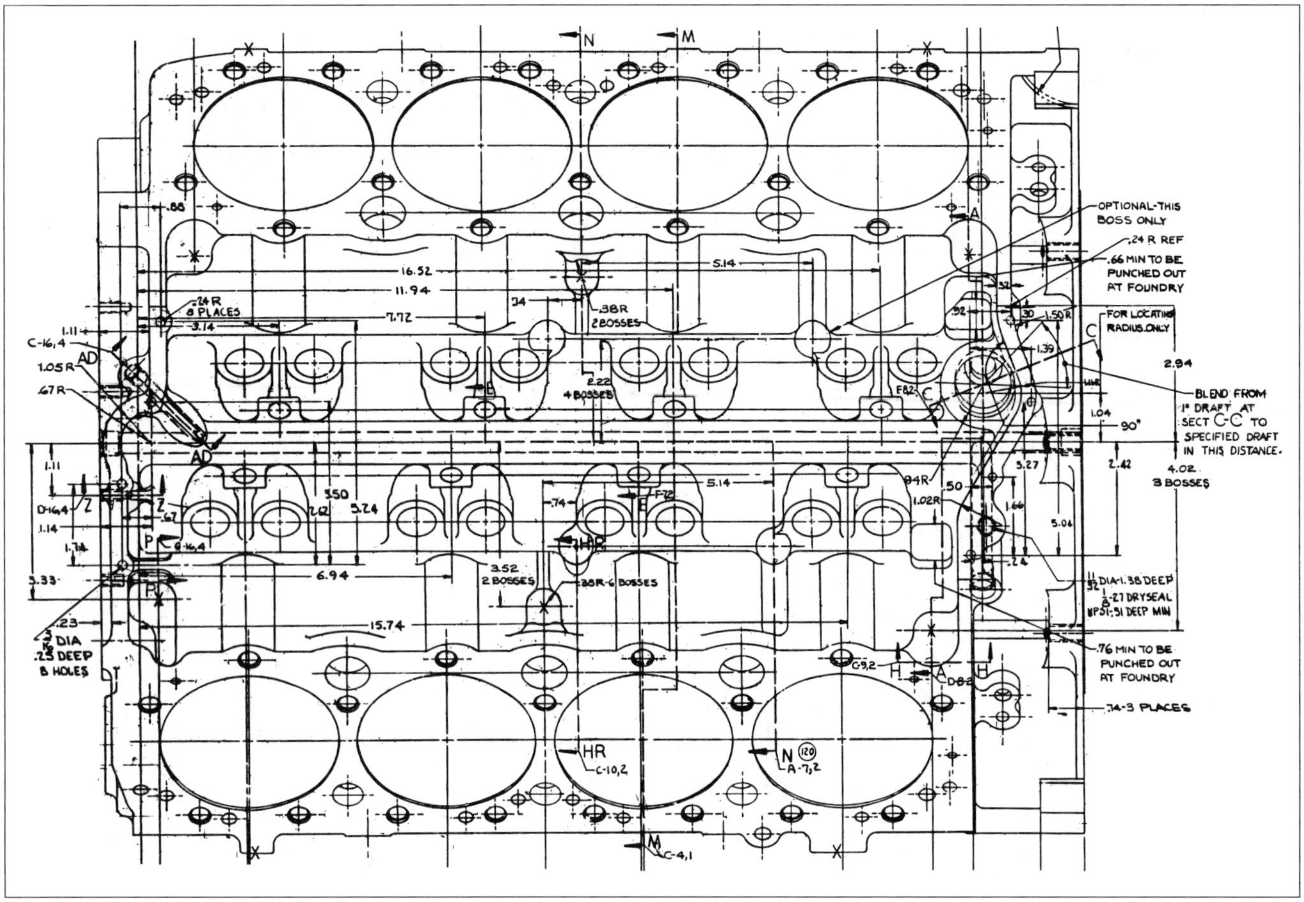

Fig. 3-10. *Top view of block #3970010.*

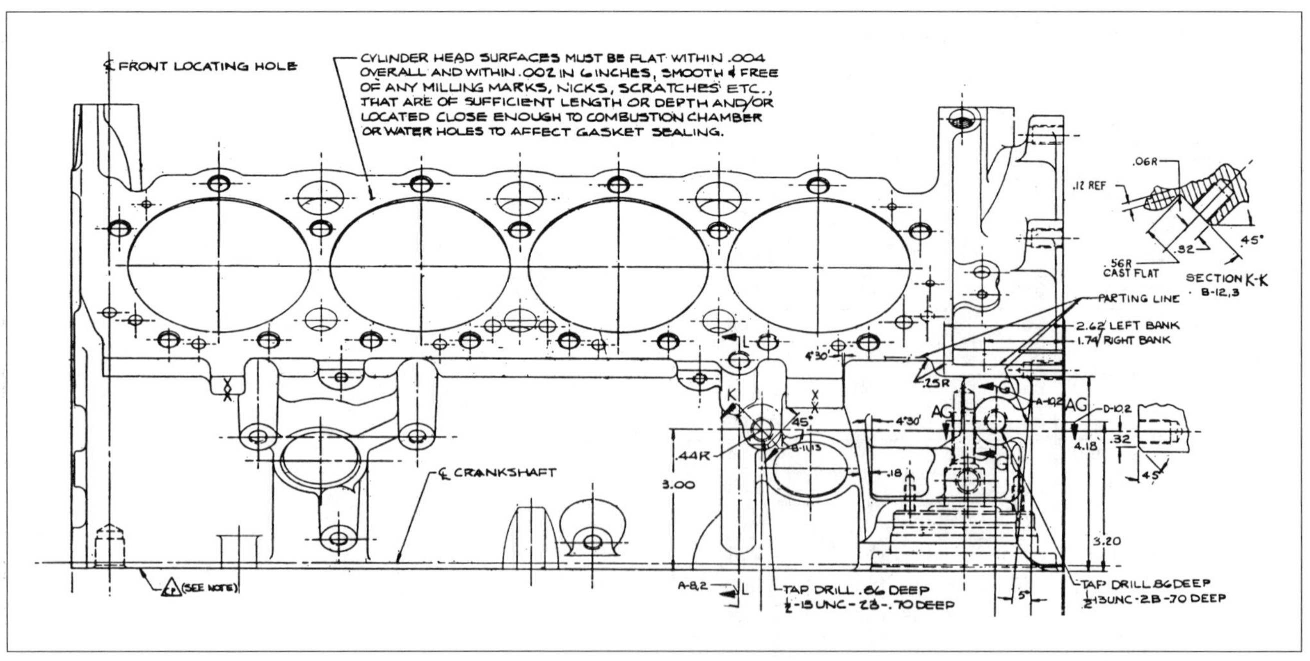

Fig. 3-11. *Side view of block #3970010.*

Block #3970014

Year	Model	Engine	Horsepower	Main	Notes
1970	Camaro	350	300	2- and 4-bolt	This block was cast and used to build engines at the Tonawanda Engine Plant. Two 1970-71 Tonawanda engines have been found that were used in Los Angeles-built Camaros. There is also published documentation which points to the possibility that some late 1972 and early 1973 Corvettes came with this block, but this is also unverified. It is unknown why Tonawanda records indicate that there were no complete engines built with this casting number at the Tonawanda Engine Plant. However, there was a Tonawanda metal casting plant where these blocks were cast in 1972. There is no Chevrolet documentation from the Flint Michigan Engine Plant to show that this block was ever built there. There were five separate engine plants producing blocks during the 1972 model year. It is possible that one of the four remaining plants produced the block.
1971	Camaro	350	245		
1972 (Late)	unknown	350	200, 255		
1973 (early)	Corvette	350	200, 255		

Block #3970020

Year	Model	Engine	Horsepower	Main	Notes
1970	Chevelle	307	200	2-bolt	This block was used exclusively for 307 applications for passenger cars and trucks from the 1970 model year through the 1973 model year. All of these blocks had 2-bolt main bearing caps. The block itself resembled the #3970010 block in certain areas, but it was definitely designed as a low performance block from day one.
	Camaro	307	200		
	Nova	307	200		
1971	Chevelle	307	200		
	Camaro	307	200		
	Nova	307	200		
1972	Chevelle	307	130		
	Camaro	307	130		
	Nova	307	130		
1973	Chevelle	307	115		
	Camaro	307	115		
	Nova	307	115		

Block #3970024

Year	Model	Engine	Horsepower	Main	Notes
1970	Chevelle	307	200	2-bolt	This block was used exclusively for 307 applications. It was cast at the Tonawanda Engine Plant, and all engines with this block identified to date were assembled at Tonawanda. 1972 engines built with this block are non-NB2 equipped, as indicated by the suffix code designations shown on the Tonawanda final build records.
	Camaro	307	200		
	Nova	307	200		
1971	Chevelle	307	200		
	Camaro	307	200		
	Nova	307	200		
1972	Chevelle	307	130		
	Camaro	307	130		
	Nova	307	130		

Block #3999289

Year	Model	Engine	Horsepower	Main	Notes
1972	Passenger	454	240, 270	2-bolt*	This block is identical with #3963512 except for minor interior and exterior casting and machining changes. This block was only available as a 454 2-bolt main block in production vehicles. This block also saw heavy truck usage until 1978. The block has the "short tower" distributor boss located in the lifter galley area. The casting date is found at the rear of the block on top of the bellhousing flange, near the casting number.
	Chevelle	454	240, 270		
	Corvette	454	270		
1973	Passenger	454	215		
	Chevelle	454	215		
	Corvette	454	245		
	Monte Carlo	454	215		
1974	Passenger	454	235		
	Chevelle	454	235		
	Corvette	454	270		
	Monte Carlo	454	235		
1975	Passenger	454	215		
	Chevelle	454	215		
	Monte Carlo	454	215		* There have been several 1973-74 #3999289 4-bolt blocks found, but they seem to be an exception.

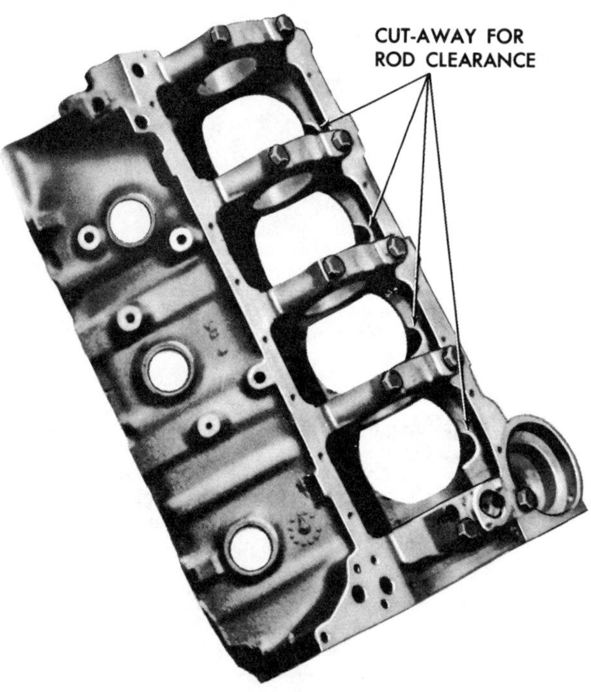

Fig. 3-12. *454 engine block was new for 1970 model year, and replaced the 427. Bore size was the same, so displacement was increased by using a longer stroke crankshaft. As a result, huge reliefs cast into bottom of cylinder bores on the 454 block were necessary for clearance of the connecting rods.*

Block #3999290

Year	Model	Engine	Horsepower	Main	Notes
1972	Passenger	402	240	2-bolt	This block was used in some late 1972 402 equipped vehicles. The changeover date from the #3969854 block is still being researched. The block has the "short tower" distributor boss located in the lifter galley area. The casting date is found at the rear of the block on top of the bellhousing flange, near the casting number. Little is known about this block. All of the above applications are not verified to date.
	Chevelle	402	240		
	Camaro	402	240		

Block #330817

Year	Model	Engine	Horsepower	Main	Notes
1972	Passenger	400	170	2-bolt	This block was used from the 1972 model year through the 1975 model year. During the 1972 and 1973 model year, it was the only 400 block that was cast for all applications. In 1974, the Flint Engine Plant started production of the 400 engine and that plant used the #3951509 block casting. Both Tonawanda and Flint produced 400 engines in 1974 through 1975. All 400 engines produced in the 1972 model year and later used a 2-bolt main configuration.
1973	Passenger	400	150		
1974	Passenger	400	150, 180		
	Chevelle	400	150, 180		
	Monte Carlo	400	150, 180		
1975	Passenger, Chevelle, Monte Carlo	400	175		

Block #346236

Year	Model	Engine	Horsepower	Main	Notes
1975	Passenger	454	215	2-bolt	This block was introduced mid-year during the 1975 model year. It is unknown at this time what changes there were to this from the #3999289 block. It is still being researched. Theses applications could have used this block after January 1, 1975, but this has not been verified.
	Chevelle	454	215		
	Monte Carlo	454	215		

Block #355909

Year	Model	Engine	Horsepower	Main	Notes
1975	Nova	262	110	2-bolt	These were the only applications for this block. It resembles block #3970010, except that #355909 has a substantially thinner water jacket. This block was produced only in 2-bolt configuration.
	Monza	262	110	2-bolt	

Chapter 4

Crankshaft Identification

1. Introduction

In this chapter I will identify all crankshafts and matching engine combinations installed in Chevrolet cars from 1970 through 1975. During this period, two types of crankshafts were manufactured by Chevrolet: forged steel and cast nodular iron. The forged steel crank was initially introduced in 1955 in the 265 engine. As production figures rose and manufacturing costs began to increase, Chevrolet decided to install a less expensive cast nodular iron crankshaft in all low and intermediate performance passenger cars. The forged steel crankshaft was reserved for all high performance applications, including Corvette.

You can identify each of these crankshafts, without having to fully disassemble the engine, by checking the parting line (or manufacturing seam) of the crankshaft. The seam was produced by the two halves of the crankshaft mold that came together to produce the part. The seam extends down the entire length of the crank. When the engine is still assembled, this parting line is still visible on the crankshaft flywheel flange.

In a cast nodular crank, the parting line is very thin, usually 1/32" wide, and it stands up above the surface of the crankshaft. The parting line of the forged steel unit is much wider, usually 1/4" to 1/2". There is no visible ridge on the forged crank. The texture of the forged crank is also much smoother than the cast iron.

Another distinguishing feature between crankshafts is the result of a special treatment called tuffriding. The treatment involved a chemical heat-treating process that was used to harden the rod and main bearing journal surfaces of most forged steel crankshafts that would be used in high performance applications. Tuffrided crankshafts have a dull gray finish.

Many small and big block crankshafts, including truck applications and all high performance applications, also have cross-drilled main bearing journals. This cross-drilling process was used to insure that all bearings and bearing journals are supplied with oil during the complete rotation of the crankshaft. All tuffrided cranks have been cross-drilled, but not all cross-drilled cranks have been tuffrided.

Finally, all crankshafts were manufactured at the foundry with a casting number. This number is located on the rough surface of one of the counterweights or between the bearing journals. The chart at the end of this chapter lists casting numbers in numerical order.

Any further information that is specific to a particular crankshaft will be explained under each individual heading.

> **NOTE—**
> Many of the crankshaft dimensions (rod and main journals) in this chapter are given in rounded numbers (i.e. 2.10, 3.00) since that is the way the dimensions are commonly described. The crankshaft illustrations give the factory dimensions, often to four decimal places, which is necessary for accurate machining.

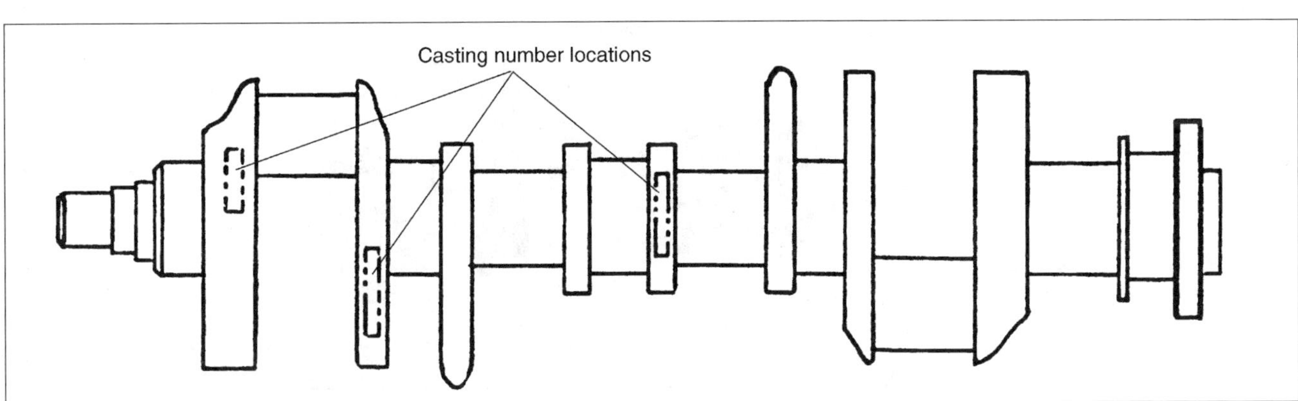

Fig. 4-1. Typical locations of crankshaft casting numbers.

2. Chevrolet Small Block Crankshafts

307 Crankshaft, 1970 Through 1973[Δ]

Engine	Year(s)	Stroke	Rod Journal	Main Journal
307	1970–73	3.25 in.	2.10 in.	2.45 in.

All 307 crankshafts are cast nodular iron. The 307 crankshaft is interchangeable with a 327 crankshaft from 1968–69. The only difference is the flywheel flange shape.

[Δ]This crank was also installed on 1968 and 1968 307 models.

Crankshaft Flange

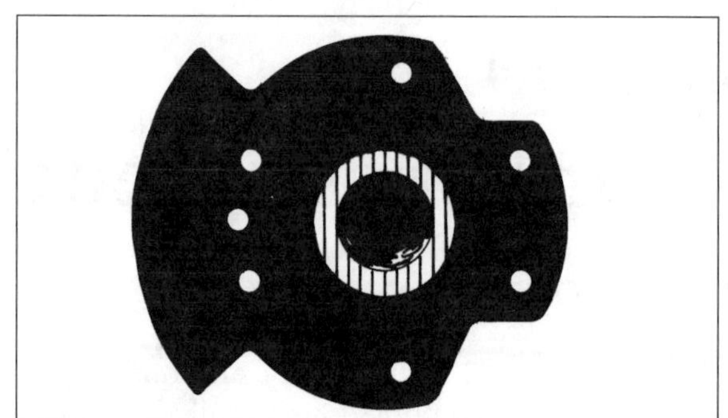

Crankshaft Dimensions

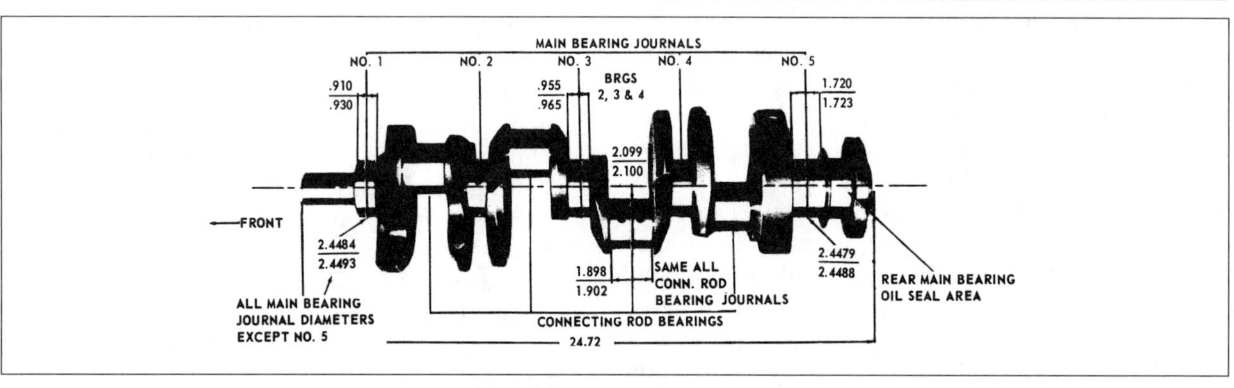

350 Crankshaft, 1970 Through 1975[Δ]

Engine	Year(s)	Stroke	Rod Journal	Main Journal
350	1970–75	3.48 in.	2.10 in.	2.45 in.

Chevrolet used both forged and cast nodular iron for 350 engines.

[Δ]The crankshaft flange was the same as the 1967 350 crankshaft and was also used on 1968 and 1969 350s.

Crankshaft Flange

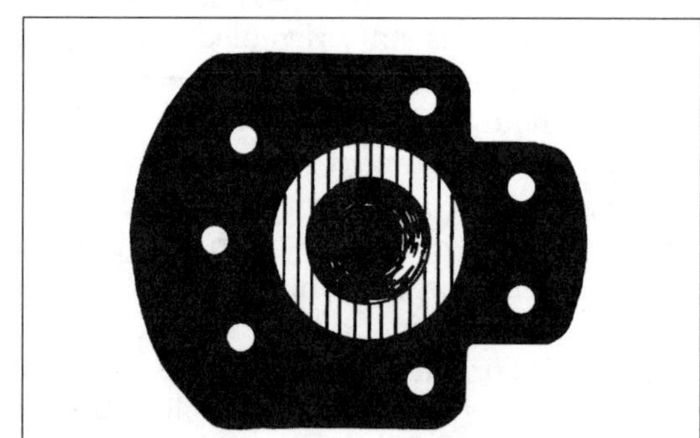

Crankshaft Dimensions

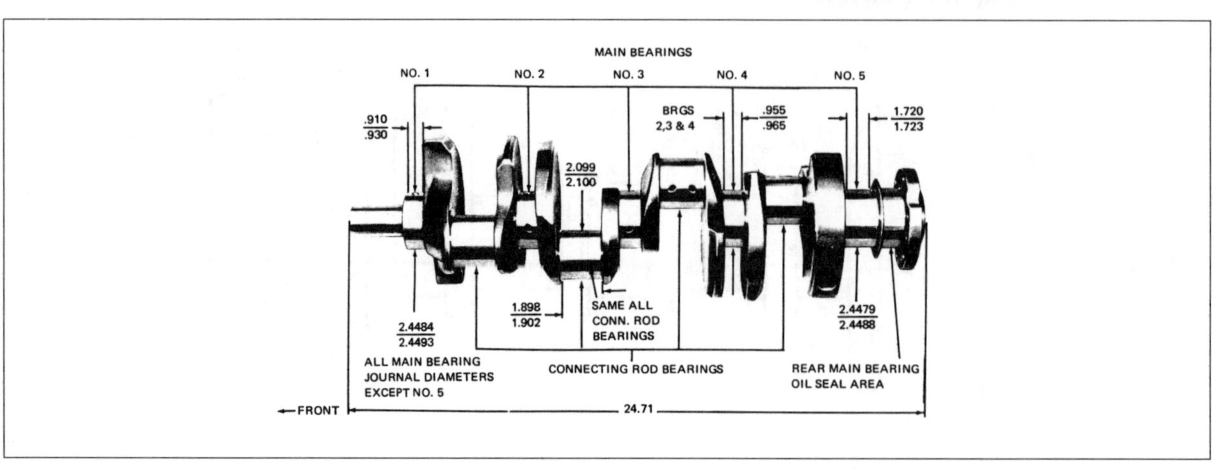

400 Crankshaft, 1970 Through 1975

Engine	Year(s)	Stroke	Rod Journal	Main Journal
400	1970–75	3.75 in.	2.10 in.	2.65 in.

All 400 crankshafts were cast nodular iron. No forged cranks were installed because the 400 motor was not designed for high-rpm use. The stroke and main bearing journal diameter are completely different from all other small block Chevrolet engines, though the connecting rod journal diameter is the same as all 1968 and later small blocks. The flywheel flange is unique to the 400 crankshaft, and it used dowel pins to locate the flywheel/flexplate.

Crankshaft Flange

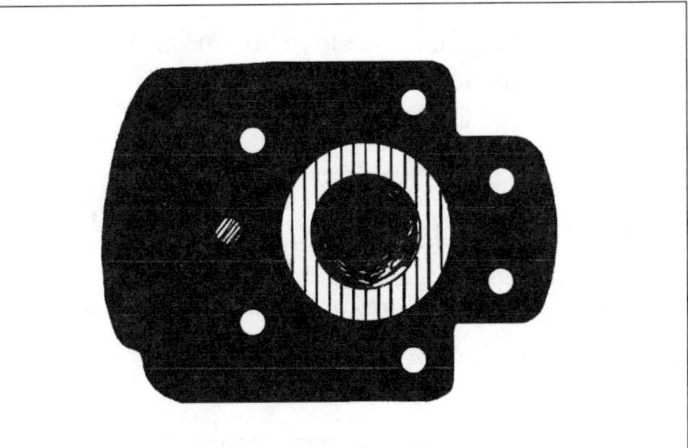

Crankshaft Dimensions

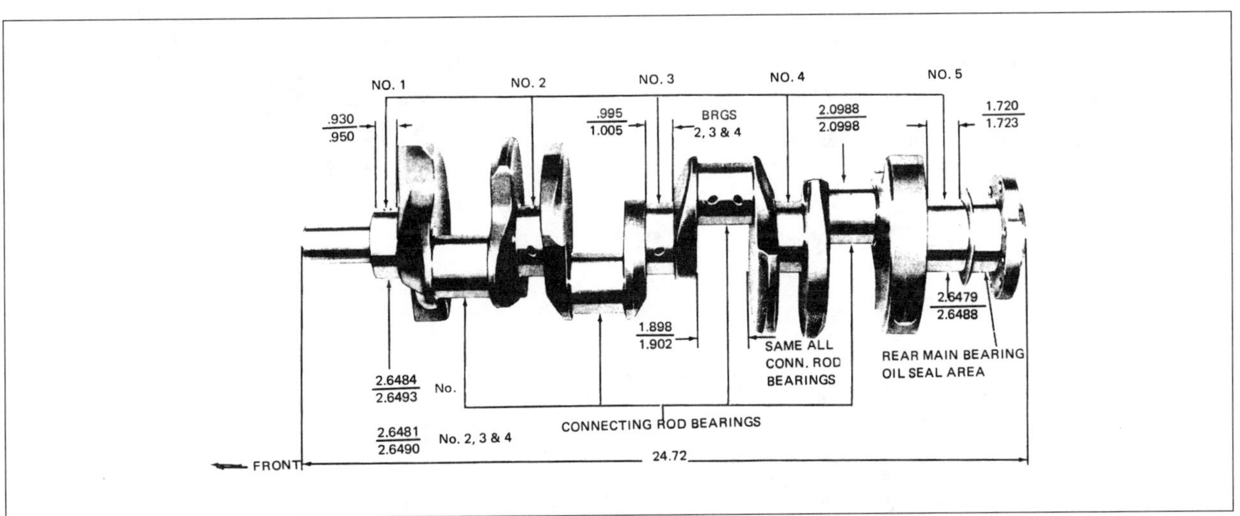

262 Crankshaft, 1975

Engine	Year(s)	Stroke	Rod Journal	Main Journal
262	1975	3.10 in.	2.10 in.	2.45 in.

All 262 crankshafts were cast nodular iron. As in the 400 crankshaft, no 262 crankshafts were produced in forged steel due to the engine not being designed for high-rpm use. While the stroke is particular to the 262 only, the main journal and connecting rod journal diameters are the same as all other small block crankshafts built after 1968, excluding the 400 crank.

Crankshaft Flange

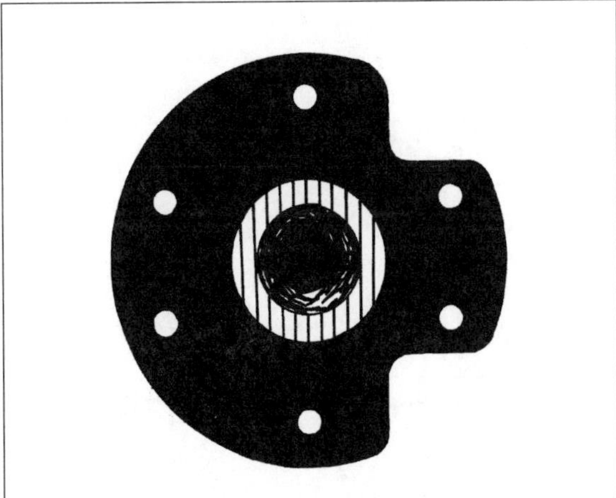

3. Chevrolet Big Block Crankshafts

Big block crankshaft identification is easier than small block crank identification because all big block cranks have the same diameter connecting rod and main journal sizes. All 396/402 and 427 crankshaft have a 3.76 inch stroke and are internally balanced. The crankshaft flywheel flanges in the 396/402 and 427 engines are the same.

402 Crankshaft, 1970 Through 1972^Δ

Engine	Year(s)	Stroke	Rod Journal	Main Journal
402	1970–72	3.76 in.	2.20 in.	1–4 2.7495; 5 2.7488 in.
The 402 crankshaft is basically the same as the 427 crankshaft used from 1966–69, except that the 402 crank is lighter, due to a different counterweight design. To tell, check the width of the third counterweight. On a 402 crank it should be 7/16" wide. You cannot tell a 402 crankshaft from a 427 crank from the shape of the flywheel flange since they are the same. Some 402 crankshafts in low-horsepower applications may be cast iron. ^ΔThis crankshaft was also used on the 1965–69 396 engine.				

Crankshaft Flange

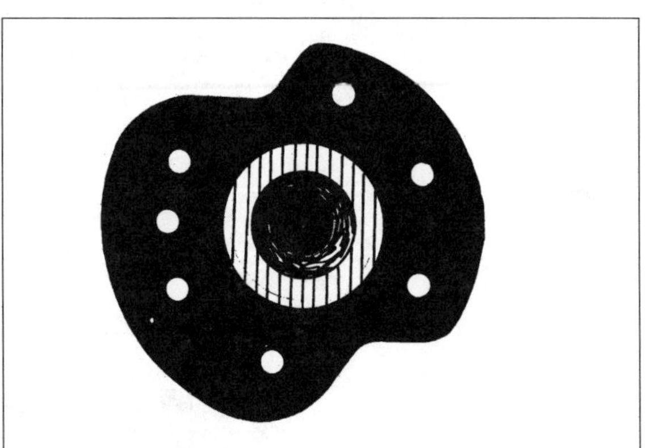

Crankshaft Dimensions

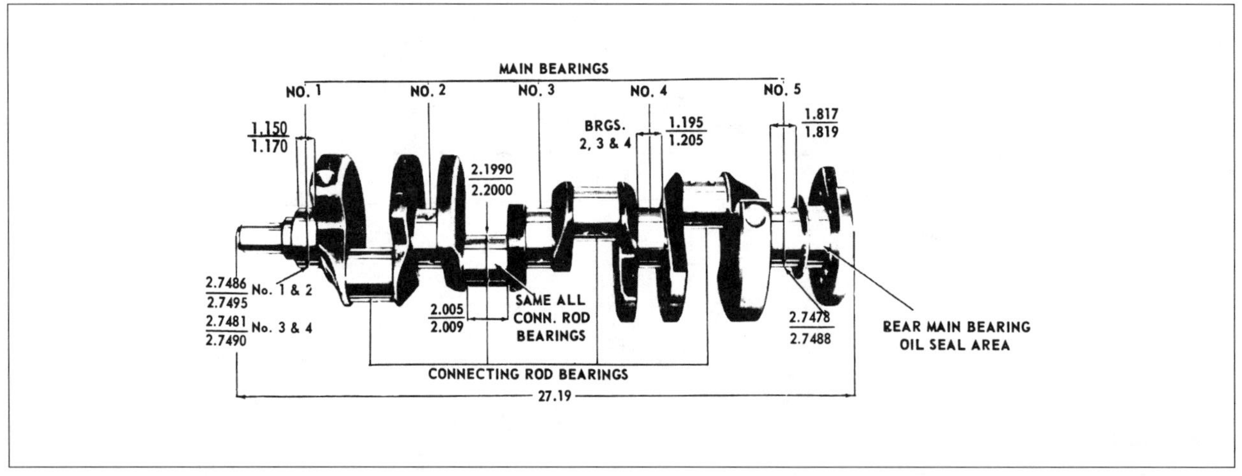

454 Crankshaft

Engine	Year(s)	Stroke	Rod Journal	Main Journal
454	1970–75	4.00 in.	2.20 in.	1–4 2.7495; 5 2.7488 in.

The 454 crankshaft is totally different from the 396/402 and 427 cranks. Unlike the other big block cranks, the 454 crank is externally balanced. External balancing is done at the crank damper and flywheel, using extra counterweights to compensate for the increased engine stroke. The 454 uses dowel pins to locate the flywheel/flexplate.

Crankshaft Flange

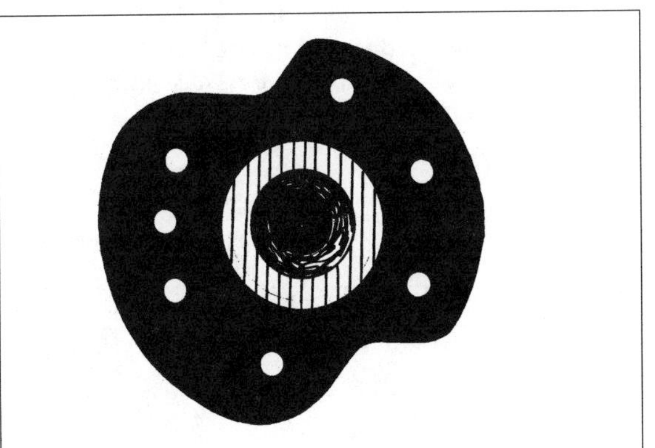

Crankshaft Dimensions

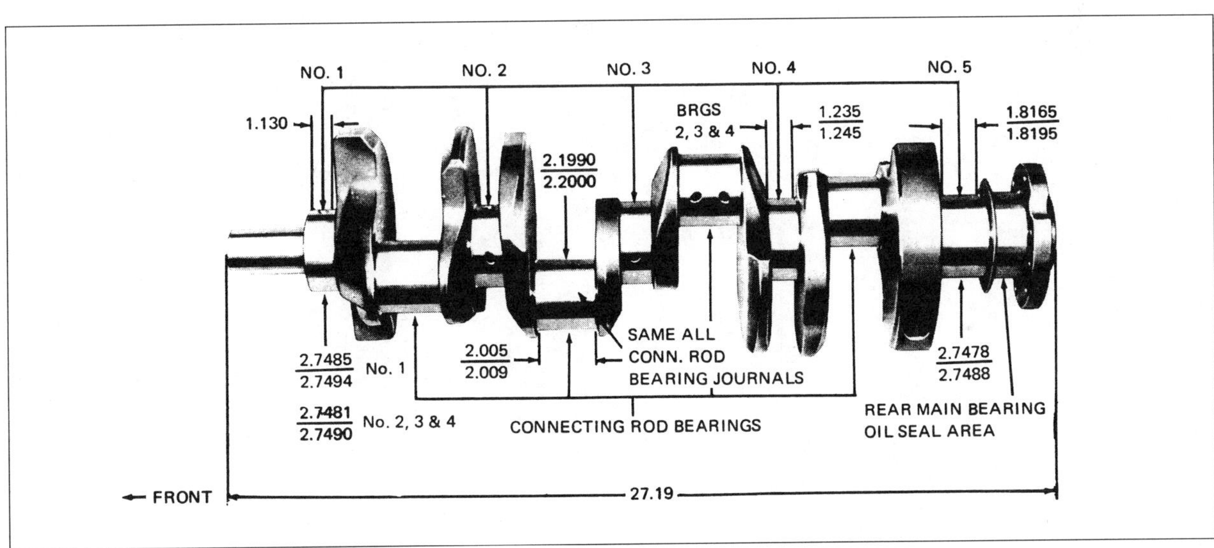

CHAPTER 4

4. CRANKSHAFT CASTING NUMBERS

> **NOTE—**
> Crankshaft stock is normally depleted in engine production during the same model year, however, there may be some crankshaft carry-over very earlier in the following model year.

Crankshaft Specifications, 1970–1975

Casting #	Year	Engine/HP	Construction	Main Journ.	Rod Journ.	Stroke	Notes
1181	1968–76	305/350	Nodular Iron	2.45	2.10	3.48	Possible Replacement
3521	1970–72	454	Forged Steel	1–4: 2.7495 5: 2.7488	2.20	4.00	
6223	1970–72	402	Forged Steel	1–4: 2.7495 5: 2.7488	2.20	3.76	
7115	1970–72	402	Forged Steel	1–4: 2.7495 5: 2.7488	2.20	3.76	
7416	1970–72	454	Forged Steel	1–4: 2.7495 5: 2.7488	2.20	4.00	LS4, LS5
310514	1977–85	350	Unverified	2.45	2.10	3.48	
330550	1973, 1974	350/245, 250HP	Forged Steel	2.45	2.10	3.48	Corvette, Camaro Only
	1975	350/205	Forged Steel	2.45	2.10	3.48	Corvette Only
353039	1973–76	454	Nodular Iron	1–4: 2.7495 5: 2.7488	2.20	4.00	
354431	1975–76	262	Nodular Iron	2.45	2.10	3.10	Monza, Nova
3804816	1970–72	402	Unverified	1–4: 2.7495 5: 2.7488	2.20	3.76	
3863144	1970–72	402	Unverified	1–4: 2.7495 5: 2.7488	2.20	3.76	
3874874	1970–72	402	Unverified	1–4: 2.7495 5: 2.7488	2.20	3.76	
3904815	1970–72	402	Nodular Iron	1–4: 2.7495 5: 2.7488	2.20	3.76	
3911011	1968–73	307/327	Nodular Iron	2.45	2.10	3.25	Replacement
3932442	1969–85	350	Nodular Iron	2.45	2.10	3.48	Possible Replacement
	1976–85	305					
3941174	1968–73	307/327	Nodular Iron	2.45	2.10	3.25	Replacement
3941182	1968–76	350	Forged Steel	2.45	2.10	3.48	Possible Replacement
3951529	1970–75	400	Nodular Iron	2.65	2.10	3.75	
3967416	1970–71	454	Forged Steel	1–4: 2.7495 5: 2.7488	2.20	4.00	LS4, LS5
14088526	1986	305	Nodular Iron	2.45	2.10	3.48	
14088535	1986 & later	305/350	Nodular Iron	2.45	2.10	3.48	
14088552	1986–88	305/350	Forged Steel	2.45	2.10	3.48	

Chapter 5

Cylinder Head Identification

1. Introduction

There are a number of ways to identify cylinder heads. The primary one is the head casting number and date, but there are also other identifying features, including port design, combustion chamber design, bosses on the head for spark plug shields and the temperature sending unit, spark plug seat design, and external casting marks on the end of the head.

Cylinder Head Casting Number

The cylinder head casting number is the single most important identifying feature on a head because it will probably be the last feature that could be altered or changed. The casting number is usually found on the top of the head, in between two valves and the rocker arm studs.

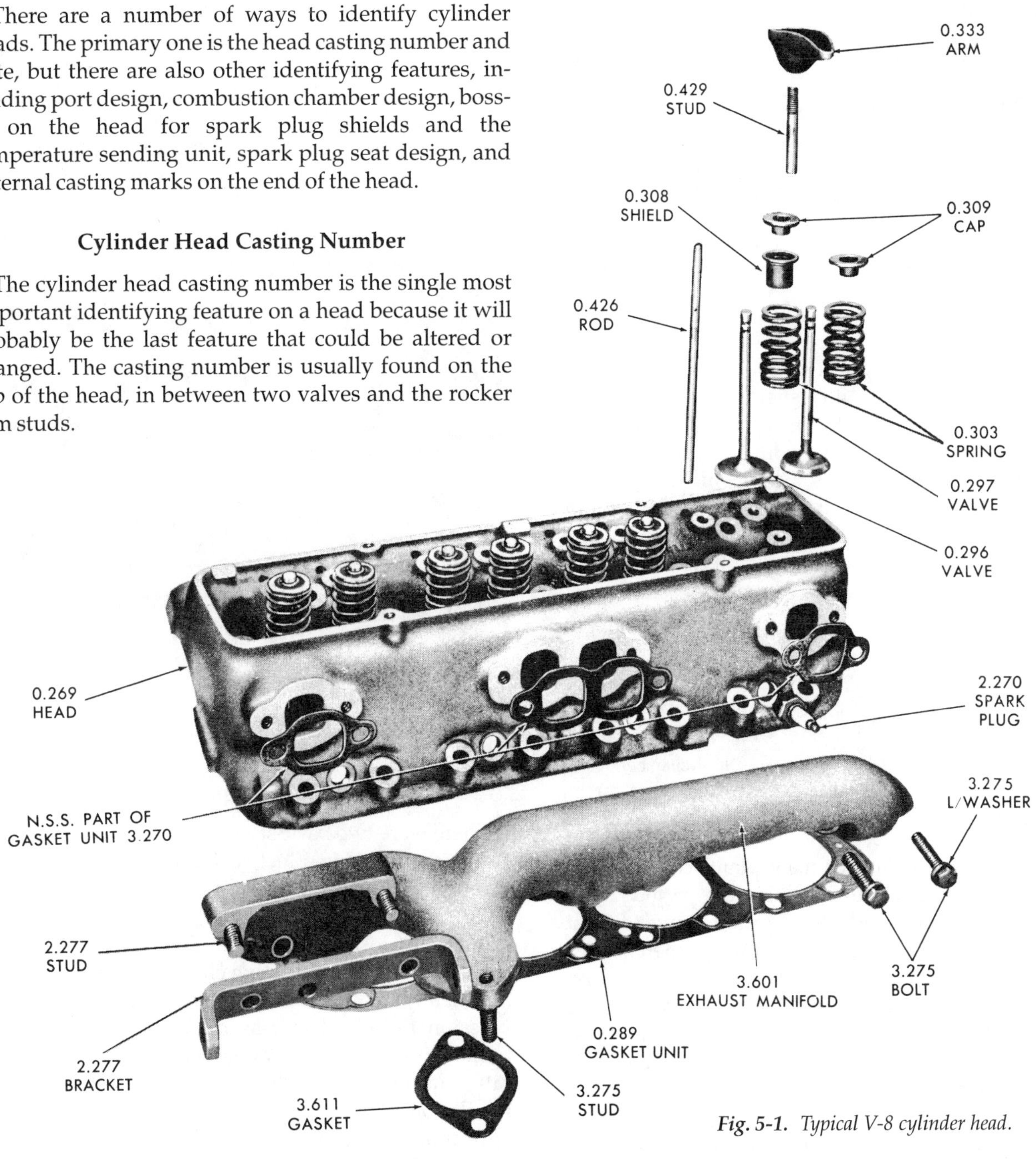

Fig. 5-1. *Typical V-8 cylinder head.*

Cylinder Head Casting Date

The casting date is usually found adjacent to the casting number. See Fig. 5-2. You should look closely at a cylinder head's casting date because many heads have been found that have been altered to represent an earlier or more expensive cylinder head.

Fig. 5-2. Casting number and casting date for head #3890462. Date code "D276" deciphers as April 27, 1966.

The casting date code is in an alphanumeric sequence. The first digit will usually be a letter code, which specifies the month the block was cast. Some casting dates have been found with all three digits represented as numbers such as "345", which decodes as March 4, 1965. These types of dates are not common in restoration circles. The table below gives month code letter designations. The remaining digits in the date refer to the day of the month and year of the casting.

Cylinder Head Month Codes (1st Letter)

A - January	E - May	I - September
B - February	F - June	J - October
C - March	G - July	K - November
D - April	H - August	L - December

Note that there were two main plants casting parts for Chevrolet engines during this time period: Flint, Michigan, and Tonawanda, New York. Tonawanda cast all components for engines assembled there. Most Tonawanda engine component castings, including most W-block components, will have a "T" cast into the surface of the part to designate it as a Tonawanda casting. In addition, all Tonawanda cast heads will have a 2-digit code to indicate the year the part was cast.

Some parts for the Flint plant (engine blocks, cylinder heads and intake manifolds) were cast in Saginaw, Michigan. These parts would have the single-digit year date code. Engines assembled in Flint with the single-digit year code were used in both passenger and Corvette applications. Also note that there were some W-block parts cast with the letters "CFD," which represented the Central Foundry Division located in Saginaw, Michigan. These parts would have the single-digit year date code the same as all other Saginaw produced parts. Most big block head change-over dates are either late E or early F. Small block head change-over dates vary from year to year.

Port Design

There are two basic designs for big block head ports, oval and square. See Fig. 5-3. Oval ports were used on low and medium performance engines, while square ports were used on high performance engines for better air flow. In general, cast iron heads with 2.06 or less diameter intake valves have oval ports, while cast iron heads with 2.19 diameter intake valves have square ports.

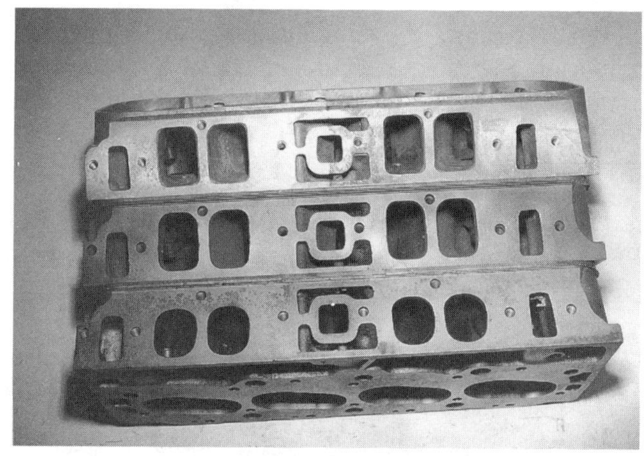

Fig. 5-3. Intake port comparison. From the top: aluminum square (open chamber), cast iron square, cast iron oval.

"Closed" and "Open" Combustion Chambers

There were two basic styles of combustion chambers were used on big block cylinder heads from 1970 through 1975, excluding the rare aluminum #3946074 ZL1/L88 cylinder head. These styles are commonly known as "closed chamber" and "open chamber," due to the size of the combustion chamber. Early heads had a generally smaller, or closed chamber for a higher compression ratio and increased performance. The ZL1 broke this rule due to its already high 12.5 compression ratio and radical camshaft. In 1971, due to emissions regulations, "open chamber" cylinder heads began to appear on more engines. See Fig. 5-4.

Fig. 5-4. Combustion chamber comparison: ZL1 aluminum open chamber (left) vs. cast iron closed chamber (right).

Spark Plug Seat Design

One spark plug seat design was used on 1970 through 1975 heads. These heads were produced with a "peanut" or tapered spark plug seat. Up through the 1969 model year, heads were produced with an "N" series, or flat gasket spark plug seat. See Fig. 5-5. It is possible, due to late model releases or fore service replacement in 1970, that some cylinder heads could have close or matching casting dates and be tapped for flat spark plug seats. Look closely at heads from early 1970.

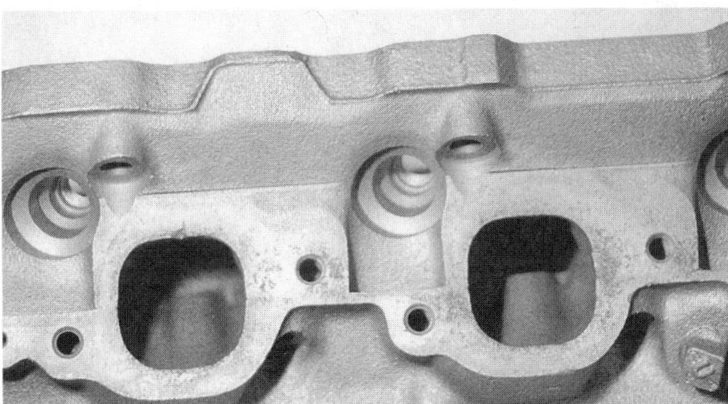

Fig. 5-5. Top: "N" series, or flat gasket type spark plug seat for years up through 1969. Bottom: "Peanut," or tapered spark plug seat for 1970 and later heads. Both of these heads are casting #3964290. See that head for more information.

External Casting Marks

All 1970 through 1975 square port big block heads have a single hump cast into the end of the head.

All small block heads had various symbols cast into the end of the head. These symbols are mentioned under each casting number. These symbols make small block and some big block identification easy without removing a valve cover.

Fig. 5-6. Typical oval port head, showing straight casting flash line.

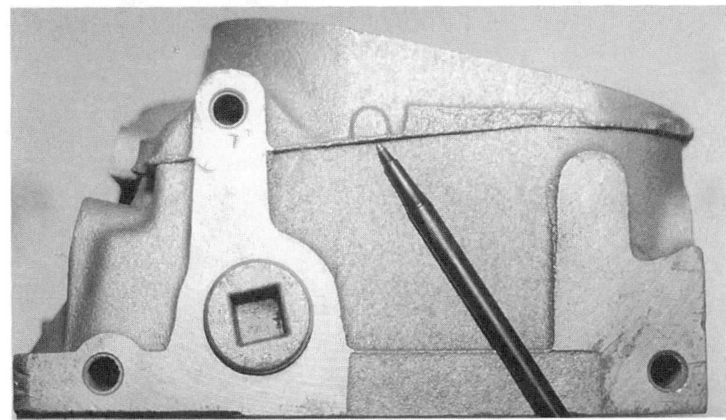

Fig. 5-7. End of square port big block heads showing lack of hump (top) on 1965 and 1966 heads, and hump (bottom) on 1967 and later heads. Hump came into production late in the 1967 model year on the #3904391 cylinder head.

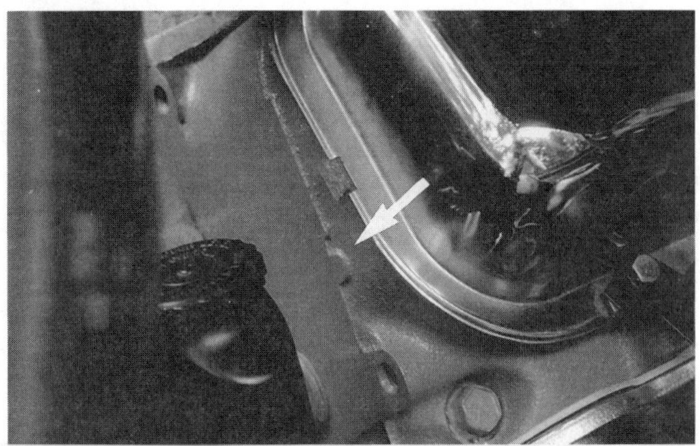

Fig. 5-8. Identification bump (arrow) found on all late 1967 and later square port big block heads. 1970 Chevelle LS6 engine shown.

2. Cylinder Head Casting Numbers

The charts on the following pages list in order of casting number the cylinder heads installed on 1970 through 1975 cars. The casting number is always found on the top, or rocker side, of the head.

Under each casting number additional information pertaining to each cylinder head is broken down into several headings to give information necessary to correctly identify the cylinder head.

The Year heading is the model year in which the casting number was used. Please note that many casting numbers were used over many model years.

In the Valve Size column the first number refers to the intake valve size, while the second number refers to the exhaust valve size. This information is very important because some engines will use the same casting number but with a different valve size. Unfortunately, the only way to validate a correct valve size is to remove the cylinder heads from the engine and measure the valve size.

The Combustion Chamber volume is included for several reasons. It is primarily an additional check to prove the originality of a cylinder head. This figure was listed on every cylinder head blueprint from Chevrolet and shows the original manufacturing specifications for the cylinder head. Second, it gives a figure of comparison between cylinder heads that are similar to one another in other aspects. Finally, no other publication has been able to procure these original combustion chamber volumes, so this should be useful reference material. These figures can be easily checked on a head at a local machine shop.

Head #3927185$^{\Delta}$

Year	Model	Engine	Horsepower	Valve Size (in.) Intake/Exhaust	Combustion Chamber (cc.)	Notes
1970	Nova	307	200	1.72/1.50	69.625	This cylinder head is similar to #3911032 (used on 1968 307 applications). It is identical to #3884520 (1966–67 283 applications) except for the addition of a temperature sending unit boss, and three accessory bolt holes at each end. The combustion chamber has been revised. The only usage after 1970 was a 307 truck application. Casting symbol: or (unverified) $^{\Delta}$This head was also used in the 1969 model year.
	Chevelle	307	200			
	Camaro	307	200			

Head #3927186^Δ

Year	Model	Engine	Horsepower	Valve Size (in.) Intake/Exhaust	Combustion Chamber (cc.)	Notes
1970	Passenger	350	300	1.94/1.50	63.305	This cylinder head is similar to #3917291. It is identical to #3782461 (a 327 head used in 1965 and 1966), but with a few changes. The combustion chamber was redesigned, a temperature sending unit boss was added, 3 accessory bolt holes were added to each end of the head, and the external identification "humps" were smaller. 2.02 applications used screw-in studs and guide plates. Casting #3991492 may appear on this part after 4/5/71. Please note that the #3947041 head was possibly used interchangeably with this head through 1969 and 1970 production. Casting symbol: (symbol not reproduced) ΔThis head was also used in the 1969 model year.
	Nova	350	300			
	Yenko Deuce	350	360	2.02/1.60		
	Chevelle	350	300	1.94/1.50		
	Camaro	350	300			
			360	2.02/1.60		
	Corvette	350	300	1.94/1.50		
			370	2.02/1.60		

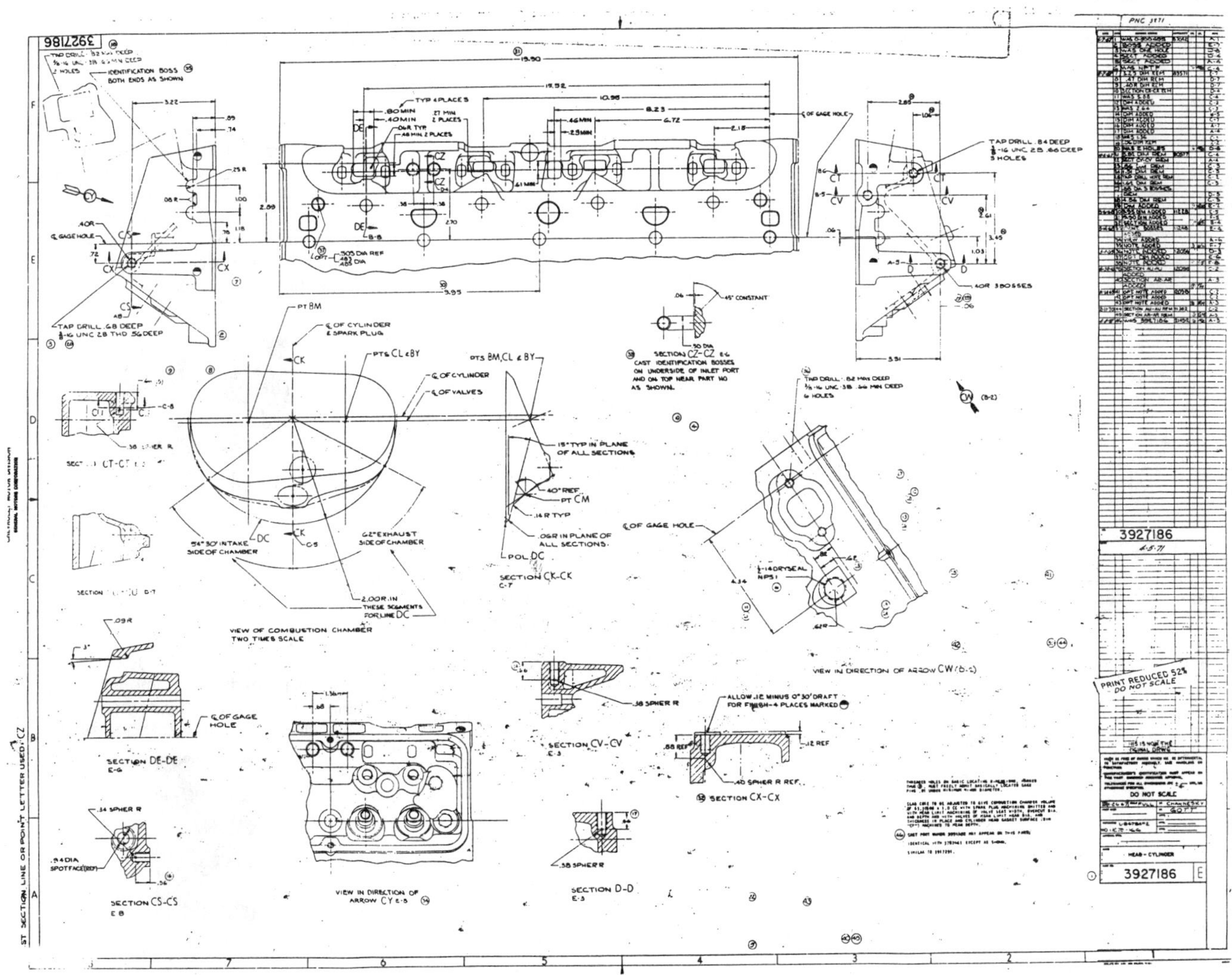

Fig. 5-9. Blueprint shows changes to head #3927186. Note double hump external casting identifier in upper right hand corner.

Head #3927187[Δ]

Year	Model	Engine	Horsepower	Valve Size (in.) Intake/Exhaust	Combustion Chamber (cc.)	Notes
1970	Corvette	350	350	2.02/1.60	63.995	This head is similar to #3917291(2). It is identical with #3782461 (a 1965–66 327 head) with a few changes. A temperature sending unit boss was added, and three accessory bolt holes were added to the end of each head. Casting #3927186 may appear on this part until 10/9/70. After that date casting #3991492 may appear on this head. Please note that #3947041 head was possibly used interchangeably with this head through 1969 production. All original equipment #3927187 cylinder heads should have 2.02/1.60 valves. Casting symbol: [Δ]This head was also used in 1969.

Head #3927188[Δ]

Year	Model	Engine	Horsepower	Valve Size (in.) Intake/Exhaust	Combustion Chamber (cc.)	Notes
1970	Chevelle	307 (low compress.)	200			This cylinder head is identical with #3932454 and #3884520 except for a redesigned combustion chamber. Also, 3 accessory bolt holes were added to each end of the head. Casting #3946813 may appear on this part. This cylinder head was used extensively on commercial trucks. The only applications in passenger cars are the low compression engines listed. Casting symbol: [Δ]This head was also used in 1969.

Head #3932441[Δ]

Year	Model	Engine	Horsepower	Valve Size (in.) Intake/Exhaust	Combustion Chamber (cc.)	Notes
1970	Passenger	350	250	1.94/1.50	76.26	This head is identical with #3927186 except for a redesigned combustion chamber and a different external identification marking. Casting symbol: [Δ]This head was also used in 1969.
	Nova	350	250			
	Chevelle	350	250			
	Monte Carlo	350	250			
	Camaro	350	250			

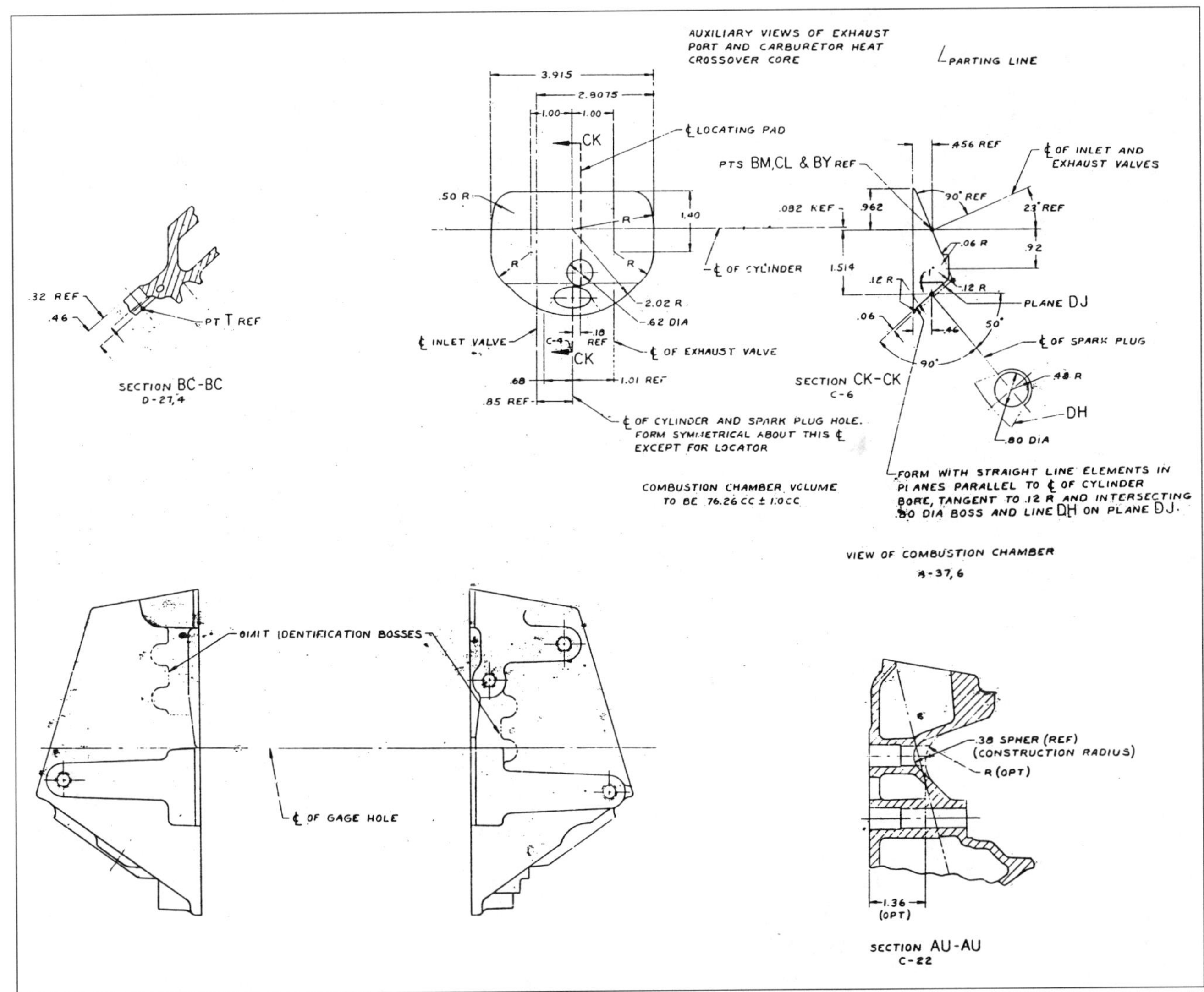

Fig. 5-10. *Casting details of head #3932441. Note omission of external identification bosses.*

Head #3946074$^{\Delta}$

Year	Model	Engine	Horsepower	Valve Size (in.) Intake/Exhaust	Combustion Chamber (cc.)	Notes
1971	Corvette	454	425 (LS6)	2.19/1.88	118.00	This aluminum cylinder head was a totally new design for the 1969 L88 Corvette. The head is similar to #3904392 . This cylinder head has a round exhaust port instead of the conventional high performance square port design. $^{\Delta}$This head was used in 1969.

see illustrations on next page

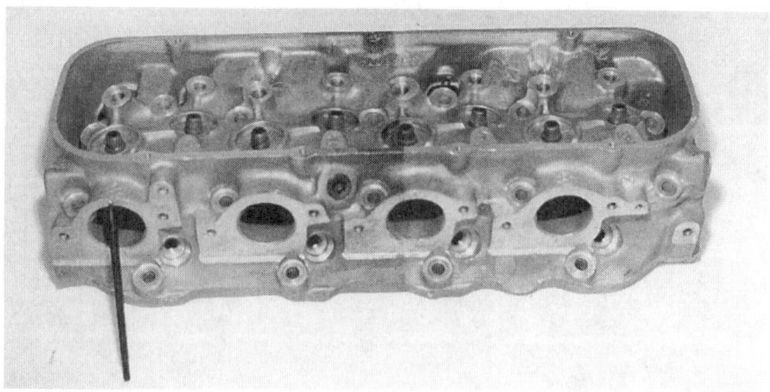

Fig. 5-11. ***Left***: *Casting number for head #3946074.* ***Right***: *Round exhaust ports.*

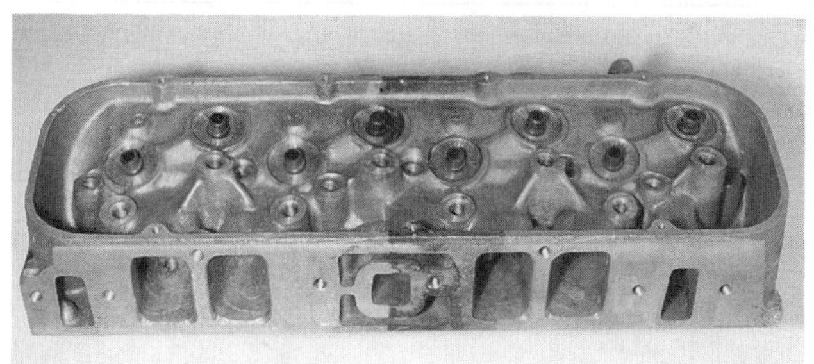

Fig. 5-12. ***Left***: *Intake ports for head #3946074.* ***Right***: *Valve side of head shows two extra tapped holes used on ZL1 applications.*

Fig. 5-13. ***Left***: *Detail of huge combustion chamber.* ***Right***: *End of aluminum head #3946074 shows that casting flash was ground off by Winters foundry.*

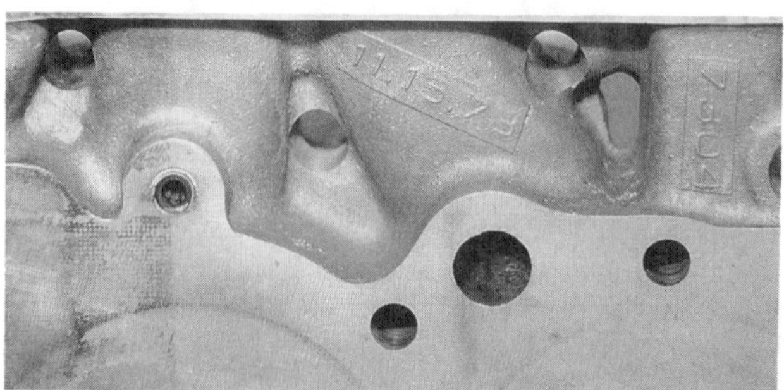

Fig. 5-14. ***Left***: *special coding from Winters foundry.* ***Right***: *casting date indicates that this #3946074 head was produced as a service/replacement part.*

Head #3947041[Δ]

Year	Model	Engine	Horsepower	Valve Size (in.) Intake/Exhaust	Combustion Chamber (cc.)	Notes
1970	Passenger	350	300	1.94/1.50	63.305	This cylinder head is identical with #3782461 (a 327 head used in 1965 and 1966) except for a redesigned combustion chamber, the addition of a temperature sending unit boss, and 3 accessory bolt holes added to the end of each head. This cylinder head was interchanged on some models with #3927186 and #3927187. Casting symbol: ◢ [Δ]This head was also used in 1969.
	Nova	350	300	1.94/1.50		
	Yenko Deuce	350	360	2.02/1.60		
	Chevelle	350	300	1.94/1.50		
	Monte Carlo	350	300	1.94/1.50		
	Camaro	350	300	1.94/1.50		
			360	2.02/1.60		
	Corvette	350	350	2.02/1.60	63.995	
			370	2.02/1.60	63.305	

Head #3951598

Year	Model	Engine	Horsepower	Valve Size (in.) Intake/Exhaust	Combustion Chamber (cc.)	Notes
1970	Passenger, Monte Carlo	400	265HP	1.94/1.60	76.0 (approx.)	This cylinder head was used on all 1970 400 engines in all applications. It was replaced with the #3973493 cylinder head in the 1971 model year.

Head #3964290

Year	Model	Engine	Horsepower	Valve Size (in.) Intake/Exhaust	Combustion Chamber (cc.)	Notes
1970	Passenger	454	345, 390	2.06/1.72	100.967	This cylinder head is identical with #3931063 (used on 396 and 427 engines in the 1969 model year) except that the spark plug seat was changed to the tapered, "peanut" type. It is possible, due to late model releases in 1970, that two cylinder heads could have close or matching casting dates and be tapped for different spark plug seats. Look closely at these heads. Casting symbol: Straight casting flashing
	Nova	402	350			
	Chevelle	402	330, 350			
		454	360			
	Monte Carlo	402	330			
		454	360			
	Camaro	402	350			
	Corvette	427	390			

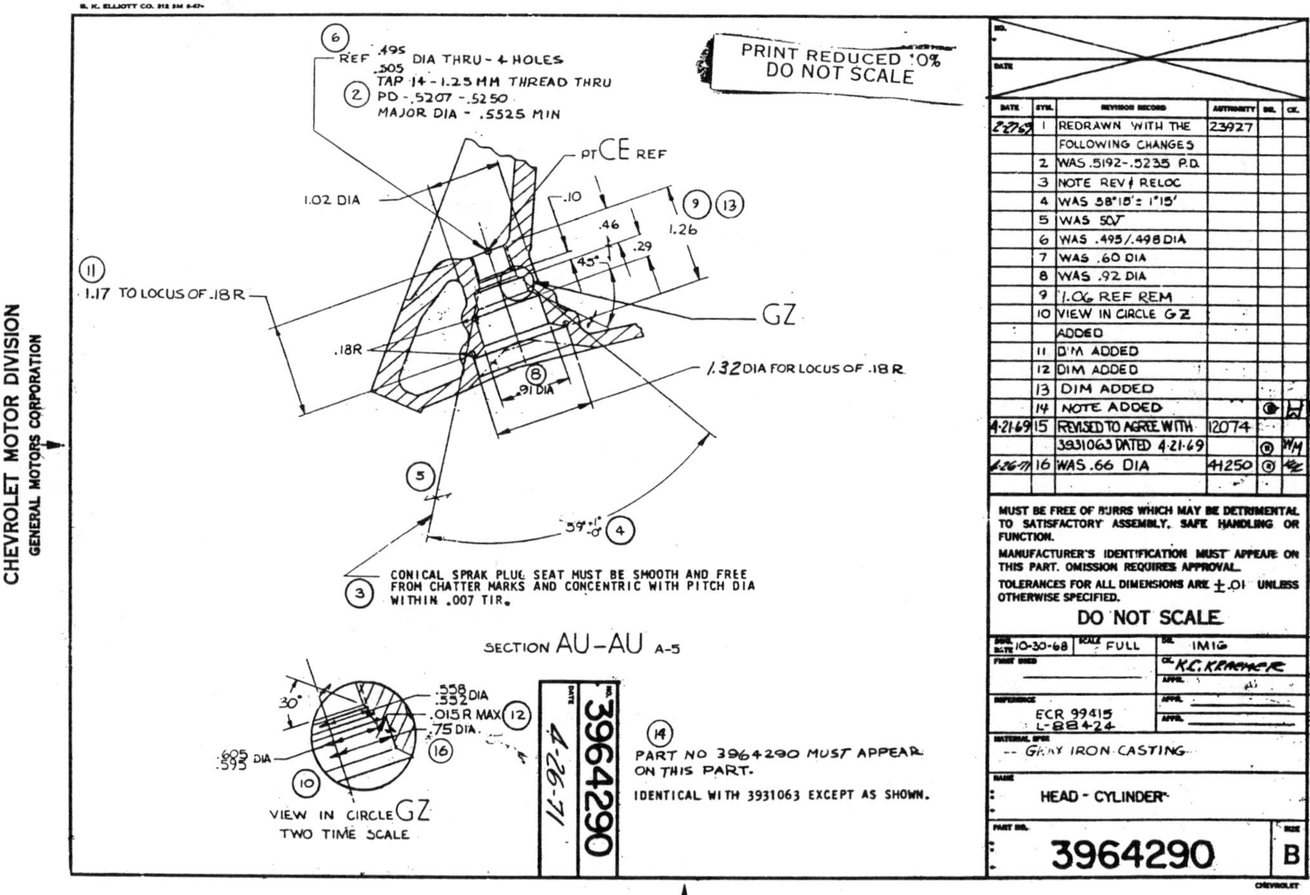

Fig. 5-15. Blueprint shows that #3964290 is identical with #3931063 except for new design tapered (conical) "peanut" type spark plug seat.

Head #3964291$^{\Delta}$

Year	Model	Engine	Horsepower	Valve Size (in.) Intake/Exhaust	Combustion Chamber (cc.)	Notes
1970	Nova	402	375	2.19/1.88	109.037	This cylinder head is identical with #3919840 (used from 1967 through 1969 on 396 and 427 engines) except that it has a tapered spark plug seat and an exhaust valve seat redesigned to accept the 1.88 exhaust valve. As with #3964290, #3964291 was produced with both "N" and "peanut" series type spark plug seats. After the 1970 model year, only the tapered seat remained. Also, this was the last closed chamber square port cast iron head produced. It was produced in both plug designs for service replacement. Casting symbol:
	Chevelle	402	375			
		454	450			
	Camaro	402	375			$^{\Delta}$This head was also used in 1969.

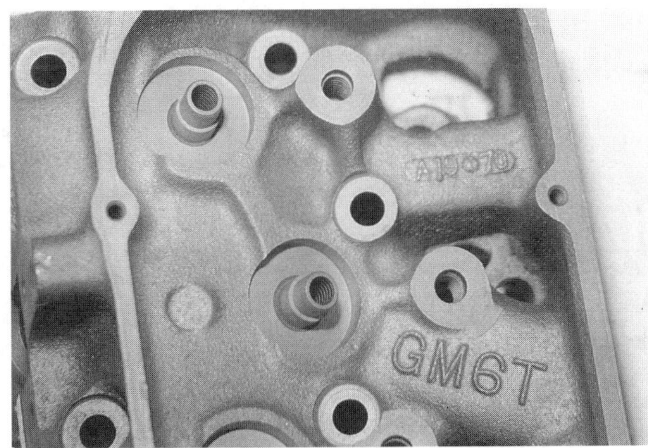

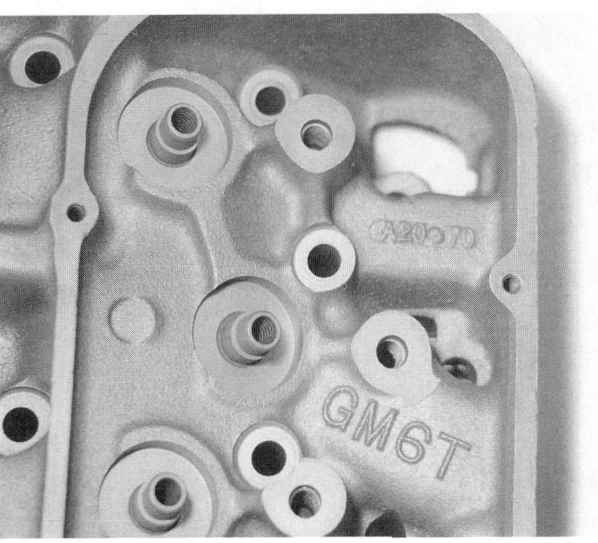

Fig. 5-16. Two #3964291 heads. Note that casting number on bottom head (left) is missing final "1". Casting dates for each of A19 70 and A20 70 (right) verify that heads were produced one day apart and do match.

CHAPTER 5

Head #3973414

Year	Model	Engine	Horsepower	Valve Size (in.) Intake/Exhaust	Combustion Chamber (cc.)	Notes
1970	Camaro Z28	350	360	2.02/1.60	63.995	This cylinder head is identical with the #3927187 cylinder head except that it has factory-installed screw-in studs and pushrod guide plates. This cylinder head was only produced with a 2.02/1.60 valve configuration. This head was an LT1 cylinder head only on Z28s and Corvettes. Casting symbol:
	Corvette	350	370			
	Yenko Deuce	350	360			

Head #3973487

Year	Model	Engine	Horsepower	Valve Size (in.) Intake/Exhaust	Combustion Chamber (cc.)	Notes
1971	Passenger	350	245, 270	1.94/1.50	75.47	This cylinder head is similar to #3932441. It is identical with #3782461 except for a redesigned combustion chamber, the addition of a temperature sending unit boss, 3 accessory bolt holes added to the end of the head, a tapered spark plug seat, and a different external identification symbol cast near the internal casting number. The 330HP versions of this head, which were installed on the LT1 Camaros and Corvettes, had several other changes made to the head. The primary difference was the addition of the 2.02/1.60 valves. Both valves were swirl polished and had chrome valve stems. The head also had factory-installed screw-in-studs and pushrod guideplates. The Passenger police and taxi 245 and 270HP engines used a 2.02/1.60 valve, but did not have swirl polished valves. Casting symbol:
	Nova	350	245, 270			
	Chevelle	350	245, 270			
	Monte Carlo	350	245, 270			
	Camaro	350	245, 270			
			330	2.02/1.60		
	Corvette	350	270	1.94/1.50		
			330	2.02/1.60		
1972	Passenger	350	165	1.94/1.50		
	Nova	350	165, 175			
	Chevelle	350	165, 175			
	Monte Carlo	350	165, 175			
	Camaro	350	165, 175			
			255*	2.02/1.60		
	Corvette	350	175	1.94/1.50		
			255	2.02/1.60		
*Unverified						

see illustration on following page

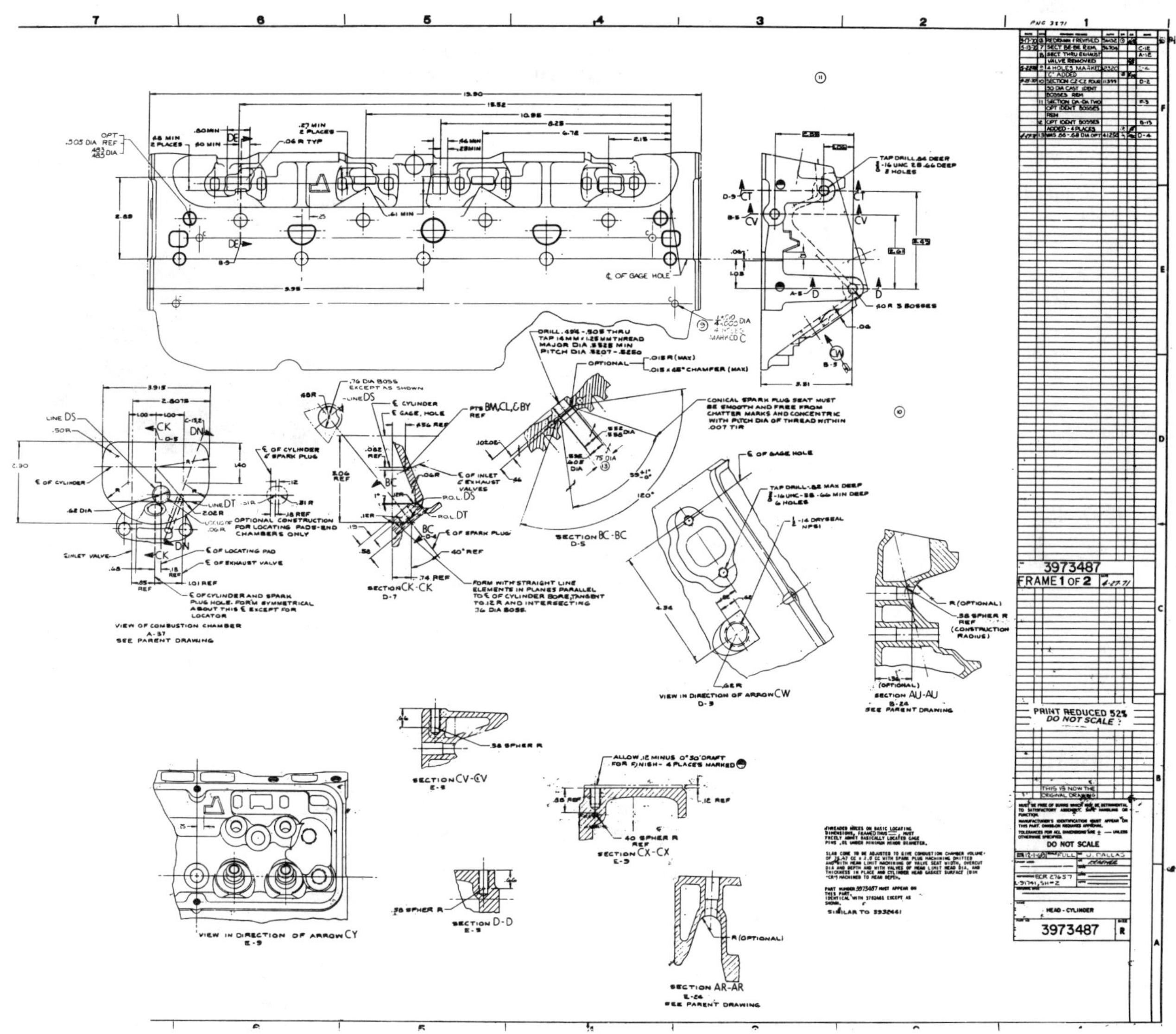

Fig. 5-17. Blueprint for head #3973487 illustrates correct external identification symbol.

Head #3973487X

Year	Model	Engine	Horsepower	Valve Size (in.) Intake/Exhaust	Combustion Chamber (cc.)	Notes
1972	Passenger	350	165	1.94/1.50	75.47	This cylinder head is identical to #3973487 except it was only used in late 1972 model year cars. It is unclear why there seems to be an overlap in usage with #3998993. #3998993 was released about January 4, 1972. Casting symbol:
	Nova	350	165, 175			
	Chevelle	350	165, 175			
	Monte Carlo	350	165, 175			
	Camaro	350	165, 175			
			255*	2.02/1.60		
	Corvette	350	175	1.94/1.50		
			255	2.02/1.60		
*Unverified						

Head #3973493

Year	Model	Engine	Horsepower	Valve Size (in.) Intake/Exhaust	Combustion Chamber (cc.)	Notes
1971	Passenger	400	255	1.94/1.60	76.0 (approx.)	This cylinder head was used on all 1971 400 engines in all applications. It was replaced with the #3998997 cylinder head for the 1972 model year.

Head #3986316

Year	Model	Engine	Horsepower	Valve Size (in.) Intake/Exhaust	Combustion Chamber (cc.)	Notes
1971	Corvette, Camaro Z28	350	255	2.02/1.60	76.18	This cylinder head is identical with #3782461 except for the following changes: a redesigned combustion chamber, the addition of a temperature sending unit boss, a tapered spark plug seat, and factory-installed screw-in studs and pushrod guideplates. This cylinder head may have casting #3973487 and should be verified by combustion chamber volume. All #3896316 heads have 3 accessory bolt holes on each of the cylinder heads. Usage unverified. Casting symbol:

Head #3986339

Year	Model	Engine	Horsepower	Valve Size (in.) Intake/Exhaust	Combustion Chamber (cc.)	Notes
1971	Passenger	350	270 (low compression)	1.72/1.50	74.56	This head is identical with #3884520 except for the following changes: a redesigned combustion chamber, a temperature sending unit boss, and all heads have a tapered spark plug seat. The exterior identification symbol is also different, and optional symbols may appear on the cylinder head. Casting symbol:
	Nova	307	200			
	Chevelle	307	200			
	Camaro	307	200			

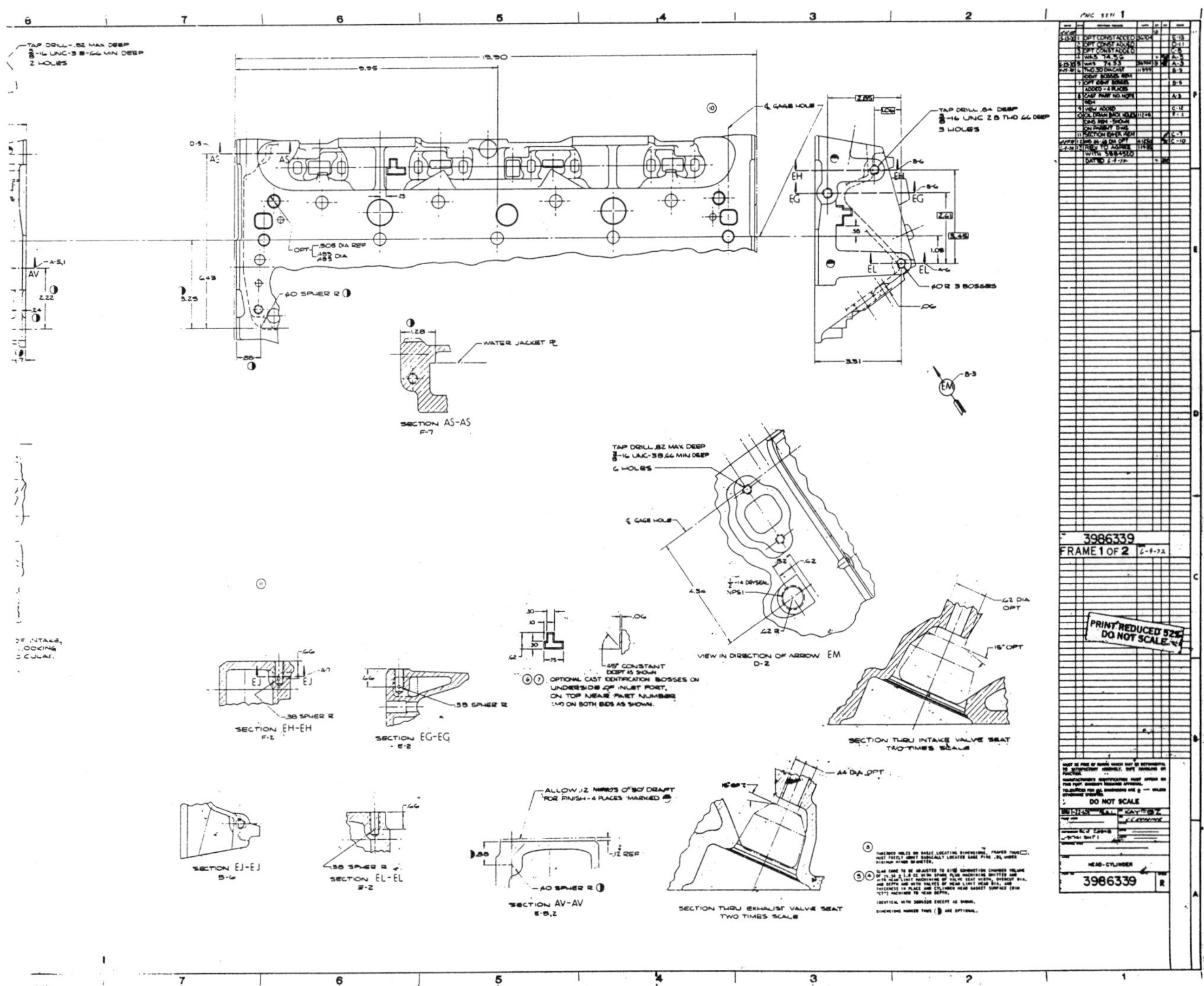

Fig. 5-18. Blueprint for head #3986339 illustrates correct external identification symbol.

CHAPTER 5

Head #3993820

Year	Model	Engine	Horsepower	Valve Size (in.) Intake/Exhaust	Combustion Chamber (cc.)	Notes
1971	Passenger	402	300	2.06/1.72	113.060	This cylinder head is identical with #3931063 except for the following differences: the cylinder head is now an open-chamber design, the intake and exhaust valve seats are redesigned and the spark plug seat is now tapered. This is an oval port design manufactured in cast iron.
		454	365			
	Chevelle	402	300			
		454	365			
	Camaro	402	300			
	Corvette	454	365			

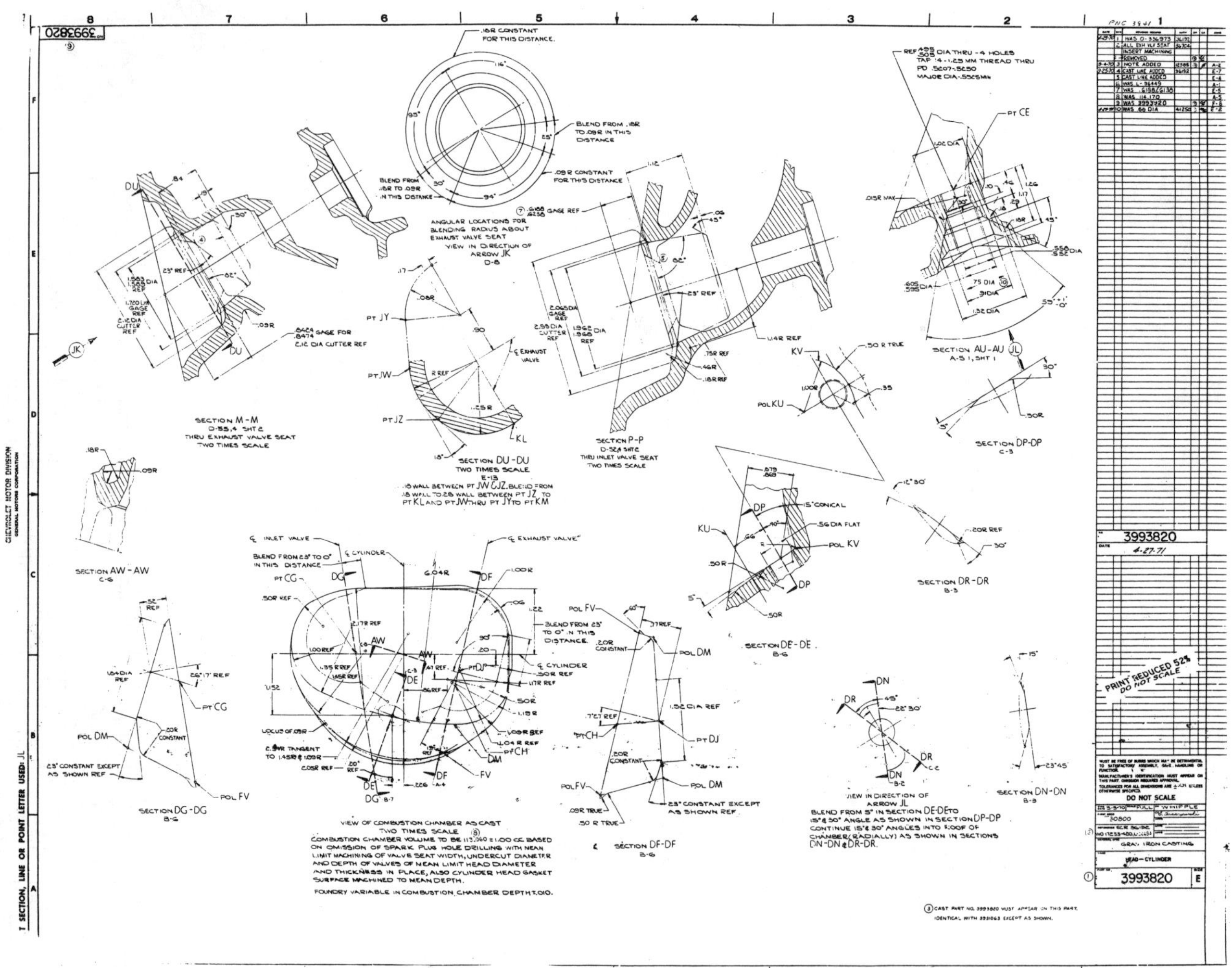

Fig. 5-19. Detail of #3993820 combustion chamber as cast.

Head #3994026

Year	Model	Engine	Horsepower	Valve Size (in.) Intake/Exhaust	Combustion Chamber (cc.)	Notes
1971	Chevelle	454	425	2.19/1.88	118.000	This is a cast iron square port design head. This cylinder head had a tapered spark plug seat. It was the last Mark IV design square port head with an open-chamber configuration used in production cars.

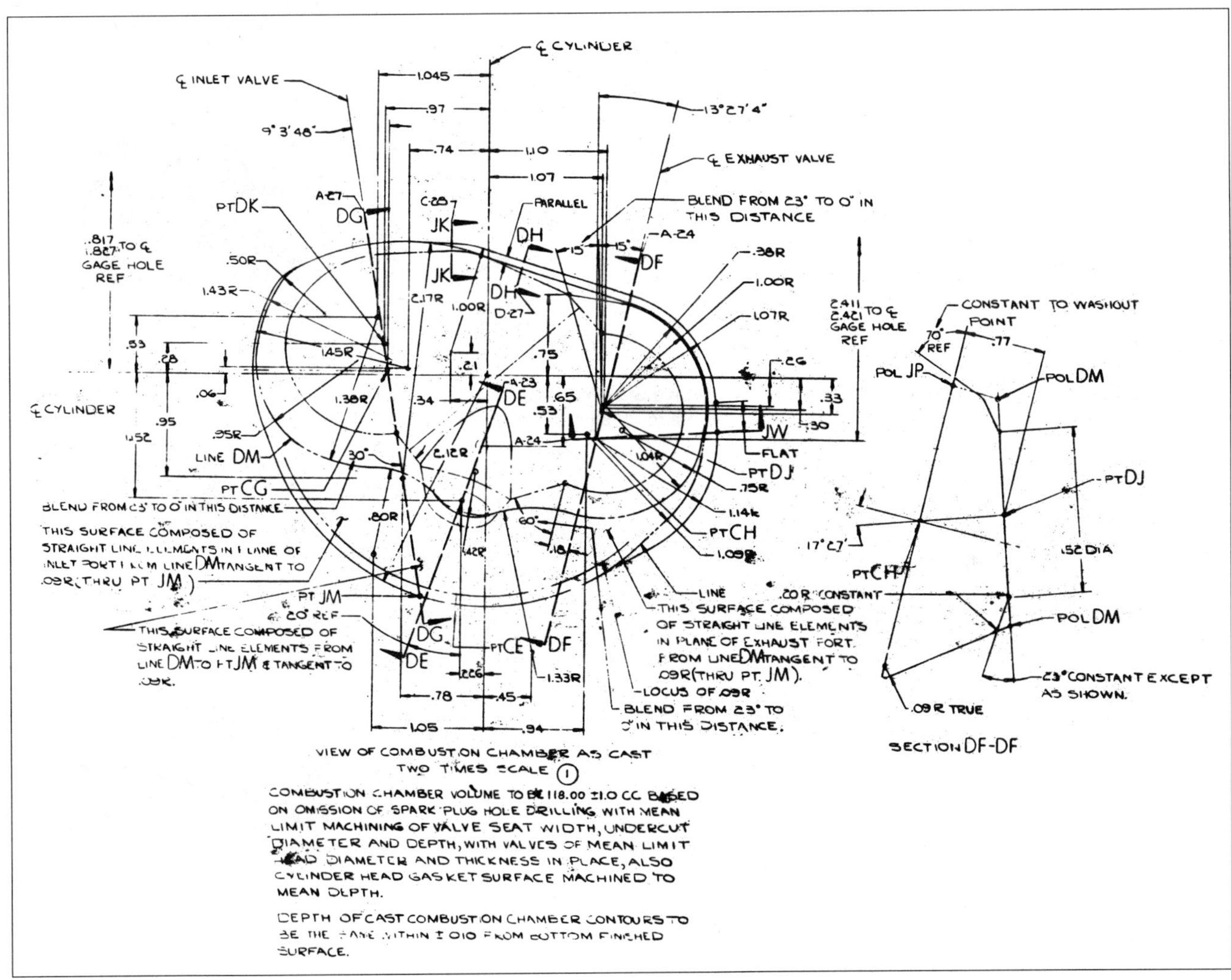

Fig. 5-20. Detail of #3994026 combustion chamber as cast.

Head #3998916

Year	Model	Engine	Horsepower	Valve Size (in.) Intake/Exhaust	Combustion Chamber (cc.)	Notes
1972	Camaro Z28	350	255	2.02/1.60	76.18	This head is identical with #3998993 except that the combustion chamber is different and swirl polished 2.02/1.60 valves are installed. These heads have screw-in studs and push rod guideplates. Casting #3998993 may appear on this part. This head has a tapered spark plug seat. This head could only be used in this application. Usage unverified. Casting symbol:
	Corvette	350	255			

Head #3998991

Year	Model	Engine	Horsepower	Valve Size (in.) Intake/Exhaust	Combustion Chamber (cc.)	Notes
1972	Passenger	350	165 (low compression)	1.72/1.50	74.56	This cylinder head is similar to #3795896 except for a few differences. It has a tapered spark plug seat, the combustion chamber has been redesigned, and now there is a temperature sending unit boss on the head. This cylinder head is the first with hardened valve seats for unleaded fuel in the 1973 model year. Casting symbol:
	Nova	307	130			
	Chevelle	307	130			
	Camaro	307	130			

Head #3998993

Year	Model	Engine	Horsepower	Valve Size (in.) Intake/Exhaust	Combustion Chamber (cc.)	Notes
1972	Passenger	350	165	1.94/1.50	75.47	This cylinder head was introduced by mid-year 1972 (about January 4) and supposedly replaced the #3973487X cylinder head. It is unclear why this took place. The cylinder head was released in the 1973 model year with hardened valve seats for emissions compliance. It has the tapered spark plug seat and a temperature sending unit boss. Casting symbol:
	Nova	350	165, 175			
	Chevelle	350	165, 175			
	Monte Carlo	350	165, 175			
	Camaro	350	165, 175			
			255*	2.06/1.72		
	Corvette	350	175	1.94/1.50		
1973	Passenger	350	145, 175			
	Nova	307	115			
		350	145, 175			
	Chevelle	307	115			
		350	145, 175			
	Monte Carlo	350	145, 175			
	Camaro	307	115			
		350	145, 175			

*Unverified

Head #3998997

Year	Model	Engine	Horsepower	Valve Size (in.) Intake/Exhaust	Combustion Chamber (cc.)	Notes
1972	Passenger	400	170	1.94/1.60	76.0 (approx.)	This cylinder head was used on all 1972 and 1973 400 engines in all applications. It was replaced by #333882 in the 1974 model year.
1973	Passenger	400	150			

Head #3999241

Year	Model	Engine	Horsepower	Valve Size (in.) Intake/Exhaust	Combustion Chamber (cc.)	Notes
1972	Passenger	402	240	2.06/1.72	113.060	This cylinder head is similar to #3993820. It has a tapered spark plug seat and an oval port head. It was used through the 1974 model year.
		454	240 (Police), 270			
	Chevelle	402	240			
		454	270			
	Camaro	402	240			
	Corvette	454	270			

see illustration on following page

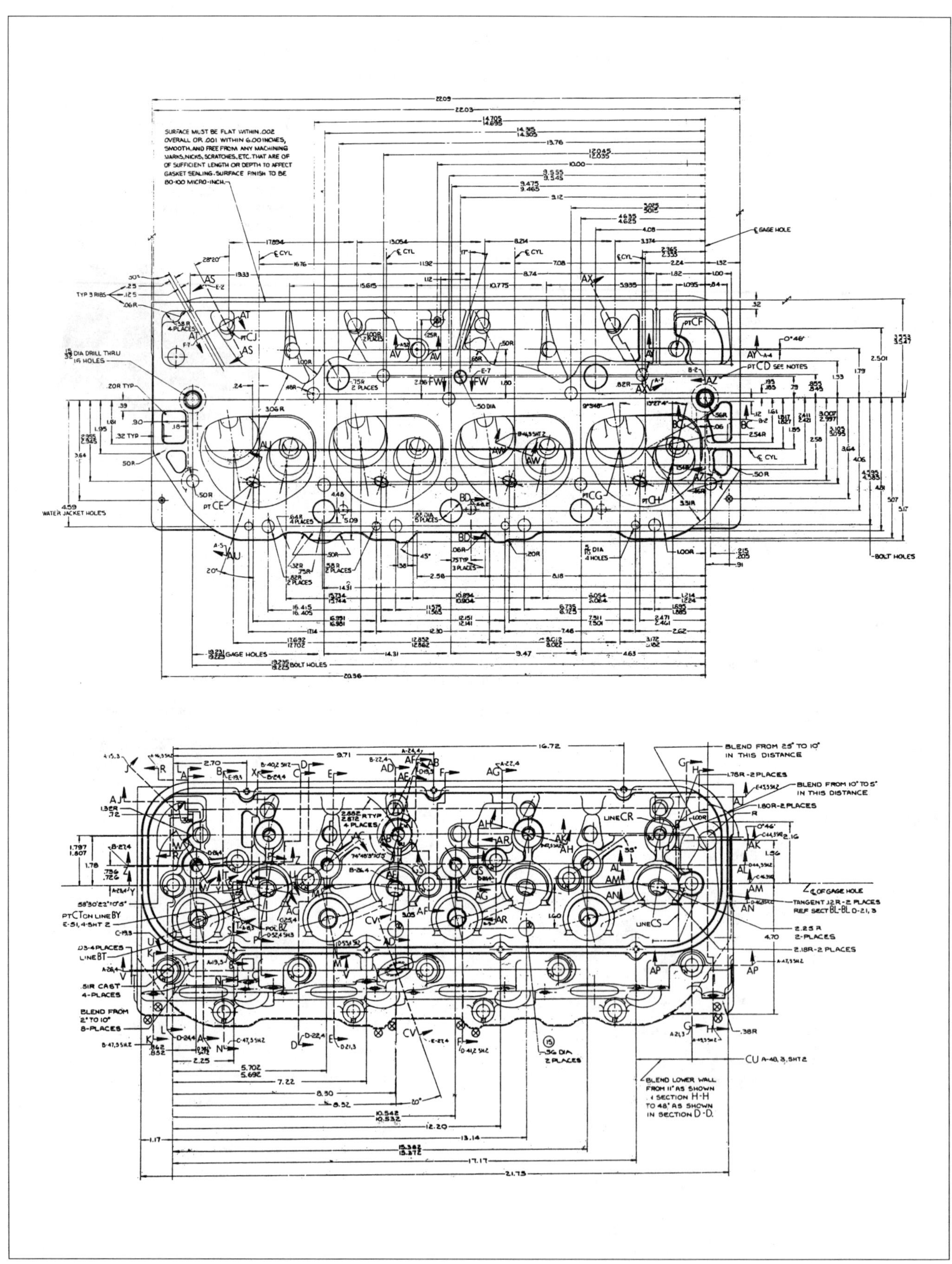

Fig. 5-21. Valve and rocker sides of head #3999241.

Head #330545

Year	Model	Engine	Horsepower	Valve Size (in.) Intake/Exhaust	Combustion Chamber (cc.)	Notes
1973	Camaro Z28	350	245	2.02/1.60	76.18	This head is identical with #3998993 except that valve seat diameters were increased to accept the 2.02/1.60 valves. Also the internal and external identification symbols have changed. The cylinder head has a tapered spark plug seat. It also has screw-in studs and push rod guideplates for high rpm usage. Casting symbol:
	Corvette	350	250			

Head #333881

Year	Model	Engine	Horsepower	Valve Size (in.) Intake/Exhaust	Combustion Chamber (cc.)	Notes
1974	Camaro Z28	350	245	2.02/1.60	76.18	This head is identical with #333882 except the valve spring seat dimension on the exhaust valves was increased to 0.84 to accept the 2.02/1.60 valves. Casting #333882 may appear on this part. The cylinder head has a tapered spark plug seat and a double heat riser passage. Casting symbol:
	Corvette	350	250			
1975	Corvette	350	205			

Head #333882

Year	Model	Engine	Horsepower	Valve Size (in.) Intake/Exhaust	Combustion Chamber (cc.)	Notes
1974–75	Passenger Nova Chevelle Monte Carlo	350	All	1.94/1.50	75.47	This head is similar to #3998993. The cylinder head has a tapered spark plug seat. If this cylinder head is found with 2.02/1.60 valves refer to #333881. This cylinder head has a double heat riser passage. Casting symbol:
	Camaro	350	All except Z28			
	Corvette	350	All except L82			
1974	Passenger Chevelle Monte Carlo	400	150, 180			
1975	Passenger Chevelle Monte Carlo	400	175			

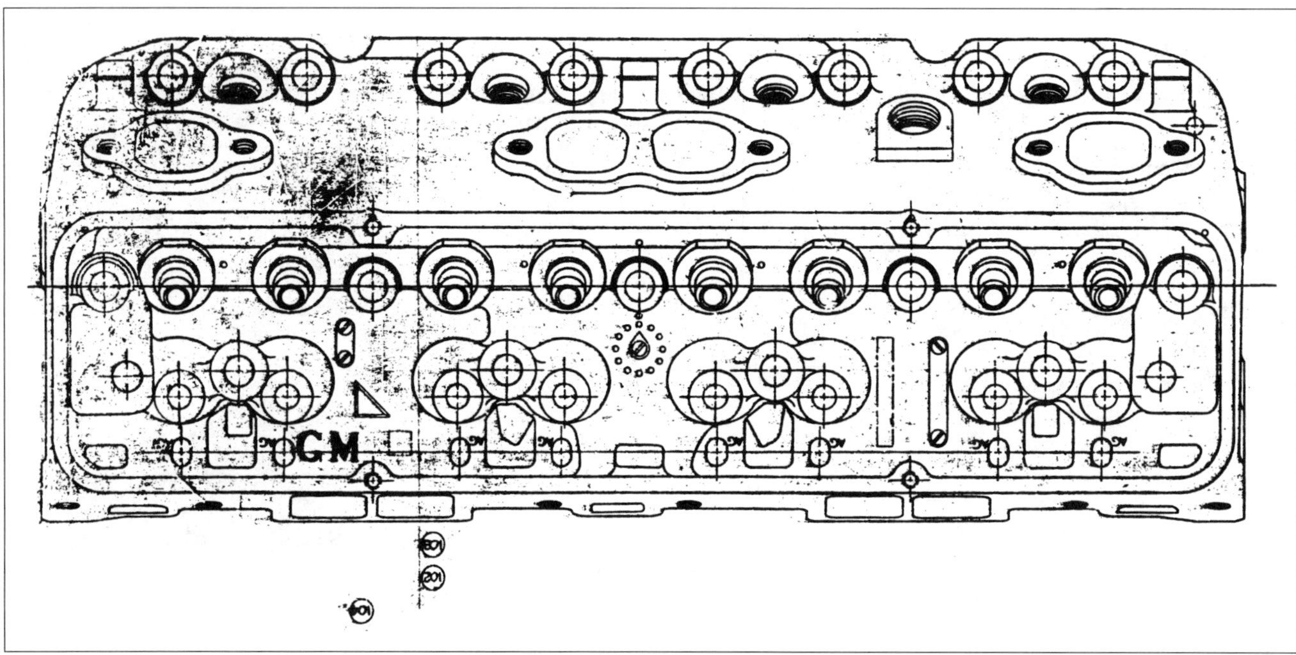

Fig. 5-22. Rocker side of #333882.

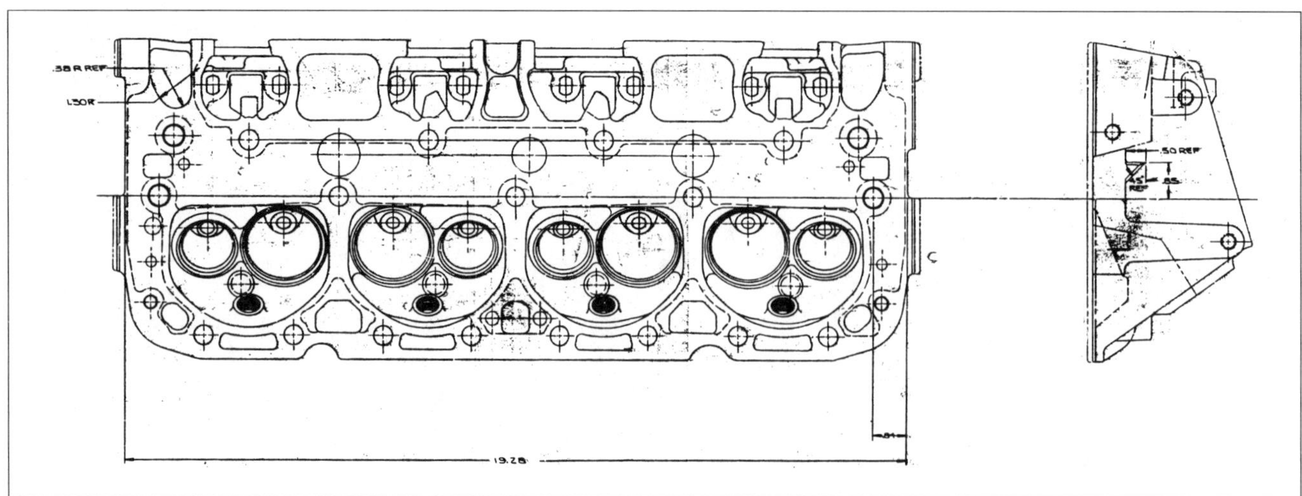

Fig. 5-23. Valve side and external identification symbol for #333882.

Head #336781

Year	Model	Engine	Horsepower	Valve Size (in.) Intake/Exhaust	Combustion Chamber (cc.)	Notes
1974	Passenger	454	235	2.06/1.72	113.06 (approx.)	This cylinder head was used for all 1974 and early 1975 454 applications. It was replaced mid-year 1975 by #346236.
	Chevelle	454	235			
	Corvette	454	270			
1975 (early)	Passenger	454	215			
	Chevelle	454	215			

Head #346236

Year	Model	Engine	Horsepower	Valve Size (in.) Intake/Exhaust	Combustion Chamber (cc.)	Notes
1975 (late)	Passenger	454	215	2.06/1.72	113.06 (approx.)	This was the second cylinder head used for the last 1975 454 applications. It replaced #336781 mid-year 1975.
	Chevelle	454	215			

Head #353049

Year	Model	Engine	Horsepower	Valve Size (in.) Intake/Exhaust	Combustion Chamber (cc.)	Notes
1973	Passenger	454	215	2.06/1.72	113.06 (approx.)	This head was used for all 1973 454 applications.
	Chevelle	454	215			
	Corvette	454	245			

Head #354434

Year	Model	Engine	Horsepower	Valve Size (in.) Intake/Exhaust	Combustion Chamber (cc.)	Notes
1975	Nova Monza	262	110	1.72/1.50	60.00 (approx.)	This head was a completely new casting for 1975. It incorporates the small valves from the #3998991 head, with the intake and exhaust ports remaining similar to the #333882 head.

Chapter 6

Connecting Rod Identification

1. Introduction

The connecting rod in an internal combustion engine is probably the most critical part. The rod transfers all the explosive power created in the combustion chamber to the crankshaft. Most catastrophic engine failures result from a connecting rod failure of some sort. In an effort to reduce rod failures and warranty claims, Chevrolet produced many variations of the original design 265 connecting rod over the years. The changes were mostly in the type of metal and/or manufacturing processes used.

The most common manufacturing processes used by the factory were shot-peening, magnafluxing, and heat-treating. In shot-peening the connecting rod is bombarded by cast iron shot or pellets. This increases the surface hardness of the rod and makes it more resistant to failure. In magnafluxing the rod is magnetized and fine iron dust is sprinkled over it. The iron dust is attracted by any imperfections or cracks, making them visible to the naked eye. In heat-treating the rod is heated to approximately 500 degrees for 10 or more hours. This allows the connecting rod to relax any torsional stress or twisting that occurred during manufacturing. Almost all of Chevrolet's high performance connecting rods were subjected to all three of these procedures.

There were a variety of connecting rod bolts used from 1970 through 1975. These bolts varied in length, type of thread, and torque settings. It is difficult to specify all the exact rod bolt usages. Fig. 6-2 correctly identifies all rod bolts from 1965 through 1968. The bolts from 1970 through 1975 were basically unchanged from previous years.

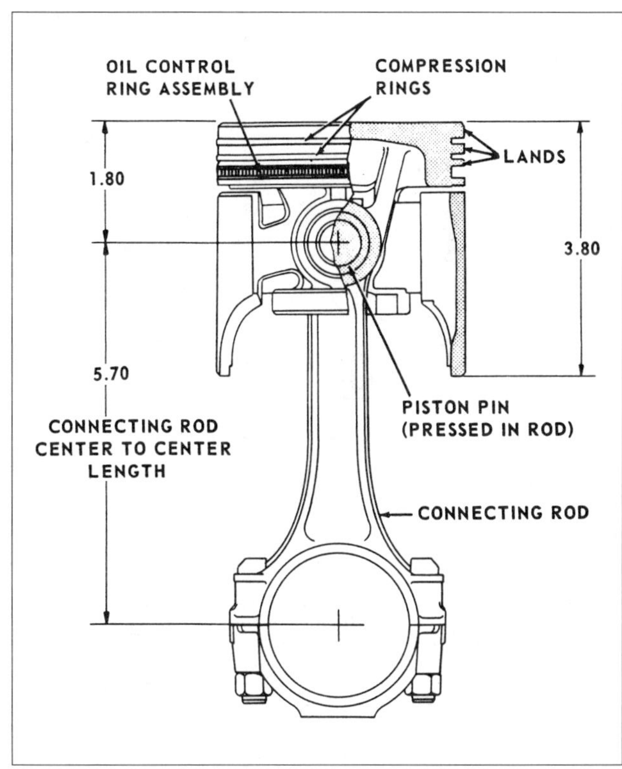

Fig. 6-1. *Typical 8-cylinder connecting rod, with piston installed.*

Because of the vast amount of small block engine combinations, rods are listed by release or design. Please note that the terms "first design," "second design," etc. do not refer to the order in which the rods were released, but are only a way to categorize the rods.

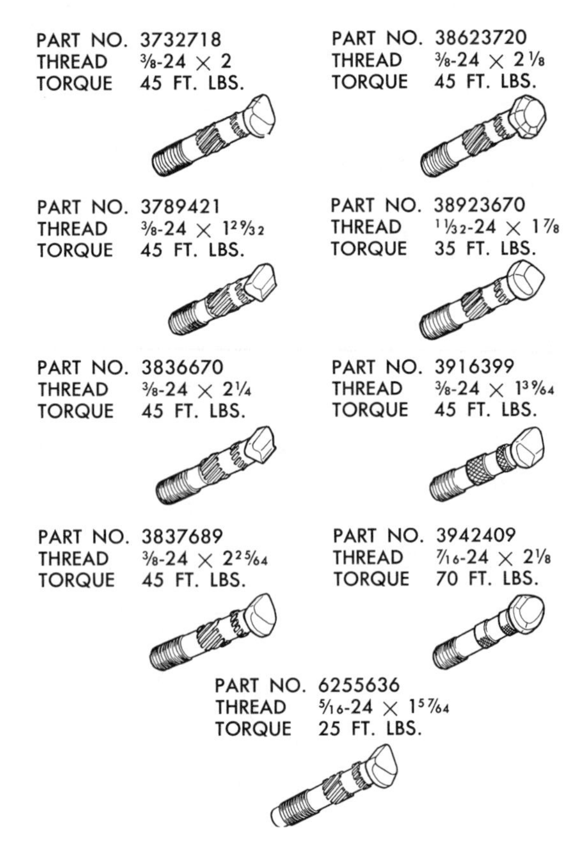

YEAR	APPLICATION	PART NO.
1968	Corvair	6255636
	4 & 6 cylinder engines (except 292)	3892670
	292 cu. in. engine	3789421
	307, 327, & 350 cu. in. engine	3916399
	366, 396 & 427 (except Corvette RPO L-88 2nd Design) cu. in. engine	3862720
	Corvette RPO L-88 2nd Design (427 cu. in., 430 H.P.)①	3942409
1967	Corvair	6255636
	4 & 6 cylinder engines (except 292)	3892670
	292 cu. in. engine	3789421
	283, 327 & 350 cu. in. engine	3892670
	366, 396 & 427 cu. in. engine	3862720
1963-1966	Corvair	6255636
	4 & 6 cylinder (except 292 engine & 1963 L-6 engine used in K Series Trucks)	3892670
	292 cu. in. engine	3789421
	L-6 engine used in 1963 K Series Trucks	3836670
	V-8 engines (except 348, 409, 366, 396 & 427)	3892670
	348 & 409 (except Special High Performance RPO Z-11)	3732718
	Special High Performance 409 engine (RPO Z-11) offered in 1963	3837689
	366, 396 & 427 cu. in. engine	3862720

①Also used in Heavy Duty M4 service engines.

Fig. 6-2. Connecting rod bolt and usage chart for 1965 through 1968 models. 1970 through 1975 usage is similar.

2. SMALL BLOCK CONNECTING RODS

All small block connecting rods, excluding the 400 engine, have a 5.70-inch center-to-center distance (the distance from the center of the piston pin hole to the center of the rod bearing hole). The 400 connecting rod has a 5.56-inch center-to-center distance.

All connecting rods produced after 1968 have a 2.10-inch rod journal diameter.

Connecting rods built until May of 1967 have V-groove holes in the rod cap, which were designed to shoot oil into the bore of the block. This design feature was discontinued because it was found to be unnecessary. This has been verified through *Chevrolet Service News*. See Fig. 6-3.

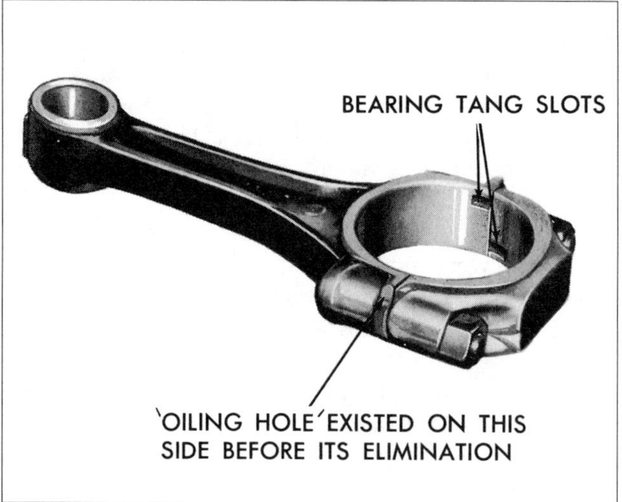

Fig. 6-3. Illustration from Chevrolet Service News, May 1967, shows new design rod without V-groove oiling holes.

First Design

- All 265 and 283 engines through 1967
- All small rod journal
- Standard forged steel construction
- Pressed-pin piston design
- No heat-treatment, magnafluxing, or shot-peening
- Small rod beam
- All had 11/32" diameter rod bolts
- A common rod

Second Design

- All 327 engines, excluding high performance applications
- Forged steel construction
- Pressed-pin piston design
- Rods produced from 1962 through 1967 had small journal diameter and 11/32" diameter rod bolts
- Rods produced in 1968 and 1969 had large journal diameter and 3/8" rod bolts
- Small rod beam

NOTE—
Approximately 6,000 327/275HP engines coupled with the Powerglide transmission, and built in early 1968 production, used the 1967 rod with a 11/32" rod bolt.

Third Design

- All 327 high performance applications (truck also)
- Forged steel construction (much stronger than the standard 327 rod)
- Pressed-pin piston design
- Heavier beam
- Journal sizes are the same as the standard size
- The standard rod for Corvettes

Fourth Design

- All 302 engines
- Forged steel construction
- Shot-peened, heat treated and magnafluxed
- Babbit dipped (a very expensive rod to manufacture)
- 1967 302 rod used the small 2.0" journal diameter
- 1968 and 1969 302 used the large 2.10" journal diameter
- 1967 302 rod used an 11/32" diameter rod bolt
- 1968 and 1969 302 rod used a 3/8" diameter rod bolt
- All 302 rod bolt P.S.I. (pounds per square inch) ratings were increased
- 1967 and early 1968 302 used a pressed-pin piston design
- Mid-year 1968, the design changed to a floating-pin piston design
- All fourth design rods are commonly called "pink rods." The name comes from the pink or purple paint used on them to identify the rods at the assembly plant

Fifth Design

- All 350 engines
- All 307 engines from 1968 through 1973
- Forged steel construction
- This rod used the standard 3/8" rod bolt
- Large rod journal diameter
- Pressed-pin piston design

Sixth Design

- All high-performance 350 engines (LT1)
- Forged steel construction
- Heat-treated, shot-peened and magnafluxed
- Originally introduced in 1970 as a pressed-pin design
- Large rod diameter journal and the high-rpm rod bolts used in the 302
- Expensive connecting rod

Seventh Design

- All 400 engines
- Drop forged steel construction
- A 2.10" rod journal diameter, but the 3.75" engine stroke, along with 2.65" main journal diameter made the rod a loner among other Chevrolet rods
- Standard 3/8" rod bolts
- A low performance rod and the main cause of engine failure

3. BIG BLOCK CONNECTING RODS

All Chevrolet big block connecting rods have a 6.135-inch center-to-center length (the distance from the center of the piston pin hole to the center of the rod bearing hole). This measurement is the same for all regardless of stroke length. Also, all rods have a 2.325-inch diameter rod journal end.

First Design

- All standard duty big block engines from 1965 through 1975:
  1965–70 396 standard
  1966–69 427 All except Special High Perf.
  1970–72 402 standard
  1970–75 454 All except Special High Perf.
- Forged steel construction
- Small 3/8" knurled-shank rod bolts. The raised cross-hatch pattern on the shank created a snug fit when the bearing cap was installed
- Pressed-pin design
- The basic weak link in most big block engines

Second Design

- All high performance applications from 1965 until 1972:
  1965–69 396
  1966–69 427
  1970–72 402
- Forged steel construction
- Immediately identified by a "double dimple bump": a single bump on each inside of the rod beam at the top of the rod (near the piston)
- Standard main beams and a stronger design at the crankshaft end of the rod
- Pressed-pin design on all except the Corvette 427/430 and 435HP engines
- Floating-pin design on Corvette 427/430 and 435HP
- 3/8" connecting rod bolts, with a higher P.S.I. rating
- Magnafluxed, heat treated

Third Design

- These rods were installed in the 454/465HP LS7 crate engines. They were also installed in:
  1969 Corvette L88 427/430HP
  1969 Corvette ZL1 427/430HP
  1969 Camaro ZL1 427/430HP
- Forged steel construction
- The same as the second design except it uses 7/16" rod bolts with *ground* shanks
- Heat-treated, shot-peened, and magnafluxed at the factory
- Floating-pin design
- Thicker main beams

Fourth Design

- 1970 Chevelle LS6 454/450HP rod
- The last big block rod design
- The same forging as the earlier L88 rods, but they had a 7/16" *knurled* shank
- This rod was not quite as strong as the L88 rod, but it is much heavier than the standard 3/8" rod

Chapter 7

Piston Identification

1. Introduction

This chapter covers the specific piston usage in all Chevrolet engines from 1970 through 1975. I have shown all popular piston shapes, but please note that piston designs changed slightly from model year to model year. The drawings indicate the *general* design of the piston, not the *final* design. However, with the description and pertinent information regarding each piston, you should be able to make a judgement call as to the originality of the piston and/or engine.

This information should be useful at the beginning of the engine restoration process. There has never been one source to which a restorer can turn to verify what piston was used to build a particular engine. Many engine rebuilders usually refer to aftermarket catalogs to supply pistons. This is fine, except that many of the pistons necessary to correctly rebuild an engine are no longer available. Although the final decision is up to the owner of the car, the information in this chapter will allow the restorer a choice in piston selection.

The piston charts are arranged in chronological order by model year. Under each year are the specific piston applications. The charts begin with each car Model in which that piston was used. Next is the Engine/Horsepower application. Many pistons were used in a variety of engines. All engines that use the piston will be listed together, beginning with the smallest V-8 engine.

The next listings are general Piston Characteristics, to further aid identification, the type of Material that was used to manufacture the piston, and the skirt type, which is the design of the piston skirt. Most pistons will be of the "slipper" design.

The Compression Ring and Oil Ring Groove Depths/Diameters are listed next. These dimensions were kept to a very close tolerance during manufacturing and should provide an accurate way of measuring and correctly identifying a piston.

The Piston Pin Type refers to the design of the piston pin. Almost all piston pins used a pressed fit. Piston Pin Offset refers to the offset of the piston pin relative to the center of piston casting. Most cast pistons will show some type of offset, while high performance forged aluminum pistons will not.

The final listing, piston Weight, will allow you to correctly identify a specific piston by weight alone if you have access to a scale. This weight figure will also give you a good idea as to the original reciprocating weight of the engine assembly as it was originally built by Chevrolet.

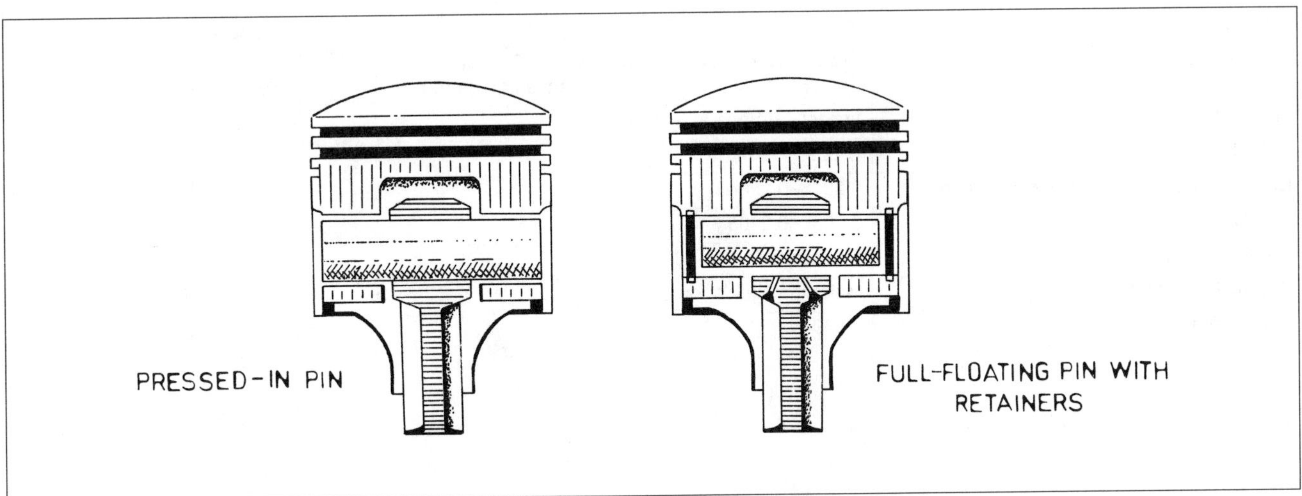

Fig. 7-1. *Pressed fit piston pin (left) compared to full-floating pin with retainers (right). Floating pin used only on 1969 302/290HP Z/28 and 427/430HP L88 and ZL1.*

2. 1970 PISTONS

Model	Nova Chevelle Camaro
Engine	307/200HP
Piston Characteristics	Flat head with reliefs for valve clearance
Material	Cast alloy aluminum
Skirt Type	Slipper
Compression Ring Groove Depth (in.)	0.2113–0.2178
Oil Ring Groove Depth (in.)	0.2053–0.2118
Piston Pin Type	Pressed fit
Piston Pin Offset	Major thrust side 0.055–0.065
Weight (oz.)	22.00

Model	Passenger car Nova Chevelle Camaro Corvette Monte Carlo
Engine	350/250, 300HP
Piston Characteristics	Flat head with reliefs for valve clearance
Material	Cast alloy aluminum
Skirt Type	Slipper
Compression Ring Groove Depth (in.)	0.2218–0.2284
Oil Ring Groove Depth (in.)	0.2038–0.2103
Piston Pin Type	Pressed fit
Piston Pin Offset	Major thrust side, 0.055–0.065
Weight (oz.)	25.76

Model	Corvette
Engine	350/350HP
Piston Characteristics	Domed head used only on 350/350HP engines. Piston has reliefs for valve clearance at high rpm
Material	Impact extruded alloy aluminum
Skirt Type	Slipper
Compression Ring Groove Depth (in.)	0.2218–0.2284
Oil Ring Groove Depth (in.)	0.2038–0.2103
Piston Pin Type	Pressed fit
Piston Pin Offset	Major thrust side, on center
Weight (oz.)	20.00

Model	Corvette Camaro
Engine	350/360HP (Camaro) 350/370HP (Corvette)
Piston Characteristics	Domed head used only on 360HP/370HP engines. Piston has reliefs for valve clearance at high rpm
Material	Impact extruded alloy aluminum
Skirt Type	Slipper
Compression Ring Groove Depth (in.)	0.2218–0.2284
Oil Ring Groove Depth (in.)	0.2038–0.2103
Piston Pin Type	Pressed fit
Piston Pin Offset	Major thrust side, on center
Weight (oz.)	20.41

Model	Passenger car Nova Chevelle Camaro Corvette
Engine	400/265HP
Piston Characteristics	Sump head for valve clearance
Material	Cast alloy aluminum
Skirt Type	Slipper
Compression Ring Groove Depth (in.)	0.2328–0.2393
Oil Ring Groove Depth (in.)	0.2183–0.2248
Piston Pin Type	Pressed fit
Piston Pin Offset	Major thrust side, 0.055–0.065
Weight (oz.)	22.59

Model	Nova Chevelle Camaro Monte Carlo
Engine	402/330HP (Chevelle, Monte Carlo) 402/350HP (Nova, Chevelle, Camaro)
Piston Characteristics	Domed head with reliefs for valve clearance
Material	Cast alloy aluminum
Skirt Type	Slipper
Compression Ring Groove Depth (in.)	0.2328–0.2392
Oil Ring Groove Depth (in.)	0.2183–0.2247
Piston Pin Type	Pressed fit
Piston Pin Offset	Major thrust side 0.055–0.065
Weight (oz.)	24.93

Model	Nova Chevelle Camaro
Engine	402/375HP
Piston Characteristics	Domed head used only in this application. Piston has reliefs for valve clearance
Material	Impact extruded alloy aluminum
Skirt Type	Slipper
Compression Ring Groove Depth (in.)	0.2278–0.2343
Oil Ring Groove Depth (in.)	0.2128–0.2143
Piston Pin Type	Pressed fit
Piston Pin Offset	Major thrust side, on center
Weight (oz.)	23.16

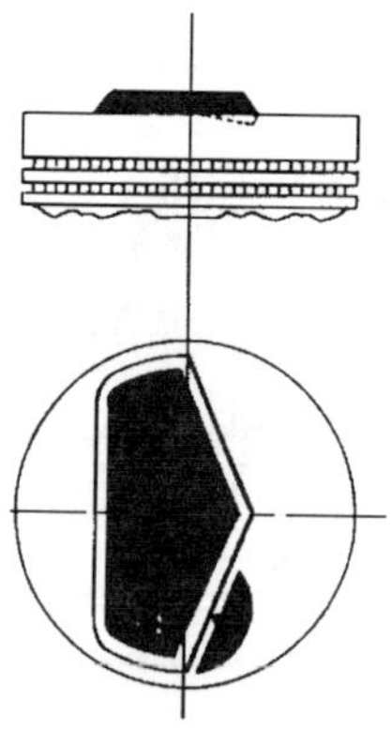

Model	Passenger car Chevelle Corvette Monte Carlo
Engine	454/345HP (Passenger car) 454/360HP (Chevelle, Monte Carlo) 454/390HP (Passenger car, Corvette)
Piston Characteristics	Domed head used only in this application. Piston has reliefs for valve clearance
Material	Cast alloy aluminum
Skirt Type	Slipper
Compression Ring Groove Depth (in.)	0.2348–0.2412
Oil Ring Groove Depth (in.)	0.2183–0.2247
Piston Pin Type	Pressed fit
Piston Pin Offset	Major thrust side, 0.055–0.065
Weight (oz.)	25.12

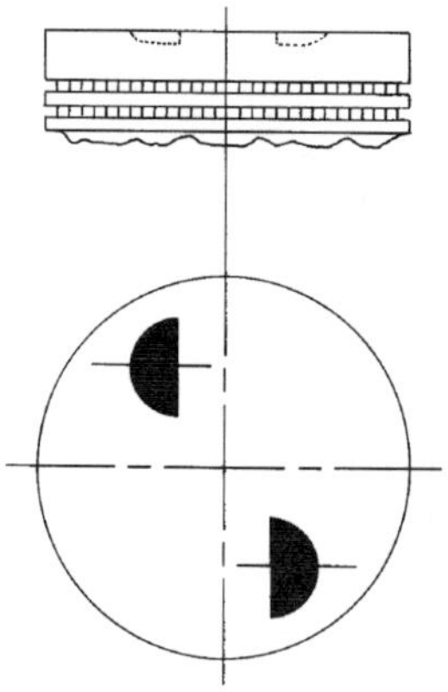

Model	Chevelle Monte Carlo (unverified)
Engine	454/450HP
Piston Characteristics	Domed head used only in this application. Piston has reliefs for valve clearance. Similar to 402/375HP piston
Material	Impact extruded alloy aluminum
Skirt Type	Slipper
Compression Ring Groove Depth (in.)	0.2373–0.2437
Oil Ring Groove Depth (in.)	0.2133–0.2197
Piston Pin Type	Pressed fit
Piston Pin Offset	Major thrust side, on center
Weight (oz.)	29.12

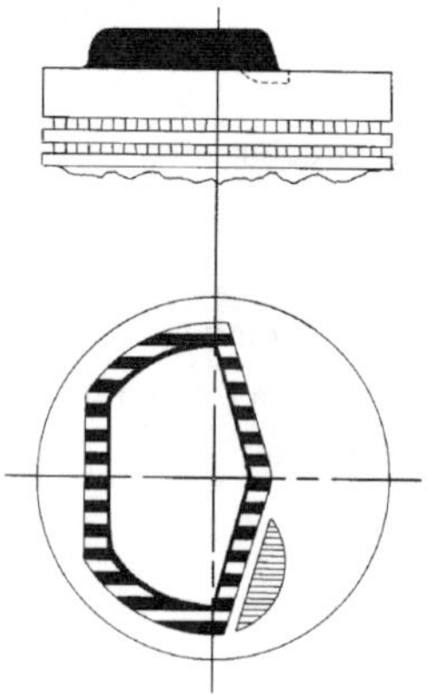

3. 1971 PISTONS

Model	Nova Chevelle Camaro
Engine	307/200HP
Piston Characteristics	Flat head with reliefs for valve clearance
Material	Cast alloy aluminum
Skirt Type	Slipper
Compression Ring Groove Diameter (in.)	3.442–3.452
Oil Ring Groove Diameter (in.)	3.454–3.464
Piston Pin Type	Pressed fit
Piston Pin Offset	Major thrust side 0.055–0.065
Weight (oz.)	22.00

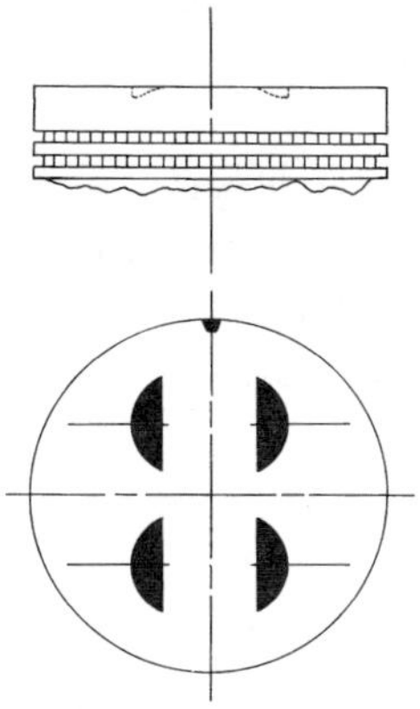

Model	Passenger car Nova Chevelle Camaro Corvette Monte Carlo
Engine	350/245HP (All except Corvette) 350/270HP (All)
Piston Characteristics	Sump head for valve clearance
Material	Cast alloy aluminum
Skirt Type	Slipper
Compression Ring Groove Diameter (in.)	3.546–3.556
Oil Ring Groove Diameter (in.)	3.582–3.592
Piston Pin Type	Pressed fit
Piston Pin Offset	Major thrust side, 0.055–0.065
Weight (oz.)	21.50

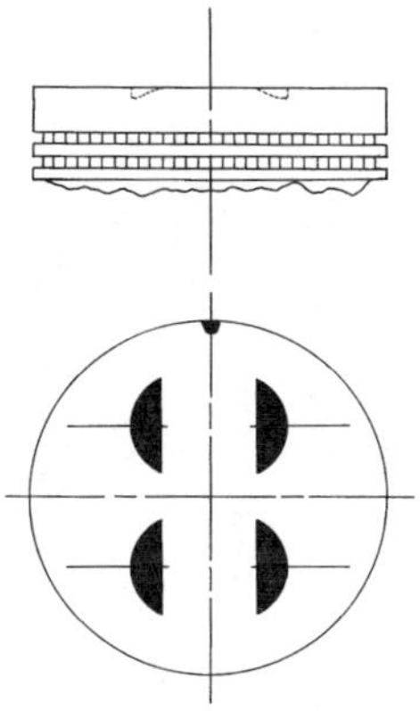

Model	Corvette Camaro
Engine	350/330HP
Piston Characteristics	Flat head used only on 350/330HP engines. Piston has notch in top for valve clearance at high rpm
Material	Impact extruded alloy aluminum
Skirt Type	Slipper
Compression Ring Groove Diameter (in.)	3.546–3.556
Oil Ring Groove Diameter (in.)	3.582–3.592
Piston Pin Type	Pressed fit
Piston Pin Offset	Major thrust side, on center
Weight (oz.)	25.68

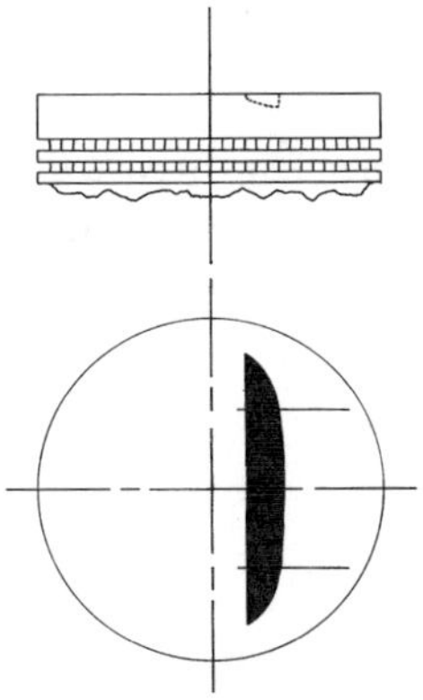

Model	Passenger car
Engine	400/255HP
Piston Characteristics	Sump head for valve clearance
Material	Cast alloy aluminum
Skirt Type	Slipper
Compression Ring Groove Diameter (in.)	3.649–3.659
Oil Ring Groove Diameter (in.)	3.678–3.688
Piston Pin Type	Pressed fit
Piston Pin Offset	Major thrust side, 0.055–0.065
Weight (oz.)	22.88

Model	Passenger car Chevelle Camaro Monte Carlo
Engine	402/300HP
Piston Characteristics	Domed head with reliefs for valve clearance
Material	Cast alloy aluminum
Skirt Type	Slipper
Compression Ring Groove Diameter (in.)	3.649–3.659
Oil Ring Groove Diameter (in.)	3.678–3.688
Piston Pin Type	Pressed fit
Piston Pin Offset	Major thrust side 0.055–0.065
Weight (oz.)	24.16

Model	Passenger car Chevelle Corvette Monte Carlo
Engine	454/365HP
Piston Characteristics	Flat head used only in this application. Piston has reliefs for valve clearance
Material	Cast alloy aluminum
Skirt Type	Slipper
Compression Ring Groove Diameter (in.)	3.770–3.780
Oil Ring Groove Diameter (in.)	3.803–3.813
Piston Pin Type	Pressed fit
Piston Pin Offset	Major thrust side, 0.055–0.065
Weight (oz.)	25.92

Model	Corvette Chevelle Monte Carlo (unverified) 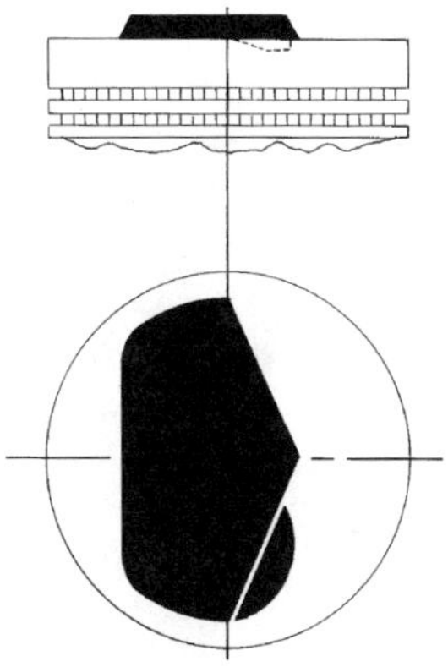
Engine	454/425HP
Piston Characteristics	Domed head used only in this application. Piston has reliefs for valve clearance
Material	Impact extruded alloy aluminum
Skirt Type	Slipper
Compression Ring Groove Diameter (in.)	3.765–3.775
Oil Ring Groove Diameter (in.)	3.816–3.820
Piston Pin Type	Pressed fit
Piston Pin Offset	Major thrust side, on center
Weight (oz.)	23.28

4. 1972 PISTONS

Model	Nova Chevelle Camaro 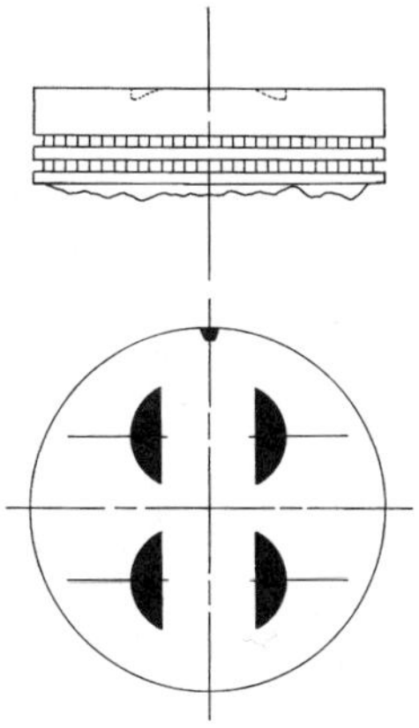
Engine	307/130HP
Piston Characteristics	Flat head with reliefs for valve clearance
Material	Cast alloy aluminum
Skirt Type	Slipper
Compression Ring Groove Diameter (in.)	3.442–3.452
Oil Ring Groove Diameter (in.)	3.454–3.464
Piston Pin Type	Pressed fit
Piston Pin Offset	Major thrust side 0.055–0.065
Weight (oz.)	22.00

Model	Passenger car Nova Chevelle Camaro Corvette Monte Carlo 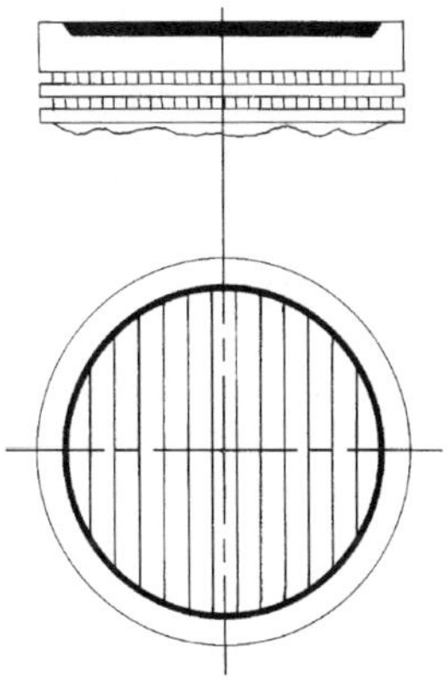
Engine	350/165HP (Passenger car, Nova, Chevelle, Camaro, Monte Carlo) 350/175HP (Nova, Chevelle, Camaro, Monte Carlo) 350/250HP (Corvette)
Piston Characteristics	Sump head for valve clearance
Material	Cast alloy aluminum
Skirt Type	Slipper
Compression Ring Groove Diameter (in.)	3.546–3.556
Oil Ring Groove Diameter (in.)	3.582–3.592
Piston Pin Type	Pressed fit
Piston Pin Offset	Major thrust side, 0.055–0.065
Weight (oz.)	21.17

Model	Corvette Camaro
Engine	350/255HP
Piston Characteristics	Flat head used only on 350/255HP engines. Piston has notch in top for valve clearance at high rpm
Material	Impact extruded alloy aluminum
Skirt Type	Slipper
Compression Ring Groove Diameter (in.)	3.546–3.556
Oil Ring Groove Diameter (in.)	3.582–3.592
Piston Pin Type	Pressed fit
Piston Pin Offset	Major thrust side, on center
Weight (oz.)	20.40

Model	Passenger car
Engine	400/170HP
Piston Characteristics	Sump head for valve clearance
Material	Cast alloy aluminum
Skirt Type	Slipper
Compression Ring Groove Diameter (in.)	3.649–3.659
Oil Ring Groove Diameter (in.)	3.678–3.688
Piston Pin Type	Pressed fit
Piston Pin Offset	Major thrust side, 0.055–0.065
Weight (oz.)	26.53

Model	Passenger car Chevelle Camaro Monte Carlo
Engine	402/240HP
Piston Characteristics	Domed head with reliefs for valve clearance
Material	Cast alloy aluminum
Skirt Type	Slipper
Compression Ring Groove Diameter (in.)	3.649–3.659
Oil Ring Groove Diameter (in.)	3.678–3.688
Piston Pin Type	Pressed fit
Piston Pin Offset	Major thrust side, 0.055–0.065
Weight (oz.)	29.70

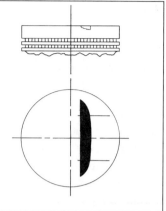

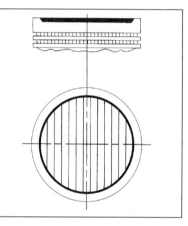

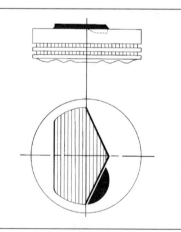

Model	Passenger car Chevelle Corvette Monte Carlo
Engine	454/240HP (Passenger car) 454/270HP (All)
Piston Characteristics	Flat head used only in this application. Piston has reliefs for valve clearance
Material	Cast alloy aluminum
Skirt Type	Slipper
Compression Ring Groove Diameter (in.)	3.770–3.780
Oil Ring Groove Diameter (in.)	3.803–3.813
Piston Pin Type	Pressed fit
Piston Pin Offset	Major thrust side, 0.055–0.065
Weight (oz.)	30.85

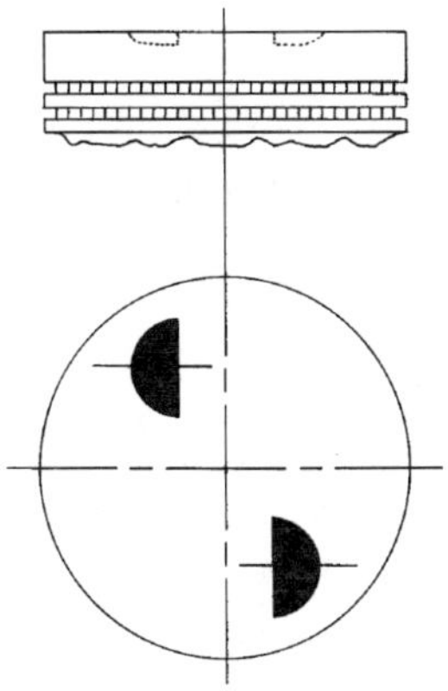

5. 1973 Pistons

Model	Nova Chevelle Camaro
Engine	307/115HP
Piston Characteristics	Flat head with reliefs for valve clearance
Material	Cast alloy aluminum
Skirt Type	Slipper
Compression Ring Groove Diameter (in.)	3.442–3.452
Oil Ring Groove Diameter (in.)	3.454–3.464
Piston Pin Type	Pressed fit
Piston Pin Offset	Major thrust side, 0.055–0.065
Weight (oz.)	22.00

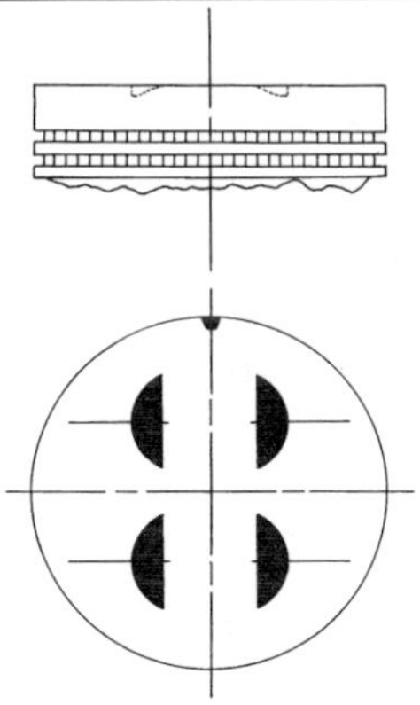

Model	Passenger car Nova Chevelle Camaro Corvette Monte Carlo
Engine	350/145HP (Passenger car, Nova, Chevelle, Camaro, Monte Carlo) 350/175HP (Passenger car, Nova, Chevelle, Camaro, Monte Carlo) 350/190HP (Corvette)
Piston Characteristics	Sump head for valve clearance
Material	Cast alloy aluminum
Skirt Type	Slipper
Compression Ring Groove Diameter (in.)	3.546–3.556
Oil Ring Groove Diameter (in.)	3.582–3.592
Piston Pin Type	Pressed fit
Piston Pin Offset	Major thrust side, 0.055–0.065
Weight (oz.)	21.17

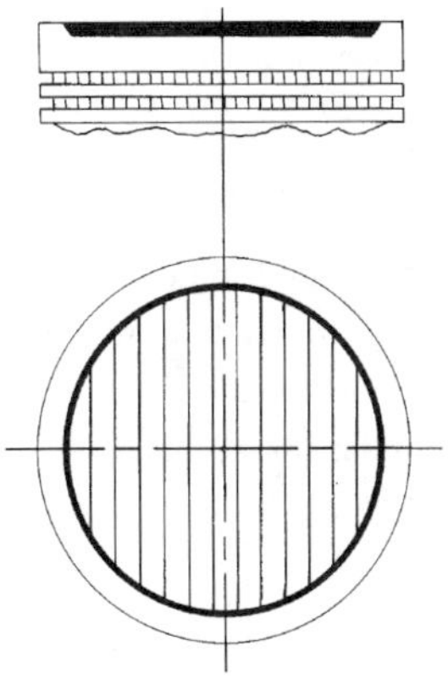

Model	Corvette Camaro
Engine	350/245HP (Camaro) 350/250HP (Corvette)
Piston Characteristics	Flat head used only on 245HP/250HP engines. Piston has notch in top for valve clearance at high rpm
Material	Impact extruded alloy aluminum
Skirt Type	Slipper
Compression Ring Groove Diameter (in.)	3.546–3.556
Oil Ring Groove Diameter (in.)	3.582–3.592
Piston Pin Type	Pressed fit
Piston Pin Offset	Major thrust side, on center
Weight (oz.)	20.40

Model	Passenger car
Engine	400/150HP
Piston Characteristics	Sump head that is notched for valve clearance
Material	Cast alloy aluminum
Skirt Type	Slipper
Compression Ring Groove Diameter (in.)	3.649–3.659
Oil Ring Groove Diameter (in.)	3.678–3.688
Piston Pin Type	Pressed fit
Piston Pin Offset	Major thrust side, 0.055–0.065
Weight (oz.)	26.53

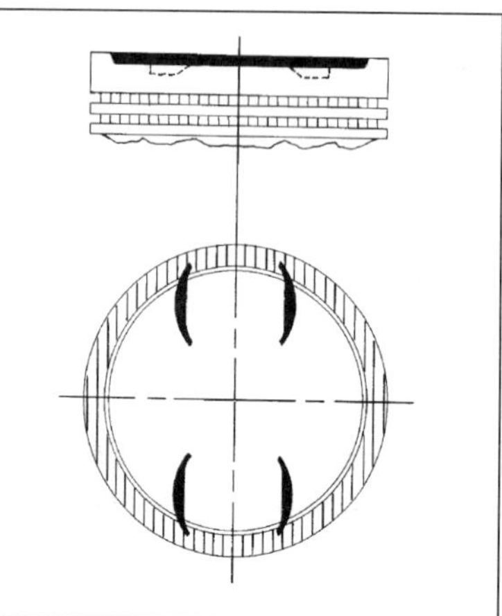

Model	Passenger car Chevelle Corvette Monte Carlo
Engine	454/215HP (All except Corvette) 454/245HP (Corvette)
Piston Characteristics	Flat head used only in this application. Piston has reliefs for valve clearance
Material	Cast alloy aluminum
Skirt Type	Slipper
Compression Ring Groove Diameter (in.)	3.770–3.780
Oil Ring Groove Diameter (in.)	3.803–3.813
Piston Pin Type	Pressed fit
Piston Pin Offset	Major thrust side, 0.055–0.065
Weight (oz.)	26.40

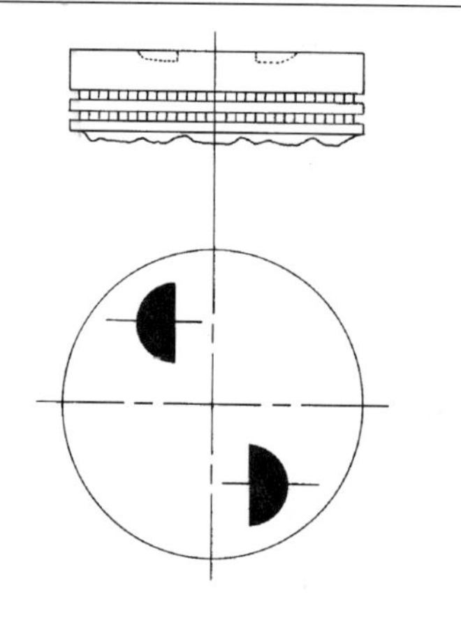

6. 1974 PISTONS

Model	Passenger car Nova Chevelle Camaro Corvette Monte Carlo
Engine	350/145HP (All except Corvette) 350/160HP (All except Corvette) 350/185HP (Nova, Camaro) 350/195HP (Corvette)
Piston Characteristics	Sump head for valve clearance
Material	Cast alloy aluminum
Skirt Type	Slipper
Compression Ring Groove Diameter (in.)	3.546–3.556
Oil Ring Groove Diameter (in.)	3.582–3.592
Piston Pin Type	Pressed fit
Piston Pin Offset	Major thrust side, 0.055–0.065
Weight (oz.)	26.02

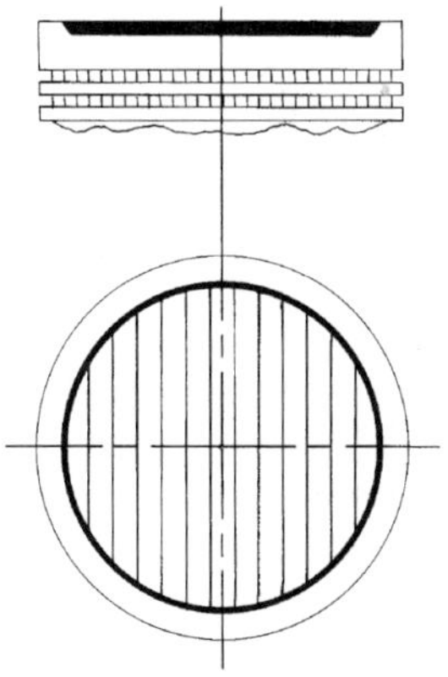

Model	Corvette Camaro
Engine	350/245HP (Camaro) 350/250HP (Corvette)
Piston Characteristics	Flat head used only on 245HP/250HP engines. Piston has notch in top for valve clearance at high rpm
Material	Impact extruded alloy aluminum
Skirt Type	Slipper
Compression Ring Groove Diameter (in.)	3.546–3.556
Oil Ring Groove Diameter (in.)	3.582–3.592
Piston Pin Type	Pressed fit
Piston Pin Offset	Major thrust side, on center
Weight (oz.)	26.08

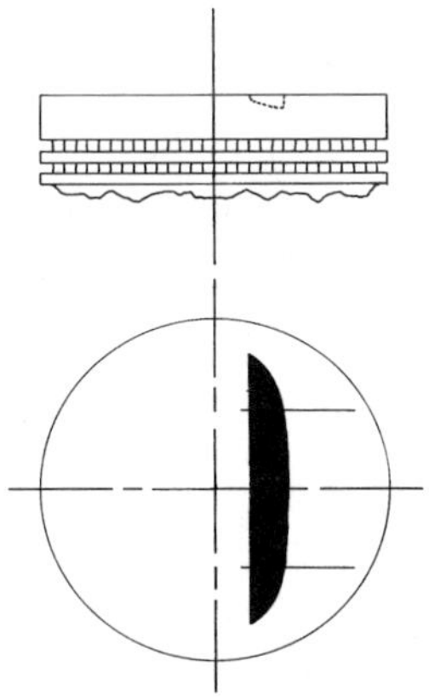

Model	Passenger car Chevelle Monte Carlo
Engine	400/150, 180HP
Piston Characteristics	Sump head that is notched for valve clearance
Material	Cast alloy aluminum
Skirt Type	Slipper
Compression Ring Groove Diameter (in.)	3.649–3.659
Oil Ring Groove Diameter (in.)	3.678–3.688
Piston Pin Type	Pressed fit
Piston Pin Offset	Major thrust side, 0.055–0.065
Weight (oz.)	21.92

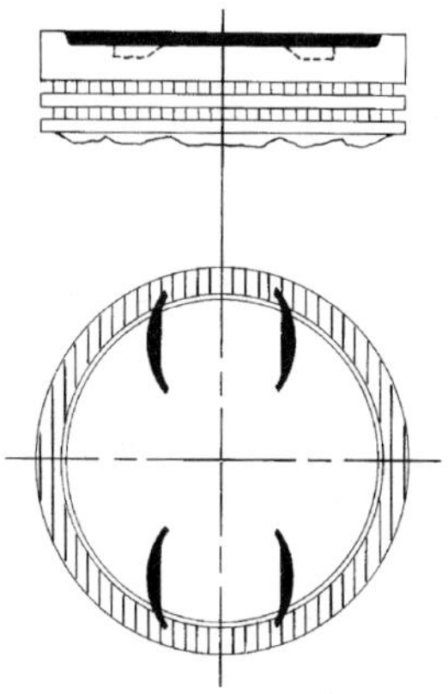

Model	Passenger car Chevelle Corvette Monte Carlo	
Engine	454/235HP (All except Corvette) 454/270HP (Corvette)	
Piston Characteristics	Flat head used only in this application. Piston has reliefs for valve clearance	
Material	Cast alloy aluminum	
Skirt Type	Slipper	
Compression Ring Groove Diameter (in.)	3.770–3.780	
Oil Ring Groove Diameter (in.)	3.803–3.813	
Piston Pin Type	Pressed fit	
Piston Pin Offset	Major thrust side, 0.055–0.065	
Weight (oz.)	25.94	

7. 1975 PISTONS

Model	Monza 2+2	
Engine	262/110HP	
Piston Characteristics	Flat head	
Material	Cast alloy aluminum	
Skirt Type	Slipper	
Compression Ring Groove Diameter (in.)	3.250–3.275	
Oil Ring Groove Diameter (in.)	3.250–3.275	
Piston Pin Type	Pressed fit	
Piston Pin Offset	Major thrust side, 0.055–0.065	
Weight (oz.)	19.30	

Model	Passenger car Nova Chevelle Camaro Corvette Monte Carlo	
Engine	350/145HP (All except Corvette) 350/155HP (All except Corvette) 350/165HP (Corvette)	
Piston Characteristics	Sump head for valve clearance	
Material	Cast alloy aluminum	
Skirt Type	Slipper	
Compression Ring Groove Diameter (in.)	3.541–3.556	
Oil Ring Groove Diameter (in.)	3.577–3.592	
Piston Pin Type	Pressed fit	
Piston Pin Offset	Major thrust side, 0.055–0.065	
Weight (oz.)	21.33	

Model	Corvette
Engine	350/205HP
Piston Characteristics	Flat head used only on 350/205HP engines. Piston has notch in top for valve clearance at high rpm
Material	Impact extruded alloy aluminum
Skirt Type	Slipper
Compression Ring Groove Diameter (in.)	3.546–3.556
Oil Ring Groove Diameter (in.)	3.582–3.592
Piston Pin Type	Pressed fit
Piston Pin Offset	Major thrust side, on center
Weight (oz.)	26.08

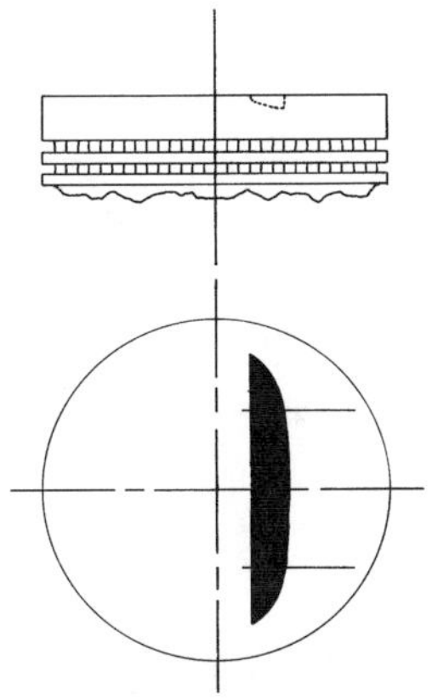

Model	Passenger car Chevelle Monte Carlo
Engine	400/175HP
Piston Characteristics	Sump head that is notched for valve clearance
Material	Cast alloy aluminum
Skirt Type	Slipper
Compression Ring Groove Diameter (in.)	3.649–3.659
Oil Ring Groove Diameter (in.)	3.678–3.688
Piston Pin Type	Pressed fit
Piston Pin Offset	Major thrust side, 0.055–0.065
Weight (oz.)	22.88

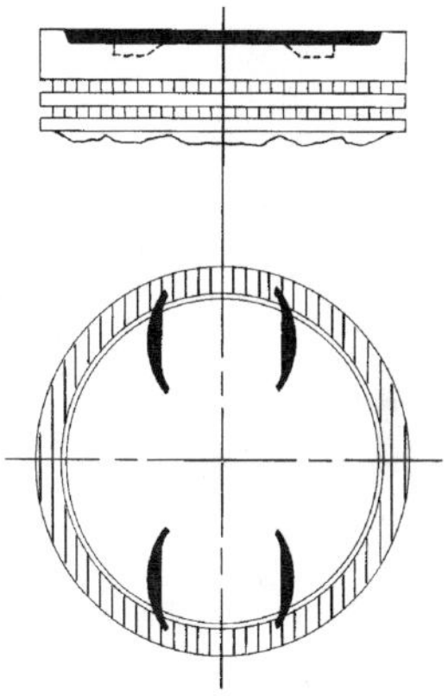

Model	Passenger car Chevelle Monte Carlo
Engine	454/215HP
Piston Characteristics	Flat head used only in this application. Piston has reliefs for valve clearance
Material	Cast alloy aluminum
Skirt Type	Slipper
Compression Ring Groove Diameter (in.)	3.770–3.780
Oil Ring Groove Diameter (in.)	3.803–3.813
Piston Pin Type	Pressed fit
Piston Pin Offset	Major thrust side, 0.055–0.065
Weight (oz.)	25.94

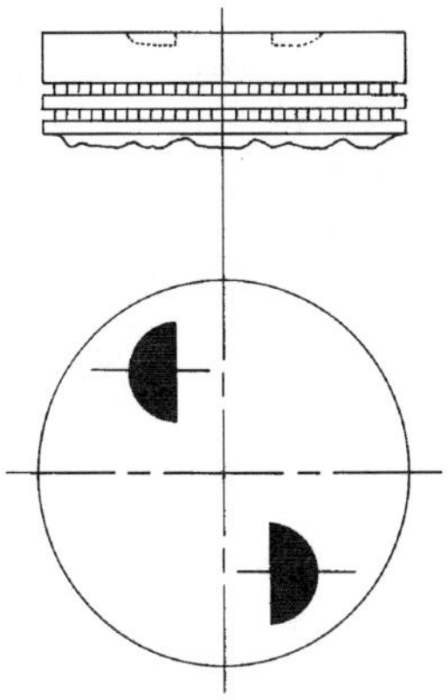

Chapter 8
Carburetor Identification

1. Introduction

This chapter will cover the identification of Holley and Rochester carburetors used from 1970 through 1975. The carburetors will be discussed and identified by manufacturer, and all specific applications will be listed.

2. Holley Carburetors

The Holley carburetor has been known as the "High Performance Carburetor" since the early 1960s. The primary reason is because most factory high performance engines were originally equipped with Holley carburetors. Most people in the high performance era were accustomed to working on Holley carburetors, which led in turn to everyone preferring that carburetor. This line of thinking has basically continued up to this day, or at least until the days of the computer-controlled and factory turbocharged engines. The majority of Holley carburetors covered here are the 4150 and 4160 4 BBL models. Also covered is the 2300 2 BBL model.

The 4150 was introduced on the 1957 312 Ford engine. It basically pioneered the "modular" design with flexibility of calibration, so that it could be used in many applications. The 4150 model features a metering block, with replaceable main jets, on both primary and secondary sides of the carburetor. Some 4150 models utilize a double accelerator pump design commonly called a "double pumper," and mechanical secondaries. These models are only used in ultra high performance applications such as the L88 Corvette. Other models use a single accelerator pump on the primary side only, and vacuum-operated secondaries.

Fig. 8-1. Typical model 4150 Holley carburetor. Arrows point to primary and secondary metering bodies.

Fig. 8-2. Metering block bodies removed from 4150 carburetor #2818 show stamping numbers. ***Top:*** *primary metering block reads 4094.* ***Bottom:*** *secondary metering block reads 4099. See Holley carburetor specification chart later in this chapter.*

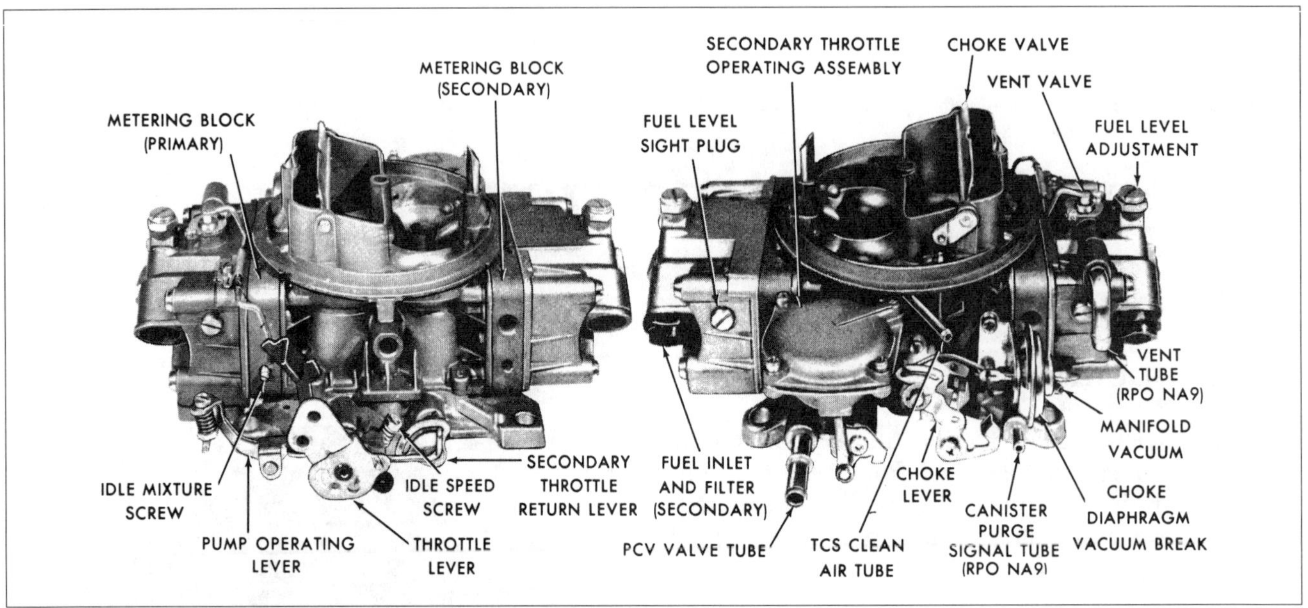

Fig. 8-3. Component details of typical Holley model 4150 center inlet carburetor.

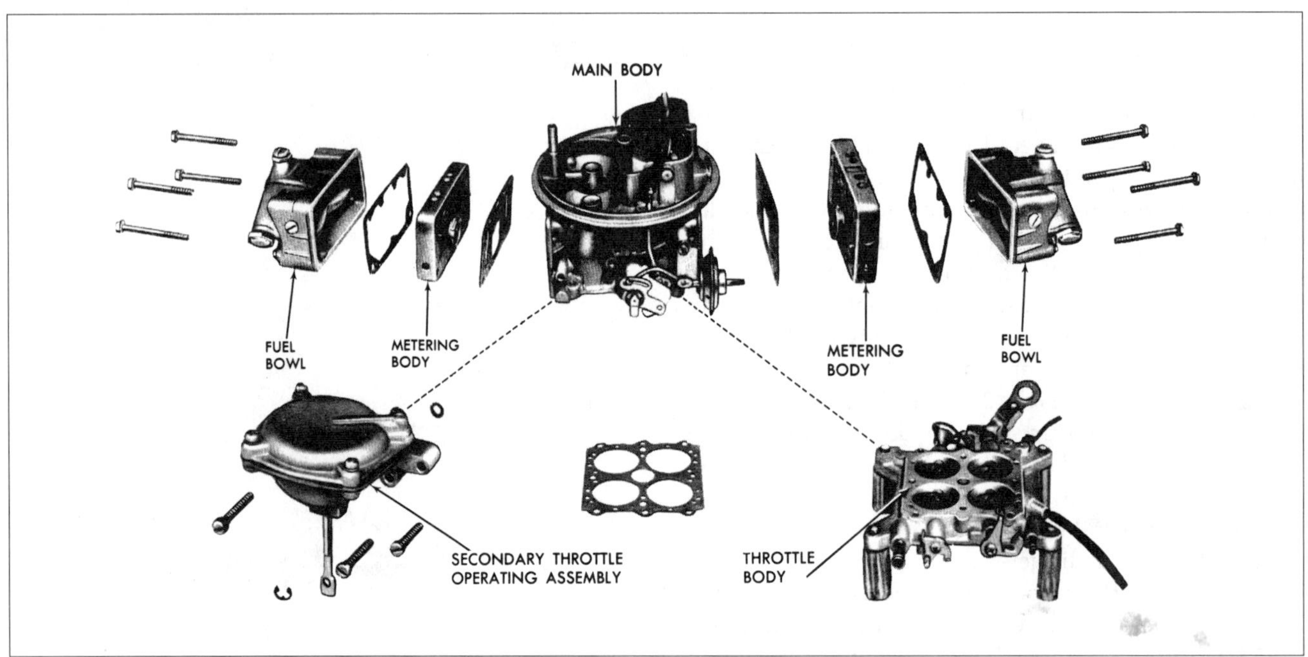

Fig. 8-4. Holley 4150 subassemblies.

2.1 Holley Carburetor Identification

All Holley carburetors are stamped with a series of numbers. These numbers are found on the air horn on the driver's side, facing toward the front of the car. All factory supplied carburetors will have a Chevrolet part number, usually followed by the letter code Chevrolet assigned to that specific application. This letter code is referred to on Chevrolet blueprints as a customer code and is the same code which is designated on late model assembly line build sheets.

Below the factory part number, the word "LIST" is stamped followed by a 4-digit number. This is the Holley list number which designates the specific parts that will make up that carburetor and its CFM (cubic feet per minute) rating.

The suffix digits and/or letters that many times follow a list number have several designations. The letter "A" suffix is shown on nearly every carburetor in the Holley numerical guide, but is almost never seen on a carburetor. Holley representatives state that the letter "A" indicated "for original equipment manufacturer" or OEM. The suffix "AAS" meant that the carburetor was an original equipment service carburetor. Holley also states that the suffix "AA" and "AAA" were after market replacement carburetors. The number digit suffixes (-1, -2, etc.) designated that a production change took place on that particular carburetor.

Below the list number is stamped the date of manufacture. This will be a 3- or 4-digit code. On 3-digit codes, the first digit indicates the year of production. The second digit indicates the month of that year of manufacture. The final digit refers to the week of the month that the carburetor was produced. In some cases the second digit is a number, in other cases a letter.

The Holley 4-digit code is based on the Julian calendar. The calendar starts with January 1 being 001 and continues through the year until 365 which is December 31, or 366 for a leap year. The first three digits indicate the day of the year. The final or fourth digit indicates the year of production. Holley used both these systems of dating but only used the 4-digit code after the 1972 model year.

Please realize that this was a manual stamping operation and was prone to human error. Also, the air horn which has all the important information stamped on it can easily be switched from carburetor to carburetor. Ask lots of questions and be as informed as you can before you start looking for that specific Holley carburetor. Following is a breakdown of the Holley date coding.

> NOTE—
> It is *very* important to match up the list number of the carburetor to the application of your car and then look for the correct date. This way, the application or list number is the priority and you are less likely to be misled.

Fig. 8-5. *List number and 3-digit date stamping for carburetor 4800.*

Fig. 8-6. *Four-digit date code for carburetor number 4802-1.*

Holley Date Coding 1970 Through 1972

Example: Date Code 084

- First Digit = Year: 1970
  0: 1970
  1: 1971
  2: 1972
  3: 1973
  4: 1974
  5: 1975
- Second Digit = Month: August

1: January	7: July
2: February	8: August
3: March	9: September
4: April	0: October
5: May	A: November
6: June	B: December

- Third Digit = Week: Second week
  1 through 5

Holley Date Coding 1973 Through 1975

Example: Date Code 2114

- First Three Digits = Month and day of manufacture: July 30

Regular Calendar:	Leap Year Calendar:
001–031 January	001–031 January
032–059 February	032–060 February
060–090 March	061–091 March
091–120 April	092–121 April
121–151 May	122–152 May
152–181 June	153–182 June
182–212 July	183–213 July
213–243 August	214–244 August
244–273 September	245–274 September
274–304 October	275–305 October
305–334 November	306–335 November
335–365 December	336–366 December

- Fourth Digit: Year of manufacture
  0: 1980
  1: 1971
  2: 1972
  3: 1973
  4: 1974
  5: 1975

Holley 4BBL Carburetors

Carburetor List #	Year	Model	Engine	Horsepower	Transmission	Carb Model	Part #
4489	1970	Camaro	350 (CA)	360	S/T	4150	3972123
		Corvette	350 (CA)	370	S/T	4150	3972123
		Yenko Deuce	350	360	S/T	4150	3972123
4490*	1970	Camaro	350 (FED)	360	A/T	4150	3972120
		Corvette (unverified)	350 (FED)	370	A/T	4150	3972120
4491	1970	Camaro	402 (CA)	375	S/T	4150	3967479 GM
		Chevelle	402 (CA)	375	S/T	4150	3967479 GM
			454 (CA)	450	S/T	4150	3967479 GM
		Nova	402 (CA)	375	S/T	4150	3967479 GM
4492	1970	Camaro	402 (FED)	375	A/T	4150	3969898 GR
		Chevelle	402 (FED)	375	A/T	4150	3969898 GR
			454 (FED)	450	A/T	4150	3969898 GR
		Nova	402 (FED)	375	A/T	4150	3969898 GR
4493**	1970	Corvette	454 (CA)	465	S/T	4150 850 CFM Dual pump	3967487
4554***	1970	Corvette	350 (CA)	370	A/T	4150	3972122
		Camaro	350 (CA)	360	A/T	4150	3972122

*This carburetor has recently been re-released by Holley due to the demand of the restoration industry. **These carburetors were manufactured by Holley for Chevrolet in full anticipation of the engine option being released. The LS7 engine option was canceled at the last minute by Chevrolet but was released as an over-the-counter parts item. ***Originally specified on Corvette for LT1 option with automatic transmission. Chevrolet production figures show that no automatic Corvettes with this option were built.

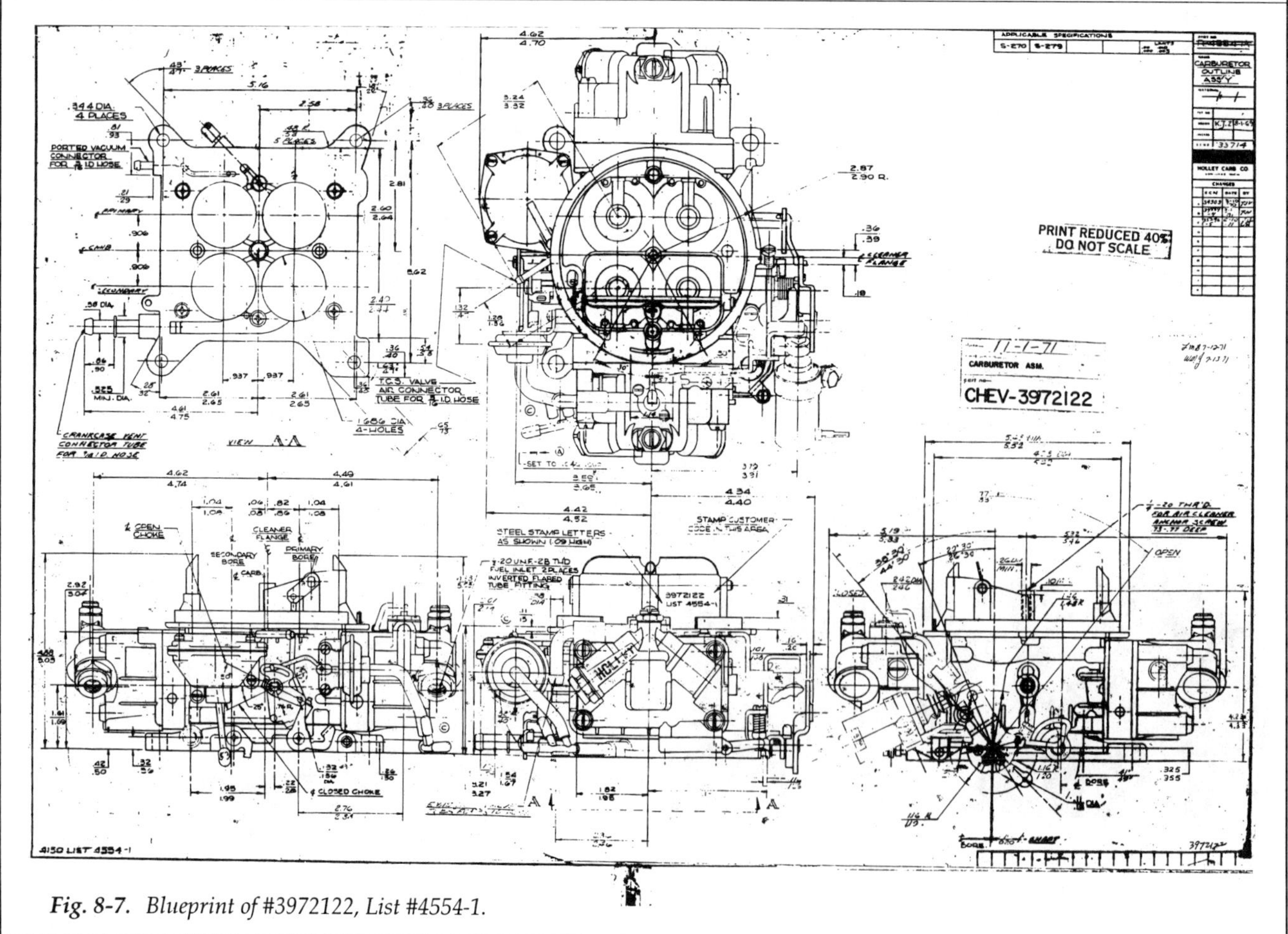

Fig. 8-7. Blueprint of #3972122, List #4554-1.

continued on next page

Holley 4BBL Carburetors (continued)

Carburetor List #	Year	Model	Engine	Horsepower	Transmission	Carb Model	Part #
4555*	1970	Camaro	350 (FED)	360	S/T	4150	3972121
		Corvette	350 (FED)	370	S/T	4150	3972121
4556	1970	Camaro, Chevelle, Nova	402 (CA)	375	A/T	4150	3969894 GP
		Chevelle	454 (CA)	450	A/T	4150	3969894 GP
4557	1970	Camaro, Chevelle, Nova	402 (FED)	375	S/T	4150	3967477GG
		Chevelle	454 (FED)	450	S/T	4150	3967477 GG
4558**	1970	Corvette	454 (CA)	465	A/T	4150	3969896
4559AAS**	1970	Corvette	454 (FED)	465	S/T	4150	3967481
4800*	1971	Camaro Z28	350	330	A/T	4150	3989022

Fig. 8-8. Overall view of carburetor 4800.

Carburetor List #	Year	Model	Engine	Horsepower	Transmission	Carb Model	Part #
4801*	1971	Camaro Z28	350	330	S/T	4150	3989021
		Corvette	350	330	S/T	4150	3989021
4802*	1971	Chevelle	454	425	A/T	4150	3986196
		Corvette	454	425	A/T	4150	3986196
4803*	1971	Chevelle	454	425	S/T	4150	3986195
		Corvette	454	425	S/T	4150	3986195
6238*	1972	Camaro Z28	350	255	A/T	4150	3997788 GB
6239*	1972	Camaro Z28	350	255	S/T	4150	3999263 GA
		Corvette	350	255	S/T	4150	3999263 GA

*This carburetor has recently been re-released by Holley due to the demand of the restoration industry.
**These carburetors were manufactured by Holley for Chevrolet in full anticipation of the engine option being released. The LS-7 engine option was canceled at the last minute by Chevrolet but was released as an over-the-counter parts item.

continued on next page

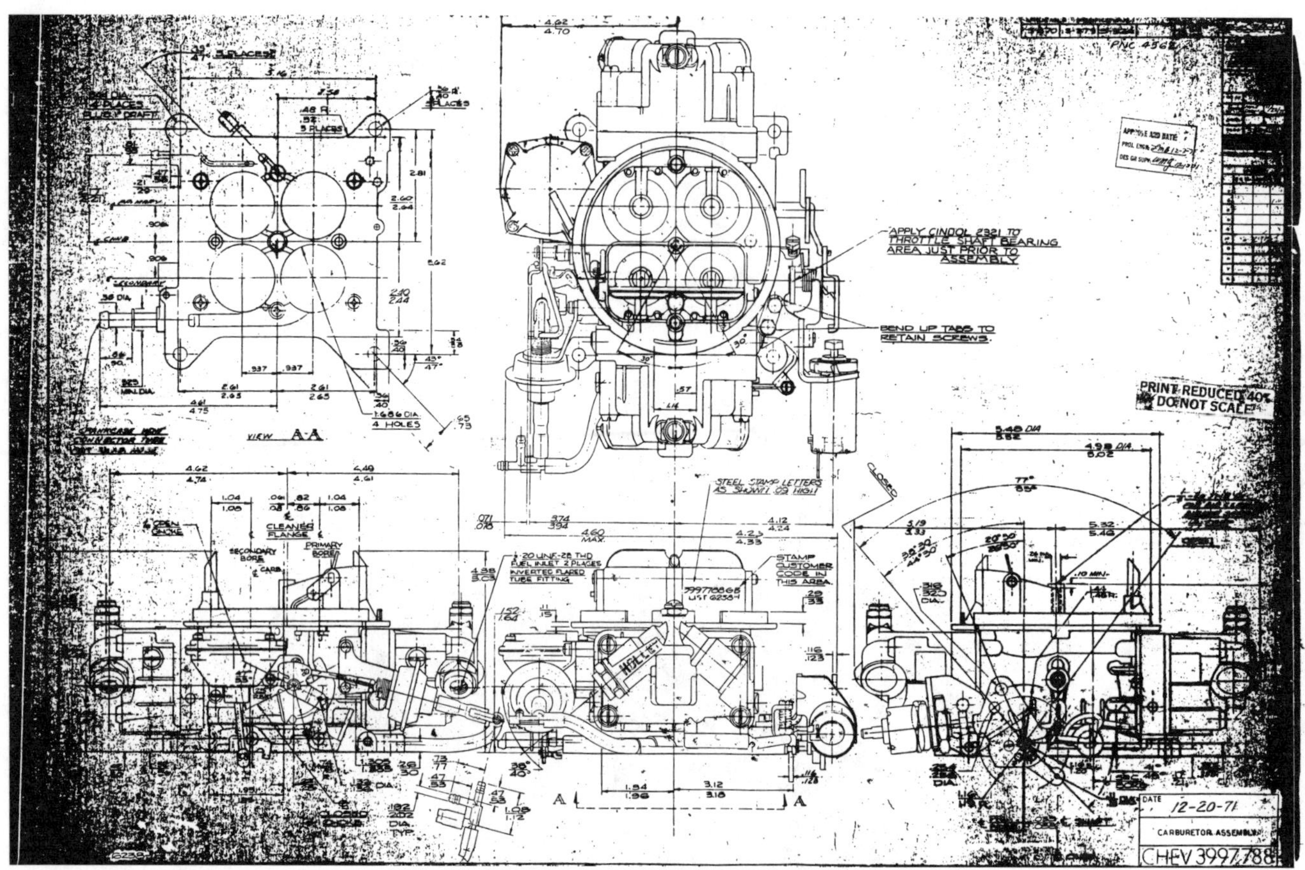

Fig. 8-9. Blueprint of #3997788, List #6238.

Holley Carburetor Specification Chart

List#	Years	Engine/HP/Transmission	Carb Model	Metering Block Stamp Primary	Secondary	Bowl	N&S	Idle Vent
4489	1970	350/360HP S/T CA 350/370HP S/T CA	4150	6335	6192	C	E	Yes
4490	1970	350/360HP A/T	4150	6333	4519	C	E	Yes
4491	1970	402/375HP S/T CA	4150	6189	6192	C	E	Yes
4492	1970	402/375HP A/T	4150	6328	4519	C	E	Yes
4493	1970	454/465HP S/T CA	4150	6203	6207	C	E	Yes
4554	1970	350/360HP A/T CA	4150	6335	6192	C	E	Yes
4555	1970	350/360HP S/T	4150	6333	4519	C	E	No
4556	1970	402/375HP A/T CA	4150	6189	6192	C	E	Yes
4557	1970	402/375HP S/T	4150	6328	4519	C	E	Yes
4558	1970	454/465HP A/T CA	4150	6203	6207	C	E	No
4559	1970	454/465HP S/T	4150	5895	5901	C	E	No
4800	1971	350/330HP A/T	4150	6671	4519	C	E	No
4801	1971	350/330HP S/T	4150	6808	4519	C	E	No
4802	1971	454/425HP A/T	4150	6671	4519	C	E	No
4803	1971	454/425HP S/T	4150	6808	4519	C	E	No
6238	1972	350/255HP A/T	4150	6825	4519	C	E	No
6239	1972	350/255HP S/T	4150	6828	4519	C	E	No

Chokes: Basically 1964-65 used integral type; 1966-72 used divorced (remote type)
Bowl Type: S = Side Pivot Float, C = Center Pivot Float
N&S Type: E = Externally Adjustable, I = Internal
*See Application for Transmission Designation

3. Rochester Carburetors

The Rochester 4MV/4MC carburetor was first introduced in 1965. It is commonly referred to as the Q-Jet or Quadrajet carburetor. There are two basic designs of this carburetor. The 4MV is an automatic choke model which was designed for use with a manifold mounted choke coil. The 4MC model is also an automatic choke model but with the choke coil mounted in a housing mounted on the side of the float bowl. Except for the aforementioned particular choke systems, both models share the same principals of operation.

There is one other Rochester carburetor model which needs mentioning here. It is the M4MC. It was released in 1975 and differs from the previous carburetors in that the "M" prefix designates "Modified," indicating that the primary side of the carburetor was revised to accommodate an adjustable metering rod assembly or aneroid rod assembly, when designated for a specific application. This aneroid feature is usually used to attain altitude compensation in air/fuel mixtures. Later modified models use separated main wells with an additional aneroid cavity insert in the float bowl. The designated models for the altitude compensation are M4MCA or M4MEA.

Starting in 1968, all models have an adjustable part throttle (APT) screw located in either the throttle body (4MV/4MC models) or in the float bowl ("M" modified models).

The thermostatic choke coil assembly is different on all carburetor models. The choke coil on 4MV models is heated by hot exhaust gases that flow through a special passage in the intake manifold. On the 4MC, M4MC and M4MCA models, the coil assembly is warmed by exhaust heated air supplied through a tube to the choke housing mounted on the float bowl. The M4ME and M4MEA models use an electrically heated thermostatic coil assembly to control choke mixtures after engine start up and cold drive away.

Rochester Carburetor Designation Breakdown

2G	Rochester 2BBL (Manual Choke)
2GC	Rochester 2BBL (Auto choke on carb)
2GV	Rochester 2BBL (Auto: Choke-Remote)
4G	Early Rochester 4BBL (Manual Choke)
4GC	Early Rochester 4BBL (Auto Choke on Carb)
4M	Late Rochester 4BBL (Manual Choke)
4MC	Late Rochester 4BBL (Auto Choke on Carb)
4MV	Late Rochester 4BBL (Auto Choke Remote)

Fig. 8-11. Carter-built Rochester 4MV Quadrajet #7027203 with a hydraulic secondary dashpot.

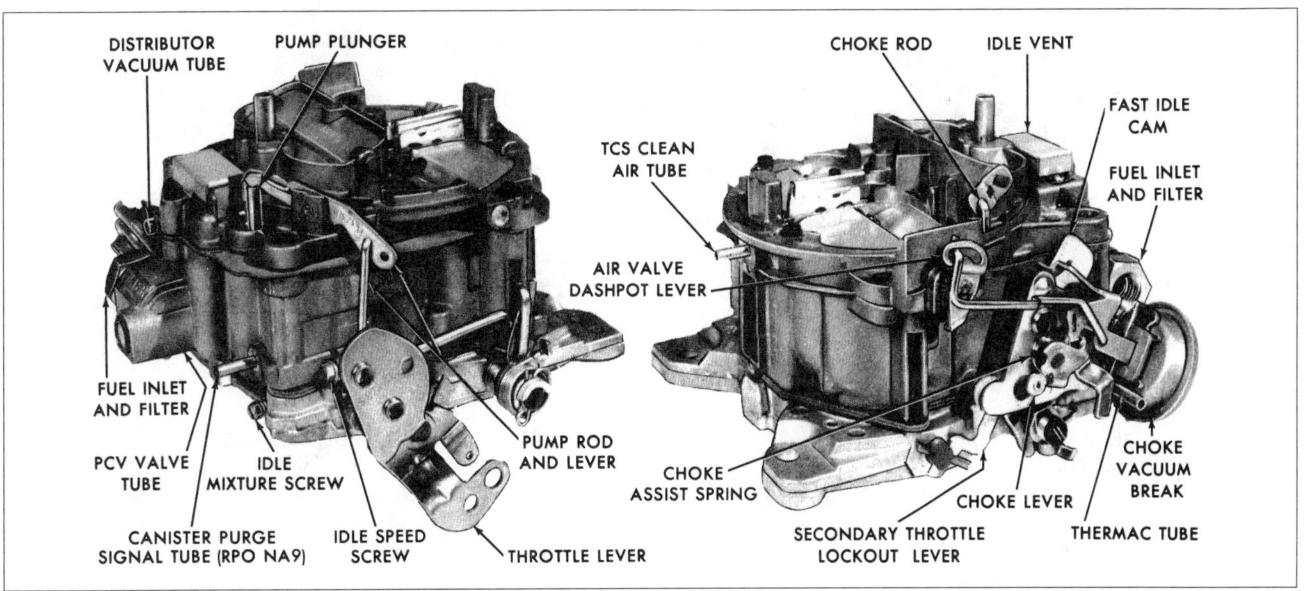

Fig. 8-10. Details of Rochester 4MV Carburetor.

NOTE—
During the production of Rochester carburetors, a number of Rochester designs were produced by Carter under license for Chevrolet. See later for more information.

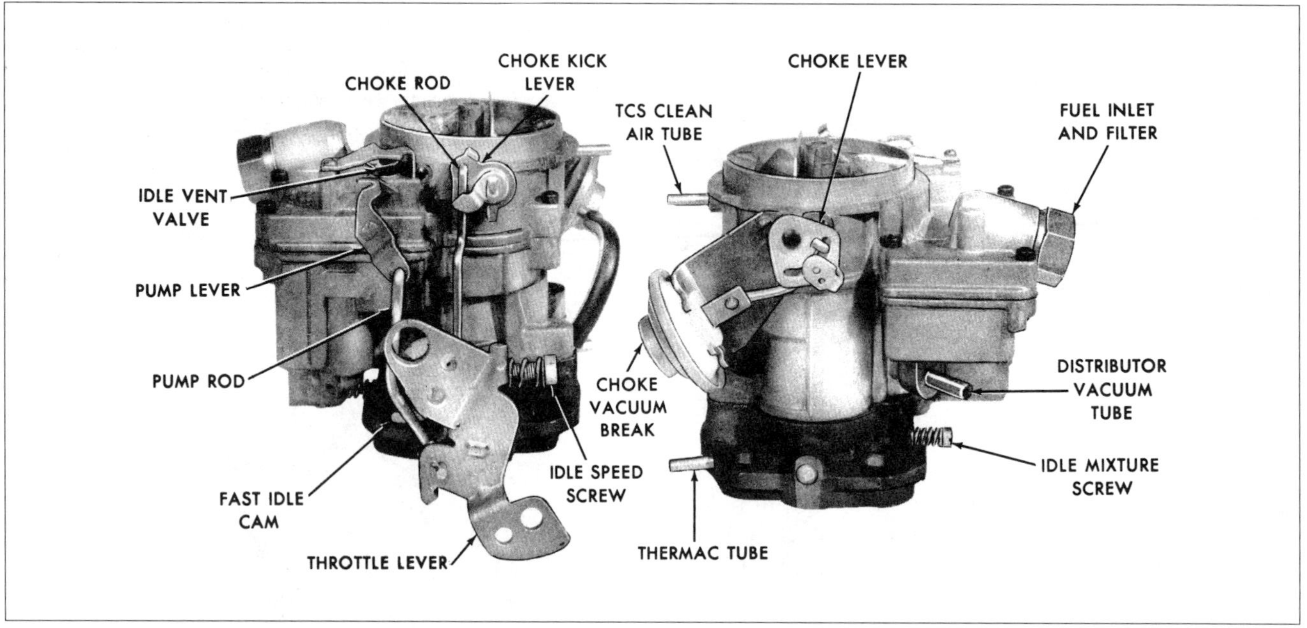

Fig. 8-12. Rochester 2GV carburetor used with a 350 or 400 C.I. engine. This carburetor has an SAE size of 1-1/2".

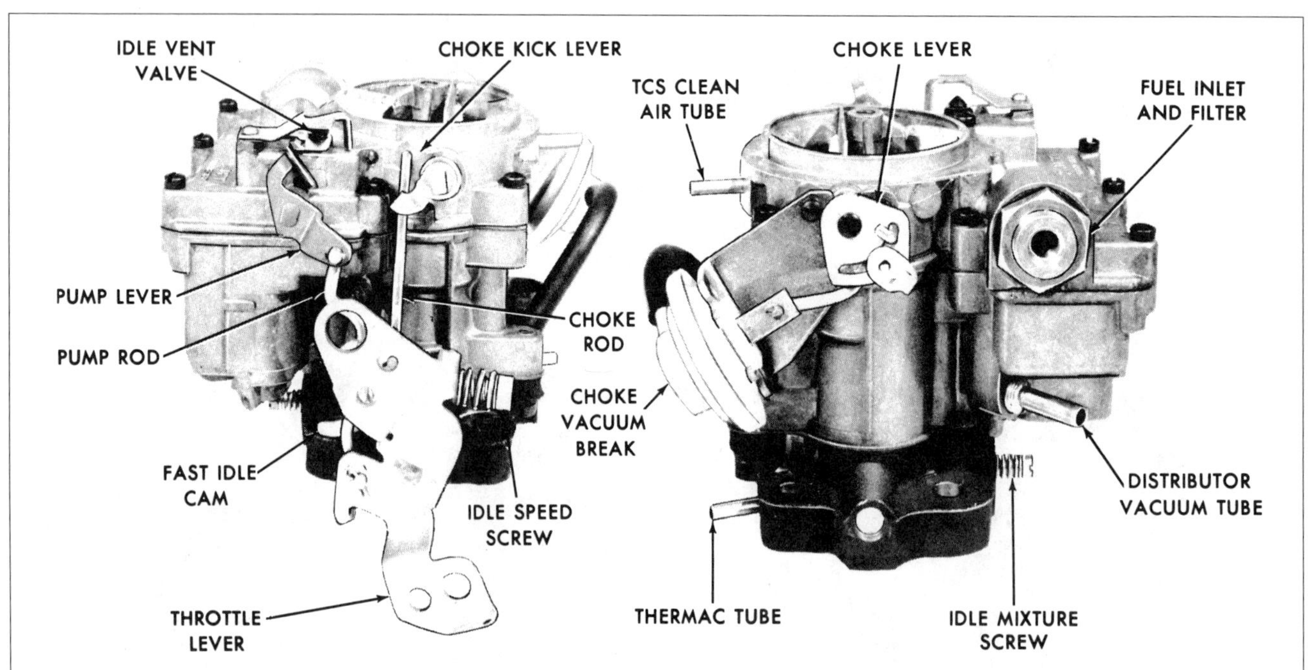

Fig. 8-13. Rochester 2GV carburetor used exclusively on the 307 C.I. engine. This carburetor has an SAE size of 1-1/4".

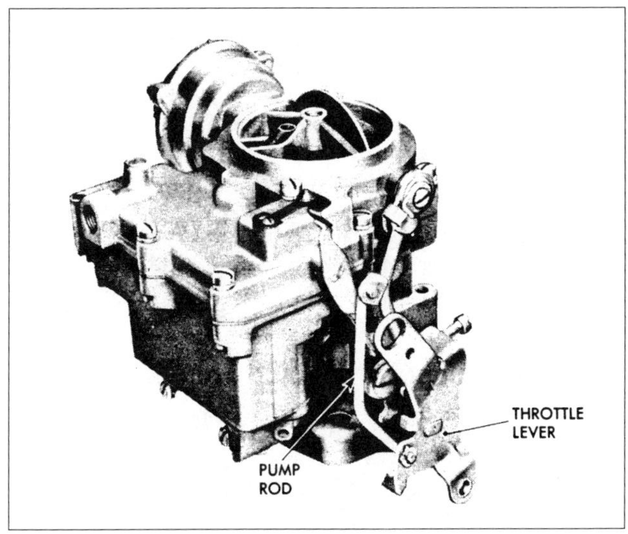

Fig. 8-14. *Overall view of Rochester 2GC carburetor.*

Fig. 8-16. *Overall view of 1975–80 modified Quadrajet M4MC.*

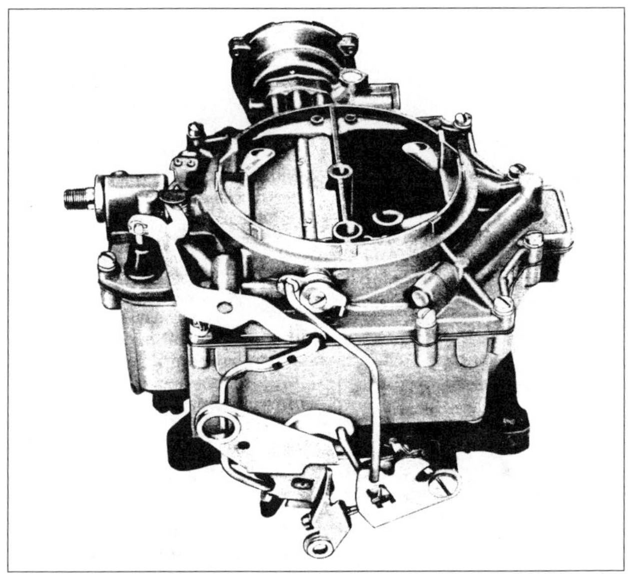

Fig. 8-15. *Rochester 4GC 4BBL carburetor.*

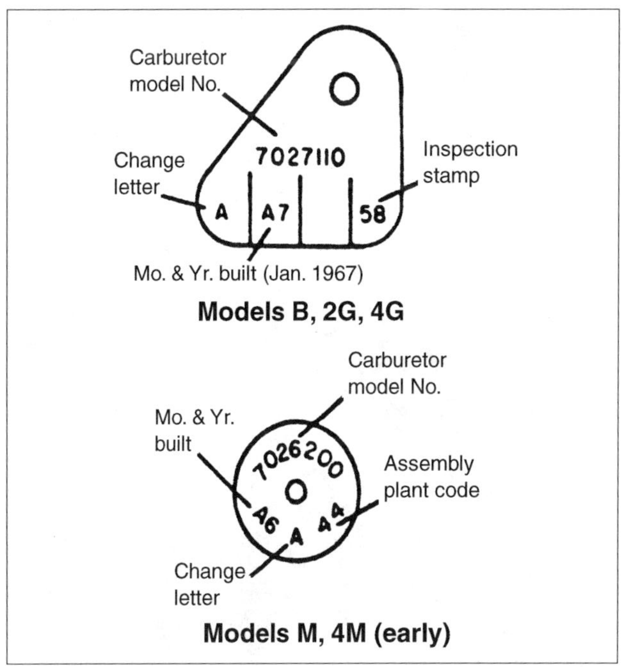

Fig. 8-17. *Two styles of carburetor identification tags used on Rochester carburetors.*

3.1 Rochester Carburetor Identification

There are three types of identifications for Rochester Carburetors. One is a triangular stamped metal tag, which is installed beneath the air horn screw. This tag was used on Models B, 2G and 4G. The second type of tag used was a circular tag, which was recessed in a cavity in the side of the float bowl. See Fig. 8-18. This tag was used on the early model M (Monojet) and 4M Quadrajet carburetors. The third type is an identification code stamped into the carburetor body.

The metal tags have several features that should be noted here. The 7-digit number is the carburetor model number. Below the model number are several other letters and numbers that denote manufacturing information. The letter that appears alone is a change letter. This letter signifies an engineering or production change. The change letter starts with "A" and goes up through the alphabet, as subsequent changes were made through the model year to that specific carburetor.

The letter and number that appear together indicate the month and year the carburetor was built. For example, "C8" indicates that the carburetor was built in March (C) of 1968 (8). Each month is assigned a consecu-

Fig. 8-18. 1967 Carter-built Rochester Quadrajet #7027203 identification tag, with an "M6" date and a "DZ" customer code.

tive letter except that the letter "I" is skipped because it can be confused with the number "1."

The 2-digit number (or letters) on the triangular tag designates a factory inspector number on the production line. On the circular tag, these numbers (letters) indicate the actual assembly plant code.

Fig. 8-19. 1967 Rochester Quadrajet #7027202 with a "C7" date and a "DB" customer code.

Decoding Stamping Numbers

The decoding of the stamping number or actual part number of Rochester Quadrajet Carburetors can be difficult to understand. The following is a breakdown of what each number inside the complete stamping number means and how that correlates to the actual carburetor and its original use. The actual decoding will be done by position number. This will enable all identification to be shown at the position rather than in text form.

NOTE—
Some carburetors may be incorrectly stamped. This operation was performed manually and was prone to human error. Also, many carburetors were used over a 2-year period, which could cause problems in the date coding. The actual carburetor numbers used in identifying specific applications were taken from General Motors documents and verified by reliable sources in the industry. Those actual application numbers should be trusted and used over the decoding process.

*Fig. 8-20. Location of stamping numbers on carburetor. Numbers at **A** (partly obscured) are 7028219 and **B** 1938. See text for decoding.*

Example: Rochester Stamping Numbers # 70 4 1 2 1 9 DG and 1676

- **70 = Prefix Code**: All Rochester Carburetors built from 1970 through 1975 should have a "70" prefix for the carburetor stamping number, though it may be missing on some carburetors. The coding is the same for 2 and 4 barrel carburetors. In 1976 the prefix changed to "170." The "170" prefix carburetors are not covered in this book.
- **4 = Decade Produced**: 4 represents the decade that the carburetor was produced. This holds true with the exception of the number "3" in this position. The number "3" designates a specific A.I.R. (Air Injection Reactor) carburetor. Most of these carburetors were installed on factory engines in 1966 and 1967. It is possible that some could have been produced for service after 1967, but this has not been verified. The decade designations are as follows:
  2 = 1960s Production
  3 = 1960s Production w/A.I.R.
  4 = 1970–75 Production
  5 = 1976–79 Production
  8 = 1980s Production

- **1 = Year Produced**: This position represents the actual year of production within the preceding decade. This position number can range from 1 through 0.
- **2 = Model**: This position shows the actual model of the carburetor. It also designates whether the carburetor was assembled for the 49 State Federal Emissions Standards or for the California Emissions Standards. The following chart is basically self- explanatory.
  0 = Monojet Carburetor (1BBL), Federal Standards
  1 = Two Jet Carburetor (2BBL), Federal Standards
  2 = Quadrajet Carburetor (4BBL), Federal Standards
  3 = Monojet Carburetor (1BBL), California Standards
  4 = Two Jet Carburetor (2BBL), California Standards
  5 = Quadrajet Carburetor (4BBL), California Standards (including high altitude)
- **1 = Division**: This position usually designates the actual General Motors Division in which the carburetor was made. Due to the variety and complications involved in giving all the General Motor codes, I only list the Chevrolet codes. The numbers 0, 1, and 2 are all used by AC-Rochester to designate Chevrolet carburetors.
- **9 = Transmission**: This position usually designates whether the carburetor was to be installed on a manual or automatic transmission engine. The identification breakdown is as follows:
  Even Numbers = Automatic Transmissions
  Odd Numbers = Manual Transmissions
- **DG = Customer Code**: The 2 or 3 letters that usually follow the stamping numbers designate the letter code Chevrolet assigned to that carburetor. There are no records to indicate which letter codes corresponded to specific plants. The correlation to the actual application of the carburetor to this code is the same code as shown on the car's original assembly-line sheet.
- **1676 = Date Code**: This position shows the actual day and year the carburetor was manufactured. It is a typical "Julian" type code. The first three digits indicate the exact day of the year. The last digit reflects the year of production.
  Example: 1676 = 167th day of production, 1976

Rochester 2BBL Carburetors

Number	Carb	Year	Model	Engine/App.
7040101	2GV	1970	Chevelle	307/200HP S/T
			Nova	
			Camaro	
7040102	2GV	1970 (Early)	Camaro	350/250HP A/T Non-CA
7040103	2GV	1970	Chevelle	307/200HP S/T, A/C
			Nova	
			Camaro	
7040104	2GV	1970 (Early)	Camaro	350/250HP A/T, A/C Non-CA
7040110	2GV	1970	Chevelle	307/200HP A/T
			Nova	
			Camaro	
7040112	2GV	1970	Chevelle	307/200HP A/T, A/C
			Nova	
			Camaro	
7040113	2GV	1970	Passenger	350/250HP S/T Non-CA
			Chevelle	
			Nova	
			Monte Carlo	
7040114	2GV	1970 (Early)	Passenger	350/250HP A/T Non-CA
			Chevelle	
			Nova	
			Monte Carlo	
7040115	2GV	1970	Passenger	350/250HP S/T, A/C Non-CA
			Chevelle	
			Nova	
			Monte Carlo	
7040116	2GV	1970 (Early)	Passenger	350/250HP A/T, A/C Non-CA
			Chevelle	
			Nova	
			Monte Carlo	
7040117	2GV	1970	Passenger	400/265HP S/T Non-CA
			Monte Carlo	
7040118	2GV	1970	Passenger	400/265HP A/T Non-CA
			Monte Carlo	
7040119	2GV	1970	Passenger	400/265HP S/T, A/C Non-CA
			Monte Carlo	
7040120	2GV	1970	Passenger	400/265HP A/T, A/C Non-CA
			Monte Carlo	
7040126	2GV	1970 (Late)	Camaro	350/250HP A/T Non-CA
7040127	2GV	1970	Camaro	350/250HP S/T Non-CA
7040128	2GV	1970 (Late)	Camaro	350/250HP A/T, A/C Non-CA
7040129	2GV	1970	Camaro	350/250HP S/T, A/C Non-CA
7040134	2GV	1970 (Late)	Passenger	350/250HP A/T Non-CA
			Chevelle	
			Nova	
			Monte Carlo	

continued on next page

Rochester 2BBL Carburetors (continued)

Number	Carb	Year	Model	Engine/App.
7040136	2GV	1970 (Late)	Passenger	350/250HP A/T, A/C non-CA
			Chevelle	
			Nova	
			Monte Carlo	
7040402	2GV	1970 (Early)	Camaro	350/250HP A/T CA
7040404	2GV	1970 (Early)	Camaro	350/250HP A/T, A/C CA
7040413	2GV	1970	Passenger	350/250HP S/T CA
			Chevelle	
			Nova	
			Monte Carlo	
7040414	2GV	1970 (Early)	Passenger	350/250HP A/T CA
			Chevelle	
			Nova	
			Monte Carlo	
7040415	2GV	1970	Passenger	350/250HP S/T, A/C CA
			Chevelle	
			Nova	
			Monte Carlo	
7040416	2GV	1970 (Early)	Passenger	350/250HP A/T, A/C CA
			Chevelle	
			Nova	
			Monte Carlo	
7040417	2GV	1970	Passenger	400/265HP S/T CA
			Monte Carlo	
7040418	2GV	1970	Passenger	400/265HP A/T CA
			Monte Carlo	
7040419	2GV	1970	Passenger	400/265HP S/T, A/C CA
			Monte Carlo	
7040420	2GV	1970	Passenger	400/265HP A/T, A/C CA
			Monte Carlo	
7040426	2GV	1970 (Late)	Camaro	350/250HP A/T CA
7040427	2GV	1970	Camaro	350/250HP S/T CA
7040428	2GV	1970 (Late)	Camaro	350/250HP A/T, A/C CA
7040429	2GV	1970	Camaro	350/250HP S/T, A/C CA
7040434	2GV	1970 (Late)	Passenger	350/250HP A/T CA
			Chevelle	
			Nova	
			Monte Carlo	
7040436	2GV	1970 (Late)	Passenger	350/250HP A/T, A/C CA
			Chevelle	
			Nova	
			Monte Carlo	
7041101	2GV	1971	Chevelle	307/200HP S/T
			Camaro	
			Nova	
7041102	2GV	1971	Camaro	350/245HP A/T
7041110	2GV	1971	Chevelle	307/200HP A/T
			Camaro	
			Nova	
7041113	2GV	1971	Passenger	350/245HP S/T
			Chevelle	
			Nova	
			Monte Carlo	
7041114	2GV	1971	Passenger	350/245HP A/T
			Chevelle	
			Nova	
			Monte Carlo	
7041118	2GV	1971	Passenger	400/255HP A/T
7041127	2GV	1971	Camaro	350/245HP S/T
7041137	2GV	1971	Passenger	400/255HP S/T
7042100	2GV	1972	Chevelle	307/130HP A/T
			Camaro	
			Nova	
7042101	2GV	1972	Chevelle	307/130HP S/T
			Camaro	
			Nova	
7042111	2GV	1972	Camaro	350/165HP S/T Non-CA
7042112	2GV	1972	Camaro	350/165HP A/T Non-CA
7042113	2GV	1972	Passenger	350/165HP S/T Non-CA
			Chevelle	
			Nova	
			Monte Carlo	
7042114	2GV	1972	Passenger	350/165HP A/T Non-CA
			Chevelle	
			Nova	
			Monte Carlo	
7042118	2GV	1972	Passenger	400/170HP A/T Non-CA
7042831	2GV	1972	Camaro	350/165HP S/T CA
7042832	2GV	1972	Camaro	350/165HP A/T CA
7042833	2GV	1972	Passenger	350/165HP S/T CA
			Chevelle	
			Nova	
			Monte Carlo	
7042834	2GV	1972	Passenger	350/165HP A/T CA
			Chevelle	
			Nova	
			Monte Carlo	
7042838	2GV	1972	Passenger	400/170HP A/T CA
7043100	2GV	1973	Chevelle	307/115HP A/T
			Nova	
			El Camino	

continued on next page

Rochester 2BBL Carburetors (continued)

Number	Carb	Year	Model	Engine/App.
7043101	2GV	1973	Chevelle	307/115HP S/T
			Nova	
			El Camino	
7043105	2GV	1973	Camaro	307/115HP S/T
7043111	2GV	1973	Camaro	350/145HP S/T
7043112	2GV	1973	Camaro	350/145HP A/T
7043113	2GV	1973	Passenger	350/145HP S/T
			Chevelle	
			Nova	
			Monte Carlo	
7043114	2GV	1973	Passenger	350/145HP A/T
			Chevelle	
			Nova	
			Monte Carlo	
7043118	2GV	1973	Passenger	400/150HP A/T
7043119	2GV	1974	Passenger	400/150HP A/T Station Wagon
7043120	2GV	1973	Camaro	307/115HP A/T
7043134	2GV	1974	Passenger	350/145HP A/T Station Wagon
7044111	2GV	1974	Camaro	350/145HP S/T
7044112	2GV	1974	Camaro	350/145HP A/T
7044113	2GV	1974	Passenger	350/145HP S/T
			Chevelle	
			Monte Carlo	
7044114	2GV	1974	Passenger	350/145HP A/T
			Chevelle	
			Monte Carlo	
7044115	2GV	1974	Nova	350/145HP S/T
7044116	2GV	1974	Nova	350/145HP A/T
7044118	2GV	1974	Passenger	400/150HP A/T
7045100	2GC	1975	Passenger	350/145HP All (Canadian Cars Only)
			Chevelle	
			Monte Carlo	
7045111	2GC	1975	Camaro	350/145HP S/T
7045112	2GC	1975	Camaro	350/145HP A/T
7045114	2GC	1975	Passenger	350/145HP A/T (U.S. Cars Only)
			Chevelle	
			Monte Carlo	
7045123	2GC	1975	Nova	350/145HP S/T
7045124	2GC	1975	Nova	350/145HP A/T

Rochester 4BBL Carburetors

Number	Carb	Year	Model	Engine/App.
7040200	4MV	1970	Passenger	402/330HP A/T Non-CA
				454/345, 360, 390HP A/T
			Chevelle Monte Carlo	402/330HP A/T
				454/360HP A/T
			Corvette	454/390HP A/T
7040201	4MV	1970	Passenger	402/330HP S/T CA
				454/360, 390HP S/T
			Chevelle	402/330HP S/T
				454/360HP S/T
			Monte Carlo	402/330HP S/T
			Corvette	454/390HP S/T
7040202 Non-CA	4MV	1970	Passenger	350/300HP A/T
			Chevelle	
			Camaro	
			Nova	
			Monte Carlo	
			Corvette	
7040203 1st design Non-CA	4MV	1970	Passenger	350/300HP S/T
			Chevelle	
			Camaro	
			Nova	
			Monte Carlo	
			Corvette	
7040204 Non-CA	4MV	1970	Chevelle	402/350HP A/T
				454/360HP A/T
			Camaro	402/350HP A/T
			Nova	402/350HP A/T
			Monte Carlo	402/330HP A/T
			Passenger	454/360, 390HP A/T
			Corvette	454/390HP A/T
7040205 Non-CA	4MV	1970	Chevelle	402/350HP S/T
			Camaro	
			Nova	
			Monte Carlo	402/330HP S/T
			Passenger	454/360, 390HP S/T
			Chevelle	454/360HP S/T
			Corvette	454/390HP S/T
7040207 Non-CA	4MV	1970	Corvette	350/350HP S/T
7040212 2nd design	4MV	1971	Corvette	350/300HP A/T
7040213 2nd design Non-CA	4MV	1970	Passenger	350/300HP S/T
			Chevelle	
			Camaro	
			Nova	
			Corvette	

continued on next page

Rochester 4BBL Carburetors (continued)

Number	Carb	Year	Model	Engine/App.
7040500 CA	4MV	1970	Passenger	402/330HP A/T
				454/345, 360, 390HP A/T
			Chevelle Monte Carlo	402/330HP A/T
				454/360HP A/T
			Corvette	454/390HP A/T
7040501 CA	4MV	1970	Passenger	402/330HP S/T
				454/360, 390HP S/T
			Chevelle	402/330HP S/T
				454/360HP S/T
			Monte Carlo	402/330HP S/T
			Corvette	454/390HP S/T
7040502 CA	4MV	1970	Passenger	350/300HP A/T
			Chevelle	
			Monte Carlo	
			Camaro	
			Nova	
			Corvette	
7040503 1st design CA	4MV	1970	Passenger	350/300HP S/T
			Chevelle	
			Monte Carlo	
			Camaro	
			Nova	
			Corvette	
7040504 CA	4MV	1970	Chevelle	402/350HP A/T
				454/360HP A/T
			Monte Carlo	402/330HP A/T
				454/360HP A/T
			Camaro	402/350HP A/T
			Nova	402/350HP A/T
			Passenger	454/360, 390HP A/T
			Corvette	454/390HP A/T
7040505 CA	4MV	1970	Chevelle	402/350HP S/T
				454/360HP S/T
			Camaro	402/350HP S/T
			Nova	402/350HP S/T
			Passenger	454/360, 390HP S/T
			Monte Carlo	402/330HP S/T
			Corvette	454/390HP S/T
7040507 CA	4MV	1970	Corvette	350/350HP S/T
7040513 2nd design CA	4MV	1970	Passenger	350/300HP S/T
			Chevelle	
			Monte Carlo	
			Camaro	
			Nova	
			Corvette	

Rochester 4BBL Carburetors (continued)

Number	Carb	Year	Model	Engine/App.
7041200	4MV	1971	Passenger	402/300HP A/T
				454/365HP A/T
			Chevelle Monte Carlo	402/300HP A/T
				454/365HP A/T
			Camaro	402/300HP A/T
7041201	4MV	1971	Passenger	402/300HP S/T
				454/365HP S/T
			Chevelle Monte Carlo	402/300HP S/T
				454/365HP S/T
			Camaro	402/300HP S/T
7041202	4MV	1971	Passenger	350/270HP A/T
			Chevelle	
			Monte Carlo	
			El Camino	
			Camaro	
			Nova	
7041203	4MV	1971	Passenger	350/270HP S/T
			Chevelle	
			Monte Carlo	
			El Camino	
			Camaro	
			Nova	
7041204	4MV	1971	Corvette	454/365HP A/T
7041205	4MV	1971	Corvette	454/365HP S/T
7041212	4MV	1971	Corvette	350/270HP A/T
7041213	4MV	1971	Corvette	350/270HP S/T
7042202	4MV	1972	Chevelle	350/175HP A/T Non-CA
			Monte Carlo	
			El Camino	
			Camaro	
			Nova	
			Corvette	350/200HP A/T Non-CA
7042203	4MV	1972	Chevelle	350/175HP S/T Non-CA
			Monte Carlo	
			El Camino	
			Camaro	
			Nova	
			Corvette	350/200HP S/T Non-CA
7042215	4MV	1972	Passenger	402/240HP S/T
			Chevelle	
			Monte Carlo	
			El Camino	
			Camaro	
			Passenger	454/270HP S/T
			Chevelle	
			Monte Carlo	
			El Camino	

continued on next page

Rochester 4BBL Carburetors (continued)

Number	Carb	Year	Model	Engine/App.
7042216	4MV	1972	Corvette	454/270HP A/T
7042217	4MV	1972	Corvette	454/270HP S/T
7042220	4MV	1972	Passenger	402/240HP A/T
			Chevelle	
			Monte Carlo	
			El Camino	
			Camaro	
		1972	Passenger	454/270HP A/T
			Chevelle	
			Monte Carlo	
			El Camino	
7042902		1972	Chevelle	350/175HP A/T CA
			Monte Carlo	
			El Camino	
			Camaro	
			Nova	
			Corvette	350/175HP A/T CA
7042903		1972	Chevelle	
			Monte Carlo	
			El Camino	
			Camaro	
			Nova	
			Corvette	350/200HP S/T CA
7043200	4MV	1973	Passenger	454/215HP A/T
			Chevelle	
			Monte Carlo	
			El Camino	
			Corvette	454/245HP A/T
7043201	4MV	1973	Passenger	454/215HP S/T
			Chevelle	
			Monte Carlo	
			El Camino	
			Corvette	454/245HP S/T
7043202	4MV	1973	Passenger	350/175HP A/T
			Chevelle	
			Monte Carlo	
			El Camino	
			Camaro	
			Nova	
			Corvette	350/190HP A/T
7043203	4MV	1973	Passenger	350/175HP S/T
			Chevelle	
			Monte Carlo	
			El Camino	
			Camaro	
			Nova	
			Corvette	350/190HP S/T
7043212	4MV	1973	Camaro	350/245HP A/T Hi Perf.
			Corvette	350/250HP L82

Rochester 4BBL Carburetors (continued)

Number	Carb	Year	Model	Engine/App.
7043213	4MV	1973	Camaro	350/245HP S/T Hi Perf.
			Corvette	350/250HP L82
7044201	4MV	1974	Chevelle	454/235HP S/T All
7044202	4MV	1974	Passenger	350/160HP A/T Non-CA
			Chevelle	
			Monte Carlo	
			Camaro	
			Nova	
7044203	4MV	1974	Passenger	350/160HP S/T Non-CA
			Chevelle	
			Monte Carlo	
			Camaro	
			Nova	
7044206	4MV	1974	Camaro	350/185HP A/T Non-CA
			Nova	
			Corvette	350/195HP S/T Non-CA
7044207	4MV	1974	Camaro	350/185HP S/T Non-CA
			Nova	
			Corvette	350/195HP S/T Non-CA
7044208	4MV	1974	Camaro Z-28	350/245HP A/T
7044209	4MV	1974	Camaro Z-28	350/245HP S/T
7044210	4MV	1974	Corvette	350/250HP A/T L-82
7044211	4MV	1974	Corvette	350/250HP S/T L-82
7044221	4MV	1974	Corvette	454/270HP S/T All
7044223	4MV	1974	Passenger	454/235HP A/T Non-CA
			Chevelle	
			Monte Carlo	
7044225		1974	Corvette	454/270HP A/T Non-CA
7044226	4MV	1974	Passenger Wagon	400/180HP A/T Non-CA
7044500	4MV	1974	Passenger	454/235HP A/T CA
			Chevelle	
			Monte Carlo	
7044502	4MV	1974	Passenger	350/160HP A/T CA
			Chevelle	
			Monte Carlo	
			Camaro	
			Nova	
7044503	4MV	1974	Passenger	350/160HP S/T CA
			Chevelle	
			Monte Carlo	
			Camaro	
			Nova	
7044505		1974	Corvette	454/270HP A/T CA

continued on next page

Rochester 4BBL Carburetors (continued)

Number	Carb	Year	Model	Engine/App.
7044506	4MV	1974	Camaro	350/185HP A/T CA
			Nova	
			Corvette	350/195HP A/T CA
7044507	4MV	1974	Camaro	350/185HP S/T CA
			Nova	
			Corvette	350/195HP S/T CA
7044526	4MV	1974	Passenger	400/180HP A/T CA
			Chevelle	400/180HP A/T CA
			Monte Carlo	400/180HP A/T CA
			El Camino	400/180HP A/T CA
			GMC Sprint	400/180HP A/T CA
7045200	M4MC	1975	Passenger	454/215HP A/T Non-CA
			Chevelle	
			Monte Carlo	
7045202	M4MC	1975	Camaro	350/155HP A/T Non-CA
7045203	M4MC	1975	Camaro	350/155HP S/T Non-CA
7045206	M4MC	1975	Nova	350/155HP A/T Non-CA
7045207	M4MC	1975	Nova	350/155HP S/T Non-CA
7045210	M4MC	1975	Corvette	350/205HP A/T Non-CA L-82
7045211	M4MC	1975	Corvette	350/205HP S/T Non-CA L-82
7045221	M4MC	1975	Passenger	454 A/T Canada
			Chevelle	454 A/T Canada
			Monte Carlo	454 A/T Canada
7045222	M4MC	1975	Corvette	350/165HP A/T
7045223	M4MC	1975	Corvette	350/165HP S/T
7045224	M4MC	1975	Passenger	400/175HP A/T CA
			Chevelle	
			Monte Carlo	
7045228	M4MC	1975	Passenger	400/175HP A/T Non-CA
			Chevelle	
			Monte Carlo	
7045294	M4MC	1975	Passenger	350 A/T Canada
			Chevelle	350 A/T Canada
			Monte Carlo	350 A/T Canada
7045502	M4MC A	1975	Camaro	350/155HP A/T CA
7045503	M4MC A	1975	Camaro	350/155HP S/T CA
7045504	M4MC	1975	Passenger	350/155HP A/T CA
			Chevelle	
			Monte Carlo	
7045506	M4MC A	1975	Nova	350/155HP A/T CA
7045507	M4MC A	1975	Nova	350/155HP S/T CA

Carter-built Rochester 4-barrel Carburetors

Although it may seem strange, Carter actually built a select group of Rochester carburetors. The reason is simple: General Motors wanted a second source from which to buy in case of a Rochester strike. Carter also built carburetors for many other GM divisions.

It is interesting that Carter built only the Quadrajet. The following listing is to date the only complete listing for all Carter-built Chevrolet carburetors.

All Carter-built Quadrajets will have "MFG by Carter" cast into the carburetor body.

Carter-built Rochester 4BBL Carburetors

Number	Carb	Year	Model	Engine/App.
7040200 Non-CA	4MV	1970	Passenger	402/330HP A/T
				454/345, 360, 390HP A/T
			Chevelle	402/330HP A/T
			Monte Carlo	454/360HP A/T
			Corvette	454/390HP A/T
7040202 Non-CA	4MV	1970	Passenger	350/300HP A/T
			Chevelle	
			Monte Carlo	
			Camaro	
			Nova	
			Corvette	
7040203 1st Design Non-CA	4MV	1970	Passenger	350/300HP S/T
			Chevelle	
			Monte Carlo	
			Camaro	
			Nova	
			Corvette	
7041200	4MV	1971	Passenger	402/300HP A/T
				454/365HP A/T
			Chevelle Monte Carlo	402/300HP A/T
				454/365HP A/T
			Camaro	402/300HP A/T
7041202	4MV	1971	Passenger	350/270HP A/T
			Chevelle	
			Monte Carlo	
			El Camino	
			Camaro	
			Nova	
7041203	4MV	1971	Passenger	350/270HP S/T
			Chevelle	
			Monte Carlo	
			El Camino	
			Camaro	
			Nova	

continued on next page

Carter-built Rochester 4BBL Carburetors (continued)

Number	Carb	Year	Model	Engine/App.
7042202	4MV	1972	Chevelle	350/175HP A/T Non-CA
			Monte Carlo	
			El Camino	
			Camaro	
			Nova	
			Corvette	350/200HP A/T Non-CA
7042203	4MV	1972	Chevelle	350/175HP S/T Non-CA
			Monte Carlo	
			El Camino	
			Camaro	
			Nova	
			Corvette	350/200HP S/T Non-CA
7042215	4MV	1972	Passenger	402/240HP S/T
			Chevelle	
			Monte Carlo	
			El Camino	
			Camaro	
			Passenger	454/270HP S/T
			Chevelle	
			Monte Carlo	
			El Camino	
7042216	4MV	1972	Corvette	454/270HP A/T
7042217	4MV	1972	Corvette	454/270HP S/T
7042220	4MV	1972	Passenger	402/240HP A/T
			Chevelle	
			Monte Carlo	
			El Camino	
			Camaro	
		1972	Passenger	454/270HP A/T
			Chevelle	
			Monte Carlo	
			El Camino	

Carter-built Rochester 4BBL Carburetors (continued)

Number	Carb	Year	Model	Engine/App.
7043200	4MV	1973	Passenger	454/215HP A/T
			Chevelle	
			Monte Carlo	
			El Camino	
			Corvette	454/245HP A/T
7043202	4MV	1973	Passenger	350/175HP A/T
			Chevelle	
			Monte Carlo	
			El Camino	
			Camaro	
			Nova	
			Corvette	350/190HP A/T
7044202	4MV	1974	Passenger	350/160HP A/T Non-CA
			Chevelle	
			Monte Carlo	
			Camaro	
			Nova	
7044206	4MV	1974	Camaro	350/185HP A/T Non-CA
			Nova	
			Corvette	350/195HP S/T Non-CA
7044226	4MV	1974	Passenger Wagon	400/180HP A/T Non-CA
7045200	M4MC	1975	Passenger	454/215HP A/T Non-CA
			Chevelle	
			Monte Carlo	
7045202	M4MC	1975	Camaro	350/155HP A/T Non-CA
7045228	M4MC	1975	Passenger	400/175HP A/T Non-CA
			Chevelle	
			Monte Carlo	

Chapter 9

Intake Manifold Identification

1. Introduction

All intake manifolds on Chevrolet engines in these years listed rest on top of the cylinder heads and underneath the carburetor. Two types of intake manifolds were installed on Chevrolet vehicles covered in this book: aluminum and cast iron. Cast iron manifolds were generally used on low performance engines. Aluminum intake manifolds, almost without exception, are found on high performance engines. Almost all Chevrolet aluminum intakes were cast by Winters Industries in Canton, Ohio and will usually carry the Winters "snowflake" logo on the intake.

All intake manifolds have a casting number on top of the intake near the carburetor. This number is raised above the actual casting of the manifold. Although relatively easy to find on aluminum manifolds, on cast iron manifolds the numbers may be somewhat corroded, so have a stiff wire brush handy. The numbers "6," "8," "5," and "3" are easily confused or mistaken for each other and should be looked at very closely.

Most aluminum intake manifolds have dates cast into the underside of the intake, usually under the oil splash shield. Most cast iron intakes have dates cast into the top of the intake, usually near the casting number. Some intakes have complete dates (2-2-65) and some have dates cast in an alpha code i.e. Jan = A, Feb = B, March = C, etc. Date codes usually follow the same pattern as engine blocks and cylinder heads. The following is a breakdown of the casting date month codes:

Intake Manifold Month Codes (1st Letter)

A - January	E - May	I - September
B - February	F - June	J - October
C - March	G - July	K - November
D - April	H - August	L - December

The number or numbers following the month code letter represent the day of the month that the manifold was cast. The last number indicates the calendar year. Never count on identifying an intake manifold by its date. Only use this as a method of narrowing down the age of the manifold. Always use the casting number for identification.

Example: A 13 0

- A = Month: January
- 13 = Day: 13th day of month
- 0 = Year: 1970

Experimental Intakes

Many experimental intakes were either installed on pre-production vehicles, given to factory-backed race teams, or stolen from the General Motors Proving Grounds. It is highly possible that you may run across one of these intakes. Almost all of Chevrolet's experimental parts were cast with a "0-" casting number or a "L-" casting number. These intakes will also carry a date code, but usually one to three years prior to the model year the manifold was designed for. Nothing is impossible, but it's fairly safe to say that no experimental intakes were intended to be released and final assembled on a factory production engine. Sometimes these intakes will carry two casting numbers. No particular "higher value" can be assigned to an experimental part, just because it is experimental.

NOTE—
When checking date codes of specific engine parts, always remember the following. First verify the build date of your car. (Refer to Chapter 1 for more information on build dates.) The date codes of the various engine components should generally be dated one to three months prior to the car build date. This time lapse allows for assembly of that engine, transport to the car assembly plant and installation in your car.

2. Aluminum Intake Manifolds

Manifold #3959594

Carb Type	Year	Model	Engine	Horsepower
4BBL Holley	1971	Corvette	350	330
		Camaro Z28	350	330
	1972	Corvette	350	255
		Camaro Z28	350	255
This intake is identical with #3917610 with a few changes. The front of the intake manifold has been totally redesigned. The thermostat housing has been centered in the front of the intake. There is now a heater outlet boss on the upper right thermostat passage and the oil filler tube boss has been deleted. There is now a "pedestal" type choke boss present instead of the "well" design on earlier manifolds. There are now intake numbers cast into the top of the runners near the cylinder head. This intake manifold used four regular silver carburetor studs. The overall height of this intake was decreased by 0.18 inches over the #3917610 intake manifold. There are other minor casting changes which are insignificant to mention here.				

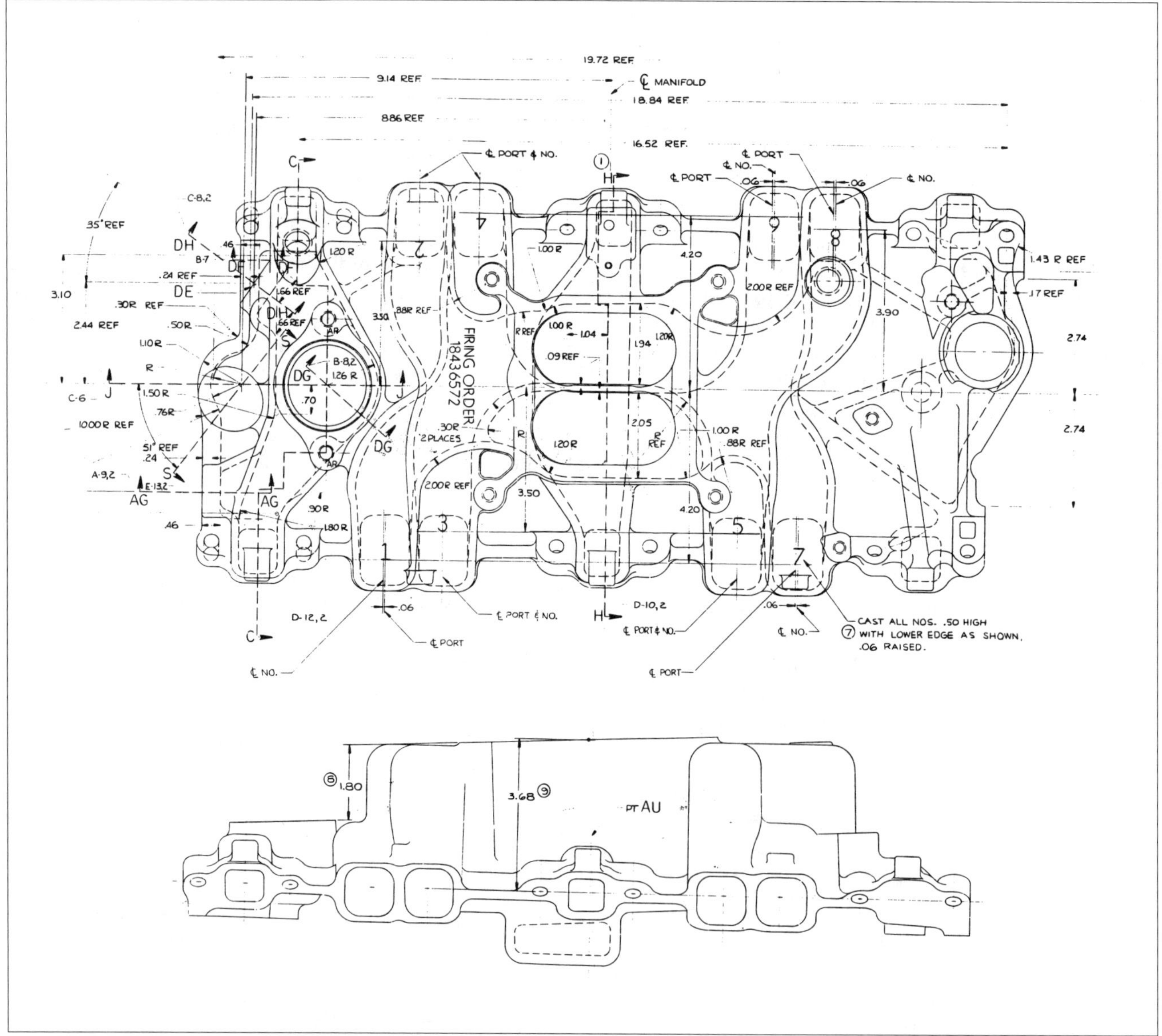

Fig. 9-1. Top and side view of #3959594.

Manifold #3963569

Carb Type	Year	Model	Engine	Horsepower
4BBL Holley	1970	Nova	402	375
		Chevelle	402	375
			454	450
		Monte Carlo (unverified)	454	450
		Camaro	402	375
	1971	Corvette	454	425
		Chevelle	454	425
		Monte Carlo (unverified)	454	425
This intake is similar to #3919852. This is the new low rise aluminum intake that was introduced for Corvette low-hood restrictions. The carburetor flange is only 1.25 inches above the cylinder head ports. This intake manifold has an oil splash shield.				

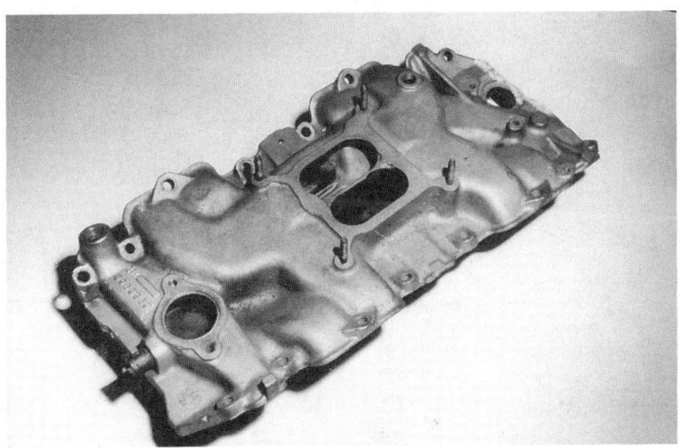

Fig. 9-2. ***Left****: overall view of #3963569.* ***Right****: close up shows casting number and Winters foundry logo (lower right).*

Manifold #3967474

Carb Type	Year	Model	Engine	Horsepower
4BBL Holley	1971	Corvette (unverified)	454	425
This intake was previously thought to be used on the 1971 Corvette 454/425HP engine, however, this is a completely different design from #3963569 that was used in most applications. This intake has an open plenum design for high rpm usage. This is a high rise design manifold with a height identical to #3866963, so it is doubtful that this was ever installed on an original 1971 Corvette. Other sources have stated this fact, but it is unverified. There is a possibility that this intake was used as a service replacement for the L88 or ZL1 engines due to the open plenum design. The front of the intake is identical to #3963569 in that there is only one water heater outlet boss underneath the thermostat. There are cast numbers above the intake port on each side of the manifold. The choke assembly pad is flat and only has two tapped holes to mount the new design choke. It is unverified if any of these manifolds had an oil splash shield.				

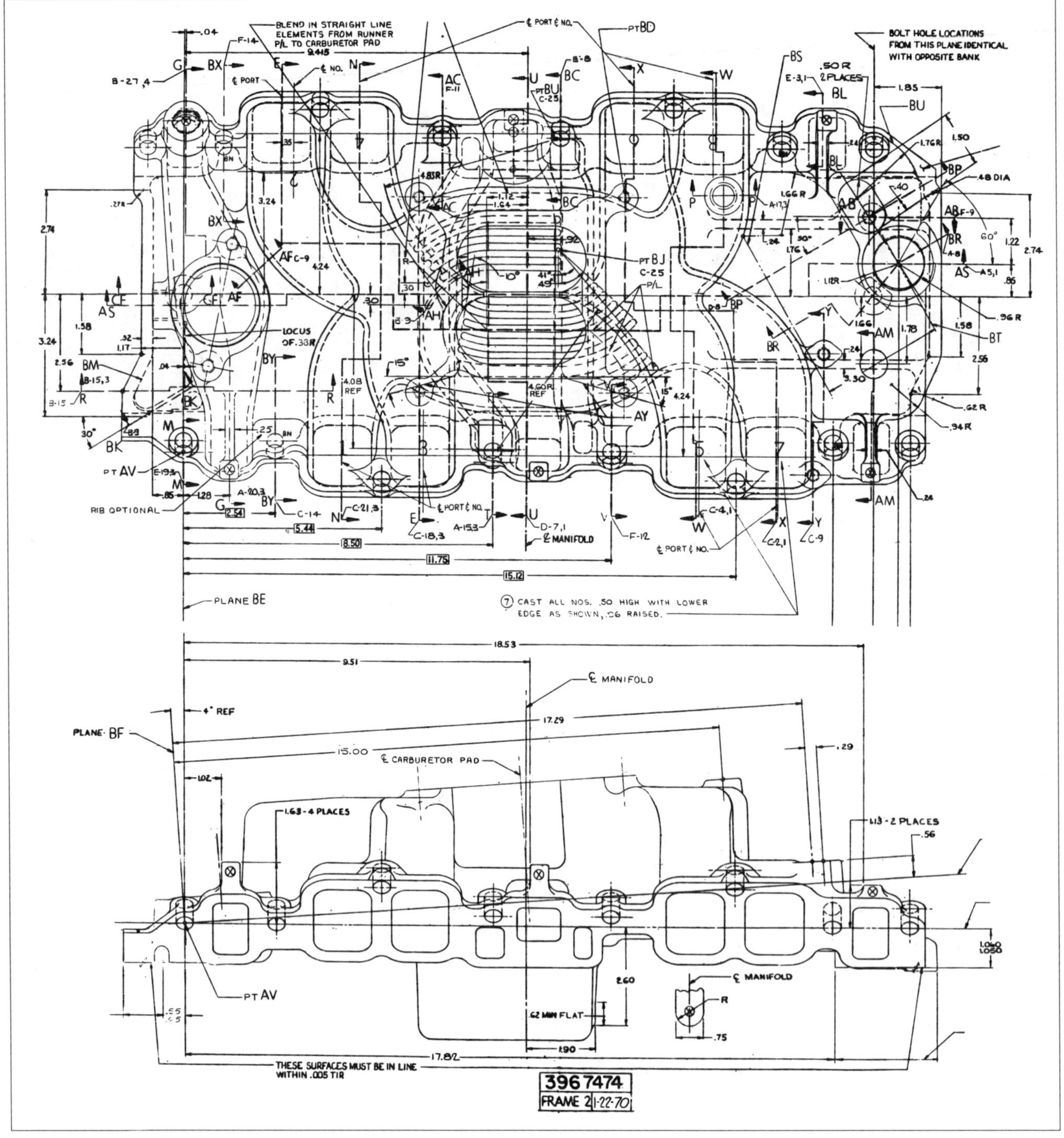

Fig. 9-3. Top and side view of #3967474.

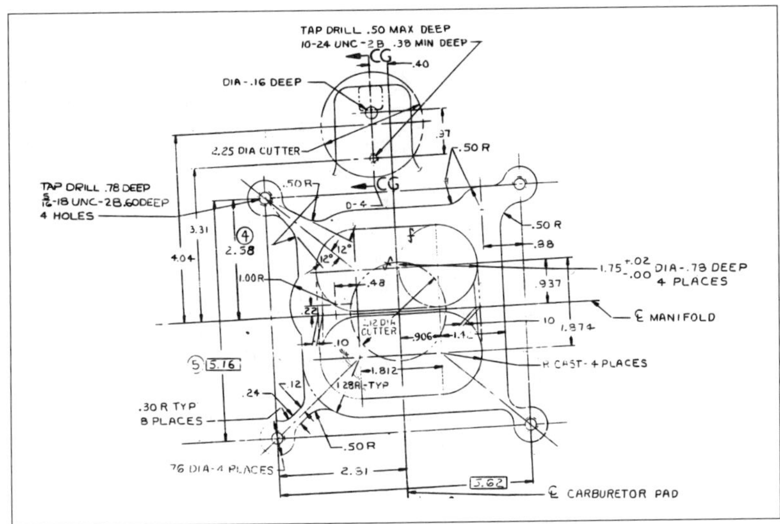

Fig. 9-4. Carb pad and plenum cut detail of #3967474.

Manifold #3972110

Carb Type	Year	Model	Engine	Horsepower
4BBL Holley	1970	Corvette	350	370
		Camaro Z28	350	360
		Yenko Duece Nova	350	360

The intake is identical with #3917610 with a few changes. All tapped water outlets at the front of the intake have been deleted. A new heater outlet boss is now on top of the right front thermostat passage. This intake has an oil splash shield. The overall height of this intake was decreased by 0.18 over the #3917610 manifold. All other casting changes are insignificant. This intake used four 1.86" carburetor studs. Many sources state that the #3972116 intake is correct for these applications. However, the #3972116 is a service only intake, and later casting dates on these parts should reflect this point.

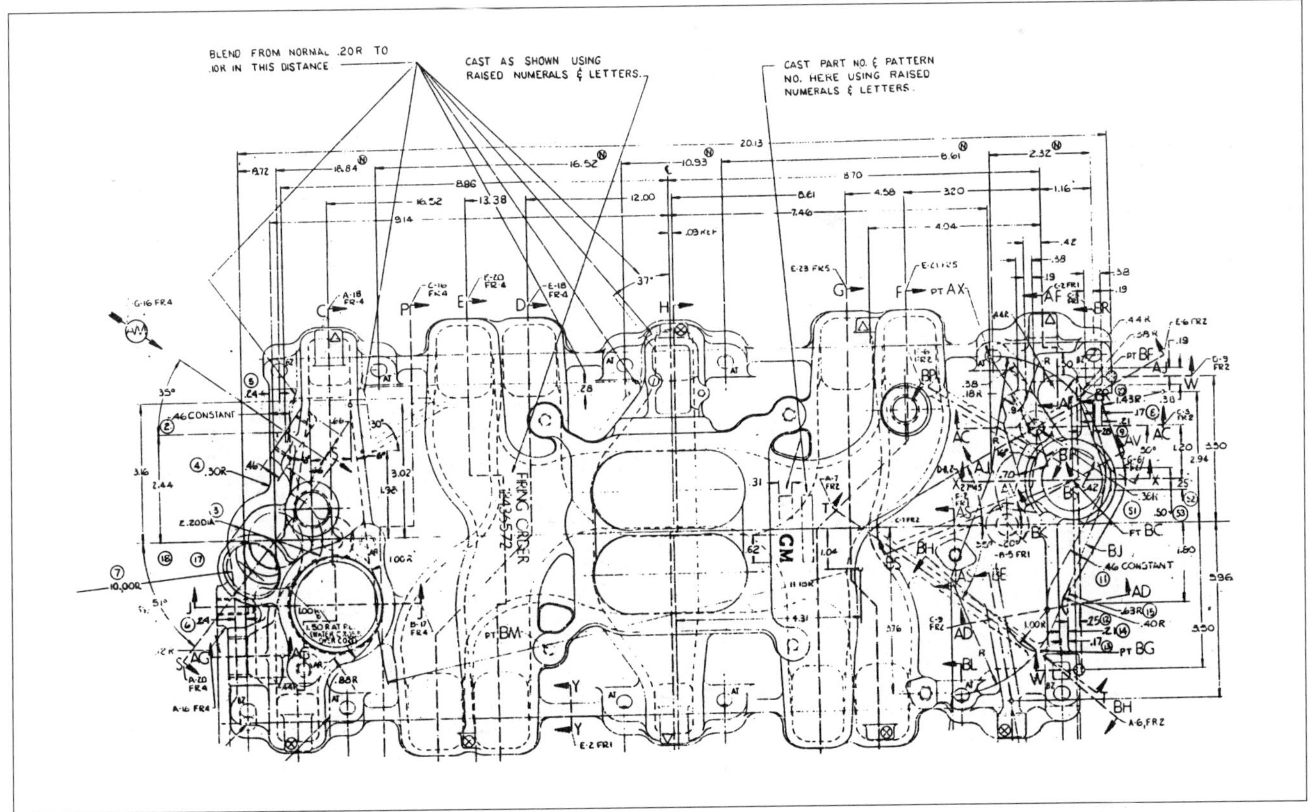

Fig. 9-5. Blueprint of #3917610 intake.

continued on next page

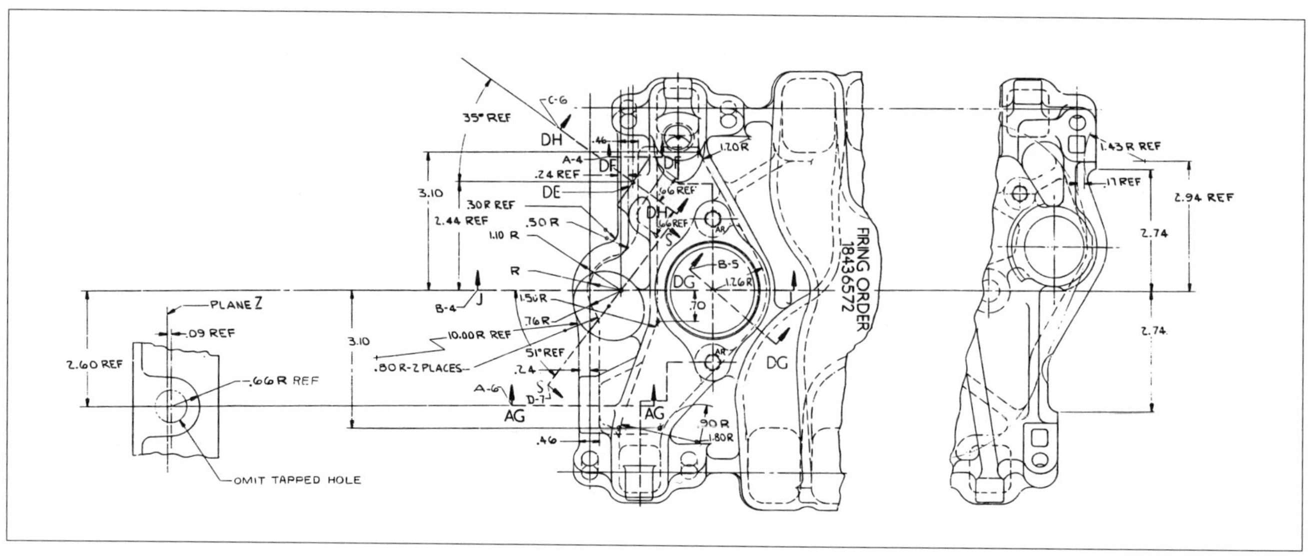

Fig. 9-5. *(cont'd) Detail of #3972110 shows changes from #3917610.*

10. Cast Iron Intake Manifolds

Manifold #3916313$^{\Delta}$

Carb Type	Year	Model	Engine	Horsepower
2BBL Rochester	1970	Passenger	350	250
			400	265
		Chevelle	350	250
		Nova	350	250
		Camaro	350	250
		Monte Carlo	350	250
			400	265
This intake manifold was primarily a low performance intake. It does not have an oil splash shield. It was used extensively as a service replacement manifold and has four 1.48" studs. $^{\Delta}$This manifold was also used in the 1969 model year.				

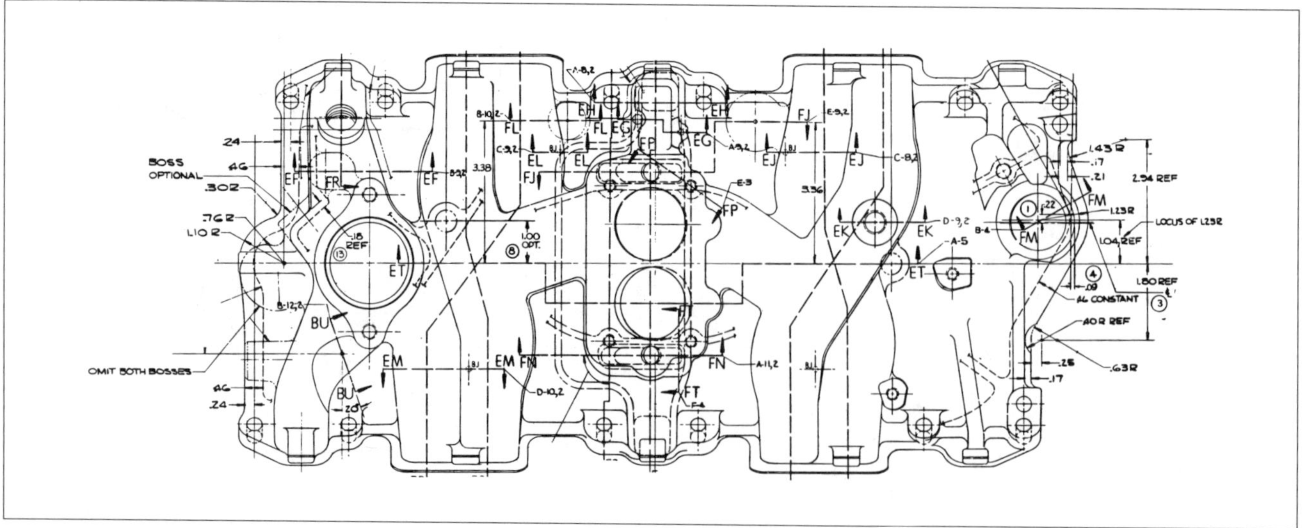

Fig. 9-6. *Top view of #3916313.*

Manifold #3927183$^{\Delta}$

Carb Type	Year	Model	Engine	Horsepower
2BBL Rochester	1970	Nova	307	200
		Chevelle	307	200
		Camaro	307	200

This intake manifold was used on low performance small block engines. It is identical with #3919801 (a 307/327 head used in 1968) except for some minor casting changes. The oil filler tube boss and the water by-pass boss have been eliminated. A new drilled and tapped heater nipple boss is on the front intake runner to the right of the thermostat housing. This intake has an oil splash shield and four 1.69" regular carburetor studs. It was used extensively as a service replacement.

$^{\Delta}$This manifold was also used in the 1969 model year.

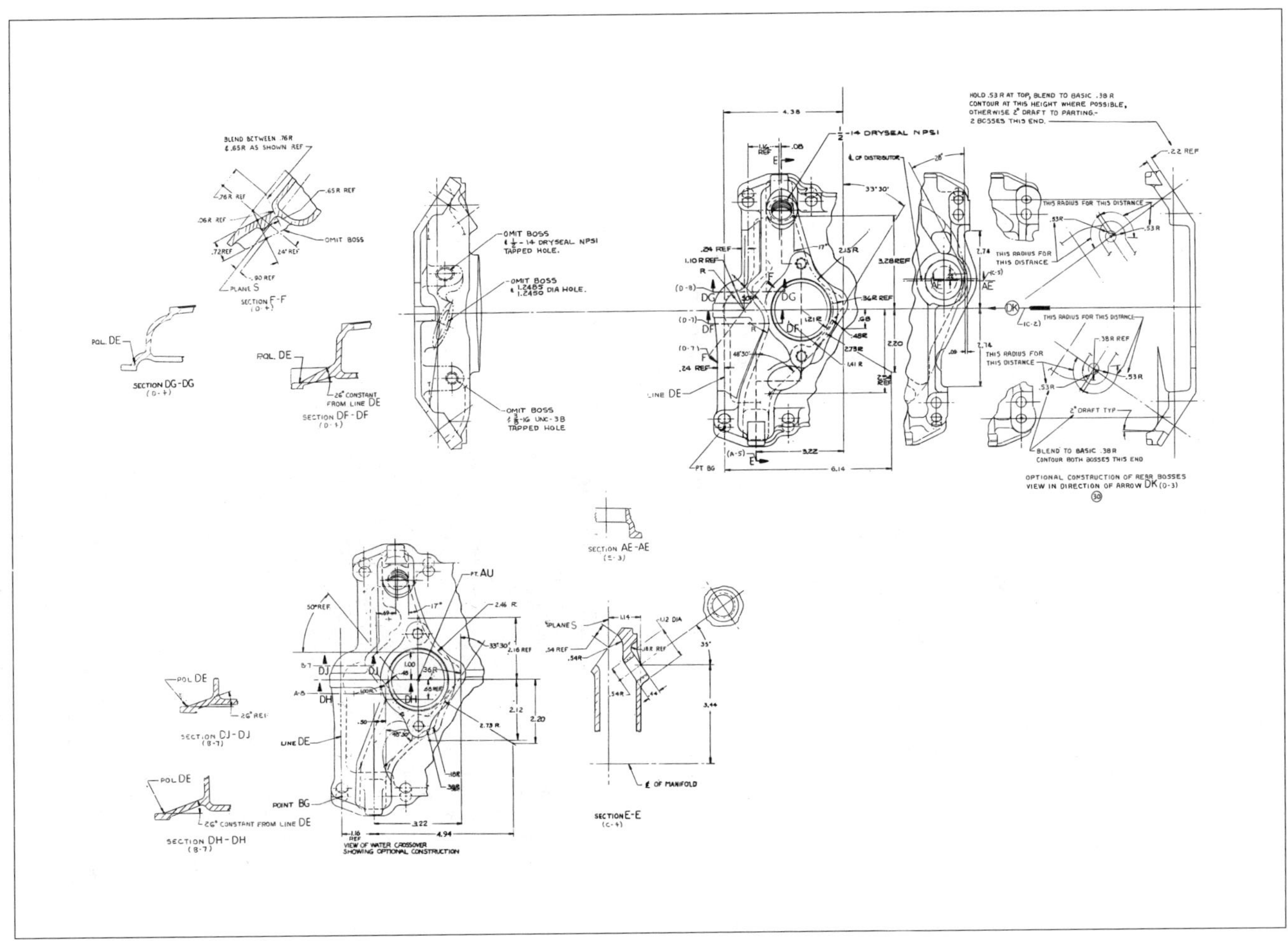

Fig. 9-7. Blueprint shows changes to #3927183 from #3919801.

Manifold #3955287

Carb Type	Year	Model	Engine	Horsepower
4BBL Rochester	1970	Passenger	454	390
		Corvette	454	390
		Nova	402	350
		Chevelle	402	330, 350
			454	360
		Monte Carlo	402	330
		Monte Carlo SS	454	360
		Camaro	402	350
	1971	Passenger	402	300
			454	365
		Corvette	454	365
		Chevelle	402	300
			454	365
		Monte Carlo	402	300
		Monte Carlo SS	454	365
		Camaro	402	300
		GMC Sprint	402	300
		GMC Sprint SP	454	365
This manifold was a completely new design for the 1970 model year. All intake manifolds were cut down due to lower hood lines. This intake does not have an oil splash shield.				

Fig. 9-8. ***Left****: overall view of #3955287.* ***Right****: detail shows casting number and date code.*

Manifold #3965577

Carb Type	Year	Model	Engine	Horsepower
4BBL Rochester	1970	Passenger	350	300
		Corvette	350	300, 350
		Nova	350	300
		Chevelle	350	300
		Monte Carlo	350	300
		Camaro	350	300
This intake is identical to #3844459 except for minor casting changes. All #3965577 intakes should have a cast raised letter "S" on the underside of the intake. It has two rear 1.69" carburetor studs. This intake has an oil splash shield.				

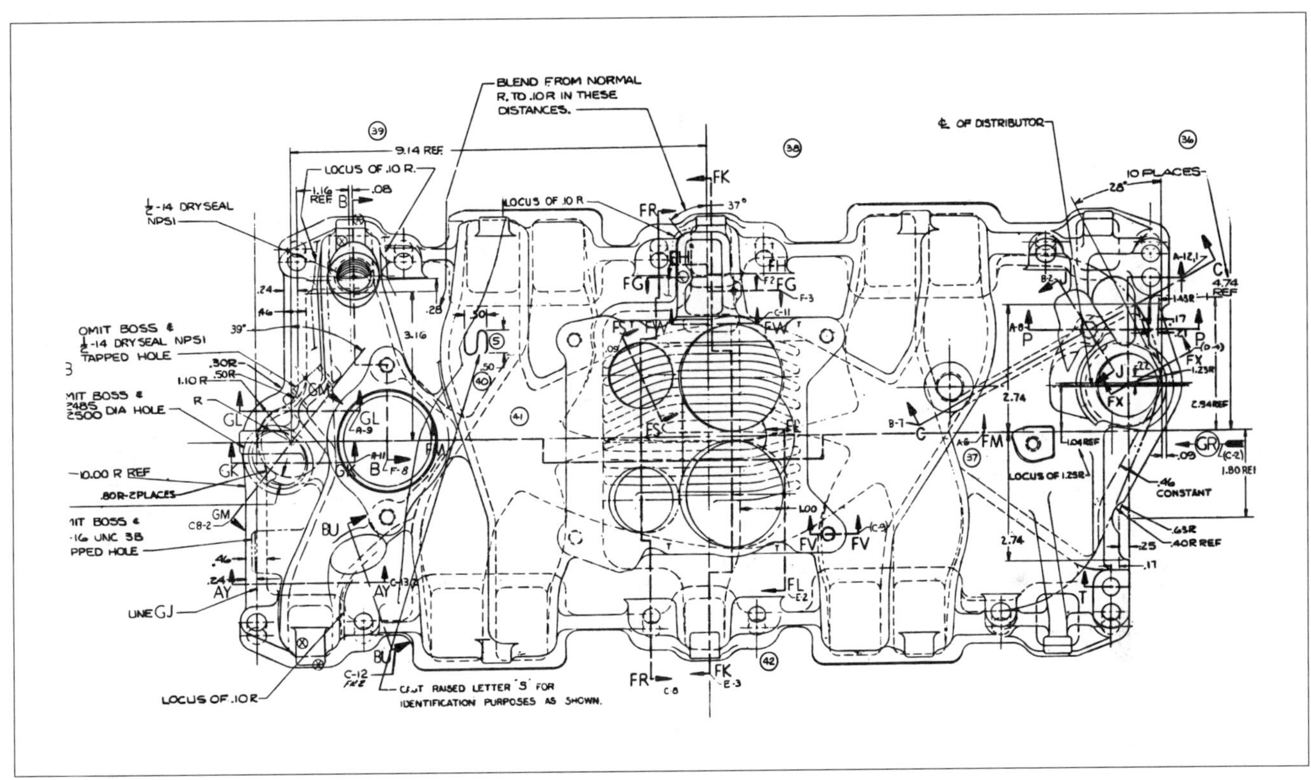

Fig. 9-9. *Top view of #3965577.*

Manifold #3973465

Carb Type	Year	Model	Engine	Horsepower
2BBL Rochester	1971	Nova	307	200
		Chevelle	307	200
		Camaro	307	200
This manifold is identical with #3919801 except for some small changes. The heater hose nipple position has been moved from the front of the intake to the top of the intake to the right of the thermostat housing. The oil tube boss is not present. Also, the intake ports have cast numbers after the 1/12/70 date. This intake has four black carburetor studs and an oil splash shield.				

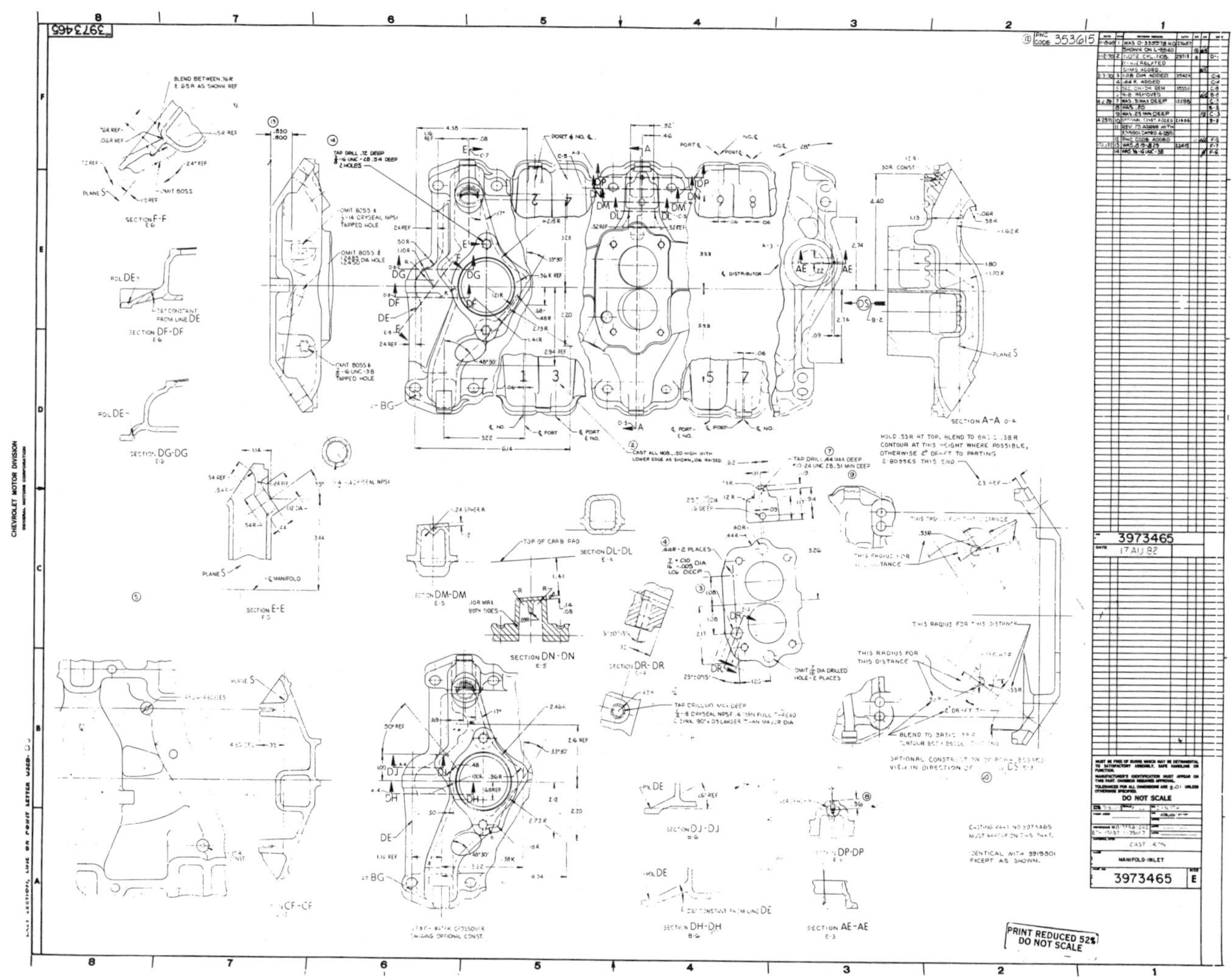

Fig. 9-10. Blueprint for #3973465 indicates it is identical with #3919801 except as shown.

Manifold #3973467

Carb Type	Year	Model	Engine	Horsepower
2BBL Rochester	1971	Passenger	350	245
			400	255
		Nova Chevelle / Monte Carlo Camaro	350	245
This manifold is identical with #3844459 except for minor changes. The heater hose nipple has been moved to the top of the intake and to the right of the thermostat housing. The oil tube boss has been omitted. This intake has four black carburetor studs and an oil splash shield.				

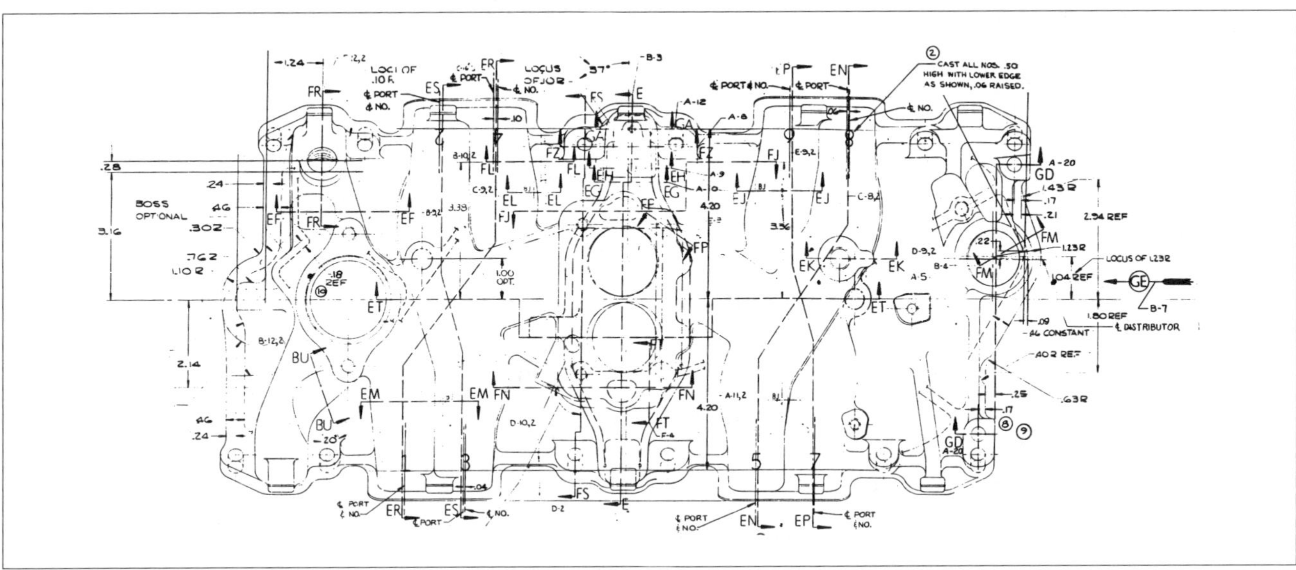

Fig. 9-11. Top view of #3973467.

Manifold #3973469

Carb Type	Year	Model	Engine	Horsepower
4BBL Rochester	1971	Passenger Corvette Nova Chevelle / Monte Carlo Camaro	350	270
This intake is identical with #3844459 except for minor casting changes. The heater hose nipple position has been moved to the top of the intake and to the right of the thermostat housing. The oil tube boss has now been omitted. Also, a cast raised letter "S" is now on the underside of the intake. This intake has two black rear carburetor studs and an oil splash shield.				

Fig. 9-12. ***Left:*** *overall view of #3973469.* ***Right:*** *highlight of casting date (K 24 0), casting number and GM mold number 8. Also note numbered intake runners.*

Manifold #3997771

Carb Type	Year	Model	Engine	Horsepower
4BBL Rochester	1973	Passenger	350	175
		Corvette	350	190, 250
		Nova	350	175
		Chevelle	350	175
		Monte Carlo	350	175
		Camaro	350	175, 245
There are the cast letters "EGR" on the underside of the manifold indicating an EGR boss on top of the intake instituted during the 1973 model year. This manifold has the intake runner numbers cast on the outside. This intake has an oil splash shield.				

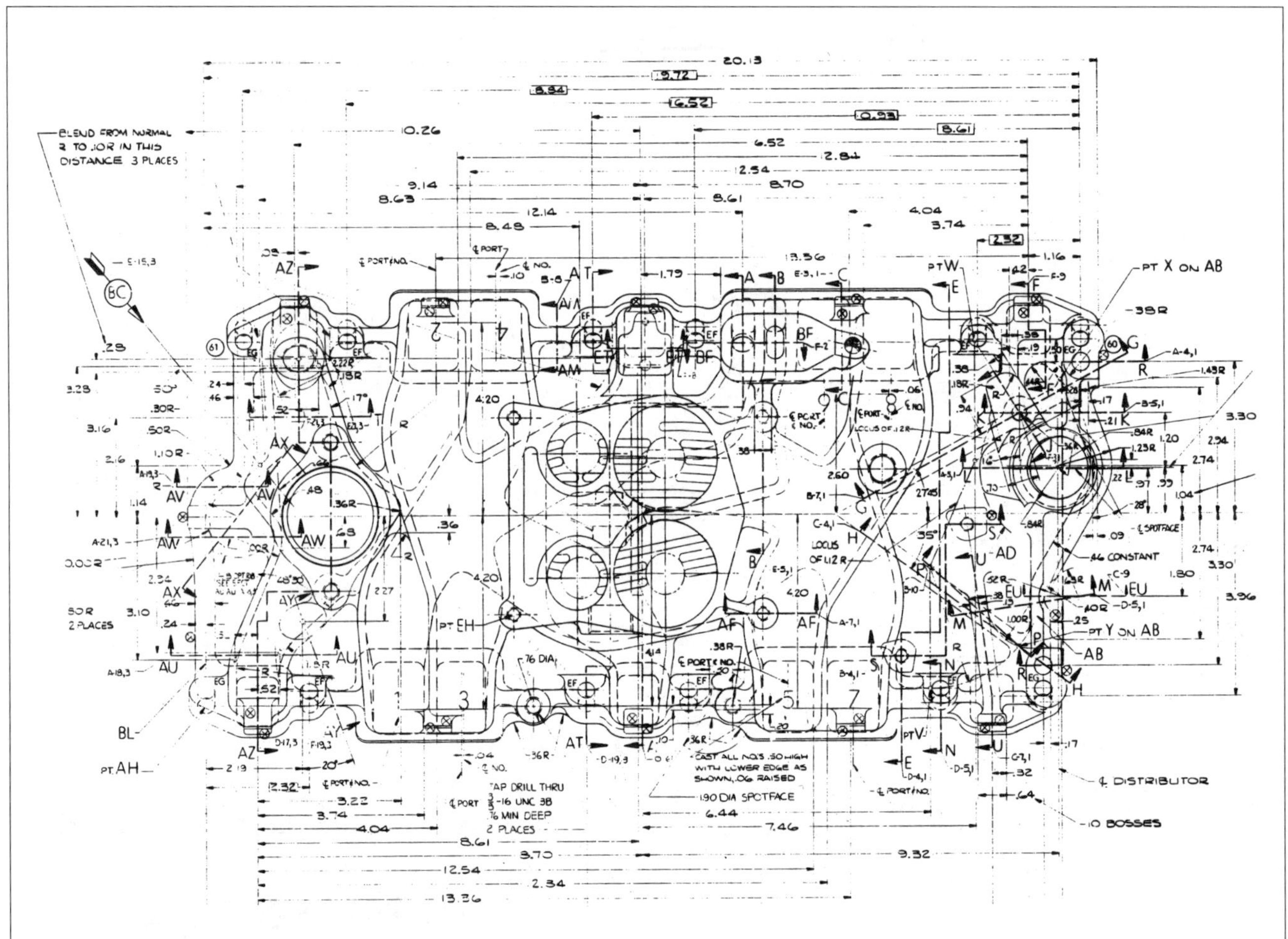

Fig. 9-13. Top view of #3997771.

Manifold #3997773

Carb Type	Year	Model	Engine	Horsepower
2BBL Rochester	1973	Passenger	350	145
			400	150
		Nova	350	145
		Chevelle	350	145
		Monte Carlo	350	145
		Camaro	350	145
This intake is identical with #3997771 except for some minor changes. This intake has the intake runners numbered. Obviously the carburetor pad has been changed to accept the 2-barrel carburetor and the interior casting also reflects that change. There is the presence of an EGR boss on top of the intake to accept the EGR fitting instituted during the 1973 model year. This intake does not have an oil splash shield.				

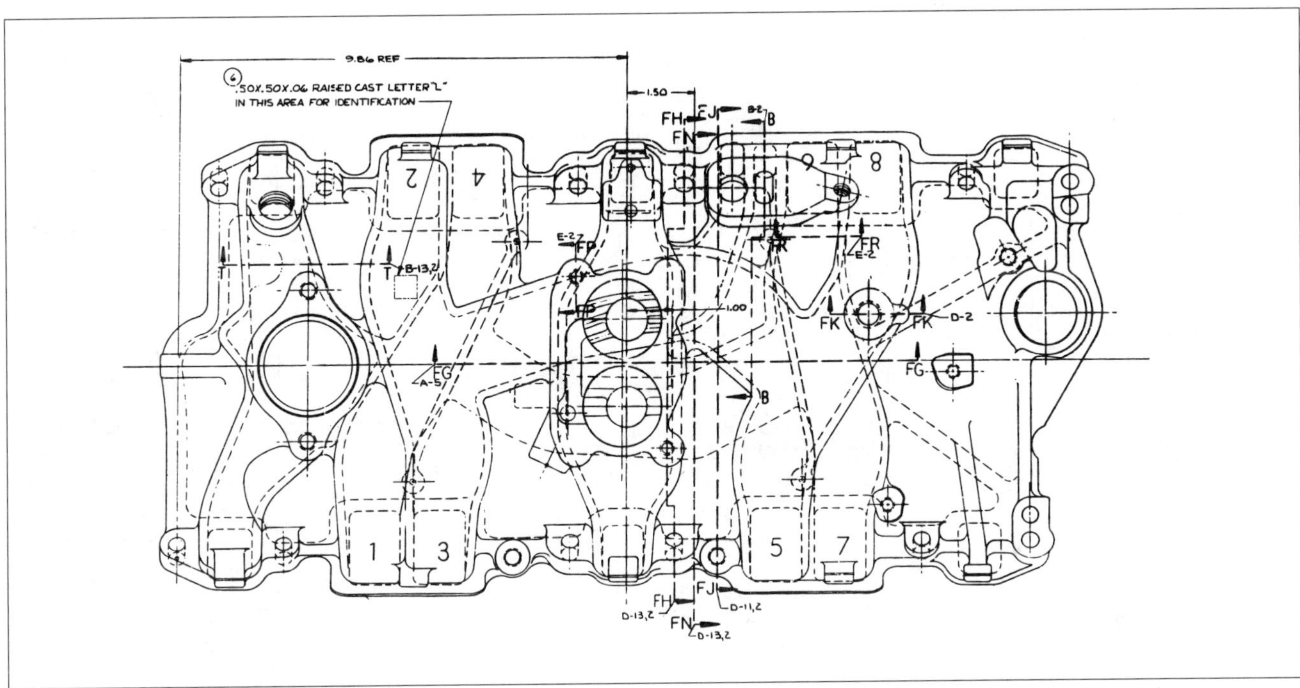

Fig. 9-14. Top view of #3997773.

Manifold #6262936

Carb Type	Year	Model	Engine	Horsepower
2BBL Rochester	1972	Nova	307	130
		Chevelle	307	130
		Camaro	307	130
This intake was used exclusively on 1972 307/130HP engines. The intake is identical with #3919801 with some minor changes. The carburetor pad and choke well have been redesigned. The heater hose boss has been relocated to the top of the intake and to the right of the thermostat housing. The oil filler tube boss and the heater hose boss at the front of the intake have been omitted. All intake runners now have cast numbers at the outside of the manifold. Finally, the last three digits of the casting number are cast into the underside of the intake below the #7 intake port. This intake has an oil splash shield.				

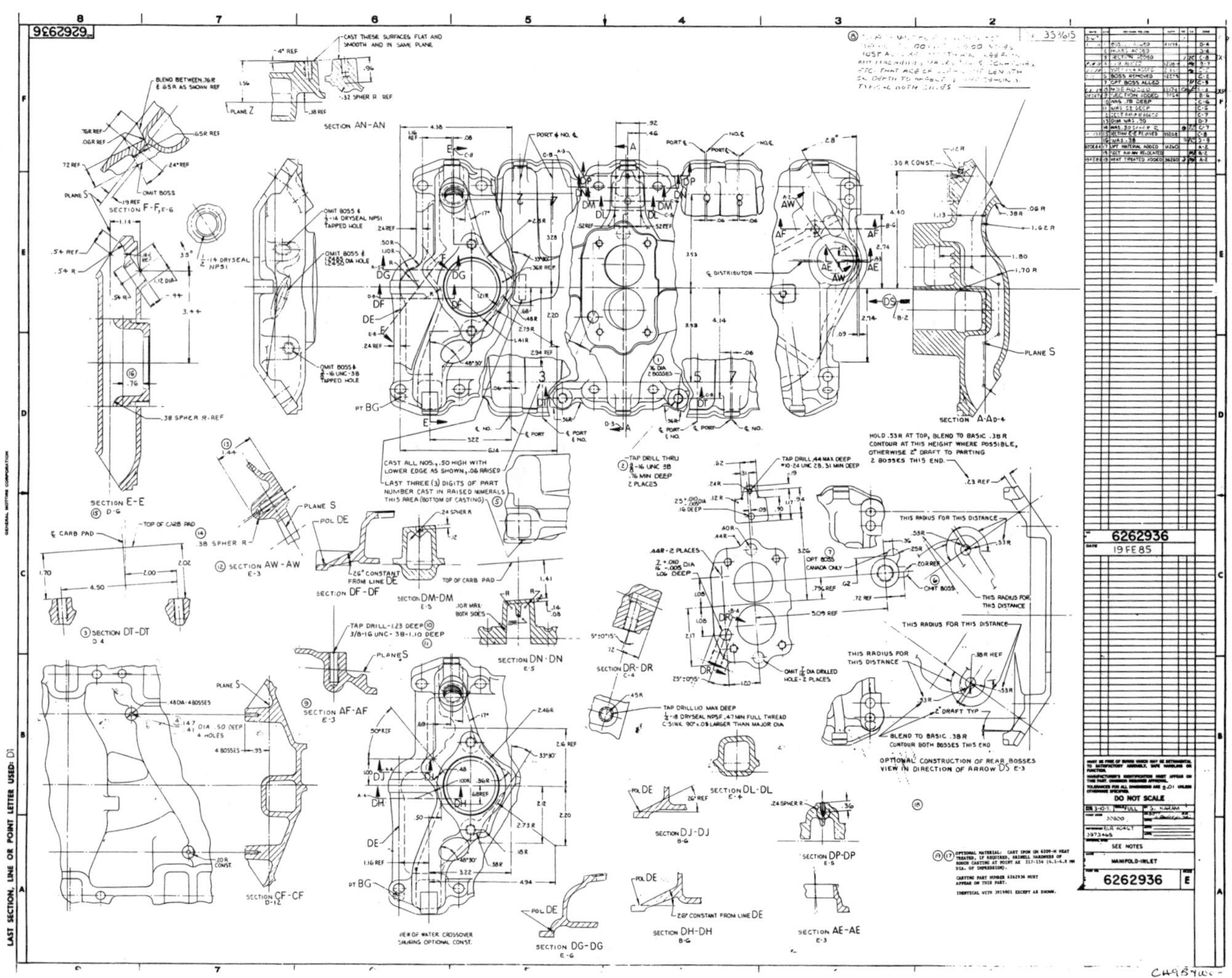

Fig. 9-15. Blueprint for #6262936 indicates it is identical with #3919801 except as shown.

Manifold #6263751

Carb Type	Year	Model	Engine	Horsepower
4BBL Rochester	1972	Corvette	350	200
		Nova	350	175
		Chevelle / Monte Carlo	350	175
		Camaro	350	175
This manifold is identical to #3844459 except for some changes. The heater hose nipple position was moved to the top of the intake. The oil filler tube boss and heater hose boss at the front of the intake have been omitted. Also the carburetor pad and the choke well have been redesigned. The last 3 digits of the casting number are cast into the bottom side of the intake. There are also intake runner numbers cast into each runner on this manifold. There are minor internal casting changes as well. This intake has an oil splash shield.				

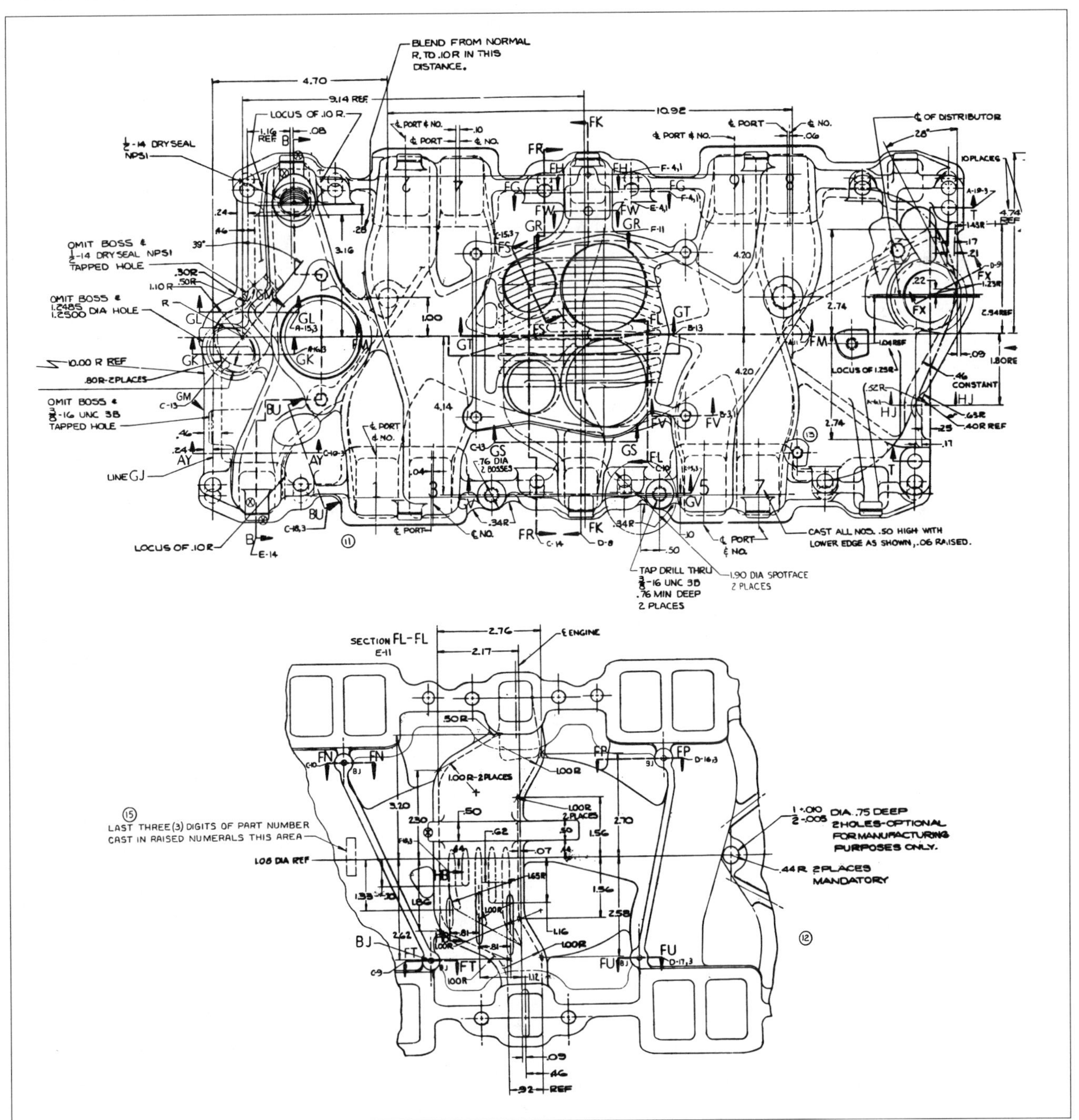

Fig. 9-16. *Top view of #6263751. Also view from below, noting casting position of last three digits of part number.*

Manifold #6263752

Carb Type	Year	Model	Engine	Horsepower
2BBL Rochester	1972	Passenger	350	165
			400	170
		Nova	350	165
		Chevelle / Monte Carlo	350	165
		Camaro	350	165
This manifold is identical with #3973467 except for some minor internal and external casting changes. On this intake, there are now 2 accessory bosses between the #3 and #5 intake ports. Internal ribbing has been added to the plenum chamber underneath the carburetor mounting pad. Also, the last three digits of the casting number are cast into the bottom of the intake. This intake has an oil splash shield.				

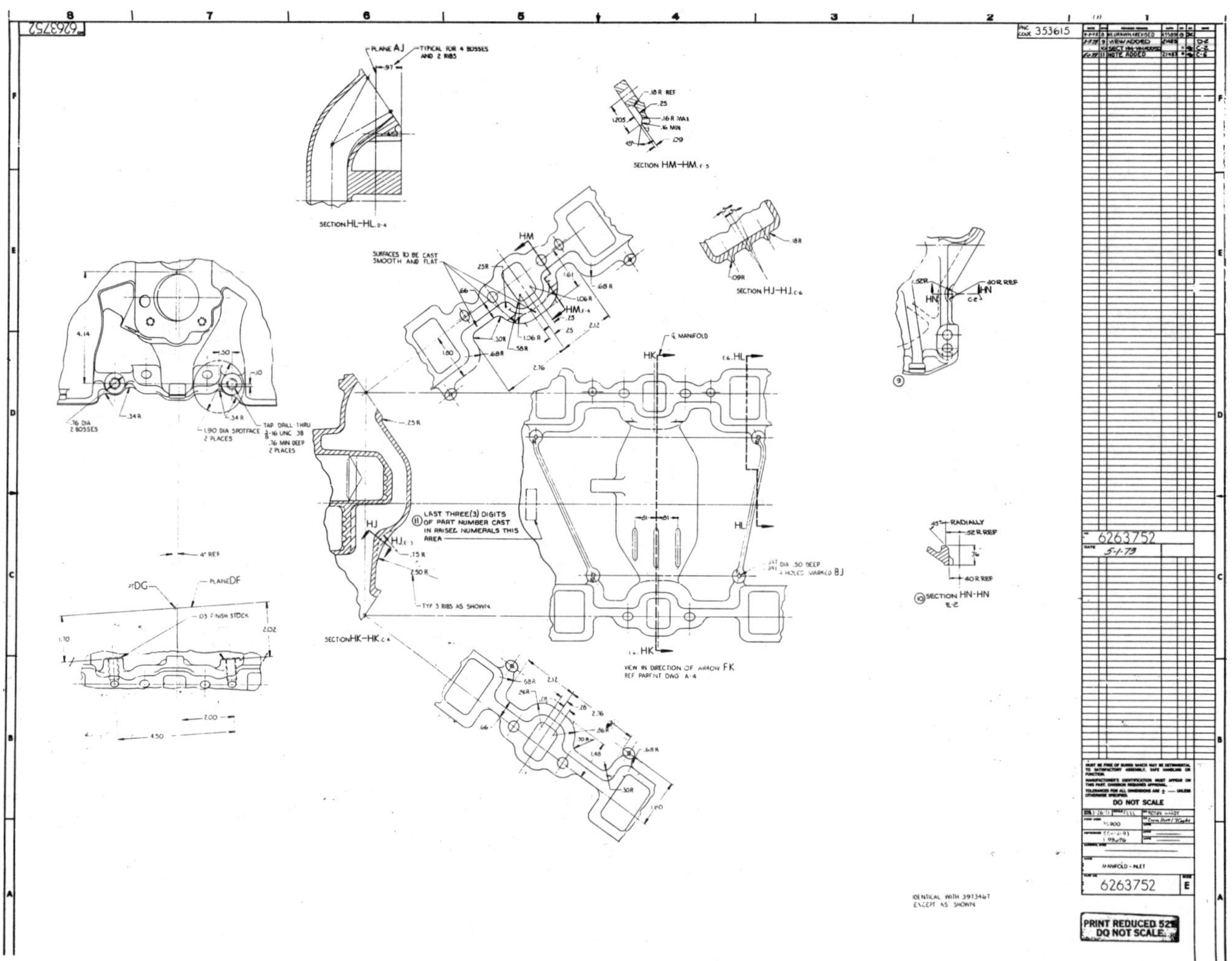

Fig. 9-17. Blueprint shows changes made to #6263752 from #3973467.

Manifold #6263753

Carb Type	Year	Model	Engine	Horsepower
4BBL Rochester	1972	Passenger	402	240
			454	240 (Police), 270
		Corvette	454	270
		Chevelle / Monte Carlo	402	240
			454	270
		Camaro	402	240
Although this intake was considered a new design, it retained the low rise style instituted in the 1970 model year. There are intake numbers cast into the top of the runners near the cylinder head. This intake has no oil splash shield.				

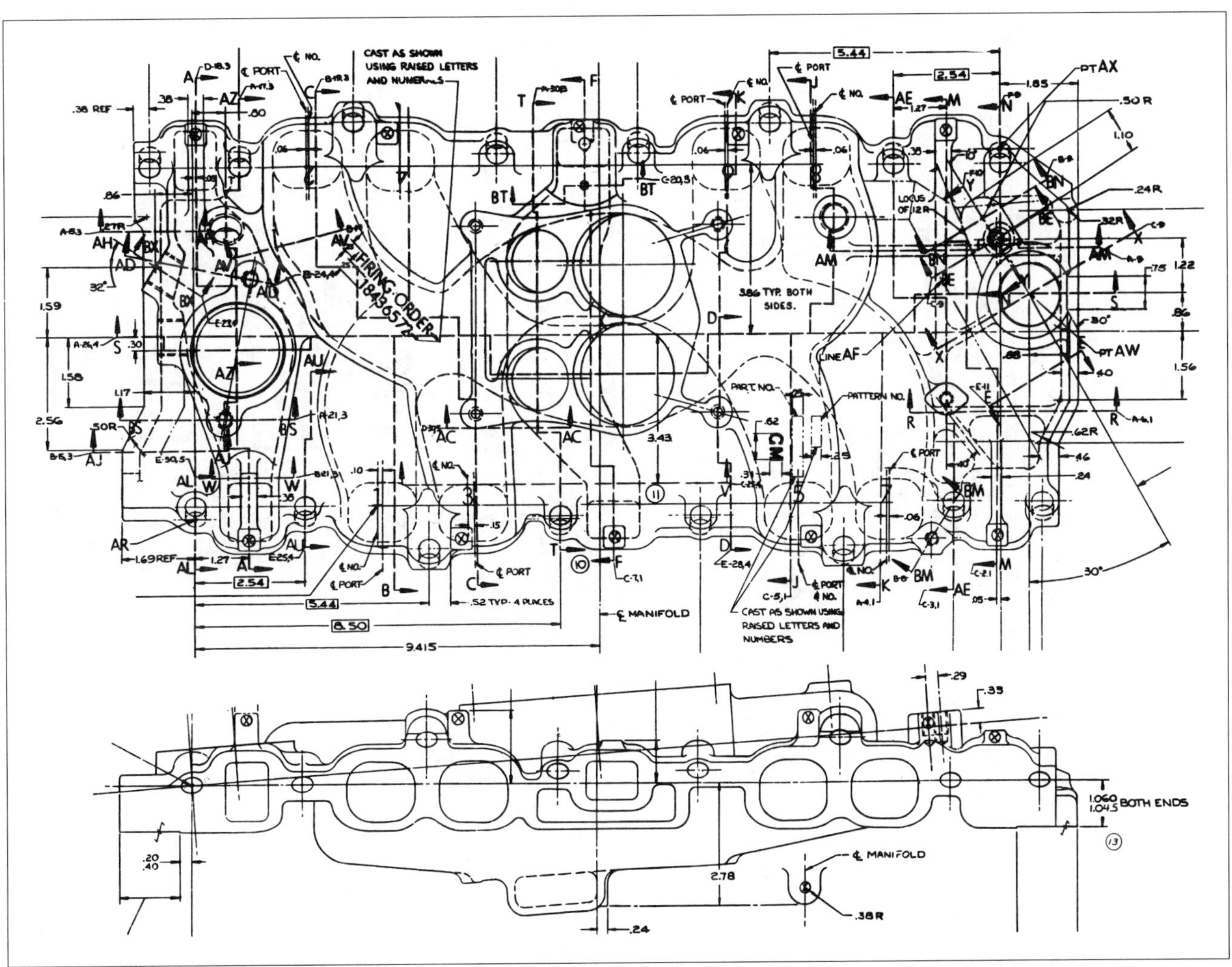

Fig. 9-18. Top and side view of #6263753.

Manifold #6271061

Carb Type	Year	Model	Engine	Horsepower
2BBL Rochester	1973	Chevelle	307	115
		Nova	307	115
		Camaro	307	115
This intake has the runner numbers cast into the top. There is an EGR boss on top to accept the EGR fitting instituted during the 1973 model year. This intake has an oil splash shield.				

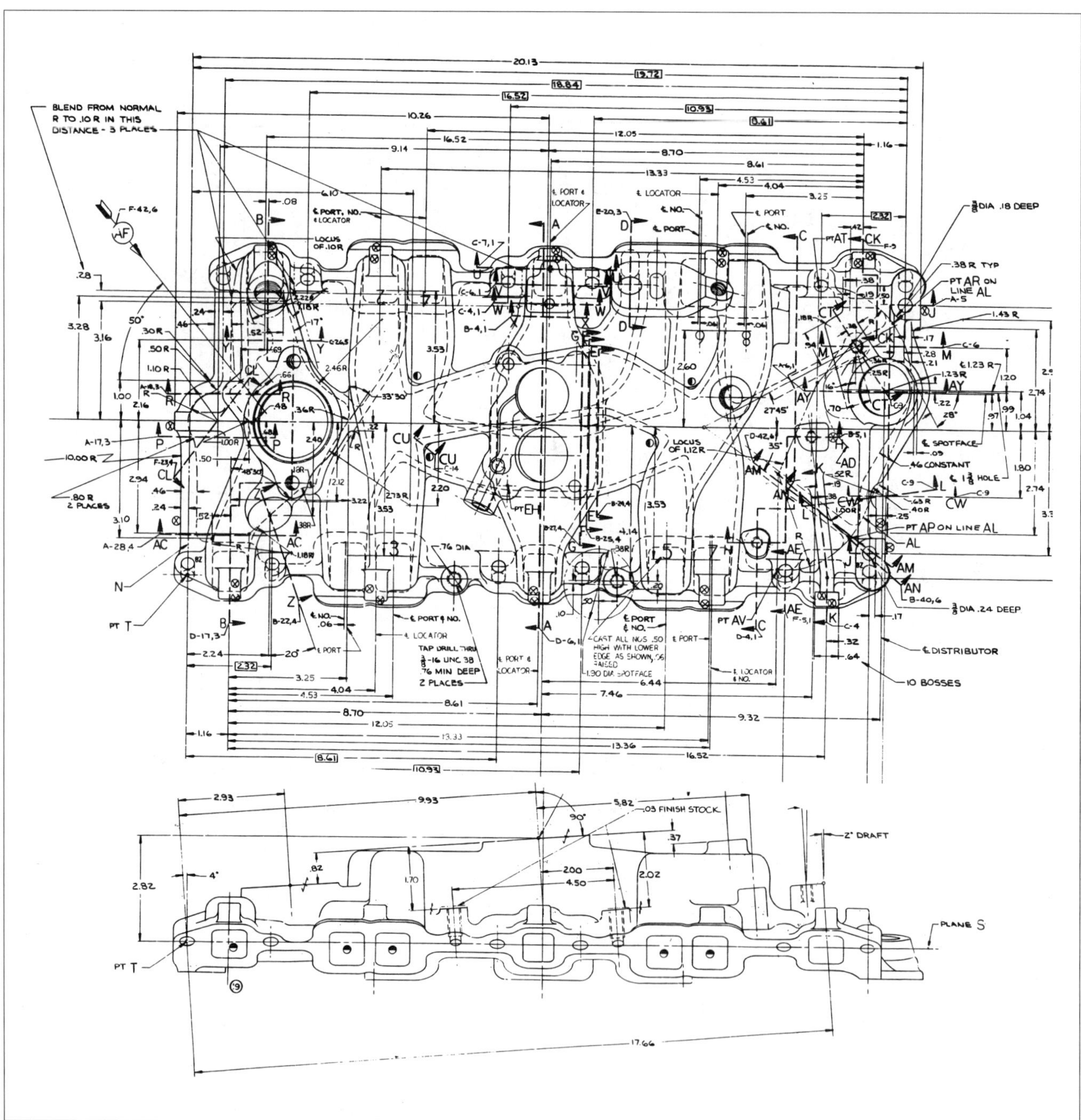

Fig. 9-19. Top and side view of #6271061.

Manifold #336789

Carb Type	Year	Model	Engine	Horsepower
4BBL Rochester	1974	Passenger	454	235
		Corvette	454	270
		Chevelle / Monte Carlo	454	235
This manifold is identical with #353015 except that the carburetor pad has been modified. Also, 4 strengthening ribs have been added at the front manifold locator points. This intake does not have an oil splash shield. There are intake numbers cast into the top of the runners.				

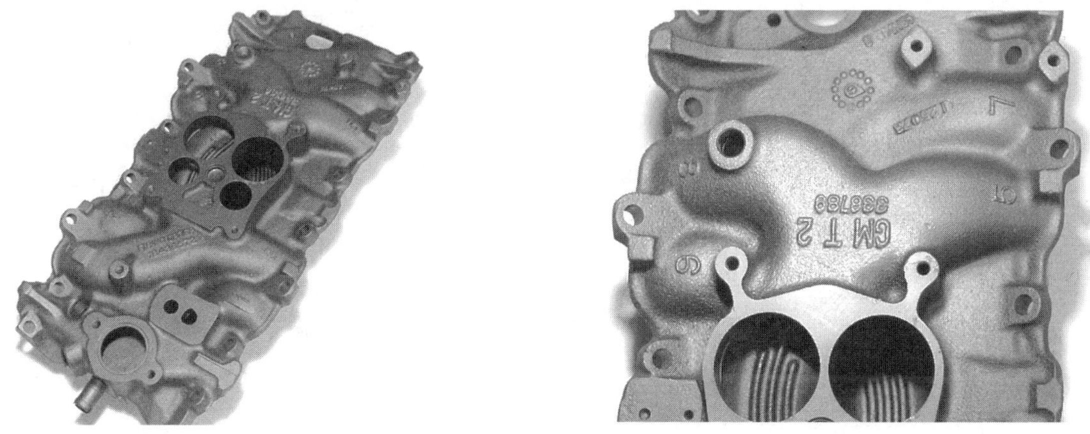

Fig. 9-20. ***Left****: overall view of #336789.* ***Right****: detail shows casting number, mold number, casting date and numbered intake runners.*

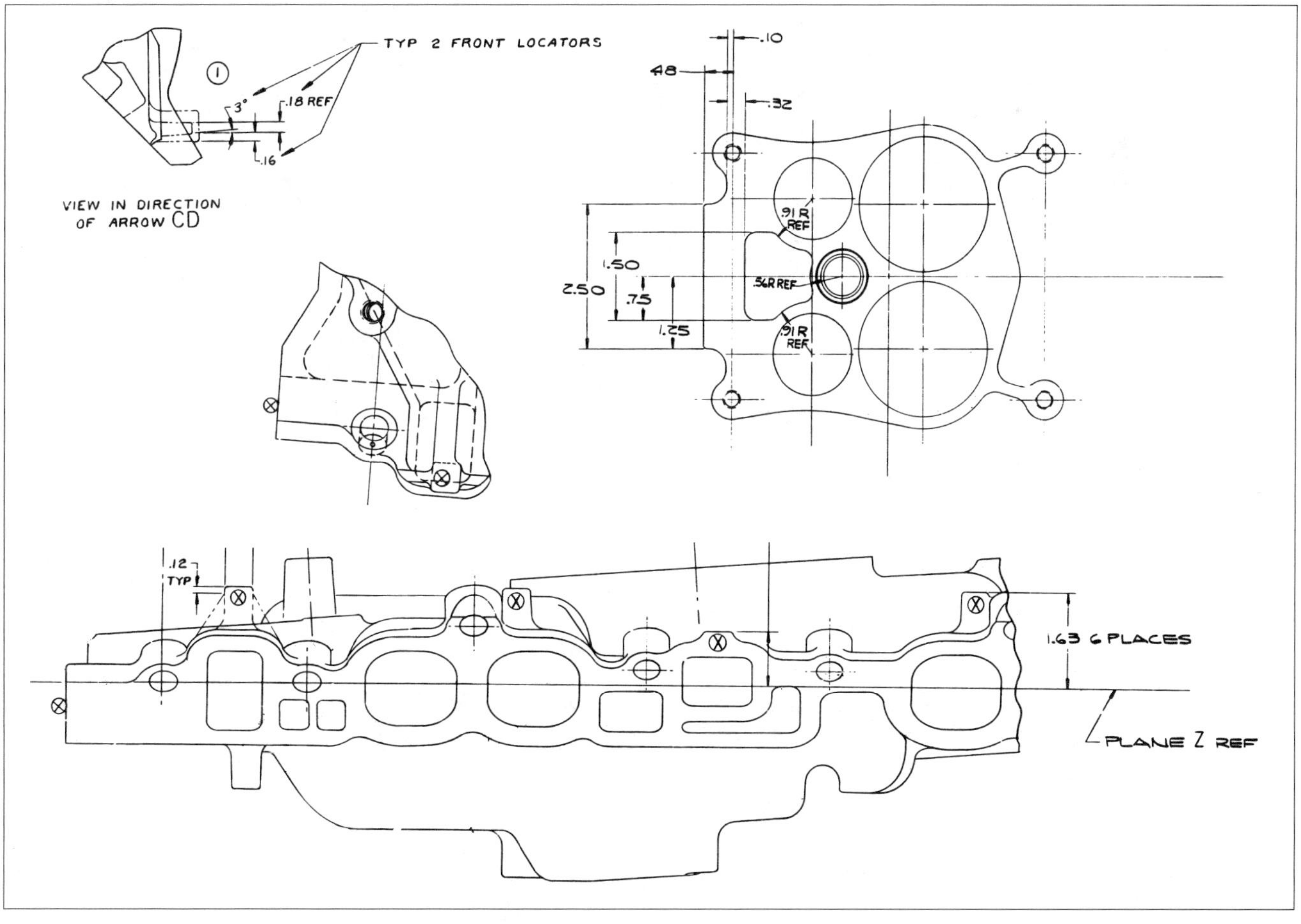

Fig. 9-21. *Detail from blueprint shows changes from #353015.*

Manifold #340261

Carb Type	Year	Model	Engine	Horsepower
4BBL Rochester	1974	Passenger	350	160
			400	180
		Corvette	350	195, 250
		Nova	350	160, 185
		Chevelle	350	160
			400	180
		Monte Carlo	350	160
			400	180
		Camaro	350	160, 185, 245
This is a new design manifold, but it is somewhat similar to #3997771 from the 1973 model year. This intake has the intake runner numbers cast into the top. There is an EGR boss on top of the intake to accept the EGR fitting instituted during the 1973 model year. This intake has an oil splash shield.				

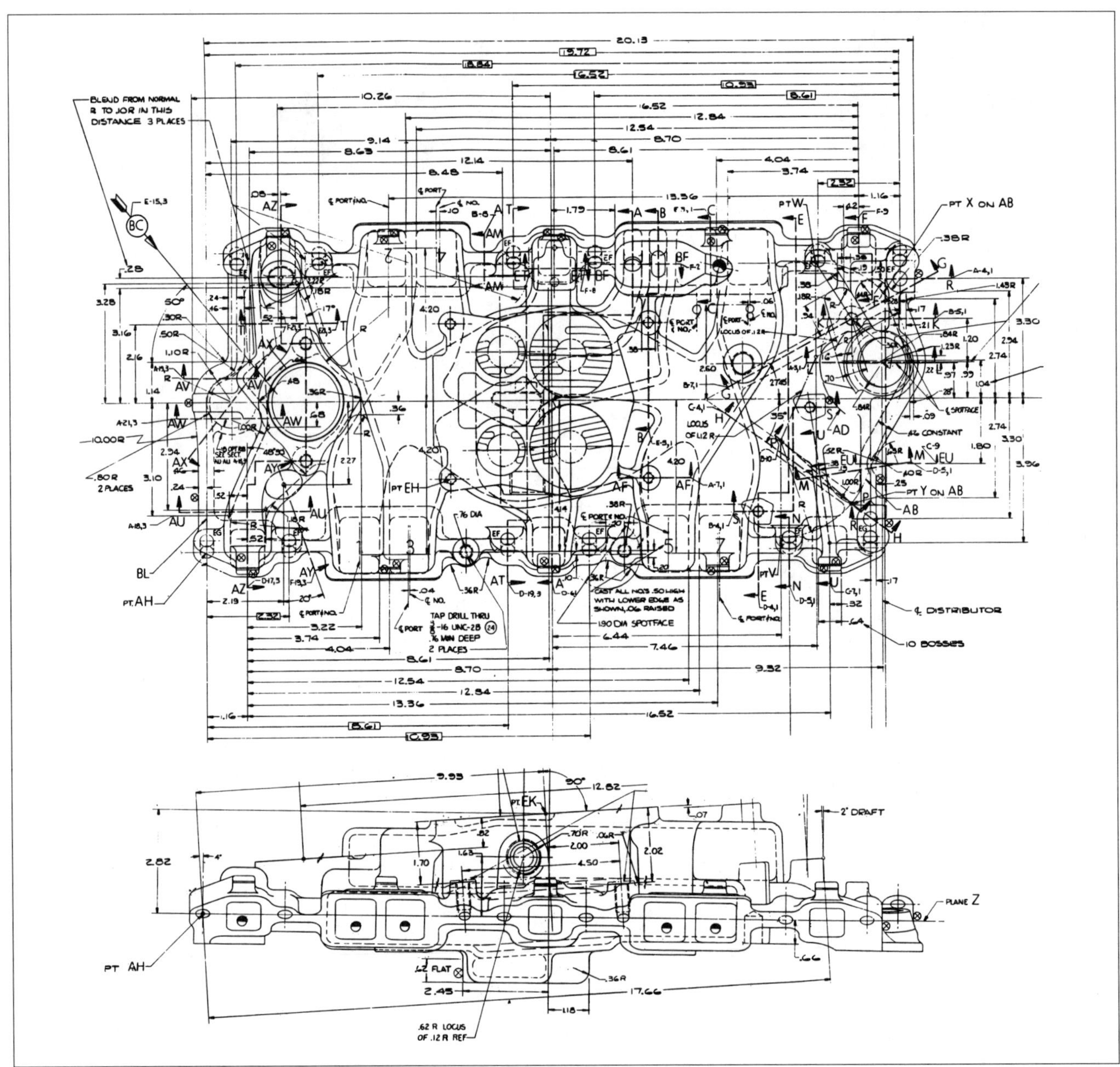

Fig. 9-22. Top and side view of #340261.

Manifold #340266

Carb Type	Year	Model	Engine	Horsepower
2BBL Rochester	1974	Passenger	350	145
			400	150
		Nova	350	145
		Chevelle	350	145
			400	150
		Monte Carlo	350	145
			400	150
		Camaro	350	145
This intake is identical to #3997771 with some minor casting and machining changes. It is similar to #3997773. This intake has the runner numbers cast into the top of the runners. There is an EGR boss on top of the intake to accept the EGR fitting instituted during the 1973 model year. This intake has an oil splash shield.				

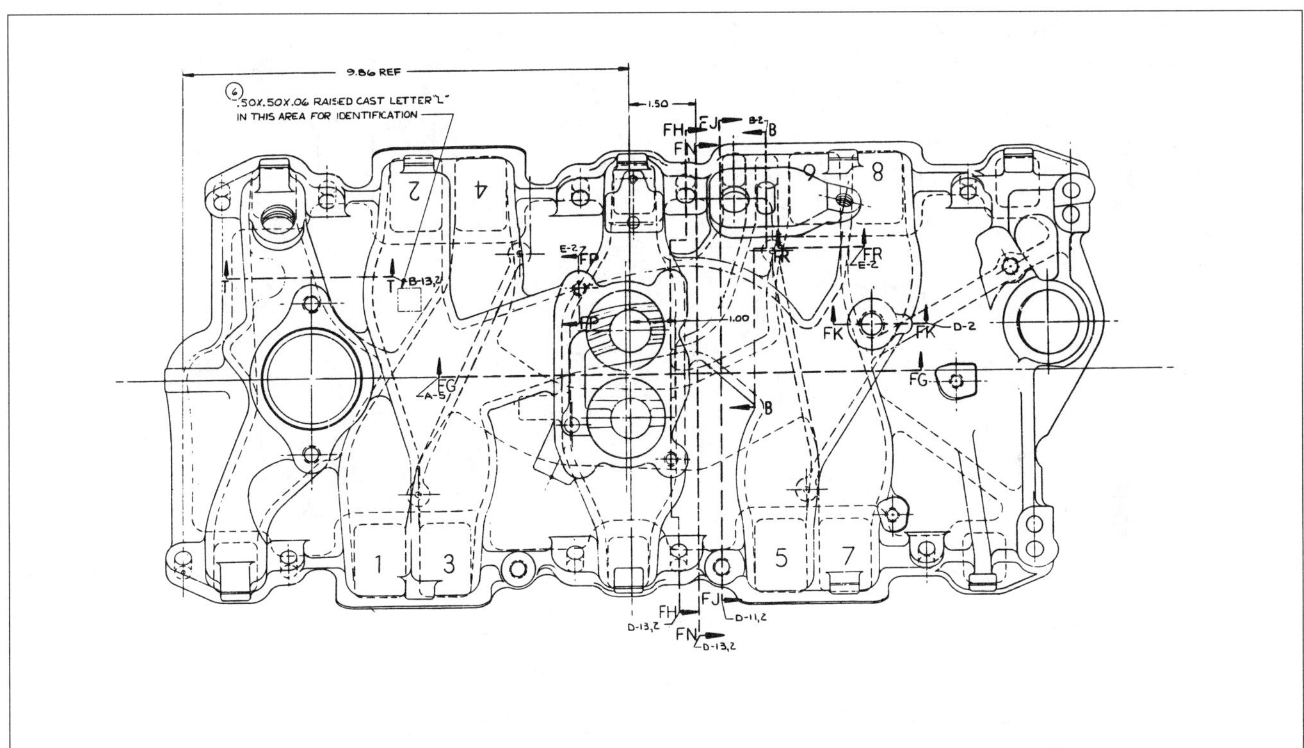

Fig. 9-23. Top view of #340266.

Manifold #346242

Carb Type	Year	Model	Engine	Horsepower
4BBL Rochester	1975	Passenger	454	215
		Chevelle	454	215
		Monte Carlo	454	215
Although this is quite similar to earlier big block intakes, this is considered a new design. This intake does not have an oil splash shield. There are intake numbers cast into the top of the runners.				

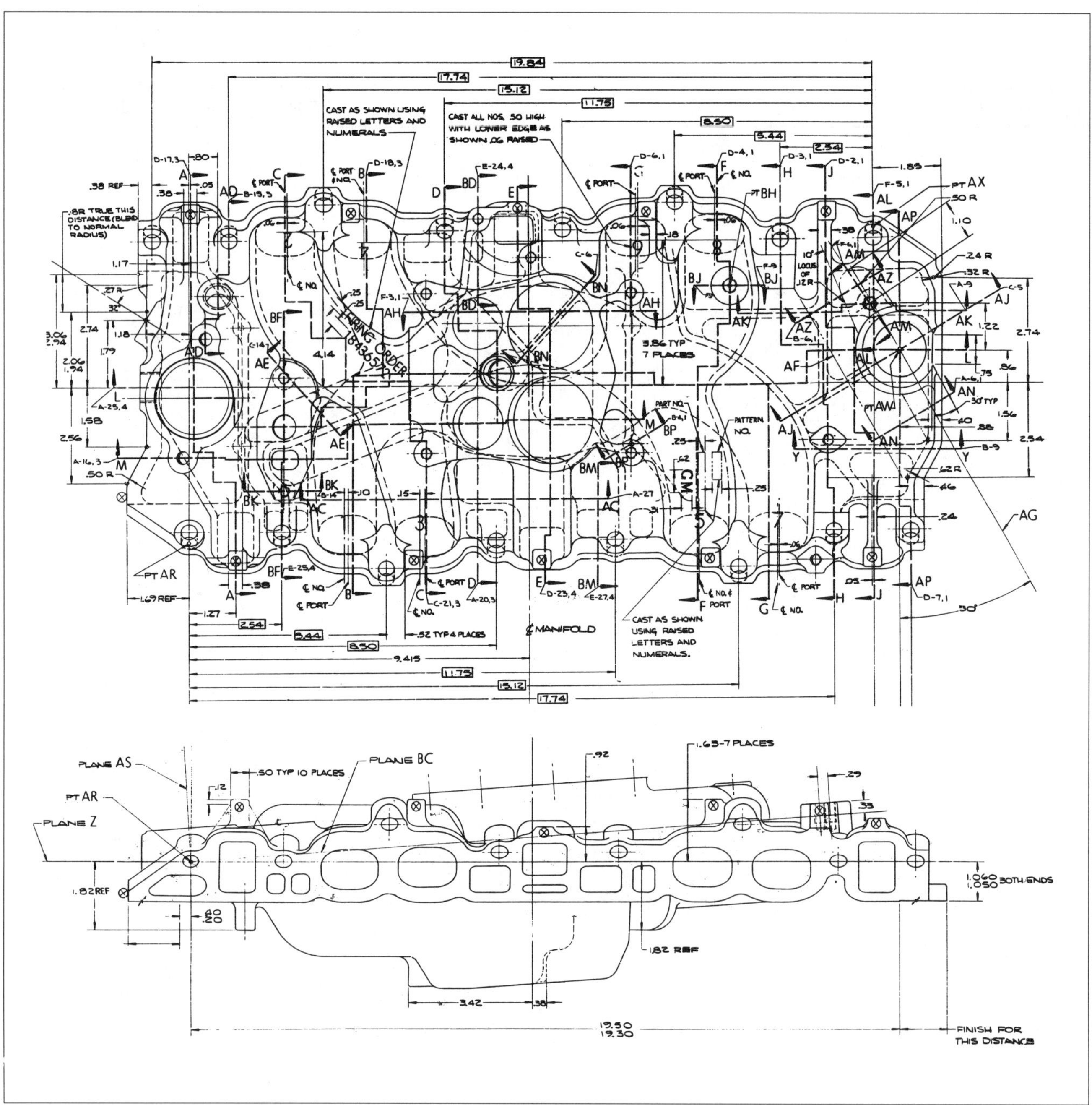

Fig. 9-24. Top and side view of #346242.

Manifold #346249

Carb Type	Year	Model	Engine	Horsepower
4BBL Rochester	1975	Passenger	350	155
			400	175
		Corvette	350	165, 205
		Nova	350	155
		Chevelle / Monte Carlo	350	155
			400	175
		Camaro	350	155
This manifold is similar to #340261. There is an EGR boss on top of the intake to accept the EGR fitting instituted during the 1973 model year. This intake has an oil splash shield. There are intake numbers cast into the top of the runners.				

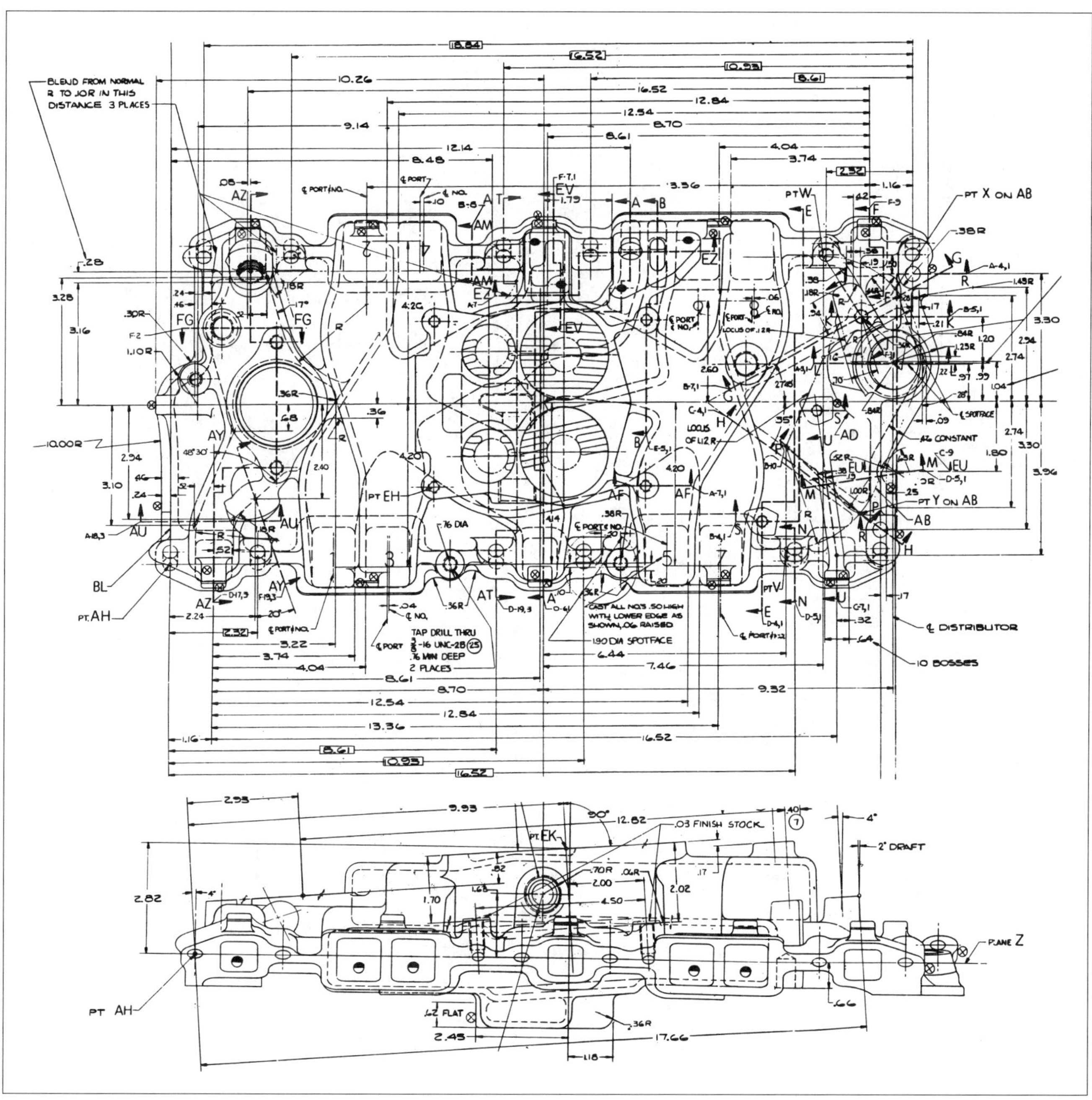

Fig. 9-25. Top and side view of #346249.

Manifold #346260

Carb Type	Year	Model	Engine	Horsepower
2BBL Rochester	1975	Passenger	350	145
		Nova	350	145
		Chevelle / Monte Carlo	350	145
		Camaro	350	145
		Monza	350 (CA only)	145
This intake is similar to #340266. There is an EGR boss on top of the intake to accept the EGR fitting instituted during the 1973 model year. This intake has an oil splash shield. There are intake numbers cast into the top of the runners.				

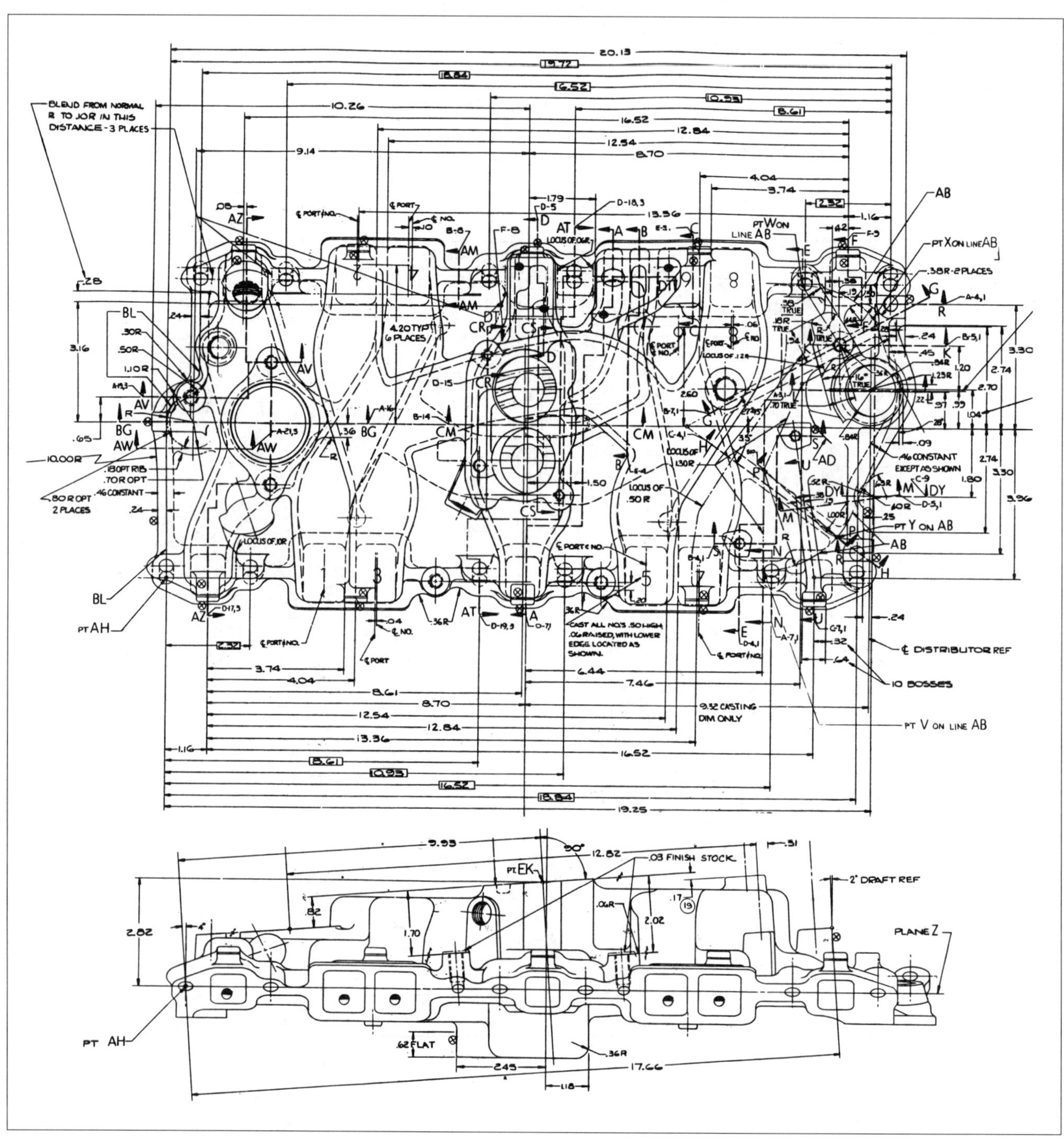

Fig. 9-26. Top and side view of #346260.

Manifold #353015

Carb Type	Year	Model	Engine	Horsepower
4BBL Rochester	1973	Passenger	454	215
		Corvette	454	245
		Chevelle / Monte Carlo	454	215
This intake was used in all 1973 454 engines. It has no oil splash shield. There are intake numbers cast into the top of the runners.				

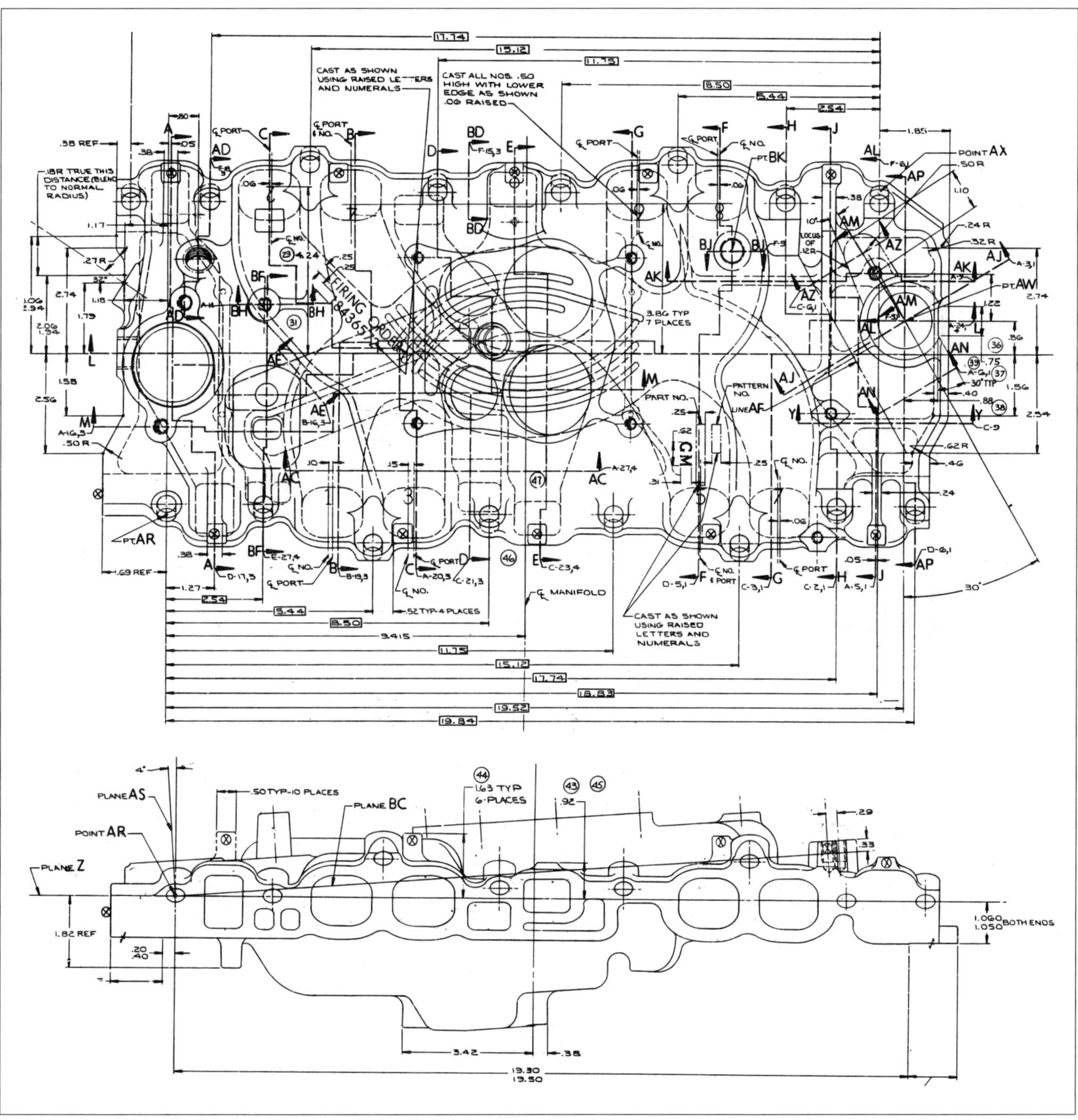

Fig. 9-27. Top and side view of #353015.

Manifold #355943

<table>
<tr><th>Carb Type</th><th>Year</th><th>Model</th><th>Engine</th><th>Horsepower</th></tr>
<tr><td rowspan="2">2BBL</td><td rowspan="2">1975</td><td>Nova</td><td>262</td><td>110</td></tr>
<tr><td>Monza</td><td>262</td><td>110</td></tr>
<tr><td colspan="5">This manifold is very similar to #346260, sharing the same style carburetor pad, mounting bosses and water outlet. The only difference are substantially smaller runners on the #355943. There are intake numbers cast into the top of the runners.</td></tr>
</table>

Chapter 10

Exhaust Manifold Identification

1. Introduction

All Chevrolet factory exhaust manifolds are cast iron. Since the manifolds are cast, the actual casting number and date are raised above the surface of the part. Most casting numbers are visible when the manifold is installed on the engine. The casting number location and casting date location will vary from year to year and sometimes manifold to manifold. Some manifolds will not carry a casting date at all. Casting date codes follow the same pattern as engine blocks. Small block exhaust manifolds usually do not carry a year designation. 2″ outlet small block manifolds will carry a casting date; most 2-1/2″ exhaust manifolds do not carry a casting date. Consult the model year calendar to verify that the exhaust manifolds for your application were cast on a weekday (Monday through Friday). The following is a breakdown of the casting date month codes:

Exhaust Manifold Month Codes (1st Letter)

A - January	E - May	I - September
B - February	F - June	J - October
C - March	G - July	K - November
D - April	H - August	L - December

The number or numbers following the month code letter represent the day of the month that the manifold was cast. A last number is sometimes present to indicate the year.

> NOTE—
> When checking date codes of specific engine parts, always remember the following. First verify the build date of your car. (Refer to Chapter 1 for more information on build dates.) The date codes of the various engine components should generally be dated one to three months prior to the car build date. This time lapse allows for assembly of that engine, transport to the car assembly plant and installation in the car.

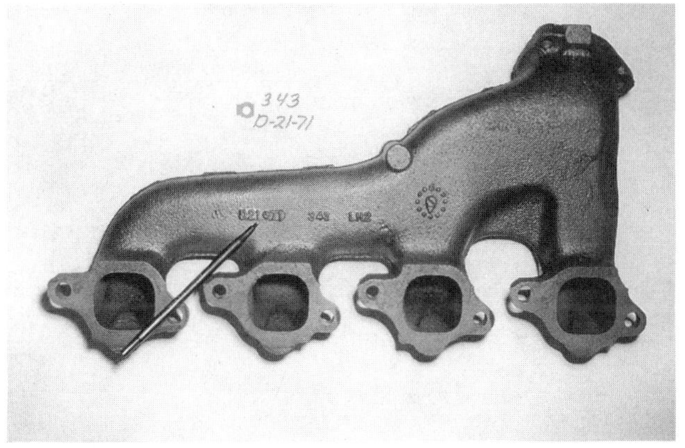

Fig. 10-1. *Rear view of #3989343 manifold with pointer indicating casting date (here upside down from normal position) and last 3 digits of casting number to side of date.*

Fig. 10-2. *Casting number for manifold #3909880 shows an error in casting date that reads "A 29 9." This should read "A296" indicating that this is a 1966 manifold, not a 1969 manifold.*

2. EXHAUST MANIFOLD CASTING NUMBERS

Manifold #3846559$^{\Delta}$

Outlet Size	Outlet Side	Year	Model	Engine	Horsepower	Notes
2.026	LH	1970	Corvette	350	300, 350	Straight outlet, 2 tapped holes on end, short studs. "Rams Horn" design. It has an odd generator brace in that the "ears" seem to have been left off the casting. Two 3/8"-16 holes have been tapped into the manifold 0.84 inches deep. $^{\Delta}$This manifold was also used from 1965 through 1967.
		1971	Corvette	350	270	

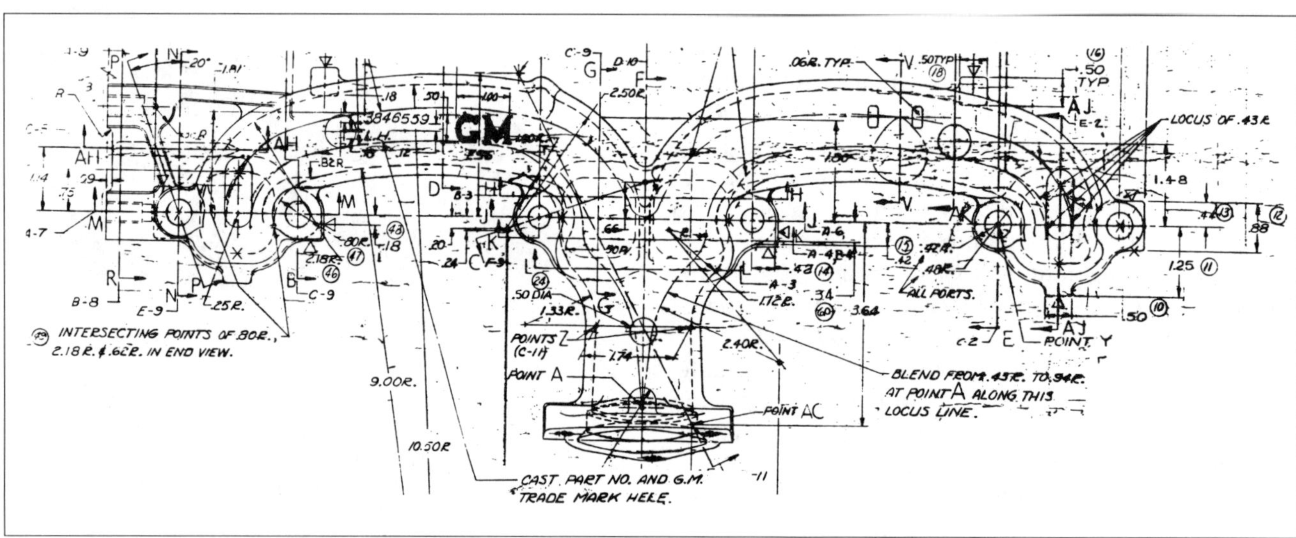

Fig. 10-3. Front view of #3846559.

Manifold #3872765$^{\Delta}$

Outlet Size	Outlet Side	Year	Model	Engine	Horsepower	Notes
2.026	LH	1970	Corvette	350	370 A.I.R.	Straight outlet, 2 tapped holes on end. "Rams Horn" design. Identical with #3846559 except 2 A.I.R. bosses added to the center of the manifold. Also, manifold has been drilled and tapped for 4 A.I.R. fittings. $^{\Delta}$This manifold was also used from 1966 through 1969.
		1971	Corvette	350	330 A.I.R.	

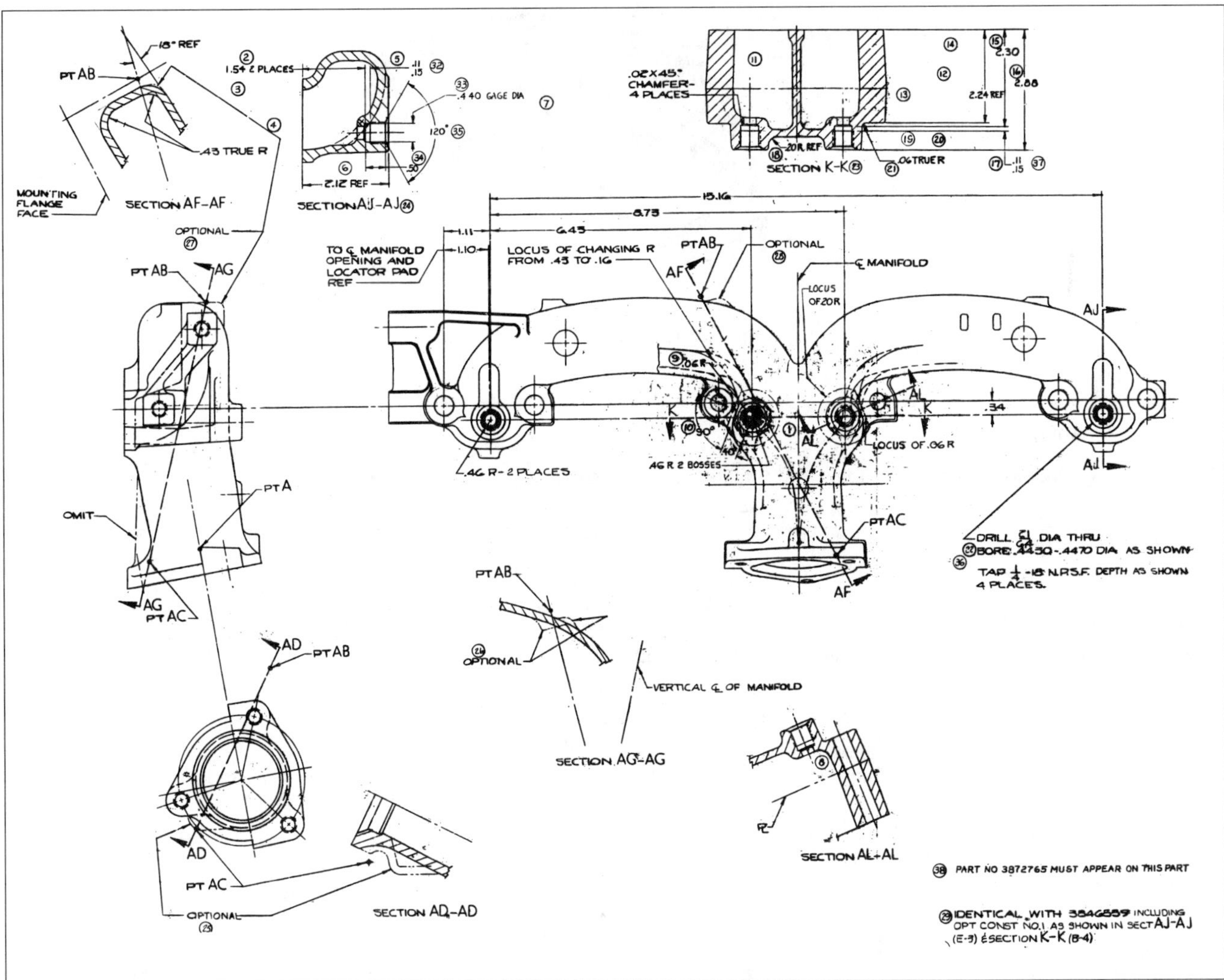

Fig. 10-4. Blueprint of #3872765 shows changes from #3846559.

Manifold #3880828$^{\Delta}$

Outlet Size	Outlet Side	Year	Model	Engine	Horsepower	Notes
2.526	RH	1970	Corvette	454	390	"Log" type design. High performance manifold, lower rear bell-bottom outlet.
		1971	Corvette	454	365	
		1972	Corvette	454	270	
		1973	Corvette	454	245	$^{\Delta}$This manifold was also used from 1966 through 1969.
		1974	Corvette	454	270	

Fig. 10-5. Front view of #3880828, drilled and tapped for A.I.R.

Manifold #3880869

Outlet Size	Outlet Side	Year	Model	Engine	Horsepower	Notes
2.526	LH	1971	Corvette	454	365, 425 A.I.R.	

Manifold #3909879$^{\Delta}$

Outlet Size	Outlet Side	Year	Model	Engine	Horsepower	Notes
2.526	LH	1970	Camaro	402	350, 375	"Log" type design. Rear outlet.
			Chevelle	402	330, 350, 375	
				454	360, 450	
			Monte Carlo	402	330	
				454	360	$^{\Delta}$This manifold was also used from 1967 through 1969.
			Nova	402	350, 375	

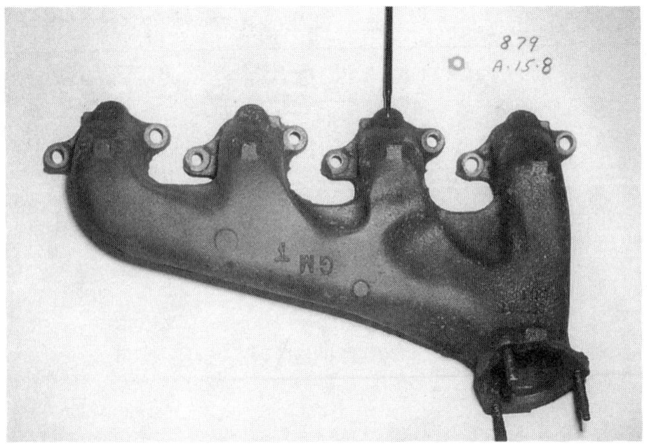

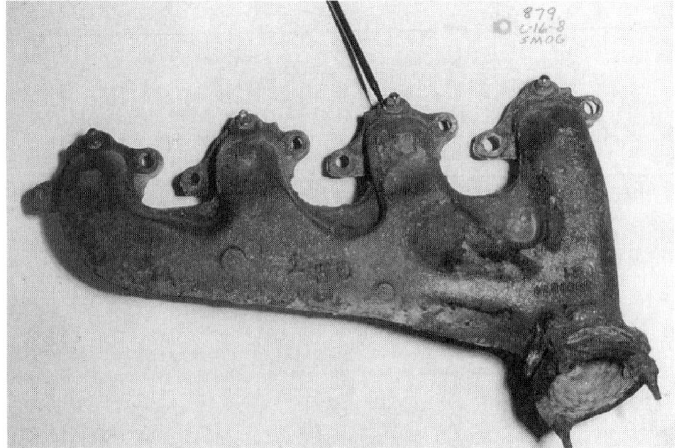

Fig. 10-6. Two views of #3909879 with non-drilled A.I.R. bosses (left) and drilled and plugged bosses (right).

Manifold #3914613$^{\Delta}$

Outlet Size	Outlet Side	Year	Model	Engine	Horsepower	Notes
2.526	LH	1970	Passenger	454	345, 390	"Log" type design. Rear outlet. $^{\Delta}$This manifold was also used in 1968 and 1969.

Fig. 10-7. *Front view of #3914613.*

Manifold #3916178$^{\Delta}$

Outlet Size	Outlet Side	Year	Model	Engine	Horsepower	Notes
2.526	RH	1970	Passenger	454	345, 390	"Log" type design, rear outlet. Manifold is identical to #3909880 except for some minor interior and exterior casting changes. $^{\Delta}$This manifold was also used in 1968 and 1969.
			Camaro	402	350, 375	
			Chevelle	402	330, 350, 375	
				454	360, 450	
			Monte Carlo	402	330	
				454	360	
			Nova	402	350, 375	

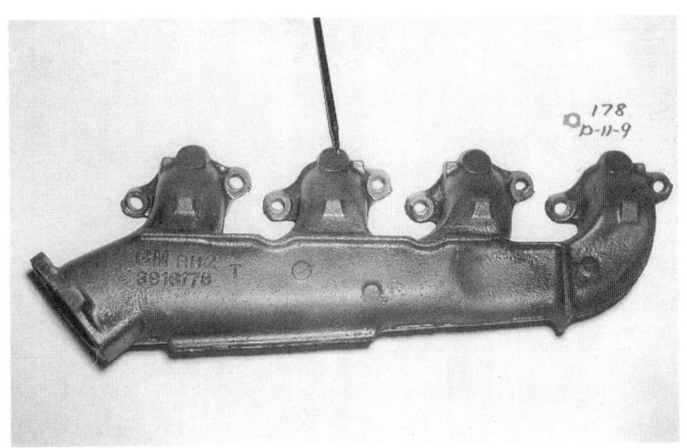

Fig. 10-8. *Two views of #3916178 with non-drilled A.I.R. bosses (left) and drilled and plugged bosses (right).*

Manifold #3932376 ^Δ^

Outlet Size	Outlet Side	Year	Model	Engine	Horsepower	Notes
1.96	RH	1970	Chevelle	307	200 w/o A.I.R.	Rear outlet. Long studs. "Log" type design.
				350	250, 300 w/o A.I.R.	
			Nova	307	200 w/o A.I.R.	
				350	250, 300 w/o A.I.R.	
			Camaro	307	200 w/o A.I.R.	
				350	250, 300 w/o A.I.R.	
			Monte Carlo	350	250, 300 w/o A.I.R.	ΔThis manifold was also used in the 1969 model year.
				400	265	

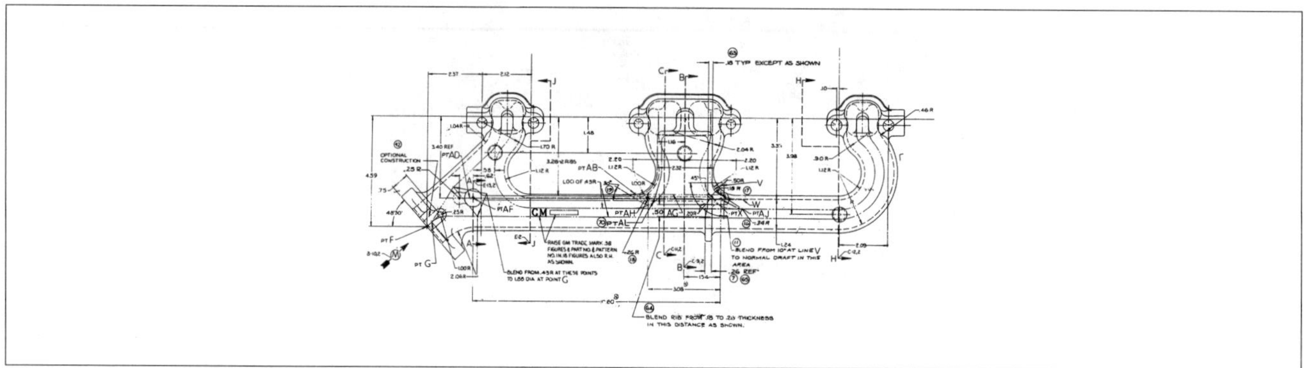

Fig. 10-9. Front view of #3932376.

Manifold #3932461^Δ^

Outlet Size	Outlet Side	Year	Model	Engine	Horsepower	Notes
1.96	RH	1970	Corvette	350	370 S/T A.I.R.	Straight outlet. Long studs. "Rams Horn" design, identical to #3932465 except that 2 A.I.R. bosses have been added to middle of manifold, drilled and tapped for 4 A.I.R. fittings. Similar to #3872778. Please see casting number #3989036 for further information.
	RH	1971	Corvette	350	330 S/T A.I.R.	
	RH	1972	Corvette	350	200 NB2	
					255 A.I.R.	
	LH	1972	Corvette	350	200 NB2	
				350	255 A.I.R.	
	RH	1973	Corvette	350	190, 250 A.I.R.	
	LH	1973	Corvette	350	190, 250 A.I.R.	
	RH	1974	Corvette	350	195, 250 A.I.R. (except THM w/o A.I.R.)	
	LH	1974	Corvette	350	195, 250 A.I.R. (except THM w/o A.I.R.)	ΔThis manifold was also used in 1969.

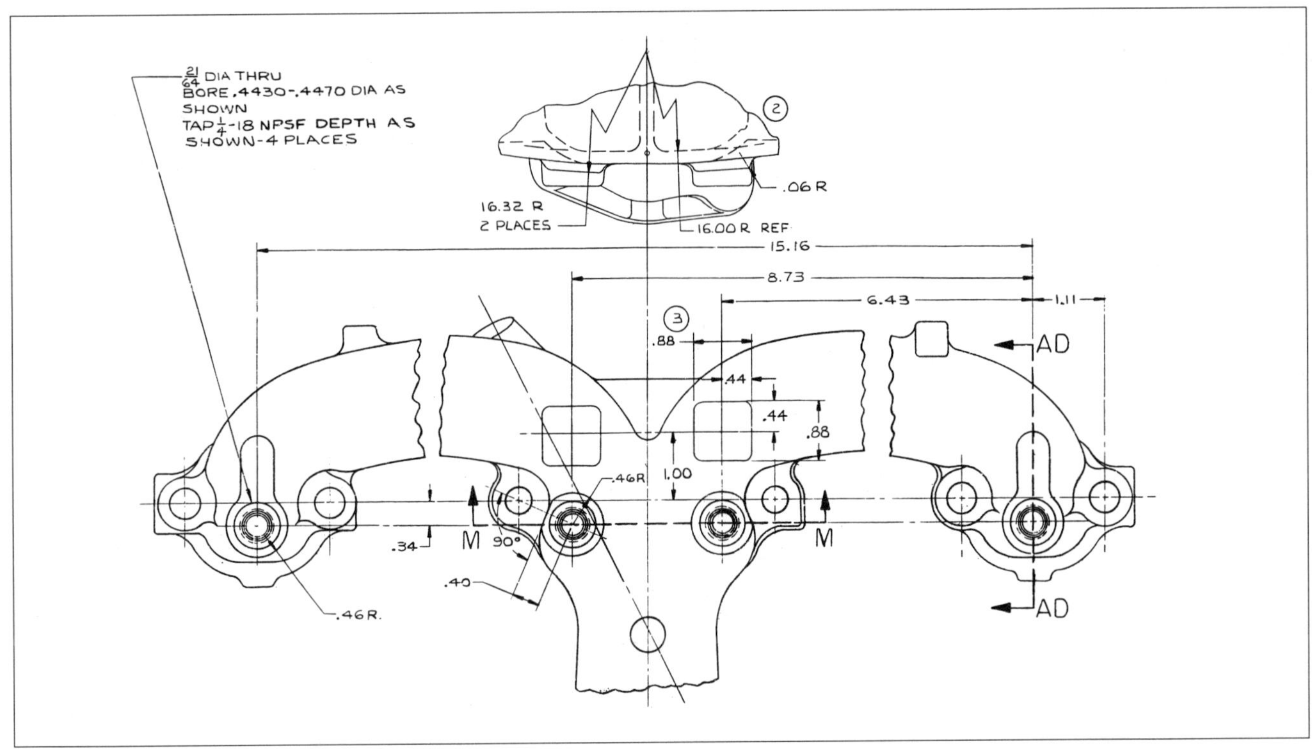

Fig. 10-10. Blueprint of #3932461 shows changes from #3932465.

Manifold #3932465$^{\Delta}$

Outlet Size	Outlet Side	Year	Model	Engine	Horsepower	Notes
1.96	RH	1970	Passenger	350	250, 300 w/o A.I.R.	Straight outlet. Long studs. "Rams Horn" design, similar to #3747042.
				400	265	
			Corvette	350	300, 350 w/o A.I.R.	$^{\Delta}$This manifold was also used in 1969.

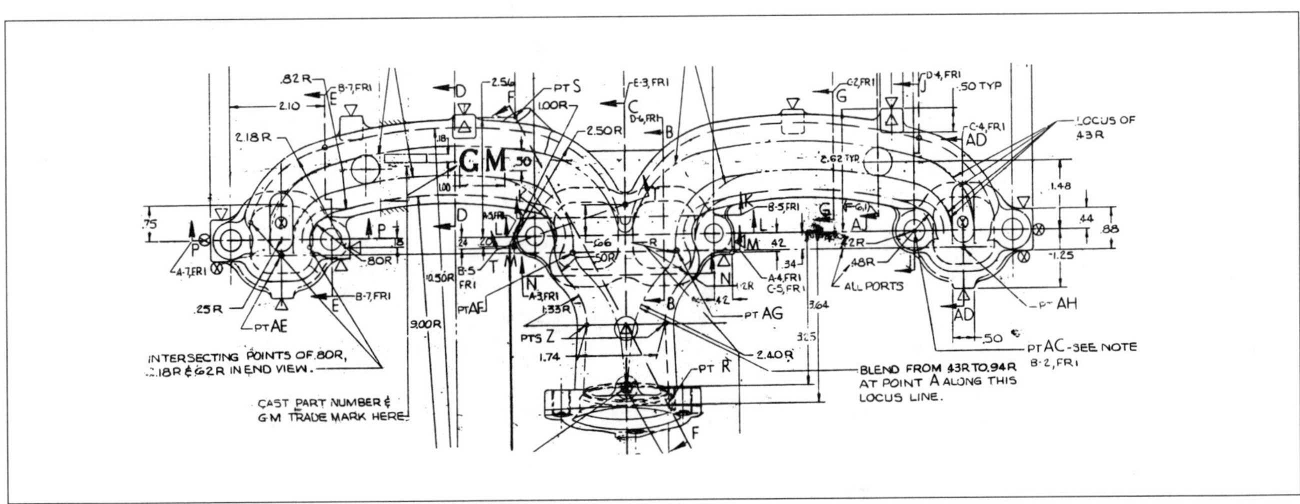

Fig. 10-11. Front view of #3932465.

Manifold #3932473$^{\Delta}$

Outlet Size	Outlet Side	Year	Model	Engine	Horsepower	Notes
2.026	LH	1970	Passenger	350	250, 300 w/o A.I.R.	Curved outlet. Short studs. "Rams Horn" design, similar to #3855163. Casting #3872741 may appear on this part. $^{\Delta}$This manifold was also used in 1969.
				400	265	

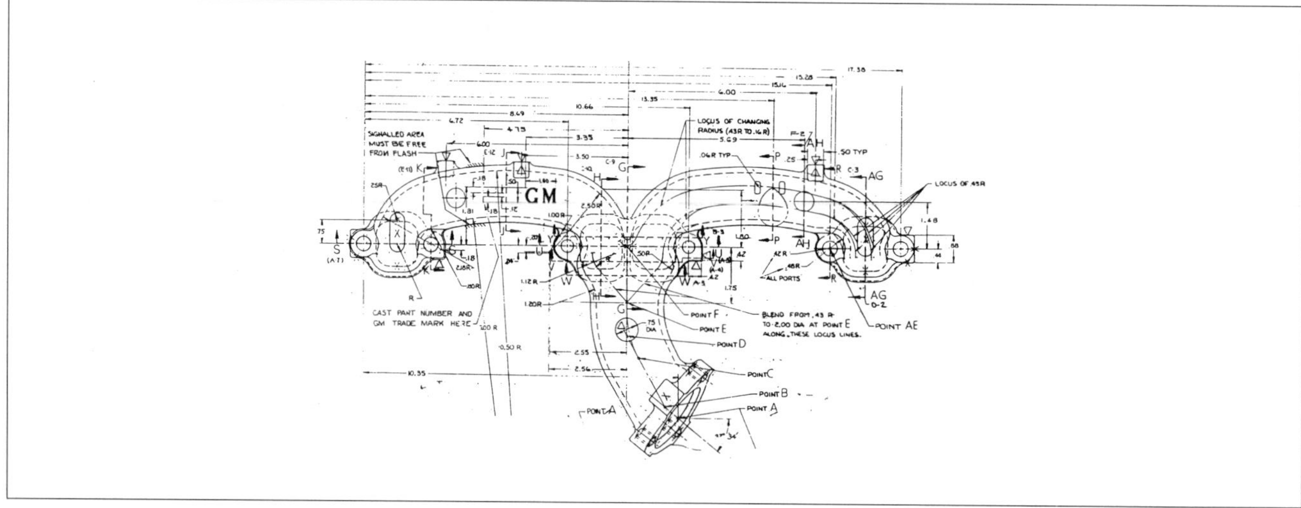

Fig. 10-12. Front view of #3932473.

Manifold #3942527$^{\Delta}$

Outlet Size	Outlet Side	Year	Model	Engine	Horsepower	Notes
2.026	LH	1970	Camaro Z28	350	360 A.I.R.	Rear outlet. Short studs. "Log" type design. Rear outlet. Identical with #3942529 except that 4 A.I.R. bosses have been added, drilled and tapped for A.I.R. fittings. $^{\Delta}$This manifold was also used in 1969.
			Yenko Duece	350	360 A.I.R.	

Manifold #3942529$^{\Delta}$

Outlet Size	Outlet Side	Year	Model	Engine	Horsepower	Notes
2.026	LH	1970	Camaro Chevelle Nova	307	200 w/o A.I.R.	Rear outlet. Short studs. "Log" type design.
				350	250, 300 w/o A.I.R.	
			Monte Carlo	350	250, 300 w/o A.I.R.	$^{\Delta}$This manifold was also used in 1969.
				400	265	

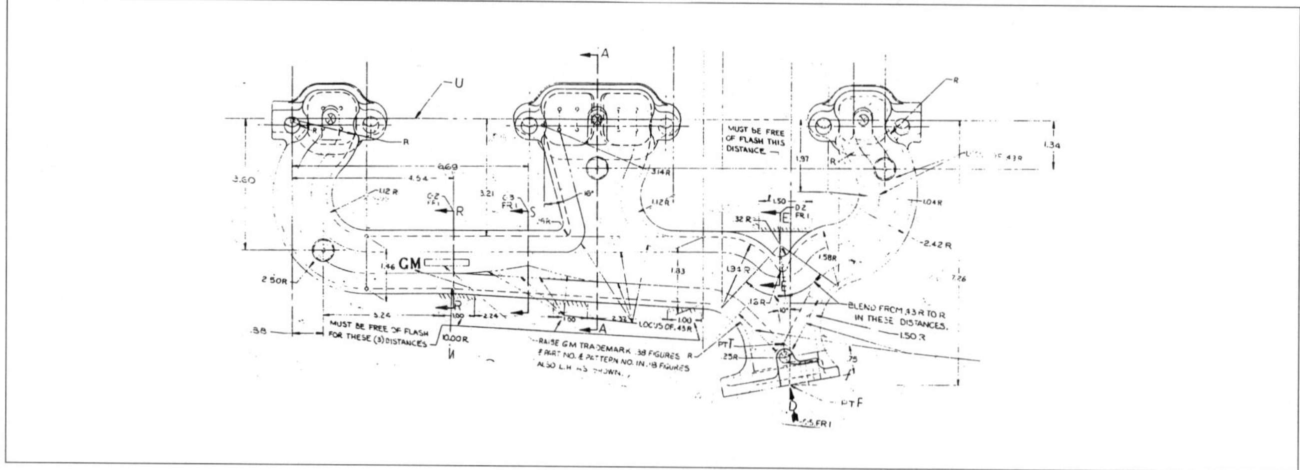

Fig. 10-13. Front view of #3942529.

Manifold #3946826$^{\Delta}$

Outlet Size	Outlet Side	Year	Model	Engine	Horsepower	Notes
1.96	RH	1970	Camaro Z28	350	360 A.I.R.	Rear outlet. Long studs. "Log" type design. Identical with #3932376 except that 4 A.I.R. bosses have been added, drilled and tapped for A.I.R. fittings. $^{\Delta}$This manifold was also used in 1969.
			Yenko Duece	350	360 A.I.R.	

Manifold #3959562

Outlet Size	Outlet Side	Year	Model	Engine	Horsepower	Notes
2.026	RH	1972	Passenger	400	170 A.I.R.	"Log" type design. Rear outlet. Identical with #3973432 except that 4 A.I.R. bosses have been added, drilled and tapped for A.I.R. fittings.
			Nova	307	130 NB2	
				350	165, 175 NB2	
			Chevelle	307	130 NB2	
				350	165, 175 NB2	
			Camaro	307	130 NB2	
				350	165, 175 NB2	
			Monte Carlo	350	165, 175 NB2	
		1973	Passenger	350	145, 175 A.I.R.	
				400	150	
			Nova	307	115 A.I.R.	
				350	145, 175 A.I.R.	
			Chevelle	307	115 A.I.R.	
				350	145, 175 A.I.R.	
			Camaro	307	115 A.I.R.	
				350	145, 175, 245 A.I.R.	
			Monte Carlo	350	145, 175 A.I.R	
		1974	Passenger	400	150, 180 A.I.R.	
			Nova	350	145, 160 A.I.R.	
				350	185 S/T A.I.R.	
			Chevelle	350	145, 160 A.I.R.	
				400	150 A.I.R.	
			Camaro	350	145, 160, 245 A.I.R.	
				350	185 S/T A.I.R.	
			Monte Carlo	350	140, 160 A.I.R.	
				400	150, 180 A.I.R.	

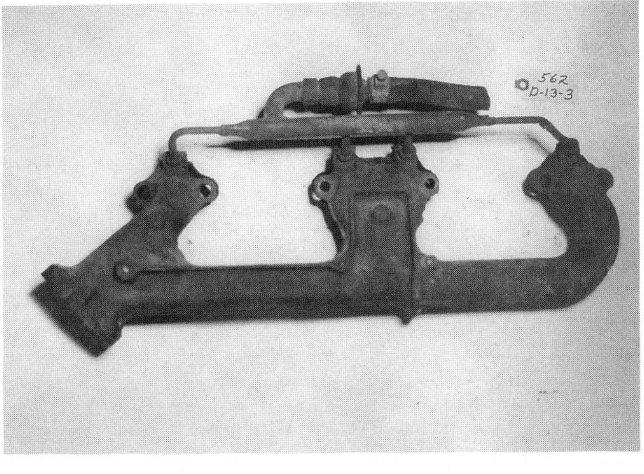

Fig. 10-14. *Front view of #3959562 with smog tube still attached.*

Manifold #3969869

Outlet Size	Outlet Side	Year	Model	Engine	Horsepower	Notes
2.026	LH	1970	Corvette	454	390	"Log" type, high performance manifold. Lower rear dump. Corvette only.
		1971	Corvette	454	365	
		1972	Corvette	454	270	
		1973	Corvette	454	245	
		1974	Corvette	454	270	

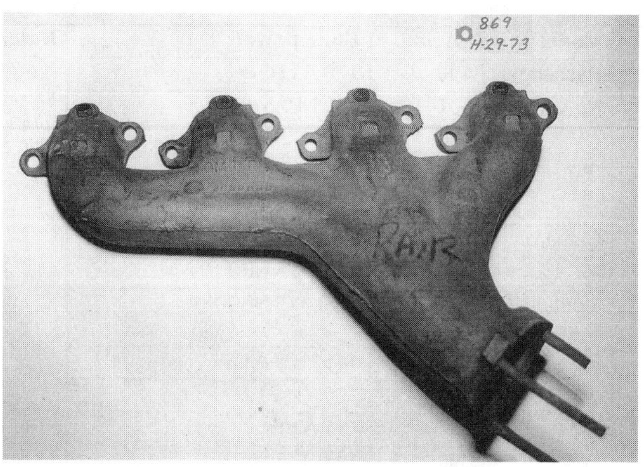

Fig. 10-15. Front view of #3969869, here drilled and tapped for A.I.R. Not all were drilled and tapped.

Manifold #3973432

Outlet Size	Outlet Side	Year	Model	Engine	Horsepower	Notes
2.026	RH	1971	Passenger	350	245 w/o A.I.R.	"Log" type. Rear outlet. Short studs. Casting number is #3959562.
				350	270 S/T w/o A.I.R.	
				400	255	
			Chevelle	307	200 w/o A.I.R.	
				350	245, 270 w/o A.I.R.	
			Nova	307	200 w/o A.I.R.	
				350	245 w/o A.I.R.	
			Camaro	307	200 w/o A.I.R.	
				350	245, 270 w/o A.I.R.	
			Monte Carlo	350	245, 270 w/o A.I.R.	
		1972	Passenger	350	165 THM w/o NB2	
				400	170 w/o A.I.R.	
			Chevelle	307	130 w/o NB2	
				350	165, 175 w/o NB2	
			Nova	307	130 w/o NB2	
				350	165, 175 w/o NB2	
			Camaro	307	130 w/o NB2	
				350	165, 175 w/o NB2	
		1974	Passenger	400	150, 180 w/o A.I.R.	
			Camaro	350	185 THM w/o A.I.R.	
			Chevelle	400	150, 180 w/o A.I.R.	
			Monte Carlo	400	150, 180 w/o A.I.R.	

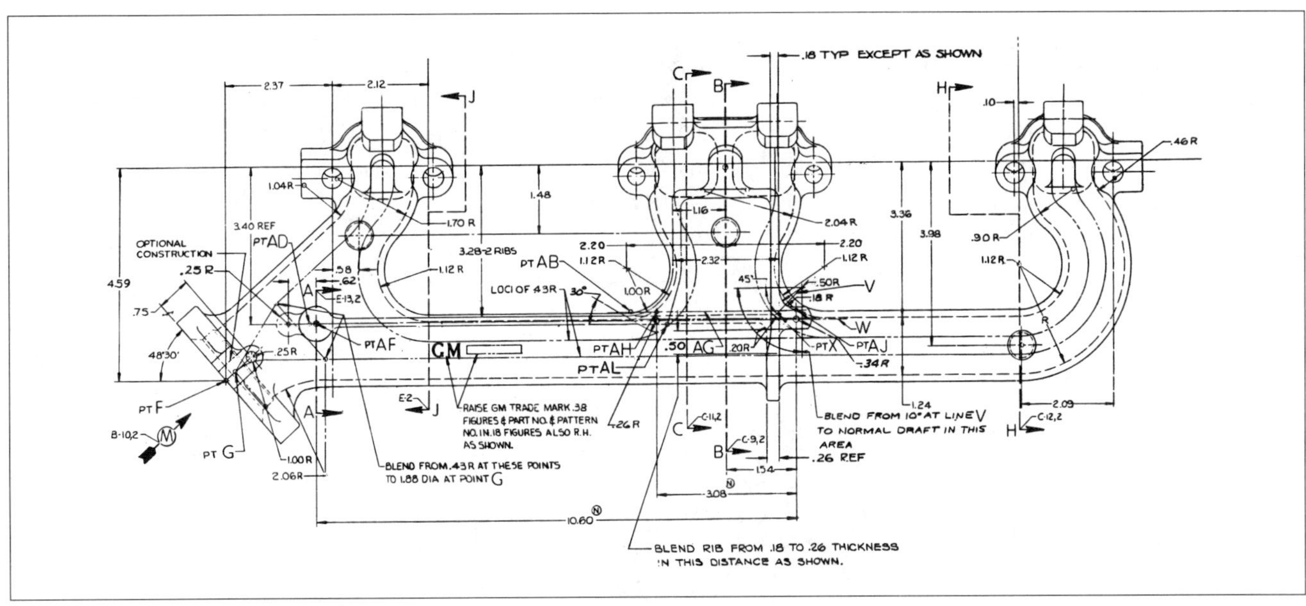

Fig. 10-16. Front view of #3973432.

Manifold #3986330

Outlet Size	Outlet Side	Year	Model	Engine	Horsepower	Notes
1.96	RH	1971	Camaro Z28	350	330 A.I.R.	"Log" type. Rear outlet. Long studs. Identical with #3932376 except that 4 A.I.R. bosses have been added, drilled and tapped for A.I.R. fittings. Exterior rib and 0.4–0.144 diameter holes have been omitted.
		1972	Camaro Z28	350	255 A.I.R.	

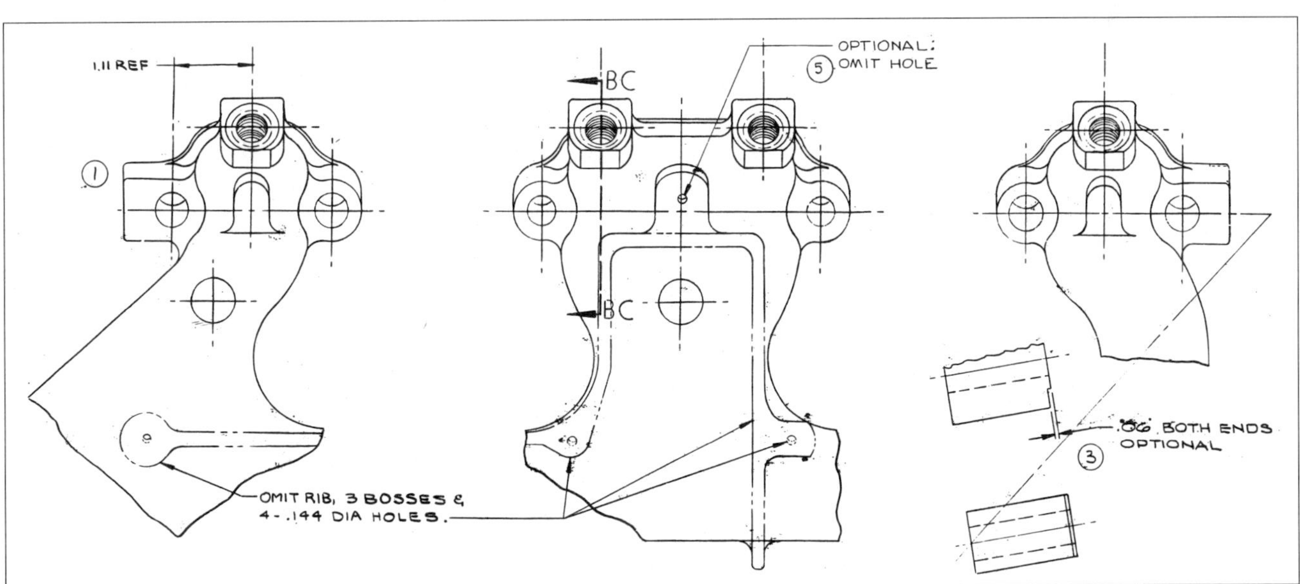

Fig. 10-17. Blueprint of #3986330 shows changes from #3932376.

Manifold #3989036

Outlet Size	Outlet Side	Year	Model	Engine	Horsepower	Notes
2.026	RH	1971	Corvette	350	270 w/o A.I.R.	Straight outlet. Long studs. “Rams Horn” design, similar to #3747042. Casting number #3932465 may appear on this part. Casting number is 3932461 after 10/19/71. Please see #3932461 for further information.
		1972	Corvette	350	200 w/o NB2	
	RH	1975	Corvette	350	165, 205	
	LH	1974	Corvette	350	195 THM w/o A.I.R.	
	LH	1975	Corvette	350	165, 205	

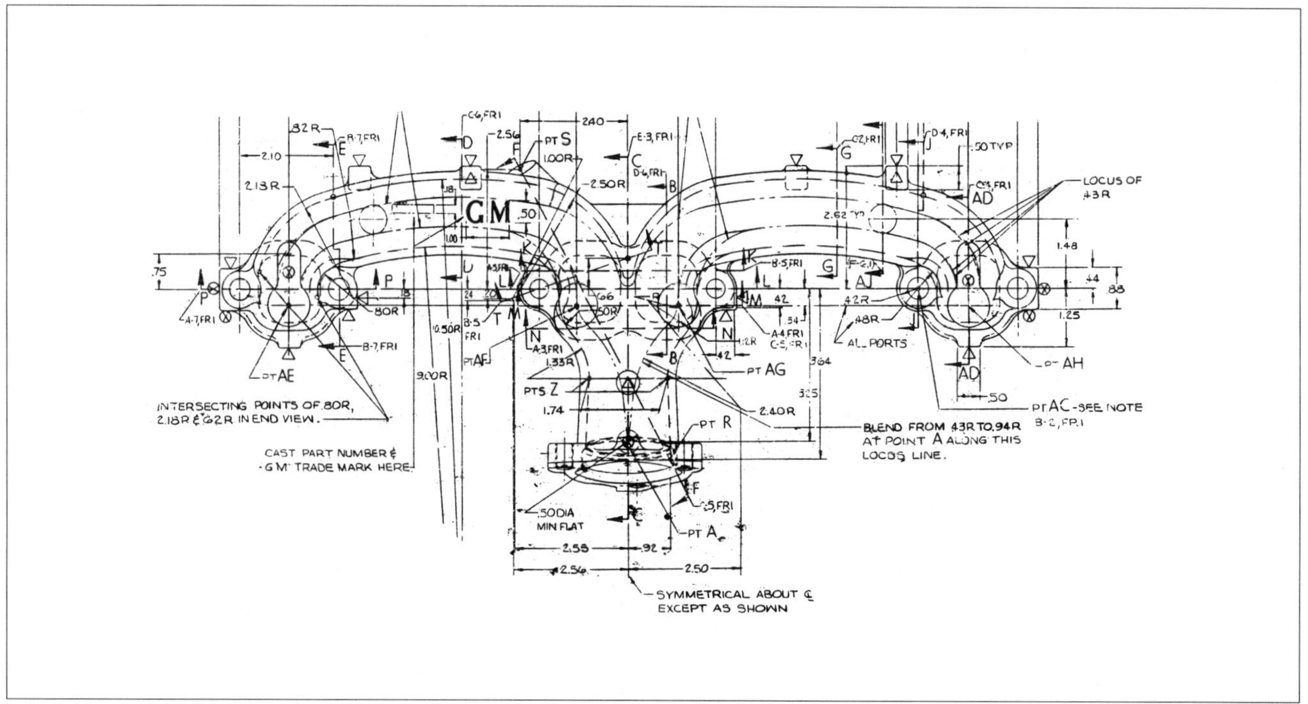

Fig. 10-18. Front view of #3989036.

Manifold #3989041

Outlet Size	Outlet Side	Year	Model	Engine	Horsepower	Notes
2.026	LH	1971	Camaro Z28	350	330 A.I.R.	Rear outlet. Short studs. "Log" type design. Identical with #3989043 except that 4 A.I.R. bosses have been added, drilled and tapped for A.I.R. fittings.
		1972	Passenger	400	170 A.I.R.	
			Chevelle	307	130 NB2	
				350	165, 175 NB2	
			Nova	307	130 NB2	
				350	165, 175 NB2	
			Camaro	307	130 NB2	
				350	165, 175 NB2, 255 All	
			Monte Carlo	350	165, 175 NB2	
		1973	Passenger	350	145, 175 A.I.R.	
				400	150 All	
			Nova	307	115 A.I.R.	
				350	145, 175 A.I.R.	
			Chevelle	307	115 A.I.R.	
				350	145, 175 A.I.R.	
			Camaro	307	115 A.I.R.	
				350	145, 175, 245 A.I.R.	
			Monte Carlo	350	145, 175 A.I.R.	
		1974	Passenger	350	145, 160 A.I.R.	
				400	150, 180 A.I.R.	
			Nova	350	145, 160 A.I.R., 185 S/T A.I.R.	
			Chevelle	350	145, 160 A.I.R.	
				400	150, 180 A.I.R.	
			Camaro	350	145, 160, 185 S/T A.I.R., 245 A.I.R.	
			Monte Carlo	350	145, 160 A.I.R.	
				400	150, 180 A.I.R.	

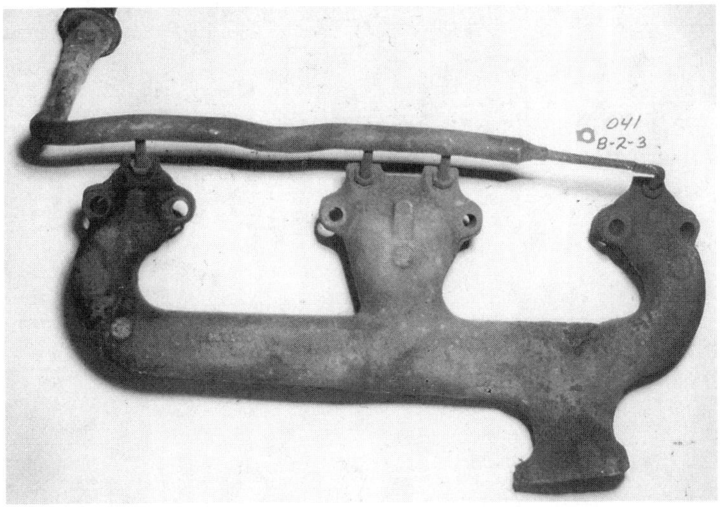

Fig. 10-19. Front view of #3989041 with smog tube still attached.

Manifold #3989043

Outlet Size	Outlet Side	Year	Model	Engine	Horsepower	Notes
2.026	LH	1971	Passenger	350	245, 270 w/o A.I.R.	Rear outlet. Short studs. "Log" type design. Casting #3989041 must appear on this part after 10/19/71. Should be identical with #3989041 except not drilled for A.I.R. fittings.
				400	255	
			Chevelle	307	200 w/o A.I.R.	
				350	245, 270 w/o A.I.R.	
			Nova	307	200 w/o A.I.R.	
				350	245, 270 w/o A.I.R.	
			Camaro	307	200 w/o A.I.R.	
				350	245, 270 w/o A.I.R.	
			Monte Carlo	350	245, 270 w/o A.I.R.	
		1972	Passenger	350	105 A/T w/o A.I.R.	
				400	170 w/o A.I.R.	
			Chevelle	307	130 w/o A.I.R.	
				350	165, 175 w/o A.I.R.	
			Nova	307	130 w/o A.I.R.	
				350	165, 175 w/o A.I.R.	
			Camaro	307	130 w/o A.I.R.	
				350	165, 175 w/o A.I.R.	
		1974	Passenger	400	150, 180 w/o A.I.R.	
			Camaro	350	185 THM w/o A.I.R.	
			Nova	350	185 THM w/o A.I.R.	
			Chevelle	400	150, 180 w/o A.I.R.	
			Monte Carlo	400	150, 180 w/o A.I.R.	

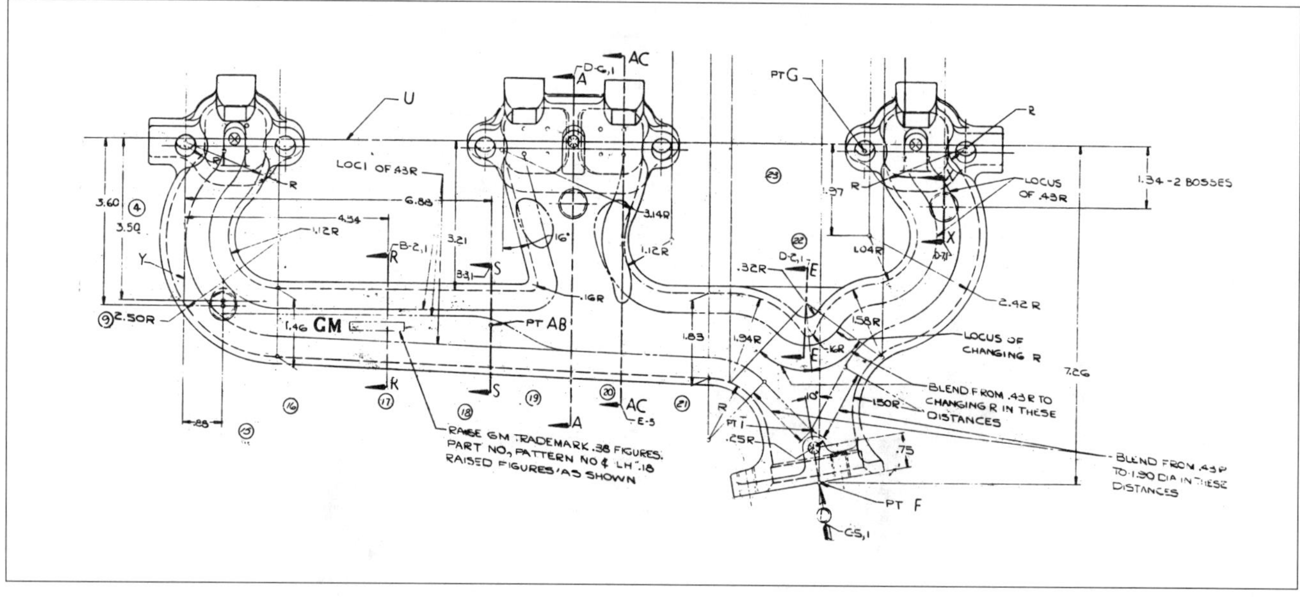

Fig. 10-20. Front view of #3989043.

Manifold #3989310

Outlet Size	Outlet Side	Year	Model	Engine	Horsepower	Notes
2.526	RH	1971	Passenger	402	300	"Log" type design. Rear outlet. Similar to #3909880.
				454	365	
			Chevelle	402	300	
				454	365, 425	
			Monte Carlo	402	300	
				454	365	
			GMC Sprint	402	300	
				454	365, 425	
			Camaro	402	300	
		1972	Passenger	402	240	
				454	240, 270	
			Chevelle	402	240	
				454	270	
			Monte Carlo	402	240	
				454	270	
			GMC Sprint	402	240	
				454	270	
			Camaro	402	240	

Fig. 10-21. *Front view of #3989310 with smog tube (damaged) still attached.*

Manifold #3989343

Outlet Size	Outlet Side	Year	Model	Engine	Horsepower	Notes
2.526	LH	1971	Passenger	402	300	Log type design. Rear outlet.
				454	365	
			Camaro	402	300	
			Chevelle	402	300	
				454	365, 425	
			Monte Carlo	402	300 SS Only	
				454	365	
			GMC Sprint	402	300	
				454	365, 425	
		1972	Passenger	402	240	
				454	240, 270	
			Chevelle	402	240	
				454	270	
			Monte Carlo	402	240	
				454	270	
			GMC Sprint	402	240	
				454	270	
			Camaro	402	240	

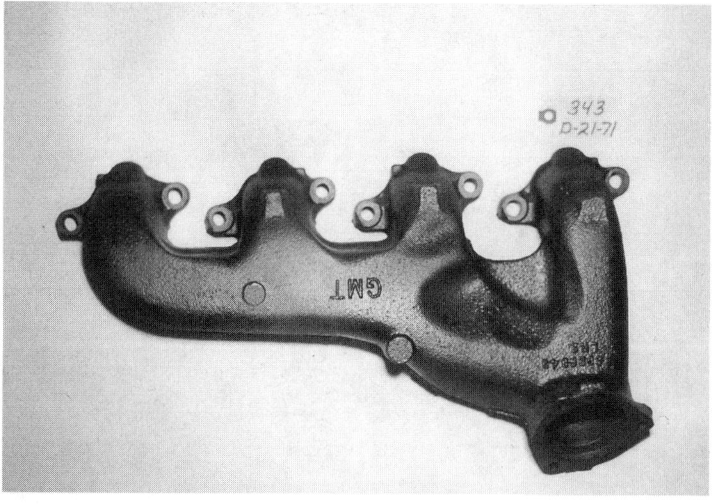

Fig. 10-22. Front view of #3989343.

Manifold #3994045

Outlet Size	Outlet Side	Year	Model	Engine	Horsepower	Notes
	LH	1973	Passenger	454	215 (Police only)	This exhaust manifold is made of nodular iron for higher material strength.
		1974	Passenger	454	235 (Police only)	
		1975	Passenger	454	215 (Police only)	

Manifold #329225

Outlet Size	Outlet Side	Year	Model	Engine	Horsepower	Notes
	LH	1973	Passenger	454	215	
			Chevelle	454	215	
		1974	Passenger	454	235	
			Chevelle	454	235	
		1975	Passenger	454	215	
			Chevelle	454	215	

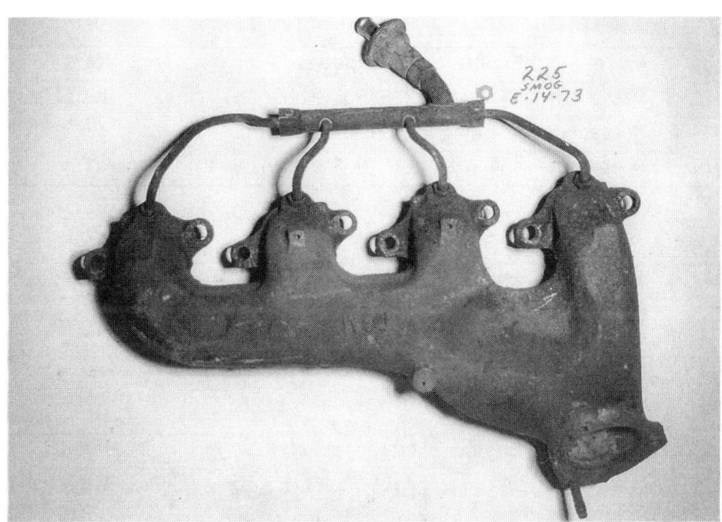

Fig. 10-23. Front view of #329225 with smog tube still attached.

Manifold #346247

Outlet Size	Outlet Side	Year	Model	Engine	Horsepower	Notes
	LH	1975	Passenger	350	145, 155	Ram's horn design.
				400	175	
			Chevelle	350	145, 155	
				400	175	
			Nova	350	145, 155	
			Nova (CA)	262	110, A.I.R.	
			Camaro	350	145, 155	
			Monte Carlo	350	145, 155	
				400	175	

Manifold #346248

Outlet Size	Outlet Side	Year	Model	Engine	Horsepower	Notes
	RH	1975	Passenger	350	145, 155	Log type.
				400	175	
			Chevelle	350	145, 155	
				400	175	
			Nova	350	145, 155	
			Nova (CA)	262	110, A.I.R.	
			Camaro	350	145, 155	
			Monte Carlo	350	145, 155	
				400	175	

Manifold #353028

Outlet Size	Outlet Side	Year	Model	Engine	Horsepower	Notes
	RH	1973	Passenger	454	215	
			Chevelle	454	215	
		1974	Passenger	454	235	
			Chevelle	454	235	
		1975	Passenger	454	215	
			Chevelle	454	215	

Manifold #353030

Outlet Size	Outlet Side	Year	Model	Engine	Horsepower	Notes
	RH	1973	Passenger	454	215 (Police only)	This exhaust manifold is made of nodular iron for higher material strength.
		1974	Passenger	454	235 (Police only)	
		1975	Passenger	454	215 (Police only)	

Manifold #354432

Outlet Size	Outlet Side	Year	Model	Engine	Horsepower	Notes
	RH	1975	Nova Monza	262	110, w/o A.I.R.	Log type design.

Manifold #354433

Outlet Size	Outlet Side	Year	Model	Engine	Horsepower	Notes
	LH	1975	Nova Monza	262	110, w/o A.I.R.	Ram's horn design.

Chapter 11
Water Pump Identification

1. Introduction

There is great difficulty in assigning the absolute correct applications of water pumps installed on Chevrolet cars from 1970 through 1975. One reason lies simply in the great variety of water pump configurations used. A second reason is that water pumps with the same design were often produced concurrently by different manufacturers, but with different casting numbers. The last and most puzzling piece of the applications puzzle is due to water pump rebuilders who altered original design features to enable a manufacturer to use a water pump on additional applications. On top of all this, water pumps are an often-replaced part. The water pump on any particular engine is as likely as not to be a replacement part, so you can see how the problem of researching and validating original casting numbers to specific models and years is very difficult.

There are two basic styles of water pumps, the "short leg" pump and the "long leg" pump. See Fig. 11-1. Application of each style depends on model and year, but generally the short leg was an earlier design and the long leg a later design.

Fig. 11-1. *Short leg style water pump (right) long leg style (left). Long leg pump was introduced on most models in 1969. These are big block pumps.*

In the following text and casting number breakdowns, please realize that this is a very reliable, but probably not perfect, chapter. Because of the complexity of this chapter, each specific engine family is listed separately and the verified casting numbers are listed chronologically.

Fig. 11-2. *Front view of pump #3856284.*

1.1 Date Coding

Casting date codes follow the same pattern as engine blocks, but some do not carry the year. The month code is always a letter, followed by a number signifying the day. See Fig. 11-3. The last number signifies the year of production. Big block water pumps, beginning in 1970, used a two-digit year code.

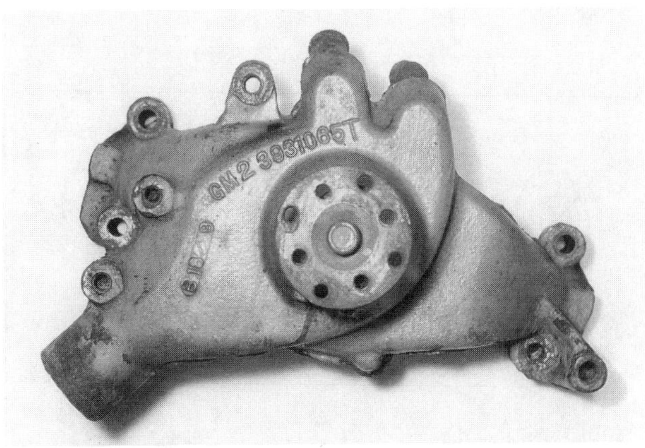

Fig. 11-3. *Casting date (left) and casting number for water pump #3931065 (a big block pump). Dual bolt pattern on hub may mean pump has been rebuilt. See text on next page for decoding of casting date B 18 0.*

Water Pump Month Codes (1st Letter)

A - January	E - May	I - September
B - February	F - June	J - October
C - March	G - July	K - November
D - April	H - August	L - December

Example:

Water pump date code B 18 0

- B = Month: February
- 18 = Casting date: 18th
- 0 = Model Year: 1970 (refer to casting number charts to confirm)

2. Small Block Water Pumps

Small block Chevrolet engines used the "short leg" water pump on Corvettes through 1970. Along with casting number changes through the years, there were also design changes due to the addition or deletion of accessory brackets.

Pump #3782608$^{\Delta}$

Year	Application	Engine	Horsepower
1970	Corvette	350	300, 350 A/C, 350 w/o A/C, 370
$^{\Delta}$This pump was also installed on some 1965–1969 models			

NOTE—
Date codes on the #3782608 water pump start in March 1964.

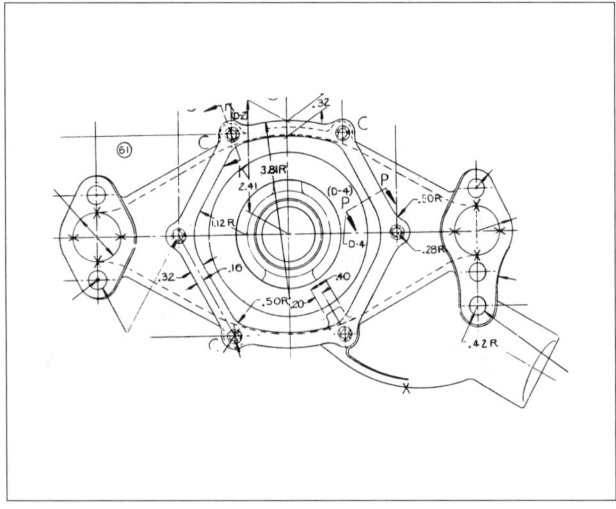

Fig. 11-4. Rear view of #3782608.

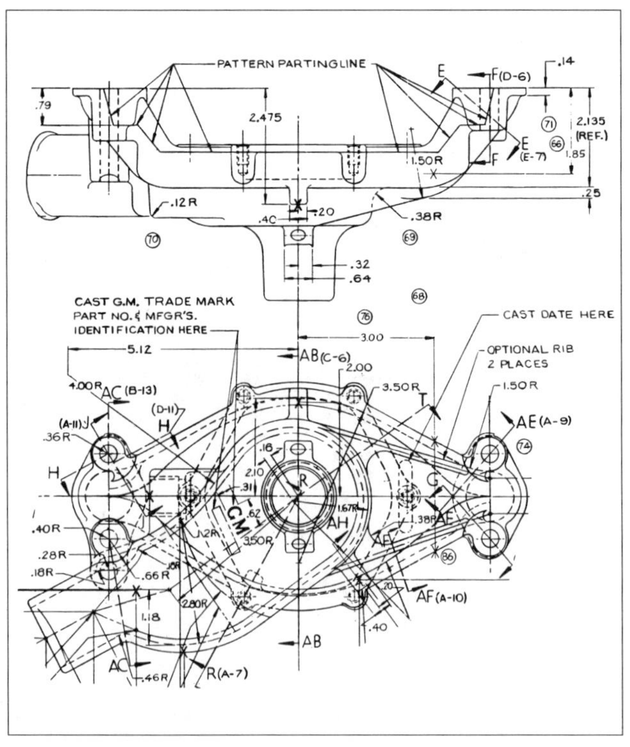

Fig. 11-5. Top and front view of #3782608.

Pump #3927170[Δ]

Year	Application	Engine	Horsepower
1970, 1971	All cars	—	—
[Δ]This pump was also installed in some 1969 models			

NOTE—

- In 1969, the water pump design changed from a "short leg" design to a "long leg" design, excluding the Corvette which changed in 1971.

- This water pump was used interchangeably with #3953692. #3953692 saw extensive usage. #3927170 saw very little usage.

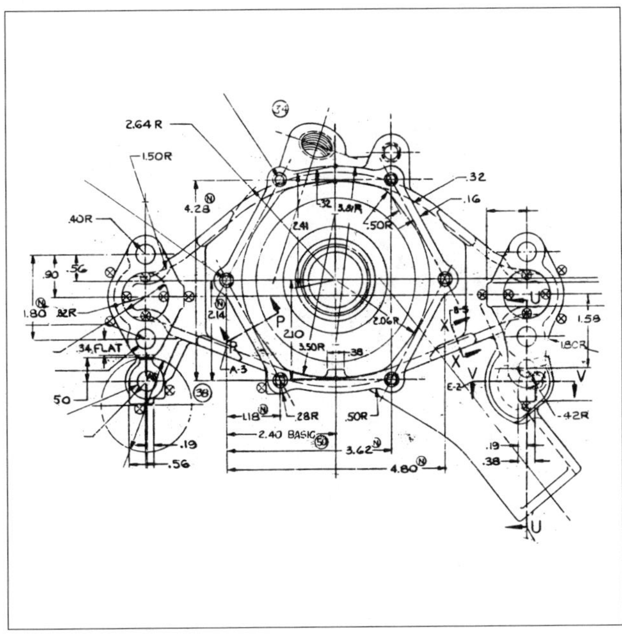

Fig. 11-6. Rear view of #3927170.

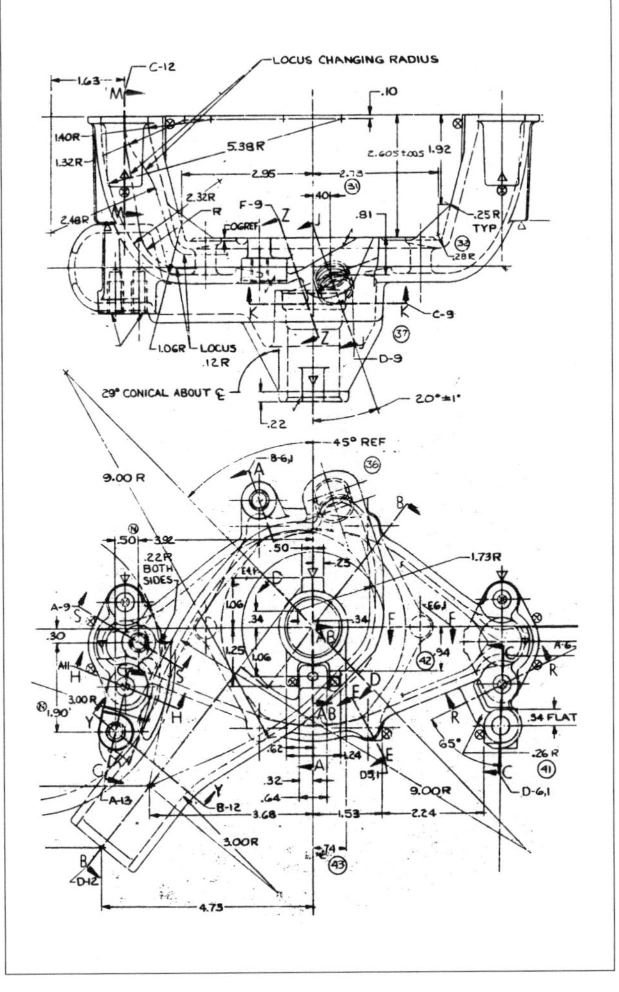

Fig. 11-7. Top and front view of #3927170.

CHAPTER 11

Pump #3953692[Δ]

Year	Application	Engine	Horsepower
1970	Passenger	350	250, 300
		400	265
	Nova	307	200
		350	250, 300
	Chevelle	307	200
		350	250, 300
	Camaro	307	200
		350	250, 300, 360
	Monte Carlo	350	250, 300
		400	265
1971	Passenger	350	245, 270
		400	255
		307	200
		350	245, 270
	Chevelle	307	200
		350	245, 270
	Camaro	307	200
		350	245, 270, 330
	Monte Carlo	350	245, 270
[Δ]This pump was also installed in some 1969 models			

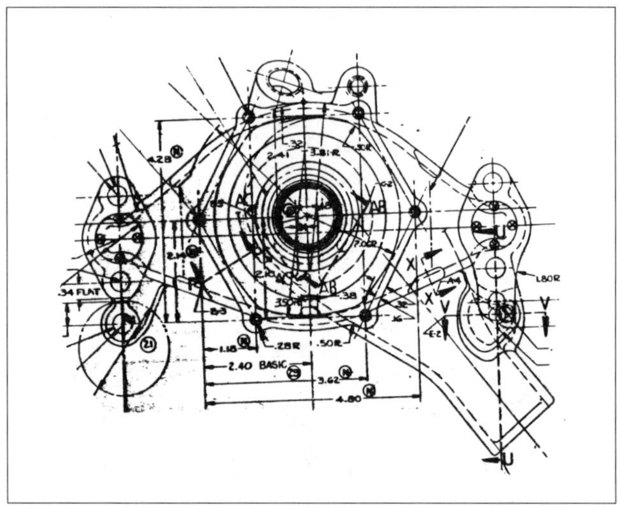

Fig. 11-8. Rear view of #3953692.

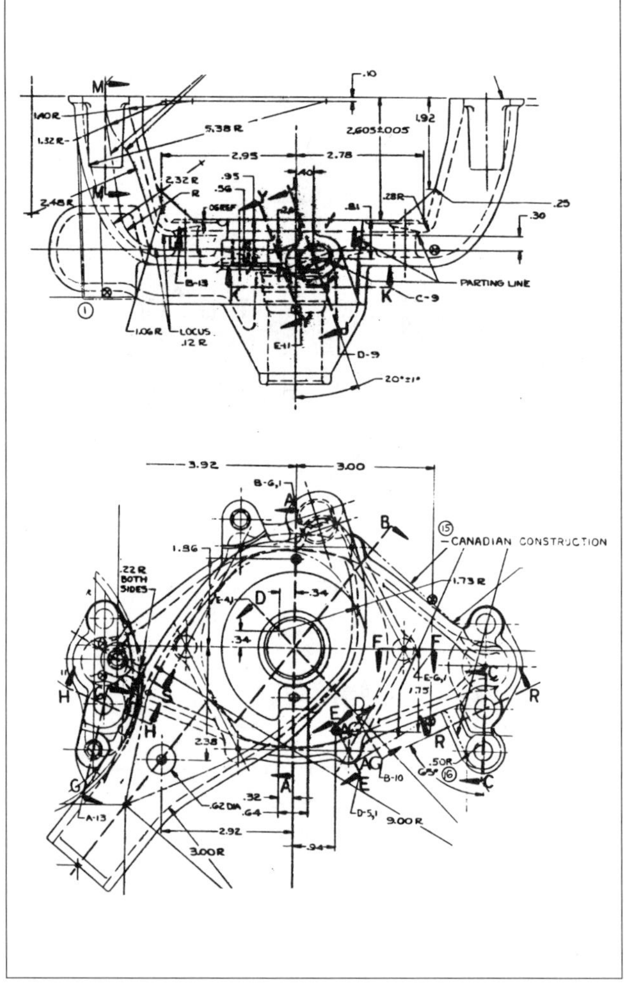

Fig. 11-9. Top and front view of #3953692.

Pump #3991399

Year	Application	Engine	Horsepower
1971	Corvette	350	270, 330
1972	Corvette*	350	200, 255
*The change-over date to the #330813 water pump is still being researched, although Flint engine plant build records show the #3991399 pump in production 11/3/71. The latest verified casting date for #3991399 is March 1972. The earliest verified casting date for #330813 is April 1972. This indicates that April could have been the change-over date between the two pumps.			

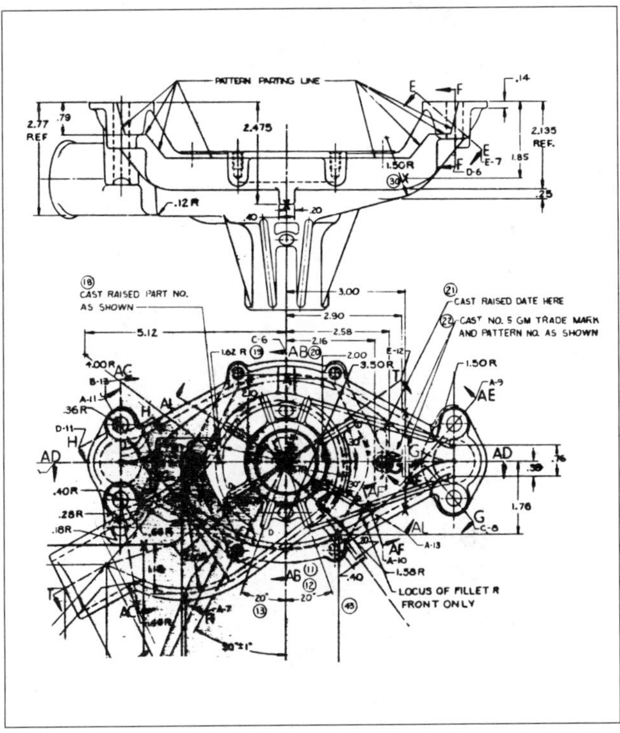

Fig. 11-10. Top and front view of #3991399.

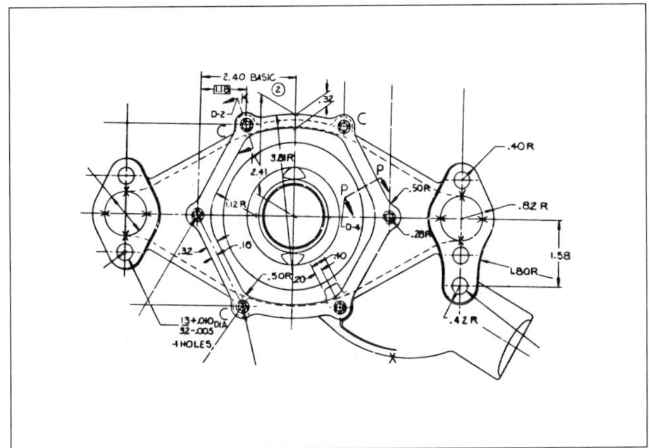

Fig. 11-11. Rear view of #3991399.

CHAPTER 11

Pump #6263701

Year	Application	Engine	Horsepower
1972	Passenger	350	165
		400	170
	Nova	307	130
		350	165, 175
	Chevelle	307	130
		350	165, 175
	Camaro	307	130
		350	165, 175, 255
	Monte Carlo	350	165, 175
		400	150
1973	Passenger	350	145, 175
		400	150
	Nova	307	115
		350	145, 175
	Chevelle	307	115
		350	145, 175
	Camaro	307	115
		350	145, 175, 245
	Monte Carlo	350	145, 175
1974	Passenger	350	145, 160
		400	150, 180
	Nova	350	145, 160, 185
	Chevelle	350	145, 160
		400	150, 180
	Camaro	350	145, 160, 185, 245
1975	Passenger	350	145, 155
		400	175
	Nova	262	110
		350	145, 155
	Chevelle	350	145, 155
		400	175
	Camaro	350	145, 155
	Monte Carlo	350	145, 155

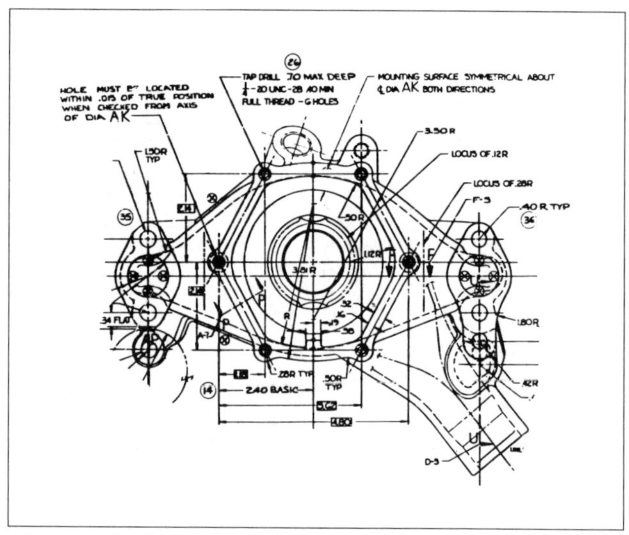

Fig. 11-12. Rear view of #6263701.

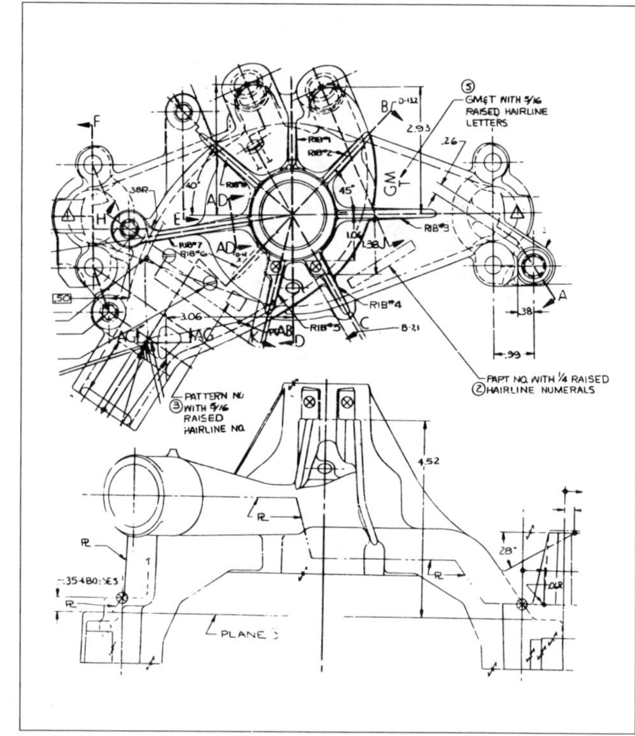

Fig. 11-13. Front and bottom view of #6263701.

Pump #330813

Year	Application	Engine	Horsepower
1972	Corvette*	350	255
1973	Corvette	350	190, 250
1974	Corvette	350	195, 250
1975	Corvette	350	165, 205
*See note at water pump #3991399			

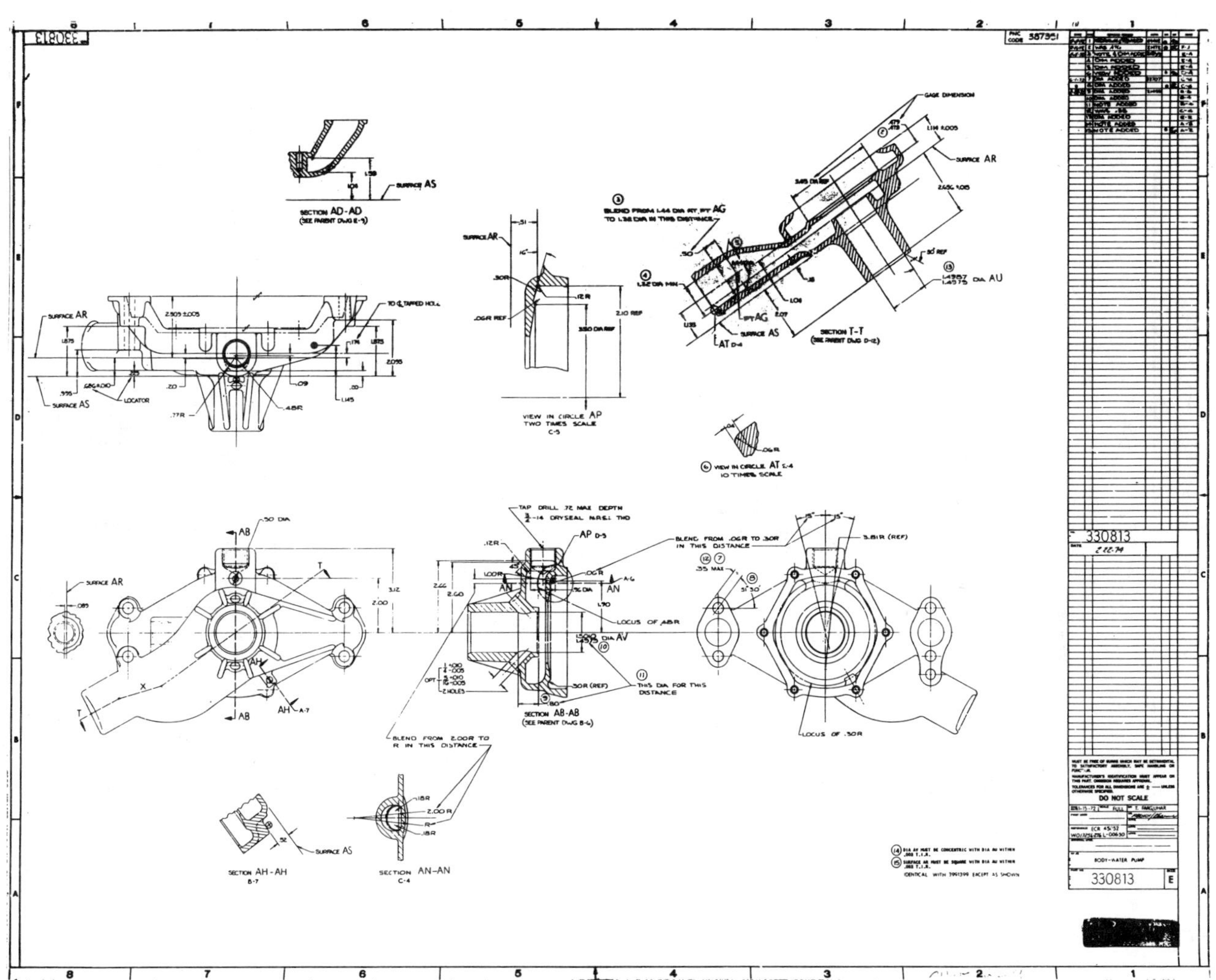

Fig. 11-14. Blueprint for #330813 shows changes from design of pump #3991399.

Pump #354495

Year	Application	Engine	Horsepower
1975	Nova	262	110
	Monza	262	110

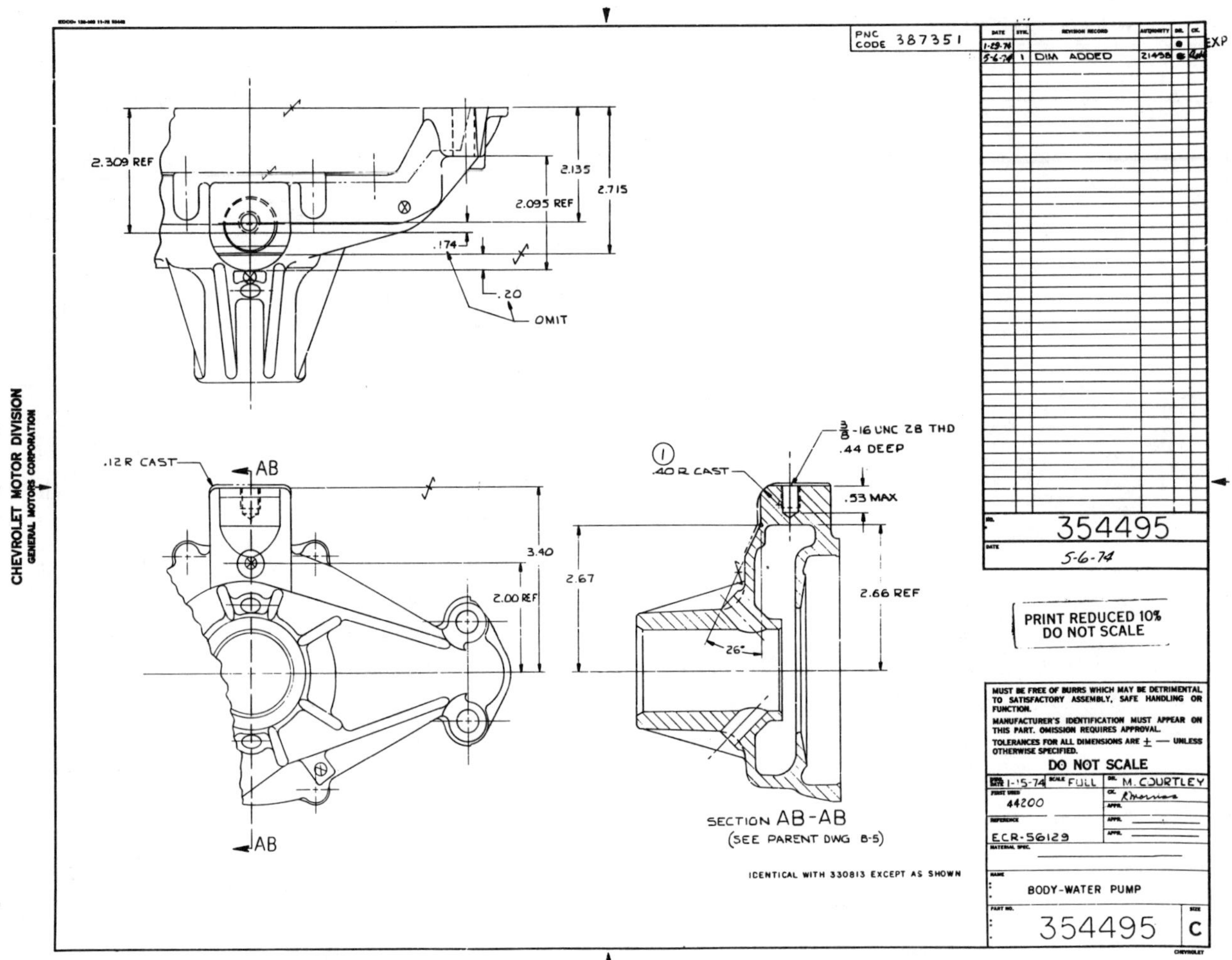

Fig. 11-15. Blueprint for #354495 shows changes from design of pump #330813.

3. Big Block Water Pumps

Big block Chevrolet engines used the "short leg" water pump on all Corvettes through the 1974 model year. All other models used the "long leg" design. Note that although the terminology used is the same as for small block water pumps, the actual water pumps do not interchange. All big block water pumps have a bypass provision on top of the pump.

Pump #3931065^Δ

Year	Application	Engine	Horsepower
1970 (early)	Passenger	454	345, 390
	Chevelle	402	330, 350, 375
		454	360, 450
	Camaro	402	350, 375
	Nova	402	350, 375
ΔThis pump was also installed on some 1969 models			

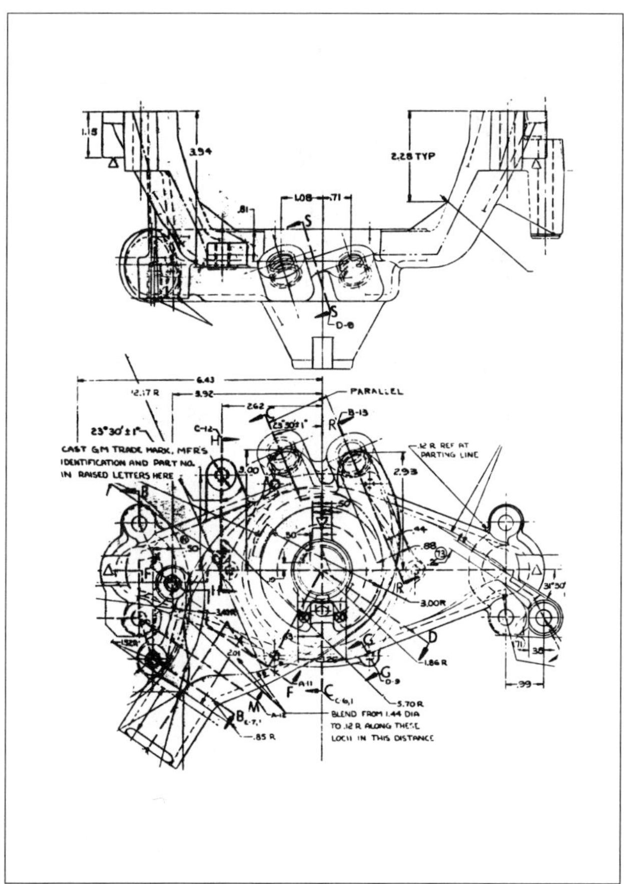

Fig. 11-16. Top and front view of #3931065.

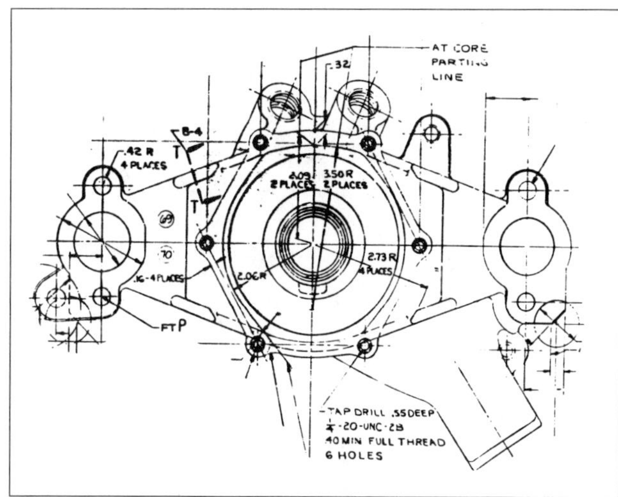

Fig. 11-17. Rear view of #3931065.

CHAPTER 11

Pump #3940960$^{\Delta}$

Year	Application	Engine	Horsepower
1970	Corvette	454	390
$^{\Delta}$This pump was also installed on some 1969 models			

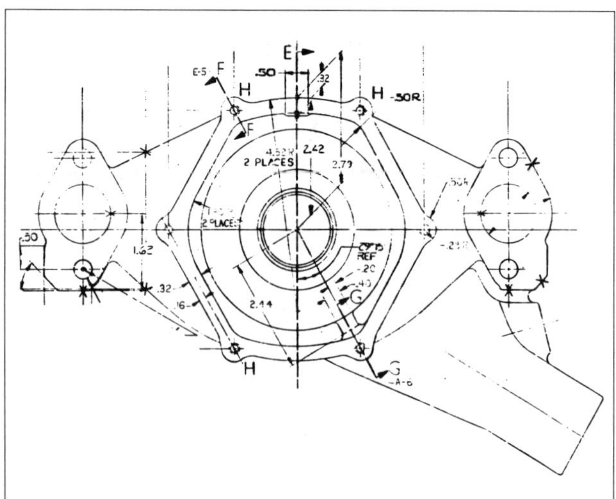

Fig. 11-18. Rear view of #3940960.

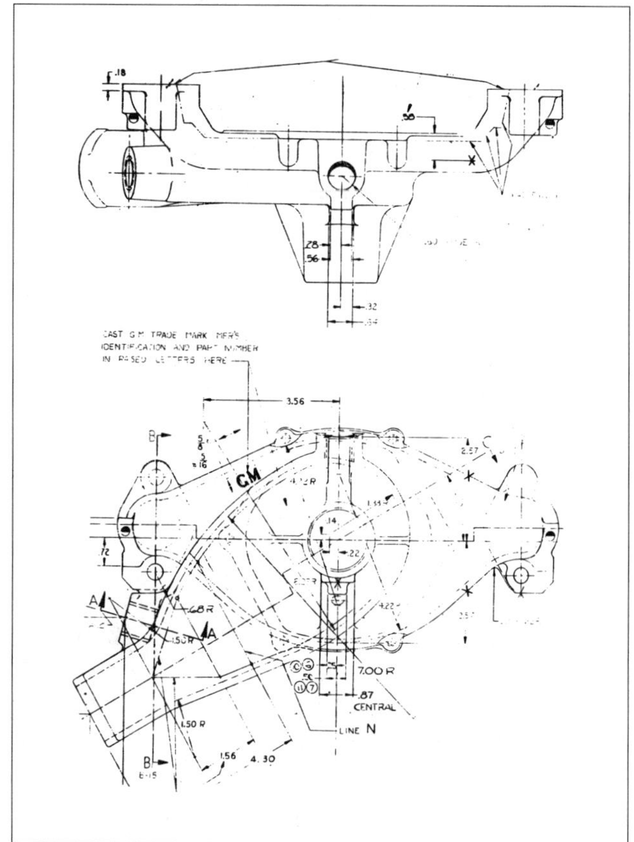

Fig. 11-19. Top and front view of #3931065.

Pump #3969811

Year	Application	Engine	Horsepower
1970 (late)	Passenger	454	345, 390
	Chevelle	402	330, 350, 375
		454	360, 450
	Camaro	402	350, 375
	Nova	402	350, 375
1971	Passenger	402	300
		454	365
	Chevelle	402	300
		454	365, 425
	Camaro	402	300

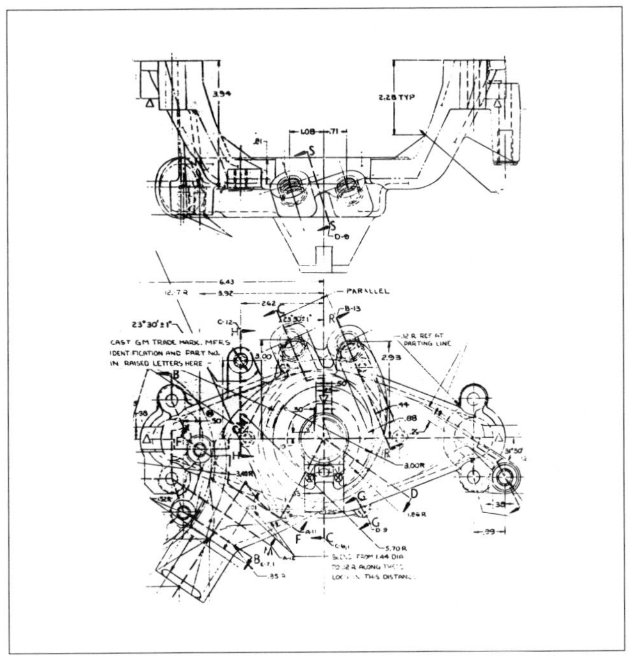

Fig. 11-20. Top and front view of #3969811.

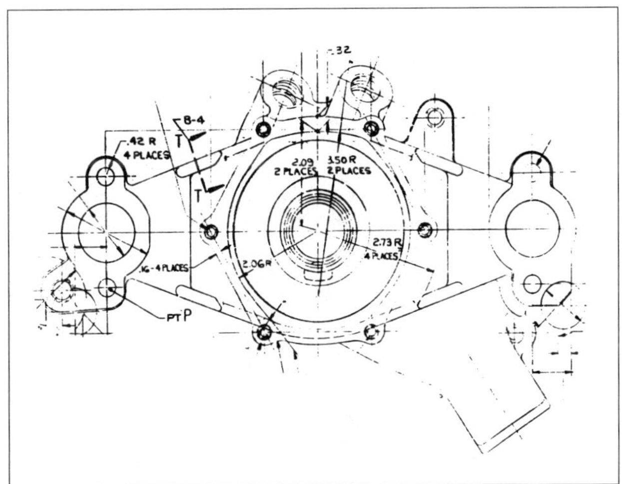

Fig. 11-21. Rear view of #3969811.

Pump #3992077

Year	Application	Engine	Horsepower
1971	Corvette	454	365, 425 Short leg
1972	Corvette	454	270

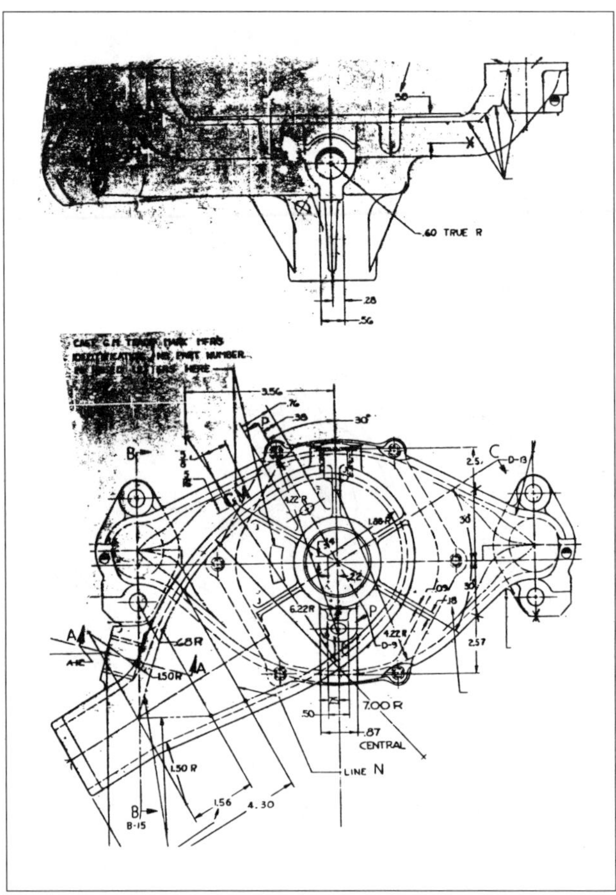

Fig. 11-22. *Top and front view of #3992077.*

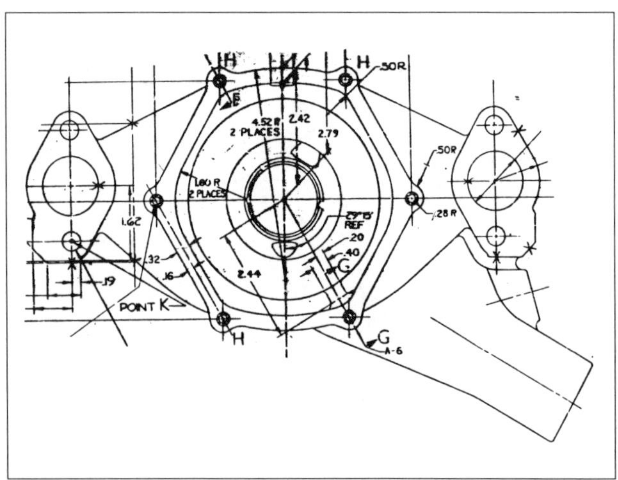

Fig. 11-23. *Rear view of #3992077.*

Pump #6263707

Year	Application	Engine	Horsepower
1972	Passenger	402	240
		454	240 (Police), 270
	Chevelle	402	240
		454	270
	Camaro	402	240
1973	Passenger	454	215
	Chevelle	454	215
1974	Passenger	454	235
	Chevelle	454	235
1975	Passenger	454	215
	Chevelle	454	215

Pump #386100

Year	Application	Engine	Horsepower
1973	Corvette*	454	245
1974	Corvette	454	270
*Some early 1973 Corvettes have been verified using the #3992077 water pump			

Chapter 12
Distributor Identification

1. Introduction

All Chevrolet distributors from 1970 through 1975 were manufactured by the Delco-Remy Division of General Motors in Anderson, Indiana. There were several plants involved in producing ignition components at Delco-Remy. Plant production was as follows:

- Plant #10: All conventional (point-type) distributors and ignition coils
- Plant #6: All ignition amplifiers and capacitor discharge ignition systems
- Plant #20: All HEI ignition systems and the newly developed (late model) Direct Ignition Systems

There are several different distributor component combinations that were used from 1970 through 1975. They were manufactured in both cast iron and die-cast aluminum. There were also "Bowl" and "Non-Bowl" distributors produced in both aluminum and cast iron. "Bowl" distributors were used primarily in 4- and 6-cylinder applications.

There were an immense number of distributor combinations across model ranges. Generally, all 1970–75 distributors were either aluminum or cast iron, and externally adjustable. All Corvette distributors produced from 1970 through 1974 were cast iron and all were equipped with tach drive; in 1975, all GM cars, including Corvette, went to the High Energy Ignition (HEI).

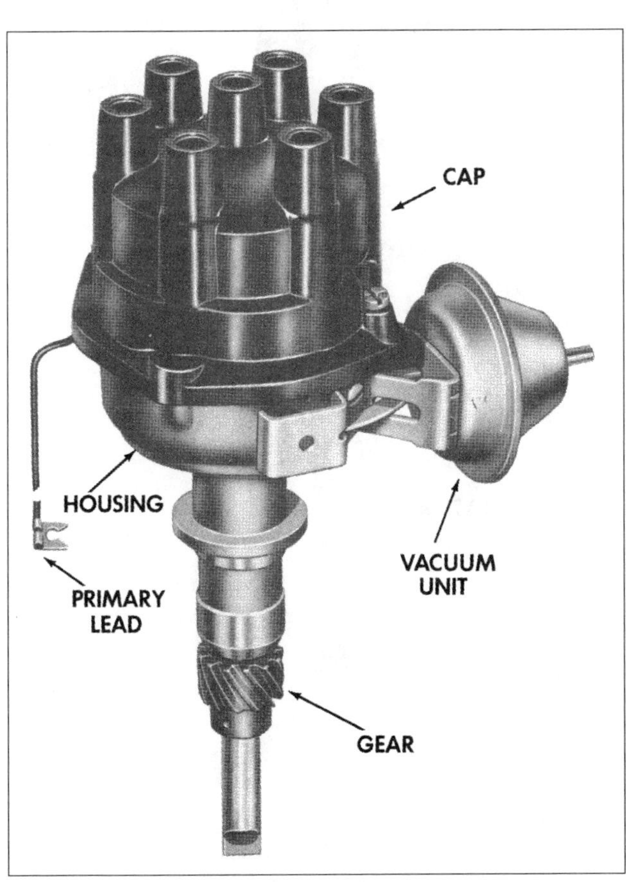

Fig. 12-1. External view of an aluminum bowl type distributor. This distributor was used primarily on 4- and 6-cylinder engines.

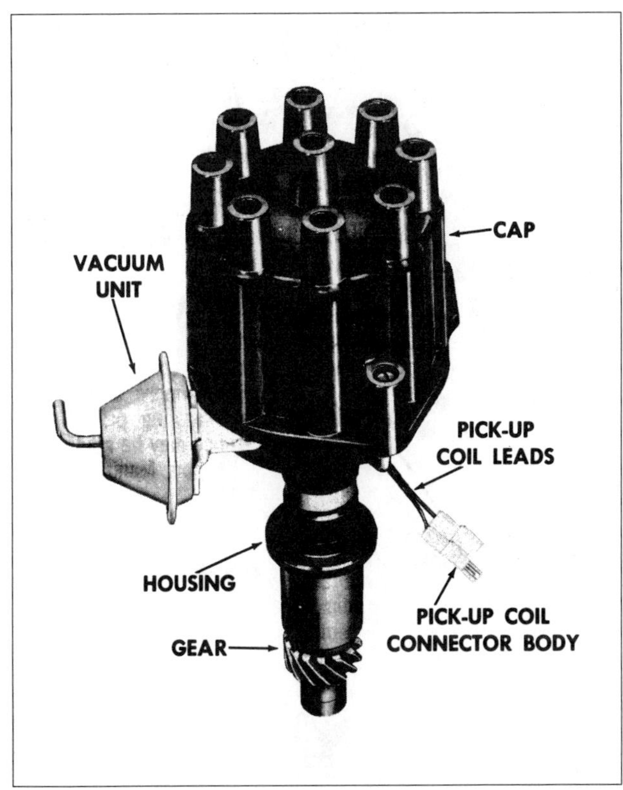

Fig. 12-2. A typical Delco-Remy magnetic pulse distributor. This is a Pontiac distributor; Chevrolet distributors are similar, except for location of gear.

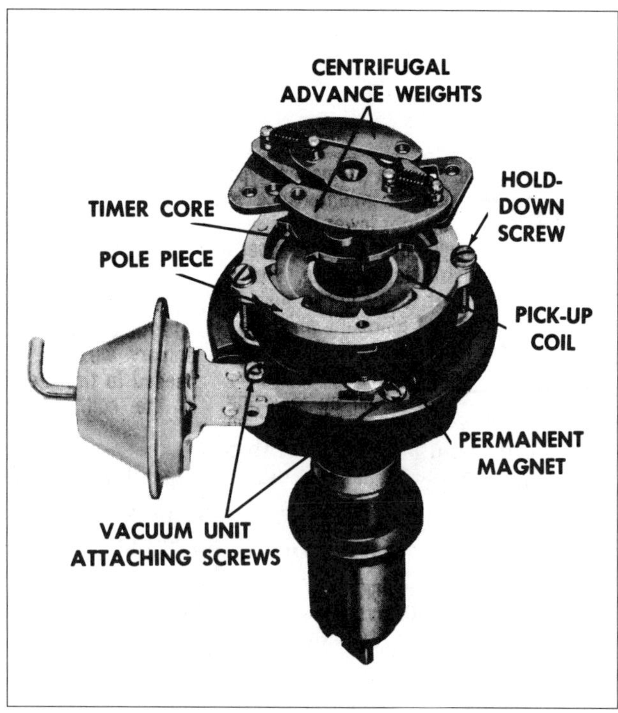

Fig. 12-3. *A Delco-Remy magnetic pulse distributor with cap removed.*

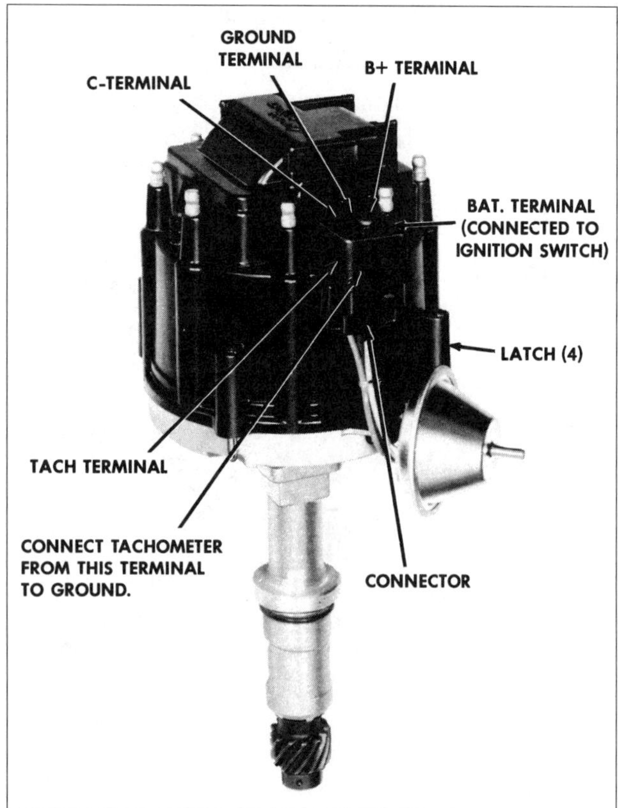

Fig. 12-4. *A Delco-Remy High Energy Ignition (HEI) distributor.*

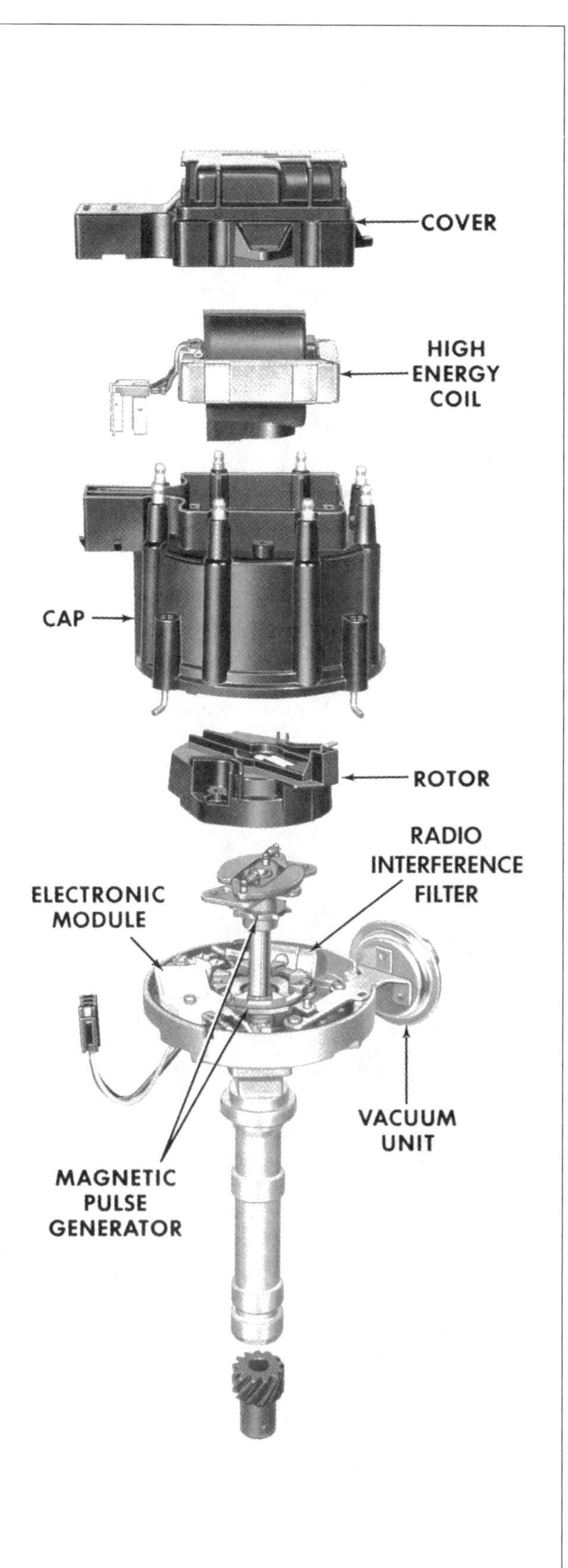

Fig. 12-5. *A partially exploded view of a typical Delco-Remy HEI distributor.*

1.1 Distributor Identification

All Delco-Remy distributors have a model number and a date code either stamped on or attached to the distributor. Generally, on 1970 through 1974 cast iron non-dual-point distributors the model number is on a small aluminum band (or tag), which wrapped around the shaft of the distributor. See Fig. 12-6 and Fig. 12-7. The late model aluminum distributor housings had the model number roll stamped right into the exterior of the housing. See Fig. 12-8.

Date code stamps are near the model number. The location varies from year to year.

Fig. 12-6. *Cast iron distributor model number (in this case 1112053 for a 1971 Corvette) is stamped on metal band on distributor shaft.*

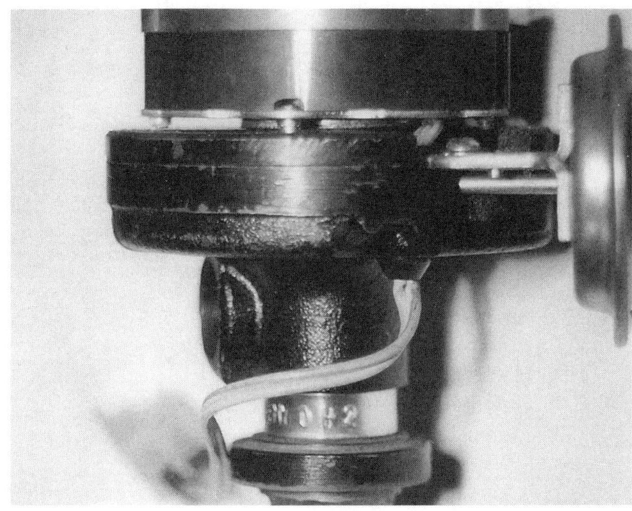

Fig. 12-7. *Cast iron distributor production date code is also on metal band.*

Fig. 12-8. *Aluminum distributor model number and date code were roll stamped into distributor housing. This 1111499 distributor (less vacuum advance control) was used exclusively on 396/350, 375HP and 427/425HP applications in the 1969 model year. Date code reads 8-L-15.*

Fig. 12-9. *Factory timing mark coincides with chisel mark on intake manifold and is used for initial engine startup.*

Date Code Deciphering

All Chevrolet distributors use the same date code style. The Julian code system is used as with many other Chevrolet parts. The actual build date is signified by a series of numbers and letters.

The date code is deciphered as follows: The first digit gives the calendar year of production. This is the last digit of the calendar year. To determine the actual *decade* of manufacture, it is necessary to inspect the distributor for common features used during that time period. Please refer to the Distributor Application charts. The second letter indicates the month of production. See the table below for month codes. ("I" was not used because it is too easily confused with the number 1.) The final two digits indicate the day of the month of production (1 through 31).

Example: 5A28

- 5 = Year: 1975
- A = Month: January
- 28 = Day: 28th

Distributor Month Codes (2nd Letter)

A - January	E - May	J - September
B - February	F - June	K - October
C - March	G - July	L - November
D - April	H - August	M - December

Distributor Color Coding

Most distributors installed at a final engine assembly plant had a color code applied to the distributor housing. See Fig. 12-10. This was to enable assemblers to identify distributors without reading the code number. Most Delco Remy blueprints call out these color codes as paint spots, but note that, in time, many of these paint marks wore off.

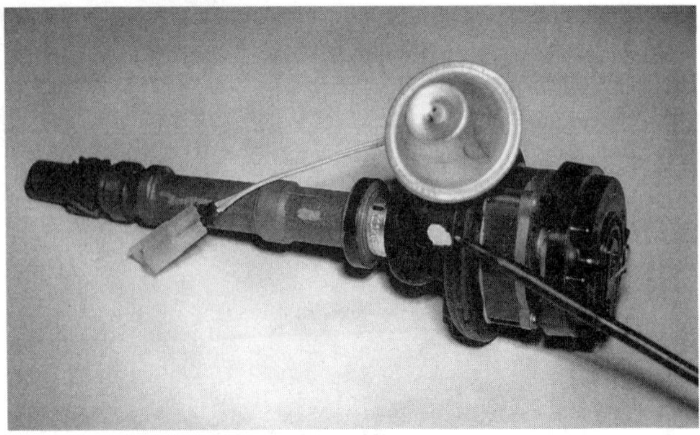

Fig. 12-10. *Distributor #1112053 shows pink identification paint dot (pointer). This distributor fits 1971 Corvette LS6 applications.*

2. DISTRIBUTOR APPLICATIONS

The charts on the following pages list the distributor applications for the years 1970 through 1975. All distributors are in numerical order within each model listing. Each distributor is listed by model and engine application, and then further distinguished by housing type, point type and other features. Be sure to check the model years before and after your car to check for other uses. The abbreviations used in the charts are listed below.

Housing Type Designations

A: Aluminum Housing Distributor
AE: Aluminum External Adjustment Distributor
C: Cast Iron Housing Distributor
CE: Cast Iron External Adjustment Distributor

Point Type Designations

EMC: Distributor model containing a uniset contact set designed for radio suppression.
HEI: High energy ignition
MP: Magnetic pulse distributor
S: Single point distributor

Letter Designations

ECC: Electro-magnetically Compatible Contact set
LW: Lead wire (with color code)
NV: No vacuum equipped distributor
RFI: Radio frequency interference shield installed
TD: Tach drive/flexible cable drive
V: Vacuum equipped distributor

Color Code Designations

1: No Paint
2: White
3: Yellow
4: Orange
5: Pink
6: Red
7: Light Blue
8: Blue
9: Light Green
10: Green
11: Gray
12: Brown
13: Black
14: Purple

Abbreviations

A.I.R.: Air Injection Reactor
A/T: Automatic Transmission
HP: Horsepower
S/T: Standard (manual) Transmission
TI: Transistorized Ignition

1970 Distributor Applications

Model	Distributor Number	Engine/HP/Application	Housing	Point	Notes
Passenger	1111436	454/345HP All	AE	S	RFI/V
	1111492	400/265HP S/T	AE	S	RFI/3-6/V
	1111494	400/265HP A/T	AE	S	RFI/3/V
	1111963	454/390HP All	AE	S	RFI/10/V
	1111996	350/300HP S/T	AE	S	RFI/2-8/V
	1111997	350/300HP A/T	AE	S	RFI/3-8/V
	1112001	350/250HP S/T	AE	S	RFI/2-12/V
	1112002	350/250HP A/T	AE	S	RFI/3-12/V
Corvette	1111464	454/390HP All	CE	S	TD/11/V
	1111490	350/300HP (Early) All (unverified)	CE	S	TD/10/V
	1111491	350/350HP	CE	MP	TD/4/LW 2-10/V
	1111493	350/350HP (Early) All (unverified)	CE	S	TD/4/V
	1111496	350/370HP All	CE	S	TD/V
	1111971	350/370HP	CE	MP	TD/LW 2-10/V
	1112020	350/300HP All	CE	S	RFI/TD/10/V
	1112021	350/350HP All	CE	S	RFI/TD/4/V
Nova	1111995	307/200HP S/T	AE	S	RFI/6-7/V
	1111996	350/300HP S/T	AE	S	RFI/2-8/V
	1111997	350/300HP A/T	AE	S	RFI/3-8/V
	1111999	402/350HP S/T	AE	S	RFI/V
	1112000	402/350HP A/T	AE	S	RFI/V
		402/375HP All	AE	S	RFI/V
	1112001	350/250HP S/T	AE	S	RFI/2-12/V
	1112002	350/250HP A/T	AE	S	RFI/3-12/V
	1112005	307/200HP A/T	AE	S	RFI/3-13/V
Yenko Duece	1112019	350/360HP S/T	AE	S	3-12/V
Chevelle	1111437	454/450HP All	AE	S	RFI/V
	1111963	454/360HP All	AE	S	RFI/10/V
	1111995	307/200HP S/T	AE	S	RFI/6-7/V
	1111996	350/300HP S/T	AE	S	RFI/2-8/V
	1111997	350/300HP A/T	AE	S	RFI/3-8/V
	1111998	402/330HP All	AE	S	RFI/V
	1111999	402/350HP S/T	AE	S	RFI/V
	1112000	402/350HP A/T	AE	S	RFI/V
		402/375HP All	AE	S	RFI/V
	1112001	350/250HP S/T	AE	S	RFI/2-12/V
	1112002	350/250HP A/T	AE	S	RFI/3-12/V
	1112005	307/200HP A/T	AE	S	RFI/3-13/V
Camaro	1111995	307/200HP S/T	AE	S	RFI/6-7/V
	1111996	350/300HP S/T	AE	S	RFI/2-8/V
	1111997	350/300HP A/T	AE	S	RFI/3-8/V
	1111999	402/350HP S/T	AE	S	RFI/V
	1112000	402/350HP A/T	AE	S	RFI/V
		402/375HP All	AE	S	RFI/V
	1112001	350/250HP S/T	AE	S	RFI/2-12/V
	1112002	350/250HP A/T	AE	S	RFI/3-12/V
	1112005	307/200HP A/T	AE	S	RFI/3-13/V
	1112019	350/360HP Z28 All	AE	S	RFI/3-11 (grey changed to red 5/71)
Monte Carlo	1111963	454/360HP All	AE	S	RFI/10/V
	1111996	350/300HP S/T	AE	S	2-8/V
	1111997	350/300HP A/T	AE	S	3-8/V
	1111998	402/330HP All	AE	S	V
	1112001	350/250HP S/T	AE	S	2-12/V
	1112002	350/250HP A/T	AE	S	3-12/V

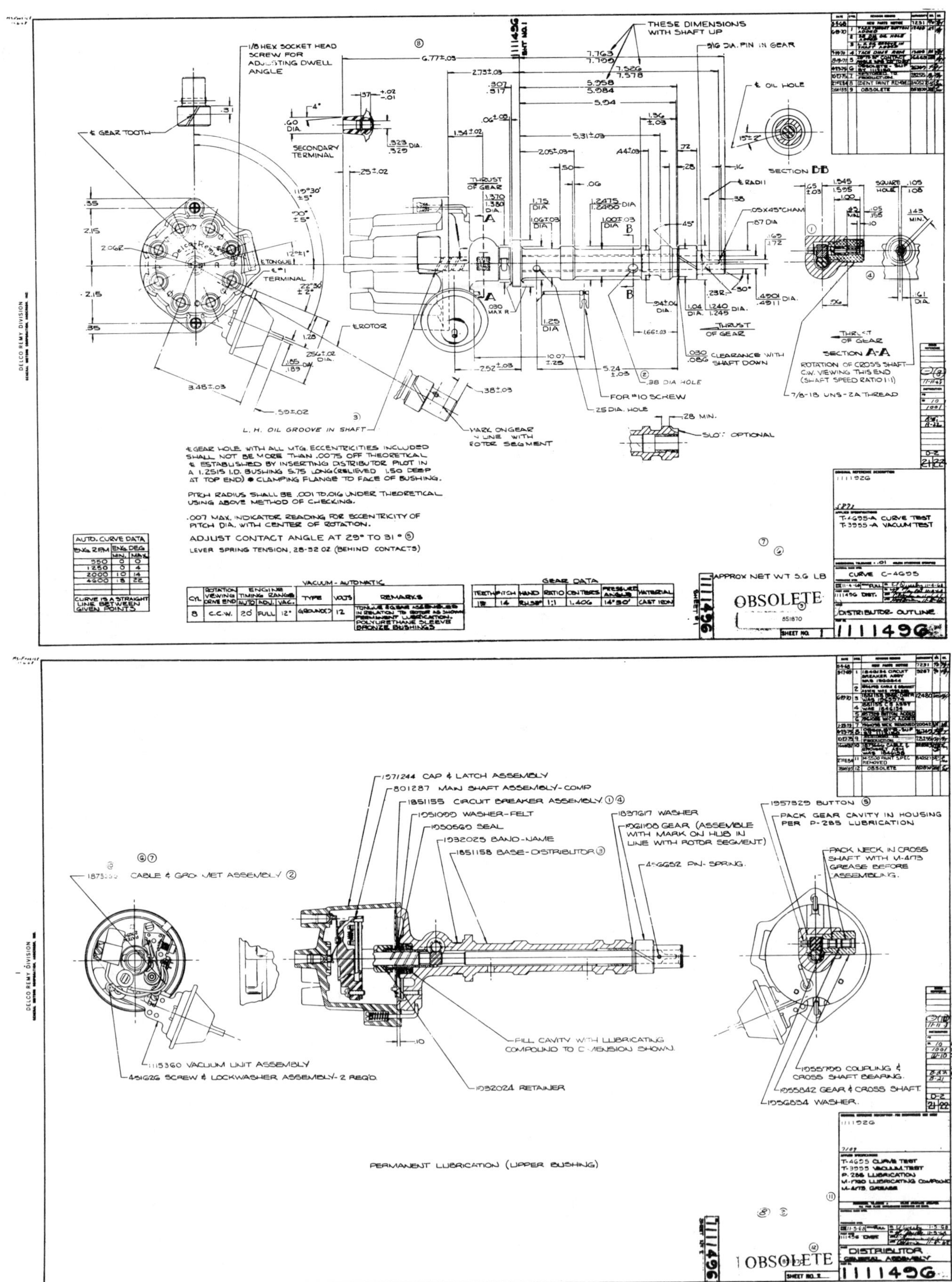

Fig. 12-11. *Views above show distributor #1111496.*

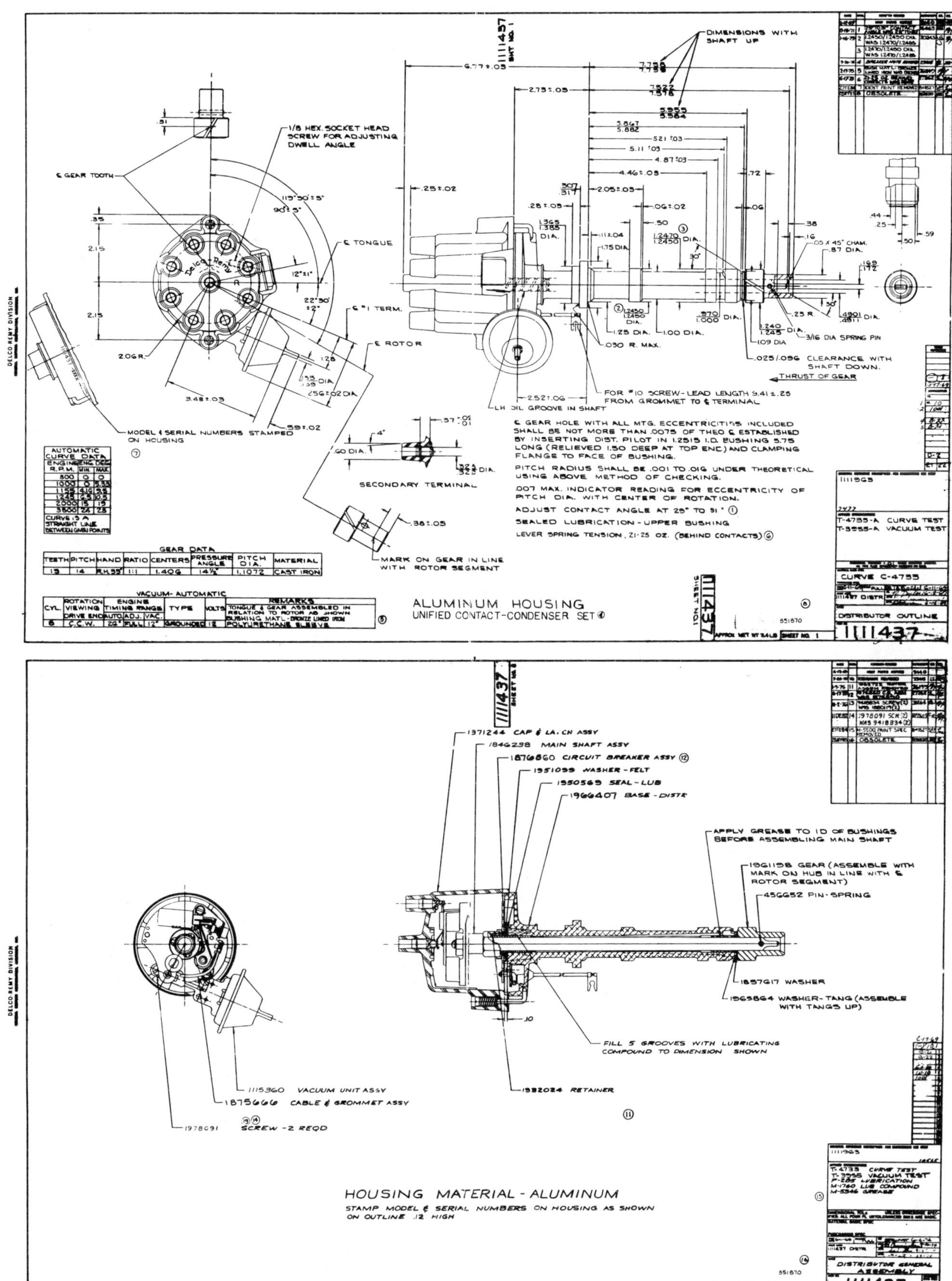

Fig. 12-12. Views above show distributor #1111437.

1971 Distributor Applications

Model	Distributor Number	Engine/HP/Application	Housing	Point	Notes
Passenger	1111968	350/245HP	AE	MP	LW 2-10/13/V
	1112005	350/245HP A/T	AE	S	3-13/V
	1112042	350/245HP S/T	AE	S/EMC	2-12/V
	1112044	350/270HP S/T	AE	S/EMC	2-8/V
	1112045	350/270HP A/T	AE	S/EMC	3-8/V
	1112052	454/365HP All	AE	S/EMC	10/V
	1112055	400/255HP S/T (unverified)	AE	S/EMC	6/V
	1112056	400/255HP A/T	AE	S/EMC	3/V
	1112057	402/300HP All	AE	S/EMC	RFI/1/V
Corvette	1112038	350/270HP	CE	MP	TD/3/LW 2-10/V
	1112050	350/270HP All	CE	S/EMC	TD/10/V
	1112051	454/365HP All	CE	S/EMC	TD/11/V
	1112053	454/425HP, A/T	CE	MP	TD/5/LW 2-10/V
	1112076	454/425HP, 4-Speed	CE	MP	TD/14/LW 2-10/V
Nova	1112005	307/200HP S/T	AE	S	3-13/V
		350/245HP A/T	AE	S	3-13/V
	1112039	307/200HP A/T	AE	S/EMC	6-7/V
	1112042	350/245HP S/T (unverified)	AE	S	2-12/V
	1112044	350/270HP S/T	AE	S	2-8/V
	1112045	350/270HP A/T	AE	S	3-8/V
Chevelle	1112005	307/200HP S/T	AE	S	3-13/V
		350/245HP A/T	AE	S	3-13/V
	1112039	307/200HP A/T	AE	S	6-7/V
	1112042	350/245HP S/T	AE	S	2-12/V
	1112044	350/270HP S/T	AE	S	2-8/V
	1112045	350/270HP A/T	AE	S	3-8/V
	1112052	454/365HP All	AE	S	10/V
	1112054	454/425HP A/T	AE	S/EMC	6-10/V
	1112057	402/300HP All	AE	S	1/V
	1112075	454/425HP S/T	AE	S	RFI/9/V
Camaro	1112005	307/200HP S/T	AE	S	3-13/V
		350/245HP A/T	AE	S	3-13/V
	1112039	307/200HP A/T	AE	S/EMC	6-7/V
	1112042	350/245HP S/T	AE	S	2-12/V
	1112044	350/270HP S/T	AE	S	2-8/V
	1112045	350/270HP A/T	AE	S	3-8/V
	1112049	350/330HP S/T	AE	S	RFI/3-11/V
	1112057	402/300HP All	AE	S/EMC	RFI/1/V
	1112074	350/330HP A/T	AE	S	RFI/11/V
Monte Carlo	1112005	350/245HP A/T	AE	S	3-13/V
	1112042	350/245HP S/T	AE	S	2-12/V
	1112044	350/270HP S/T	AE	S	2-8/V
	1112045	350/270HP A/T	AE	S	3-8/V
	1112052	454/365HP All	AE	S/EMC	10/V
	1112054	454/425HP A/T (unverified)	AE	S/EMC	6-10/V
	1112057	402/300HP All	AE	S	1/V
	1112075	454/425HP S/T (unverified)	AE	S	RFI/9/V

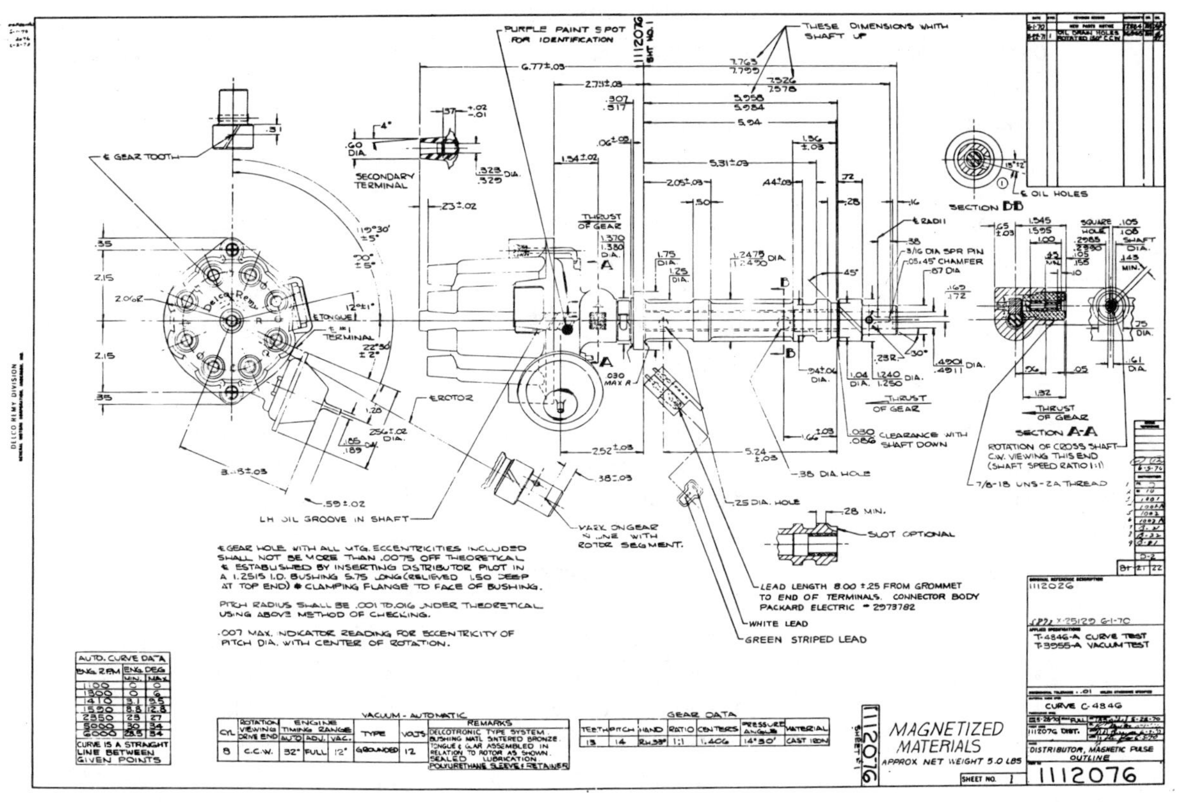

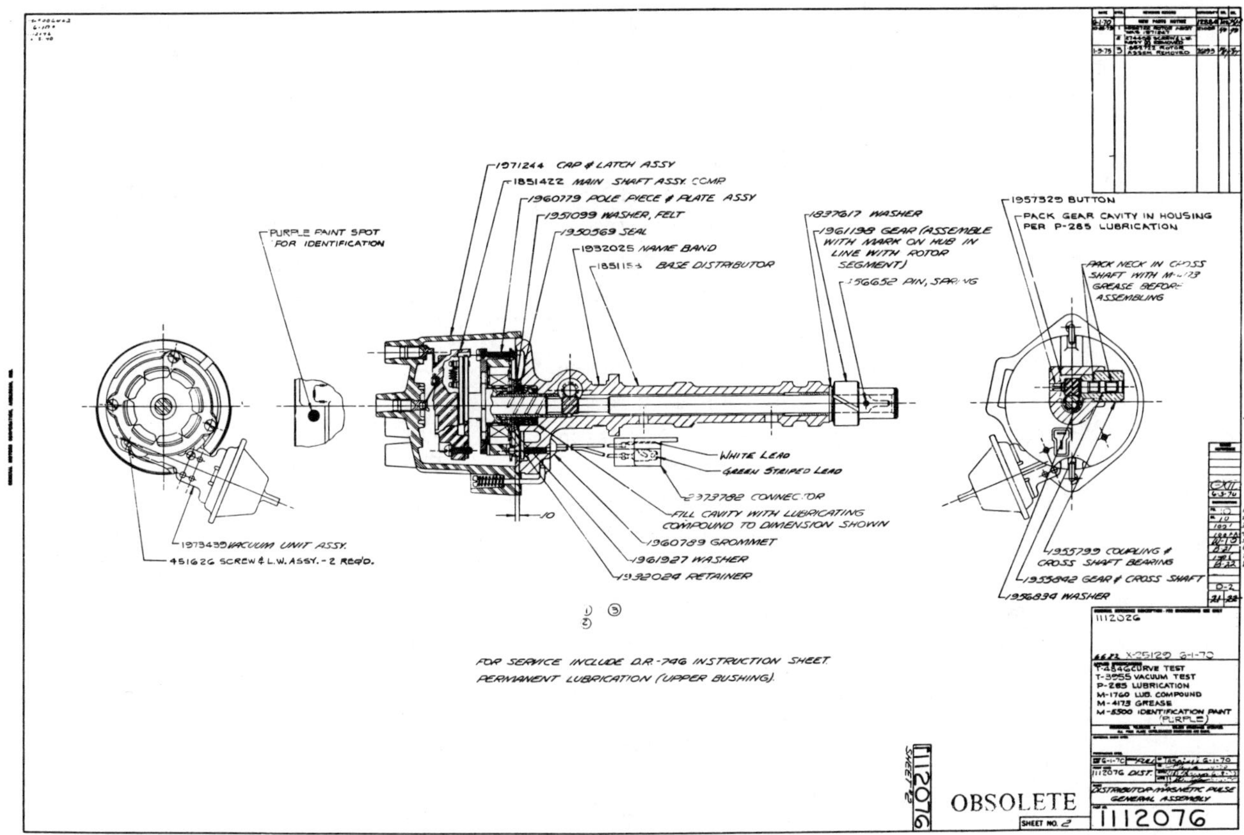

Fig. 12-13. *Views above show distributor #1112076.*

1972 Distributor Applications

Model	Distributor Number	Engine/HP/Application	Housing	Point	Notes
Passenger	1112005	350/165HP All	AE	S	13/V
	1112052	454/240HP All	AE	S	10/V
		454/270HP All	AE	S	10/V
	1112057	402/240HP All 1st Design	AE	S	1/V
	1112099	400/170HP All 1st Design	AE	S/EMC	RFI/3/V
	1112161	400/170HP All 2nd Design	AE	S/EMC	RFI/3/V
Corvette	1112050	350/200HP All	CE	S/EMC	TD/10/V
	1112051	454/270HP All	CE	S/EMC	TD/11/V
	1112101	350/255HP LT1 All	CE	S/EMC	TD/3/V
	1112165	350/200HP 2nd Design	CE	S/EMC	TD/10/ECC/V
	1112167	350/255HP LT1 All 2nd Design	CE	S/EMC	TD/3/ECC/V
	1112169	454/270HP All 2nd Design	CE	S/EMC	TD/11/V
Nova	1112005	307/130HP All	AE	S	13/V
		350/165HP All	AE	S	13/V
	1112039	307/130HP A/T 1st Design	AE	S/EMC	7/V
	1112044	350/175HP S/T 1st Design	AE	S	8/V
	1112045	350/175HP A/T 1st Design	AE	S/EMC	8/V
	1112134	307/130HP S/T	AE	S/EMC	3-13/V
		350/165HP All 2nd Design	AE	S/EMC	3-13/V
	1112147	307/130HP A/T 2nd Design	AE	S/EMC	6-7/V
	1112152	350/175HP S/T 2nd Design	AE	S/EMC	2-8/V
	1112154	350/175HP A/T 2nd Design	AE	S/EMC	3-8/V
Chevelle	1112005	307/130HP S/T 1st Design	AE	S	13/V
		350/165HP All 1st Design	AE	S	13/V
	1112039	307/130HP A/T 1st Design	AE	S/EMC	7/V
	1112044	350/175HP S/T 1st Design	AE	S	8/V
	1112045	350/175HP A/T 1st Design	AE	S/EMC	8/V
	1112052	454/270HP All	AE	S	10/V
	1112057	402/240HP All	AE	S	1/V
	1112134	307/130HP S/T 2nd Design	AE	S/EMC	13/V
		350/165HP All 2nd Design	AE	S/EMC	13/V
	1112147	307/130HP A/T 2nd Design	AE	S/EMC	7/V
	1112152	350/175HP S/T 2nd Design	AE	S/EMC	8/V
	1112154	350/175HP A/T 2nd Design	AE	S/EMC	8/V
Camaro	1112005	307/130HP S/T 1st Design	AE	S	13/V
		350/165HP All 1st Design	AE	S	13/V
	1112039	307/130HP A/T 1st Design	AE	S/EMC	7/V
	1112044	350/175HP S/T 1st Design	AE	S	8/V
	1112045	350/175HP A/T 1st Design	AE	S/EMC	8/V
	1112049	350/255HP A/T 1st Design	AE	S/EMC	RFI/3-11/V
	1112057	402/240HP All	AE	S	1/V
	1112095	350/255HP S/T 1st Design	AE	S/EMC	RFI/12/V
	1112134	307/130HP S/T 2nd Design	AE	S/EMC	13/V
		350/165HP All 2nd Design	AE	S/EMC	13/V
	1112147	307/130HP A/T 2nd Design	AE	S/EMC	7/V
	1112152	350/175HP S/T 2nd Design	AE	S/EMC	8/V
	1112153	350/255HP S/T 2nd Design	AE	S/EMC	ECC/12/V
	1112154	350/175HP A/T 2nd Design	AE	S/EMC	8/V
	1112156	350/255HP A/T 2nd Design	AE	S/EMC	ECC/3-11/V

continued on 2nd page following

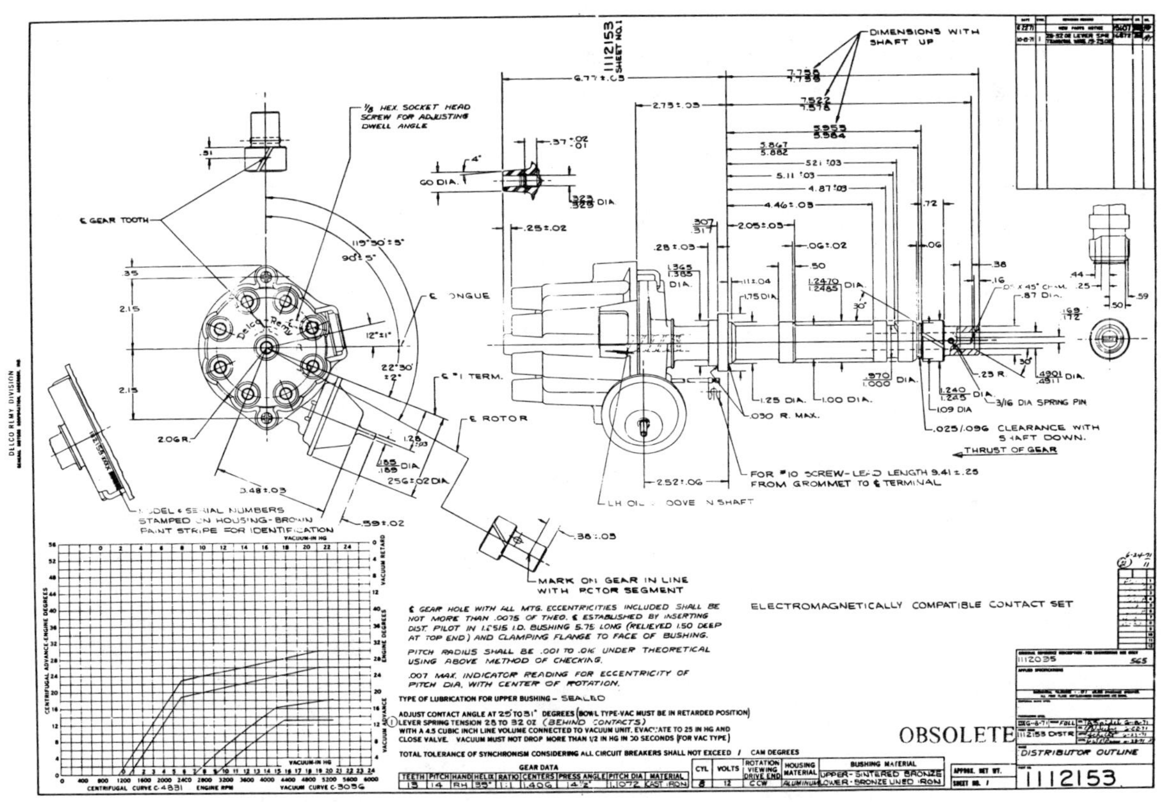

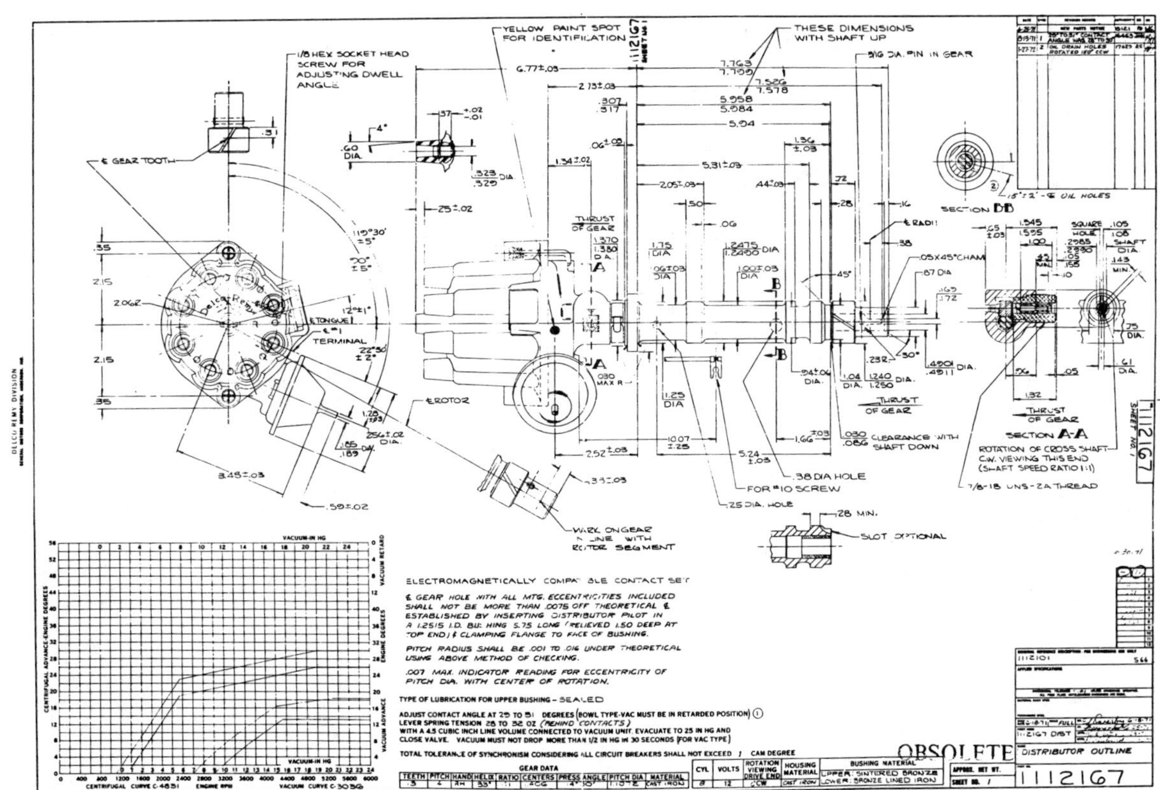

Fig. 12-14. *Views above show that #1112153 (top) aluminum distributor was installed in Camaro LT1, while #1112167 (bottom) cast iron distributor was installed in Corvette LT1.*

1972 Distributor Applications (continued)

Model	Distributor Number	Engine/HP/Application	Housing	Point	Notes
Monte Carlo	1112005	350/165HP All 1st Design	AE	S	13/V
	1112044	350/175HP S/T 1st Design	AE	S	8/V
	1112045	350/175HP A/T 1st Design	AE	S/EMC	8/V
	1112052	454/270HP All	AE	S	10/V
	1112057	402/240HP All	AE	S	1/V
	1112134	350/165HP All 2nd Design	AE	S/EMC	13/V
	1112152	350/175HP S/T 2nd Design	AE	S/EMC	8/V
	1112154	350/175HP A/T 2nd Design	AE	S/EMC	8/V

1973 Distributor Applications

Model	Distributor Number	Engine/HP/Application	Housing	Point	Notes
Passenger	1112094	350/175HP All	AE	S/EMC (Aft. 3/73)	RFI/3-8/V
	1112113	454/215HP All	AE	S/EMC (Aft. 3/73)	RFI/10/V
	1112166	400/150HP All	AE	S/EMC (Aft. 7/73)	RFI/3/V
	1112168	350/145HP All exc. Wagon	AE	S/EMC (Aft. 7/73)	RFI/13/V
	1112230	350/145HP Station Wagon	AE	S/EMC	4-13/V
Corvette	1112098	350/190HP All	CE	S	TD/10/V
	1112114	454/245HP All	CE	S/EMC (Aft. 7/73)	TD/RFI/11/V
	1112150	350/250HP L82 All	CE	S/EMC (Aft. 7/73)	TD/RFI/5 (7 after 4/73)
Nova	1112093	350/175HP S/T	AE	S/EMC (Aft. 3/73)	RFI/2-8/V
	1112094	350/175HP A/T	AE	S/EMC (Aft. 3/73)	RFI/3-8/V
	1112102	307/115HP A/T	AE	S/EMC	6-8/V
	1112168	350/145HP All	AE	S/EMC (Aft. 7/73)	RFI/13/V
	1112227	307/115HP S/T	AE	S/EMC	3-13/V
Chevelle	1112093	350/175HP S/T	AE	S/EMC (Aft. 3/73)	RFI/2-8/V
	1112094	350/175HP A/T	AE	S/EMC (Aft. 3/73)	RFI/3-8/V
	1112102	307/115HP A/T	AE	S/EMC	6-8/V
	1112113	454/215HP All	AE	S/EMC (Aft. 7/73)	RFI/10/V
	1112168	350/145HP All	AE	S/EMC (Aft. 7/73)	RFI/13/V
	1112227	307/115HP A/T	AE	S	3-13/V
Camaro	1112093	350/175HP S/T	AE	S/EMC (Aft. 3/73)	RFI/2-8/V
	1112094	350/175HP A/T	AE	S/EMC (Aft. 3/73)	RFI/3-8/V
	1112102	307/115HP A/T	AE	S/EMC	6-8/V
	1112148	350/245HP Z28 All	AE	S/EMC (Aft. 7/73)	RFI/7/V
	1112168	350/145HP All	AE	S/EMC (Aft. 7/73)	RFI/13/V
	1112227	307/115HP S/T	AE	S	3-13/V
Monte Carlo	1112113	454/215HP All	AE	S/EMC (Aft. 7/73)	RFI/10/V
	1112168	350/145HP All	AE	S/EMC (Aft. 7/73)	RFI/13/V
	1112094	350/175HP A/T	AE	S/EMC (Aft. 3/73)	RFI/3-8/V

1974 Distributor Applications

Model	Distributor Number	Engine/HP/Application	Housing	Point	Notes
Passenger	1112093	350/160HP S/T	AE	S/EMC (Aft. 3/73)	RFI/2-8/V
	1112094	350/160HP A/T	AE	S/EMC (Aft. 3/73)	RFI/3-8/V/
	1112113	454/235HP All	AE	S/EMC (Aft. 3/73)	RFI/10/V
	1112250	400/180HP All 1st Design	AE	S/EMC (Aft. 7/73)	RFI/3/V
	1112527	454/235HP All CA HEI	A	HEI	10/V
	1112543	350/160HP S/T CA	AE	S/EMC (Aft. 7/73)	RFI/8-8/V
	1112545	400/180HP All CA 1st Design	AE	S/EMC (Aft. 7/73)	RFI/3-10/V
	1112843	350/145HP S/T	AE	S/EMC (Aft. 7/73)	RFI/6-13/V
	1112844	350/145HP A/T	AE	S/EMC (Aft. 7/73)	RFI/13/V
	1112846	400/150HP All	AE	S/EMC (Aft. 7/73)	RFI/7-13/V
	1112864	400/180HP All 2nd Design Wagon	A	HEI	3/V
	1112865	400/180HP All CA 2nd Design	A	HEI	3-10/V
Corvette	1112150	350/250HP L82 All	CE	S/EMC (Aft. 7/73)	RFI/TD/7/V
	1112247	350/195HP All exc. CA, S/T	CE	S	TD/2/V
	1112526	454/270HP All	CE	S	TD/10/V
	1112544	350/195HP S/T CA	CE	S	TD/4/V
Nova	1112093	350/160HP S/T exc. CA	AE	S/EMC (Aft. 3/73)	RFI/2-8/V
		350/185HP	AE	S/EMC (Aft. 3/73)	RFI/2-8/V
	1112094	350/160HP A/T	AE	S/EMC (Aft. 3/73)	RFI/3-8/V
		350/185HP A/T	AE	S/EMC (Aft. 3/73)	RFI/3-8/V
	1112543	350/160HP S/T CA	AE	S/EMC (Aft. 7/73)	RFI/8-8/V
	1112843	350/145HP S/T	AE	S/EMC (Aft. 7/73)	RFI/6-13/V
	1112844	350/145HP A/T	AE	S/EMC (Aft. 7/73)	RFI/13/V
Chevelle	1112093	350/160HP S/T	AE	S/EMC (Aft. 3/73)	RFI/2-8/V
	1112094	350/160HP A/T	AE	S/EMC (Aft. 7/73)	RFI/3-8/V
	1112113	454/235HP All	AE	S/EMC (Aft. 7/73)	RFI/10/V
	1112250	400/180HP All 1st Design	AE	S/EMC (Aft. 7/73)	RFI/3/V
	1112543	350/160HP S/T CA	AE	S/EMC (Aft. 7/73)	RFI/8-8/V
	1112545	400/180HP All CA	AE	S/EMC (Aft. 7/73)	RFI/3-10/V
	1112843	350/145HP S/T	AE	S/EMC (Aft. 7/73)	RFI/6-13/V
	1112844	350/145HP A/T	AE	S/EMC (Aft. 7/73)	RFI/13/V
	1112846	400/150HP All A/T	AE	S/EMC (Aft. 7/73)	RFI/7-13/V
	1112865	400/180HP All 2nd Design	A	HEI	3-10/V
Camaro	1112093	350/185HP S/T exc. CA	AE	S/EMC (Aft. 3/73)	RFI/2-8/V
	1112094	350/160HP All	AE	S/EMC (Aft. 3/73)	RFI/3-8/V
		350/185HP All	AE	S/EMC (Aft. 3/73)	RFI/3-8/V
	1112148*	350/245HP Z28, 1st Design	AE	S/EMC (before 1/74)	7/V
	1112528	350/245HP Z28, HEI, 2nd Design	A	HEI (Aft. 1/74)	7/V
	1112543	350/160HP S/T CA	AE	S/EMC (Aft. 7/73)	RFI/8-8/V
		350/185HP S/T CA	AE	S/EMC (Aft. 7/73)	RFI/8-8/V
	1112843	350/145HP S/T	AE	S/EMC (Aft. 7/73)	RFI/6-13/V
	1112844	350/145HP A/T	AEE	S/EMC (Aft. 7/73)	RFI/13/V
Monte Carlo	1112093	350/160HP S/T CA	AE	S/EMC (Aft. 3/73)	RFI/2-8/V
	1112094	350/160HP A/T	AE	S/EMC (Aft. 3/73)	RFI/3-8/V
	1112113	454/235HP All	AE	S/EMC (Aft. 7/73)	RFI/10/V
	1112250	400/180HP All CA 1st Design	AE	S/EMC (Aft. 7/73)	RFI/13/V
	1112545	400/180HP All CA	AE	S/EMC (Aft. 7/73)	RFI/3-10/V
	1112843	350/145HP S/T	AE	S/EMC (Aft. 7/73)	RFI/6-13/V
	1112844	350/145HP S/T	AE	S/EMC (Aft. 7/73)	RFI/13/V
	1112846	400/150HP All A/T	AE	S/EMC (Aft. 7/73)	RFI/7-13/V
	1112865	400/180HP All CA 2nd Design	A	HEI	3-10/V

* 3123 Z28s were built after Jan., 1974 with this distributor, contradicting the Feb., 1974 CSN concerning the release of the new HEI distributor.

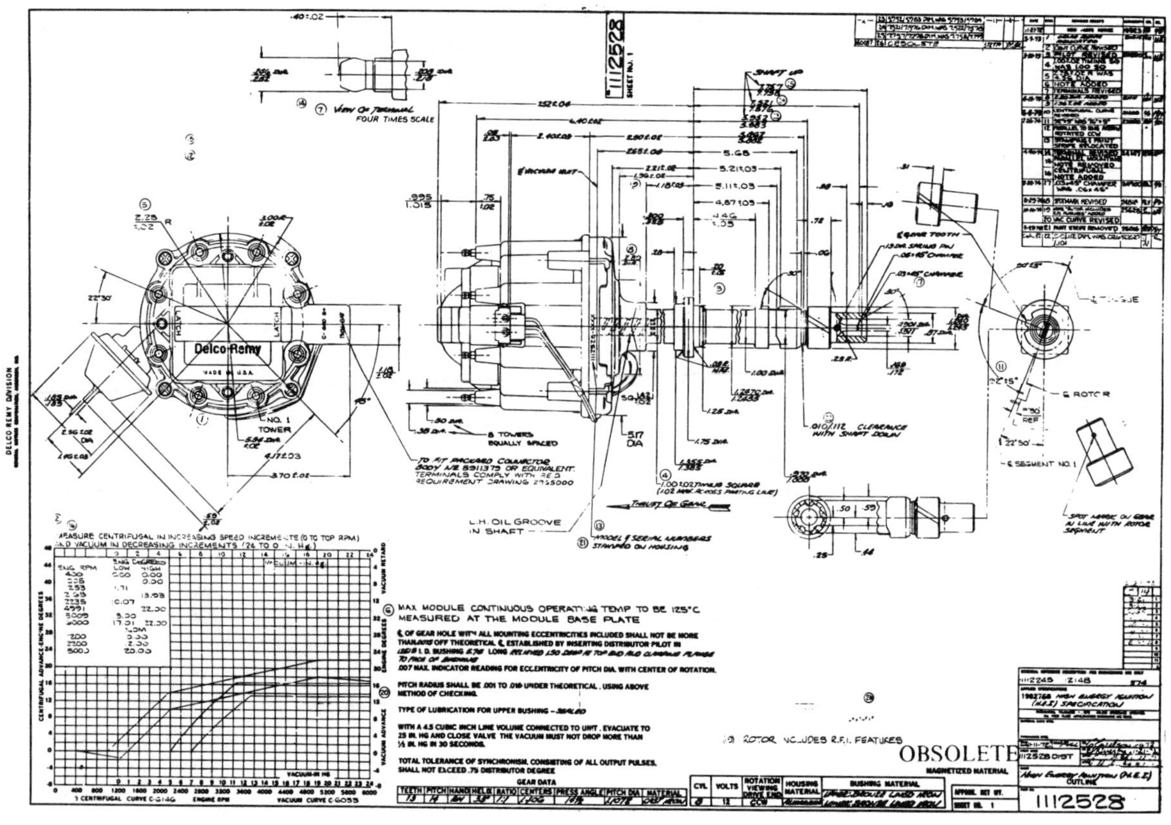

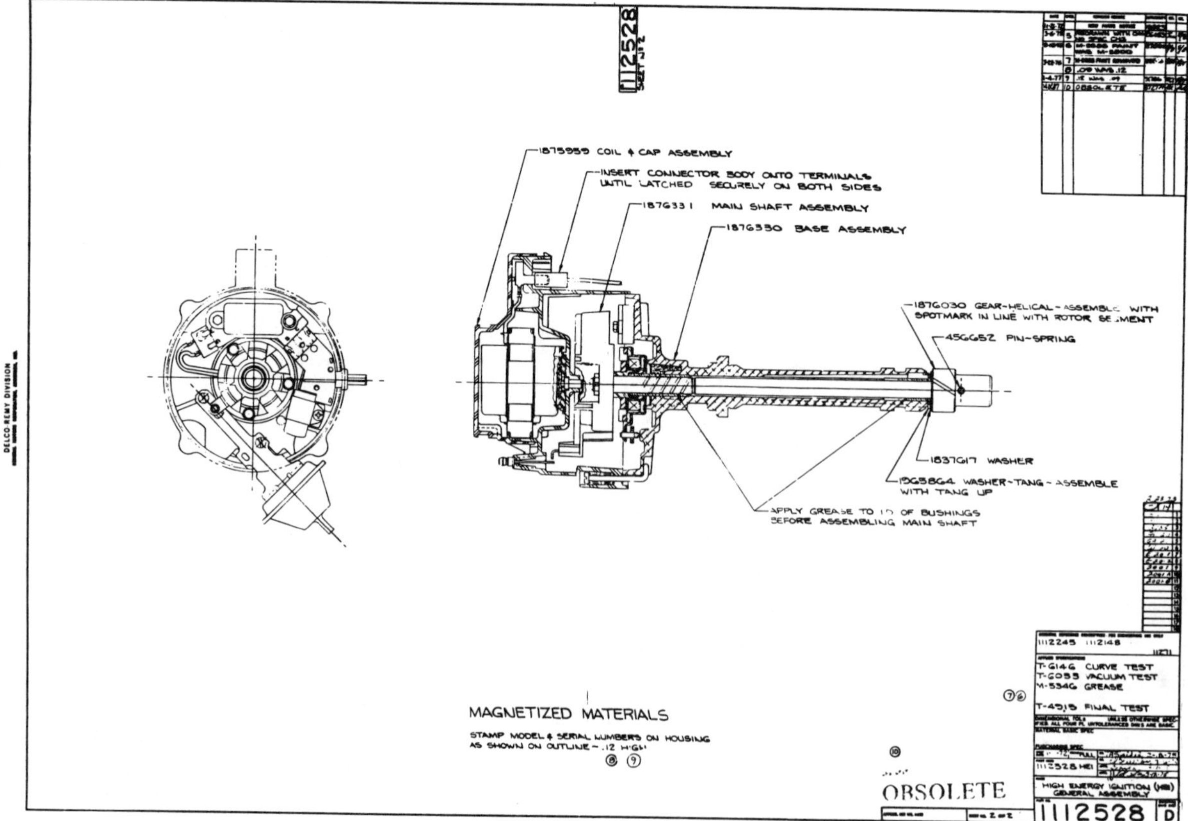

Fig. 12-15. *Views above show typical #1112528 aluminum High Energy Ignition (HEI) distributor used on all 1974 Z28 Camaro applications after Jan., 1974 as detailed in Chevrolet Service News, Feb., 1974.*

1975 Distributor Applications

Model	Distributor Number	Engine/HP/Application	Housing	Point	Notes
Passenger	1112880	350/145HP All	A	HEI	13/V
	1112882	400/175HP All	A	HEI	3-10/V
	1112886	454/215HP All	A	HEI	10/V
	1112888	350/155HP All	A	HEI	8-8/V
Corvette	1112880	350/165HP All CA	A	HEI	13/V
	1112883	350/205HP L82 All 1st Design	A	HEI	7/V
	1112888	350/165HP All exc. CA	A	HEI	8-8/V
	1112979	350/205HP L82 All 2nd Design	A	HEI	9/V
Nova	1112880	350/145HP All	A	HEI	13/V
		350/155HP S/T CA	A	HEI	13/V
		350/155HP A/T CA 1st Design	A	HEI	13/V
	1112888	350/155HP S/T exc. CA	A	HEI	8-8/V
		350/155HP A/T exc. CA	A	HEI	8-8/V
	1112933	262/110HP All	A	HEI	3/V
	1112959	350/155HP A/T CA 2nd Design	A	HEI	12/V
Chevelle	1112880	350/145HP All	A	HEI	13/V
		350/155HP S/T CA	A	HEI	13/V
		350/155HP A/T CA 1st Design	A	HEI	13/V
	1112882	400/175HP All	A	HEI	3-10/V
	1112886	454/215HP All	A	HEI	10/V
	1112888	350/155HP S/T exc. CA	A	HEI	8-8/V
		350/155HP A/T exc. CA	A	HEI	8-8/V
	1112959	350/155HP A/T CA 2nd Design	A	HEI	12/V
Camaro	1112880	350/145HP All	A	HEI	13/V
		350/155HP S/T CA	A	HEI	13/V
		350/155HP A/T CA 1st Design	A	HEI	13/V
	1112888	350/155HP S/T exc. CA	A	HEI	8-8/V
		350/155HP A/T exc. CA	A	HEI	8-8/V
	1112959	350/155HP A/T CA 2nd Design	A	HEI	12/V
Monte Carlo	1112880	350/145HP All	A	HEI	13/V
		350/155HP S/T CA	A	HEI	13/V
		350/155HP A/T CA 1st Design	A	HEI	13/V
	1112882	400/175HP All	A	HEI	3-10/V
	1112886	454/215HP All	A	HEI	10/V
	1112888	350/155HP S/T exc. CA	A	HEI	8-8/V
		350/155HP A/T exc. CA	A	HEI	8-8/V
	1112959	350/155HP A/T CA 2nd Design	A	HEI	12/V
Monza	1112933	262/110HP, All	A	HEI	V
	1112880	350/145HP A/T CA	A	HEI	13/V

3. DISTRIBUTOR VACUUM UNITS

Almost all distributors used a vacuum advance unit. Up until recently, all data pertaining to original vacuum unit applications had to be gleaned from Delco-Remy Parts Replacement Sheets, which only gave the current replacement vacuum unit. The following vacuum unit numbers were taken directly from the original Delco-Remy blueprints.

Vacuum Unit Decoding

The vacuum unit usually has two sets of numbers stamped into the flat of the mounting bracket.

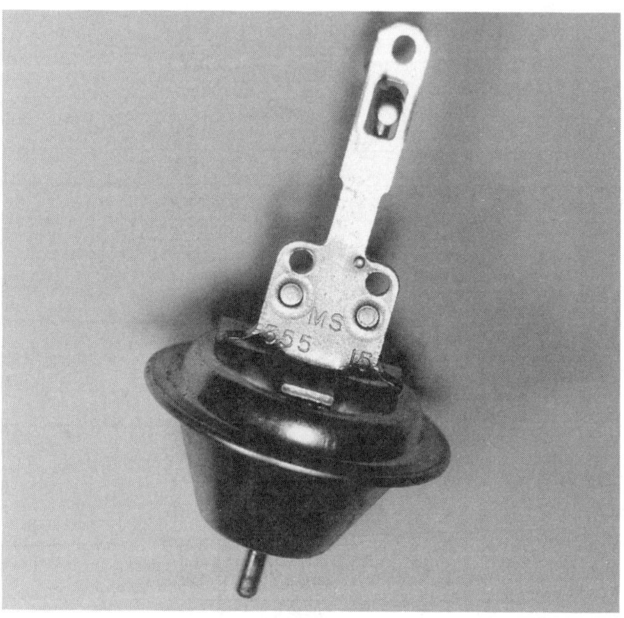

Fig. 12-16. Vacuum unit #1115355. Note Letters and numbers stamped into flat portion of the advance arm.

The first two-digits letter code signifies the original manufacturer for the vacuum unit.

The first three numbers usually refer to the last three numbers of the Delco-Remy part number. Occasionally, a vacuum unit will be stamped with a different number for reasons currently unknown. One example of this is the 1968861 unit, which is stamped "400."

The final two digits represent the number of crankshaft degrees of advance built into the vacuum unit. Typically the units are rated at 10, 15, or 20 degrees of advance.

Many vacuum units were used on a variety of distributors. There were often two or three units on the same distributor over its usage period. This is reflected in the applications listed below.

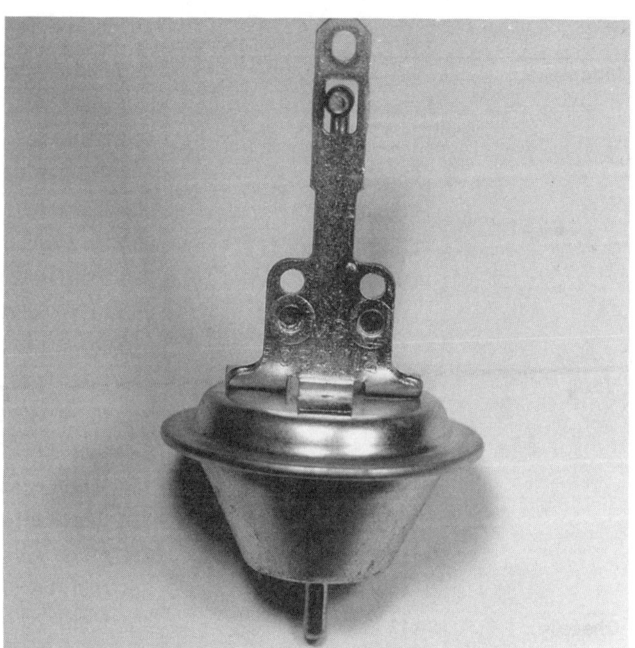

Fig. 12-17. Vacuum unit #1115360.

Distributor/Vacuum Unit Applications

Distributor	Vacuum Unit
1111436	1973437
1111437	1115360
1111464	1115360
1111490	1115357
1111491	1116201/1973437 after 2/72
1111492	1973437
1111493	1115360
1111494	1973437
1111496	1115360
1111963	1973437
1111968	1115357/1973436 after 4/70
1111971	1115360
1111995	1115355
1111996	1968861
1111997	1115357
1111998	1973437
1111999	1115355
1112000	1115355
1112001	1973421
1112002	1973421
1112005	1973436
1112019	1973437

Distributor/Vacuum Unit Applications

Distributor	Vacuum Unit
1112020	1115357
1112021	1115360
1112038	1973437
1112039	1973436
1112042	1973436
1112044	1973437
1112045	1973437
1112049	1973437
1112050	1973437
1112051	1973436
1112052	1973436
1112053	1973439
1112054	1973439
1112055	1973438
1112056	1973438
1112057	1973436
1112074	1973437
1112075	1973439
1112076	1973439
1112093	1973446
1112094	1973446
1112095	1973437
1112098	1973446
1112099	1973436
1112101	1973437
1112102	1973448
1112113	1116212
1112114	1116212
1112134	1973436
1112147	1973436
1112148	1973448
1112150	1973448
1112152	1973437

Distributor/Vacuum Unit Applications (cont'd)

Distributor	Vacuum Unit
1112153	1973437
1112154	1973437
1112156	1973437
1112161	1973436
1112165	1973437
1112166	1973437
1112167	1973437
1112168	1973469
1112169	1973436
1112227	1973448
1112230	1973472
1112247	1973446
1112250	1973459
1112526	1973437
1112527	1973481
1112528	1973482
1112543	1973446
1112544	1973446
1112545	1973437
1112843	1973502
1112844	1973502
1112846	1973503
1112864	1973507
1112865	1973492
1112880	1973517
1112882	1973492
1112883	1973508
1112886	1973519
1112888	1973517
1112933	1973567
1112959	1973482
1112979	1973508

Chapter 13

Camshaft Identification

1. INTRODUCTION

The camshaft is the one part of the internal combustion engine which has the most bearing on how that engine will operate. The basic function of the camshaft is to control the timing, the length, the speed, and the height of the intake and exhaust valve openings inside the cylinder head. The camshaft in all Chevrolet engines is located within its own bearing chamber below the cylinder head face and above the oil pan rails. There have been some minor changes in rear camshaft bearing face design, but for the most part the camshaft remained the same from 1970 through 1975. It is important to verify which type of block, rear bearing face and camshaft bearing you need before you invest in a camshaft.

Please note that Chevrolet always includes clearance ramps in their valve timing specifications for hydraulic camshafts. The clearance ramp is the portion of the camshaft that gradually takes up the clearance, or lash, of the valvetrain. It begins the acceleration of the lifter on the opening side and slows the lifter on the closing side until the valve is seated. Since this distance is quite a bit longer than the actual valve timing event, true valve timing is much milder in many cases than the theoretical timing specs on the blueprints indicate. See Fig. 13-2.

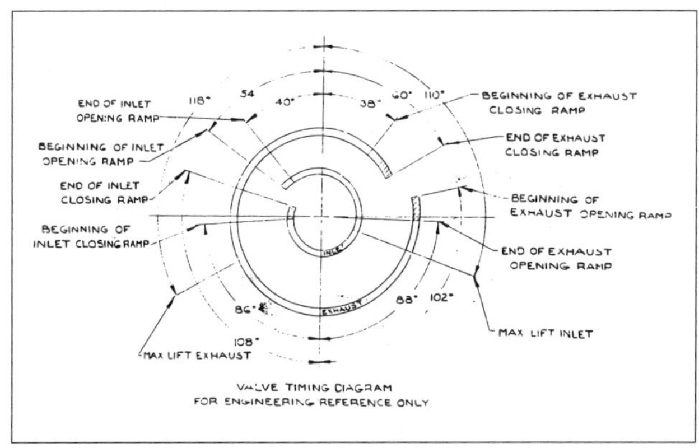

Fig. 13-2. *Blueprint of camshaft #3863152 illustrates how camshaft timing specifications are relative to opening and closing ramps on hydraulic cam lobes.*

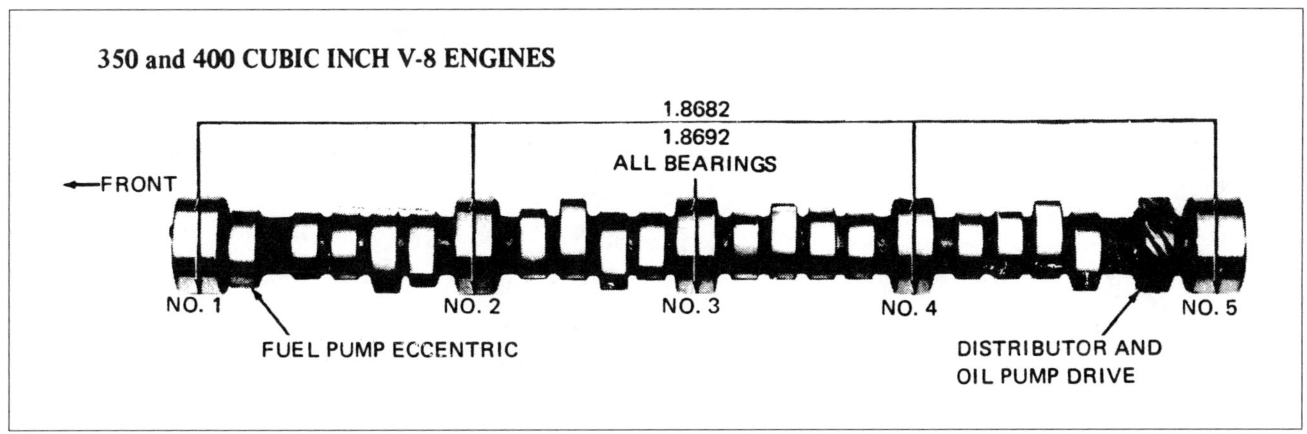

Fig. 13-1. *Engine camshaft and bearings diagram.*

2. CAMSHAFT IDENTIFICATION CHARTS

All of the following cam specifications are listed at "0" lash setting. This is done to avoid confusion of comparing original Chevrolet camshaft figures and actual specifications. Also note that in the Lifter column, "H" stands for Hydraulic and "M" stands for mechanical. The column named Casting Symbol relates to the symbols cast into many of the camshafts. Fig. 13-3 shows the specifications for one of these symbols.

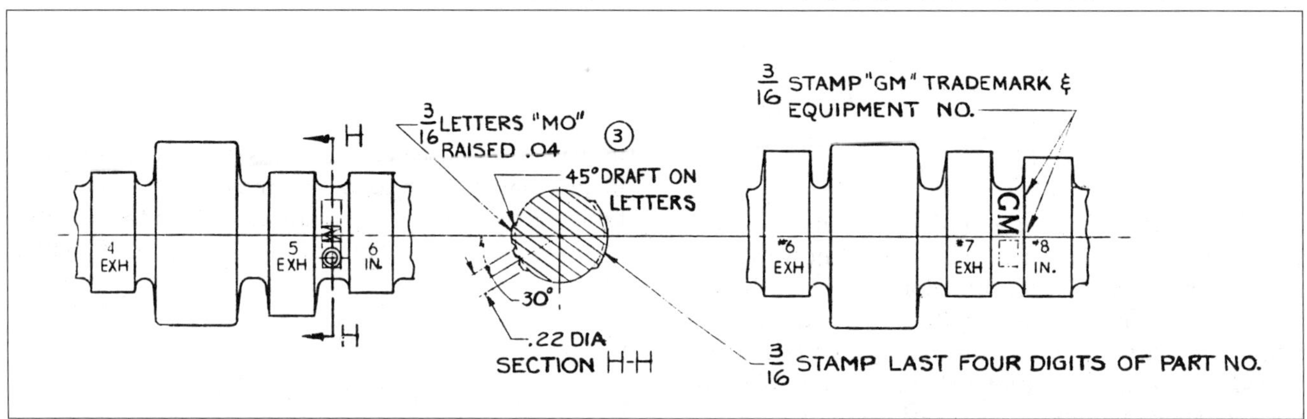

Fig. 13-3. Detail of blueprint shows casting letters, numbers and GM trademark information. This also illustrates that most casting numbers consist of only last four digits of casting number.

1970 Camshaft Identification

Engine	Horsepower	Lifter	Intake Lift	Exhaust Lift	Intake Duration	Exhaust Duration	Rocker Ratio	Part Number	Casting Number	Casting Symbol
307 350 400	200 250, 300 265	H	.390	.410	310	320	1.50	3896929	3896930	Horizontal Diamond
350	350	H	.447	.447	346	340	1.50	3896962	3896964	Vertical Diamond
350	360, 370	M	.458	.484	317	346	1.50	3972178	3972182	(1) Square
402	330	H	.398	.398	322	322	1.70	3904365	3904365	"M" In a circle
402 454	350 360, 390	H	.461	.480	350	352	1.70	3904359	3904364	OM
402 454	375 450	M	.520	.520	316	302	1.70	3904362	3904366	OMO
454	345	H	.398	.430	316	334	1.70	3963544	3963545	"M" In a circle

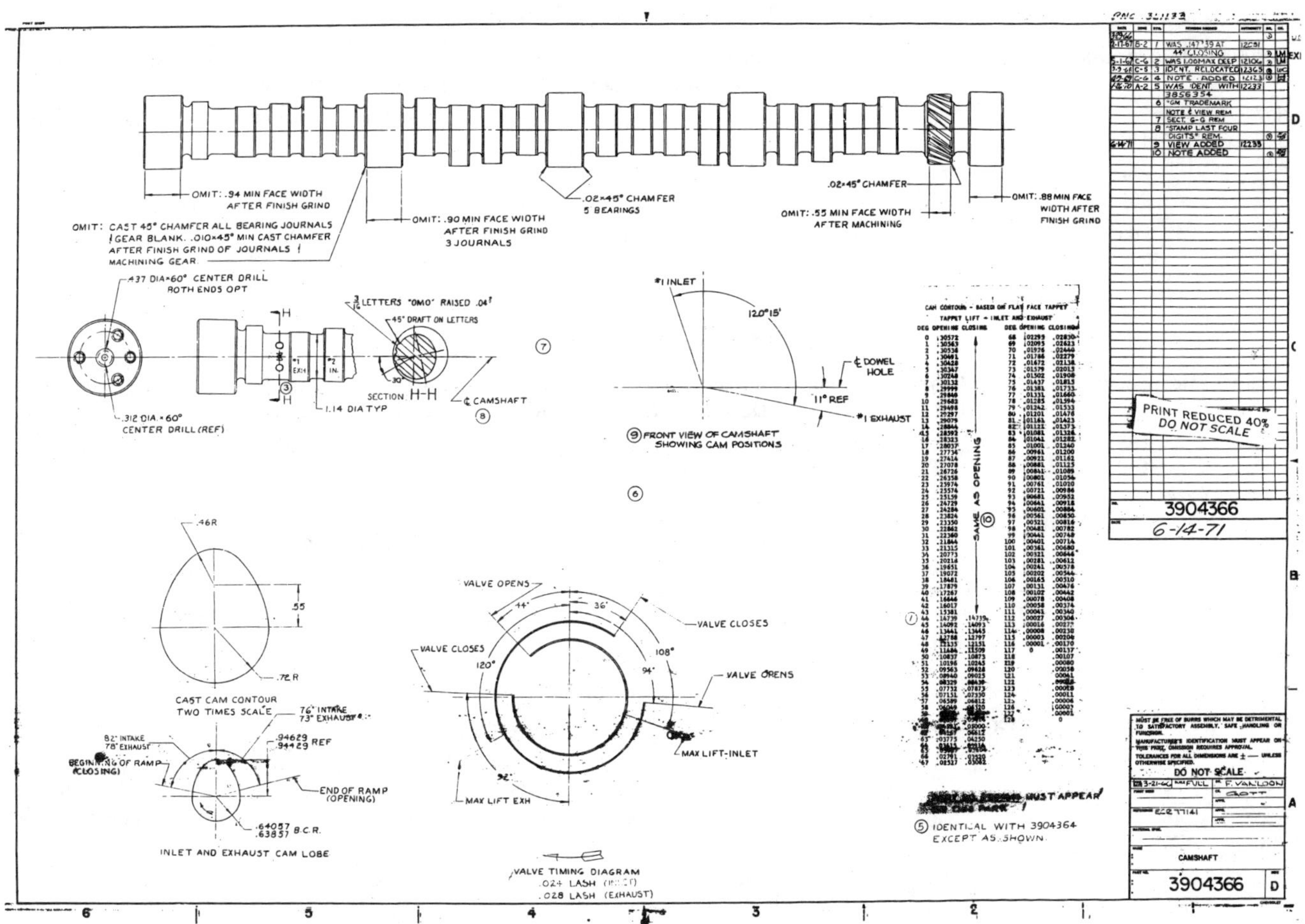

Fig. 13-4. Blueprint for camshaft #3904366. Note "OMO" casting symbol on sectional view.

1971 Camshaft Identification

Engine	Horsepower	Lifter	Intake Lift	Exhaust Lift	Intake Duration	Exhaust Duration	Rocker Ratio	Part Number	Casting Number	Casting Symbol
302 350 400	200 245, 270 255	H	.390	.410	310	320	1.50	3896929	3896930	Horizontal Diamond
350	330	M	.458	.484	317	346	1.50	3972178	3972182	(1) Square
402	300	H	.398	.430	316	334	1.70	3963544	3863545	M
454	365	H	.461	.480	350	352	1.70	3904359	3904364	OM
454	425	M	.520	.520	316	302	1.70	3904362	3904366	OMO

1972 Camshaft Identification

Engine	Horsepower	Lifter	Intake Lift	Exhaust Lift	Intake Duration	Exhaust Duration	Rocker Ratio	Part Number	Casting Number	Casting Symbol
307 350 400	130 165, 175, 200* 170*	H	.390	.410	310	320	1.50	3896929	3896930	Horizontal Diamond
350	255	M	.459	.485	317	346	1.50	3972178	3972182	(1) Square
402	240	H	.398	.430	316	334	1.70	3963544	3863545	
454	240, 270	H	.461	.480	350	352	1.70	3904359	3904364	OM
350 400	165, 175, 200 170	H	.401	.410	320	334	1.50	340284	6262944	

* Optional camshaft

1973 Camshaft Identification

Engine	Horsepower	Lifter	Intake Lift	Exhaust Lift	Intake Duration	Exhaust Duration	Rocker Ratio	Part Number	Casting Number	Casting Symbol
307 350 400	115 145, 175, 190 150	H	.390	.410	310	320	1.50	3896929	3896930	Horizontal Diamond
350	245, 250	H	.450	.460	346	360	1.50	3896962	3896964	Vertical Diamond
454	215, 245	H	.440	.440	346	348	1.70	353040	353041	Square

1974 Camshaft Identification

Engine	Horsepower	Lifter	Intake Lift	Exhaust Lift	Intake Duration	Exhaust Duration	Rocker Ratio	Part Number	Casting Number	Casting Symbol
350 400	145, 185, 195 150, 180	H	.390	.410	310	320	1.50	3896929	3896930	Horizontal Diamond
350	160	H	.401	.401	320	334	1.50	340284	6262944	
350	245, 250	H	.450	.460	346	360	1.50	3896962	3896964	Vertical Diamond
454	235, 270	H	.440	.440	346	348	1.70	353040	353041	Square

1975 Camshaft Identification

Engine	Horsepower	Lifter	Intake Lift	Exhaust Lift	Intake Duration	Exhaust Duration	Rocker Ratio	Part Number	Casting Number	Casting Symbol
262	110	H	.373	.390	272	280	1.50	357149	357148	Vertical Rectangle
350 400	145, 155, 165 175	H	.390	.410	310	320	1.50	3896929	3896930	Horizontal Diamond
350	205	H	.450	.460	346	360	1.50	3896962	3896964	Vertical Diamond
454	215	H	.440	.440	346	348	1.70	353040	353041	Square

Chapter 14

Alternator Identification

1. Introduction

This chapter covers 1970 through 1975 alternator model numbers. All alternators have the part number, ampere rating, voltage, and date of manufacture stamped on top of the unit, usually under or below the alternator bracket or top brace mounting. See Fig. 14-1.

Fig. 14-1. *Alternator stamping number includes part number (1100696), amp rating (40A), date code (see text) and voltage rating (12 Volt, negative ground).*

The date code is deciphered as follows: The first digit gives the calendar year of production. This is the last digit of the calendar year, 1966 in the example above. The following letter indicates the month of production. See the table below for month codes. The final two digits indicate the day of the month of production (1 through 31). The code 6 J22 in Fig.14-1 decodes as September 22, 1966.

Alternator Month Codes (2nd Letter)

A - January	E - May	J - September
B - February	F - June	K - October
C - March	G - July	L - November
D - April	H - August	M - December

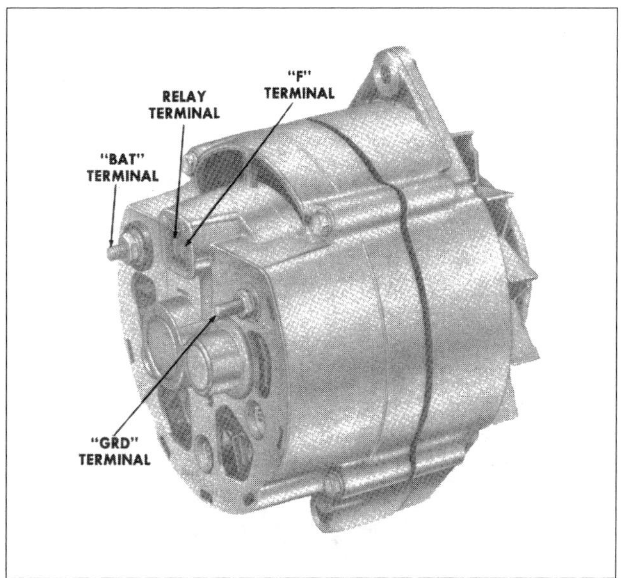

Fig. 14-2. *Typical Delcotron 10-DN Series Alternator. this alternator was used in 1970 on almost all standard amp cars.*

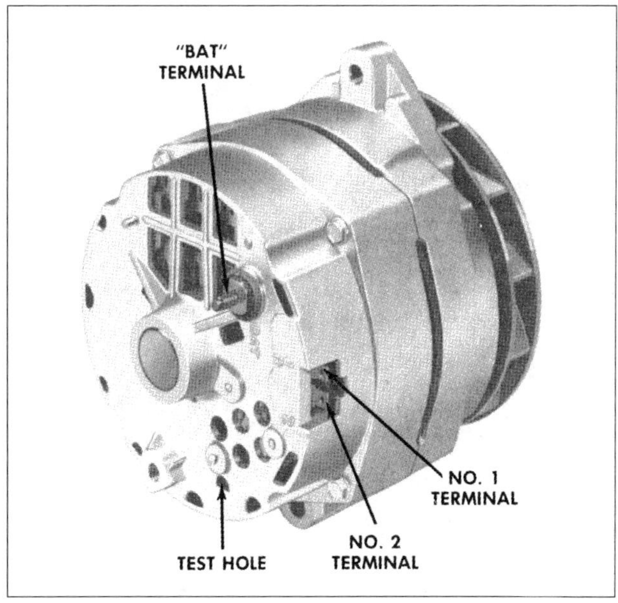

Fig. 14-3. *Typical Delcotron 10-SI Series Alternator, used almost exclusively on all 1973 through 1975 passenger cars.*

2. ALTERNATOR APPLICATIONS

1970 Delcotron Alternators

Model	Style	Engine	Type	Part No.	Notes
Passenger	Biscayne Bel Air Impala Caprice	L6 250 Opt. 350 400, 454	37 Amp	1100834	Base unit
			37 Amp	1100836	6-Cyl. P.S.
			37 Amp	1100837	454/390HP
			42 Amp	1100841	6-Cyl. P.S.
			42 Amp	1100839	All V-8
			61 Amp	1100845	6-Cyl. A/C P.S., K85 option
			61 Amp	1100843	All, K85 option
Corvette	Corvette		42 Amp	1100901	Base 300HP
			42 Amp	1100900	350 & 390HP
			61 Amp	1100884	A/C or Mag Pulse
Nova	Nova	L4 153 L6 230, 250 307, 350, 402	37 Amp	1100834	Base unit
			37 Amp	1100836	6-Cyl. Smog Pump or P.S.
	Acadian	L6 230, 250 307, 350, 402	61 Amp	1100845	6-Cyl. P.S., A/C
			61 Amp	1100843	All A/C Ex. 6-Cyl. P.S.
Nova	Yenko Duece	350/360 HP	37 Amp	1100837	350/360HP, 402/375HP
Chevelle	Nomad Chevelle El Camino Greenbrier Malibu El Camino Cust. Concours Wagon Super Sport	L6 250 307, 350, 402, 454	37 Amp	1100834	Base unit
			37 Amp	1100836	6-Cyl. P.S.
			37 Amp	1100837	402/375HP, 454/450HP
			61 Amp	1100843	All A/C Ex. 6-Cyl. P.S., K85 option
			61 Amp	1100845	6-Cyl. P.S., A/C, K85 option
	Monte Carlo	350, 400, 402, 454			
Camaro	Std. & Deluxe	L6 250 307, 350, 402	37 Amp	1100834	Base unit
			37 Amp	1100836	6-Cyl. P.S.
			37 Amp	1100837	350/360HP, 402/375HP
			61 Amp	1100843	All A/C Ex. 6-Cyl. Smog Control or P.S.
			61 Amp	1100845	6-Cyl. P.S., A/C

1971 Delcotron Alternators

Model	Style	Engine	Type	Part No.	Notes
Passenger	Biscayne, Bel Air, Impala, Caprice	L6 250, 350, 400, 402, 454	37 Amp	1100566	Base unit
			37 Amp	1100836	L6 250 P.S.
			42 Amp	1100841	L6 250 P.S.
			42 Amp	1100567	V-8 All
			63 Amp	1100917	All A/C, K85 option
Corvette	Corvette	350, 454	42 Amp	1100950	350/270, 330HP
			42 Amp	1100543	454/365, 425HP
			61 Amp	1100544	A/C & TI
Nova	Nova, Acadian	L6 250, 307, 350	37 Amp	1100566	Base unit
			37 Amp	1100836	L6 250 Smog Pump & P.S.
			61 Amp	1100843	A/C

continued on next page

1971 Delcotron Alternators (continued)

Model	Style	Engine	Type	Part No.	Notes
Chevelle & Monte Carlo	Nomad, Chevelle, El Camino, Malibu, Concours Estate Wagon	L6 250, 307, 350, 402, 454	37 Amp	1100566	Base unit
			37 Amp	1100836	L6 250 P.S.
			37 Amp	1100837	454/425HP
	Monte Carlo	350, 402, 454	61 Amp	1100843	A/C
			63 Amp	1100917	All, K85 option
Camaro		L6 250, 307, 350, 402	37 Amp	1100566	Base unit
			37 Amp.	1100836	L6 250 P.S.
			37 Amp	1100837	350/330HP (4-BBL), Z28
			61 Amp	1100843	A/C All

1972 Delcotron Alternators

Model	Style	Engine	Type	Part No.	Notes
Passenger	Biscayne, Bel Air, Impala, Caprice	L6 250, 350, 400, 402, 454	37 Amp	1102452	6-Cyl.
				1102453	6-Cyl. P.S. or Smog Pump
				1102456	6-Cyl. P.S. and Smog Pump
				1102440	350, 400
				1102454	402,454
			63 Amp	1102464	A/C or Heavy Duty Output, K85 option
Corvette	Corvette	350, 454	42 Amp	1100950	350
			42 Amp	1100543	454
			61 Amp	1100544	A/C
Nova	Nova	L6 250, 307, 350	37 Amp	1102452	6-Cyl.
				1102453	6-Cyl. P.S. or Smog Pump
				1102456	6-Cyl. P.S. & Smog Pump
			37 Amp	1102440	8-Cyl.
			61 Amp	1102463	A/C
Chevelle & Monte Carlo	Chevelle	L6 250, 307, 350, 402, 454	37 Amp	1102452	6-Cyl.
			37 Amp	1102453	6-Cyl. P.S. or Smog Pump
	Monte Carlo	350, 402, 454		1102456	6-Cyl. P.S. & Smog Pump
				1102440	307,350
				1102454	402,454
			61 Amp	1102463	A/C
			63 Amp	1102464	A/C or Heavy Duty Cool, K85 option
Camaro		L6 250, 307, 350, 402	37 Amp	1102452	6-Cyl.
				1102453	6-Cyl. P.S. or Smog Pump
				1102456	6-Cyl. P.S. & Smog Pump
			37 Amp	1102440	307, 350
				1102454	402 or Z28
			61 Amp	1102463	A/C

1973 Delcotron Alternators

Model	Style	Engine	Type	Part No.	Notes
Passenger	Bel Air, Impala, Caprice, Classic; Townsman, Kingswood, Caprice Estate	350, 400, 454	37 Amp	1100934	All
			63 Amp	1100542	A/C or Heavy Duty, K85 option
			42 Amp	1100573	Police & Taxi
Corvette	Corvette	350, 454	42 Amp	1100950	350
			42 Amp	1102353	454 P.S.
			61 Amp	1100544	A/C
Nova	Nova, Nova Custom	L6 250, 307, 350	37 Amp	1100497	6-Cyl.
			42 Amp	1102346	6-Cyl. Police & Taxi
			37 Amp	1100934	V-8
			42 Amp	1100573	Opt. Police & Taxi
			61 Amp	1100597	A/C or Heavy Duty
Chevelle	Chevelle, El Camino, El Camino Custom, Malibu, Laguna; Greenbrier, Concours, Malibu, Laguna Estate	L6 250, 307, 350,454	37 Amp	1100497	6-Cyl.
			63 Amp	1102354	6-Cyl. A/C, K85 option
			42 Amp	1102346	6-Cyl. Police & Taxi
			37 Amp	1100934	V-8
			63 Amp	1100542	A/C, K85 option
			42 Amp	1100573	Opt. Police & Taxi
Monte Carlo		350, 454	37 Amp	1100934	All
			63 Amp	1100542	A/C, K85 option
Camaro*	Camaro, Camaro LT	L6 250, 307, 350	37 Amp	1100497	6-Cyl.
			37 Amp	1100934	V-8
			61 Amp	1100597	A/C

*Some 1973 Camaros were built using a 1972-type Delcotron with external voltage regulator.

1973 Camaro Models Utilizing 1972 External Voltage Regulator

Some 1973 Camaro models were built using the 1972 type delcotron and external voltage regulator. The wiring harness was modified by the addition of a jumper harness necessary to adapt the 1972 system in a 1973 vehicle.

All Camaro models built after February, 1973 until end of production may have the previously outlined system. Vehicles commencing with the serial numbers listed below are affected.

V-8 Engine N146488
L-6 Engine N154788

1972 Diagnostic and Service procedures should be used on subject vehicles.

Fig. 14-4. *Partial page from* Chevrolet Service News *for October, 1973, shows usage of 1972-type alternator in some 1973 Camaro applications.*

1974 Delcotron Alternators

Model	Style	Engine	Type	Part No.	Notes
Passenger	Bel Air Sedan & Wagon, Impala Sedan, Coupe & Wagon, Caprice Sedan & Coupe, Caprice Classic Sedan, Coupe & Estate Wagon	350, 400, 454	37 Amp	1100934	All
			61 Amp	1100597	A/C or Heavy Duty, K76 option
			42 Amp	1100573	Police or Taxi
Corvette	Corvette	350, 454	37 Amp	1100934	350 Ex. L82
			42 Amp	1100950	454, 350, L82 Opt.
			42 Amp	1102353	454 P.S.
			61 Amp	1100544	A/C or Heavy Duty
Nova	Nova, Nova Custom	L6 250, 350	37 Amp	1100497	L6 250
			55 Amp	1102839	6-Cyl. A/C, K77 option
			37 Amp	1100934	350
			55 Amp	1100575	A/C or Heavy Duty
Chevelle	Deluxe Sedan, Coupe, Wagon, El Camino, Malibu, Wagon, El Camino Custom, Estate Wagon, Laguna Wagon, Custom Estate Wagon	L6 250, 350, 400, 454	37 Amp	1100497	6-Cyl.
			55 Amp	1102839	6-Cyl. A/C
			37 Amp	1100934	All V-8
			61 Amp	1100597	A/C & Heavy Duty, K76 option
Monte Carlo		350, 400, 454	37 Amp	1100934	All
			61 Amp	1100597	A/C & Heavy Duty, K76 option
Camaro	Camaro, Camaro LT	L6 250, 350	37 Amp	1100497	L6 250
				1100934	350 Ex. Z28
				1102397	350 Z28
			61 Amp	1100597	A/C & Heavy Duty, K76 option

1975 Delcotron Alternators

Model	Style	Engine	Type	Part No.	Notes
Passenger	Bel Air Sedan & Wagon, Impala Sedan, Coupe & Wagon, Caprice Sedan, Coupe, Caprice Classic Sedan, Coupe & Estate Wagon	350, 400, 454	37 Amp	1102483	Base unit
				1102394	2nd Production
			61 Amp	1100597	A/C or Heavy Duty, K76 option
				1102480	2nd Production
			42 Amp	1102493	Police & Taxi
				1102841	2nd Production
Corvette	Corvette	350	37 Amp	1102483	All Ex. L82
				1102394	2nd Production
			42 Amp	1100950	L82 Opt.
				1102484	2nd Production
			61 Amp	1100597	Heavy Duty
				1102480	2nd Production
				1100544	A/C
				1102474	2nd Production
Nova	Nova, Nova Custom	L6 250, 262, 350	37 Amp	1100497	L6 250
				1102491	2nd Production
			55 Amp	1100575	L6 250 A/C
				1102479	2nd Production
			42 Amp	1102493	L6 250 Police & Taxi
				1102841	2nd Production
			61 Amp	1102347	Heavy Duty
				1102486	2nd Production
			37 Amp	1102483	262
				1102394	2nd Production
			55 Amp	1100560	262 A/C
				1102478	2nd Production
			42 Amp	1102493	262 Police & Taxi
				1102841	2nd Production
			55 Amp	1100560	Heavy Duty, K77 option
				1102478	2nd Production
			37 Amp	1102483	350
				1102394	2nd Production
			55 Amp	1100575	350 A/C
				1102479	2nd Production
			42 Amp	1102493	350 Police & Taxi
				1102841	2nd Production
			61 Amp	1100597	Heavy Duty
				1102480	2nd Production
Chevelle	Deluxe Sedan, Coupe, Wagon, El Camino, Malibu, Wagon, El Camino Custom, Estate Wagon	L6 250, 350, 400, 454	37 Amp	1100497	L6 250
				1102491	2nd Production
			61 Amp	1100597	L6 250 A/C
				1102480	2nd Production
			61 Amp	1102347	K76 option
				1102486	2nd Production
			37 Amp	1102483	V-8 All
				1102394	2nd Production
			61 Amp	1100597	V-8 A/C
				1102480	2nd Production
			42 Amp	1102493	V-8 Police & Taxi
				1102841	2nd Production

continued on next page

1975 Delcotron Alternators (continued)

Model	Style	Engine	Type	Part No.	Notes
Monte Carlo		350, 454	37 Amp	1102483	All V-8
				1102394	2nd Production
			61 Amp	1100597	A/C or Heavy Duty, K76 option
				1102480	2nd Production
Camaro	Camaro, Camaro LT	L6 250, 350	37 Amp	1100497	L6 250
				1102491	2nd Production
			61 Amp	1100597	L6 250 A/C
				1102480	2nd Production
			61 Amp	1102347	Heavy Duty
				1102486	2nd Production
			37 Amp	1102483	350
				1102394	2nd Production
			61 Amp	1100597	A/C or Heavy Duty
				1102480	2nd Production
Monza	Town Coupe, 2 + 2	262, 350	37 Amp	1102483	Base unit
				1102394	2nd Production
			55 Amp	1100575	Optional
				1102479	2nd Production
			63 Amp	1102857	A/C
				1102854	A/C, 2nd Production
			55 Amp	1100560	Heavy Duty option
				1102478	Heavy Duty, 2nd Production

Chapter 15
Transmission Identification

1. Introduction

This chapter covers all transmissions from 1970 through 1975. This introduction gives a brief overview of the transmissions, while the rest of the chapter is structured by model year to allow you to quickly and easily determine transmission applications. Under each year heading there is a quick-access section, transmission specifications with parts casting numbers, and stamping number decoding. At the end of this chapter are specific transmission casting number charts, which will allow you to access individual casting numbers without hunting through the entire chapter.

Casting Date Codes

Casting date codes can be found on almost all maincases, extension housings, and sidecovers. Most casting dates are in an alpha-numeric style, and usually follow the same pattern as blocks and cylinder heads. Many casting dates are difficult to read.

The first digit of a casting date code is usually a letter, to designate the month. The second digit will be a letter, designating the month. The third digit designates the day of the month, while the fourth (or last) digit designates the calendar year.

Assembly Date Code Stamping

All of the transmissions have an assembly date code stamped on the maincase. This stamping is different from the casting numbers of the individual parts that make up the entire transmission. Remember that any casting date codes on parts must always precede the transmission assembly date.

The location of the stamped code differs slightly from year to year and from application to application. This is very important to remember. For example, two similar Saginaw transmissions, one for a truck application and one for a car application, often have different date code stamping locations.

The date code typically identifies the plant where the transmission was assembled, the date of assembly, and usually application information. Please note that the assembly date code will reflect the *model* year of stamping, not the calendar year. Some transmission plants did not begin to stamp the model year until 1967.

Fig. 15-1. *Sidecover #3919365 used for 1968 and 1969 production. Note C 17 9 casting date code (March 17, 1969). Also transmission assembly date code S9C19 (Saginaw, 1969, March 19th) stamped into maincase below sidecover.*

Fig. 15-2. *Maincase #3925647 shows casting date code C 10 9 (March 10, 1969). Also note vehicle identification number on oval pad above casting date. After 1968 VIN was more uniformly stamped on parts to foil theft and reselling. Do not confuse with assembly date code.*

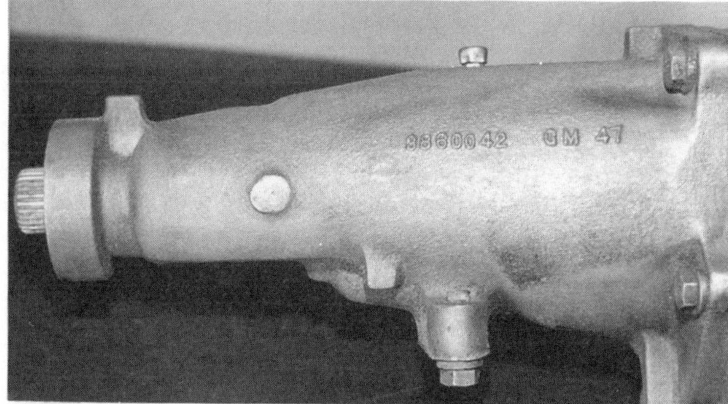

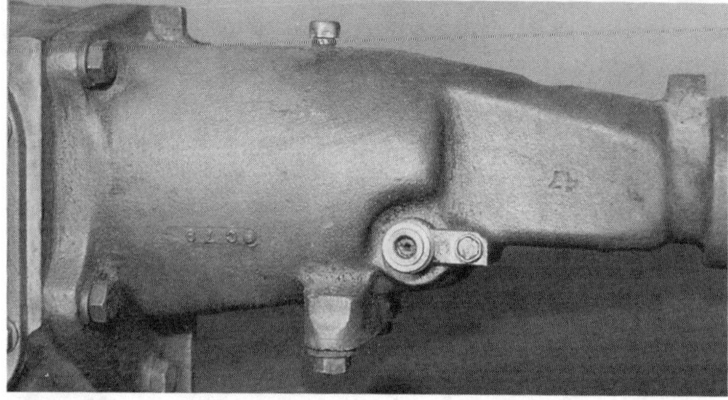

Fig. 15-3. Two views of extension housing #3860042 used for 1966–70 Saginaw 3-speeds. Note GM 47 mold number (top), and casting date code C 7 9 (March 7, 1969) (bottom).

Fig. 15-4. 1968 Muncie transmission shows VIN stamping near the assembly build date (arrows). Assembly date reads P8E09 (Muncie, 1968 model year, May, 9th day). VIN reads 28R305374 (2 = division (Pontiac), 8 = 1968 model year, R = Arlington, TX, assembly plant, 305374 is sequential portion of VIN. This transmission was originally installed in a 1968 GTO. The R designation for Chevrolet was only applicable to a passenger car, which would have had a sequence number of 100001. See Chapter 1 for more information on VIN decoding.

Transmission VIN Stamping

Most transmissions originally installed in Chevrolet vehicles from the 1962 model year on should have a VIN (vehicle identification number) stamped on them. The VIN will be located on the top or side of the maincase. Most passenger car plants stamped the VIN on the top, while other plants stamped it on the side, near the assembly date code. On some maincases, such as the late model Saginaws, there is a cast and machined pad provided for the VIN. Characteristics of the VIN stamp, including the location of the pad, the type size of the stamp, and the stamping method (gang or individual), was chosen by the final assembly plant.

The total number of characters in the VIN stamp were variable. It is documented that from 1962 through 1964, Corvettes did not use an assembly plant designation for the first digit. Instead, they used the model year number, for example 4 for 1964. The remainder of the Corvette VIN stamp was the last six digits of VIN, i.e. the car's sequential assembly number. On the other hand, St. Louis-built passenger cars had the letter "S" as the first digit. Starting with the 1965 model year, Corvettes used the letter "S" as the plant designation. Many other assembly plants stamped only the sequential number, with no prefix.

Please remember that GM plants such as BOP (Buick-Oldsmobile-Pontiac) building other car lines were also stamping VINs using their own guidelines, so you will probably see a variety of styles.

1.1 Chevrolet 3-Speed Transmissions

1970 Through 1975 Saginaw 3-Speed

The 1970 Chevrolet 3-Speed, fully synchronized in all forward gears, was first released in 1966. Heavy duty features of the transmission include wide helical gears, larger synchronizers, and higher capacity front and rear carrier bearings. This side-loaded transmission had a four-step countershaft cluster, 30-tooth synchronizer rings, and was used in all light-duty applications. It also used several gear ratios depending on model application.

There were several design changes that were made over the years, resulting in the use of two specific maincase casting numbers, six major extension housing casting numbers, and three major sidecover casting numbers. The reasons behind these changes are still being researched, but all casting number applications are listed in chart form in this chapter.

The Saginaw 3-speed was built at the Saginaw plant from 1966 through 1969. In 1970, Muncie took over production, however, the prefix code letter "S" did not change.

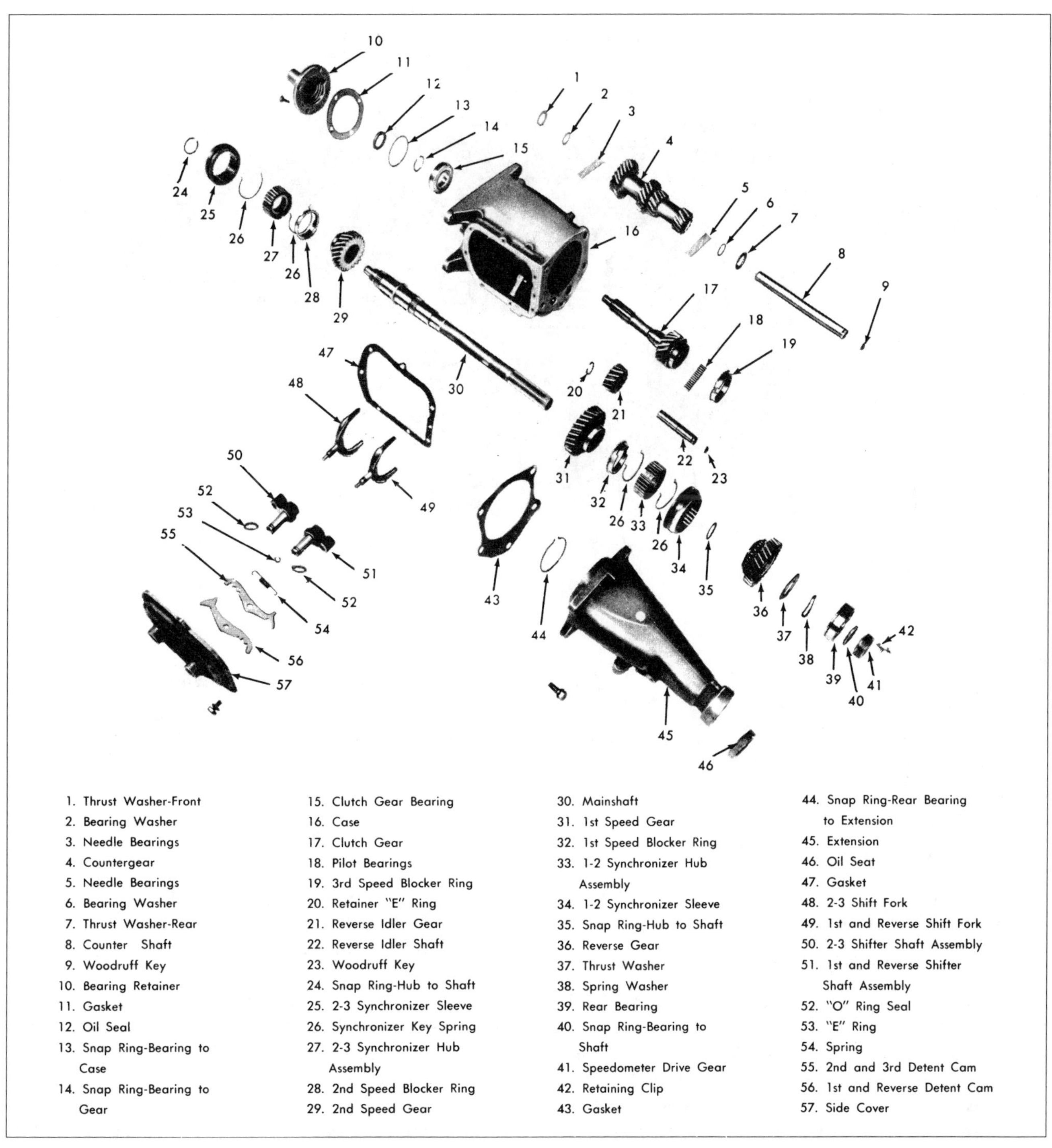

1. Thrust Washer-Front
2. Bearing Washer
3. Needle Bearings
4. Countergear
5. Needle Bearings
6. Bearing Washer
7. Thrust Washer-Rear
8. Counter Shaft
9. Woodruff Key
10. Bearing Retainer
11. Gasket
12. Oil Seal
13. Snap Ring-Bearing to Case
14. Snap Ring-Bearing to Gear
15. Clutch Gear Bearing
16. Case
17. Clutch Gear
18. Pilot Bearings
19. 3rd Speed Blocker Ring
20. Retainer "E" Ring
21. Reverse Idler Gear
22. Reverse Idler Shaft
23. Woodruff Key
24. Snap Ring-Hub to Shaft
25. 2-3 Synchronizer Sleeve
26. Synchronizer Key Spring
27. 2-3 Synchronizer Hub Assembly
28. 2nd Speed Blocker Ring
29. 2nd Speed Gear
30. Mainshaft
31. 1st Speed Gear
32. 1st Speed Blocker Ring
33. 1-2 Synchronizer Hub Assembly
34. 1-2 Synchronizer Sleeve
35. Snap Ring-Hub to Shaft
36. Reverse Gear
37. Thrust Washer
38. Spring Washer
39. Rear Bearing
40. Snap Ring-Bearing to Shaft
41. Speedometer Drive Gear
42. Retaining Clip
43. Gasket
44. Snap Ring-Rear Bearing to Extension
45. Extension
46. Oil Seat
47. Gasket
48. 2-3 Shift Fork
49. 1st and Reverse Shift Fork
50. 2-3 Shifter Shaft Assembly
51. 1st and Reverse Shifter Shaft Assembly
52. "O" Ring Seal
53. "E" Ring
54. Spring
55. 2nd and 3rd Detent Cam
56. 1st and Reverse Detent Cam
57. Side Cover

Fig. 15-5. *Exploded view of 1970—75 Saginaw 3-speed.*

Muncie 3-Speed Heavy Duty Transmissions

The Muncie 3-speed heavy duty transmission was General Motors' answer to replacing the excellent Borg Warner T16. It was introduced for the 1969 model year, and was a fully synchronized, side-loaded transmission with a side lever shift mechanism. The Muncie was used in all heavy duty performance applications.

This transmission is completely different from previous Muncie models, and component parts are not interchangeable. It is very similar to the 1966–69 Saginaw, but it has a center distance of 3.25, compared to 3.00 for the Saginaw. It also has larger bearings, output shaft, mainshaft, and gearset. The last year for a Muncie heavy duty 3-speed production installation was 1972.

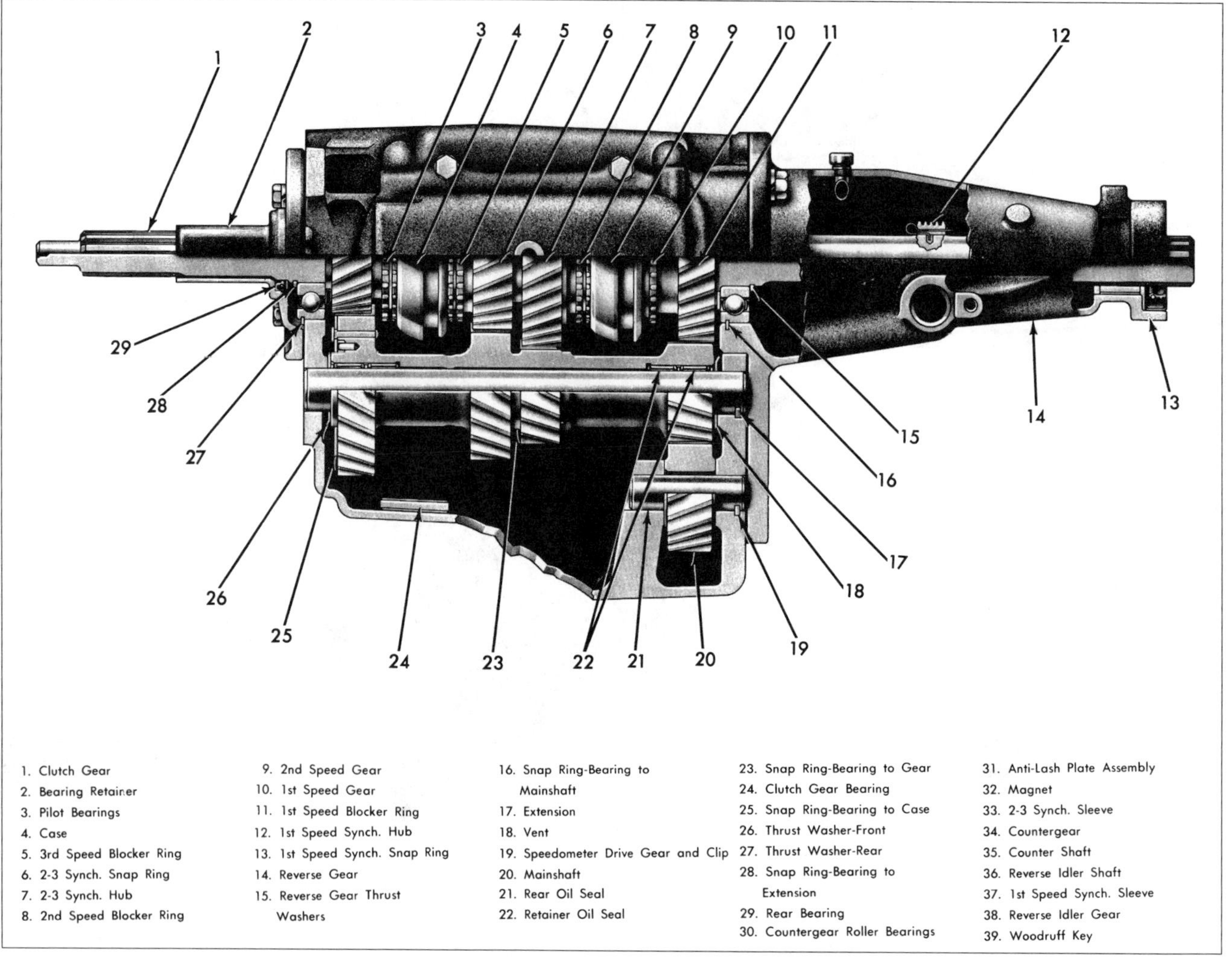

Fig. 15-6. *Muncie 3-speed heavy duty transmission cutaway.*

1.2 4-Speed Transmissions

Saginaw 4-Speed Transmissions

The Saginaw 4-speed is basically of the same family as the Saginaw 3-speeds introduced in 1966. It is a side-loaded transmission with a side lever shift linkage. It can be identified by its five-step cluster gear, by the reverse gear incorporated into the 1st/2nd synchronizer, by the three-lever sidecover, or by the 30-tooth synchronizer rings. It was introduced to provide a suitable 4-speed for all light duty (under 300 HP) applications.

There were two distinct designs of the Saginaw 4-speed. "First designs" were built from the start of production through early 1967. These had narrow reverse teeth that did not extend through the fork flange and proved to be inadequate. First designs also have the cluster gear spur step midway between the two helical steps, and the reverse idler has a length of 1-1/2 inches.

"Second designs" were used from late 1967 through 1977. These have wider teeth on the reverse steps, and the reverse teeth extend through the fork flange. On second designs, the cluster-gear spur step is adjacent to the second gear step, and the reverse idler is 2-1/2 inches long.

This transmission was built at the Saginaw plant from 1966 through 1969. In 1970, Muncie took over production, however, from all indications the prefix letter "R" was not changed.

A great deal of interchangeability exists between 3- and 4-speed Saginaws. Please see the data charts at the end of this chapter for more information.

Note that the same M20 RPO (Regular Production Option) code was used for many years to designate the Saginaw 4-speed for ordering. To reduce confusion, all wide ratio Muncie 4-speeds are noted M20 throughout the book. Saginaws are referred to only by name.

Muncie 4-Speed Transmissions

The Muncie transmission was an aluminum main-case/extension housing, side-loaded transmission with side-lever shift linkage. This transmission was similar to, and based on, the successful Borg Warner T-

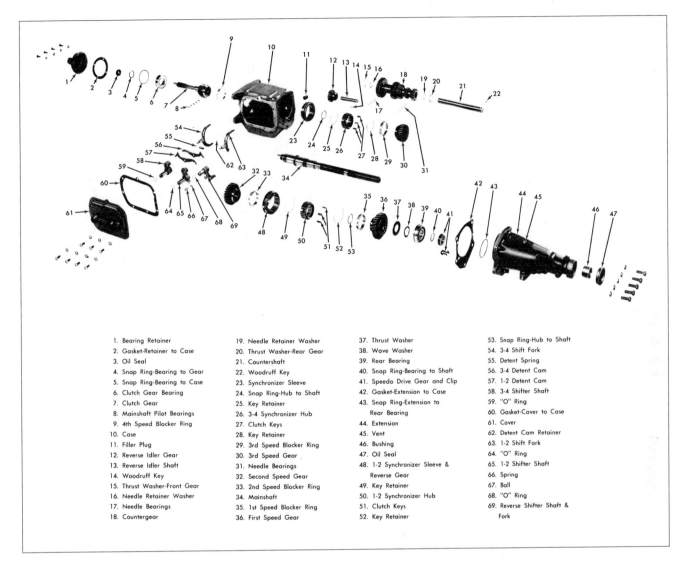

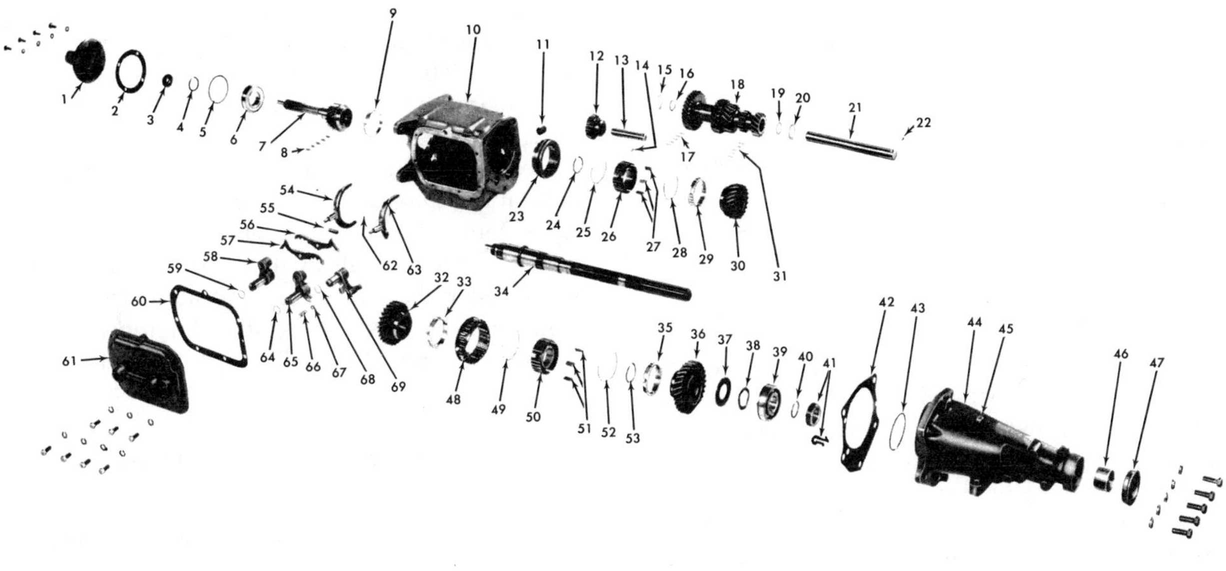

1. Bearing Retainer
2. Gasket-Retainer to Case
3. Oil Seal
4. Snap Ring-Bearing to Gear
5. Snap Ring-Bearing to Case
6. Clutch Gear Bearing
7. Clutch Gear
8. Mainshaft Pilot Bearings
9. 4th Speed Blocker Ring
10. Case
11. Filler Plug
12. Reverse Idler Gear
13. Reverse Idler Shaft
14. Woodruff Key
15. Thrust Washer-Front Gear
16. Needle Retainer Washer
17. Needle Bearings
18. Countergear
19. Needle Retainer Washer
20. Thrust Washer-Rear Gear
21. Countershaft
22. Woodruff Key
23. Synchronizer Sleeve
24. Snap Ring-Hub to Shaft
25. Key Retainer
26. 3-4 Synchronizer Hub
27. Clutch Keys
28. Key Retainer
29. 3rd Speed Blocker Ring
30. 3rd Speed Gear
31. Needle Bearings
32. Second Speed Gear
33. 2nd Speed Blocker Ring
34. Mainshaft
35. 1st Speed Blocker Ring
36. First Speed Gear
37. Thrust Washer
38. Wave Washer
39. Rear Bearing
40. Snap Ring-Bearing to Shaft
41. Speedo Drive Gear and Clip
42. Gasket-Extension to Case
43. Snap Ring-Extension to Rear Bearing
44. Extension
45. Vent
46. Bushing
47. Oil Seal
48. 1-2 Synchronizer Sleeve & Reverse Gear
49. Key Retainer
50. 1-2 Synchronizer Hub
51. Clutch Keys
52. Key Retainer
53. Snap Ring-Hub to Shaft
54. 3-4 Shift Fork
55. Detent Spring
56. 3-4 Detent Cam
57. 1-2 Detent Cam
58. 3-4 Shifter Shaft
59. "O" Ring
60. Gasket-Cover to Case
61. Cover
62. Detent Cam Retainer
63. 1-2 Shift Fork
64. "O" Ring
65. 1-2 Shifter Shaft
66. Spring
67. Ball
68. "O" Ring
69. Reverse Shifter Shaft & Fork

Fig. 15-7. Exploded view of Saginaw 4-speed transmission.

10. General Motors decided to develop a 4-speed in-house to eliminate dependency on the T-10. This was accomplished with minimal changes to the overall design. The Muncie was used in all high performance applications until the Borg Warner Second Design Super T-10 began replacing it in 1974.

Muncie transmissions have probably been the most popular among the hot rodding set since their introduction in 1963. This section will clarify all information on Muncie and Borg-Warner transmissions.

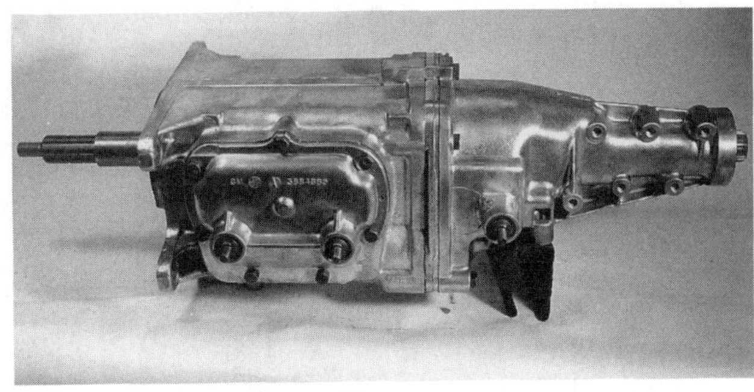

Fig. 15-8. Typical 1968 Muncie 4-speed M20.

Muncie Date Coding

Many Muncie 4-speed maincases, extension housings, and sidecovers have a casting date code. On maincases, the code is usually found on the passenger side of the case, below the casting number. The extension housing code is usually within a few inches of the casting number, also on the passenger side.

Muncie casting date codes are very different from other transmission manufacturers. The code consists of two circles, both 1/2 inch in diameter and divided in half. One circle is called the date marker, the other the status marker. See Fig. 15-9.

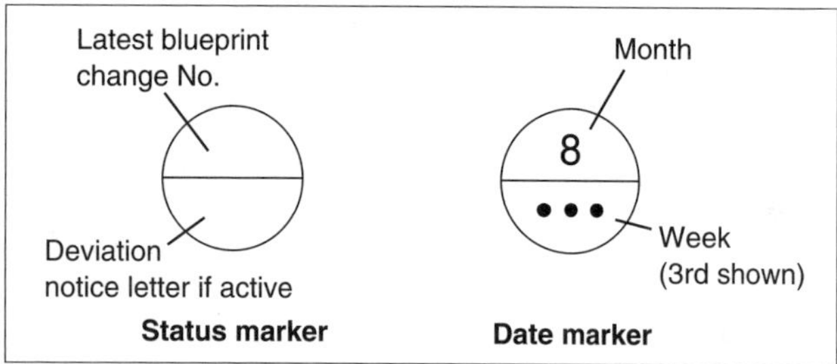

Fig. 15-9. Muncie date coding system.

The date marker has a month designator for when the part was cast or manufactured. This is represented by the numbers 1 through 12 (Jan. – Dec.). The opposite side of the date marker has between one and five dots, representing the week of the month. (Please refer to the component casting chart and the location of the transmission build date to determine the correct model year and application for the part.) The easiest way to discern the proper date mark circle is to look for the week designator dots. Always check to see that the date marked precedes the final assembly stamp code.

The status marker has the latest blueprint change number on one side of the circle, and a deviation notice letter on the other side if the part change letter is active. This information was only useful to the Muncie plant by allowing the tracking of problem parts. Often this circle is blank.

All original Muncie transmissions have ring grooves on the input shaft and counter gear. These grooves were put on for the Muncie assembly line workers to readily identify which input shaft to install. Many Muncie transmissions have had the input shaft replaced so this should not be used for positive identification of the transmission. See **Muncie Parts Identification** for more information.

Oddball Muncie Casting Numbers

Several Muncie parts—primarily the maincase—with "oddball" casting numbers have been found and documented on production vehicles. None of these maincases are shown on the original build records from the Muncie plant. Due to their rarity, these oddball numbers have not been listed in the component casting charts at the back of this chapter.

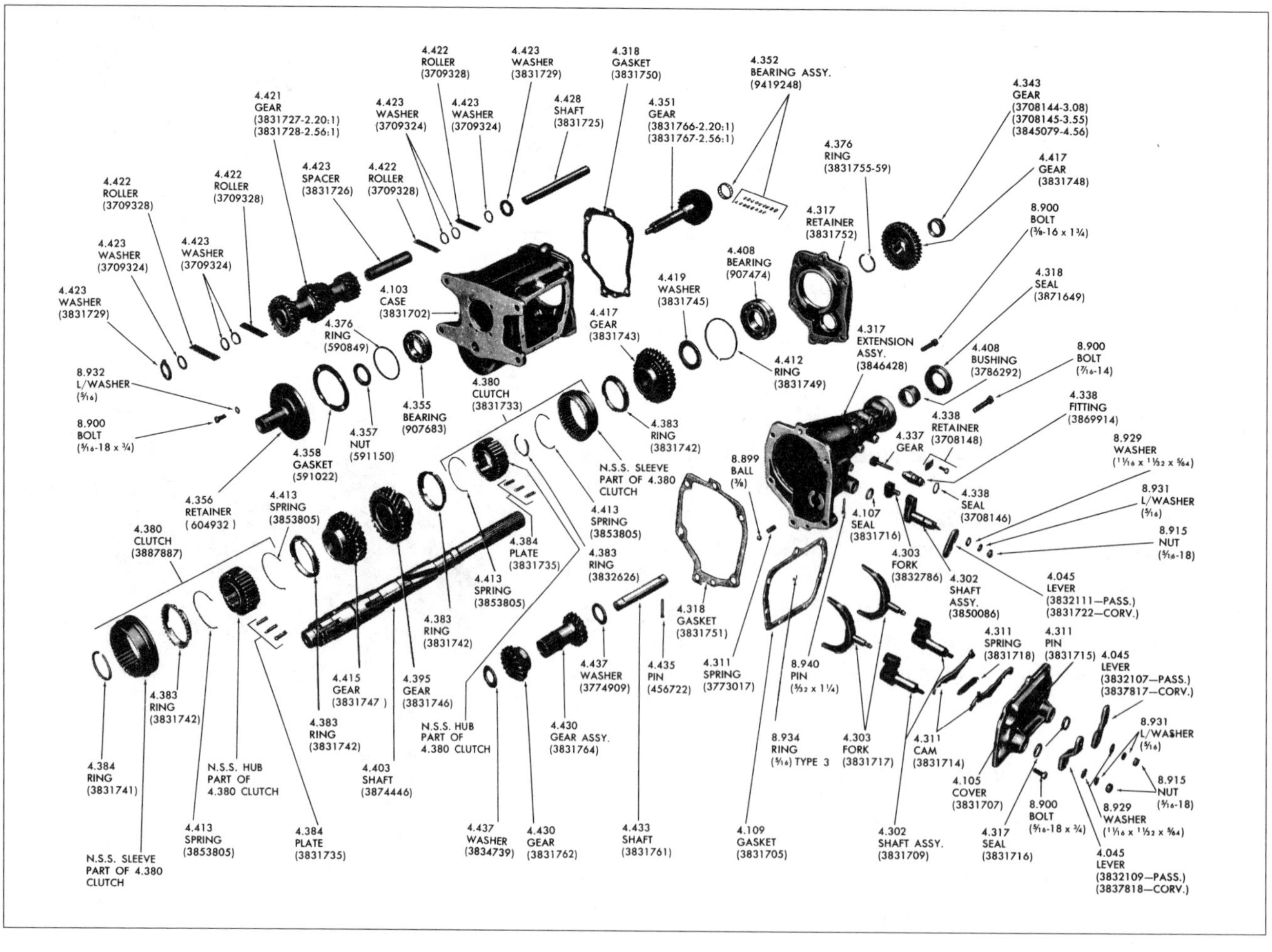

Fig. 15-10. Exploded view of typical 1970 through 1974 Muncie 4-speed transmission.

1970 Through 1974 Muncie 4-Speed

The 1970 Muncie 4-speed was a basic carryover from the 1969 version, with two major changes. The first was the addition of a transmission drain plug to all transmissions. (In previous years only the M22 Muncie transmission had a drain plug.) The second change was the addition of a fine-spline output shaft for Chevelle M22 applications. (All other transmission assemblies used a course spline output shaft.) This dictated the use of a new extension housing, which was specific to the Chevelle M22 applications for the 1970 model year.

It is worth noting that with the 1969 4-speed, Muncie changed the sidecover and shifter arm attachment design. The new design wide ratio sidecovers used an externally pressed pivot pin with a "nail" head on the outside to secure the sifter arms. This was done to solve the problem of the internally pressed pivot pin occasionally falling out and leaving the transmission stuck in gear. This design was used through the 1974 model year. Also, on all Muncie transmissions in 1969 the method of attaching the shifting rods to the transmission was changed from a 3/8-inch fine thread male stud to a 3/8-inch coarse thread female socket.

The M22 Close Ratio 4-Speed utilized a stronger alloy steel along with a straighter helix angle on the main gearset. This straight angle gearset was used to produce less thrust load, and ultimately a cooler-running transmission. This gearset creates a whining sound which is where Chevrolet came up with the nickname "Rockcrusher." All original M22 transmission cases had the front drain plug boss drilled and tapped for a magnetic drainplug. Almost all *original* drainplugs are magnetic and are stamped with the letter "P" which signifies the code letter for passenger car Muncie transmissions.

The 1971 model year marked the last of the major changes to the Muncie 4-speed. On all transmissions the input and output shafts were changed from coarse spline to fine spline.

Finally, on October 21, 1968 (1969 model year), a suffix letter was added to the Assembly Date Code on each Muncie transmission to aid in the identification of transmission ratios for the 1969 model year. This was carried through the 1974 model year.

3-Speed:
A = 3.03:1,
B = 2.42:1
4-Speed:
A = 2.52:1 Wide Ratio,
B = 2.20:1 Close Ratio,
C= 2.20:1 M22 close ratio.

Muncie Identification

Muncie transmission parts are easily identified when the transmission is apart. This is because Muncie used a series of rings or circles on the parts to make identification easier at the assembly line. The following figures show the external differences between Muncie transmission parts to aid identification.

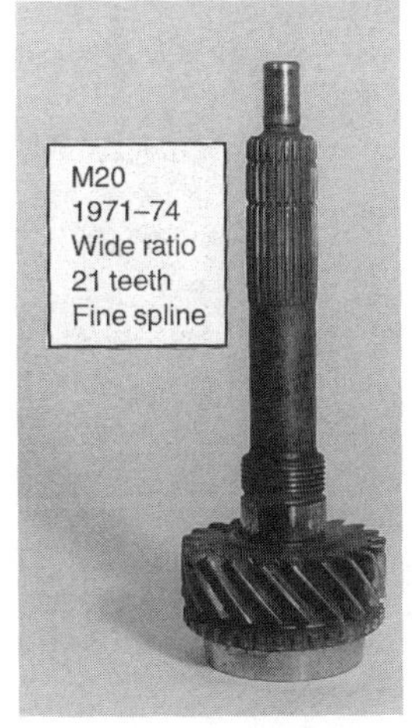

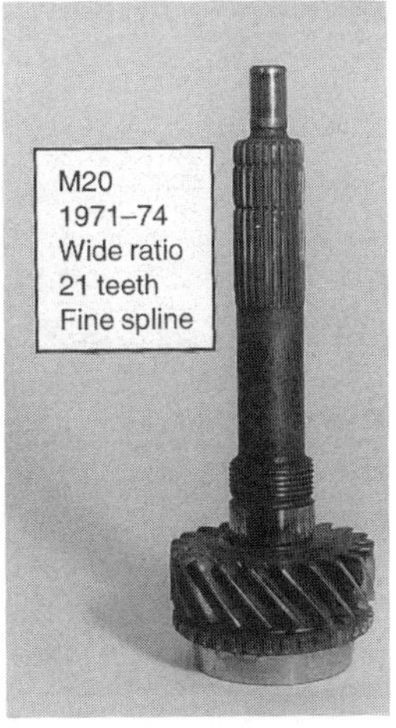

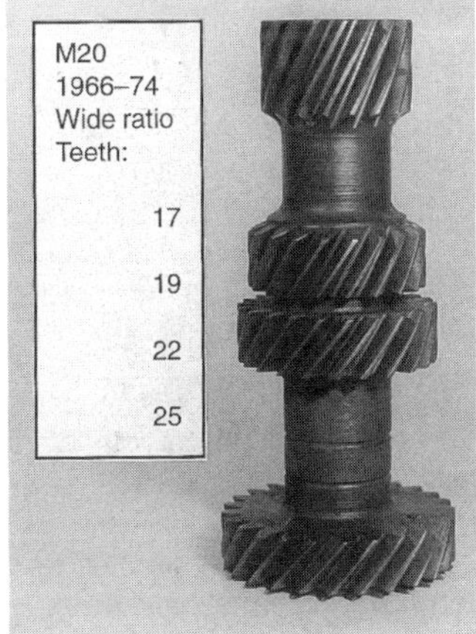

Fig. 15-11. *Identification of Muncie M20 wide ratio main drive gears and countergear.*

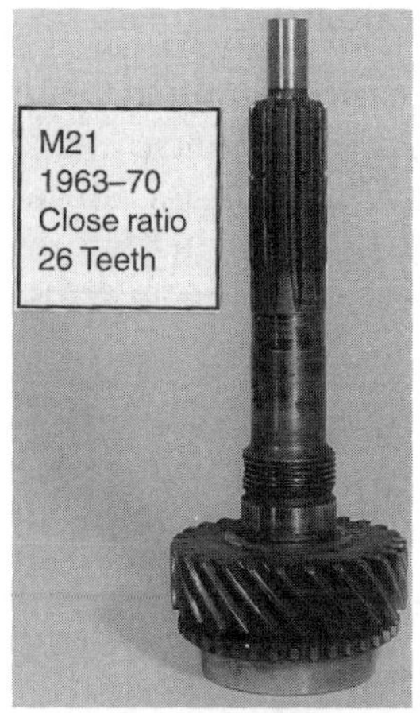

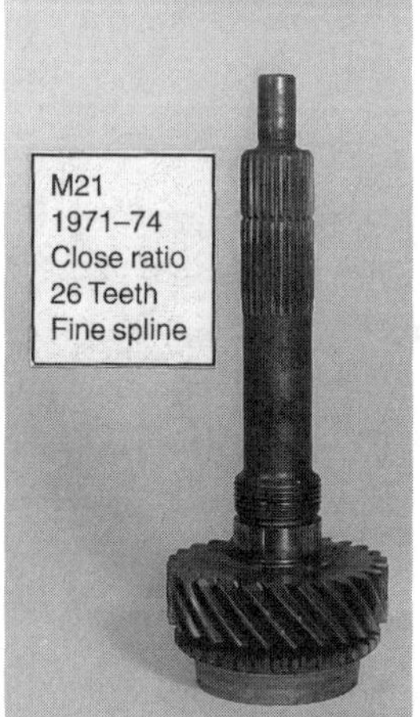

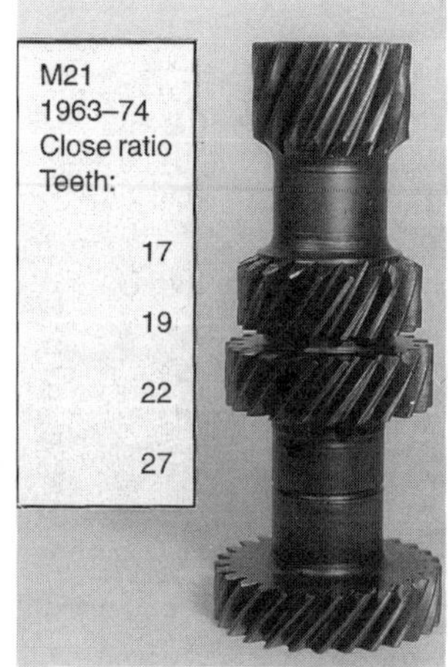
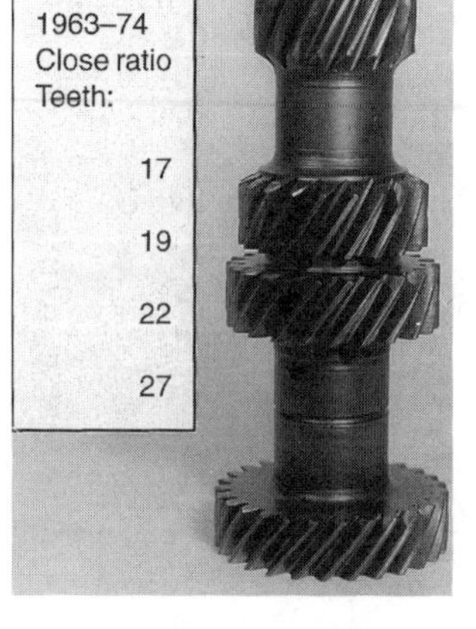

Fig. 15-12. *Identification of Muncie M21 close ratio main drive gears and countergear. Note that from 1963 through 1965 the countergear bore size was 7/8". From 1966 on the bore size was 1".*

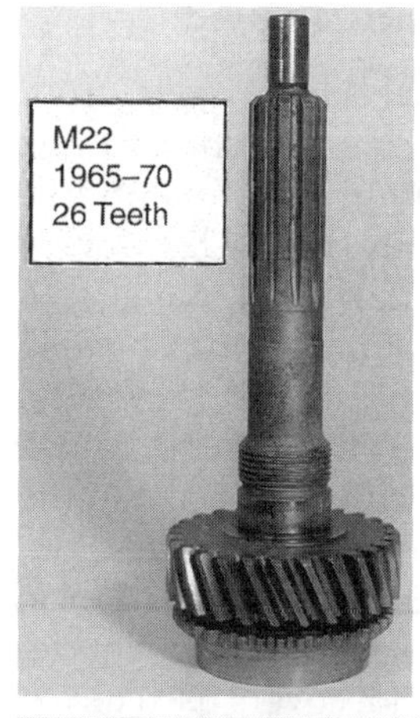

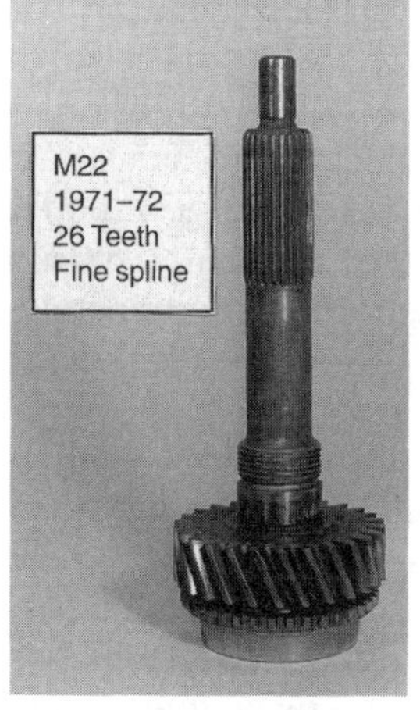

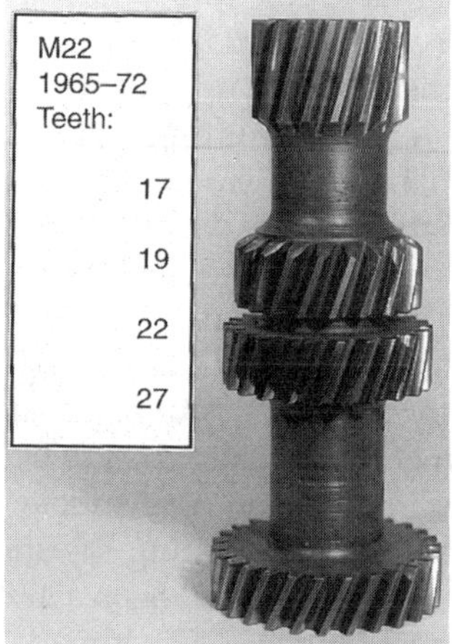

Fig. 15-13. *Identification of Muncie M22 close ratio main drive gears and countergear.*

Borg-Warner 4-Speed Transmissions

The Borg-Warner T10 4-speed was introduced in the Camaro and Corvette in January 1974. In all applications except the Chevelle 454/235HP it replaced the close and wide ratio Muncie. The Chevelle 454/235HP continued to use a Muncie for the complete 1974 model year. By 1974, the muscle car era was basically over, and General Motors decided to out-source transmissions for those few models that still needed a high performance gearbox. The T10 had been offered in a broad range of models and ratios since 1957. This version is considered the sixth, or final, design, and is more commonly known as the Second Design Super T10.

The Borg-Warner 4-speed offered two new gear ratios, a low wide ratio of 2.64:1 and low close ratio of 2.43:1. This transmission was significantly stronger in several key areas over the Muncie gearbox and the new gear ratios were more suited to lower elapsed times.

The Super T10 is a side-loaded transmission with a side-lever shift linkage based on earlier T10 designs. It

Fig. 15-14. *Borg Warner Second Design Super T10. Detail shows build date WD 2892, which decodes as Warner, April, 28th day, 1979, 2nd shift. Note casting date on sidecover, C 8 79, which precedes build date and can be considered correct.*

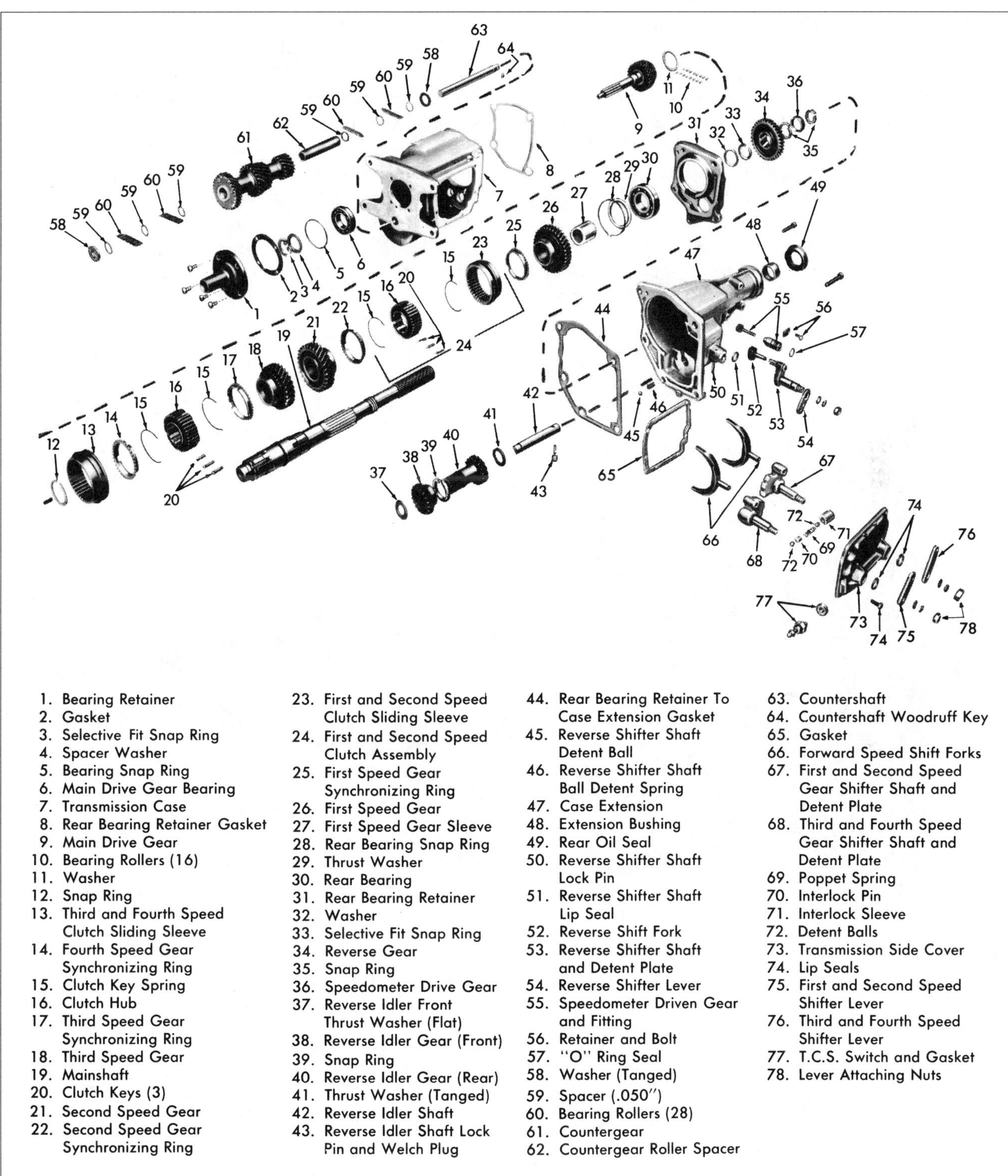

1. Bearing Retainer
2. Gasket
3. Selective Fit Snap Ring
4. Spacer Washer
5. Bearing Snap Ring
6. Main Drive Gear Bearing
7. Transmission Case
8. Rear Bearing Retainer Gasket
9. Main Drive Gear
10. Bearing Rollers (16)
11. Washer
12. Snap Ring
13. Third and Fourth Speed Clutch Sliding Sleeve
14. Fourth Speed Gear Synchronizing Ring
15. Clutch Key Spring
16. Clutch Hub
17. Third Speed Gear Synchronizing Ring
18. Third Speed Gear
19. Mainshaft
20. Clutch Keys (3)
21. Second Speed Gear
22. Second Speed Gear Synchronizing Ring
23. First and Second Speed Clutch Sliding Sleeve
24. First and Second Speed Clutch Assembly
25. First Speed Gear Synchronizing Ring
26. First Speed Gear
27. First Speed Gear Sleeve
28. Rear Bearing Snap Ring
29. Thrust Washer
30. Rear Bearing
31. Rear Bearing Retainer
32. Washer
33. Selective Fit Snap Ring
34. Reverse Gear
35. Snap Ring
36. Speedometer Drive Gear
37. Reverse Idler Front Thrust Washer (Flat)
38. Reverse Idler Gear (Front)
39. Snap Ring
40. Reverse Idler Gear (Rear)
41. Thrust Washer (Tanged)
42. Reverse Idler Shaft
43. Reverse Idler Shaft Lock Pin and Welch Plug
44. Rear Bearing Retainer To Case Extension Gasket
45. Reverse Shifter Shaft Detent Ball
46. Reverse Shifter Shaft Ball Detent Spring
47. Case Extension
48. Extension Bushing
49. Rear Oil Seal
50. Reverse Shifter Shaft Lock Pin
51. Reverse Shifter Shaft Lip Seal
52. Reverse Shift Fork
53. Reverse Shifter Shaft and Detent Plate
54. Reverse Shifter Lever
55. Speedometer Driven Gear and Fitting
56. Retainer and Bolt
57. "O" Ring Seal
58. Washer (Tanged)
59. Spacer (.050")
60. Bearing Rollers (28)
61. Countergear
62. Countergear Roller Spacer
63. Countershaft
64. Countershaft Woodruff Key
65. Gasket
66. Forward Speed Shift Forks
67. First and Second Speed Gear Shifter Shaft and Detent Plate
68. Third and Fourth Speed Gear Shifter Shaft and Detent Plate
69. Poppet Spring
70. Interlock Pin
71. Interlock Sleeve
72. Detent Balls
73. Transmission Side Cover
74. Lip Seals
75. First and Second Speed Shifter Lever
76. Third and Fourth Speed Shifter Lever
77. T.C.S. Switch and Gasket
78. Lever Attaching Nuts

Fig. 15-15. *Exploded view of Borg-Warner T10 transmission.*

is fully synchronized in all forward gears. A spur sliding gear in the extension housing engages the rear of a two-step reverse idler to provide reverse. The countershaft was enlarged from an 0.870-inch diameter to a 1.00-inch diameter, while the mainshaft was redesigned for a larger 1st gear journal. The reverse gear spline count is 32. All factory original Chevrolet Second Design Super T10s had an aluminum maincase and extension housing. Aftermarket Super T10s generally used a cast or nodular iron case.

1.3 Powerglide Automatic Transmissions

The Powerglide was a two-speed transmission with an automatic hydraulic torque converter and a planetary gear system for reverse and low. There were several external design changes made to the 1970 through 1975 Powerglide transmissions. These changes are discussed in detail underneath each model year heading in this chapter.

Many oil filler tubes and fluid level gauges are specific to passenger car, Corvette or truck applications. For example, the Corvette oil filler tubes are designed to clear the body floor pan shapes. Many external parts such as linkages, vacuum modulator lines, park-neutral safety switches, and dipsticks are also unique to the Corvette models. Be very careful and do your research when looking for these parts.

There were two production sources for the Powerglide transmission, the Cleveland, Ohio, and Toledo, Ohio plants. According to Chevrolet Technical Service Bulletins and Parts Catalog Identification charts, all 327, 409, 396, and 427 V-8 aluminum Powerglides were supplied by the Toledo plant. Thus, all Corvette transmissions will have a "T" (Toledo) plant code. The

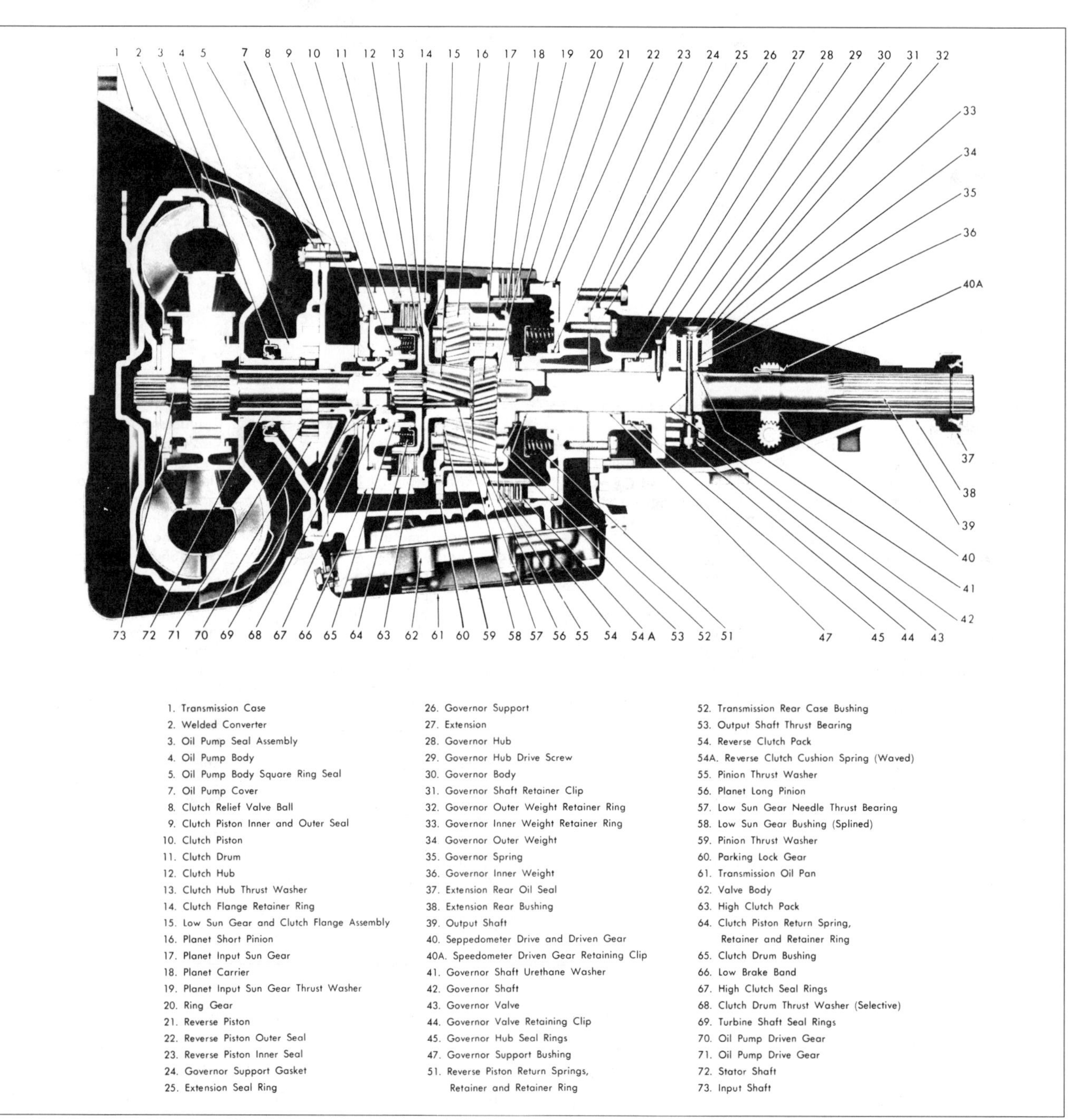

***Fig. 15-16.** Cutaway of typical Powerglide transmission.*

Cleveland plant, supplied only the 230 L6 and 283 V-8 Powerglide transmissions.

1.4 Turbohydramatic Automatic Transmissions

Turbohydramatic 350 Transmission

The Turbohydramatic 350 transmission entered full production for all models in the 1969 model year. Although it was installed in some 1968 Chevrolet test vehicles, the option was not available until 1969. The Turbohydramatic 350 was the next step up the automatic transmission design ladder, in that the Powerglide could not be efficiently improved. More vehicles were being built with smaller V-8s, and those cars needed an efficient 3-speed automatic that could also help the powertrain pass the coming emission regulations. Because the Turbohydramatic 400 was regarded as a heavy duty transmission, it was deemed inappropriate for these cars. The 350 took the best features of the 400 and combined them into a more cost-efficient base transmission. The Turbohydramatic 350 was used behind engines up to, but not including, the 396.

The Turbo 350 is a fully automatic 3-speed encased in a two-piece aluminum main housing and extension. The transmission consists primarily of a hydraulic torque converter and a compound planetary gearset. Four multi-disc clutches, two roller clutch assemblies, and one band provide the friction elements required to manipulate the planetary gearset.

A Turbo 350 can be identified by checking the throttle cable, either from the engine compartment or from underneath the car. The transmission is connected by cable to the throttle to make the transmission responsive to engine load. The cable runs from the accelerator control lever to the *right* side of the transmission. In contrast, throttle control of the Turbohydramatic 400 is electric; the cable runs from a switch at the carburetor to the *left* side of the transmission. In addition, the Turbo 350 has a 7/8-inch diameter speedometer driven gear bore in the transmission extension.

Further identification points are the oil pans, as shown later, and the transmission modulator. On 350s, the modulator is at the rear of the transmission. On 400s, the modulator is at the right front of the transmission.

Turbohydramatic 400 Transmission

The Turbohydramatic 400 was introduced in 1965 in the passenger car line in conjunction with the 396/325HP engine. This transmission has been used

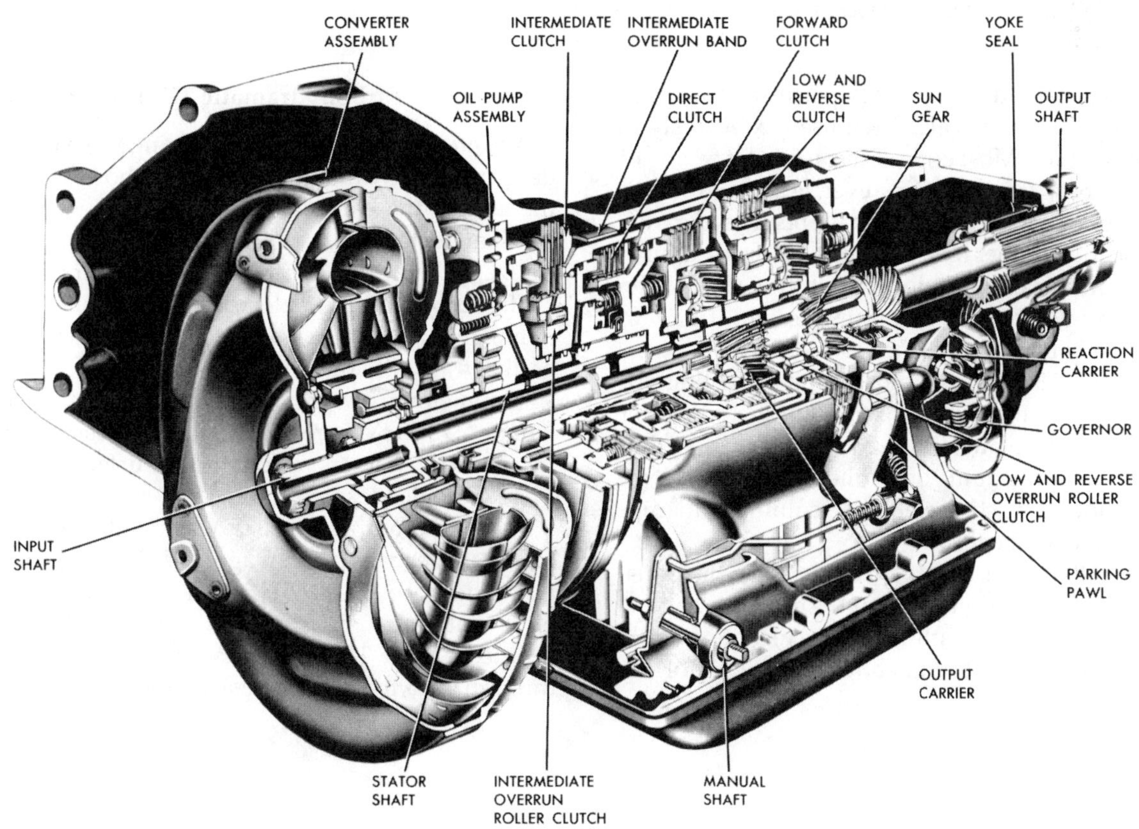

Fig. 15-17. *Sectional view of Turbohydramatic 350.*

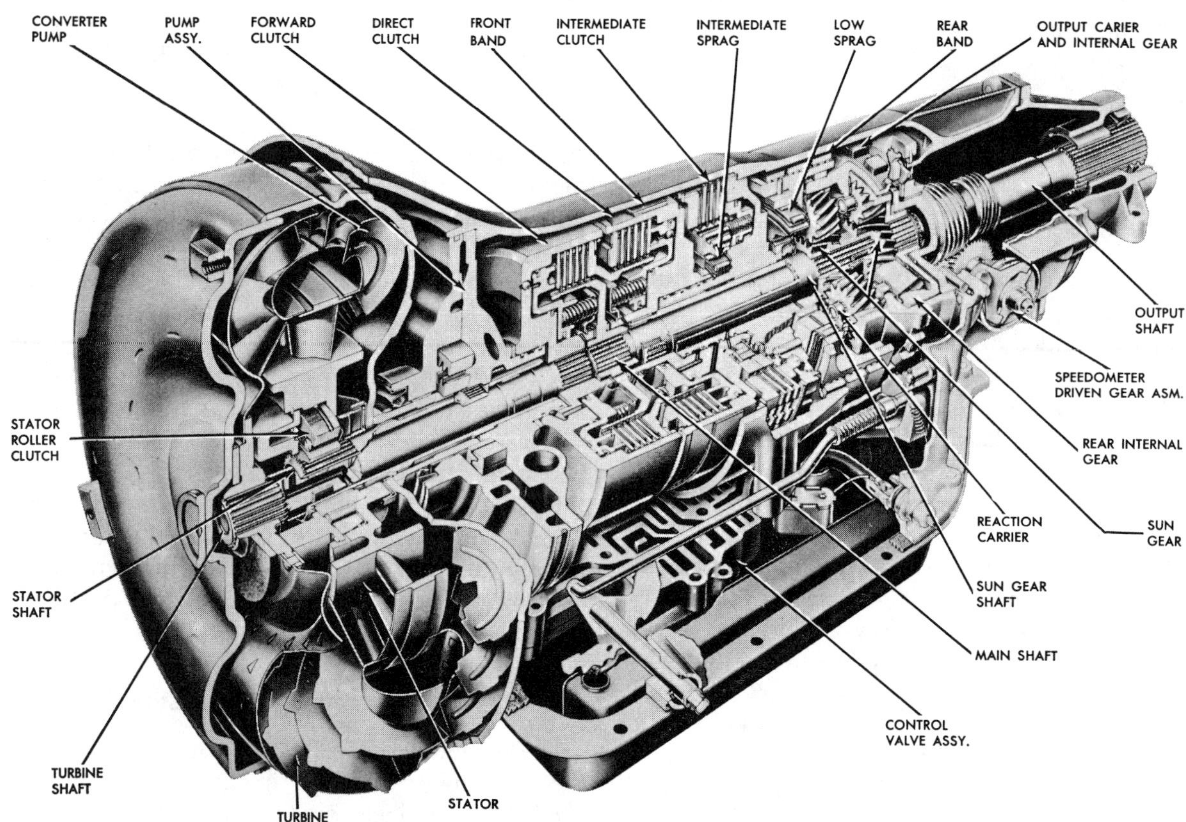

Fig. 15-18. *Sectional view of Turbohydramatic 400 transmission.*

behind most heavy duty and high performance applications since then. It has also been used extensively in truck applications. Most enthusiasts regard it as one of Chevrolet's best transmissions ever. Although modified Powerglides and Turbo 350s have been used in racing applications, the stock Turbo 400 was almost unbeatable in stock applications. While there have been several improvements to this transmission, it has remained largely unchanged since 1965.

The Turbo 400 is a fully automatic unit consisting primarily of a three-element hydraulic torque converter and a compound planetary gearset. Three multi-disc clutches, one sprag unit, one roller clutch, and two bands provide the friction elements required to manipulate the planetary gearset.

The Turbo 400 can be identified by checking the transmission throttle cable, either from the engine compartment or from underneath the car. Please see the Turbohydramatic 350 section above for more information.

Special Turbohydramatic 375 Transmission

An interim 1972 production change released a new design Turbohydramatic 375. The Turbo 375 is basically the same as the 400, with some minor changes. The output shaft, extension, and related parts were modified to utilize the same driveshaft yoke as the Turbo 350.

The Turbo 375 has an electrically activated detent system with the electrical connector located on the left side of the transmission. The 375 has a 2-inch diameter speedometer driven gear bore in the extension, and the letters "375 THM" are cast on the underside of the extension in characters raised off the surface 0.60 inches. The 375 model designation is CB

The Turbohydramatic 375 was available optionally on Passenger car station wagons (125" wheelbase only) with the base 350/165HP and 400/170HP engines. Note that Turbo 350 transmissions were also installed in these cars. This information has been verified through *Chevrolet Service News*, August 1972.

2. 1970 TRANSMISSIONS

1970 Transmission Applications

Transmission	Model & Engine
3-Speed Saginaw (Low Performance)	Passenger 250 Chevelle 250, 307 Nova 153, 230, 250, 307 Camaro 250, 307
3-Speed Saginaw	Passenger 350/250HP Nova 350/250HP Chevelle 350/250HP Monte Carlo 350/250HP
3-Speed Heavy Duty Muncie MC1**	Camaro 350/255, 300HP, 396/325, 350, 375HP
4-Speed Wide Ratio Saginaw (Low Performance)	Chevelle 307/200HP
4-Speed Wide Ratio Saginaw (Low Performance)	Nova 350/250HP Chevelle 350/250HP Camaro 350/250HP Monte Carlo 350/250HP
4-Speed Wide Ratio Muncie M20	Corvette 350/300, 350, 370HP 454/390 Nova 350/300HP, 402/350, 375HP* Chevelle 350/300HP 402/330, 350, 375HP* Camaro 350/300, 360HP, 402/350, 375HP Monte Carlo 350/300HP 400/265HP 402/330HP
4-Speed Close Ratio Muncie M21	Corvette 350/350, 370HP 454/390HP Nova 402/350, 375HP* Chevelle 402/350, 375HP* Camaro 350/360HP 402/350, 375HP Yenko Duece 350/360 HP
4-Speed Close Ratio Muncie M22	Corvette 350/370HP Chevelle 454/360, 450HP Camaro 350/360HP 402/375HP* Yenko Duece 350/360 HP
2-Speed Powerglide	Passenger 250/155HP 350/250, 300HP Nova 230, 250 307/200HP 350/250, 300HP Chevelle 250/155HP 307/200HP 350/250, 300HP Camaro 250/155HP 307/200HP Monte Carlo 350/250, 300HP
3-Speed Turbohydramatic 350	Passenger 350/250, 300HP 400/265HP Nova 230/140HP 250/155HP 307/200HP 350/250, 300HP Chevelle 250/155HP 307/200HP 350/250, 300HP Camaro 307/200HP 350/250, 300HP Monte Carlo 350/250, 300HP 400/265HP
3-Speed Turbohydramatic 400	Passenger 454/345, 390HP Corvette 350/300HP 454/390HP Nova 402/350HP* Chevelle 402/330, 350HP 454/360, 450HP Camaro 350/360HP 402/350HP Monte Carlo 402/330HP 454/360HP Yenko Duece 350/360 HP
* Unverified **The MC1 option was never available for the 1970 model year. The 1969 Camaro line ran until Jan. 1970. Muncie plant shipping records show that a substantial number of heavy duty 3-speeds were sent to assembly plants. Since only the Camaro and Corvette had long model runs in 1969, it is highly likely these transmissions were installed in Camaros. Corvettes never received the MC1.	

2.1 Date Code

1970 Assembly Date Code Location (Car)

Transmission	Code Location
3-Speed	Left side of maincase, on boss below and to rear of sidecover
4-Speed (Muncie Cast Iron Case)	Left side of maincase, on boss below and to rear of sidecover
4-Speed (Muncie Aluminum Case)	Right side of maincase, just in front of extension housing
Powerglide	Transmission oil pan, right side
Turbohydramatic 350	Transmission oil pan, right side
Turbohydramatic 400	Identification plate, right side

3-, 4-Speed, Powerglide, Turbohydramatic 350
Example: N 0 E 03

- N: Prefix = 4-Speed, Muncie (Truck)
- 0: Model Year = 1970
- E: Month = May
- 03: Day = day 3

1970 Transmission Letter Prefix Identification

Prefix	Plant	Transmission and Engine
B	Cleveland	Turbohydramatic 350
C	Cleveland	Powerglide
E	McKinnon	Powerglide
K	McKinnon	3-Speed (Passenger)
M	Muncie	3-Speed (Truck, heavy duty)
N	Muncie	4-Speed (Truck)
P	Muncie	4-Speed (Passenger, Heavy Duty, Aluminum Case)
R	Muncie	4-Speed (Passenger, Light Duty, Cast Iron Case)
S	Muncie	3-Speed (Passenger, Truck Light Duty)

NOTE—
Powerglide and Turbohydramatic 350 transmissions built at Cleveland have an additional identification code, stamped on the front pump seal flange. This code was instituted approximately 12/1/68. Example: C9T. C = Cleveland, 9 = model year, T = month (December).

NOTE—
1970 Muncie 3- and 4-Speed car transmissions have a suffix letter added to the date code that further identifies the first gear ratio:
3-Speed: A = 3.03:1, B = 2.42:1
4-Speed: A = 2.52:1 Wide Ratio, B = 2.20:1 Close Ratio, C= 2.20:1 M22.

Assembly Month Code

A - January	E - May	P - September
B - February	H - June	R - October
C - March	K - July	S - November
D - April	M - August	T - December

Turbohydramatic 400 Example: 70 A 372

- 70: Model Year = 1970
- A: Engine identification = 400
  A = 400 (Chevrolet)
  B = 454 (Chevrolet)
  D = 400 (Chevelle & Monte Carlo)
  F = 402 (Chevelle, Camaro, Nova)
  G = 454 (Police)
  J = 402 (Truck 10-30 Series)
  K = 350 (Corvette)
  R = 454 (Chevelle)
  S = 454 (Chevelle, Monte Carlo, Corvette)
  W = 402 (Chevelle, Camaro, Nova)
  Y* = 454 (Chevelle, Corvette)
  *High shift point
- 372: Assembly date = the assembly date code for the 1970 model year starts with the first day of the calendar year in 1969 and continues through the 1970 calendar year. "372" is January 7, 1970.

2.2 Transmission Specifications

3-Speed Saginaw (Low Performance)

Maincase	Cast Iron
Extension Housing	Cast Iron
Type	Synchromesh, all forward gears
Gear Ratios	1st: 2.85:1 2nd: 1.68:1 3rd: Direct Reverse: 2.95:1
Maincase Casting No.	3925647
Extension Housing Casting No.	3860042
Sidecover Casting No.	3952645
Special Information	None

NOTE—
Starting 7/21/69, the Muncie transmission plant took over production of the 3-speed Saginaw transmissions, formerly built at the Saginaw plant. On 8/26/69, 58,813 light duty transmissions were shipped from Saginaw to Muncie. These transmissions were shipped to assembly plants from a central Indiana warehouse and were finally depleted on 8/14/70.

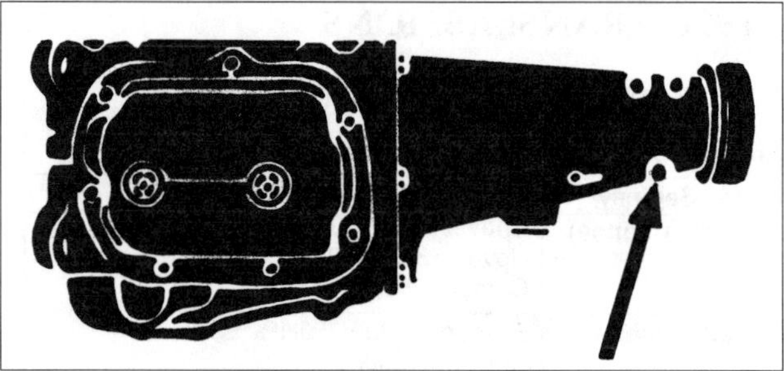

Fig. 15-19. 1966 and later Saginaw 3-speed transmission. Sidecover is held by seven bolts. Holes for shifter mounting (arrow) not tapped on all models.

3-Speed Heavy Duty Muncie

Maincase	Cast Iron
Extension Housing	Cast Iron
Type	Synchromesh, all forward gears
Gear Ratios	1st: 2.42:1 2nd: 1.58:1 3rd: Direct Reverse: 2.41:1
Maincase Casting No.	3911940
Extension Housing Casting No.	3911942
Sidecover Casting No.	3911947
Special Information	This transmission was a new heavy duty design that was more durable than previous 3-Speed Transmissions. The gear ratio spread was similar to the 1968 Borg Warner version

3-Speed Saginaw

Maincase	Cast Iron
Extension Housing	Cast Iron
Type	Synchromesh, all forward gears
Gear Ratios	1st: 2.54:1 2nd: 1.50:1 3rd: Direct Reverse: 2.63:1
Maincase Casting No.	3925647
Extension Housing Casting No.	3860042
Sidecover Casting No.	3952645
Special Information	None

4-Speed Wide Ratio (Chevelle, Low Performance)

Maincase	Cast Iron
Extension Housing	Cast Iron
Type	Synchromesh, all forward gears
Gear Ratios	1st: 2.85:1 2nd: 2.02:1 3rd: 1.35:1 4th: Direct Reverse: 2.85:1
Maincase Casting No.	3925656
Extension Housing Casting No.	3860042
Sidecover Casting No.	3952647
Special Information	This transmission is a carry-over from 1969. It was only used in the Chevelle model line and only behind the 307/200HP engine. This was the last year that this transmission was used

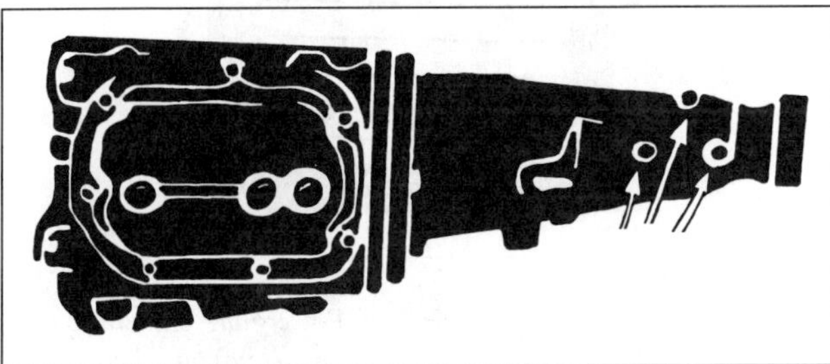

Fig. 15-20. Saginaw 4-speed cast iron transmission. Sidecover is held by seven bolts. Holes for shifter mounting (arrow) not tapped on all models. Also note three-lever sidecover.

4-Speed Wide Ratio Saginaw (Standard)

Maincase	Cast Iron
Extension Housing	Cast Iron
Type	Synchromesh, all forward gears
Gear Ratios	1st: 2.54:1 2nd: 1.80:1 3rd: 1.44:1 4th: Direct Reverse: 2.54:1
Maincase Casting No.	3925656
Extension Housing Casting No.	3860042 All except Camaro 3873886 Camaro
Sidecover Casting No.	3952647
Special Information	None

4-Speed Wide Ratio Muncie M20

Maincase	Aluminum
Extension Housing	Aluminum
Type	Synchromesh, all forward gears
Gear Ratios	1st: 2.52:1 2nd: 1.88:1 3rd: 1.46:1 4th: Direct Reverse: 2.59:1
Maincase Casting No.	3925661
Extension Housing Casting No.	3857584
Sidecover Casting No.	3952648
Special Information	This transmission was a basic carry-over from the 1969 model year with the following exception: The gear ratio was changed slightly in 3rd and reverse. The "A" suffix code letter continued to be added to the plant build date code to designate a wide ratio transmission, as in the 1969 model year. All 1970 and later M20 Muncie 4-speeds have drain plugs

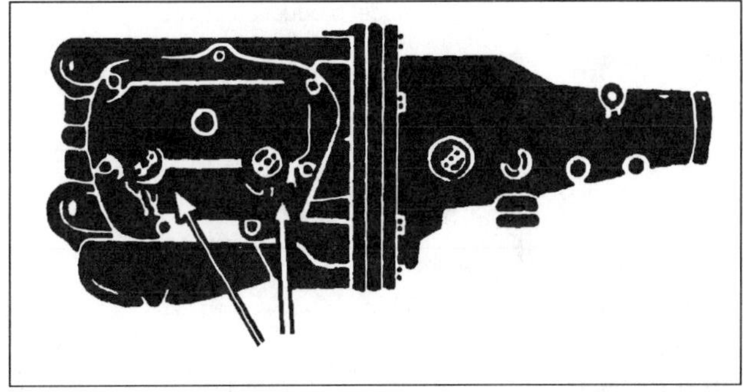

Fig. 15-21. Typical 1969 and later Muncie 4-speed. Shifter arms attach (arrows) with bolt.

4-Speed Close Ratio Muncie M21

Maincase	Aluminum
Extension Housing	Aluminum
Type	Synchromesh, all forward gears
Gear Ratios	1st: 2.20:1 2nd: 1.64:1 3rd: 1.28:1 4th: Direct Reverse: 2.26:1
Maincase Casting No.	3925661
Extension Housing Casting No.	3857584
Sidecover Casting No.	3952648
Special Information	This transmission was a complete carry-over from the 1969 model year including the "B" suffix letter code, which was added to the plant build date code to aid in identification. All 1970 and later M21 4-speeds have drain plugs

4-Speed Close Ratio Muncie M22

Maincase	Aluminum
Extension Housing	Aluminum
Type	Synchromesh, all forward gears
Gear Ratios	1st: 2.20:1 2nd: 1.64:1 3rd: 1.28:1 4th: Direct Reverse: 2.26:1
Maincase Casting No.	3925661
Extension Housing Casting No.	3857584 (All except Chevelle) 3978764 (Chevelle only)
Sidecover Casting No.	3952648
Special Information	The M22 transmission was carried over with no changes in design for 1970. This also included the "C" suffix letter code, which was added to the plant build date code to aid in identification. Although the production figures of the M22 increased, the overall model usage decreased, with the Passenger and Nova dropping the option in 1970. This is reflected in the Chevrolet Accumulative Production Report below, which shows the complete M22 model production usage: Corvette (ZR1): 25 Chevelle: 5,410 Camaro: 1,185 Total: 6,620

2-Speed Powerglide

Maincase	Aluminum
Extension Housing	Aluminum
Application (1)	307
Gear Ratios (1)	Drive Range 1:1 Direct Drive Low Range 1.82:1 Reverse 1.82:1
Application (2)	327, 350, 396
Gear Ratios (2)	Drive Range 1:1 Direct Drive Low Range 1.76:1 Reverse 1.76:1
Maincase Casting No.	Unknown
Extension Housing Casting No.	Unknown
Special Information	None

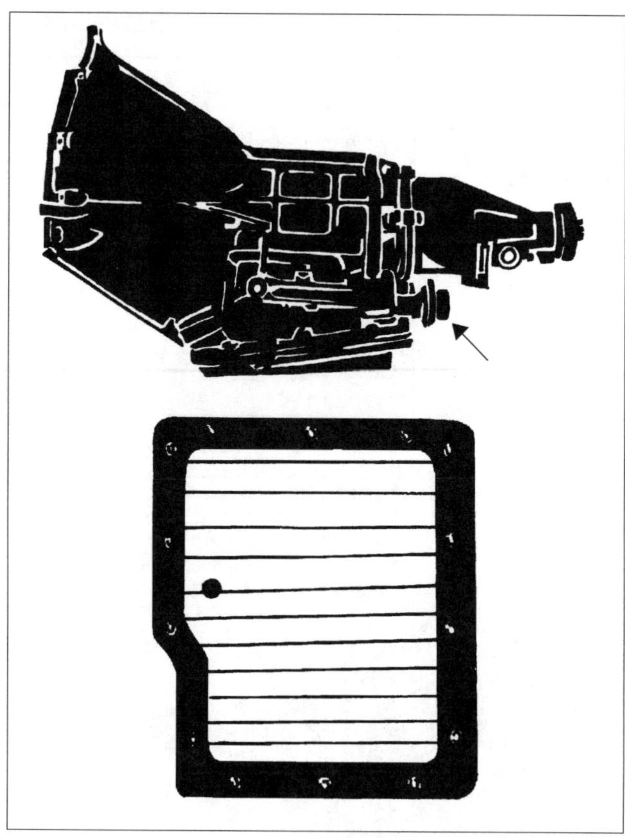

Fig. 15-22. *Top: External view of Powerglide transmission. Note position of modulator (arrow) and distinctive ribbing on case.* ***Bottom:*** *Powerglide oil pan is the same for aluminum or cast iron case.*

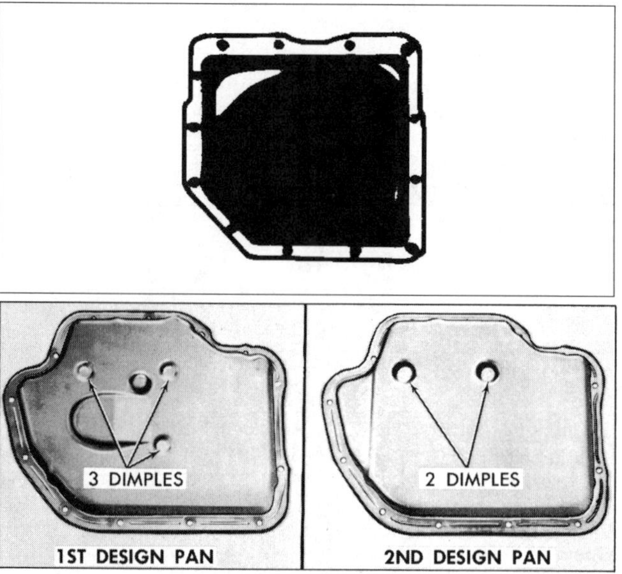

Fig. 15-23. *Top: Turbo 350 oil pan.* ***Bottom:*** *Illustration from Chevrolet Service News, July 1967, shows changes to Turbohydramatic 400 oil pan. Left is 1965 to late 1967 pan. Right is late 1967 and later pan*

3-Speed Turbohydramatic 350

Maincase	Aluminum
Extension Housing	Aluminum
Gear Ratios	Drive Range: 1:1 Direct Drive Low 2 Range: 1.52:1 Low 1 Range: 2.52:1 Reverse: 1.93:1
Maincase Casting No.	Unknown
Extension Housing Casting No.	Unknown
Special Information	A second design valve body transfer plate gasket and valve body gasket were released mid-year in production for 1970 vehicles equipped with the Turbo 350. This change is due to the redesign of the transmission case in the modulator bore area to reduce porosity. The transmission case is identified by an "X" on the side

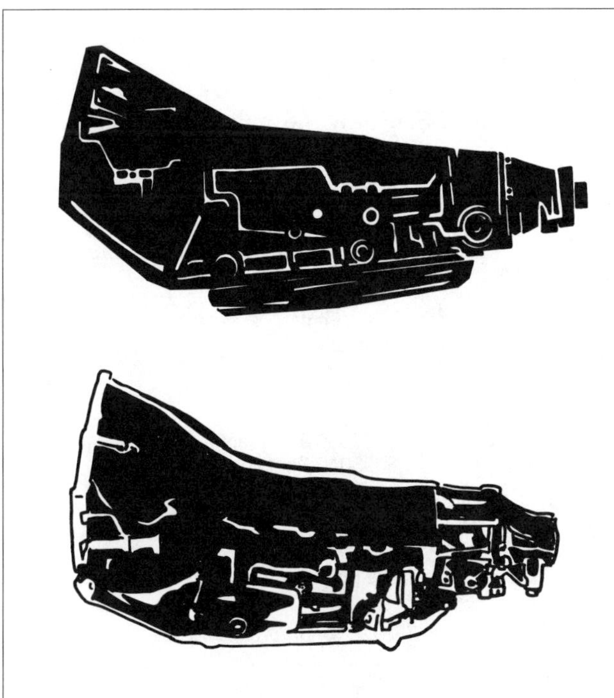

*Fig. 15-24. Top: Turbohydramatic 350 transmission. **Bottom:** Turbohydramatic 400 transmission.*

3-Speed Turbohydramatic 400

Maincase	Aluminum
Extension Housing	Aluminum
Gear Ratios	Drive: 2.48:1, 1. 48:1, 1.00:1 Low 2: 2.48:1 Low 1: 2.48:1 Reverse: 2.08:1
Maincase Casting No.	Unknown
Special Information	The Turbo 400 was a carry-over from the 1969 model year

3. 1971 TRANSMISSIONS

1971 Transmission Applications

Transmission	Model & Engine
3-Speed Saginaw (Low Performance)	Passenger 250 Chevelle 250, 307 Nova 250, 307 Camaro 250, 307
3-Speed Saginaw	Passenger 350/245HP 400/255HP Nova 350/245HP Chevelle 350/245*, 270HP Monte Carlo 350/245HP
3-Speed Heavy Duty Muncie	Chevelle 402/300HP
4-Speed Wide Ratio Saginaw	Chevelle 350/245HP Camaro 350/245HP
4-Speed Wide Ratio Muncie M20	Corvette 350/270, 330HP 454/365HP Nova 350/270HP Chevelle 350/270HP Camaro 350/270, 330HP 402/300HP Monte Carlo 350/270HP 402/300HP
4-Speed Close Ratio Muncie M21	Corvette 350/330HP 454/365, 425HP Camaro 350/330HP 402/300HP
4-Speed Close Ratio Muncie M22	Corvette 350/330HP 454/425HP Chevelle 454/365, 425HP Camaro 350/330HP Monte Carlo 454/425HP
2-Speed Powerglide	Passenger 250/145HP 350/245HP Nova 250/145HP 307/200HP Chevelle 250/145HP 307/200HP Camaro 250/145HP 307/200HP Monte Carlo 350/245HP
3-Speed Turbohydramatic 350	Passenger 350/245, 270HP 400/255HP Nova 307/200HP 350/245, 270HP Chevelle 307/200HP 350/245, 270HP Camaro 307/200HP 350/245, 270HP Monte Carlo 350/245, 270HP
3-Speed Turbohydramatic 400	Passenger 402/300HP 454/365HP Corvette 350/270HP 454/365, 425HP Chevelle 402/300HP 454/365, 425HP Camaro 350/330HP 402/300HP Monte Carlo 402/300HP 454/365, 425HP
*Available until December 1970	

3.1 Date Code

1971 Assembly Date Code Location (Car)

Transmission	Code Location
3-Speed	Left side of maincase, on boss below and to rear of sidecover
4-Speed (Muncie Cast Iron Case)	Left side of maincase, on boss below and to rear of sidecover
4-Speed (Muncie Aluminum Case)	Right side of maincase, just in front of extension housing
Powerglide	Transmission oil pan, right side
Turbohydramatic 350	Transmission oil pan, right side
Turbohydramatic 400	Identification plate, right side

3-, 4-Speed, Powerglide, Turbohydramatic 350 Example: N 1 E 03

- N: Prefix = 4-Speed, Muncie (Truck)
- 1: Model Year = 1971
- E: Month = May
- 03: Day = day 3

1971 Transmission Letter Prefix Identification

Prefix	Plant	Transmission and Engine
B	Cleveland	Turbohydramatic 350
C	Cleveland	Powerglide
E	McKinnon	Powerglide
H	Muncie	3-Speed Chevelle (Heavy Duty)
J	GM Canada	Turbohydramatic 350
M	Muncie	3-Speed (Truck, heavy duty)
N	Muncie	4-Speed (Truck)
P	Muncie	4-Speed (Heavy Duty, Aluminum Case)
R	Muncie	4-Speed (Light Duty, Cast Iron Case)
S	Muncie	3-Speed (Passenger, Truck Light Duty)
Y	Toledo	Turbohydramatic 350

NOTE—
Powerglide and Turbohydramatic 350 transmissions built at Cleveland have an additional identification code, stamped on the front pump seal flange. This code was instituted approximately 12/1/68. Example: C9T. C = Cleveland, 9 = model year, T = month (December).

NOTE—
1971 Muncie 3- and 4-Speed car transmissions have a suffix letter added to the date code that further identifies the first gear ratio:
3-Speed: A = 3.03:1, B = 2.42:1
4-Speed: A = 2.52:1 Wide Ratio, B = 2.20:1 Close Ratio, C= 2.20:1 M22.

Assembly Month Code

A - January	E - May	P - September
B - February	H - June	R - October
C - March	K - July	S - November
D - April	M - August	T - December

Turbohydramatic 400 Example: 71 A 372

- 71: Model Year = 1971
- A: Engine identification = 400
  A = 400 (Chevrolet)
  B = 454 (Chevrolet)
  D = 400 (Chevelle & Monte Carlo)
  F = 402 (Chevelle, Camaro, Nova)
  G = 454 (Police)
  J = 402 (Truck 10-30 Series)
  K = 350 (Corvette)
  R = 454 (Chevelle)
  S = 454 (Chevelle, Monte Carlo, Corvette)
  W = 402 (Chevelle, Camaro, Nova)
  Y* = 454 (Chevelle, Corvette)
  *High shift point
- 372: Assembly date = the assembly date code for the 1971 model year starts with the first day of the calendar year in 1970 and continues through the 1971 calendar year. "372" is January 7, 1971.

3.2 Transmission Specifications

3-Speed Saginaw (Low Performance)

Maincase	Cast Iron
Extension Housing	Cast Iron
Type	Synchromesh, all forward gears
Gear Ratios	1st: 2.85:1 2nd: 1.68:1 3rd: Direct Reverse: 2.95:1
Maincase Casting No.	3925647
Extension Housing Casting No.	3873886 All except Passenger Wagon 3993045 Passenger Wagon
Sidecover Casting No.	3952645
Special Information	None

3-Speed Saginaw

Maincase	Cast Iron
Extension Housing	Cast Iron
Type	Synchromesh, all forward gears
Gear Ratios	1st: 2.54:1 2nd: 1.50:1 3rd: Direct Reverse: 2.63:1
Maincase Casting No.	3925647
Extension Housing Casting No.	3873886 All except Passenger Wagon 3993045 Passenger Wagon
Sidecover Casting No.	3952645
Special Information	None

3-Speed Muncie Heavy Duty (Chevelle Only)

Maincase	Cast Iron
Extension Housing	Cast Iron
Type	Synchromesh, all forward gears
Gear Ratios	1st: 2.42:1 2nd: 1.58:1 3rd: Direct Reverse: 2.41:1
Maincase Casting No.	3911940
Extension Housing Casting No.	3911942
Sidecover Casting No.	3952646
Special Information	This transmission is new for the 1971 model year and was only used in the Chevelle with the 402/300Hp engine

4-Speed Wide Ratio Saginaw

Maincase	Cast Iron
Extension Housing	Cast Iron
Type	Synchromesh, all forward gears
Gear Ratios	1st: 2.54:1 2nd: 1.80:1 3rd: 1.44:1 4th: Direct Reverse: 2.54:1
Maincase Casting No.	3925656
Extension Housing Casting No.	3873886
Sidecover Casting No.	3952647
Special Information	None

4-Speed Wide Ratio Muncie M20

Maincase	Aluminum
Extension Housing	Aluminum
Type	Synchromesh, all forward gears
Gear Ratios	1st: 2.52:1 2nd: 1.88:1 3rd: 1.46:1 4th: Direct Reverse: 2.59:1
Maincase Casting No.	3925661
Extension Housing Casting No.	3978764
Sidecover Casting No.	3952648
Special Information	The 1971 model year marked the last of the major changes to the Muncie 4-speed. The input and output shaft both changed from coarse spline to fine spline. The input shaft identification rings remained the same as 1966–70: two rings. The output shaft now required a yoke similar to the Turbo 400 yoke, although the manual was slightly shorter. The "A" suffix code letter continued to designate a 2.52:1 wide ratio from the plant build date code. All Muncie 4-speeds now had a drain plug

4-Speed Close Ratio Muncie M21

Maincase	Aluminum
Extension Housing	Aluminum
Type	Synchromesh, all forward gears
Gear Ratios	1st: 2.20:1 2nd: 1.64:1 3rd: 1.28:1 4th: Direct Reverse: 2.26:1
Maincase Casting No.	3925661
Extension Housing Casting No.	3978764
Sidecover Casting No.	3952648
Special Information	This transmission had the same spline changes as the previously mentioned M20 gearbox. The input shaft identification rings remained the same: one. The "B" suffix letter code continued to be used to designate a 2.20:1 close ratio. All Muncie 4-speeds now had a drain plug

4-Speed Close Ratio Muncie M22

Maincase	Aluminum
Extension Housing	Aluminum
Type	Synchromesh, all forward gears
Gear Ratios	1st: 2.20:1 2nd: 1.64:1 3rd: 1.28:1 4th: Direct Reverse: 2.26:1
Maincase Casting No.	3925661
Extension Housing Casting No.	3978764
Sidecover Casting No.	3952648
Special Information	The M22 transmission was also changed for 1971. The input and output were changed to fine spline. The M22 continued to carry no identification rings on the input shaft. The "C" suffix letter date code continued to be used. All Muncie 4-speeds now carried a drain plug. M22 production dropped in 1971. The primary difference was 2375 fewer Chevelles ordered with the option. Corvette and Camaro totals actually went up. Production: Corvette 130 Chevelle 3,035 Camaro 1,290 Total: 4,455

2-Speed Powerglide

Maincase	Aluminum
Extension Housing	Aluminum
Application (1)	307
Gear Ratios (1)	Drive Range 1:1 Direct Drive Low Range 1.82:1 Reverse 1.82:1
Application (2)	350
Gear Ratios (2)	Drive Range 1:1 Direct Drive Low Range 1.76:1 Reverse 1.76:1
Maincase Casting No.	Unknown
Extension Housing Casting No.	Unknown
Special Information	Patent numbers cast on the right side of the case are: 2,430,258; 2,762,384; 2,625,056; 2,821,095; 2,633,760; 2,853,167; 2,733,797; 2,865,227; 2,733,798; RE 25,180; 2,740,512; 3,003,368

3-Speed Turbohydramatic 350

Maincase	Aluminum
Extension Housing	Aluminum
Application (1)	307, 327, 350
Gear Ratios (1)	Drive Range: 1:1 Direct Drive Low 2 Range: 1.52:1 Low 1 Range: 2.52:1 Reverse: 1.93:1
Maincase Casting No.	Unknown
Extension Housing Casting No.	Unknown
Special Information	Special Monte Carlo applications. See Fig. 15-25.

3-Speed Turbohydramatic 400

Maincase	Aluminum
Gear Ratios	Drive: 2.48:1, 1. 48:1, 1.00:1 Low 2: 2.48:1 Low 1: 2.48:1 Reverse: 2.08:1
Maincase Casting No.	Unknown
Special Information	The Turbo 400 was a carry-over from the 1970 model year

4. 1972 TRANSMISSIONS

1972 Transmission Applications

Transmission	Model & Engine
3-Speed Saginaw (Low Performance)	Passenger 250* Chevelle 250, 307 Nova 250, 307 Camaro 250, 307
3-Speed Saginaw	Nova 350/165HP Chevelle 350/165, 175HP Camaro 350/165HP** Monte Carlo 350/165HP
3-Speed Heavy Duty Muncie	Chevelle 402/240HP
4-Speed Wide Ratio Saginaw	Nova 350/175HP Chevelle 350/165, 175HP Camaro 350/165HP 350/175HP***
4-Speed Wide Ratio Muncie M20	Corvette 350/200, 255HP 454/270HP Chevelle 402/240HP Camaro 350/175HP**** 350/255HP 402/240HP
4-Speed Close Ratio Muncie M21	Corvette 350/255HP 454/270HP Camaro 350/255HP 402/240HP
4-Speed Close Ratio Muncie M22	Corvette 350/255HP Chevelle 454/270HP Camaro 350/255HP
2-Speed Powerglide	Passenger 250/110HP Nova 250, 307 Chevelle 250, 307 Camaro 250, 307 Monte Carlo 350/165HP
3-Speed Turbohydramatic 350	Passenger 350/165HP 400/170HP Nova 307/130HP 350/165, 175HP Chevelle 307/130HP 350/165, 175HP Camaro 307/130HP 350/165, 175HP Monte Carlo 350/165, 175HP
3-Speed Turbohydramatic 400	Passenger 402/240HP 454/240, 270HP Corvette 350/200HP 454/270HP Chevelle 402/240HP 454/270HP Camaro 350/255HP 402/240HP Monte Carlo 402/240HP 454/270HP
*Offered only until January 1972 **California Only ***The Saginaw 2.54 wide ratio transmission replaced the Muncie 2.52 wide ratio in this application in December 1971 ****The Muncie 2.52 wide ratio was only used until December 1971 in this application	

4.1 Date Code

1972 Assembly Date Code Location (Car)

Transmission	Code Location
3-Speed	Left side of maincase, on boss below and to rear of sidecover
4-Speed (Muncie Cast Iron Case)	Left side of maincase, on boss below and to rear of sidecover
4-Speed (Muncie Aluminum Case)	Right side of maincase, just in front of extension housing
Powerglide	Transmission oil pan, right side
Turbohydramatic 350	Transmission oil pan, right side
Turbohydramatic 375, 400	Identification plate, right side

3-, 4-Speed, Powerglide, Turbohydramatic 350 Example: C 2 E 03

- C: Prefix = Powerglide, Cleveland
- 2: Model Year = 1972
- E: Month = May
- 03: Day = day 3

1972 Transmission Letter Prefix Identification

Prefix	Plant	Transmission and Engine
B	Cleveland	Turbohydramatic 350
C	Cleveland	Powerglide
H	Muncie	3-Speed Chevelle (Heavy Duty)
J	GM Canada	Turbohydramatic 350
M	Muncie	3-Speed (Truck, heavy duty)
N	Muncie	4-Speed (Truck)
P	Muncie	4-Speed (Heavy Duty, Aluminum Case)
R	Muncie	4-Speed (Light Duty, Cast Iron Case)
S	Muncie	3-Speed (Passenger, Truck Light Duty)

NOTE—
Powerglide and Turbohydramatic 350 transmissions built at Cleveland have an additional identification code, stamped on the front pump seal flange. This code was instituted approximately 12/1/68. Example: C9T. C = Cleveland, 9 = model year, T = month (December).

NOTE—
1972 Muncie 3- and 4-Speed car transmissions have a suffix letter added to the date code that further identifies the first gear ratio:
3-Speed: A = 3.03:1, B = 2.42:1
4-Speed: A = 2.52:1 Wide Ratio, B = 2.20:1 Close Ratio, C= 2.20:1 M22.

Assembly Month Code

A - January	E - May	P - September
B - February	H - June	R - October
C - March	K - July	S - November
D - April	M - August	T - December

Turbohydramatic 400 Example: 72 K 372

- 72: Model Year = 1972
- A: Engine identification
  A = 350/165HP, 400/170HP, 402/240HP (Chevrolet)
  D = 402/240HP (Chevelle & Monte Carlo)
  F = 454/270HP (Chevelle & Monte Carlo)
  J = 402/240HP (Truck 10-30 Series)
  K = 350/200HP (Corvette)
  R = 454/240, 270HP (Passenger, Police), 360/165HP (Police), 400/170HP (Police), 402/240HP (Police)
  S = 454/270HP (Corvette)
  Y = 350/255HP (Camaro)
- 372: Assembly date = the assembly date code for the 1972 model year starts with the first day of the calendar year in 1971 and continues through the 1972 calendar year. "372" is January 7, 1972.

4.2 Transmission Specifications

3-Speed Saginaw (Low Performance)

Maincase	Cast Iron
Extension Housing	Cast Iron
Type	Synchromesh, all forward gears
Gear Ratios	1st: 2.85:1 2nd: 1.68:1 3rd: Direct Reverse: 2.95:1
Maincase Casting No.	3925647
Extension Housing Casting No.	3873886
Sidecover Casting No.	3952645
Special Information	None

3-Speed Saginaw

Maincase	Cast Iron
Extension Housing	Cast Iron
Type	Synchromesh, all forward gears
Gear Ratios	1st: 2.54:1 2nd: 1.50:1 3rd: Direct Reverse: 2.63:1
Maincase Casting No.	3925647
Extension Housing Casting No.	3873886
Sidecover Casting No.	3952645
Special Information	None

3-Speed Heavy Duty Muncie (Chevelle Only)

Maincase	Cast Iron
Extension Housing	Cast Iron
Type	Synchromesh, all forward gears
Gear Ratios	1st: 2.42:1 2nd: 1.58:1 3rd: Direct Reverse: 2.41:1
Maincase Casting No.	3911940
Extension Housing Casting No.	3911942
Sidecover Casting No.	3952646
Special Information	This was the last year that this transmission was offered

4-Speed Wide Ratio Saginaw

Maincase	Cast Iron
Extension Housing	Cast Iron
Type	Synchromesh, all forward gears
Gear Ratios	1st: 2.54:1 2nd: 1.80:1 3rd: 1.44:1 4th: Direct Reverse: 2.54:1
Maincase Casting No.	3925656
Extension Housing Casting No.	3873886
Sidecover Casting No.	3952647
Special Information	None

4-Speed Wide Ratio Muncie M20

Maincase	Aluminum
Extension Housing	Aluminum
Type	Synchromesh, all forward gears
Gear Ratios	1st: 2.52:1 2nd: 1.88:1 3rd: 1.46:1 4th: Direct Reverse: 2.59:1
Maincase Casting No.	3925661
Extension Housing Casting No.	3978764
Sidecover Casting No.	3952648
Special Information	This transmission was a direct carry-over from 1971 with no changes

4-Speed Close Ratio Muncie M21

Maincase	Aluminum
Extension Housing	Aluminum
Type	Synchromesh, all forward gears
Gear Ratios	1st: 2.20:1 2nd: 1.64:1 3rd: 1.28:1 4th: Direct Reverse: 2.26:1
Maincase Casting No.	3925661
Extension Housing Casting No.	3978764
Sidecover Casting No.	3952648
Special Information	This transmission was a direct carry-over from 1971 with no changes

4-Speed Close Ratio Muncie M22

Maincase	Aluminum
Extension Housing	Aluminum
Type	Synchromesh, all forward gears
Gear Ratios	1st: 2.20:1 2nd: 1.64:1 3rd: 1.28:1 4th: Direct Reverse: 2.26:1
Maincase Casting No.	3925661
Extension Housing Casting No.	3978764
Sidecover Casting No.	3952648
Special Information	The M22 was only available in three body styles during 1972, and it was the last year the M22 was available as a factory ordered option. The Chevrolet Accumulative Production Report is as follows: Corvette: 20 Chevelle: 1,513 Camaro: 767 Total: 2,300

2-Speed Powerglide Transmission

Maincase	Aluminum
Extension Housing	Aluminum
Application (1)	250, 307
Gear Ratios (1)	Drive Range 1:1 Direct Drive Low Range 1.82:1 Reverse 1.82:1
Application (2)	350
Gear Ratios (2)	Drive Range 1:1 Direct Drive Low Range 1.76:1 Reverse 1.76:1
Maincase Casting No.	Unknown
Extension Housing Casting No.	Unknown
Special Information	None

3-Speed Turbohydramatic 350

Maincase	Aluminum
Extension Housing	Aluminum
Application (1)	230, 250, 307, 327, 350
Gear Ratios (2)	Drive Range: 1:1 Direct Drive Low 2 Range: 1.52:1 Low 1 Range: 2.52:1 Reverse: 1.93:1
Maincase Casting No.	Unknown
Extension Housing Casting No.	Unknown
Special Information	Special Monte Carlo applications. See Fig. 15-25

3-Speed Turbohydramatic 400

Maincase	Aluminum
Extension Housing	Aluminum
Gear Ratios	Drive: 2.48:1, 1. 48:1, 1.00:1 Low 2: 2.48:1 Low 1: 2.48:1 Reverse: 2.08:1
Maincase Casting No.	Unknown
Special Information	The Turbo 400 was a carry-over from 1971

Turbo Hydra-Matic 350 Transmission Identification — 1972 Monte Carlo

Early built 1972 Monte Carlo models equipped with Turbo Hydra-Matic 350 transmissions were assembled with the Chevrolet built THM—350 transmission PN 6261841. After approximately the first six weeks of production, the Buick built transmission assembly PN 6260362 took over all Monte Carlo THM 350 production requirements. The reason for this change-over is the heavy production requirements for Monte Carlo models with this transmission. Transmission assembly 6261841 remains in production for Nova, Camaro and Chevelle models.

The Buick built transmission incorporates different speedometer drive design than those built by Chevrolet, using a larger speedometer driven gear fitting. Also, the speedometer drive and driven gears are not interchangeable between the two designs. Identification of the transmission may be made by observing the speedometer gear area of the transmission extension. The driven gear bore on Buick built transmissions is 2 inches in diameter as compared to 7/8 inch on Chevrolet built transmissions. Speedometer related serviceable parts are as follows:

DESCRIPTION	CHEVROLET	BUICK
Transmission Asm.	6261841	6260362
Extension Asm.	6261369	6260035
Gear, Speedo Drive	6261785 (10T-Purple)	6260037 (18T-Green)
Gear, Speedo Driven	3987918 (A)	1359271 (C)
Gear, Speedo Driven	3987921 (B)	9775187 (D)
Adaptor, Speedo Driven Gear	3932220 (E)	Not Required
Seal, Speedo Driven Gear Fitting	6264903	6264904
Retainer, Speedo Driven Gear Fitting	3708148	1362215
Fitting Asm., Driven Gear	3869912	1362284

A. 18 teeth–color brown–used with 2.73:1 axle
B. 21 teeth–color red–used with 3.31:1 axle
C. 37 teeth–color red–used with 2.73:1 axle
D. 45 teeth–color blue–used with 3.31:1 axle
E. Used with 3.31:1 axle only (trailer option)

NOTE: *The parts described here are of the latest design at the time of publication. An early production transmission may contain a different color gear than listed above, however, only the latest service parts should be installed.*

Fig. 15-25. April 1972 Chevrolet Service News shows special Monte Carlo Turbo 350 applications.

5. 1973 TRANSMISSIONS

1973 Transmission Applications

Transmission	Application
3-Speed Saginaw (Low Performance)	Passenger 250 Chevelle 250, 307* Nova 250, 307 Camaro 250, 307
3-Speed Saginaw	Nova 350/145HP Chevelle 350/145 Camaro 350/145, 175HP Monte Carlo 350/145HP
4-Speed Wide Ratio Saginaw	Nova 350/175HP Chevelle 350/175HP Camaro 350/145, 175HP
4-Speed Wide Ratio Muncie M20	Corvette 350/190, 250HP 454/245HP Camaro 350/245HP
4-Speed Close Ratio Muncie M21	Corvette 350/250HP 454/245HP Chevelle 454/215HP Camaro 350/245HP
3-Speed Turbohydramatic 350	Passenger 350/165, 175HP 400/150HP Nova 307/115HP 350/165, 175HP Chevelle 250/100HP 307/115HP** 350/165, 175HP Camaro 250/100HP 307/115HP 350/165, 175HP Monte Carlo 350/165, 175HP
3-Speed Turbohydramatic 400	Passenger 454/215HP Corvette 350/190, 250HP 454/245HP Chevelle 454/215HP Camaro 350/245HP Monte Carlo 454/215HP
*This 3-speed transmission was the only transmission available in the 307 Chevelle until January, 1973, when the turbo 350 transmission was made available **Turbohydramatic 350 not available in this application until January 1973	

5.1 Date Code

1973 Assembly Date Code Location (Car)

Transmission	Code Location
3-Speed	Left side of maincase, on boss below and to rear of sidecover
4-Speed (Muncie Cast Iron Case)	Left side of maincase, on boss below and to rear of sidecover
4-Speed (Muncie Aluminum Case)	Right side of maincase, just in front of extension housing
Powerglide	Transmission oil pan, right side
Turbohydramatic 350	Transmission oil pan, right side
Turbohydramatic 375, 400	Identification plate, right side

3-, 4-Speed, Powerglide, Turbohydramatic 350 Example: C 3 E 03

- C: Prefix = Powerglide, Cleveland
- 3: Model Year = 1973
- E: Month = May
- 03: Day = day 3

1973 Transmission Letter Prefix Identification

Prefix	Plant	Transmission and Engine
B	Cleveland	Turbohydramatic 350
C	Cleveland	Powerglide (Nova)
J	GM Canada	Turbohydramatic 350
M	Muncie	3-Speed (Truck, heavy duty)
N	Muncie	4-Speed (Truck)
P	Muncie	4-Speed (Heavy Duty, Aluminum Case)
R	Muncie	4-Speed (Light Duty, Saginaw type)
S	Muncie	3-Speed (Passenger, Truck Light Duty, Saginaw Type)
Y	Toledo	Turbohydramatic 350

NOTE—
Powerglide and Turbohydramatic 350 transmissions built at Cleveland have an additional identification code, stamped on the front pump seal flange. This code was instituted approximately 12/1/68. Example: C9T. C = Cleveland, 9 = model year, T = month (December).

NOTE—
1973 Muncie 3- and 4-Speed car transmissions have a suffix letter added to the date code that further identifies the first gear ratio:
3-Speed: A = 3.03:1, B = 2.42:1
4-Speed: A = 2.52:1 Wide Ratio, B = 2.20:1 Close Ratio.

Assembly Month Code

A - January	E - May	P - September
B - February	H - June	R - October
C - March	K - July	S - November
D - April	M - August	T - December

Turbohydramatic 375, 400 Example: 73 A 245

- 73: Model Year = 1973
- A: Engine identification
  A = 350/145, 175HP, 400/150HP 375 (Chevrolet)
  F = 454/215HP 400 (Chevelle & Monte Carlo)
  J = 402/240HP 400 (Truck 10, 20, 30 Series)
  K = 350/190HP 400 (Corvette)
  R = 454/215HP 400
  S = 454/245HP 400 (Corvette)
  Y = 350/245HP 400 (Z28 Camaro)
  Z = 350/250HP 400 (L82 Corvette)
- 245: Assembly date = the assembly date code for the 1973 model year starts with the first day of the calendar year in 1972 and continues through the 1973 calendar year. “245” is December 11, 1972.

NOTE—
1973 Turbohydramatic transmissions also have a transmission model and production sequence number stamped below the build date code. Example: 73CA6997. "C" stands for Chevrolet, "A" for engine application. The last four digits are the sequence number.

5.2 Transmission Specifications

3-Speed Saginaw (Low Performance)

Maincase	Cast Iron
Extension Housing	Cast Iron
Type	Synchromesh, all forward gears
Gear Ratios	1st: 2.85:1 2nd: 1.68:1 3rd: Direct Reverse: 2.95:1
Maincase Casting No.	3925647
Extension Housing Casting No.	326558
Sidecover Casting No.	3952645
Special Information	New extension housing casting number

3-Speed Saginaw

Maincase	Cast Iron
Extension Housing	Cast Iron
Type	Synchromesh, all forward gears
Gear Ratios	1st: 2.54:1 2nd: 1.50:1 3rd: Direct Reverse: 2.63:1
Maincase Casting No.	3925647
Extension Housing Casting No.	326558
Sidecover Casting No.	3952645
Special Information	New extension housing casting number

4-Speed Wide Ratio Saginaw

Maincase	Cast Iron
Extension Housing	Cast Iron
Type	Synchromesh, all forward gears
Gear Ratios	1st: 2.54:1 2nd: 1.80:1 3rd: 1.44:1 4th: Direct Reverse: 2.54:1
Maincase Casting No.	3925656
Extension Housing Casting No.	326558
Sidecover Casting No.	3952647

continued

Special Information	A 1973 interim production change revised all Saginaw 4-speed 1st, 2nd and Reverse shifter shaft assemblies in the interlock area. The shifter shaft fork lever material was changed from malleable to sintered iron. See Fig. 15-26

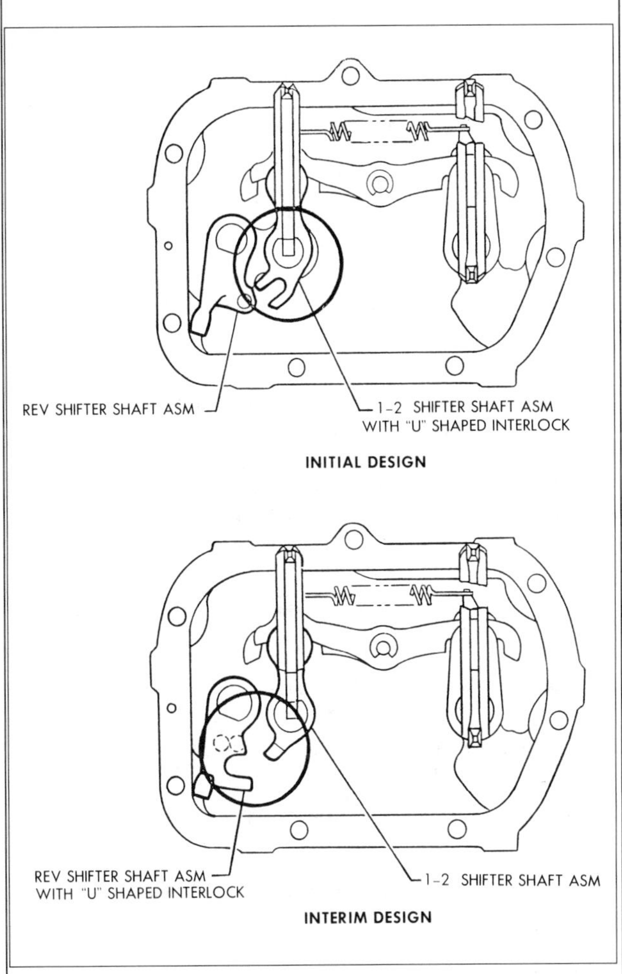

Fig. 15-26. Initial and interim design 1973 Saginaw-type 4-speed shifter shafts.

4-Speed Wide Ratio Muncie M20

Maincase	Aluminum
Extension Housing	Aluminum
Type	Synchromesh, all forward gears
Gear Ratios	1st: 2.52:1 2nd: 1.88:1 3rd: 1.46:1 4th: Direct Reverse: 2.59:1
Maincase Casting No.	3925661
Extension Housing Casting No.	3978764
Sidecover Casting No.	3952648
Special Information	This transmission was a direct carry-over from 1972

4-Speed Close Ratio Muncie M21

Maincase	Aluminum
Extension Housing	Aluminum
Type	Synchromesh, all forward gears
Gear Ratios	1st: 2.20:1 2nd: 1.64:1 3rd: 1.28:1 4th: Direct Reverse: 2.26:1
Maincase Casting No.	3925661
Extension Housing Casting No.	3978764
Sidecover Casting No.	3952648
Special Information	This transmission was a direct carry-over from 1972

3-Speed Turbohydramatic 350

Maincase	Aluminum
Extension Housing	Aluminum
Gear Ratios	Drive Range: 1:1 Direct Drive Low 2 Range: 1.52:1 Low 1 Range: 2.52:1 Reverse: 1.93:1
Maincase Casting No.	Unknown
Extension Housing Casting No.	Unknown
Special Information	This transmission had only one change from the 1972 Turbo 350 transmission: the torque converter stall ratio was changed from 2.10 to 2.00.

3-Speed Turbohydramatic 400

Maincase	Aluminum
Extension Housing	Aluminum
Gear Ratios	Drive: 2.48:1, 1. 48:1, 1.00:1 Low 2: 2.48:1 Low 1: 2.48:1 Reverse: 2.08:1
Maincase Casting No.	Unknown
Special Information	The Turbo 400 was a carry-over from 1972

6. 1974 TRANSMISSIONS

1974 Transmission Applications

Transmission	Application
3-Speed Saginaw (Low Performance)	Nova 250/100HP 350/145, 160HP Chevelle 250/100HP Camaro 250/100HP
3-Speed Saginaw	Chevelle 350/145, 160HP Camaro 350/145, 160, 185HP Monte Carlo 350/145, 160HP
4-Speed Wide Ratio Saginaw	Nova 350/185HP Camaro 350/145, 160, 185HP
4-Speed Wide Ratio Muncie* M20	Corvette 350/195, 250HP 454/270HP Camaro Z28 350/245HP
4-Speed Wide Ratio Warner**	Corvette 350/195, 250HP Camaro Z28 350/245HP
4-Speed Close Ratio Muncie* M21**	Corvette 350/250HP 454/270HP Chevelle 454/235HP Camaro Z28 350/245HP
4-Speed Close Ratio Warner	Corvette 350/250HP 454/270 Camaro Z28 350/245HP
3-Speed Turbohydramatic 350	Passenger 350/145, 160HP 400/150, 180HP Nova 250/100HP 350/145, 160, 185HP Chevelle 250/100HP 350/145, 160HP 400/150, 180HP Camaro 250/100HP 350/145, 160, 185HP Monte Carlo 350/145, 160HP 400/150, 180HP
3-Speed Turbohydramatic 400	Passenger 454/235HP Corvette 350/195, 250HP 454/270HP Chevelle 454/235HP Camaro Z28 350/245HP Monte Carlo 454/235HP
*This transmission was only used in these vehicles until January 1974, when the Warner 4-speed replaced the Muncie **The Warner 4-speed was instituted into production in January 1974, to replace the Muncie 4-speed. The Warner 2.43 gearbox was only available on the Corvette 454/270HP after January 1974 ***This transmission was only used in these vehicles until January 1974, when the Warner 4-speed replaced the Muncie. The Chevelle 454/235HP application used the Muncie the complete 1974 model year	

NOTE—
The Muncie/Warner changeover was officially to take place in January. Due to production run-outs, this may not have happened on some applications until April or May.

NOTE—
All 1974 transmissions originally installed in vehicles have a portion of the Vehicle Identification Number (VIN) stamped on them. The location is usually near the date code or, on some automatic transmissions, on the bellhousing. Example: 14T00025. See Chapter 1 for more information on decoding VINs.

6.1 Date Code

1974 Assembly Date Code Location (Car)

Transmission	Code Location
3-Speed	Left side of maincase, on boss below and to rear of sidecover
4-Speed (Saginaw Cast Iron Case)	Left side of maincase, on boss below and to rear of sidecover
4-Speed (Muncie Aluminum Case)	Right side of maincase, just in front of extension housing
4-Speed (Warner)	Left side of maincase, top rear
Turbohydramatic 350 (Except Monte Carlo)	Transmission oil pan, right side
Turbohydramatic 350 (Monte Carlo*)	Transmission governor cover
Turbohydramatic 375, 400	Identification plate, right side
*Supplied by Buick Motor Division;	

1974 Transmission Letter Prefix Identification

Prefix	Plant	Transmission and Engine
B	Cleveland*	Turbohydramatic 350
J	GM Canada	Turbohydramatic 350
P	Muncie	4-Speed (Heavy Duty, Aluminum Case)
R	Muncie	4-Speed (Light Duty, Saginaw type)
S	Muncie	3-Speed (Passenger, Truck Light Duty, Saginaw Type)
W	Warner	4-Speed (Heavy Duty, Aluminum Case)
Y	Toledo	Turbohydramatic 350
JA / JH	Buick Division	Turbohydramatic 350 (Monte Carlo)
*Cleveland plant renamed as Parma		

3-, 4-Speed (Muncie)
Example: P 4 H 03

- P: Prefix = 4-Speed, Muncie
- 4: Model Year = 1974
- H: Month = June
- 03: Day = day 3

NOTE—
1974 Muncie 3- and 4-Speed car transmissions have a suffix letter added to the date code that further identifies the first gear ratio:
3-Speed: A = 3.03:1, B = 2.42:1
4-Speed: A = 2.52:1 Wide Ratio, B = 2.20:1 Close Ratio.

4-Speed (Warner)
Example: W A 2041

- W: Source = Warner
- A: Month = January
- 20: Day = day 20
- 4: Year = 1974
- 1: Shift = 1st shift

NOTE—
All Warner transmissions have an additional 2-digit code painted on the maincase, below the sidecover, to identify the first gear ratio: HS = 2.64:1, HW = 2.43:1.

Turbohydramatic 350 (All except Monte Carlo)
Example: B 4 A 10D

- B: Source = Cleveland
- 4: Model Year = 1974
- A: Month = January
- 10: Day = day 10
- D: Shift = Day shift

Turbohydramatic 350 (Monte Carlo)
Example: JA 001 D 74

- JA: Source = Buick
- 001: Production day = first day of year
- D: Shift = Day shift
- 74: Year = 1974

Assembly Month Code (All except Warner)

A - January	E - May	P - September
B - February	H - June	R - October
C - March	K - July	S - November
D - April	M - August	T - December

Assembly Month Code (Warner)

A - January	E - May	J - September
B - February	F - June	K - October
C - March	G - July	L - November
D - April	H - August	M - December

Turbohydramatic 375, 400 Example: 74 A 234

- 74: Model Year = 1974
- A: Engine identification
  A = 350/160HP (LM1), 400/150HP (LF6) 375 (Chevrolet)

continued on next page

B = 400/180HP (LT4) 400 (Chevrolet)
F = 454/235HP (LS4) 400 (Chevelle & Monte Carlo)
K = 350/195HP (L48) 400 (Corvette)
R = 454/235HP (LS4) 400 (Chevrolet)
S = 454/270HP (LS4) 400 (Corvette)
Y = 350/245HP 400 (Z28 Camaro)
Z = 350/250HP 400 (L82 Corvette)

- 234: Assembly date = the assembly date code for the 1974 model year starts with the first day of the calendar year in 1973 and continues through the 1974 calendar year. "234" is August 22, 1973.

NOTE—
1974 Turbohydramatic transmissions also have a transmission model and production sequence number stamped below the build date code. Example: 74CA6997. "C" stands for Chevrolet, "A" for engine application. The last four digits are the sequence number.

6.2 Transmission Specifications

3-Speed Saginaw (Low Performance)

Maincase	Cast Iron
Extension Housing	Cast Iron
Type	Synchromesh, all forward gears
Gear Ratios	1st: 2.85:1 2nd: 1.68:1 3rd: Direct ; Reverse: 2.95:1
Maincase Casting No.	3925647
Extension Housing Casting No.	326558
Sidecover Casting No.	3952645
Special Information	None

3-Speed Saginaw

Maincase	Cast Iron
Extension Housing	Cast Iron
Type	Synchromesh, all forward gears
Gear Ratios	1st: 2.54:1 2nd: 1.50:1 3rd: Direct ; Reverse: 2.63:1
Maincase Casting No.	3925647
Extension Housing Casting No.	326558
Sidecover Casting No.	3952645
Special Information	None

4-Speed Wide Ratio Saginaw

Maincase	Cast Iron
Extension Housing	Cast Iron
Type	Synchromesh, all forward gears
Gear Ratios	1st: 2.54:1 2nd: 1.80:1 3rd: 1.44:1 4th: Direct ; Reverse: 2.54:1
Maincase Casting No.	3925656
Extension Housing Casting No.	326558
Sidecover Casting No.	3952647
Special Information	None

4-Speed Wide Ratio Muncie M20

Maincase	Aluminum
Extension Housing	Aluminum
Type	Synchromesh, all forward gears
Gear Ratios	1st: 2.52:1 2nd: 1.88:1 3rd: 1.46:1 4th: Direct ; Reverse: 2.59:1
Maincase Casting No.	3925661
Extension Housing Casting No.	3978764
Sidecover Casting No.	3952648
Special Information	This transmission was a direct carry-over from 1973 with no changes.

4-Speed Wide Ratio Warner

Maincase	Aluminum
Extension Housing	Aluminum
Type	Synchromesh, all forward gears
Gear Ratios	1st: 2.64:1 2nd: 1.75:1 3rd: 1.33:1 4th: Direct ; Reverse: 2.55:1
Maincase Casting No.	1304 065 903
Extension Housing Casting No.	13.04.066.901
Sidecover Casting No.	13-04-097-901
Special Information	This transmission was brought into production in January 1974 in the Corvette and Camaro. This transmission is notable in that the gear ratio spread is much more advantageous to lower elapsed times

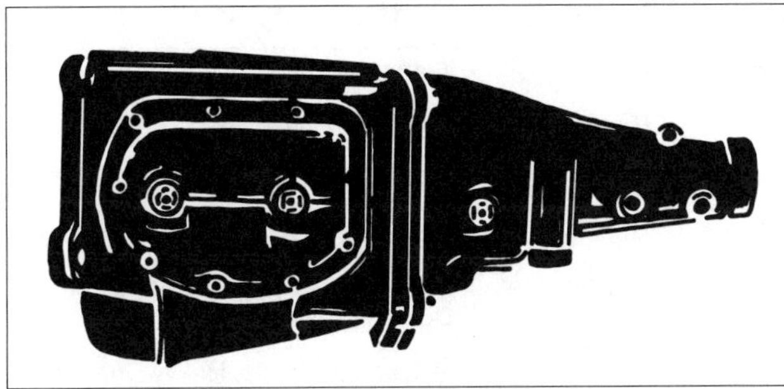

Fig. 15-27. 1974 and later Borg-Warner T-10 transmission. Note sidecover, with 9 securing bolts and curved bottom.

4-Speed Close Ratio Muncie M21

Maincase	Aluminum
Extension Housing	Aluminum
Type	Synchromesh, all forward gears
Gear Ratios	1st: 2.20:1 2nd: 1.64:1 3rd: 1.28:1 4th: Direct ; Reverse: 2.26:1
Maincase Casting No.	3925661
Extension Housing Casting No.	3978764
Sidecover Casting No.	3952648
Special Information	This was a carry-over from 1973

4-Speed Close Ratio Warner

Maincase	Aluminum
Extension Housing	Aluminum
Type	Synchromesh, all forward gears
Gear Ratios	1st: 2.43:1 2nd: 1.61:1 3rd: 1.23:1 4th: Direct ; Reverse: 2.35:1
Maincase Casting No.	1304 065 903
Extension Housing Casting No.	13.04.066.901
Sidecover Casting No.	13-04-097-901
Special Information	This transmission was new for 1974 (mid-year). It replaced the aging Muncie 4-speed, which had changed very little since 1963. The Chevelle 454/235HP *did not* use this transmission in 1974. It is not clear why

3-Speed Turbohydramatic 350

Maincase	Aluminum
Extension Housing	Aluminum
Gear Ratios	Drive Range: 1:1 Direct Drive Low 2 Range: 1.52:1 Low 1 Range: 2.52:1 ; Reverse: 1.93:1
Maincase Casting No.	Unknown
Extension Housing Casting No.	Unknown
Special Information	This was a direct carry-over from 1973

3-Speed Turbohydramatic 400

Maincase	Aluminum
Extension Housing	Aluminum
Gear Ratios	Drive: 2.48:1, 1. 48:1, 1.00:1 Low 2: 2.48:1 Low 1: 2.48:1 ; Reverse: 2.08:1
Maincase Casting No.	Unknown
Special Information	This was a carry-over from 1973

7. 1975 TRANSMISSIONS

1975 Transmission Applications

Transmission	Application
3-Speed Saginaw (Low Performance)	Nova 250/105HP* 262/110HP Chevelle 250/105HP* Camaro 250/105HP*
3-Speed Saginaw	Nova 350/145HP* Chevelle 350/145HP* 350/155HP**@ Camaro 350/145HP* 350/155HP**$ Monte Carlo 350/145HP*@ 350/155HP** Monza 140/87HP, 262/110HP
4-Speed Wide Ratio (Saginaw)	Nova 350/155HP* Camaro 350/155HP*
4-Speed Wide Ratio (Warner)	Corvette 350/165HP 350/205HP
4-Speed Close Ratio (Warner)	Corvette 350/205HP
3-Speed Turbohydramatic 350	Passenger 350/145HP* 350/155HP** Nova 250/105HP 262/110HP* 350/145HP* 350/155HP Chevelle 250/110HP 350/145HP* 350/155HP** 400/175HP Camaro 250/105HP 350/145HP* 350/155HP** Monte Carlo 350/145HP* 350/155HP** 400/175HP Monza 140/87HP, 262/110HP
3-Speed Turbohydramatic 400	Passenger 400/175HP^ 454/215HP Corvette 350/165, 205HP Chevelle 454/215HP Monte Carlo 454/215HP
^This is considered a 375 transmission *Not available in California **California Only @Powerteam available only until March 1975 $Powerteam available only after March 1975	

NOTE—
All 1975 transmissions have a portion of the Vehicle Identification Number (VIN) stamped on them. The location is usually near the date code or, on some automatic transmissions, on the bellhousing. Example: 15J100025. See Chapter 1 for more information on decoding VINs.

7.1 Date Code

1975 Assembly Date Code Location (Car)

Transmission	Code Location
3-Speed	Left side of maincase, on boss below and to rear of sidecover
4-Speed (Saginaw Cast Iron Case)	Left side of maincase, on boss below and to rear of sidecover
4-Speed (Warner)	Left side of maincase, top rear
Turbohydramatic 350 (Except Monte Carlo)	Transmission oil pan, right side
Turbohydramatic 350 (Monte Carlo*)	Transmission governor cover
Turbohydramatic 375, 400	Identification plate, right side
*Supplied by Buick Motor Division	

1975 Transmission Letter Prefix Identification

Prefix	Plant	Transmission and Engine
B	Parma	Turbohydramatic 350
J	GM Canada	Turbohydramatic 350
R	Muncie	4-Speed (Light Duty, Saginaw type)
S	Muncie	3-Speed (Passenger, Truck Light Duty, Saginaw Type)
W	Warner	4-Speed (Corvette, Heavy Duty, Aluminum Case)
Y	Toledo	Turbohydramatic 350

3-, 4-Speed (Muncie)
Example: S 5 R 03

- S: Prefix = 3-Speed, Muncie
- 5: Model Year = 1975
- R: Month = October
- 03: Day = day 3

4-Speed (Warner)
Example: W A 2051

- W: Source = Warner
- A: Month = January
- 20: Day = day 20
- 5: Year = 1975
- 1: Shift = 1st shift

NOTE—
All Warner transmissions have an additional 2-digit code painted on the maincase, below the sidecover, to identify the first gear ratio: HS = 2.64:1, HW = 2.43:1.

Turbohydramatic 350
Example: Y 5 A 10N

- Y: Source = Toledo
- 5: Model Year = 1975
- A: Month = January
- 10: Day = day 10
- N: Shift = Night shift

Assembly Month Code (All except Warner)

A - January	E - May	P - September
B - February	H - June	R - October
C - March	K - July	S - November
D - April	M - August	T - December

Assembly Month Code (Warner)

A - January	E - May	J - September
B - February	F - June	K - October
C - March	G - July	L - November
D - April	H - August	M - December

Turbohydramatic 375, 400 Example: 75 A 234

- 75: Model Year = 1975
- A: Engine identification
  A = 400/175HP 375 (Chevrolet)
  B = 400/175HP 400 (Chevrolet)
  D = 454/215HP 400 (Chevelle & Monte Carlo)
  F = 454/215HP 400 (Chevelle & Monte Carlo)
  K = 350/165HP 400 (Corvette)
  R = 454/215HP 400 (Chevrolet)
  Z = 350/205HP 400 (Corvette)
- 234: Assembly date = the assembly date code for the 1975 model year starts with the first day of the calendar year in 1974 and continues through the 1975 calendar year. "234" is August 22, 1974.

NOTE—
1975 Turbohydramatic transmissions also have a transmission model and production sequence number stamped below the build date code. Example: 74CA6997. "C" stands for Chevrolet, "A" for engine application. The last four digits are the sequence number.

7.2 Transmission Specifications

3-Speed (Low Performance)

Maincase	Cast Iron
Extension Housing	Cast Iron
Type	Synchromesh, all forward gears
Gear Ratios	1st: 3.11:1 2nd 1.84:1 3rd: Direct Reverse: 3.22:1
Maincase Casting No.	3925647
Extension Housing Casting No.	326558
Sidecover Casting No.	3952645
Special Information	This transmission was brand new for 1975. It was only used behind the 250/105HP and the 262/110HP engines

3-Speed (Low Performance)

Maincase	Cast Iron
Extension Housing	Cast Iron
Type	Synchromesh, all forward gears
Gear Ratios	1st: 2.85:1 2nd: 1.68:1 3rd: Direct Reverse: 2.95:1
Maincase Casting No.	3925647
Extension Housing Casting No.	326558
Sidecover Casting No.	3952645
Special Information	None

4-Speed Wide Ratio Saginaw

Maincase	Cast Iron
Extension Housing	Cast Iron
Type	Synchromesh, all forward gears
Gear Ratios	1st: 2.54:1 2nd: 1.80:1 3rd: 1.44:1 4th: Direct Reverse: 2.54:1
Maincase Casting No.	3925656
Extension Housing Casting No.	326558
Sidecover Casting No.	3952647
Special Information	None

4-Speed Wide Ratio Warner

Maincase	Aluminum
Extension Housing	Aluminum
Type	Synchromesh, all forward gears
Gear Ratios	1st: 2.64:1 2nd: 1.75:1 3rd: 1.33:1 4th: Direct Reverse: 2.55:1
Maincase Casting No.	1304 065 903
Extension Housing Casting No.	13.04.066.901
Sidecover Casting No.	13-04-097-901
Special Information	This transmission was a carry-over from the late 1974 Warner. It was only used in the Corvette application because the Z28 Camaro was no longer available

CHAPTER 15

4-Speed Close Ratio Warner

Maincase	Aluminum
Extension Housing	Aluminum
Type	Synchromesh, all forward gears
Gear Ratios	1st: 2.43:1 2nd: 1.61:1 3rd: 1.23:1 4th: Direct Reverse: 2.35:1
Maincase Casting No.	1304 065 903
Extension Housing Casting No.	13.04.066.901
Sidecover Casting No.	13-04-097-901
Special Information	This transmission was a carry-over from the late 1974 Warner. It was only used in the Corvette application because the Z28 Camaro was no longer available

3-Speed Turbohydramatic 350

Maincase	Aluminum
Extension Housing	Aluminum
Gear Ratios	Drive Range: 1:1 Direct Drive Low 2 Range: 1.52:1 Low 1 Range: 2.52:1 Reverse: 1.93:1
Maincase Casting No.	Unknown
Extension Housing Casting No.	Unknown
Special Information	This was a direct carry-over from 1974

3-Speed Turbohydramatic 400

Maincase	Aluminum
Extension Housing	Aluminum
Gear Ratios	Drive: 2.48:1, 1. 48:1, 1.00:1 Low 2: 2.48:1 Low 1: 2.48:1 Reverse: 2.08:1
Maincase Casting No.	Unknown
Special Information	This was a carry-over from 1974

8. TRANSMISSION DATA CHARTS

Saginaw 3-Speed Component Casting Numbers

Year	Application	Maincase Casting #	Extension Housing Casting #	Sidecover Casting #	Front Bearing Retainer Casting #
1970	Passenger Corvette Nova Chevelle Camaro Monte Carlo	3925647	3860042 3860042 3860042 3860042 3873886 3873886	3952645	3859033
1971	Passenger Nova Chevelle Camaro Monte Carlo	3925647	3873886 Except wagon 3993045 Wagon 3873886	3952645	3859033
1972	Passenger Nova Chevelle Camaro Monte Carlo	3925647	3873886	3952645	3859033
1973	Passenger Nova Chevelle Camaro Monte Carlo	3925647	326558	3952645	3859033
1974	Nova Chevelle Camaro Monte Carlo	3925647	326558	3952645	3859033
1975	Nova Chevelle Camaro Monte Carlo	3925647	326558	3952645	3859033

Muncie Heavy Duty 3-Speed Component Casting Numbers

Year	Application	Maincase Casting #	Extension Housing Casting #	Sidecover Casting #	Front Bearing Retainer Casting #
1970 (late 1969)	Camaro	3911940	3911942	3911947	3911977
1971	Chevelle	3911940	3911942	3952646	3911977
1972	Chevelle	3911940	3911942	3952646	3911977

Saginaw 4-Speed (Cast Iron) Component Casting Numbers

Year	Application	Maincase Casting #	Extension Housing Casting #	Sidecover Casting #	Front Bearing Retainer Casting #
1970	Nova, Chevelle, Monte Carlo Camaro	3925656 3925656	3860042 3873886	3952647 3952647	3859033 3859033
1971	Chevelle Camaro	3925656	3873886	3952647	3859033
1972	Nova Chevelle Camaro	3925656	3873886	3952647	3859033
1973	Nova Chevelle Camaro	3925656	326558	3952647	3859033
1974	Nova Camaro	3925656	326558	3952647	3859033
1975	Nova Camaro	3925656	326558	3952647	3859033

Muncie 4-Speed Specifications

Type	RPO	Model Year	Gear Ratios				Input Splines		Output Spline Teeth	Count-ershaft pin dia.	Main Drive Teeth	Synch. Hub Width	Synch. Ring Shldr.	Cluster Gear Teeth	Helix Gear Angle
			1st	2nd	3rd	4th	Teeth	Grooves							
Wide ratio	M20	1963–65	2.56	1.91	1.48	1.00	10	None	27	7/8	24	Wide	No	29	39
		1966–70	2.52	1.88	1.46	1.00	10	2	27	1	21	Narrow	Yes	25	39
		1971–74	2.52	1.88	1.46	1.00	26	2	32	1	21	Narrow	Yes	25	39
Close ratio	M20	1963–65	2.20	1.64	1.28	1.00	10	1	27	7/8	26	Wide	No	27	39
	M21	1966–70	2.20	1.64	1.28	1.00	10	1	27	1	26	Narrow	Yes	27	39
		1971–74	2.20	1.64	1.28	1.00	26	1	32	1	26	Narrow	Yes	27	39
	M22	1965–70*	2.20	1.64	1.28	1.00	10	None	27	1	26	Narrow	Yes	27	21
		1970**	2.20	1.64	1.28	1.00	26	None	32	1	26	Narrow	Yes	27	21
		1971–72***	2.20	1.64	1.28	1.00	26	None	32	1	26	Narrow	Yes	27	21

*All M22 applications except 454 Chevelle. **454 Chevelle applications. ***M22 transmissions were produced in 1973 and 1974 for other GM divisions and Chevrolet service applications only.

Please note that the RPO column in the Muncie 4-speed specifications chart designates how the transmission option was ordered. All Muncie wide ratio transmissions are considered M20s. All close ratio Muncies are considered either M21 or M22, depending on the gearset installed. Note that in 1963–65, the close ratio M21 had to be ordered under the RPO M20, with the factory deciding whether you received and M20 or M21 gearbox on the rear axle ratio specified. In 1966, the customer could designate transmission choice.

Muncie 4-Speed (Aluminum) Component Casting Numbers

Year	Application	Maincase Casting #	Extension Housing Casting #	Sidecover Casting #	Front Bearing Retainer Casting #
1970	Corvette, Nova, Chevelle, Camaro, Monte Carlo	3925661	3857584 (All except A-Body M22) 3978764 (A-Body M22)	3952648	3915020
1971	Corvette, Nova, Chevelle, Camaro, Monte Carlo	3925661	3978764	3952648	3915020
1972	Corvette, Nova, Chevelle, Camaro	3925661	3978764	3952648	3915020
1973	Corvette, Chevelle, Camaro	3925661	3978764	3952648	3915020
1974	Corvette, Camaro	3925661	3978764	3952648	3915020

Borg-Warner 4-Speed Component Casting Numbers

Year	Application	Maincase Casting #	Extension Housing Casting #	Sidecover Casting #	Front Bearing Retainer Casting #
1974	Corvette, Camaro	1304 065 903	13.04.066.901	13-04-097-901	T89C-6A
1975	Corvette	1304 065 903	13.04.066.901	13-04-097-901	T89C-6A

Manual Transmission Dimensions*

Dimension / Transmission	Saginaw/Muncie 3-Speed	Saginaw 4-Speed	Muncie 4-Speed (M20/21 1970)	Muncie 4-Speed (M20/21, M22)	Borg-Warner Super T-10 4-Speed
Front of input shaft to front of transmission case **(A)**	6-1/2	6-1/2	6-1/2	6-1/2	6-1/2
Front of transmission case to mount location **(B)**	14	14	14	14	14
Overall length **(C)**	21-1/2	21-1/2	21-1/2	22-1/4	22-1/4
End of transmission case to end of output spline **(D)**	1/2	1/2	1/2	1/2	1/2
Transmission Mount Bolt Spacing	3-3/4	3-3/4	3-3/4	3-3/4	3-3/4
Spline Count: Input Shaft/Output Shaft	10/27	10/27	10/27	26/32	26/32

*Dimensions in inches; some converted from metric system

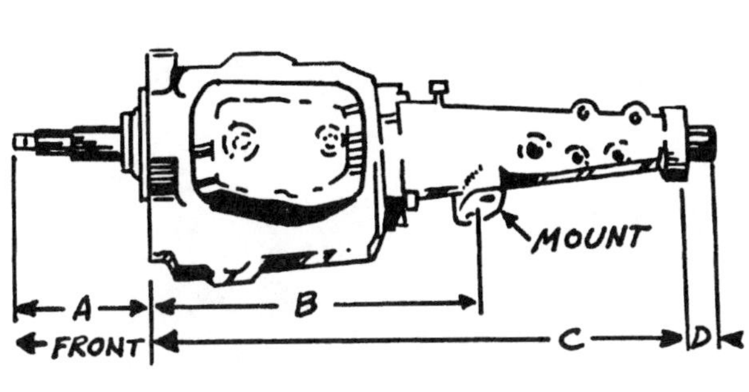

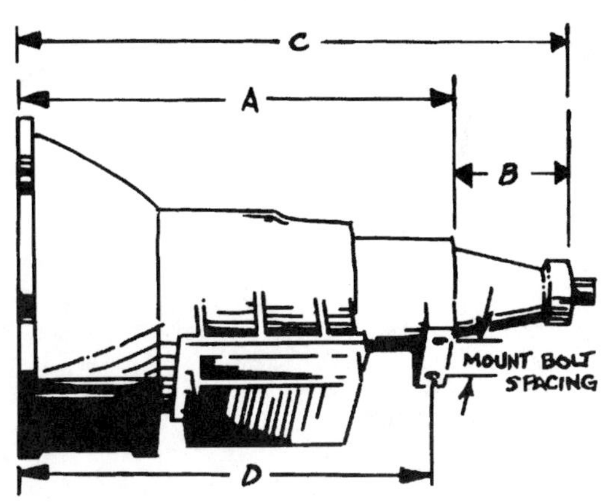

Automatic Transmission Dimensions***

Transmission	Case-to-Block Mounting Pattern	Case Length (A)	Tailshaft Length (B)	Overall Length (C)	Mount Location (D)	# Of Splines On Output Shaft	Mount Bolt Spacing
Powerglide (Cast Iron)	Chevrolet	22	5 or 7-1/4	27 or 29-1/4	Varies	16	3-3/4
Powerglide (Aluminum)	Chevrolet	16	9 or 11-1/4	27-1/4	21-1/4	27	3-3/4
TH-350*	Chevrolet B-O-P Composite	21-1/4	4 9-1/2 13-1/2	A+B	End Of Case minus 1-1/2	27	3-3/4
TH-400**	Chevrolet BOP	21-1/4	4 9-1/2 13-1/2	A+B	End Of Case minus 1-1/2	27/32	3-3/4 or 4-1/4

*Turbohydramatic 350 transmissions came with either a Chevrolet or BOP (Buick-Oldsmobile-Pontiac) bolt pattern. Some late model transmissions have a composite pattern which contains both Chevrolet and BOP bolt patterns
**Turbohydramatic 400 transmissions came in a variety of bolt patterns including Cadillac
***All dimensions in inches. Late model dimensions converted from the metric system

Chapter 16
Rear Axle/Differential Identification

1. Introduction

This chapter will focus on the different types of Chevrolet rear axle designs and differentials (together called the "rear end") used in the years from 1970 through 1975. All rear end s are grouped under model headings: Passenger, Corvette, Chevy II/Nova, Chevelle/Monte Carlo, and Camaro.

Most rear ends were built in both 10-bolt and 12-bolt versions. The bolt designation refers to the number of bolts that secure the differential ring gear to the carrier. Purely by coincidence, the same number of bolts are used to retain the rear inspection cover, which makes for easy identification.

1.1 Passenger Rear Ends

1970 Passenger

This Salisbury-type rear end was introduced as a new design for the 1965 Passenger model line, although a similar design was released on 1964 Chevelles and Chevy IIs. This rear end is a link suspension.

Two- and four-door sedans with the base 350, and two- and four-door hardtops with the base 350 and manual transmission, received a 3-link suspension with one upper control arm. Of these, those with a 3.36:1 or 2.56:1 axle ratio have provision for mounting a second upper control arm. All other engine/transmission/model combinations received a 4-link suspension. See Fig. 16-1. This has been verified through *Chevrolet Service News*, June 1970.

In all cases the upper control arm links are connected to the rear axle via upright steel brackets welded to the axle tube. The axle tubes are pressed and welded into the cast differential carrier housing. The differential is a two-pinion type. The axle shafts are forged and heat-treated steel with the wheel drive flange forged integral with the axle. This rear end was built in both 10-bolt and 12-bolt versions.

Spring mounting varied by model. On all except 116" wheelbase wagons, the springs are mounted between the frame and the lower control arm (Fig. 16-1). On 116" wheelbase wagons, which used the Chevelle/Monte Carlo rear suspension, the springs are mounted between the frame and brackets welded to the axle tubes. (See later Fig. 16-6.)

The specifications for the 1970 rear end are as follows:

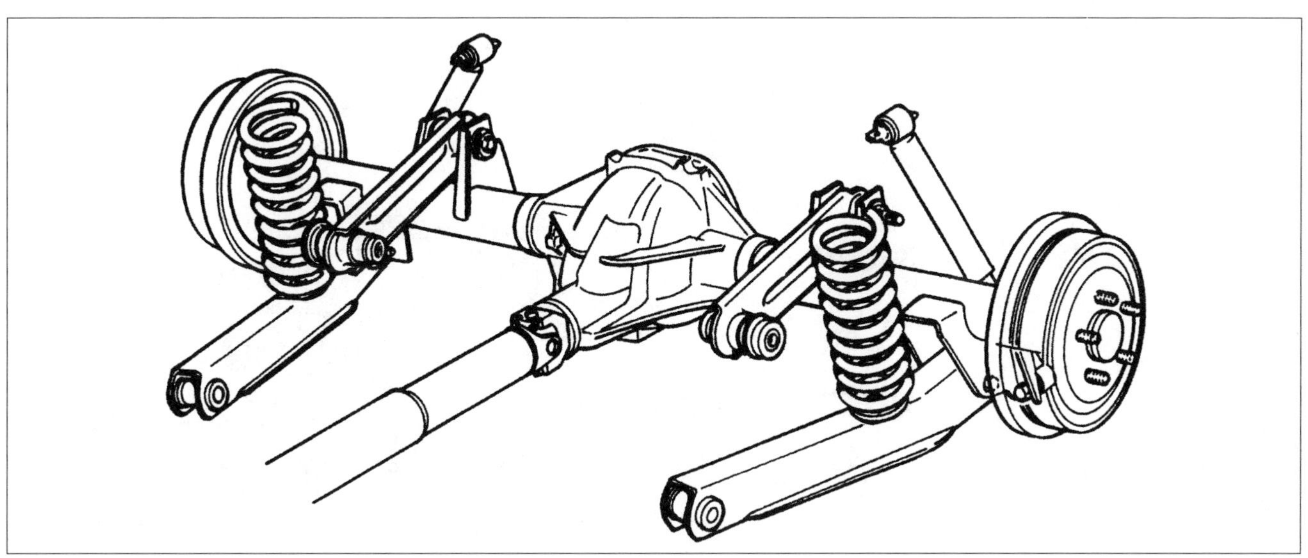

Fig. 16-1. *Passenger 4-link rear end for all except 116" wheelbase station wagons.*

Passenger, 1970*

	10-Bolt	12-Bolt
Bolt Diameter (in.)	3/8	3/8
Ring Gear Diameter (in.)	8.20	8.875
Pinion Diameter (in.)	1.438	1.625
Axle Splines	28	30
Overall Dimensions:		
Axle tube flange to axle tube flange	58 1/4	58 1/4
Between centerlines of control arm brackets	43 1/8	43 1/8
Axle shaft length	31 15/32	31 15/32
This axle was also used in some 1965 through 1969 models *For 116" wheelbase wagons, see the Chevelle specifications		

1971 Through 1975 Passenger

This rear end was a new design for 1971 Passenger cars. With this design, General Motors started to institute a standardized "corporate" rear axle (it also appeared in 1971 on Camaro models). This rear end continues the Salisbury axle design with either a 3- or 4-link suspension. On most sedans and coupes, the two upper control arms are bias mounted and the two lower control arms are parallel mounted.

Spring installation varies by model. On all except 125" wheelbase station wagons, coil springs are positioned between the frame and the axle tube. See Fig. 16-2. On 125" wheelbase station wagons, six multiple leaf springs are used. This is the first time a different axle design was used just for the Passenger station wagon model.

Both axles have a cast differential carrier housing with the axle tubes pressed and welded into the center section. Non-wagon models have "ears" cast into the carrier housing for the upper control arms. Wagon models do not have the "ears." The differential is a two-pinion design. The axle shafts are forged and heat-treated steel with the wheel drive flange forged integral with the axle.

This rear end was built in both 10-bolt and 12-bolt versions. All Passenger cars except the 125-in. wheelbase station wagons received the 8.50" ring gear/10-bolt rear end, built by either Buick, Oldsmobile, Chevrolet or GM of Canada. The 125-in. wheelbase station wagon used the 8.875" ring gear/12 bolt rear end built by either Pontiac or GM of Canada. The 12-bolt was available as an option in the sedan, coupe and convertible models with the 454 engine during the 1975 model year.

Rear ends built by Buick and Oldsmobile are identical. These rear ends have wheel bearings pressed *onto* the axle shafts and the axle shafts are retained by a retaining plate. All other rear ends have wheel bearings

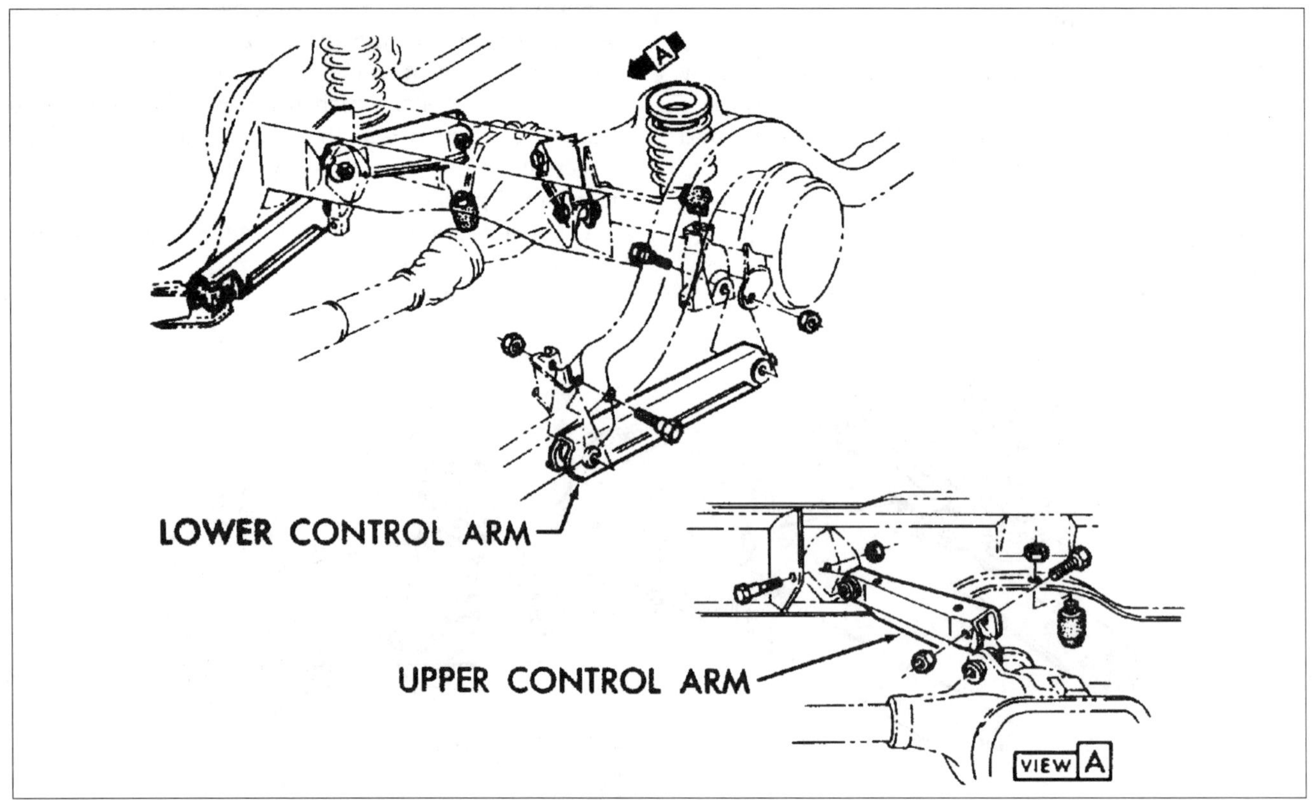

Fig. 16-2. 1971 and later Passenger rear suspension attachment (excluding station wagons).

pressed *into* the axle tube and the axle shafts are retained with a C-clip design.

The specifications for the 10- and 12-bolt rear axles are as follows:

Passenger, 1971–75

	10-Bolt	12-Bolt
Bolt Diameter (in.)	7/16 LH	7/16 LH
Ring Gear Diameter (in.)	8.50	8.875
Pinion Diameter (in.)	1.625	1.625
Axle Splines	28	31
Overall Dimensions:		
Axle tube flange to axle tube flange	59 3/4	59 3/4
Between centerlines of spring seats	37 1/2	37 1/2
Axle shaft length	31 53/64	31 1/2

1.2 1970 Through 1975 Corvette Rear End

This was a carry-over from 1963 of the fully independent rear suspension that featured a frame-anchored differential. (This rear end was actually used until 1979.) The location of each wheel is established by 3 links. The links are the universally-jointed drive shaft, the adjacent strut, and the control arm that pivots at the frame side rail. All vertical suspension loads are taken by the shock absorbers and the transverse leaf spring. The leaf spring uses 9 separate leaves made of hardened and tempered chrome carbon steel. The differential carrier is a semi-floating design with an overhung pinion gear supported by two tapered roller bearings. The differential housing is of cast nodular iron construction. The primary change in this differential over its full production was the switch in 1965 from a Dana differential carrier to an Eaton positraction unit.

The attachment of the U-joint joining the side yokes to the half shafts depends upon engine application. On big block cars, bolts with caps attach the U-joint (heavy duty axle). On small block cars, the U-joint is attached to the half shaft by U-bolts. In later years, the heavy duty axle could be ordered on small block cars.

Corvette Axle Center Section Casting Numbers

Model Year	Casting Number
1970–75	3899143

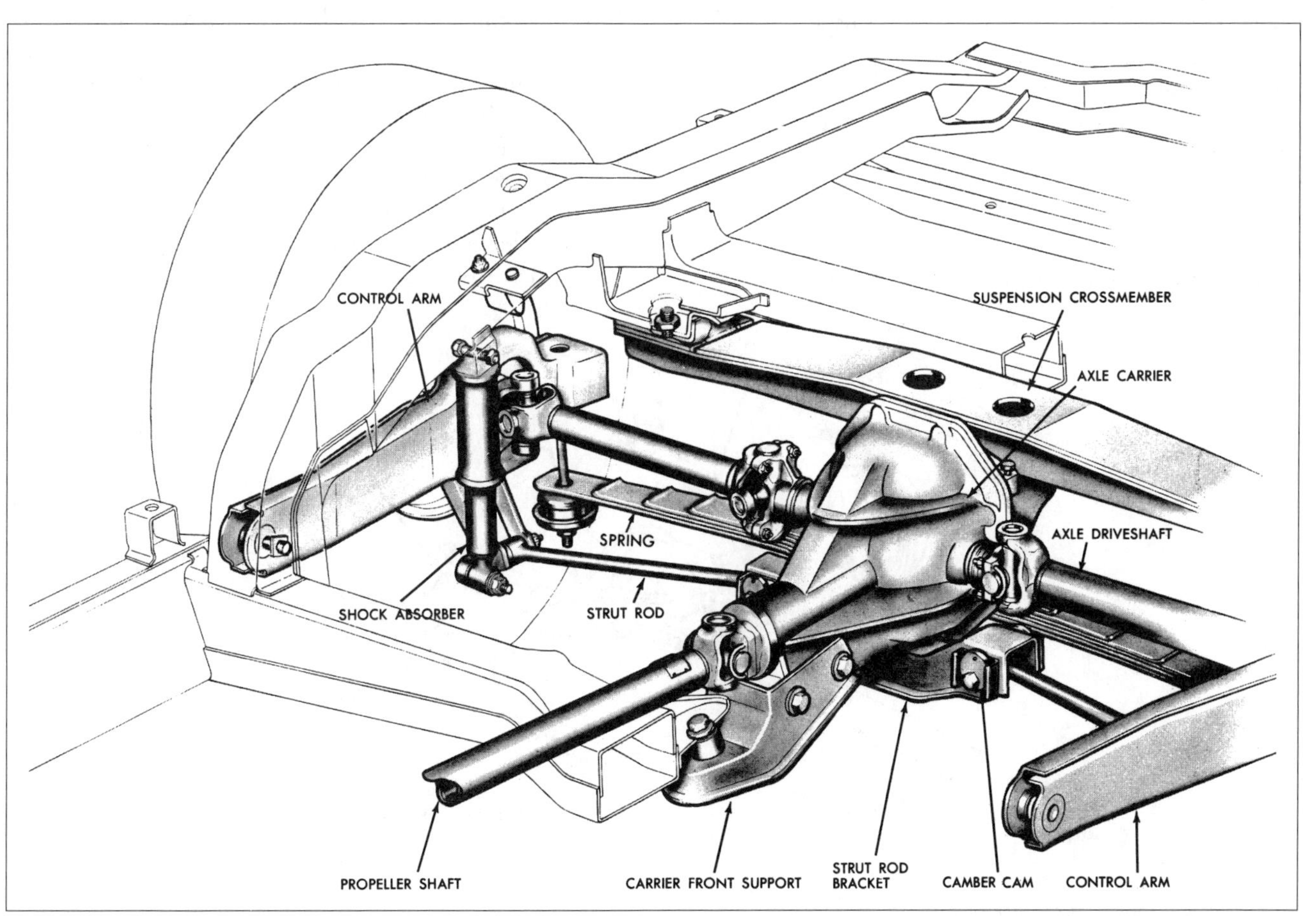

Fig. 16-3. 1970 through 1975 Corvette rear end.

1.3 Nova Rear Ends

1970 Through 1971 Nova

This rear end is a Salisbury design similar to the Chevelle/Monte Carlo unit, though it does not have the upper control arm mounting "ears" cast into the Chevelle center section. Also, a pedestal type mounting plate is used to mount the springs. Both mono-leaf and multi-leaf springs were available. The rear end is constructed of a cast iron differential carrier housing with pressed-in and welded axle tubes. The axle shafts are forged and heat-treated steel with the wheel drive flange forged integral with the axle. The axle shaft lengths are the same for both the left and right side.

This rear end is similar to the 1968–69 Camaro rear end and was introduced in the 1968 model year. The differential was produced in both 10- and 12-bolt versions. The specifications for the 1970–71 Nova rear end are as follows:

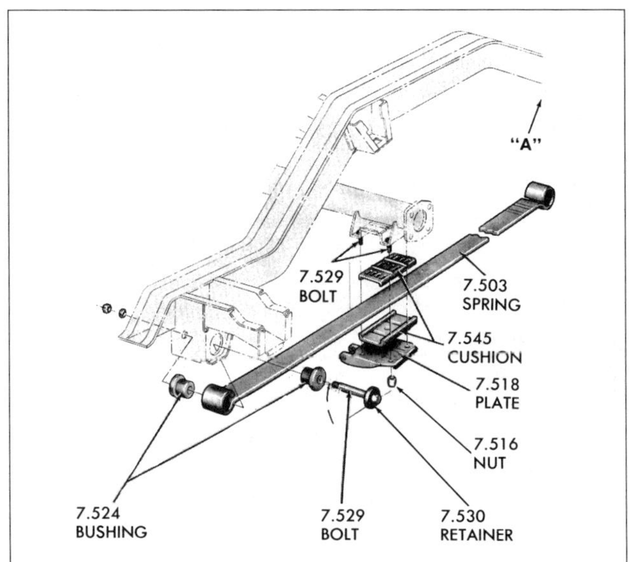

Fig. 16-5. Typical spring mounting for Nova rear axle. Mono leaf spring shown.

Nova, 1970–71

	10-Bolt	12-Bolt
Casting Number	unknown	3969341
Bolt Diameter (in.)	3/8	3/8
Ring Gear Diameter (in.)	8.20	8.875
Pinion Diameter (in.)	1.438	1.625
Axle Splines	28	30
Overall Dimensions:		
Axle tube flange to axle tube flange	54 1/4	54 1/4
Between centerlines of spring seats	42 7/16	42 7/16
Axle shaft length	29 33/64	29 9/16
This axle was also used in some 1968 and 1969 models		

1972 Through 1975 Nova

This rear end was a new design for the Nova, although it was the "corporate" rear axle first used in the 1971 Passenger and Camaro models. This rear end continues the Salisbury axle design with a leaf spring suspension. It has a cast differential carrier housing with the axle tubes pressed in and welded into the center section. The differential is a two-pinion design. The axle shafts are forged and heat-treated steel with the wheel drive flange forged integral with the axle. This rear end was built in only a 10-bolt version.

The specifications for the 1972 through 1975 Nova rear end are as follows:

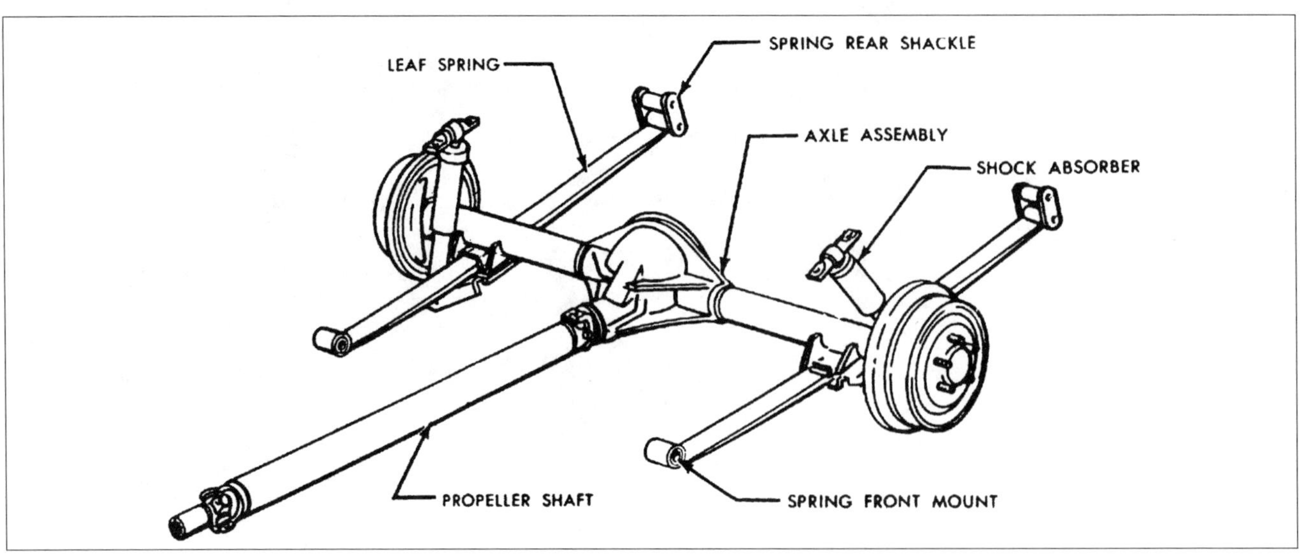

Fig. 16-4. Typical Nova rear suspension components.

Nova, 1972–75

	10-Bolt
Casting Number	unknown
Bolt Diameter (in.)	7/16
Ring Gear Diameter (in.)	8.50
Pinion Diameter (in.)	1.625
Axle Splines	28
Overall Dimensions:	
Axle tube flange to axle tube flange	54 1/4
Between centerlines spring seats	42 7/16
Axle shaft length	29 5/8

1.4 Chevelle/Monte Carlo Rear Ends

1970 Through 1972 Chevelle/Monte Carlo

This rear end is a Salisbury-type 4-link suspension with two cross-member-hinged upper control arms and two frame-hinged lower control arms. There are two mounting "ears" cast into the center section of the housing that are mounting points for the rear of each upper control arm. This rear end has the axle tubes pressed and welded into a cast differential carrier housing. A circular pad spring seat is welded to the forward edge of each axle tube, slightly inboard of the attachment for the lower control arms. The differential is a two-pinion type. The axle shafts are forged and heat-treated steel with the wheel drive flange forged integral with the axle. This rear end was introduced in the 1968 model year. The differential was produced in both 10- and 12-bolt versions.

There were some 1970 Monte Carlo models built with Pontiac Tempest rear axles and brake assemblies. These axles can be identified by the differential cover. The Tempest axle has two cut-outs on the circumference of the cover, while the Chevrolet cover has none. The Pontiac Tempest brakes may be identified by the rivets used to secure the linings to the brake shoes. See Fig. 16-7. Chevrolet brake linings are bonded to the brake shoes. The backing plate, the primary and secondary brake shoes and the adjusting nut are specific to this rear end application. All other parts of the brake assembly were standard Chevrolet stock.

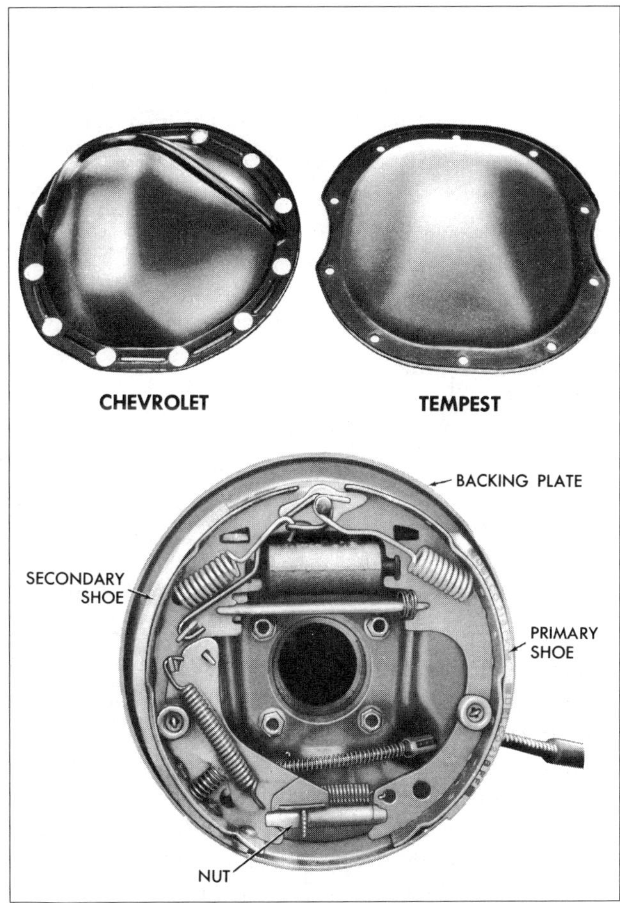

Fig. 16-7. *Top: 1970 Pontiac Tempest rear differential cover identifier. Bottom: parts unique to 1970 Monte Carlo rear brakes.*

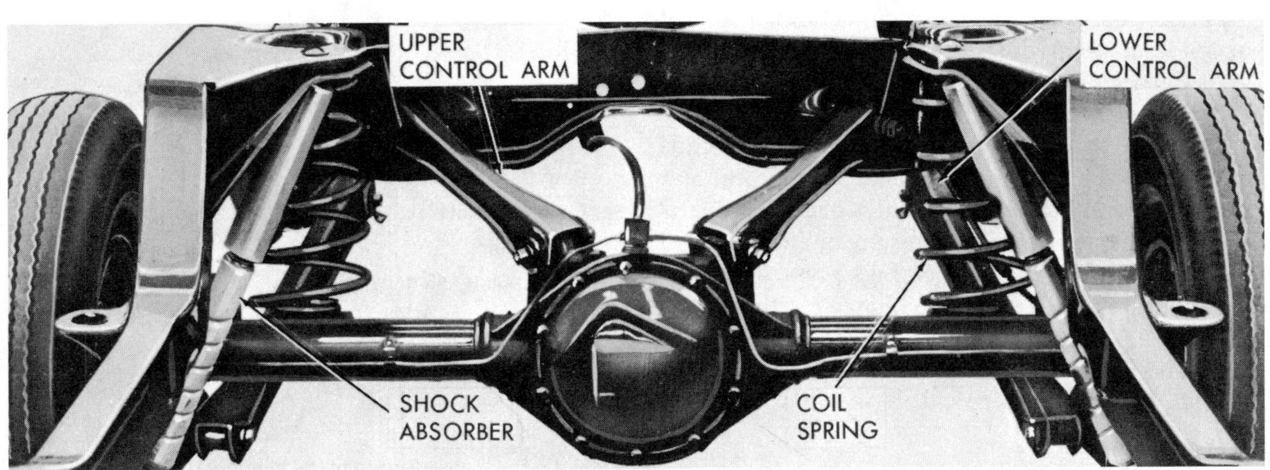

Fig. 16-6. *Typical Chevelle rear axle assembly.*

Due to the change-over to the "corporate" rear axle assembly for the 1973 model year, some late 1972 Chevelle models could have received the 1973 "corporate" rear axle. These cars would have a May 1,1972 build date or later. This is verified through Chevrolet Service News, Volume 44, Number 6.

The specifications for the 1970 through 1972 Chevelle/Monte Carlo rear end are as follows:

Chevelle/Monte Carlo, 1970–72

	10-Bolt	12-Bolt
Bolt Diameter (in.)	3/8	3/8
Ring Gear Diameter (in.)	8.20	8.875
Pinion Diameter (in.)	1.438	1.625
Axle Splines	28	30
Overall Dimensions:		
Axle tube flange to axle tube flange	55 1/4	55 1/4
Between centerlines of spring seats	34 31/32	34 31/32
Axle shaft length	30 5/32	30 1/8
This axle was also used in some 1968 and 1969 models		

1973 Through 1975 Chevelle/Monte Carlo

This rear end was the first application of the General Motors standardized "corporate" rear axle to Chevelle/Monte Carlo model line. (The standard axle was first introduced in the 1971 Passenger and Camaro models.) This rear end continues the Salisbury axle design with a 4-link suspension as used in previous years. This axle has a cast differential carrier housing with the axle tubes welded into the center section. The differential is a two-pinion design. The axle shafts are forged and heat-treated steel with the wheel drive flange forged integral with the axle. This rear end was built in both 10-bolt and 12-bolt versions.

All Chevelles and Monte Carlos except the Chevelle station wagons received the 8.50" ring gear/10-bolt "corporate" rear end that were manufactured by one of four manufacturers: Buick, Oldsmobile, Chevrolet, or GM of Canada. The Chevelle station wagon used the 8.875" ring gear/12 bolt "corporate" rear end built by either Pontiac or GM of Canada. Chevrolet rear ends built by Buick and Oldsmobile are identical. These rear ends have wheel bearings pressed *onto* the axle shafts and the axle shafts are retained by a retaining plate. All other rear ends have wheel bearings pressed *into* the axle tube and the axle shafts are retained with a C-clip design.

The specifications for the 1973 through 1975 Chevelle/Monte Carlo rear end are as follows:

Chevelle/Monte Carlo, 1973–75

	10-Bolt	12-Bolt
Bolt Diameter (in.)	7/16 LH	7/16 LH
Ring Gear Diameter (in.)	8.50	8.875
Pinion Diameter (in.)	1.625	1.625
Axle Splines	28	31
Overall Dimensions:		
Axle tube flange to axle tube flange	56 1/16	56 1/16
Between centerlines of spring seats	34 3/4	34 3/4
Axle shaft length	30 7/16	30 7/16

1.5 Camaro Rear Ends

1970 Camaro

This rear axle assembly is a Salisbury design similar to the 1970 Nova rear end. It does not have upper control arm mounting "ears" on the differential carrier housing. This rear end is the same width as the 1970–72 Chevelle/Monte Carlo rear end and uses the same axles, although all 1970 Camaro rear ends were mounted on multi-leaf springs. (The mounting is the same as that used in the 1968–69 Camaro.)

The 1970 rear shock design continues as a staggered-mount setup. The right side shock is located in front of the axle tube and the left side shock is behind the axle tube. This shock setup greatly enhanced the handling of the car and reduced high-rpm wheel hop.

The rear end is constructed of a cast iron differential carrier with pressed-in and welded axle tube housings. The axle shafts are forged and heat-treated steel with the wheel drive flange forged integral with the axle. The axle shaft lengths are the same for both the left and right side. This rear end was built in both 10-bolt and 12-bolt versions.

The specifications for the 1970 Camaro rear end are as follows:

Camaro, 1970

	10-Bolt	12-Bolt
Bolt Diameter (in.)	3/8	3/8
Ring Gear Diameter (in.)	8.20	8.875
Pinion Diameter (in.)	1.438	1.625
Axle Splines	28	30
Overall Dimensions:		
Axle tube flange to axle tube flange	55 1/4	55 1/4
Between centerlines of spring seats	45 3/8	45 3/8
Axle shaft length	30 5/32	30 5/32
Note: The 12-bolt version of this rear axle is a direct bolt-in to all Camaros built through the 1981 model year for non-original high performance applications.		

Camaro Axle Center Section Casting Numbers

Model Year	10-Bolt	12-Bolt
1970	Unknown	3969341NF
1971–72	Unknown	Not applicable
1973–74	1235542B	
1975	1249518	

1971 Through 1975 Camaro

This rear end was a new design for the 1971 Camaro. With this design, General Motors started to institute a standardized "corporate" rear axle (it also appeared in 1971 on Passenger models). By the 1972 model wreathes program was fully in place. The design of this rear end is the same as for 1971 through 1975 Passenger cars. This rear end was built in only 10-bolt versions.

The specifications for the 1971 through 1975 Camaro rear end are as follows:

Camaro, 1971–75

	10-Bolt
Bolt Diameter (in.)	7/16 LH
Ring Gear Diameter (in.)	8.50
Pinion Diameter (in.)	1.625
Axle Splines	28
Overall Dimensions:	
Axle tube flange to axle tube flange	55 1/4
Between centerlines of spring seats	45 3/8
Axle shaft length	30 5/32

1.6 1975 Monza Rear End

This Salisbury design rear axle was the only one installed in the Vega/Monza H-body cars. It consisted of a cast differential carrier housing with the axle tubes pressed and welded into the center section. The axle shafts were forged and heat-treated steel with the drive flange forged integral with the axle.

This axle was mounted in a torque arm rear suspension with a track bar and two parallel lower control arms. The positraction differential was a cone-clutch type manufactured by Borg-Warner. The date code should be stamped on the posi case on a non-functional surface. The ring gear diameter should be 7.50 on all V-8 Monza applications.

Monza/Monza 2 + 2, 1975

	10-Bolt
Bolt Diameter (in.)	7/16 LH
Ring Gear Diameter (in.)	7.50
Pinion Diameter (in.)	1.375
Axle Splines	26
Overall Dimensions:	
Axle tube flange to axle tube flange	49 51/64
Axle shaft length	26 7/8

2. REAR AXLE IDENTIFICATION

The rear axle of a car has two separate date codes. The most commonly known code is the axle build date. This code is usually stamped on the axle tube near the center section or carrier. On earlier vehicles and Corvettes, this code is stamped on the carrier of the axle assembly. This stamping designates the month/day axle assembly date, axle plant code, and model usage suffix code.

Secondly, almost all rear axles carry a casting date on the carrier. It is always a smart idea to compare this casting date code to the build date code of the axle assembly, always remembering that the carrier had to be manufactured prior to the final building of the axle.

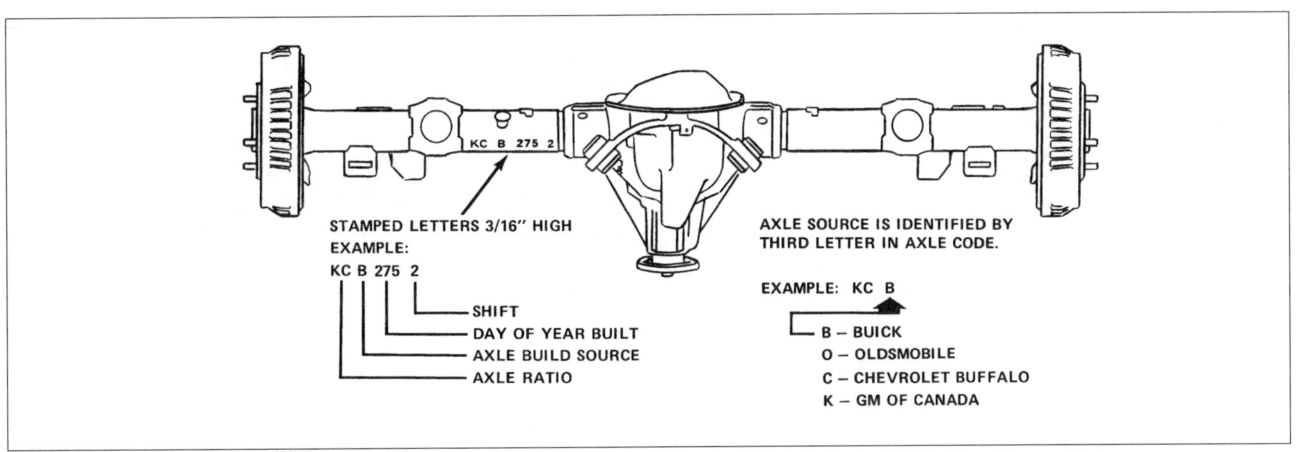

Fig. 16-8. Typical axle build date location.

Ring and Pinion Identification

The plant source for the differential pinion in the rear axle can be found by checking the characteristics of the pinion head. Fig. 16-9 shows the pinion heads for the rear axles manufactured at the plants covered by this book. Note that while Detroit and Buick pinion heads are similar, their part number series are different, Also, while Pontiac and Oldsmobile are similar, Pontiac stamps pinion identification information on the pinion stem. This information is vital in determining the originality of the ring and pinion gear.

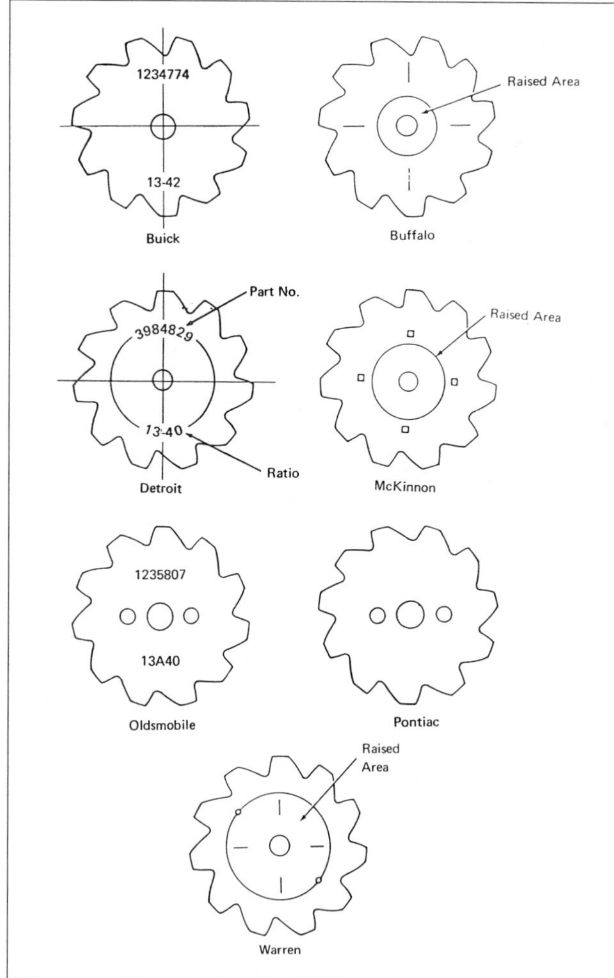

Fig. 16-9. Identification of differential pinion heads.

Positraction Unit Casting Numbers

The following table lists casting numbers for positraction units. The notation "up" or "down" indicates that the positraction unit is applicable to gearing numerically higher or lower.

Positraction Casting Numbers

Axle	Casting Number	Series	Gearing
12-bolt Passenger	ED 32088	2	2.73:1 and down
	30140PM1	3	3.08 to 3.73:1
	EDB 30174	4	3.90:1 and up
Corvette	ED 32297 PW 3	3	2.73 to 3.70:
	EDB 32298	4	3.90:1 and up
8.5 corporate	410408N	3	2.73:1 and up
	410409N	2	2.56:1 and down
8.2 10-bolt	ED 32118	2	2.73:1 and down
	EDB 30116	3	3.08:1 and up

Rear Axle Gear Ratios

The gear tooth ratio of the ring and pinion, for example 10-41, is stamped on the pinion head or stem, and also on the ring gear. Dividing the ring gear tooth count (41) by the pinion tooth count (10) gives you the final rear axle ratio. The following are the more popular tooth combination counts.

Tooth Combinations	Ratio
16-41	2.56:1
15-41	2.73:1
14-43	3.07:1
13-40	3.08:1
13-43	3.31:1
12-37	3.08:1
12-41	3.42:1
11-37	3.36:1
11-39	3.55:1
11-41	3.73:1
10-41	4.10:1
9-37	4.11:1

All Chevy-built gearsets should incorporate a date code stamped into the ring gear, and the pinion head or stem. This date code will indicate the month and year (calendar) of gear manufacture. Example: 11-70 means November, 1970. Pontiac date codes their pinions, but Buick and Oldsmobile do not.

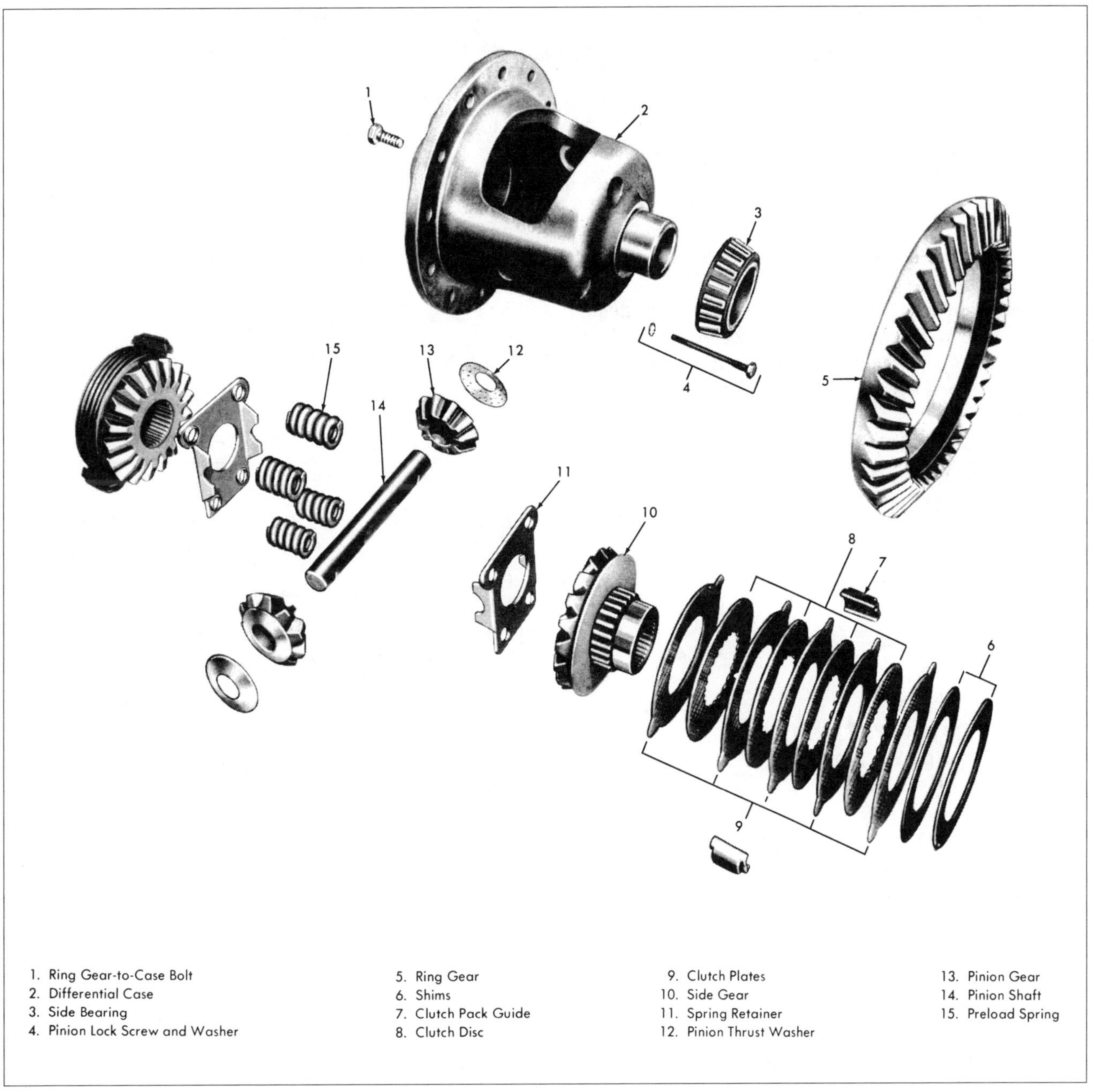

Fig. 16-10. *Exploded view of Eaton positraction differential.*

3. 1970 REAR AXLES

All 1970 Passenger, Chevelle, Nova, Camaro and Monte Carlo rear axles are stamped with an alpha-numeric identification code. The 8-digit code contains the axle code prefix, the month and day build code, an axle plant letter suffix code, and, on positraction axles, a letter code stamped below the axle code to provide source information.

The axle code is located on the forward-facing part of the passenger side (or left) axle tube. The axle code reads from left to right. The three-letter prefix designates the gear ratio and any other specific information about the axle. The calendar month is designated by a two number code from January (01) through December (12).

On the 1970 Corvette IRS rear suspension the differential code is stamped on the bottom of the differential carrier housing just forward of the rear end cover.

Plant Codes:

- G = Detroit Gear & Axle
- B = Buffalo NY
- W = Warren MI

Positraction Codes:

- D = Dana positraction differential
- E = Eaton positraction differential
- W = Warren Motive

Example: COZ-04 09 G
E

- COZ = Axle Prefix: 3.73:1 Camaro positraction axle
- 04 = Month: April
- 09 = Day: 9th day
- G = Assembly Plant: Detroit Gear and Axle
- E = Positraction Source: Eaton

1970 Passenger Rear Axle Codes

Gear Ratio	Code
3.08:1	CDA
3.55:1	CDC
3.31:1	CDD
3.31:1	CDE
Posi 3.07:1	CDF
Posi 3.08:1	CDG
Posi 3.31:1	CDH
Posi 3.55:1	CDK
Posi Heavy Duty 2.73:1	CDR
Posi 2.73:1	CDX
Posi 2.73:1	CDY
2.73:1	CDZ
2.56:1	CEA
2.29:1	CEC

1970 Passenger Rear Axle Codes (cont'd)

Gear Ratio	Code
Posi 2.56:1	CED
Heavy Duty 2.73:1	CEK
3.07:1	CEM
3.07:1	CEN
Heavy Duty 3.08:1	CES
Posi 3.08:1	CET
3.36:1	CEU
Heavy Duty 3.36:1	CEV
Posi 3.36:1	CEW
2.73:1	CEZ
2.73:1	CE3
2.56:1	CFW
Posi 2.56:1	CFX
Posi 3.31:1	CGH
2.73:1	CGK
Posi 2.73:1	CGM
3.08:1	CGQ
Posi 3.08:1	CGR
Posi 3.36:1	CGU
Posi 3.07:1	CGW
Posi 2.56:1	CLJ
Posi 2.73:1	CLK
Posi 3.07:1	CLN
2.56:1	CMY
2.73:1	CNA
3.07:1	CND
3.07:1	CWK
2.29:1	CWO
Posi 3.07:1	CWP
Heavy Duty 3.31:	CWT
Posi 3.31:1	CWU
3.31:1	CWY
Posi 3.31:1	CWZ
3.55:1	CXA
Posi 3.55:1	CXB

1970 Corvette Rear Axle Codes

Gear Ratio	Code
3.36:1	CAK
3.08:1	CAL
Posi 3.36:1	CAM
3.55:1	CAN
Posi 3.70:1	CAO
4.11:1	CAP
3.70:1	CAS
Heavy Duty 3.08:1	CAT
Heavy Duty 3.36:1	CAU
3.08:1	CAV
3.08:1	CAW
Heavy Duty 3.36:1	CAX
Posi 2.73:1	CAY
Heavy Duty 3.55:1	CAZ
Posi 3.70:1	CFA

1970 Corvette Rear Axle Codes (cont'd)

Gear Ratio	Code
Heavy Duty 4.11:1	CFB
Posi 4.56:1	CFC
3.36:1	CLR

1970 Nova Rear Axle Codes

Gear Ratio	Code
2.56:1	CBA
Posi 2.56:1	CBB
3.36:1	CBC
Posi 3.36:1	CBD
2.73:1	CBI
3.07:1	CBL
3.31:1	CBM
3.55:1	CBN
2.73:1	CBP
2.73:1	CBQ
Posi 3.07:1	CBR
Posi 3.31:1	CBS
Posi 3.55:1	CBT
3.08:1	CPA
Posi 3.08:1	CPE
2.56:1	CPI
Posi 2.56:1	CPJ
Heavy Duty 2.73:1	CPL
Posi Heavy Duty 2.73:1	CPM
Heavy Duty 3.08:1	CPO
Posi 3.08:1	CPR
Heavy Duty 3.36:1	CPT
Posi Heavy Duty 3.36:1	CPU
Posi 2.73:1	CPX

1970 Chevelle/Monte Carlo Rear Axle Codes

Gear Ratio	Code
3.08:1	CCA
3.36:1	CCB
Posi 3.07:1	CCD
Posi 3.08:1	CCE
Posi 3.31:1	CCF
Posi 3.36:1	CCG
Posi 2.73:1	CCH
2.56:1	CCL
Posi 2.56:1	CCM
2.56:1	CCN
Posi 2.56:1	CCO
2.73:1	CCP
3.31:1	CCW
3.07:1	CCX
2.56:1	CGA
Posi Heavy Duty 2.56:1	CGB
Heavy Duty 2.73:1	CGC
Heavy Duty Posi 2.73:1	CGD
Heavy Duty 3.08:1	CGE
Posi Heavy Duty 3.08:1	CGF

1970 Chevelle/Monte Carlo Rear Axle Codes (cont'd)

Gear Ratio	Code
Heavy Duty 3.36:1	CGG
Posi Heavy Duty 3.36:1	CGI
Posi 2.73:1	CKC
2.73:1	CKD
Posi 3.55:1	CKF
3.55:1	CKJ
Posi 4.10:1	CKK
2.56:1	CRJ
Posi 2.56:1	CRK
3.07:1	CRL
3.07:1	CRM
3.31:1	CRU
Posi 3.31:1	CRV
Heavy Duty 4.10:1	CRW

1970 Camaro Rear Axle Codes

Gear Ratio	Code
2.56:1	COA
2.56:1	COB
2.73:1	COC
Posi 2.73:1	COD
3.08:1	COE
Posi 3.08:1	COF
3.36:1	COG
Posi 3.36:1	COH
Heavy Duty 3.08:1	COI
Posi Heavy Duty 3.08:1	COJ
Heavy Duty 3.36:1	COK
Posi Heavy Duty 3.36:1	COL
2.56:1	COM
Posi 2.56:1	CON
4.10:1	COO
2.73:1	COP
Posi 2.73:1	COR
3.07:1	COS
Posi 3.07:1	COT
3.31:1	COU
Posi 3.31:1	COV
3.55:1	COW
Posi 3.55:1	COX
3.73:1	COY
Posi 3.73:1	COZ
3.07:1	CRA
3.31:1	CRB
3.55:1	CRC
3.73:1	CRD
4.10:1	CRE
2.56:1	CRF
Posi 2.56:1	CRU
Heavy Duty 3.08:1	CRH
Posi Heavy Duty 3.08:1	CRI
2.73:1	CRX
Posi 2.73:1	CRY

4. 1971 REAR AXLES

All 1971 Passenger, Nova, Chevelle, Camaro and Monte Carlo rear axles are stamped with an alpha-numeric production code. The 8-digit code contains the axle code prefix, manufacturing plant code, a date code, the build shift code and the positraction source (if applicable).

The axle code is located on the forward-facing part of the passenger side (or left) axle tube. The axle code reads from left to right. The two-letter prefix designates the gear ratio and any other specific information about the axle. The third digit is the plant code. The next three numbers designate the actual day of the year this axle was built (001-365). The seventh digit represents the shift the axle was manufactured on. The last character letter is the positraction source. If a space or no letter follows the shift code, the axle did not originally come equipped with a positraction axle.

On the 1971 Corvette IRS rear suspension the differential code is stamped on the bottom of the differential carrier housing just forward of the rear end cover.

Plant Codes:

- B = Buick
- C = Buffalo
- G = Detroit Gear & Axle
- K = GM of Canada
- O = Oldsmobile
- P = Pontiac
- W = Warren MI

Positraction Codes:

- (-) = No positraction
- D = Dana positraction differential
- E = Eaton positraction differential
- W = Warner Motive Positraction Carrier

Example: CJ G 218 1 E

- CJ = Axle Prefix: 3.42:1 Camaro positraction axle
- G = Assembly Plant: Detroit Gear and Axle
- 218 = Day of Year: August 6, 1971
- 1 = Shift: First
- E = Positraction Source: Eaton

Some early axles from Buffalo and Detroit Gear and Axle were coded differently. On theses axles, the positraction and shift codes were transposed (CJ G 218 **E 1**). Also, early Buffalo axles may be have an alpha character instead of a numerical character for the shift code (CJ C 218 E **A**).

1971 Passenger Rear Axle Codes

Gear Ratio	Code
3.08:1	NA
2.73:1	NK
Posi 3.08:1	NP
Posi 2.73:1	NT
2.73:1	UD
3.08:1	UF
3.42:1	UH
Posi 2.73:1	VD
Posi 3.08:1	VF
Posi 3.42:1	VH
3.42:1	WJ
3.08:1	WR
Posi 3.08:1	XJ
Posi 3.42:1	X3
2.73:1	YD
3.08:1	YF
Posi 3.42:1	YH
Posi 2.73:1	ZD
Posi 3.08:1	ZF
Posi 3.42:1	ZH

1971 Corvette Rear Axle Codes

Gear Ratio	Code
Posi 3.55:1	AA
Posi 3.70:1	AB
Posi 4.11:1	AC
Posi 4.56:1	AD
Posi 3.08:1	AW
Posi 3.36:1	AX
Posi 3.36:1	LR

1971 Nova Rear Axle Codes

Gear Ratio	Code
3.07:1	BL
3.31:1	BM
Posi 3.07:1	BR
Posi 3.31:1	BS
2.56:1	GJ
Posi 2.56:1	GK
3.08:1	GR
Posi 3.08:1	GS
3.36:1	GT
Posi 3.36:1	GW
2.56:1	PI
Posi 2.56:1	PJ
3.08:1	PO
Posi 3.08:1	PR

1971 Chevelle/Monte Carlo Rear Axle Codes

Gear Ratio	Code
Posi 3.31:1	CF
Posi 2.73:1	CH
3.31:1	CW
2.56:1	GA
Posi 2.56:1	GB
2.73:1	GC
Posi 2.73:1	GD
3.08:1	GF
3.36:1	GG
2.73:1	GH
Posi 3.36:1	GI
3.08:1	GN
2.73:1	KD
3.31:1	RU
Posi 3.31:1	RV
4.10:1	RW

1971 Camaro Rear Axle Codes

Gear Ratio	Code
Posi 2.73:1	CA
4.10:1	CB
3.73:1	CG
Posi 3.42:1	CJ
3.42:1	CK
3.08:1	GX
Posi 3.08:1	GY
2.73:1	GZ
3.42:1	2L
3.08:1	2M

5. 1972 Rear Axles

All 1972 Passenger, Nova, Chevelle, Camaro and Monte Carlo rear axles are stamped with an alpha-numeric production code. The 8-digit code contains the axle code prefix, manufacturing plant code, a date code, the build shift code and the positraction source (if applicable).

The axle code is located on the forward-facing part of the passenger side (or left) axle tube. The axle code reads from left to right. The two-letter prefix designates the gear ratio and any other specific information about the axle. The third digit is the plant code. The next three numbers designate the actual day of the year this axle was built (001–365). The seventh digit represents the shift the axle was manufactured on. The last character letter is the positraction source. If a space or no letter follows the shift code, the axle did not originally come equipped with a positraction axle.

On the 1972 Corvette IRS rear suspension the differential code is stamped on the bottom of the differential carrier housing just forward of the rear end cover.

Plant Codes:

- B = Buick
- C = Buffalo
- G = Detroit Gear & Axle
- K = McKinnon Industries
- M = Pontiac of Canada
- O = Oldsmobile
- P = Pontiac
- W = Warren MI

Positraction Codes:

- (-) = No positraction
- D = Dana positraction differential
- E = Eaton positraction differential
- W = Warner Motive Positraction Carrier

Example: CJ G 218 1 E

- CJ = Axle Prefix: 3.42:1 Camaro positraction axle
- G = Assembly Plant: Detroit Gear and Axle
- 218 = Day of Year: August 6, 1972
- 1 = Shift: First
- E = Positraction Source: Eaton

1972 Passenger Rear Axle Codes

Gear Ratio	Code
3.08:1	NA
3.23:1	NJ
2.73:1	NK
Posi 3.08:1	NP
Posi 3.23:1	NR
Posi 2.73:1	NT
2.73:1	UD
3.08:1	UF
3.42:1	UH
Posi 2.73:1	VD
Posi 3.08:1	VF
Posi 3.42:1	VH
3.08:1	WP
Posi 3.08:1	XJ
3.42:1	X3
2.73:1	YD
3.08:1	YF
3.42:1	YH
Posi 2.73:1	ZD
Posi 3.08:1	ZF
Posi 3.42:1	ZH

1972 Corvette Rear Axle Codes

Gear Ratio	Code
Posi 3.55:1	AA
Posi 3.70:1	AB
Posi 4.11:1	AC
Posi 3.36:1	AX
Posi 3.36:1	LR

1972 Nova Rear Axle Codes

Gear Ratio	Code
2.73:1	JB
3.08:1	JC
3.42:1	JE
2.73:1	JG
3.08:1	JI
3.42:1	JK
Posi 2.73:1	JN
Posi 3.08:1	JQ
Posi 3.42:1	JS
Posi 2.73:1	JV
Posi 3.08:1	JW
Posi 3.42:1	JY
3.08:1	4T

1972 Camaro Rear Axle Codes

Gear Ratio	Code
2.73:1	CA
4.10:1	CB
3.73:1	CG
Posi 3.42:1	CJ
3.42:1	CK
3.42:1	CL
Posi 3.42:1	CM
3.08:1	GX
Posi 3.08:1	GY
2.73:1	GZ
3.23:1	2M
3.42:1	4S

1972 Chevelle/Monte Carlo Rear Axle Codes

Gear Ratio	Code
Posi 3.31:1	CF
Posi 2.73:1	CH
3.31:1	CW
2.73:1	GC
Posi 2.73:1	GD
3.08:1	GF
3.36:1	GG
2.73:1	GH
Posi 3.36:1	GI
3.08:1	GN
2.73:1	KD
3.31:1	RU
Posi 3.31:1	RV

6. 1973 REAR AXLES

All 1973 Passenger, Nova, Chevelle, Camaro and Monte Carlo rear axles are stamped with an alpha-numeric production code. The 8-digit code contains the axle code prefix, manufacturing plant code, a date code, the build shift code and the positraction source (if applicable).

The axle code is located on the forward-facing part of the passenger side (or left) axle tube. The axle code reads from left to right. The two-letter prefix designates the gear ratio and any other specific information about the axle. The third digit is the plant code. The next three numbers designate the actual day of the year this axle was built (001–365). The seventh digit represents the shift the axle was manufactured on. The last character letter is the positraction source. If a space or no letter follows the shift code, the axle did not originally come equipped with a positraction axle.

On the 1972 Corvette IRS rear suspension the differential code is stamped on the bottom of the differential carrier housing just forward of the rear end cover.

> NOTE—
> Beginning with the 1973 model year on Chevelle and Monte Carlo models, black chassis paint was no longer applied to the axle assembly.

Plant Codes:

- B = Buick
- C = Buffalo
- D = Cadillac
- G = Detroit Gear & Axle
- K = McKinnon Industries
- M = Pontiac of Canada
- O = Oldsmobile
- P = Pontiac
- W = Warren MI

Positraction Codes:

- (-) = No positraction
- D = Dana positraction differential
- E = Eaton positraction differential
- G = Chevrolet Gear and Axle Positraction Carrier
- O = Oldsmobile Positraction Carrier
- W = Warner Motive Positraction Carrier

Example: CM G 218 1 E

- CM = Axle Prefix: 3.42:1 Camaro positraction axle
- G = Assembly Plant: Detroit Gear and Axle
- 218 = Day of Year: August 6, 1973
- 1 = Shift: First
- E = Positraction Source: Eaton

1973 Passenger Rear Axle Codes

Gear Ratio	Code
2.73:1	KA
3.08:1	KC
3.42:1	KE
Posi 2.73:1	LA
Posi 3.08:1	LC
Posi 3.42:1	LE
2.73:1	UA
3.08:1	UC
3.42:1	UE
3.08:1	UL
Posi 2.73:1	VB
Posi 3.08:1	VC
Posi 3.42:1	VE
Posi 3.08:1	VL
2.73:1	YA
3.08:1	YC
3.42:1	YE
Posi 2.73:1	ZB
Posi 3.08:1	ZC
Posi 3.42:1	ZE

1973 Corvette Rear Axle Codes

Gear Ratio	Code
Posi 3.55:1	AA
Posi 3.70:1	AB
Posi 4.11:1	AC
Posi 3.08:1	AW
Posi 3.36:1	AX
Posi 3.36:1	LR

1973 Nova Rear Axle Codes

Gear Ratio	Code
2.73:1	JA
3.08:1	JB
3.42:1	JC
Posi 2.73:1	JM
Posi 3.08:1	JN
Posi 3.42:1	JP

1973 Chevelle/Monte Carlo Rear Axle Codes

Gear Ratio	Code
2.73:1	AC
3.08:1	AD
3.42:1	AJ
Posi 2.73:1	CC
Posi 3.08:1	CD
Posi 3.42:1	CJ
2.73:1	WA
3.08:1	WC
3.42:1	WE
Posi 2.73:1	XB
Posi 3.08:1	XC
Posi 3.42:1	XE

1973 Camaro Rear Axle Codes

Gear Ratio	Code
Posi 2.73:1	CA
Posi 4.10:1	CB
Posi 3.73:1	CG
3.42:1	CL
Posi 3.42:1	CM
3.08:1	GX
Posi 3.08:1	GY
2.73:1	GZ
3.36:1	HC
Posi 3.36:1	HH

7. 1974 Rear Axles

All 1974 Passenger, Nova, Chevelle, Camaro and Monte Carlo rear axles are stamped with an alpha-numeric production code. The 8-digit code contains the axle code prefix, manufacturing plant code, a date code, the build shift code and the positraction source (if applicable).

The axle code is located on the forward-facing part of the passenger side (or left) axle tube. The axle code reads from left to right. The two-letter prefix designates the gear ratio and any other specific information about the axle. The third digit is the plant code. The next three numbers designate the actual day of the year this axle was built (001–365). The seventh digit represents the shift the axle was manufactured on. The last character letter is the positraction source. If a space or no letter follows the shift code, the axle did not originally come equipped with a positraction axle.

> NOTE—
> Positraction source code stamping was deleted mid-year and may not appear on late production axles.

On the 1974 Corvette IRS rear suspension the differential code is stamped on the bottom of the differential carrier housing just forward of the rear end cover.

Plant Codes:

- B = Buick
- C = Buffalo
- G = Detroit Gear & Axle
- K = McKinnon Industries
- M = Pontiac of Canada
- O = Oldsmobile
- P = Pontiac
- W = Warren MI

Positraction Codes:

- (-) = No positraction
- E = Eaton positraction differential
- G = Chevrolet Gear and Axle Positraction Carrier
- O = Oldsmobile Positraction Carrier
- W = Warner Motive Positraction Carrier

Example: CM C 218 1 E

- CM = Axle Prefix: 3.42:1 Camaro positraction axle
- C = Assembly Plant: Buffalo Axle
- 218 = Day of Year: August 6, 1974
- 1 = Shift: First
- E = Positraction Source: Eaton

1974 Passenger Rear Axle Codes

Gear Ratio	Code
2.73:1	KA
3.08:1	KC
Posi 2.73:1	LA
Posi 3.08:1	LC
2.73:1	UB
3.08:1	UC
3.42:1	UE
3.08:1	UL
Posi 2.73:1	VA
Posi 3.08:1	VC
Posi 3.42:1	VE
Posi 3.08:1	VL
Posi 2.73:1	YA
2.73:1	YB
3.08:1	YC
3.42:1	YE
Posi 2.73:1	ZA
Posi 3.08:1	ZC
Posi 3.42:1	ZE

1974 Corvette Rear Axle Codes

Gear Ratio	Code
Posi 3.55:1	AA
Posi 3.70:1	AB
Posi 4.11:1	AC
Posi 3.36:1	AX
Posi 3.36:1	LR

1974 Nova Rear Axle Codes

Gear Ratio	Code
2.73:1	JA
3.08:1	JB
3.42:1	JC
Posi 2.73:1	JM
Posi 3.08:1	JN
Posi 3.42:1	JP

1974 Chevelle/Monte Carlo Rear Axle Codes

Gear Ratio	Code
2.73:1	AC
3.08:1	AD
3.42:1	AJ
Posi 2.73:1	CC
Posi 3.08:1	CD
Posi 3.42:1	CJ
2.73:1	WB
3.08:1	WC
3.42:1	WE
Posi 2.73:1	XA
Posi 3.08:1	XC
Posi 3.42:1	XE

1974 Camaro Rear Axle Codes

Gear Ratio	Code
Posi 2.73:1	CA
3.73:1	CG*
3.42:1	CL
Posi 3.42:1	CM
3.08:1	GX
Posi 3.08:1	GY
2.73:1	GZ

* Chevrolet records do not indicate that the CG-code axle is a Positraction assembly, but verified examples have been found in 1974 Z28s, which were all Positraction-equipped from the factory.

8. 1975 REAR AXLES

All 1975 Passenger, Nova, Chevelle, Camaro and Monte Carlo rear axles are stamped with an alpha-numeric production code. The 7-digit code contains the axle code prefix, manufacturing plant code, a date code, and the build shift code.

The axle code is located on the forward-facing part of the passenger side (or left) axle tube. The axle code reads from left to right. The two-letter prefix designates the gear ratio and any other specific information about the axle. The third digit is the plant code. The next three numbers designate the actual day of the year this axle was built (001–365). The seventh digit represents the shift the axle was manufactured on.

On the 1975 Corvette IRS rear suspension the differential code is stamped on the bottom of the differential carrier housing just forward of the rear end cover.

Plant Codes:

- B = Buick
- C = Buffalo
- D = Cadillac
- G = Detroit Gear & Axle
- K = McKinnon Industries
- M = Pontiac of Canada
- O = Oldsmobile
- P = Pontiac
- W = Warren MI

Example: PT C 218 1

- PT = Axle Prefix: 2.56:1 Camaro positraction axle
- C = Assembly Plant: Buffalo Axle
- 218 = Day of Year: August 6, 1975
- 1 = Shift: First

1975 Passenger Rear Axle Codes

Gear Ratio	Code
2.56:1	KF
Posi 2.56:1	LF
2.73:1	UA, YA, UJ, KA
3.08:1	UC, UL, YC, CL, KC
Posi 3.08:1	VL, ZC, LC, VC
Posi 2.73:1	ZA, LA, VA, VJ

1975 Corvette Rear Axle Codes

Gear Ratio	Code
Posi 3.55:1	AA
Posi 3.70:1	AB
Posi 3.08:1	AW
Posi 3.36:1	AX
Posi 2.73:1	AY
Posi 3.36:1	LR

1975 Nova Rear Axle Codes

Gear Ratio	Code
2.56:1	GA
2.73:1	GB
3.08:1	GD
Posi 2.56:1	JU
Posi 2.73:1	JV
Posi 3.08:1	JX

1975 Chevelle/Monte Carlo Rear Axle Codes

Gear Ratio	Code
Posi 2.56:1	AH
Posi 2.73:1	CC, XA
Posi 3.08:1	CD, XC
2.56:1	CH
2.73:1	WA,AC
3.08:1	WC,AD

1975 Camaro Rear Axle Codes

Gear Ratio	Code
2.73:1	PA
3.08:1	PC
2.56:1	PH
Posi 2.56:1	PT
Posi 2.73:1	PU
Posi 3.08:1	PW

1975 Monza Rear Axle Codes

Gear Ratio	Code
3.42:1	DE, DK, DV
Posi 3.42:1	EE, EK, EV
2.93:1	DC, DJ, DX
Posi 2.93:1	EC, EJ, EX
2.56:1	DB, DH
Posi 2.56:1	EB, EH

Chapter 17

Wheel Identification

1. Introduction

Usually, what you look for in a wheel is only one thing: rim size. You can usually find the correct rim size for your car in your owner's manual, shop manual or other factory literature. This is a great start, but what you need to realize is that other factors affect wheel choice. For example, two wheels manufactured for different divisions may have the same rim size and bolt pattern but a different offset.

This chapter will focus on the cryptic coding found on almost all Chevrolet wheels. Most of the difficulty in identifying wheels relates to the decoding of the specific stampings. For this reason, Kelsey-Hayes was used as a source for this chapter. Kelsey-Hayes produced almost all of Chevrolet's production wheels, along with wheels for almost every other manufacturer.

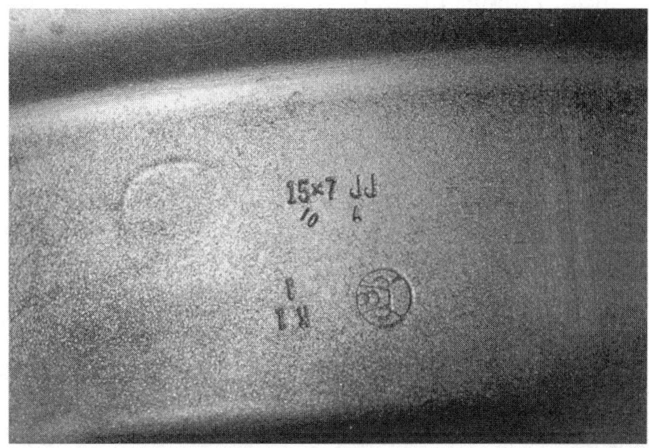

Fig. 17-1. *Inside of wheel (tire side) shows various code stampings. See text for decoding.*

1.1 Interior Wheel Stampings

All wheels should at least have stamped into them the size of the wheel and some type of manufacturer's trademark. You will usually find the size stamping on the inside (tire side) of the rim. You will also find a series of numbers stamped inside the wheel. Fig. 17-1 shows an example of several different stampings all in the same area.

Most obvious at the lower right of the photo is the Kelsey-Hayes logo. Immediately to the left of the Kelsey-Hayes logo is the code K-1-1 (upside down in the photo), stamped in a triangular pattern. The K-1-1 code is deciphered as follows:

- K: Kelsey-Hayes designation
- 1: Plant:
  1 = Romulus, MI
  2 = Windsor, ONT Canada
  3 = Philadelphia, PA
- 1: Last digit of year, in this case 1971

Please note that there were three plants that were producing wheels for Kelsey-Hayes during this period.

Of the group of numbers and letters above the K-1-1 code, the most obvious is the rim size, in this case "15x7 JJ." The letters JJ signify the type of rim contour of the wheel. Other rim contour type designations which appear on Chevrolet wheels are K, J, JK and many others.

The number "10" stamped below the size signifies the actual day of the month this rim *part* was run. In the same manner, the letter "A" stamped below signifies that this rim *part* was built during the first production run of the year. In some cases, this letter designation coincided with the corresponding month of the year, i.e. A = first production run = January, but this was not always the case.

Please note that the date code(s) on the inside (tire side) of the rim pertain only to the part or parts of the rim that were manufactured. The actual production date code for the rim as an assembled whole is found on the exterior of the wheel, near the valve stem. In many cases the dates on the inside and exterior will match, without any significance. Neither date has any reference to the other except that the exterior (assembled) date should never precede the inner (parts) date.

1.2 Exterior Wheel Stampings

Fig. 17-2 shows a typical Kelsey-Hayes exterior wheel stamping. These codes indicate the final assembly date of the whole wheel. Starting at the left and reading right, you first read the K-1-1 code. This is decoded exactly like the interior code given above. The next number to the right, "10," represents the month of wheel assembly, in this case the 10th month of the year, or October. It does not represent the actual day of the month as indicated on the inside of the rim. The stamped number on the opposite side of the valve stem hole, "4," represents the day of the month of the final wheel assembly. In this case the 4th day of the month. To the right of the "4" is the actual letter code of the wheel, which in this example is the letters "AG."

Fig. 17-2. Exterior of wheel shows various code stampings. See text for decoding.

The wheel codes were assigned by Chevrolet to each specific wheel, and the manufacturer was required to stamp the code onto that wheel. These codes were usually used on one specific vehicle in a particular model year, but in some cases could possibly be used on another model during that year or possibly the next model year. In the example above, AG stands for a 1968 Corvette 15x7 Rally Wheel. Note that this wheel was made on October 4, 1971, but was coded AG as a factory replacement.

Fig. 17-3 shows the K-1-1 code again, stamped on the "spider" or center section of the wheel. This code is read the same as previous K-1-1 codes. The code can differ from the final assembly code stamped near the valve stem. Many Kelsey-Hayes wheels were built all in one day, but this would depend on plant scheduling, car sales, wheel demand, and so on.

Fig. 17-3. Additional exterior stamping is often found on "spider" section of wheel.

NOTE—
Some factory aluminum wheels could have a different date coding sequence. On these wheels, a typical date code would be 11 13 72, which decodes month/day/year, or November 13, 1972.

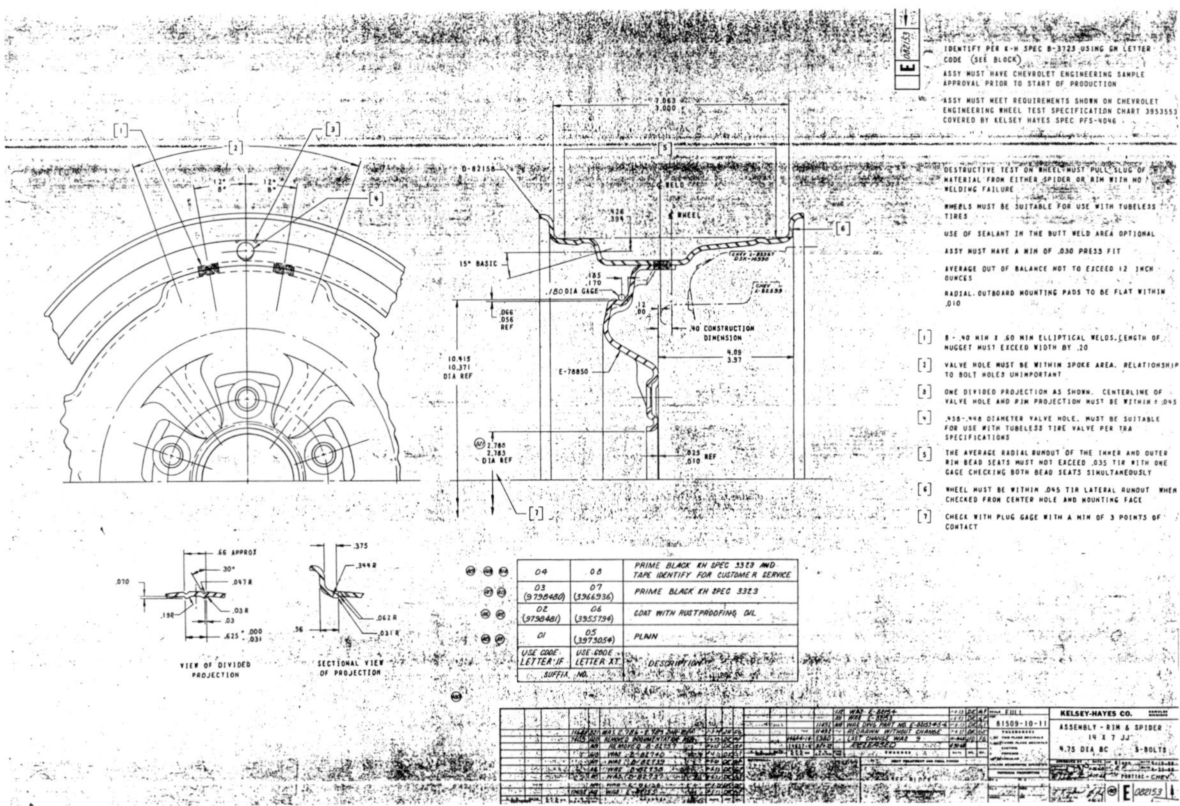

Fig. 17-4. *1969 14x7 JJ standard wheel used on all high performance 14x7 applications. Arrow indicates letter code "XT" coding of wheel.*

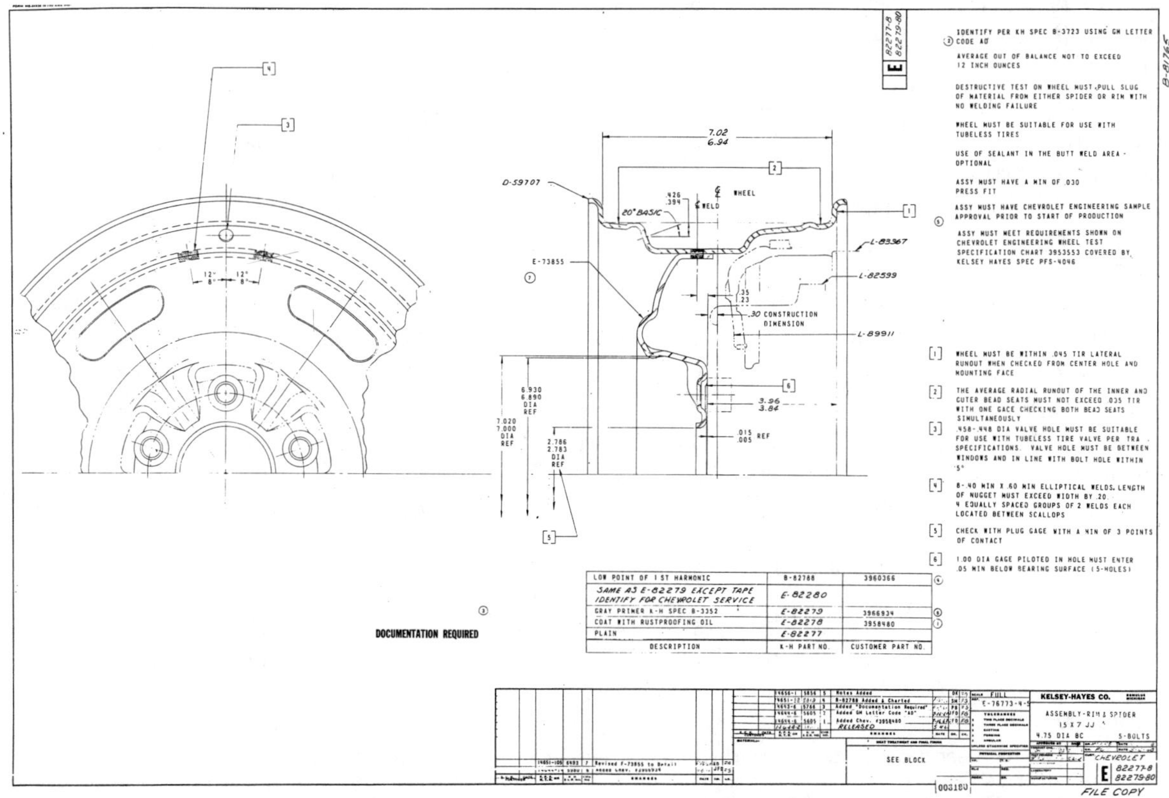

Fig. 17-5. *1969 Z28 Camaro 15x7 rally wheel was used initially for 1969 model year but was later superseded by E-82742 rally wheel which was designed to be used with 4-wheel disc brake option.*

2. 1970 THROUGH 1975 WHEELS

Included in the chart below are all Chevrolet wheels produced from 1965 through 1975. The chart designates the specific model year, model usage, wheel size, wheel code, number of bolts, bolt center, center hole size, offset, type of construction, rim inside diameter, and wheel manufacturer. Some wheels had riveted construction and these particular wheels will have the letter "R" in that column.

Abbreviations	D/B: Disc Brakes Ex.: Except Opt.: Optional RPO: Regular Production Option	SS: Super Sport SST: Space Saver Tire application Std.: Standard
Code	—: No Code/Not Used –C–: Canceled	( ): Number of spokes
Wheel Construction	A: Aluminum CA: Cast Aluminum FA: Forged Aluminum P: Polycast	R: Riveted SW: Steel Welded TC: Trued Center W: Welded
Wheel Manufacturer	C: Chevrolet Warren KH: Kelsey-Hayes MW: Motor Wheel	NI: Norris Industries NT: Norris Technologies

1970 Through 1975 Wheel Applications

Year	Model	Size	Code	Bolts	Bolt Center	Bolt Size	Center Hole	Offset	Const.	Rim I.D.	Mfg.
1970	Camaro RPO ex. SS Z28	14x6 JJ	AM	5	4-3/4	7/16	2.783	.50	W	12.328	KH
	Camaro RPO SS	14x7 JJ	CL	5	4-3/4	7/16	2.783	.34	W	12.328	KH
	Camaro RPO Rally	14x7 JJ	AV	5	4-3/4	7/16	2.783	.34	W	12.328	KH
	Camaro Z28, Trans-Am	15x7 JJ	AU	5	4-3/4	7/16	2.783	.30	W	13.156	KH
	Chevelle, ex. SS & Wagon	14x5	YD	5	4-3/4	7/16	2.783	.60	W	12.328	C
	Chevelle RPO ex. SS & Wagon, Rally	14x6 JJ	YW	5	4-3/4	7/16	2.783	.88	W	12.328	KH
	Chevelle RPO and Wagon	14x6 JJ	YB	5	4-3/4	7/16	2.783	.88	W	12.328	KH
	Chevelle RPO and Wagon, replaces YB	14x6 JJ	CZ	5	4-3/4	7/16	2.783	.88	W	12.328	KH
	Chevelle Wagon, Rally	14x6 JJ	AE	5	4-3/4	7/16	2.783	.88	W	12.328	KH
	Chevelle SS, Super Sport	14x7	AO*	5	4-3/4	7/16	2.783	.34	W	12.328	MW
	Chevelle SS, Super Sport	14x7	YA	5	4-3/4	7/16	2.783	.34	W	12.328	MW
	Chevy II, ex. SS	14x5	YD	5	4-3/4	7/16	2.783	.60	W	12.328	C
	Chevy II, RPO ex. SS	14x6 JJ	XF	5	4-3/4	7/16	2.783	.50	W	12.328	KH
	Chevy II SS	14x7 JJ	XT	5	4-3/4	7/16	2.783	.40	W	12.328	KH
	Chevy II RPO Rally ex. SS	14x6 JJ	XG	5	4-3/4	7/16	2.783	.50	W	12.328	KH
	Chevy II RPO Rally SS	14x7 JJ	YJ	5	4-3/4	7/16	2.783	.40	W	12.328	KH
	Chevy II RPO SS, Super Sport	14x7	AO*	5	4-3/4	7/16	2.783	.34	W	12.328	MW
	Chevy II SS, Super Sport	14x7	YA	5	4-3/4	7/16	2.783	.34	W	12.328	MW
	Corvette	15x8 JJ	AZ	5	4-3/4	7/16	2.783	-.50	W	13.156	KH
	Monte Carlo "G", Std.	15x6	CI	5	4-3/4	7/16	2.783	.85	W	13.156	C
	Monte Carlo RPO	15x7 JJ	AF	5	4-3/4	7/16	2.783	.30	W	13.156	KH
	Monte Carlo RPO Rally	15x7 JJ	YH	5	4-3/4	7/16	2.783	.30	W	13.156	KH
	Chevrolet "B" ex. Wagon	15x5 JJ	YM	5	4-3/4	7/16	2.783	.12	W	13.156	KH
	Chevrolet "B" RPO ex. Wagon, Rally	15x6 JK	YS	5	4-3/4	7/16	2.783	.06	W	13.156	KH
	Chevrolet "B" RPO Wagon, Rally	15x6 JK	FI	5	4-3/4	7/16	2.783	.06	W	13.156	KH
	RPO ex. Wagon	15x6 JK	DH	5	4-3/4	7/16	2.783	.06	W	13.156	KH
	RPO Wagon	15x6 JK	DJ	5	4-3/4	7/16	2.783	.06	W	13.156	KH
	Chevrolet "B" Wagon, replaces DJ	15x6 JK	DL	5	4-3/4	7/16	2.783	.06	W	13.172	KH
	* The YA wheel has been documented as being built from November 4, 1968, through July 17, 1969 (1969 model year). Motor Wheel has no record of the YA wheel being used, although wheels do exist. It is possible that the AO wheel could have been used during the 1969 model year. The earliest dated AO wheel found to date is September 23, 1969 (1970 model year, excluding Camaro and Corvette). Both codes are listed here due to lack of confirming information.										

continued on next page

1970 Through 1975 Wheel Applications (continued)

Year	Model	Size	Code	Bolts	Bolt Center	Bolt Size	Center Hole	Offset	Const.	Rim I.D.	Mfg.
1971	Camaro ex. SS, Z28	14x6 JJ	AM	5	4-3/4	7/16	2.783	.50	W	12.328	KH, NI
	Camaro RPO SS	14x7 JJ	CL	5	4-3/4	7/16	2.783	.34	W	12.328	KH, NI
	Camaro RPO Rally (6)	14x7 JJ	AV	5	4-3/4	7/16	2.783	.34	W	12.328	KH
	Camaro Z28, Trans-Am	15X7 JJ	AU	5	4-3/4	7/16	2.783	.30	W	13.156	KH
	Chevelle Std.	14x5	DD	5	4-3/4	7/16	2.783	.60	W	12.328	C, NI
	Chevelle RPO, Wagon	14X6 JJ	CZ	5	4-3/4	7/16	2.783	.88	W	12.328	KH, NI
	Chevelle RPO Rally, ex. SS	14x6 JJ	DE	5	4-3/4	7/16	2.783	.50	W	12.328	KH
	Chevelle Trans-Am RPO	15x7 JJ	AU	5	4-3/4	7/16	2.783	.30	W	13.156	KH
	Chevy II Std.	14x5	DD	5	4-3/4	7/16	2.783	.60	W	12.328	C, NI
	Chevy II RPO Rally Ex. SS	14x6 JJ	DE	5	4-3/4	7/16	2.783	.50	W	12.328	KH
	Chevy II RPO SS	14X7 JJ	CL	5	4-3/4	7/16	2.783	.34	W	12.328	KH, NI
	Chevy II Rally (6)	14x7 JJ	AV	5	4-3/4	7/16	2.783	.34	W	12.328	KH
	Corvette	15X8 JJ	AZ	5	4-3/4	7/16	2.783	-.50	W	13.156	KH
	Monte Carlo "G" Std.	15x6 JJ	XX	5	4-3/4	7/16	2.783	.85	W	13.156	C, NI
	Monte Carlo Opt., SS	15x7 JJ	XY	5	4-3/4	7/16	2.783	.30	W	13.156	KH, NI
	Monte Carlo Rally (5)	15X7 JJ	FW	5	4-3/4	7/16	2.783	.30	W	13.156	KH
	Vega Std.	13x5 JJ	AS	4	4	7/16	2.343	.20	W	11.248	KH
	Vega Opt.	13X6 JJ	AT	4	4	7/16	2.343	.45	W	11.248	KH
	Vega GT	13x6 JJ	FF	4	4	7/16	2.343	.45	A	11.248	KH
	Chevrolet, all Light	15x6 JJ	BX	5	5	1/2	3.0645	.34	W	13.156	C, KH, NI, MW
	Chevrolet, all Heavy	15X6 JJ	AK	5	5	1/2	3.0645	.34	W	13.156	C, KH, NI
1972	Vega	13x5 JJ	AS	4	4	7/16	2.343	.45	SW	11.248	KH
	Vega	13X6 JJ	AT	4	4	7/16	2.343	.45	SW	11.248	KH
	Vega GT	13x6 JJ	FF	4	4	7/16	2.343	.45	SW	11.248	KH
	Nova, Camaro, SS	14x7 JJ	CL	5	4-3/4	7/16	2.783	.34	SW	12.328	KH, NI
	Nova, Chevelle, Std.	14x5	DD	5	4-3/4	7/16	2.783	.60	SW	12.328	C, NI
	Nova, Chevelle Rally (6)	14X6 JJ	DE	5	4-3/4	7/16	2.783	.50	SW	12.328	KH
	Nova, Camaro Rally (6)	14x7 JJ	AV	5	4-3/4	7/16	2.783	.34	SW	12.328	KH
	Camaro, Std.	14x6 JJ	AM	5	4-3/4	7/16	2.783	.50	SW	12.328	KH, NI
	Camaro, Chevelle, Trans-Am	15x7 JJ	AU	5	4-3/4	7/16	2.783	.30	SW	13.156	KH
	Chevelle Wagon	14X6 JJ	CZ	5	4-3/4	7/16	2.783	.88	SW	12.328	KH, NI
	Monte Carlo Std.	15x6 JJ	XX	5	4-3/4	7/16	2.783	.85	SW	13.156	Heintz
	Chevrolet	15X6 JJ	BA	5	5	1/2	3.0645	.34	SW	13.156	C
	Chevrolet, Monte Carlo	15x7 JJ	AH	5	4-3/4	7/16	2.783	.30	SW	13.156	KH, NI
	Monte Carlo Rally	15x7 JJ	FW	5	4-3/4	7/16	2.783	.30	SW	13.156	KH
	Chevy, all Light	15X6 JJ	BX	5	5	1/2	3.0645	.34	SW	13.156	KH, NI, MW
	Chevy, all Heavy	15x6 JJ	AK	5	5	1/2	3.0645	.34	SW	13.156	KH, NI
	Corvette	15x8 JJ	AZ	5	4-3/4	7/16	2.783	-.50	SW	13.156	KH
1973	Vega	13x5 JJ	AS	4	4	7/16	2.343	.20	S/TC	11.248	KH
	Vega	13X6 JJ	AT	4	4	7/16	2.343	.45	S/TC	11.248	KH
	Vega GT	13X6	FF	4	4	7/16	2.343	.45	S/TC	11.248	KH, MW
	Nova	14x5	XA	5	4-3/4	7/16	2.783	.20	S/TC	12.328	KH, NI, MW
	Chevelle, Camaro	14x6	EL	5	4-3/4	7/16	2.783	.50	S/TC	12.328	C, KH, NI, MW
	Chevelle	14x6	FM	5	4-3/4	7/16	2.783	.50	S/TC	12.328	KH, NI, MW
	Nova Rally	14x6	XW	5	4-3/4	7/16	2.783	.50	S/TC	12.328	KH
	Nova, Camaro, SS	14x7	EM	5	4-3/4	7/16	2.783	.34	S/TC	12.328	KH, NI, MW
	Nova, Camaro, Chevelle Rally	14x7	XZ	5	4-3/4	7/16	2.783	.34	S/TC	12.328	KH
	Camaro, Chevelle, Turbine I	14x7 JJ	AN	5	4-3/4	7/16	2.783	.34	P	12.328	MW

continued on next page

1970 Through 1975 Wheel Applications (continued)

Year	Model	Size	Code	Bolts	Bolt Center	Bolt Size	Center Hole	Offset	Const.	Rim I.D.	Mfg.
1973 cont'd	Chevy, all Light	15x6	BX	5	5	1/2	3.0645	.34	S/TC	13.156	KH, NI, MW
	Chevy, all Heavy	15x6	AK	5	5	1/2	3.0645	.34	S/TC	13.156	KH, NI
	Chevrolet	15x6	BA	5	5	1/2	3.0645	.34	S/TC	13.156	C
	Monte Carlo, Chevelle Rally	15x7	FW	5	4-3/4	7/16	2.783	.30	S/TC	13.156	KH
	Monte Carlo, Std.	15x7	AE	5	4-3/4	7/16	2.783	.30	S/TC	13.156	KH, NI
	Monte Carlo, Turbine II	15x7	AG	5	4-3/4	7/16	2.783	.30	P	13.156	MW
	Camaro Z28 (Trans-Am)	15x7	AU	5	4-3/4	7/16	2.783	.30	S/TC	13.156	KH
	Corvette	15x8	AZ	5	4-3/4	7/16	2.783	-.50	S/TC	13.156	KH
	Corvette Cast Aluminum	15x8	XM	5	4-3/4	7/16	2.783	-.50	A/TC	13.156	AM RACING
1974	Vega Std.	13x5	AS	4	4	7/16	2.343	.20	W/TC	11.248	KH
	Vega Opt.	13x6	AT	4	4	7/16	2.348	.45	S/TC	11.248	KH
	Vega GT	13x6	FF	4	4	7/16	2.343	.45	S/TC	11.248	KH, MW
	Vega Cast Aluminum	13x6	-	4	4	7/16	2.343	.45	A/TC	11.248	GKN
	Nova, Std.	14x5	XA	5	4-3/4	7/16	2.783	.20	S/TC	12.328	KH, NI, MW
	Nova, Camaro, Chevelle Lt.	14x6	EL	5	4-3/4	7/16	2.783	.50	S/TC	12.328	C, KH, NI, MW
	Chevelle Heavy	14x6	FM	5	4-3/4	7/16	2.783	.50	S/TC	12.328	KH, NI, MW
	Nova, Camaro Rally	14x6	XW	5	4-3/4	7/16	2.783	.50	S/TC	12.328	KH
	Nova, Camaro	14x7	EM	5	4-3/4	7/16	2.783	.34	S/TC	12.328	KH, NI, MW
	Nova, Camaro Rally	14x7	XZ	5	4-3/4	7/16	2.783	.34	S/TC	12.328	KH
	Camaro, Chevelle, Turbine I	14x7	AN	5	4-3/4	7/16	2.783	.34	P	12.328	MW
	Chevrolet, Light	15x6	BX	5	5	1/2	3.0645	.34	S/TC	13.156	KH, NI, MW
	"B" Wagons, Heavy	15x6	AK	5	5	1/2	3.0645	.34	S/TC	13.156	KH, NI, MW
	Chevrolet	15x6	XH	5	5	1/2	3.0645	.34	S/TC	13.156	C
	Chevelle Rally	15x7	FW	5	4-3/4	7/16	2.783	.30	S/TC	13.156	KH
	Chevelle, Std.	15x7	AE	5	4-3/4	7/16	2.783	.30	S/TC	13.156	KH, NI
	Monte Carlo, Turbine II*	15x7	AG	5	4-3/4	7/16	2.783	.30	P	13.156	MW
	Camaro Z28 (Trans-Am)	15x7	AU	5	4-3/4	7/16	2.783	.30	A/TC	13.156	KH
	Chevelle, Monte Carlo	15x7	FN	5	4-3/4	7/16	2.783	.30	S/TC	13.156	KH
	Corvette	15x8	AZ	5	4-3/4	7/16	2.783	.50	S/TC	13.156	KH
1975	Vega, Monza, SST	13x5	AS	4	4	7/16	2.343	.20	S/TC	11.248	KH, NI
	Vega, Monza	13x6	AT	4	4	7/16	2.348	.45	S/TC	11.248	KH, NI
	Vega GT	13x6	FF	4	4	7/16	2.343	.45	A/TC	11.248	KH, NI, MW
	Cosworth Vega	13x6		4	4	7/16	2.343	.45	CA	11.248	GKN
	Monza 2 + 2	13x6		4	4	7/16	2.343	.45	FA	11.248	Alcoa
	Nova, Camaro	14x5	XA	5	4-3/4	7/16	2.783	.20	S/TC	12.328	KH, NI
	Nova, Camaro, Light	14x6	UA	5	4-3/4	7/16	2.783	.50	S/TC	12.328	C, KH, NI
	Chevelle, Heavy	14x6	FM	5	4-3/4	7/16	2.783	.50	S/TC	12.328	KH, NI, MW
	Nova, Camaro Rally	14x6	UB	5	4-3/4	7/16	2.783	.50	S/TC	12.328	KH
	Nova, Camaro, SST	14x7	UC	5	4-3/4	7/16	2.783	.34	S/TC	12.328	KH, NI, MW
	Nova, Camaro Rally	14x7	UD	5	4-3/4	7/16	2.783	.34	S/TC	12.328	KH
	Chevelle	15x6	FL	5	4-3/4	7/16	2.783	.50	S/TC	13.156	KH, MW, C
	Chevrolet, Light	15x6	BX	5	5	1/2	3.0645	.34	S/TC	13.156	KH, MW
	Chevrolet, Heavy	15x6	AK	5	5	1/2	3.0645	.34	S/TC	13.156	KH, MW
	Chevelle, Monte Carlo	15x7	AE	5	4-3/4	7/16	2.783	.30	S/TC	13.156	KH, MW
	Chevelle	15x7	FN	5	4-3/4	7/16	2.783	.30	S/TC	13.156	KH
	Chevelle, Monte Carlo Rally	15x7	FW	5	4-3/4	7/16	2.783	.30	S/TC	13.156	KH
	Monte Carlo, Turbine II	15x7	CB/XU	5	4-3/4	7/16	2.783	.30	P	15	MW
	Camaro Z28 (Trans-Am)	15x7	AU	5	4-3/4	7/16	2.783	.30	S/TC	13.156	KH
	Corvette	15x8	AZ	5	4-3/4	7/16	2.783	-.50	S/TC	13.156	KH

* To meet production needs, some Monte Carlo Landau and "S" coupes built before Nov. 9, 1973 were shipped with 15" x 7" Rally wheels instead of the Turbine II.